TRADE UNIONS OF THE WORLD
5th edition (2001)

Trade Unions of the World, 5th edition

Published by John Harper Publishing
Editorial enquiries: 27 Palace Gates Road, London N22 7BW, UK. E-mail: jhpublish@aol.com
Sales enquiries: Turpin Distribution Services Ltd, Blackhorse Road, Letchworth, SG6 1HN, UK. E-mail: books@turpinltd.com

Distributed exclusively in the United States and Canada, and non-exclusively outside North America, by Gale Group Inc., 27500 Drake Rd., Farmington Hills, Michigan 48331, USA

1st edition (1987), Longman Group UK Ltd
2nd edition (1989), Longman Group UK Ltd
3rd edition (1991), Longman Group UK Ltd
4th edition (1996), Cartermill International Ltd

This edition first published 2001
© John Harper Publishing 2001
ISBN 0-9536278-4-5

Page makeup by Fakenham Photosetting Ltd
Printed in Great Britain by Bookcraft (Bath) Ltd

Contents

TRADE UNIONS OF THE WORLD

Other current affairs reference titles from John Harper Publishing include:

Border and Territorial Disputes
The Council of the European Union
Directory of European Union Political Parties
Directory of Pressure Groups in the EU
The European Commission
The European Courts
The European Parliament
Political Parties of Eastern Europe, Russia and the Successor States
Political Parties of the World
Treaties and Alliances of the World

Foreword

The first edition of *Trade Unions of the World* was published in 1987. Since then, the world trade union movement has experienced more wide-ranging and fundamental change than in any period since the 1940s. In each country, inevitably, the course of change has been shaped by local circumstances, but two recurrent underlying themes are apparent in the pages that follow.

The first is the impact of the general collapse of communism in the period 1989–91, culminating in the dissolution of the Soviet Union. This set in motion a wholesale reconstruction of the trade union movement in Eastern Europe and (parts of) the former Soviet Union, including the creation of a unified German trade union centre, and the appearance in many countries of entirely new independent unions or reformation of old structures. This is a process that still continues. The collapse of single-party rule in Europe also sent a shock wave through the developing world, most notably in Africa, where the early 1990s saw a strong surge towards political pluralism sweep across the continent. While the momentum of reform in many countries petered out as the 1990s went by, it left a considerable legacy. These global trends also underlay a reconfiguration of the trade union movement at the international level. Until the late 1980s, the world trade union movement was polarized between the World Federation of Trade Unions (WFTU), dominated by the official trade unions of the Soviet bloc, and the International Confederation of Free Trade Unions (ICFTU), dominated by the centres of Western Europe and North America. In the 1990s, however, the WFTU declined to a minor force at the global level, while the ICFTU unequivocally emerged as the voice of the world trade union mainstream, increasing from 87 million members in 1988 to 155 million by the end of 2000. The ICFTU's continuing expansion was underscored by its affiliation of three Russian centres for the first time in Nov. 2000.

The second theme is the impact of structural economic changes that have posed a serious challenge to the position of unions in the developed Western world and to their claim to speak for workers as a whole. Manufacturing industries with high union density have suffered many job losses and new jobs have been created mainly in private sector services where the unions have generally found it difficult to secure a base. Unions have lost members, density has fallen, and the profile of union membership has become increasingly unrepresentative of the profile of the workforce as a whole. In many Western countries the largest and most influential individual unions are now in the public sector whereas the active workforce is concentrated in the private sector. In the USA, the bastion of free enterprise, by 1999 some 43% of union members were in the public sector. With unions increasingly representing workers in occupations funded by the public purse rather than private profit, this has been reflected in the ever-growing emphasis on issues such as opposition to privatization and maintenance of public sector spending programmes.

In a few countries, notably in Scandinavia, the unions have seemed impervious to the impact of structural economic change. The Scandinavian unions have exceptional strength in white-collar, professional and service areas, and they have capitalized on a perception that they are responsible and important social partners and bedrock institutions in their national lives. By the end of the 1990s, trade union movements in other countries were increasingly re-focusing their efforts to try to build their appeal to workers in economic growth sectors, and in some respects re-inventing themselves. There was a new emphasis on combining robust organizing at shop floor level with an approach that underlined the role of unions as "partners" with employers and communities in creating and building productive businesses and social cohesion. In some leading countries, including the US and UK, unions believed by the end of the 1990s that they had begun to turn the corner after years of decline. In the US, where union membership fell continuously for two decades from the end of the 1970s, the period 1998–99 saw increasing union membership, albeit against the background of a booming economy. In Aug. 2000 the AFL-CIO executive council, reflecting a new buoyancy, adopted a target of adding new members at the rate of one million per annum. A similar trend and mood was apparent in the UK, where the Trades Union Congress (TUC) in June 2000 predicted that its affiliates could add one million members to the existing 6.8 million membership over the next five years.

Trade Unions of the World has always recorded the position of each country in respect of ratification of the fundamental ILO conventions relating to trade union rights. These are No.87 (Freedom of Association and Protection of the Right to Organize, 1948) and No.98 (Right to Organize and Collective Bargaining, 1949). It is the case that those countries with the most firmly established and freely functioning trade unions have nearly always ratified both conventions, and likewise that many of the countries in which trade unions have few rights or are not permitted at all have ratified neither. However, there has always been a substantial mismatch between ratification and practical implementation and respect. Many single-party states with controlled unions have ratified the conventions and to the end of the 1980s it was widely if tacitly accepted that free and independent trade unionism was a luxury in the main of Western developed countries. In the Soviet bloc the unions were controlled by the ruling party and this pattern had been imitated by much of the developing world. During the 1990s, however, the break-up of communism and the advance of economic globalization, with its implication of a single integrated world economy, have increasingly opened the way to demands for, and the opportunity to create, a more inclusive and truly global approach. Much of the effort of trade unions internationally is now focusing on ensuring the world-wide adoption, and above all practical observance, of the core labour standards of the ILO, which include ILO conventions 87 and 98.

Layout of entries. The basic layout of country entries has been simplified to some degree from previous editions. For each country an introductory section provides outline data on the national political and economic context within which trade unions operate (*Political and Economic Background*). This is followed by an overview of the history, structure, scale and influence of the trade union movement, including information on ratification of ILO conventions No.87 and No.98 and how these are observed in practice (*Trade Unionism*). A third section describes the various trade union centres, including detailed information on affiliates for some countries where the trade union movement is highly developed and industry-level affiliates are of independent significance (*Trade Union Centres*). Finally, where there are major organizations standing outside the principal trade union centre or centres these are described in a further section (*Other Trade Union Organizations*).

International affiliations of trade union centres are systematically recorded in respect of the following organizations: International Confederation of Free Trade Unions (ICFTU); World Confederation of Labour (WCL); World Federation of Trade Unions (WFTU); European Trade Union Confederation (ETUC); Commonwealth Trade Union Council (CTUC); and Trade Union Advisory Committee to the OECD (TUAC). In addition to postal address, telephone and fax numbers, e-mail addresses are now included wherever available. It should be noted that e-mail addresses are proving more volatile than postal addresses, with the complication that, unlike with post, e-mails are not re-directed. Websites are reported for the first time. Where the language of the website is not English, this is noted, including whether some data in English is provided.

Acknowledgements and sources of further information. Thanks are due to the many trade union officers who took the trouble to answer queries concerning their organizations. Since the publication of the last edition of *Trade Unions of the World*, in 1996, most trade unions in Western Europe, North America, East Asia and Australasia, and a scattering of unions elsewhere, have created websites and these now provide a major source of updated information on those unions and their national context.

A number of more general sources should also be noted. Population and GDP data in country introductions have been derived from the CIA *World Factbook*. An essential reference point is the ICFTU's *Annual Survey of Trade Union Rights* (including about two-thirds of countries) which is included on the ICFTU website (www.icftu.org). The *Country Reports on Human Rights Practices* of the Bureau of Democracy, Human Rights and Labor of the US State Department cover all countries (except the US) and all contain an overview of the position of unions (www.state.gov). The European Industrial Relations Observatory (EIRO) online database (www.eiro.eurofound.ie) of the European Foundation for the Improvement of Living and Working Conditions, provides extensive objective news and analysis relating to trade unions in the 15 EU member states and Norway. There are several sites that gather up labour-related news from a range of sources and which are useful for checking on recent developments, especially in more high-profile countries. These include the Global Unions Website, which combines the resources of all ten international trade secretariats as well as the ETUC, ICFTU and TUAC. It can be found at www.global-unions.org. Other updating sites include www.labourstart.org, which collates labour-related stories from a wide range of news sources, and www.labournet.org. The Cyber Picket Line (www.cf.ac.uk/ccin/union) includes links to many trade union sites around the world.

John Harper
London
Feb. 2001

Afghanistan

Capital: Kabul
Population: 25.84 m. (2000 est.)

1 Political and Economic Background

The (communist) People's Democratic Party of Afghanistan (PDPA) took power in 1978 as the sole political party. The Soviet Union intervened militarily in Dec. 1979 to sustain the faltering regime and remained for ten years in the face of escalating resistance from the mujaheddin ("holy warriors"). President Najibullah outlasted the Soviet withdrawal until 1992, when he was deposed, the mujaheddin entered Kabul and the Islamic State of Afghanistan was proclaimed. The various mujaheddin factions agreed to revolve the presidency among them, but the first holder of the office, President Burhannuddin Rabbani, clung onto power and was ultimately overthrown by the Taliban militia in 1996. The Taliban control most of the country, including Kabul. Most other countries continue to recognize the Rabbani government, however, and fighting continues within the country at varying levels of intensity.

Agriculture, based mainly on livestock rearing and herding and on the growing of cotton and fruits, is the dominant activity of the Afghan economy. There is some small-scale industry. Unrelenting civil war for two decades and fundamentalist rule in recent years have contributed to a substantial decline in GDP and Afghanistan is one of the world's poorest countries.

GDP (purchasing power parity) $21bn. (1999 est.); GDP per capita (purchasing power parity) $800 (1999 est.).

2 Trade Unionism

Afghanistan has ratified neither ILO Convention No.87 (Freedom of Association and Protection of the Right to Organize, 1948) nor Convention No.98 (Right to Organize and Collective Bargaining, 1949).

Afghanistan's first unions were reportedly formed in 1967. Following the 1978 revolution, when the (communist) People's Democratic Party of Afghanistan took power, the new regime established the Central Council of Afghan Trade Unions (CCATU) which began to organize a trade union structure. In Dec. 1979 the Soviet Union intervened in Afghanistan and the CCATU was purged and restructured. There were no trade unions outside the CCATU.

The CCATU defined its main policies as: (i) providing leadership for the nation's trade union movement; (ii) improving the working and living conditions of wage earners; (iii) strengthening the state sector and the national economy; and (iv) "defending the gains made by the Sowr (i.e. 1978) Revolution". After the Soviet withdrawal, at a 1990 congress (the first for nine years) it transformed itself into the National Workers' Union of Afghanistan (NUWA) though under a mostly unchanged leadership. Since the capture of Kabul by the mujaheddin in 1992, and the declaration of an Islamic Republic, this structure has ceased to exist, although the NUWA is still recorded as a WFTU affiliate. There is no indication of continuing trade union activity, and there are no labour courts or collective bargaining mechanisms. There are no reports of strikes or other forms of organized industrial activity.

Albania

Capital: Tirana
Population: 3.49 m. (2000 est.)

1 Political and Economic Background

From the end of World War II until 1990, Albania was a one-party state under the (communist) Albanian Party of Labour (APL) of Enver Hoxha. Albania was a closed society, sealed off from both Eastern and Western Europe, with a rigid Stalinist ideology combined with tribal social structures. However, the reform movement consuming the communist world also found expression in Albania. In March 1991 multi-party elections were won by the reformed APL (subsequently known as the Socialist Party of Albania, PSS), though the results were disputed by the new opposition Democratic Party (DP) which campaigned with union support for new elections;

industrial agitation culminated in a general strike. In June the government resigned and was replaced by a succession of temporary administrations.

New elections in March 1992 brought victory to the DP and its leader Sali Berisha became President. The DP again won elections in 1996. In early 1997, however, the collapse of financial pyramid selling schemes precipitated social chaos, resulting in 1500 deaths and the virtual disintegration of the country, with an armed rebellion in the South, wholesale destruction of businesses and public buildings, pursuit of blood feuds, and looting by criminal gangs. Berisha resigned and a new PSS-led coalition government took office following elections in June–July 1997. The government struggled thereafter to restore central control to parts of the country. The Democratic Party sustained a boycott of Parliament for long periods after losing power in 1997, and has accused the government of assassinating some of its members.

The PSS-led government that took power in June 1991 took the first steps away from the command economy of the communist era, under which Albania had been Europe's most backward economy. It legalized foreign investment, liberalized prices and introduced private home ownership. A Privatization Act of Aug. 1991 envisaged the sale of some 25,000 state enterprises. Subsidies were virtually eliminated. The abolition of collective farms (begun with a law of May 1991) paved the way for redistribution of the land in small plots to the (majority) rural population.

The collapse of the state planned system brought a steep decline in GDP, estimated at some 35 per cent in the period 1989–92. From 1993 this was followed by a recovery, but further crisis resulted from the pyramid selling debacle of 1997. Despite GDP growth of 8% in 1999, Albania remains a poor, technologically backward country, with high unemployment, considerable legal and illegal economic migration, and dependence on foreign aid and remittances from workers abroad. Modern development is frustrated by rampant corruption and widespread crime encouraged by lack of enforcement of laws. The mainstays of the Albanian economy are agriculture and mining, with agriculture providing a living (much of it at subsistence level) for perhaps two-thirds of the population; tobacco and cotton are grown as well as food crops. There are major mineral deposits, and Albania is the world's second largest exporter of chromite (chromium ore). Industry includes the processing of agricultural and mineral raw materials, chemicals and fertilizers. Locally extracted petroleum is refined and there are considerable hydroelectric resources.

GDP (purchasing power parity) $5.6bn. (1999 est.); GDP per capita (purchasing power parity) $1,650 (1999 est.).

Bargaining, 1949) in 1957. It withdrew from the ILO in 1967 but returned in 1991.

The Albanian trade union movement was organized after 1945 on the communist model, with unions coordinated by the Central Council of Albanian Trade Unions (TUA). Independent unions in Albania made their presence felt from the beginning of 1991. They started in the mines, where strikes had already taken place, recruiting 7,000 miners in 200 enterprises. The formation of the United Independent Albanian Trade Unions (BSPSh) was announced soon after. On April 4 it raised a call for a general strike to protest against post-election violence. On May 15 a general strike was launched, led by the miners – now organized in the Independent United Mineworkers' Union (SBPM) – to press demands, (matching those of the DP), for fresh elections. The independent unions were prominent in the demonstrations in Tirana, Shkoder and other cities that forced replacement of the APL government by an "administration of national salvation".

A new labour code was adopted in 1993. Under this and other legislation all workers, except police and security forces and some officers in the judicial system, may join unions, bargain collectively and strike. However, high unemployment and the parlous state of enterprises make meaningful bargaining and enforcement of contracts impossible in much of the economy and in the public sector pay is set administratively. Political strikes are not lawful. Major private sector areas of employment in Albania are agriculture, small shops and craft enterprises and restaurants, but unions are not significant in those areas.

The Albanian labour movement has reflected the unstable national political, social and economic environment of the 1990s. The WCL recently noted that the situation was "confused", although it wished to "encourage the setting up of democratic structures in a country where this seems particularly difficult". Neither the ICFTU nor the WCL has an affiliate. Two centres exist, the BSPSh and KSSh (Confederation of Trade Unions, also sometimes called the KS). They have reportedly agreed in some areas not to work against each other. According to the US State Department Human Rights report for 1999, the BSPSh has 127,000 members, and the Confederation of Trade Unions has 80,000, representing a sharp fall from levels in the mid-1990s. Some unions are not affiliated to either. While the centres are not politically affiliated, they have been embroiled in the complex and conspiratorial world of Albanian politics.

A key issue for unions since 1997 has been the recovery of public order and stability and the lack of social protection in the face of extreme levels of unemployment, exacerbated by wholesale destruction of enterprises in the 1997 disorder. However, the unions have complained of a lack of access to government and tripartism does not function.

2 Trade Unionism

Albania ratified both ILO Convention No.87 (Freedom of Association and Protection of the Right to Organize, 1948) and No.98 (Right to Organize and Collective

3 Trade Union Centres

United Independent Albanian Trade Unions (BSPSh)

Membership. 127,000 (estimated)

History and character. The BSPSh (variously referred to in English as the United Independent Albanian Trade Unions, the Union of Independent Trade Unions and the Independent Confederation of Trade Unions of Albania) emerged in 1991 in opposition to the official trade unions established in the communist period. Under the leadership of Valer Xheka it became the leading voice of independent trade unionism, with the mineworkers its most important affiliate. It held its first national conference in Feb. 1992.

The BSPSh became riven by factionalism. An emergency congress in Durres in Nov. 1996 elected Democratic Party legislator Azem Hajdari as president and Fatmir Musaku, a former BSPSh deputy leader, as general secretary. Hajdari, the head of the parliamentary control commission for the secret service, claimed that BSPSh leader Valer Xheka was corrupt and had spied for the secret service in the communist era. The BSPSh steering council said that the Durres congress had no legitimacy and opponents said it represented a political takeover, while President Berisha gave his support to Valer Xheka, even though Hajdari was a former close ally in the creation of the Democratic Party. In September 1997 Hajdari was shot four times by a Socialist Party MP inside the parliament building, but survived.

On Oct. 26, 1997, Astrit Balluku, the chairman of the Teachers' Federation in Tirana and a member of the BSPSh executive committee, was shot dead at BSPSh hedquarters. On Nov. 18, 1997, the Court of Appeal recognized Fatmir Musaku as BSPSh general secretary. On Dec. 8, 1997, police occupied BSPSh headquarters to expel the leadership under Xhevdet Lubani. In June 1998, however, the Supreme Court confirmed Lubani as the legitimate leader.

Hajdari was shot dead on Sept. 12, 1998, triggering anti-government riots in Tirana. Sali Berisha accused the Socialist Party of being behind the assassination.

Confederation of Trade Unions (KSSh)

Leadership. Kastriot Muco (president)

Membership. 80,000 (estimated)

History and character. The KSSh (sometimes referred to as KS) has recruited members in the school, food, petroleum, postal and telecommunications, and railroad sectors.

Algeria

Capital: Algiers
Population: 31.19 m. (2000 est.)

1 Political and Economic Background

Algeria achieved independence from France in 1962 following a lengthy armed struggle spearheaded by the Front de Libération Nationale (FLN). Until 1989, the FLN was the sole permitted political party, but riots and severe unrest precipitated constitutional changes that foresaw a market economy and a more liberal and pluralist society.

In the first round of National Assembly elections in Dec. 1991, the fundamentalist Islamic Salvation Front (FIS) took 47.5% of the vote, compared with 23.5% for the FLN. In consequence, in Jan. 1992 the FLN government canceled the second round of voting and declared a state of emergency. Since then fighting between government forces and FIS rebels has led to the loss of an estimated 100,000 lives in a conflict notable for the barbarism of the atrocities committed by the rebels and the thousands of "disappearances" blamed on security forces. Following elections to the National Assembly in 1997, the National Democratic Rally (RND) is the largest party; both it and the FLN supported the candidacy of Abdelaziz Bouteflika in 1999 presidential elections, which Bouteflika won after all his opponents withdrew, claiming electoral fraud. In Sept. 1999 a national referendum resulted in a massive majority for a peace plan that included an amnesty for rebels who laid down their arms; the FIS's armed wing was subsequently dissolved but not all its members abandoned conflict.

Despite some moves to a market-oriented system, the state continues to control key sectors of the economy, including the oil and gas sector, which generates one-quarter of national income and 96% of exports. Most of the industrial sector is state-controlled and considered inefficient. Unemployment is reported as high as 30%.

GDP (purchasing power parity) $147.6bn. (1999 est.); GDP per capita (purchasing power parity) $4,700 (1999 est.).

2 Trade Unionism

Prior to independence the French trade union centres maintained regional organizations in Algeria and there were also independent federations. Following independence, however, the Union Générale des Travailleurs Algériens (UGTA), which was linked with the FLN, became the sole centre. It remained the sole legal (non-peasant) labour organization until the constitutional changes of 1989. Three laws of 1990 laid down a new framework for industrial relations and the rights of trade unions.

Despite the loss of its status as the sole legal centre, the UGTA has in practice remained the only trade union centre, with only a few unions not affiliated. Under 1990 legislation the Labour Ministry must approve the registration of any union. An Independent Trade Union Confederation (CSA) has been in development since 1996, but has yet to receive approval by the Labour Ministry. In addition the FIS's labour front, the Islamic Union of Workers (SIT), was banned in 1992 along with the FIS. The UGTA itself has established a role as a politically autonomous trade union organization focused on the economic interests of its members. Pre-emergency legislation bans unions from associating with political parties or receiving funds from abroad.

Under the 1990 Law on Industrial Relations, strikes are legal provided mandatory conciliation, mediation, and arbitration procedures are followed. Where arbitration fails, workers may strike legally subject to a secret ballot and the maintenance of basic public services in the case of public sector strikes. However, under the state of emergency, in force since 1992, the government has powers to force workers to stay at their jobs in the event of an unauthorized or illegal strike. There have been frequent strikes in recent years over issues such as job losses, inadequate redundancy payments, pay arrears and failure by the government to consult the unions.

The trade union movement has been caught in the crossfire of the conflict between the government and FIS fundamentalist rebels. The UGTA general secretary was killed in 1997, apparently by a member of FIS, although in Algeria the attribution of killings is often uncertain. To FIS extremists the secular, civil character of trade unions makes them anathema. However, the degree to which the many union members who have died has been because of their union activities, or because they were engaged in activities intolerable to the fundamentalists (e.g. women teachers), or simply because they were random victims of indiscriminate violence, is unclear.

Algeria ratified both ILO Convention No.87 (Freedom of Association and Protection of the Right to Organize, 1948) and No.98 (Right to Organize and Collective Bargaining, 1949) in 1962.

3 Trade Union Centre

Union Générale des Travailleurs Algériens (UGTA) General Union of Algerian Workers

Address. Maison du Peuple, Place du 1er Mai, Algiers

Phone. +213 2 67 21 67

Fax. +213 2 66 61 63

Leadership. Madjid Sid-Said (secretary general)

Membership. 1 million

History and character. The UGTA was created in 1956 as part of the FLN, and after independence replaced all existing union federations. Legislation adopted in 1971 named the UGTA as the sole recognized labour organization and provided that it should set up a trade union section in any work unit with more than nine workers. A 1975 ordinance made UGTA the sole bargaining agent, and a provision of the 1976 Constitution placed all mass organizations under the protection and control of the party. This provision was rescinded by the country's 1989 Constitutional amendments.

At the 8th (June 1990) congress new statutes and regulations were adopted and a new leadership elected, headed by Abdelhak Benhamouda. The UGTA successfully campaigned for better pay for the low paid, called a widely observed general strike in Mar. 1991, and in Nov. 1991 led for the union side in Algeria's first tripartite consultations. In 1993, the UGTA was given responsibility in the administration of social security assets. It has campaigned against privatization of state enterprises.

The UGTA secretary general, Abdelhak Benhamouda, was assassinated on Jan. 28, 1997, outside UGTA headquarters in Algiers. He was regarded as strongly opposed to the Islamic fundamentalists. A member of the FIS made a televised confession to the murder, but he was found dead in prison before a trial.

The UGTA urged members to vote "yes" in the Sept. 1999 referendum on the President's peace plan (which was overwhelmingly endorsed by the electorate).

Under pressure from the ruling FLN, the UGTA disaffiliated from the ICFTU in 1963. In 1991 it resumed contacts, and it re-affiliated in 1994.

International affiliation. ICFTU

Andorra

Capital: Andorra la Vella
Population: 67,000 (2000 est.)

1 Political and Economic Background

Under its constitution of May 1993, Andorra is a sovereign parliamentary co-principality with the President of France and Bishop of Urgel (Spain) as joint heads of state. Following elections in 1997, the Liberal Union holds a majority in the legislature. 80% of GDP is derived from tourism.

GDP (purchasing power parity) $1.2bn. (1996 est.);
GDP per capita (purchasing power parity) $18,000 (1996 est.).

2 Trade Unionism

The first trade union, the Andorran Workers' Union was formed in 1990, claiming several hundred members. The 1993 Constitution recognizes the right to form and join trade unions, although there is no legal protection against anti-union discrimination. The right to strike is not specifically recognized or denied. Andorra is not a member of the ILO.

Angola

Capital: Luanda
Population: 10.15 m. (2000 est.)

1 Political and Economic Background

The former Portuguese province of Angola became independent in 1975 and was ruled as a Marxist state for 15 years by the Popular Movement for the Liberation of Angola (MPLA), with large-scale Cuban military support. Parts of the country continued to be controlled by the National Union for the Total Independence of Angola (UNITA), which received South African support across the border from Namibia and engaged the MPLA in a protracted military struggle.

The MPLA decided at its 1990 Congress to adopt a new ideology of "democratic socialism". After the last Cubans left in 1991, a series of attempts to make peace between the MPLA and UNITA was undertaken, culminating in the Lusaka protocol of 1994 which brought about an element of power-sharing with UNITA. This failed to produce a permanent peace, however, and intermittent fighting between the factions increased at the end of the decade. Some 1.5 million lives may have been lost in the past quarter century of conflict. There have been no elections since 1992 for either the president (nominally elected for 5 years) or the National Assembly (nominally elected for four years).

In the 1990s the MPLA has moved away from the policies that led in the post-independence era to the expropriation of foreign-owned enterprises and a command economy, but its economic stability has been undermined by two decades of civil war aggravated by mismanagement and corruption. Other than a small elite, mainly in Luanda, most of the population lives in poverty. Subsistence agriculture in the main livelihood of 85% of the population with coffee and sugar as export commodities. Industry is based around oil production, which accounts for 45% of GDP.

GDP (purchasing power parity) $11.6bn. (1999 est.); GDP per capita (purchasing power parity) $1,030 (1999 est.).

2 Trade Unionism

Under Portuguese rule to 1975 there existed "occupational syndicates"; these organizations functioned mainly to provide welfare services, and free collective bargaining and strikes were banned. Members of these syndicates were predominantly Europeans and assimalados, and independent African trade unionism was illegal. However, several underground or exiled unions gave their support to the independence struggle, these becoming identified with the rival factions among the independence forces. Following the winning of power by the MPLA, the União Nacional de Trabalhadores Angolanos (UNTA) became and remained the sole union centre although there is now an independent centre, affiliated to the ICFTU, the Central Geral de Sindicatos Independentes e Livres de Angola. Trade union organization is limited by the small scale of the formal economy, in which there is also massive unemployment. Collective bargaining and the right to strike are formally guaranteed by the Constitution, although collective bargaining is little developed. Strikes have occurred in recent years in the state sector where salaries were undermined by inflation and in 2000 many salaries were in arrears despite rising oil production and buoyant oil prices.

Angola ratified ILO Convention No.98 (Right to Organize and Collective Bargaining, 1949) in 1976 but has not ratified Convention No.87 (Freedom of Association and Protection of the Right to Organize, 1948).

3 Trade Union Centres

Central Geral de Sindicatos Independentes e Livres de Angola (CGSILA)
General Centre of Independent and Free Unions of Angola

Address. CP 10603, Luanda

Phone. +244 39 55 39

Fax. +244 33 83 31

E-mail. cgsiladis@netangola.com

Membership. 50,000

History and character. Led a strike in March 1997 over 6-month wage arrears due to public servants and in support of a minimum wage. Complained it had not been represented in tripartite discussions on reform of the labour law.

International affiliation. ICFTU

União Nacional de Trabalhadores Angolanos (UNTA)
National Union of Angolan Workers

History and character. The UNTA was formed in the late 1950s, and through the 1960s worked both in exile abroad and underground at home, organizing cooperative production in areas held by MPLA forces. Other trade union centres, linked to the rival liberation movements, also existed in the 19605 and early 1970s, but following independence in 1975 and the assumption of control of most of the country by the MPLA, these ceased to function.

International affiliation. WFTU

Antigua and Barbuda

Capital: St. John's
Population: 66,000 (2000 est.)

1 Political and Economic Background

Antigua and Barbuda, formerly a West Indian Associated State, became independent in 1981 as a full member of the Commonwealth, with the British sovereign as head of state. The Antigua Labour Party (ALP), and previously the Antigua Trades and Labour Union (ATLU) to which it is linked, has been the dominant political force since the 1940s, being most recently re-elected to power under Prime Minister Lester Bird, in Mar. 1999. Only in 1971–76 was the administration formed by the Progressive Labour Movement, now the opposition United Progressive Party (UPP).

Antigua's economy is heavily dependent on (mainly United States) tourism, which accounts for more than half of GDP. Agriculture is based mainly on locally consumed crops; there is a little light industry.

GDP (purchasing power parity), $524m. (1999 est.); GDP per capita (purchasing power parity), $8,200 (1999 est.).

2 Trade Unionism

Provision for the registration of trade unions was first made in 1939, and the Antigua Trades and Labour Union (ATLU) dates from that year. Unions are well established, representing a majority of the workforce, and operate freely and engage in collective bargaining. As an independent country Antigua and Barbuda ratified both ILO Convention No.87 (Freedom of Association and Protection of the Right to Organize, 1948) and No.98 (Right to Organize and Collective Bargaining, 1949) in 1983. The two rival centres are politically aligned, the ATLU with the ruling ALP, and the AWU with the UPP. Vere Bird, Prime Minister until 1992 was co-founder and president of ATLU. The Leader of the

(UPP) Opposition Baldwin Spencer is also first vice-president and assistant general secretary of AWU.

The ATLU is affiliated to the WCL, while the ICFTU affiliates are the AWU and the Antigua and Barbuda Public Service Association (ABPSA).

3 Trade Union Centres

Antigua Trades and Labour Union (ATLU)

Address. Emancipation House, PO Box 3, 46 North Street, St John's

Phone. +1268 46 200 90

Fax. +1268 46 240 56

E-mail. atandlu@candw.ag

Leadership. Wigley George (president); Nathalie Payne (general secretary)

Membership. 7,000

History and character. The ATLU was founded in 1939 and functioned for many years as both a trade union and a political party. It founded and remains close to the ALP. The ATLU represents most non-established workers in the civil service and in statutory bodies but also has membership in the private sector.

Publications. Workers' Voice

International affiliatons. WCL; CTUC

Antigua Workers' Union (AWU)

Address. Freedom Hall, PO Box 940, Newgate Street, St John's

Phone. +1268 462 0442

Fax. +1268 462 5220

E-mail. awu@candw.ag

Leadership. Keithlyn Smith (general secretary)

History and character: Originated from a split in the ATLU in 1967 and founded the Progressive Labour Movement (now the UPP) in 1970. The AWU is strongest in the highly unionized tourist industry.

Publication. Trumpet

International affiliatons. ICFTU; CTUC

4 Other Trade Union Organizations

Antigua and Barbuda Public Service Association (ABPSA)

Address. PO Box 1285, St. John's

Phone. +1268 461 5821

Fax. +1268 461 5821

E-mail. abpsa@candw.ag

History and character. Gained recognition as bargaining agent for civil servants in the 1980s but is rivaled in the public service sector by other unions. It now bargains for some 1,500 civil servants though its membership is little more than one-fifth of this.

International affiliation. ICFTU

Argentina

Capital: Buenos Aires
Population: 36.96 m. (2000 est.)

1 Political and Economic Background

From the overthrow of President María Estela (Isabelita) Perón in 1976 to 1983 Argentina was under military rule. In 1983 the military handed power to a civilian administration under Raúl Alfonsín. The Peronist Carlos Menem who succeeded him in 1989 remained in office until standing down after elections in Oct. 1999 in which Fernando de la Rúa became president as the leader of a coalition of centre-left forces, although lacking a majority in either house of the bi-cameral legislature

(Congress). The Oct. 1999 election represented the first occasion on which the Peronists had handed over power other than in the event of a military coup and was seen as an indication of the increasing stability of the Argentine state and society. Peronists continued to govern the major provinces.

Under Menem the Peronists had largely turned their backs on their corporatist, populist past (in which they had been closely linked with the CGT labour confederation) in favour of more conventional centre-right free market policies. The Menem government sought to reverse years of economic decline in which Argentina had experienced hyper-inflation, an escalating burden of foreign debt and a progressive erosion of the position it had enjoyed in the 1930s as one of the leading economies of the western hemisphere. Menem's programme of "major surgery without anaesthetic" included trade liberalization, austerity packages and privatization, with major cutbacks in the public sector. In the three years 1997–99 prices rose by less than 1 per cent and the real GDP growth rate reached 9 per cent in 1997. However, the economy contracted by up to 4 per cent in 1999, affected by the fall in prices of export commodities and a major January 1999 devaluation in Brazil. In the poorer provinces public sector workers went unpaid for periods leading to strikes and other action in 1999. In Dec. 2000 an aid package of $40bn. from the IMF and other donors was unveiled, aimed at assisting recovery and averting default on the foreign debt.

GDP (purchasing power parity) $367bn. (1999 est.); GDP per capita (purchasing power parity) $10,000 (1999 est.).

2 Trade Unionism

Argentina ratified ILO Convention No.87 (Freedom of Association and Protection of the Right to Organize, 1948) in 1960 and No.98 (Right to Organize and Collective Bargaining, 1949) in 1956.

In the twentieth century successive attempts to form a national centre culminated in 1930 in the formation of the CGT. Since the 1940s it has been a major force in Argentine politics. Although trade unionism was suppressed by the military after 1976 it resurfaced strongly through demonstrations and general strikes in the transitional phase preceding the restoration of full civilian rule at the end of 1983. The formal right to belong to a trade union was restored in 1982 and the right to strike in 1983 (although the government retained powers to ban individual strikes). Unions were brought into tripartite discussions with government and business on questions relating to the transition to democracy and the economic crisis. An Act of March 23, 1988 recognized the right of workers to form or be (or not to be) members of a union of their choice and for trade unions to become members of their preferred federations and confederations, and to affiliate to international union organizations. Unions were allowed to set up mutual benefit societies and cooperatives and were allowed to retain their controversial role of administering social welfare (a vast system of health provision, education, tourism, sports facilities).

In a review presented to the World Trade Organization in January 1999, the ICFTU concluded that the situation in respect of trade union rights had "improved immeasurably" since the 1970s and 1980s, although some measures intended to increase labour market flexibility had weakened union rights. All workers except military personnel have the legal right to form and join trade unions and about 40 per cent of the formal workforce are unionized. There is no state interference in the internal affairs of unions. However, there are restrictions on granting legal recognition to enter-

prise-level unions where another union is already established.

Workers enjoy the right to strike and are in law protected from recriminations by employers. A 1990 report found that two-thirds of disputes between 1986 and 1989 occurred in the public sector. In 1990 Menem restricted the right to strike in "essential industries", namely public health, transport, water supply, gas, oil, phones, education and the judiciary. In 1991 the decree was tested by a major rail strike; when the government proposed to privatize the steel firm SOMISA and impose mass dismissals, a general strike threat was issued by the metalworkers' union UOM. The outcome was that compulsory redundancies were replaced by more generous voluntary severance terms. Legal challenges and union action have since limited the impact of restrictions in the public sector.

While strikes are legal, unauthorized demonstrations and assemblies have led to violent clashes with police on occasions in recent years. Death threats and intimidation have been reported in some disputes.

Argentina's relatively inflexible labour market has been seen as a factor in persistent high unemployment. In the early 1990s the government passed a series of decrees that sought to limit pay increases to those justified by productivity. In Aug. 1996 Menem proposed wide-ranging labour law reforms that broadly aimed to restrict collective bargaining to the enterprise level and encourage flexibility of labour contracts. The unions forcefully opposed the reforms, and there were two general strikes organized by the CGT in September and December 1996. Faced with opposition in Congress, Menem attempted to introduce elements of the reforms by decree, but the decrees were overturned in the courts in 1997. After extended discussions with employers and the CGT a further package of measures was adopted in Sept. 1998. This package confirmed the status of industry-wide collective bargaining and banned future temporary contracts under which workers had no social benefits. Collective agreements that extended beyond the enterprise level required approval by the Ministry of Labour. The role of industry-wide collective agreements has declined, however, and by 1998 64 per cent of workers in the private sector were either employed on individual employment contracts without social security coverage or were not registered at all.

3 Trade Union Centre

Confederación General del Trabajo de la Républica Argentina (CGT)
General Conferation of Labour

Address. Azopardo 802, CP 1107, Buenos Aires

Phone. +54 11 4343 1883

Fax. +54 11 4343 1883

E-mail. secgral@cgtra.org.ar

Website. www.cgtra.org.ar (Spanish only)

Leadership. Rodolfo Daer (secretary general)

History and character. The CGT was founded in 1930, but its position was challenged by competing syndicalist, anarchist and socialist federations for a further decade. After becoming Minister of Labour and Social Welfare in a 1943 coup, Col. Juan Domingo Perón nurtured his relationship with it as part of a new politics of charismatic, authoritarian populism. Perón was dismissed in October 1945, but a CGT strike forced his release and paved the way for his election as President in 1946. From then, until Perón's fall and exile in 1955, the CGT leadership consolidated its position in Argentinian society in concert with the Peronist movement. His overthrow was resisted by the unions, and several hundred workers were killed in an abortive Peronist uprising of June 1956.

Government-appointed officials now administered the unions; the CGT was officially disbanded, though continuing clandestinely. This period saw internal differences over the question of its relationship to successive civilian and military governments and even to the exiled Perón. In 1961 union control was restored and two years later the CGT held its first open congress since Perón's fall. Under Augusto Vandor, its secretary general, who advocated "Peronism without Perón", the CGT reached an accommodation with the military regime of 1966. But bitterly disputed union elections of 1968 shattered its unity with the dissidents forming the "CGT of the Argentines".

Perón himself returned to power in September 1973, and was succeeded by his widow, María Estela (Isabelita), on his death in July 1974. Relations were undermined by worsening economic conditions and wage restraint which in 1975 provoked the first CGT-led strikes against a Peronist government and the resignation and flight from the country of the Minister of Social Welfare. Following the March 1976 coup in which Isabelita Perón was deposed, government officials again seized the CGT, and it was officially dissolved in 1979.

As before, however, the organization continued in being. At first underground but later increasingly openly, the CGT was already leading protests and strikes by 1982, even before the 1983 restoration of the right to strike and restoration of civilian government. The CGT found itself in conflict with the new administration of President Raúl Alfonsín, who had repeatedly criticized the close links between the CGT leadership and hard-line members of the previous military government. The CGT's legal status was restored in 1986 but only after ILO mediation.

After the Peronist Carlos Menem came into office in 1989, his free market policies provoked a crisis in Peronism and in the CGT. By Nov. 1989 it had split into two factions, for and against the austerity programme, opposition to which was led by CGT general secretary Saul Ubaldini. The Ubaldini faction fiercely resisted government calls for a voluntary two-year strike ban and was displaced by a "Menemista" group at the head of the official CGT apparatus. For two-and-a-half years the main trade union centre was organizationally split into the (Menemista) CGT–San Martín and the CGT–Azarpado, which was not officially recognized. When reunification occurred in 1992 it was largely on the CGT–San Martín's terms.

The CGT split again in March 2000. A congress staged by the "combative" unions elected Hugo Moyano as secretary general. The "official" CGT remained under the leadership of Rodolfo Daer. Both the dissident and official factions joined strike action in June 2000 to protest against IMF-backed austerity measures introduced against a background of economic stagnation and unemployment rising to 16%.

International affiliation. ICFTU

4 Other Trade Union Organization

Consejo Coordinador Argentino Sindical (CCAS)

Address. Combate de Los Pozos 235, CP 1080 Buenos Aires

Phone. +54 11 4952 77 88

Fax. +54 11 4952 77 94

E-mail. inforcas@ntdate.com.ar

Leadership. Victor R. Huerta (secretary-general)

History and character. Also referred to as the Congreso or Central de Trabajadores Argentinos (CTA) it became prominent in mid-1990s protests against anti-union policies of the Menem government.

International affiliation. WCL

Armenia

Capital: Yerevan
Population: 3.34 m. (2000 est.)

1 Political and Economic Background

The Soviet Republic of Armenia declared its independence in Aug. 1990. President Levon Ter-Petrossian, who had led Armenia to independence, was forced from office in Feb. 1998 and was succeeded by Robert Kocharian, also of the Pan-Armenian National Movement. The Unity group holds a majority in the legislature. The Prime Minister, Vazgen Sarkissian, was among those killed by terrorists when they seized the legislature in Oct. 1999 (being succeeded by his brother, Aram Sarkissian).

Armenia experienced a severe economic contraction following the loss of its Soviet-era markets and the collapse of its central command economy, this being exacerbated by military conflict with neighbouring Azerbaijan over the enclave of Nagorno–Karabakh, prior to a cease fire in May 1994. Positive growth occurred from 1995, although GDP contracted slightly in 1999 as a result of the Russian economic crisis. Most small and medium sized enterprises are now in private control, but much of the inherited Soviet heavy industry is closed. Unemployment may be as high as 50%.

GDP (purchasing power parity) $9.9bn. (1999 est.); GDP per capita (purchasing power parity) $2,900 (1999 est.).

2 Trade Unionism

The 1995 Constitution accords the right to form unions but the collapsed state of major enterprises and high unemployment has resulted in a low level of organization and activity.

There is little development of collective bargaining. There is a constitutional right to strike and an Arbitration Commission. The Soviet era unions reformed as the Confederation of Trade Unions of Armenia. An independent labour federation was reportedly created in Dec. 1997 but has not been active.

Australia

Capital: Canberra
Population: 19.17 m. (2000 est.)

1 Political and Economic Background

The Commonwealth of Australia dates from 1901 and comprises six states and two territories. From 1949 to 1972 and again from 1975 to 1983 the federal government was formed by the Liberal/National (Country) Party coalition. The Australian Labour Party (ALP), led by Bob Hawke, a former Australian Council of Trade Unions (ACTU) president, came to power in 1983. In 1993, now led by Paul Keating, the ALP won an historic fifth consecutive term of office. In March 1996, however, the ALP was defeated in a general election and a Liberal–National Party coalition government came into office under Liberal leader John Howard. The Howard government was re-elected in Oct. 1998.

The Australian economy was built on the surpluses generated by commodity exports, such as meat, wool, minerals and metals, allowing the growth of tariff-protected industries and a high-wage economy. By the 1980s, however, most commodity prices were on a downward path and Australia faced pressures arising from the need to modernize its economy. In 1992 unemployment reached a record 11 per cent. There has been a shift to the services sector and the government emphasizes the need for Australian industries to remain competitive in world markets. However, commodities still account for 57% of the value of exports. The latter half of the 1990s saw improved economic performance, with GDP growth averaging 4% per annum 1995–99, low inflation (1.8% in 1999) and a lower level of unemployment (running below 7% in 2000).

GDP (purchasing power parity) $416.2bn. (1999 est.); GDP per capita (purchasing power parity) $22,000 (1999 est.).

2 Trade Unionism

Australia ratified both ILO Convention No.87 (Freedom of Association and Protection of the Right to Organize, 1948) and No.98 (Right to Organize and Collective Bargaining, 1949) in 1973.

Trade unionism developed strongly among the nineteenth century British settlers, and there were some 200 unions operating by 1890. The Australian Council of Trade Unions (ACTU), the national centre, dates from 1927. The pattern was traditionally one of craft unionism. As recently as 1988 there were still 308 unions, and nearly half of these had fewer than 1,000 members. The pressure to amalgamate increased after the 1988 Industrial Relations Act extended legal standing only to unions with 1,000 or more members. The number of ACTU affiliates (146 in 1989) fell to 119 in 1991 and to 50 by 1999.

Blue-collar unions have lost much of their earlier preeminence in the face of the rise of white-collar and public sector unionism. Indeed, union density in the public sector is now 52.9% compared with only 21.4% in the private sector. However, the overall position has been one of decline. Factors have been the shift from public to private sector employment; the decline of highly unionized "old economy" industries in the face of the growth of services, where unionization rates are generally lower; the increase in part-time working (27% of the workforce now being part-time, with only 20.2% of part-timers in unions, compared with 31.2% of full-timers); and the shift from large to small-scale enterprises. In 1976 union density stood as high as 51 per cent, but it has fallen steadily since then and by 1999 was 28 per cent.

The major focus of concern for unions in the 1990s has been the development of enterprise unionism and the encouragement of greater labour flexibility at the expense of industry-wide collective bargaining. From the establishment of the Commonwealth Conciliation and Arbitration Commission (CAC) in 1904, Australian industrial relations were dominated by its unique highly structured collective bargaining and quasi-judicial conciliation and settlement systems. These resulted in legally enforceable federal and state "awards" defining pay and conditions in detail for each industry and helped the unions, as negotiators, build a strong position. Enterprise unionism, although not unknown previously, was generally strongly opposed by the unions, which supported the practice of negotiating industry-wide agreements regardless of the varying circumstances of individual employers.

The consensus in favour of this system began to break down in the 1980s as increasing numbers of employers sought the right to manage their own business costs and as free market sentiment increased. By the 1990s the political consensus had fundamentally shifted and the traditionally pro-union ALP had largely adopted policies which accepted the need for greater market liberalization and labour flexibility if Australia was to remain competitive in world markets. The Howard government since 1996 has continued to aggressively press policy objectives that are widely seen as aimed at reducing the power of the unions and ending rigid bargaining and award structures.

Under Labour, the industry-wide system was first modified by the Industrial Relations Act of 1988. While maintaining the (constitutionally prescribed) involvement of the state at each level it strengthened the role of the Industrial Relations Commission (IRC) and its counterparts in the states. To its power to resolve industrial disputes, demarcation disputes at the national level, and to register unions, the Commission now added the power (under Section 115) to certify agreements which were unique and thus inconsistent with broader awards. This was a very important consideration in Australia, where the pay of some 85% of employees traditionally was regulated by state or federal awards. The really revolutionary step was taken in 1991, when the IRC ruled that direct collective bargaining should be permitted between companies and their employees.

Section 115 had proved important in opening up the path for enterprise agreements. Section 118 facilitated the right of unions to cover a wide range of workers at a single plant. Another section precipitated radical structural change among Australia's unions by effectively requiring them to have membership of at least 10,000 by 1991.

In 1993 the government unveiled a second major industrial relations package, adopted in 1994. It included new national minimum standards of employment, a legal right to strike (not previously formally enshrined in law, although in practice recognized), and – if unions broke laws forbidding secondary boycotts – a conciliation period of up to 72 hours during which an employer must refrain from legal action. The employers' organization, the Australian Chamber of Commerce and Industry (ACCI), claimed that it was "95 per cent an ACTU agenda, 5 per cent a government agenda and zero per cent an employer agenda".

However, the measures also contained provisions for non-union workers to strike "enterprise deals" through the use of flexibility clauses incorporated into national wage awards, though unions would have the right to scrutinize such deals. This provision was seen as opening up the possibility of "enterprise bargaining" as potentially a rival channel of wage settlement to that offered by the unions; already some 11 per cent of the workforce was thought to be covered by enterprise deals. The ACTU failed to obtain the agreement of the Industrial Relations minister Lawrie Brereton that enterprise bargaining should only take place via a union vehicle. In November 1994 the Industrial Relations Commission ruled that the transport union had forfeited its immunity from civil action by pursuing an industry-wide pay claim for aircraft refuellers and oil tanker drivers -in effect that it had avoided enterprise bargaining. By the end of 1994, the number of enterprise agreements in force numbered 2,700, covering one-fifth of the workforce.

Following the election of the centre-right government

in March 1996, the 1996 Workplace Relations Act gave strong backing to enterprise bargaining and gave enterprise-level "Australian Workplace Agreements" (AWAs) primacy over federal and state awards on statutory minimum pay and over certified collective agreements. The Act directed the Industrial Relations Commission to encourage enterprise-level agreements and put union and non-union collective agreements on the same basis.

AWAs are in effect individual contracts, although employers must offer comparable terms to comparable employees. No current employee can be forced to sign an AWA, or be sacked or discriminated against for refusing to do so, and their existing terms and conditions must be respected. AWAs have to be approved by the Office of the Employment Advocate (set up under the Act), and may be referred to the Australian Industrial Relations Commission if their terms are detrimental. The unions have objected to AWAs as weakening collective bargaining and a way of eroding terms and conditions but have also increasingly sought to position themselves as acting as a bargaining agent for employees signing AWAs. Some major employers have preferred to remain with the system of collective bargaining.

In June 1999, the government announced plans to make changes to the Workplace Relations Act. These would end the requirement for comparable terms to be offered to comparable employees, and remove the Industrial Relations Commission's backstop role. In all cases, AWAs would prevail over certified collective agreements. The proposals were strongly opposed by the unions and the ALP.

While the 1996 Workplace Relations Act left intact protections against anti-union discrimination and rights to take industrial action, it weakened union power, curtailing closed shops and narrowing the scope of legal strikes. Under the Act strikes are only legally protected during the period of bargaining and fines may be imposed where action takes place during the term of a collective agreement. In the view of the ICFTU, "the operation of the law effectively denies the right to strike in the negotiation of multi-employer, industry-wide or national level agreements". The Act likewise banned strikes triggered by demarcation disputes and in effect banned sympathy strikes, secondary boycotts and strikes threatening to cause "significant damage" to the economy.

In March 2000, the ILO called on the government to amend the Workplace Relations Act to ensure that AWAs do not undermine collective bargaining, and to amend the Trade Practices Act to allow workers to take sympathy action in support of a legal strike. ACTU secretary Greg Combet stated in response: "the Workplace Relations Act has been found in breach of so many international conventions that there will surely be a day of reckoning".

While the unions have complained bitterly about the 1996 Act, its impact has been blunted by several factors. Unions have won a series of injunctions and court cases frustrating its implementation, and snap strikes and secondary boycotts do in practice occur. Most employers have tended to avoid recourse to legal remedies in trying to reach settlements with unions. While opposing the shift to workplace level bargaining in principle, in practice unions have also shifted resources and expertise into dealing with the changed bargaining context as they try to carve out a clear position for themselves in the changing industrial relations context. Nonetheless, the decline in union density continues. From 1996-98 union density declined from 55.4% to 52.9% in the public sector and from 24% to 21.4% in the private sector. In 1999 there were 2,037,000 union members, with an overall density of 28.1%.

3 Trade Union Centre

Australian Council of Trade Unions (ACTU)

Address. North Wing, 54 Victoria Street, Carlton South, VIC 3053

Phone. +61 3 9663 5655

Fax. +61 3 9663 4051

E-mail. mailbox@actu.asn.au

Website. www.actu.asn.au

Leadership. Sharan Burrow (president); Greg Combet (general secretary)

Membership. 2 million

History and character. The ACTU was founded in 1927 and is the only trade union centre in Australia.

While the ACTU has no formal political affiliation, it has traditionally enjoyed a close and at one time dominating relationship with the ALP, as seen in the period of Labour government from 1983–96. Bob Hawke, Prime Minister 1983–91, was a former ACTU president (as had been his predecessor as party leader, Bill Hayden). His successor as Prime Minister, Paul Keating (1991–96), began his working life as a research officer of the Municipal Employees' Union, now the Australian Services Union (ASU), while his Employment Minister, Simon Crean, was a former ACTU president. In the ALP, 50% of congress delegates must be union members, although the unions do not vote or participate as a bloc.

Through the period of Labour Party rule from 1983–96, the ACTU was party to a series of 13 tripartite Prices and Incomes Accords with the Confederation of Australian Industry (CAI) and the government. Each accord had at its heart a commitment to wage restraint in return for certain welfare or desired fiscal measures. Achievement of the accords was widely seen as strengthening the position of the ALP and the ACTU and the relationship between them.

Into the 1980s, the ACTU was at least nominally committed to a programme of sweeping socialization but this has been abandoned as it focuses on defending its members from the erosion of union power. It has strongly supported the campaign for a republic, but in

Nov. 1999 a national referendum narrowly decided not to replace the Queen by a President as Head of State.

Even under Labour, the ACTU was apprehensive about the impact of enterprise bargaining and sought to persuade Labour to give it a veto over the recognition process for bargaining units, a quest in which it was only partially successful. Since passage of the 1996 Workplace Relations Act, the ACTU has claimed the Howard government is determined to break the unions. However, it is also aware that the unions face deep-seated challenges arising from underlying structural changes in the economy that go beyond the policies of individual governments. During 1985–95, a period of Labour government, union membership fell faster than in any comparable country except New Zealand (where special factors applied), including countries such as the USA and Britain with conservative governments committed to curbing union power. The ACTU is looking to increase its support in weakly-organized growth sectors such as services and part-time working, and among women, who have a lower unionization rate than do men, and general secretary Greg Combet has said that the service industries must be the union base for the future. It is also encouraging the shift of resources to workplace level to reflect the reality of workplace level agreements.

ACTU's policy has been for many years to encourage amalgamation of existing member unions, in part to reduce disruptive demarcation disputes and in part to assist in the development of powerful, professionally managed and institutionally sophisticated unions able to deal with modern companies on a more equivalent footing. Industry-wide unions are also seen as better fitted to cope with the problems posed for narrowly recruited skill-based craft unions by new technology. Although resisted to some degree by the smaller unions, this process has resulted in the number of affiliated unions falling from 170 in the mid-1980s to 49 by early 2000.

The ACTU and its affiliates operate a wide range of member services and discount schemes. The ACTU also has a training body, Trade Union Training Australia (TUTA Ltd.).

The supreme policy-making body of the ACTU is the biennial congress. Following a policy adopted in 1989 the mandatory proportion of women on the executive has been increased in stages and in Oct. 2000 the target of 50% was reached with an expanded 64-member executive. There are ACTU state branches (known as trades and labour councils) for each of the six states of Australia, which have wide discretion in dealing with intrastate industrial and political issues.

The ACTU has a strong international dimension to its work. APHEDA (Australian People for Health Education and Development Abroad) is its overseas humanitarian agency, running 60 projects at any one time. The ACTU is the major trade union centre in the South-East Asia and Pacific region and has taken a leading role in recent campaigns for human and trade union rights in East Timor, Burma and Fiji. It participates in the ILO and has accused the Howard government of seeking to downgrade Australia's commitment to the ILO.

International affiliatons. ICFTU; TUAC; CTUC
Affiliates.

1. Ansett Pilots Association (APA)
Address. 19 Napier St, Essendon 3040
Phone. +61 3 9375 1941
Fax. +61 3 9375 7405

2. Association of Professional Engineers, Scientists and Managers, Australia (APESMA)
Address. GPO Box 1272L, Melbourne, VIC 3001
Phone. +61 3 9695 8842
Fax. +61 3 9696 9312
E-mail. info@apesma.asn.au
Website. www.apesma.asn.au
Leadership. Robert Allen (general president)
Membership. 23,000
Publications. Professional Update (monthly)

3. Association of Professional Teachers (APT)
Address. PO Box 7644, Melbourne, VIC 3004
Phone. +61 3 9820 0766
Fax. +61 9820 0322
E-mail. aapt@netlink.com.au
Website. www.apt.org.au
Leadership. Robert Fenton (president)
History and character. Members are teachers in public education in Victoria. Was founded in 1976 as "an alternative to the then extreme teacher militancy" and is non-party political.

4. Australasian Meat Industry Employees' Union (AMIEU)
Address. 377–383 Sussex Street, Sydney NSW 2000
Phone. +61 2 9264 2041
Fax. +61 2 9261 1970

5. Australian Airline Flight Engineers' Association (AAFEA)
Address. 3/87 Buckley Street, Essendon 3040
Phone. +61 3 9375 7590
Fax. +61 3 9375 7590

6. Australian Colleries Staff Association (ACSA)
Address. PO Box 21, Merewether, NSW 2291
Phone. +61 2 4963 5656
Fax. +61 2 4963 3425
E-mail. acsa@acsa.org.au
Website. www.acsa.org.au
Leadership. Mick Burgess (general president); Wendy Clews (general secretary)
Membership. Represents technical, supervisory and professional staff in the coal industry.

7. Australian Education Union (AEU)
Address. PO Box 1158, South Melbourne, VIC 3205
Phone. +61 3 9254 1800
Fax. +61 3 9254 1805
E-mail. aeu@edunions.labor.net.au

8. Australian Institute of Marine and Power Engineers (AIMPE)
Address. 52 Buckingham Street, Surry Hills 2010
Phone. +61 2 9698 3999
Fax. +61 2 9319 7505
E-mail. aimpe@ozemail.com.au

9. Australian Licensed Aircraft Engineers' Association (ALAEA)
Address. 25 Stoney Creek Road, Bexley 2207
Phone. +61 2 9554 9399
Fax. +61 9554 9644
E-mail. alaea@alaea.asn.au
Website. www.alaea.asn.au
Leadership. Iain Lang (federal president); Peter Melhuish (federal secretary)
Membership. 3,000

10. Australian Manufacturing Workers' Union (AMWU)
Address. PO Box 160, Granville, NSW 2142
Phone. +61 2 9897 9133
Fax. +61 2 9897 9274
E-mail. amwu2@amwu.asn.au
Website. www.amwu.asn.au
Leadership. Doug Cameron (national secretary)
Membership. About 200,000
History and character. Formed by the amalgamation of unions with widespread coverage in metals and engineering, manufacturing, vehicle building, food and printing industries. It also includes some trade, technical and supervisory employees in government agencies.

The union says that average enterprise bargaining wage increases obtained by AMWU members are significantly higher than those obtained by direct negotiation between employees and employers. It has an Education Department that runs courses around the country to help members keep up-to-date with industrial relations developments and develop negotiating skills, and an active Research Department. Members can develop workplace skills through MISTAS, the Manufacturing Industry Skills Training and Assessment Service.

AMWU has a militant tradition. Its national secretary Doug Cameron has been sharply critical of what is seen as the adoption by the Australian Labour Party of free market economic policies, and has called on the ALP to re-discover its working class base. The union has called on the government to give tax breaks to Australian manufacturing companies facing competition from low-wage countries such as China, saying that 60,000 Australian manufacturing jobs have been lost in the last two years. It welcomed the collapse of the Seattle WTO talks, and has called for "fair trade" not "free trade" with a focus on core labour standards. Internationally it is affiliated to the ITF.
Publications. The Manufacturing Worker (4 times per year); sectoral publications (also 4 times per year), *The Metal Worker, The Auto Worker, The Food Worker,* and *The Printing Worker.*

11. Australian Maritime Officers' Union (AMOU)
Address. PO Box 407, Haymarket, NSW 1240
Phone. +61 2 9264 2388
Fax. +61 2 9267 4766

12. Australian Nursing Federation (ANF)
Address. Level 2, 21 Victoria Street, Melbourne, VIC 3000
Phone +61 3 9639 5211
Fax. +61 3 9652 0567
E-mail. anfresources@c031.aone.net.au
Website. www.anf.org.au
Membership. 115,000
Leadership. Ged Cowin (federal president); Jill Iliffe (federal secretary)

Publications. Australian Nursing Journal; Australian Journal of Advanced Nursing

13. Australian Salaried Medical Officers' Federation (ASMOF)
Address. Locked Mail Bag No. 13, Glebe, NSW 2037
Phone. +61 2 9212 6900
Fax. +61 2 9212 6911
E-mail. peters@asmof.labor.net.au

14. Australian Services Union (ASU)
Address. 116–124 Queensberry Street, Carlton South, VIC 3053
Phone. +61 3 9342 1400
Fax. +61 3 9342 1499
E-mail. mosullivan@asu.asn.au
Website. www.asn.au
Leadership. Michael O'Sullivan (national executive president); Paul Slape (national secretary)
Membership. 130,000
History and character. The ASU was formed by the amalgamation in July 1993 of the Federated Clerks Union of Australia, the Federated Municipal and Shire Council Employees' Union of Australia, and the Australian Services Union, and established a unitary organization in 1995. Its 130,000 members work in local government, energy, water, public transport, airlines, shipping, travel, ports, social and community services, information technology and private sector clerical and administrative employment.

15. Australian Workers' Union (AWU)
Address. Suite 15, 245 Chalmers Street, Redfern, NSW 2016
Phone. +61 2 9690 1022
Fax. +61 2 9690 1020
E-mail. nat.office@awu.net.au
Website. www.awu.net.au
Leadership. Graeme Roberts (national president); Terry Muscat (national secretary)
Membership. 170,000
History and character. The AWU was founded in 1886 as the Amalgamated Shearers' Union, based in the wool shearing industry. Its Pastoral Industry Award, still in existence (most recently re-negotiated in 1998), was the first federal award achieved by a union under the Commonwealth conciliation and arbitration system set up at the start of the 20th Century and set the precedent for Australian industrial relations practice for most of the century. The AWU is committed to defending this system against the encroachment of AWAs and the reduction of awards to basic provisions.

In 1993 the AWU amalgamated with the Federation of Industrial, Manufacturing and Engineering Employees (FIMEE). The AWU, once the "union of the bush", is now a general union and has recently recruited successfully in such diverse areas as horse racing and aviation. It is affiliated internationally to IUF, IMF and ICEM.
Publications. The Australian Worker (accessible via website)

16. Blind Workers' Union of Victoria (BWU)
Address. 201 High Street, Prahan VIC 3181
Phone. +61 3 9521 3050
Fax. +61 3 9521 3050

17. Breweries and Bottleyards Employees' Industrial Union of Workers WA (BBEIUW (WA))
Address. PO Box 1455 Canning Vale, WA 6970

Phone. +61 8 9455 4633
Fax. +61 8 9455 4733

18. Civil Air Operations Officers Association of Australia (CAOOAA)
Address. PO Box 394, Port Melbourne, VIC 33207
Phone. +61 3 9646 9277
Fax. +61 3 9646 6799
E-mail. civilair@civilair.asn.au

19. Club Managers' Association Australia (CMAA)
Address. PO Box 845, Auburn, NSW 1835
Phone. +61 2 9643 2300
Fax. +61 2 9643 2400
E-mail. cmaa@cmaa.asn.au

20. Communications, Electrical and Plumbing Union of Australia (CEPU)
Address. PO Box 812, Rockdale, NSW 2216
Phone. +61 2 9597 4499
Fax. +61 2 9597 6354
E-mail. edno@cepu.mpx.com.au
Plumbing Division:
Address. 52 Victoria Street, Carlton South, VIC 3053.
Phone. +61 3 9662 1400
Fax. +61 3 9663 7516

21. Community and Public Sector Union (CPSU)
Address. 191–199 Thomas Street, Haymarket, Sydney, NSW 2000
Phone. +61 2 9334 9200
Fax. +61 2 9334 9250
E-mail. cpsu@cpsu.org
Website. www.cpsu.org
Leadership. Matthew Reynolds (national president); Wendy Caird (national secretary)
Membership. 250,000

22. Construction, Forestry, Mining and Engineering Union (CFMEU)
Address. 361 Kent Street, Sydney, NSW 2000
Phone. +61 2 9290 3699
Fax. +61 2 9299 1685

23. Dental Technicians' Union of New South Wales (DTA)
Address. PO Box A261, Sydney, NSW 2001
Phone. +61 2 9713 7580
Fax. +61 2 9713 1409

24. Finance Sector Union of Australia (FSU)
Address. GPO Box 2829 AA, Melbourne, VIC 3001
Phone. +61 3 9261 5461
Fax. +61 3 9670 2940
E-mail. fsuinfo@fsunion.org.au
Leadership. Anthony J. Beck (national secretary)
Membership. 85,000
History and character. The FSU was amalgamated in July 1991 with the Australian Bank Employees Union, the Australian Insurance Employees Union, the AMP Society Staff Association, the Trustee Companies Officers Association, and the Wool Brokers Staffs Association, and increased its strength further by amalgamating with the Commonwealth Bank Officers Association in March 1994. Affiliated internationally to UNI.

25. Flight Attendants' Association of Australia (FAAA)
Address. 388–390 Sussex Street, Sydney, NSW 2000
Phone. +61 2 9267 2533
Fax. +61 2 9267 9663
E-mail. info@faaa.net

26. Funeral and Allied Industries Union of New South Wales (F&AI)
Address. 4 Goulburn Street, Sydney, NSW 2000
Phone. +61 2 9283 3277
Fax. +61 2 9283 3279

27. Health Services Union of Australia (HSUA)
Address. PO Box 560, Flemington, VIC 3031
Phone. +61 3 9376 8242
Fax. +61 3 9376 8243

28. Independent Education Union of Australia (IEU)
Address. PO Box 1301, South Melbourne, VIC 3205
Phone. +61 3 9254 1830
Fax. +61 3 9254 1835
E-mail. ieu@edunions.labor.net.au
Membership. 44,000
Leadership. Richard Shearman (president), Lynne Rolley (general secretary)

29. Independent Schools Staff Association ACT (ISSA ACT)
Address. PO Box 916, Fyshwick, ACT 2609
Phone. +61 2 6280 7677
Fax. +61 2 6280 5263

30. Liquor, Hospitality and Miscellaneous Workers' Union (LHMU)
Address. 187 Thomas Street, Haymarket, Sydney, NSW 2000
Phone. +61 2 9281 9511
Fax. +61 2 9281 4480
E-mail. lhmu@lhmu.org.au
Website. www.lhmu.org.au
Leadership. Jeff Lawrence (national secretary)
Membership. 150,000. The diverse membership is in four areas: (1) hospitality and leisure (e.g. hotels, motels, restaurants, clubs, casinos, theme parks); (2) contracting and property services (e.g. cleaning, security, contract catering, parking attendants, gardeners); (3) mining and manufacturing (e.g. paints, plastics, chemicals, tanneries, and mining in the Northern Territories)); (4) community and health workers (e.g. children's services, hospital workers, aged care, aboriginal health workers).
Publications. Union News

31. Maritime Union of Australia (MUA)
Address. 365–375 Sussex Street, Sydney, NSW 2000
Phone. +61 2 9267 9134
E-mail. muano@mua.asn.au
Website. www.mua.tcp.net.au
Leadership. John Coombs (national secretary)
Membership. 10,000 dock workers and seafarers. Formed by the amalgamation of the Waterside Workers' Federation of Australia (WWF) and the Seamen's Union of Australia on July 1, 1993

32. Media, Entertainment and Arts Alliance (MEAA)
Address. PO Box 723, Strawberry Hills, NSW 2016
Phone. +61 2 9333 0999

Fax. +61 2 9333 0933
E-mail. mail@meaa.aust.com
Website. www.alliance.org.au
Leadership. Alan Kennedy (federal president); Christopher Warren (federal secretary)
Membership. 25,000

33. Medical Scientists' Association of Victoria (MSAV)

Address. Mail Box 98 Trades Hall, 54 Victoria Street, Carlton South, VIC 3053
Phone. +61 3 9663 8122
Fax. +61 3 9663 8109
E-mail. msav@c031.aone.net.au

34. Musicians' Union of Australia (MUA (Music))

Address. PO Box 360, Strawberry Hills, NSW 2012
Phone. +61 2 9690 0866
Fax. +61 2 9690 0844

35. National Tertiary Education Union (NTEU)

Address. PO Box 1323, South Melbourne, VIC 3205
Phone. +61 3 9254 1910
Fax. +61 3 9254 1915
E-mail. nteunat@nteu.org.au
Website. www.nteu.org.au
Leadership. Carolyn Allport (president); Grahame McCulloch (general secretary)
Membership. 25,000

36. National Union of Workers (NUW)

Address. 552 Victoria Street, North Melbourne, VIC 3051
Phone. +61 3 9287 1850
Fax. +61 9287 1818
E-mail. nuw@c031.aone.net.au

37. New South Wales Nurses' Association (NSWNA)

Address. 43 Australia Street, Camperdown, NSW 2050
E-mail. gensec@nswnurses.asn.au
Website. www.nswnurses.asn.au

38. Police Federation of Australia and New Zealand (PFANZ)

Address. 157 Liverpool Street, Sydney, NSW 2000
Phone. +61 2 9283 5299
Fax. +61 2 9283 5105

39. Public Transport Union (RBTU)

Address. 428 Upper Edward Street, Brisbane 4000
Phone. +61 7 3831 8350
Fax. +61 7 3832 5335

40. Rail, Tram and Bus Union (RTBU)

Address. 83–89 Renwick Street, Redfern, NSW 2016
Phone. +61 2 9310 3966
Fax. +61 2 9319 2096
E-mail. publictu@magna.com.au

41. Salaried Pharmacists' Association of Western Australia (SPA of WA)

Address. PO Box 8204 Perth Business Centre, Perth, WA 6000
Phone. +61 8 9328 5155

Fax. +61 8 9328 9107

42. Shop, Distributive and Allied Employees' Association (SDA)

Address. 53 Queen Street, Melbourne, VIC 2000
Phone. +61 3 9629 2299
Fax. +61 9629 2646
E-mail. sdanat@c031.aone.net.au

43. Textile, Clothing and Footwear Union of Australia (TCFUA)

Address. 28 Anglo Road, Campsie 2194
Phone. +61 2 9789 4188
Fax. +61 2 9789 6510
E-mail. tcfua@tcfua.org.au

44. Transport Workers' Union of Australia (TWU)

Address. 18–20 Lincoln Square North, Carlton, VIC 3053
Phone. +61 3 9347 0099
Fax. +61 3 9347 2502
E-mail. info@twu-federal.asn.au
Website. www.twu-federal.asn.au
Leadership. John Allan (federal secretary)
Membership. 82,000. Members are in road transport, airlines, oil and gas distribution, armoured vehicles, distribution facilities, air/express freight etc. Affiliated internationally to ITF.

45. Union of Christmas Island Workers (UCIW)

Address. PO Box 84, Christmas Island, Indian Ocean, WA 6798
Phone. +61 8 9164 8471
Fax. +61 8 9164 8470
E-mail. uciw@iocomm.com.au
History and character. Christmas Island is an Australian territory with a population of under 3,000. The UCIW represents most of the work force.

46. United Firefighters' Union of Australia (UFU of A)

Address. PO Box 289, Torrensville, SA 5031
Phone. +61 8 8352 7211
Fax. +61 8 8234 1031
E-mail. ufua@senet.com.au

47. Western Australian Dental Technicians' Union (DTEU)

Address. PO Box 8204, Perth Business Centre, Perth, WA 6001
Phone. +61 8 9328 5155
Fax. +8 9328 9107

48. Western Australian Prison Officers' Union of Workers (WAPOUW)

Address. 63 Railway Parade, Mt. Lawley 6050
Phone. +61 8 9272 3222
Fax. +61 8 9271 2666

49. Woolclassers' Association of Australia

Address. Box 1855, Ballarat Mail Centre, VIC 3354
Phone. +61 3 5333 4011
Fax. +61 3 5333 4012

Austria

Capital: Vienna
Population: 8.13 m. (2000 est.)

1 Political and Economic Background

Austria's republican Constitution was restored in 1945 immediately following the defeat of German forces in World War II, although the country remained under Allied occupation until 1955. Since 1945 the major political parties have been the Social Democrats (SPÖ) and the conservative Austrian People's Party (ÖVP). These have at times governed in coalition with each other, including for most of the period since 1987. In elections in Oct. 1999, the SPÖ won the largest number of seats (65) but a coalition government was subsequently formed in Feb. 2000 by the ÖVP and the right-wing Freedom Movement (DF/FPÖ) of Jörg Haider, which had won 52 seats each. The Federal Chancellor, Wolfgang Schüssel, comes from the ÖVP. Opposition to the xenephobic Freedom Movement's participation in government led all other EU member states to suspend bilateral relations with Austria, which had joined the EU in 1995, for a period of several months in 2000.

Austria has a developed modern market economy and a high standard of living. Most of the workforce is employed in industry and services. It has low inflation (around 1% per annum for most of the 1990s) and at 4.2% unemployment in 1999 was half the EU average. Growth in 1999 was 2.2%. The state sector has been reduced with the privatization of large manufacturing enterprises, but key basic services remain in state hands. Austria joined the single European currency in 1999.

GDP (purchasing power parity) $190.6bn. (1999 est.); GDP per capita (purchasing power parity) $23,400 (1999 est.).

2 Trade Unionism

Austria ratified ILO Convention No.87 (Freedom of Association and Protection of the Right to Organize, 1948) in 1950 and No.98 (Right to Organize and Collective Bargaining, 1949) in 1951.

Organized trade union activity in Austria developed in the second half of the nineteenth century, with legal protection for the formation of trade unions being extended in 1870. The first federation of trade unions (the Provisional Committee of the Austrian Trade Unions) was established in 1893. While many unions were closely associated with the Social Democratic Party, the Christian Social Party from around 1900 also contributed to the development of Christian trade unions. After the civil war of Feb. 1934, the Social Democratic Party and its allied trade unions were dissolved and a United Trade Union was founded, controlled by the Christian groups. This organization was itself dissolved following the Anschluss (German annexation) in 1938, and workers and employers were brought into the German Labour Front. Only three weeks after the capture of Vienna by Soviet troops on April 13, 1945, the Österreichischer Gewerkschaftsbund (ÖGB -the Austrian Federation of Trade Unions) was formed, uniting former members of Christian, Socialist and Communist unions.

The pattern of trade unionism established after 1945 was one of industrial unionism, whereby all manual workers in a plant belong to one union regardless of job demarcation lines. However, blue-collar and white-collar workers are traditionally organized in separate unions, and there are residual formal differences between the two categories of workers embedded in law. There are 13 national trade unions, all of which are affiliated to the ÖGB. Union density has declined somewhat since the early 1980s but still stands at 48%. Many large enterprises were formerly in state ownership, and are highly unionized. The unions are less strong in small and medium-sized enterprises and in private sector services.

The reputation of Austrian trade unions since 1945 has been one of a moderate and disciplined reformism, with the ÖGB cooperating with government in the pursuit of policies of balanced growth. Austria's social partnership system sets the context for management-union relations. The social partnership is a phrase used to depict the informal consensus of employers, unions, agriculture and government surrounding the formulation of economic and social policy.

As part of the system of social partnership a parallel structure of Chambers of Labour exists alongside the unions. The Chambers of Labour (AK), the Chambers of Economy (WK – the equivalent of the Chambers of Labour on the employers' side), the Federation of Austrian Industry, and the ÖGB constitute the main social partners in the Austrian system. Chambers of Labour are established by law and funded by compulsory contributions from the wages and salaries of employees. There is a Chamber of Labour in each of the nine Austrian provinces and an umbrella Federal Chamber of Labour (Bundesarbeitskammer, BAK). The Chambers of Labour are involved in practically every aspect of Austrian daily life, and their main role is to serve the interests of employees at both provincial and federal level. The chambers carry out a wide range of functions including advice on employment, legislation, housing, urban policies, education, transport, health, and the provision of training, cultural activities, statistical and technical information, health and safety, etc. They provide assistance in legal proceedings, dealing with 10,000 cases per annum. All proposals for legislation at local, provincial and federal level must be submitted to the Chambers of Labour for expert appraisal before being considered by the appropriate legislature. In addition, the Chambers of Labour play an important role in nominating representatives on to a wide range of public bodies. While the Chambers' existence is predicated on representing the interests of the whole working population of Austria, they work very closely with the trade unions. The relationship is broadly complementary, with the Chambers structured regionally while the unions are organized sectorally and the Federal Chamber of Labour acts as a "think tank" for the ÖGB. The unions have sole responsibility for collective bargaining. However, as the Chambers provide many member services performed by unions in other countries, this has limited that element of the unions' value to members. The role of the Chambers has been questioned on the political right, and the new ÖVP/FPÖ coalition government has proposed reducing the dues payable to the Chambers, in an effort to reduce their activities.

Elections to the general assemblies of the Chambers of Labour are held every five years and are contested by the political factions. The leadership and administration of the BAK and provincial Chambers of Labour are traditionally dominated by supporters of the Social Democrats (SPÖ). In the most recent elections, in the Spring of 2000, the faction linked to the SPÖ won 57.5% of the vote, while that linked to the conservative ÖVP got 26.2% (but the majority in the western provinces of Vorarlberg and Tirol). The faction allied to the FPÖ got under 10% of the vote. In contrast, in parallel elections to the employers' representative bodies, the Chambers of Economy, the ÖVP remained the leading force, with two-thirds of the vote, while the FPÖ affiliate took 19.6% and the SPÖ under 10%.

More than 95% of private sector employees are covered by collective agreements, which are nearly always negotiated at national sectoral level, between the appropriate ÖGB affiliate and its opposite number employer association. Traditionally the agreements for blue-collar and white-collar workers in the metalworking sector set the pattern for industry as a whole and are the first to be negotiated in each pay round. There are some 400 collective agreements, many of them applying to a narrow occupational field. Collective bargaining agreements are signed by the ÖGB with the employer organizations and are governed by law. When a wage agreement is negotiated between unions and employers it is applied to the whole industry whether the workers are organized or not. By law the right to engage in collective bargaining is reserved to the unions, but in companies with well established works councils agreements may in practice be supplemented by informal secondary negotiations at the company level. In the public sector the unions negotiate with government officials and settlements are legislated for by Parliament.

A paradox of Austrian legislation is that there is no law that explicitly permits strikes, although the right to strike is assumed. In practice strikes are most uncommon, and for two consecutive years in 1998–99 there were no strikes at all. "Staff meetings" are employed as a way of temporarily withdrawing labour as a warning, but industrial peace is prevalent. The last really serious strike wave was in 1965.

3 Trade Union Centre

Österreichischer Gewerkschaftsbund (ÖGB)
Austrian Federation of Trade Unions

Address. Postfach 155, Hohenstaufengasse 10–12, 1010 Vienna

Phone. +43 1 53 444 222

Fax. +43 1 534 44 349

E-mail. oegb@oegb.or.at

Website. www.oegb.or.at (German only)

Leadership. Friedrich (Fritz) Verzetnitsch (president)

Membership. 1,465,164

History and character. The ÖGB was formed in Vienna in 1945 as a federation of 16 occupational unions, eight regional organizations and three fractions (socialist, communist and Popular Party, the last becoming the Christian fraction in 1951). It played an active role in the post-war emergence of Austria as a democratic, neutral nation. It has emphasized policies of cooperation with government to achieve orderly growth. In the 1930s Austria experienced civil war as a result of the conflict between communism, socialism and fascism and the ÖGB has adopted a non-partisan position. However, the major political forces (Christian Democrats, Social Democrats and, formerly, the Communists) have been given a formal position as "fractions" within its structure and are represented on the National Board (Bundesvorstand), as are members of other minority groups. Fractions similarly exist within the member unions. While the ÖGB as a whole is affiliated to the ICFTU the minority Christian fraction has a parallel affiliation to the WCL. The Social Democrats have traditionally been the predominant voice within the ÖGB and many union officials have sat in Parliament for the Social Democrats. However, the pluralist nature of the federation has been reflected in its cautious approach to the inclusion of Haider's Freedom Party in government since Feb. 2000, recognizing that Haider's populist platform has some supporters within the unions. The ÖGB was critical of the diplomatic boycott mounted against Austria in 2000 by other EU member states.

The ÖGB has, however, opposed the policies of the new coalition at the domestic level, on issues such as pension and welfare reform. On June 28, 2000, it organized a "day of action" against government plans on these issues and there were brief work stoppages on the railways. Since the 1999 elections the unions have been under increased pressure to concede more deregulation of working practices. Other issues for the ÖGB include the call (opposed by the employers) for harmonization of the legal status of blue-collar and white-collar employees (residual differences lying in the areas of rules concerning dismissal and sick leave payment). It is campaigning for the 35-hour week (which it prefers to see won through collective bargaining rather than by law); average normal working hours under collective agreements are 38.5. The pending enlargement of the EU by admitting states from former Eastern Europe is a sensitive issue in Austria and the ÖGB argues that the creation of European wide norms to prevent "social dumping" by countries with lower wage and social costs must be an essential element of such enlargement. It wishes to see the development of European wide collective bargaining.

Total ÖGB membership peaked at 1.67 million in 1981 and has declined only slowly in the subsequent two decades, to the 1999 level of 1.46 million. The membership is 68% male, a proportion that has remained little changed for the last two decades. Although not affected by the sharp declines that have affected trade unions in some other countries, the ÖGB is seeking to build union membership in under-represented sectors, such as part-time and "non-standard" working and in services.

The highest forum is the quadrennial national congress (held most recently in Oct. 1999), the delegates to which are elected by the members of the national unions affiliated to the federation in accordance with their membership strength. Between congresses the highest policy-making body is the Bundesvorstand, comprising the presidium, delegates of the unions and representatives of minority groups. Day-to-day work is done by the presidium, led by the president. There is also an audit commission elected by the national congress to monitor the financial activities of the ÖGB and adherence to congress resolutions. There are provincial and district offices throughout the country.

As a voluntary occupational association the ÖGB is financed primarily by its membership. It concludes collective bargaining agreements (its affiliated unions being empowered only to negotiate such agreements), represents the interests of its membership in the legislative sphere, and offers welfare and social insurance programmes and occupational training.

The 1995 congress decided on a plan to reduce the Austrian unions to three super-unions, for manufacturing, services and the public sector. However, little has resulted from this. Following the merger of the Metal, Miners and Energy Workers' union with the Textile, Garment and Leather Workers' union, to form Gewerkschaft Metall-Textil (Austria's biggest blue-collar union) in June 2000, there are 13 member unions. Metall-Textil and the Commercial, Clerical and Technical Employees, with about 300,000 members each, are the largest unions. The structure in practice has been fairly stable, with the last previous merger being in 1992, when the Agriculture and Forestry Workers merged with the Food, Beverage and Tobacco Workers.

Publications. Solidarität; Arbeit und Wirtschaft; Hallo International affiliatons. ICFTU, ETUC, TUAC

Christian Democratic Fraction (FCG- ÖGB)
Address. Hohenstaufengasse 10–12, Vienna 1010

Phone. +43 1 53444 210

E-mail. j.kastner@fcg.at (press office)

Website. www.fcg.at (German only)

Leadership. Fritz Neugebauer (president)

History and character. The Christian fraction of the ÖGB was formed in 1951, replacing the Popular Party fraction, which had been formed in 1945. It has fractions within each of the member unions. It is non-confessional and independent of political parties, although many officials have links with the Christian Democratic ÖVP. It is separately affiliated to the WCL.

Affiliated unions.
1. Gewerkschaft Bau-Holz (Construction and Woodworkers)
Address. Ebendorferstrasse 7. 1010 Vienna
Phone. +43 1 401 47 0
Fax. +43 1 401 47 258
E-mail. bau.holz@gbh.oegb.or.at
Website. www.oegb.or.at/gbh (German only)
Leadership. Johann Driemer (president)
Membership. 161,812

2. Gewerkschaft der Chemiearbeiter (Chemical Workers)
Address. Stumpergasse 60, 1060 Vienna
Phone. +43 1 577 15 01
Fax. +43 1 597 21 01 23
Website. www.oegb.or.at/chemie (German only)
Leadership. Wilhelm Beck (president)

3. Gewerkschaft Druck und Papier (DUP, Printing and Paper Trade Workers)
Address. Seidengasse 15–17, 1072 Vienna
Phone. +43 1 523 82 31
Fax. +43 523 82 31 28
Website. www.dup.or.at (German only)

4. Gewerkschaft der Eisenbahner (GDE, Railway Workers)
Address. Margaretenstrasse 166, 1050 Vienna
Phone. +43 1 546 41 511
Fax. +43 1 546 41 513
E-mail. zentralsekretaer@gde.oegb.or.at
Website. www.oegb.at/gde (German only)
Leadership. Wilhelm Haberzettl (president)
Publication. Der Eisenbahner

5. Gewerkschaft der Gemeindebedriensteten (GDG, Municipal Employees)
Address. Maria-Theresien Strasse 11, 1090 Vienna
Phone. +43 1 313 16 8300
E-mail. gdg@gdg.oegb.or.at
Website. www.oegb.or.at/gdg (German only)
Leadership. Günter Weninger (president)

6. Gewerkschaft Handel, Transport, Verkehr (HTV, Workers in Commerce and Transport)
Address. Teinfaltstrasse 7, 1010 Vienna
Phone. +43 1 534 54
Fax. +43 1 534 54 325
E-mail. htv@htv.oegb.or.at
Website. www.oegb.or.at/gewerkschaften/htv (German only)
Leadership. Peter Schneider

7. Gewerkschaft Hotel, Gastgewerbe, Personlicher Dienst (HGPD, Hotel, Restaurant and Personal Services)
Address. Hohenstaufengasse 10, 1013 Vienna
Phone. +43 1 534 44 501
Fax. +43 1 534 44 505
E-mail. hgpd@hgpd.oegb.or.at
Website. www.oegb.or.at/gewerkschaften/hgpd (German only)
Leadership. Rudolf Kaske (president)
Membership. 52,280

8. Gewerkschaft Kunst, Medien, Freie Berufe (KMFB, Artists, Media and Freelance Workers)
Address. Maria Theresien-Strasse 11, A-1090 Vienna
Phone. +43 1 31316 83800
Fax. +43 1 313 16 7700
E-mail. t.linzbauer@magnet.at
Website. www.oegb.or.at/gewerkschaften/kmfb (German only)
Leadership. Thomas Linzbauer (president)
Membership. 16,000
Publications. Dabei

9. Gewerkschaft Agrar, Nahrung, Genuss (ANG, Agricultural, Food, Beverage and Tobacco Workers)
Address. Albertgasse 35, 1081 Vienna
Phone. +43 1 401 49
Fax. +43 1 40 49 20
E-mail. ang@ang.oegb.or.at
Website. www.oegb.or.at/gewerkschaften/ang (German only)

10. Gewerkschaft Metall-Textil (Metalworkers and Textiles)
Address. Plösslgasse 15, 1040 Vienna
Phone. +43 1 501 46 0
Fax. +43 1 50146 13300
Website. www.oegb.or.at.gmbe (German only)
Leadership. Rudolf Nürnberger (president)
Membership. 300,000
History and character. Metall-Textil was formed in June 2000 by the merger of Metall-Bergbau-Energie (Metalworkers, Mining and Energy) with Textil-Bekleidung-Leder (Textiles, Garment and Leatherworkers).

11. Gewerkschaft Öffentlicher Dienst (GÖD, Public Employees)
Address. Teinfaltstrasse 7, 1010 Vienna
Phone. +43 1 53454 0
E-mail. goed@goed.or.at
Website. www.oegb.or.at/gewerkschaften/goed (German only)
Leadership. Fritz Neugebauer (president)
Membership. 230,000
Publication. GÖD Magazin

12. Gewerkschaft der Post und Fernmeldebediensteten (Postal and Telegraph Workers)
Address. Biberstrasse 5, PF 343, 1010 Vienna
Phone. +43 1 512 55 11
Fax +43 1 512 55 11/52
E-mail. gpf@gpf.oegb.or.at
Leadership. Hans-Georg Dörfler (president), Rudolf Randus (national secretary)
Membership. 78,436
Publication. Post- u. Telegraphie

13. Gewerkschaft der Privatangestellten (GPA, Commercial, Clerical and Technical Employees)
Address. Deutschmeisterplatz 2, A-1013 Vienna.
Phone. +43 1 313 930
Fax. +43) 1 313 93 566
E-mail. gpa@gpa.at (German only)
Website. www.gpa.at
Leadership. Hans Sallmutter (president)
Membership. 300,000
History and character. This is Austria's biggest white-collar union, covering all private sector white-collar employees.
Publications. Kompetenz

Azerbaijan

Capital: Baku
Population: 7.75 m. (2000 est.)

1 Political and Economic Background

The Azerbaijan Republic declared independence from the USSR in 1991. The government is formed by a coalition led by the New Azerbaijan party of the President, Heydar Aliyev, a former KGB general who assumed power amid civil strife in 1993. His re-election in 1998 was marked by ballot-rigging. Azerbaijan's political progress since independence has been held back by a still unresolved territorial conflict with Armenia over Nagorno-Karabakh (although a cease fire since 1994 has generally held) and bitter political factionalism.

Azerbaijan is a producer of oil, cotton and natural gas. It has major oil reserves which remain to be properly exploited. The private sector comprises mainly small-scale enterprises, and most employees in the formal sector work for larger enterprises, which remain in state hands. However, as a condition of further IMF credits, plans to begin privatization of large enterprises were announced in Aug. 2000. Output remains far below

Soviet levels and corruption and patronage are considered major obstacles to economic progress.

GDP (purchasing power parity) $14bn. (1999 est.); GDP per capita (purchasing power parity) $1,770 (1999 est.).

2 Trade Unionism

The 1994 Trade Union Act provides for the right to form unions and for these to bargain collectively. However, trade unions have remained closely controlled by the government. Azerbaijan ratified ILO Conventions No. 87 (Freedom of Association and Protection of the Right to Organize, 1948) and No. 98 (Right to Organize and Collective Bargaining, 1949) in 1992. Unions are prohibited from engaging in political activity. A 1996 law provides for collective bargaining in state owned enterprises but this has not developed. There is a right to strike but the penal code effectively bans strikes in the public sector.

3 Trade Union Centre

Azerbaijan Trade Union Confederation

Address. 3 Youth Square, Baku

Phone. +994 12 92 66 59

Fax.. +994 12 92 72 68

E-mail. ahik@azern.com

History and character. This organizes nearly all employees in the formal economy. The US State Department Human Rights report for 1999 characterized it as "government-run", noting that the "overwhelming majority of labour unions still operate as they did under the Soviet system and remain tightly linked to the government". However, in Nov. 2000 the ICFTU announced it had accepted the Confederation into affiliation.

International affiliation. ICFTU

Bahamas

Capital: Nassau
Population: 295,000 (2000 est.)

1 Political and Economic Background

The Bahamas became independent from the United Kingdom in 1973. From 1967 until 1992, Sir Lynden Pindling's populist Progressive Liberal Party (PLP) formed the government, deriving its main support from the black community. The 1992 general election ended the PLP's run of five consecutive victories and put in power the conservative Free National Movement (FNM) with Hubert Ingraham as Prime Minister. The FNM was re-elected at the most recent elections in 1997.

Tourism is the mainstay of the economy, employing 40 per cent of the workforce and generating 60 per cent of GDP. There is also offshore banking and finance. Industry and agriculture are relatively undeveloped. Despite some unemployment (around 8 per cent in 1999), the general standard of living is one of the highest in the Caribbean. There is relatively little difference in economic approach between the FNM and PLP.

GDP (purchasing power parity) $5.58bn. (1998 est.); GDP per capita (purchasing power parity) $20,000 (1998 est.).

2 Trade Unionism

Trade unions developed after World War II. The first union centre was the Bahamas Federation of Labour, founded in 1942, but this ceased to function as a federation in 1969. The principal trade union centre is now known as the Commonwealth of the Bahamas Trade Union Congress. The Bahamas ratified ILO Convention No.98 (Right to Organize and Collective Bargaining, 1949) in 1976. It has not ratified Convention No.87 (Freedom of Association and Protection of the Right to Organize, 1948) but under domestic law all private sector and most public sector workers (with the exception of police, defence, fire brigade and prison officers) may join unions. About one-quarter of the work force is unionized and the hotel sector is highly organized.

Collective bargaining is widely practiced. Strikes must be approved by a majority vote of the work force, supervised by the Department of Labour. In 1996, with union support, the Industrial Relations Act was amended to set up an Industrial Tribunal. Disputes may be referred to this for a binding decision.

3 Trade Union Centres

Commonwealth of the Bahamas Trade Union Congress (CBTUC)

Address. PO Box CB 10992, Nassau, New Providence

Phone. +1242 394 6301

Fax. +1242 394 7401

E-mail. tuc@bahamas.net.bs

Leadership. Obie Ferguson Jr. (president); Timothy Moore (secretary general)

History and character. The Commonwealth of the Bahamas Trade Union Congress was established in its present form in 1976. In 1996 it played a leading role in discussions leading to adoption of the Industrial Relations (Amendment) Act and the creation of the

Industrial Tribunal. In 1998 it was awarded a medal struck by the government for service to the community.

International affiliations. ICFTU; CTUC

National Congress of Trade Unions

Address. PO Box GT 2887, Nassau

Phone. +1242 356 7459

Fax. +1242 356 7457

Leadership. Kingsley Black (general secretary)

International affiliation. CTUC

Bahrain

Capital: Manama
Population: 634,000 (2000 est.)

1 Political and Economic Background

Bahrain became fully independent in 1971 having previously been a British protected state. It is an hereditary emirate, in which the al-Khalifa family has ruled since the 18th Century. The National Assembly was dissolved in 1975, although an advisory Consultative Council, with government-nominated representatives from different sectors of society, has existed since 1993. The ruling family and dominant elite are Sunni Muslim, and there was unrest in 1994–96 among the Shia Muslim majority. Political parties are prohibited and anti-government activities tightly controlled. More than 1,000 people were reportedly still in detention in 1999 for security-related offences.

Bahrain was the first Arab oil producer but its wells are small. Despite efforts at diversification into light manufacturing and services, its economy still largely depends upon petroleum production and processing, which account for 60% of government revenues and 30% of GDP. The oil sector is government-controlled. A large number of multi-national firms with business in the Gulf have Bahrain as a base. Two-thirds of the workforce is foreign (mainly manual labourers from the Indian sub-continent), though foreigners comprise only a third of the total population. Government policy is to displace as many foreigners as possible with nationals, but this has had little impact in view of the welfare system for nationals and the generally lower wages paid to non-nationals.

GDP (purchasing power parity) $8.6bn. (1999 est.); GDP per capita (purchasing power parity) $13,700 (1999 est.).

2 Trade Unionism

Bahrain has ratified neither ILO Convention No.87 (Freedom of Association and Protection of the Right to Organize, 1948) nor Convention No.98 (Right to Organize and Collective Bargaining, 1949).

Independent trade unionism is not permitted in Bahrain. A system of Joint Labour-Management Committees (JLCs), established by ministerial decree, provides a form of employee representation in larger enterprises. A total of 19 JLCs had been set up by 1999. Each JLC is chaired alternately by the management and worker representative and comprises equal numbers of appointed management representatives and elected worker representatives. The Ministry of Interior may exclude worker candidates considered a threat to national security, although this has not happened in recent years. This system covers approximately 70% of the indigenous work force, but a lesser proportion of foreign workers.

The worker representatives on the JLCs elect the 11 members of the General Committee of Bahrain Workers (GCBW), set up in 1983, which oversees and coordinates the work of the JLCs. The GCBW hears complaints from Bahraini and foreign workers and assists in referring these to the Ministry of Labour or the courts. The government and employers are not represented on the GCBW but the Labour Ministry closely supervises the work of the GCBW, controlling its disbursal of funds. Although foreign workers comprise two-thirds of the total in Bahrain, there are no foreign workers on the GCBW committee, although there are a few on JLCs. The GCBW represents workers in the Arab Labour Organization, but has no international trade union affiliations. In 1995 it asked the government to allow trade unions to be set up, but this was refused. According to the ICFTU 1998 report, "The Ministry of Labour has always kept a close eye on the GCBW, and there is evidence that the government has tightened up its surveillance and is tapping the organization's telephone". In addition, some worker representatives on the JLCs and GCBW had been "harassed, arrested and detained for several months without charge or trial, or had their passports taken away by the authorities because of their trade union activities".

While the JLCs provide a forum for the discussion of pay and conditions, there is no collective bargaining. The government generally sets public sector rates administratively and these provide benchmarks for the private sector. There is no formal prohibition on the right to strike, although acts considered detrimental to employee-employer relationships or the economic condition of the country are banned by the 1974 Security Act. There have been no recent major strikes, but occasional walkouts and other protests occur.

The WFTU affiliates a Bahrain Workers' Union (BWU), which the government considers illegal, but this does not appear to have any real presence in Bahrain.

A variety of abuses of foreign workers are reported. Many are present illegally, no longer working for their sponsoring employers and are vulnerable to late or non-payment of wages and in some cases continue to pay fees to their original sponsor. In 1998 38,000 illegal workers participated in a government amnesty whereby they could legalize their status or leave the country without punishment. Domestic servants are not protected by the labour laws.

Bangladesh

Capital: Dhaka
Population: 129.19 m. (2000 est.)

1 Political and Economic Background

Bangladesh (formerly East Pakistan) broke away from Pakistan in 1971, with the assistance of the Indian Army, under the leadership of Sheikh Mujibur Rahman and his Awami (People's) League. Bangladesh's history since then has been characterized by the inability of successive governments to build a democratic consensus, military interventions in government, and periods of virtual paralysis when opposition parties have made effective administration of the country impossible.

At elections in June 1996 the Awami League returned to power for the first time since the assassination of its leader, Sheikh Mujib, in a military coup in 1975. However, the government of the League's leader, Prime Minister Sheikh Hasina Wajed has faced a sustained campaign of strikes and demonstrations led by the major opposition party, the Bangladesh Nationalist Party (BNP), which from mid-1999 boycotted parliament. The BNP had itself previously faced a similar campaign of protests, strikes and boycotts by the Awami League and its allies when in office 1990–96. Prime Minister Hasina is the daughter of Sheikh Mujib, while the leader of the BNP is Begum Khaleda Zia, the widow of Gen. Ziaur Rahman, who had come to power as a result of the overthrow and death of Sheikh Mujib.

Bangladesh's economy is primarily based on subsistence agriculture, with the cultivation of rice the most important activity. Bangladesh is routinely subject to catastrophic cyclones and floods. The country is densely populated and cannot generate jobs for the expanding population: there is high unemployment and underemployment. Some 65 per cent of the workforce are engaged in agriculture and less than 10 per cent in manufacturing and industry, with the jute industry as the largest single industrial source of employment. State-owned enterprises are considered highly inefficient but the government has struggled to implement reforms in the face of entrenched and highly politicized resistance. There is a heavy reliance on international aid.

GDP (purchasing power parity) $187bn. (1999 est.); GDP per capita (purchasing power parity) $1,470 (1999 est.).

2 Trade Unionism

Pakistan ratified ILO Convention No.87 (Freedom of Association and Protection of the Right to Organize, 1948) in 1951 and Convention No.98 (Right to Organize and Collective Bargaining, 1949) in 1952; Bangladesh in turn ratified both Conventions in June 1972. The rights embodied in these conventions have been almost continuously threatened or weakened by contradictory national legislation, and periodic martial law. However, in practice a degree of union activity has persisted throughout the last 50 years regardless of the edicts of military and other governments, often serving as a vehicle for political dissent.

Trade union activity in Bangladesh has a long and at times bloody history, dating back to a revolt by tea plantation workers in 1920 (when the country was part of British-ruled India) and the formation in that year of the All-India Trade Union Congress. The East Pakistan Trade Union Federation was formed following the creation of Pakistan in 1947, and split into five factions shortly before the achievement of independence by Bangladesh in 1971.

There is no accepted national trade union centre, and there has been considerable fluidity and confusion in respect of the status of trade union confederations. The ICFTU-APRO Committee on Affiliation Questions found in April 1987 that there were "17 or more trade union centres, and also 10 labour fronts" linked to political parties, and that trade union leaders often seemed to "shift their loyalties for various considerations". This situation has not changed and there is a proliferation of centres whose status is doubtful. The ICFTU itself says it has no less than five affiliates in Bangladesh: the Bangladesh Jatio Sramik League (BJSL), the Bangladesh Jatiyatabadi Sramik Dal (BJSD), the Jatiya Sramik Party (JSP), the Bangladesh Free Trade Union Congress (BFTUC) and the Jatio Sramik League (JSL). The ICFTU reported in Feb. 2000 that these would henceforth function as one organization, the Bangladesh Confederation of Trade Unions (BCTU), with 900,000 members, although they appear to have retained separate identities. The WCL records one affiliate, the Bangladesh Sanjunkta Sramik Federation (BSSF). The WFTU claims to have five affiliates: the Bangladesh Trade Union Kendra (BTUK), the Jatio Sramik Jote, the Jatio Sramik League, the Ganotantrik Sramik Federation, and the Jato Sramik Federation. Some of the confederations associate for campaigning purposes in the umbrella SKOP.

Union density in Bangladesh is low relative to the size of the total labour force, although unions are strongly entrenched in some parts of the formal economy, especially state-owned enterprises. In 1989 there were 3,905 unions with a total membership of 1,175,878 putting unionization at only 3 per cent. This low rate was not improved by government repression: in 1988–89 the registration of no less than 80 unions was canceled for violations of the Industrial Relations Ordinance. Ten years later, the ICFTU reported that about 1.8 million of the country's 5 million workers in the formal sector belong to unions, out of a total work force of approximately 58 million. The ICFTU noted, however, that "many so-called 'unions' are not controlled by workers but are directed by political factions or criminal elements, a situation that has been tolerated by successive governments. Partly as a result, there are nowadays a total of 23 national trade union centres in Bangladesh and approximately 5,450 trade unions". Only 15% of unions are in any case affiliated to one of the 23 registered centres.

Unions are highly politicized. Virtually all federations are associated with political parties, and it is normal for a party to have a union wing. Political relationships can advance or retard a federation's cause. The relationship between the various unions is often hostile and there are frequently violent clashes between supporters of different unions.

General strikes are not uncommon, and are usually called on political rather than industrial grounds. Strikes indeed were a major component of the opposition parties' resistance to the rule of Khaleda Zia, who was Prime Minister after the overthrow of Ershad in 1990 until elections in 1996. This pattern has continued in the period of Awami League government since 1996. A strike called by Khaleda Zia's Bangladesh Nationalist Party (BNP) and its allies in mid-February 2000 was the 55th national stoppage since 1996 in a campaign aimed at toppling the government of Prime Minister Sheikh Hasina.

There are many restrictions on union activities. Thirty per cent of workers in any workplace must belong to a union before it can be registered, and a union can be wound up if membership falls below this level. Registration of a union is mandatory, but the government may refuse registration on a variety of grounds and such refusals do occur. Unions cannot be registered on a nationwide basis. The ICFTU says that: "would-be unionists are forbidden to engage in many activities prior to registration, and legally are not protected from employer retaliation during this period. Employers usually discourage registration or any union activity, sometimes with violence or working in collaboration with local police. Requests for registration frequently result in the names of union members being given to the employers concerned, who immediately dismiss them. In consequence, trade unions are rare and there is little collective bargaining." A particular problem is reported in the garment sector, where the ICFTU believes, the government has actively worked with employers to prevent unions from being set up.

In the public sector, only those employed on the railways and in posts and telecommunications may legally form unions. Teachers, nurses, supervisory staff, and workers in export processing zones may not form unions, and although unregistered unions exist they cannot legally bargain collectively. The Registrar of Trade Unions has wide powers to investigate the internal affairs of unions and cancel registrations.

Under the 1980 Bangladesh Export Processing Zones Authority Act, workers in the zones, where 90,000 are employed (90% of them women), do not have the protection of the labour laws and trade unions do not exist. The Government in 1992 said it would end restrictions on the formation of unions in the zones by 1997, and apply the labour law in full by 2000, but this has not happened.

The support of 75% of the workforce is needed to make a strike legal. Workers in broadly defined essential services are prohibited from striking. Strikes lasting more than 30 days may be banned by the government and referred to the labour court for adjudication. Special Powers legislation enables the authorities to detain union activists without charge and under a Public Safety

Act effective Feb. 15, 2000, jail terms of up to 14 years' hard labour may be imposed for crimes including obstruction and damaging property during strike action.

In the public sector, wages and conditions are generally set by government-appointed commissions. In the private sector organized collective bargaining is uncommon. There is a Labour Court but according to the ICFTU it has a backlog of cases and "there are indications that many of its decisions have been the result of corrupt intervention by employers". Bangladesh has been regularly criticized by the ILO for non-observance of the conventions. In Feb. 1998 the government and the union umbrella SKOP signed an agreement that included a commitment to implementation of the conventions.

3 Trade Union Centres

Bangladesh Free Trade Union Congress (BFTUC)

Address. Section 6, Block A, Lane 1, House 19, Mirpur, Dhaka-1216

Phone. +880 2 801 7001

Fax. +880 2 801 5919

E-mail. bftuc@dhaka.agni.com

Leadership. M.S. Alom Mendu Mia (president); Mamunur Rashid Chowdhury (general secretary); A.R. Chowdhury Repon (international secretary)

Membership. 175,000

History and character. The BFTUC was established in 1983 by national unions and industrial federations that believed in the concept of free, independent, non-partisan and democratic trade unionism. It continues to emphasize those values. The BFTUC has 35 affiliated national industrial federations and unions.

The BFTUC describes its objectives as including providing support to the formation of unions among unorganized workers, advancing women's equality, providing education, training and welfare programmes, and offering self-employment training and income generating and cooperative activities for unemployed workers and BFTUC members.

The BFTUC has been campaigning to organize women in the informal sector and has 55,000 women members. Its Workers' Cooperative programme and self-employment training programme, started in 1998, provide an opportunity for unemployed members and women to be self-reliant with BFTUC assistance. The BFTUC child labour elimination programme gives the opportunity to 200 children per year working in hazardous occupations to receive non-formal education and training instead of working.

Publications. Naybarta (weekly)

International affiliation. ICFTU

Bangladesh Jatio Sramik League (BJSL)

Address. GPO Box 2730, Dhaka

Phone. +880 2 8613470

History and character. The Bangladesh Jatio Sramik League was founded in 1969, its first conference being opened by Sheikh Mujibur Rahman. It played an active role in the 1971 war for independence, training 40,000 Sramik League fighters. In 1974 the government declared a state of emergency, banning strikes and restricting trade union activities. In 1975 the rival centres – Bangladesh Trade Union Kendra (BTUK) and the Bangladesh Sanjukta Sramik Federation (BSSF) – were dissolved by the government of Sheikh Mujibur. The BJSL became the only recognized trade union centre in the country (and the Bangladesh Krishak Sramik Awami League became the only legal political party); many thousands of trade unionists belonging to anti-government groups were imprisoned. In 1975 a new government dissolved all national trade union centres, although grass-roots trade unionism continued. After 1978, a breakaway group from the BJSL formed an organization affiliated to the WFTU, but the main body affirms its belief in a free and democratic trade union movement.

In 1999, ten BJSL members, including its president Nashu Miah, were arrested in connection with a dispute over nonpayment of wages at a jute mill. They remained in prison for four months until the courts ordered their release.

International affiliation. ICFTU

Bangladesh Sanjunkta Sramic Federation (BSSF)

Address. 23/2 Topkhana Road (Ground Floor), Dhaka 1000

Phone. +880 2 25 1819

Fax. +880 2 81 6152

E-mail. bssf@citechno.net

Leadership. Mukhlesur Rahman (president)

International affiliation. WCL

Barbados

Capital: Bridgetown
Population: 275,000 (2000 est.)

1 Political and Economic Background

Barbados gained independence from the United Kingdom in 1966. The Barbados Labour Party defeated the governing Democratic Labour Party (DLP) in elections in 1994, and in Jan. 1999 was re-elected with a large majority in Parliament. Owen Arthur has been Prime Minister since 1994.

75% of the labour force are in the services sector, including tourism and offshore finance. There is also some light manufacturing and the agricultural sector is traditionally based on sugar cane cultivation, although agriculture only employs 10% of the workforce and generates 6% of GDP. Under rigorous IMF-backed austerity measures unemployment rose to one-quarter of the workforce in the early 1990s but fell to 12% by 1998. The government has carried out a programme of privatizing state-owned enterprises.

GDP (purchasing power parity) $2.9bn. (1998 est.); GDP per capita (purchasing power parity) $11,200 (1998 est.).

2 Trade Unionism

Following riots in 1937, the British government in 1939 passed legislation, the Trades Disputes (Arbitration and Equity) Act, legalizing the formation of trade unions. Barbados ratified ILO Convention No.87 (Freedom of Association and Protection of the Right to Organize, 1948) and Convention No.98 (Right to Organize and Collective Bargaining, 1949) in 1967.

About 30 per cent of the work force are organized. The Barbados Workers' Union (BWU) includes in membership a majority of the country's trade unionists. A significant union outside the BWU is the National Union of Public Workers (NUPW), the largest public service union.

While there is no law on recognition for collective bargaining purposes, custom and practice has been for employers to give recognition when 50 per cent of employees are in a union. In the late 1990s, however, the BWU reported that some foreign-owned companies were breaking this custom. This led to strikes in 1998 against six foreign-owned companies; in five cases the companies ultimately said they would recognize the union, while in a sixth, the company said it would relocate to Trinidad and Tobago.

The government meets the social partners in the National Economic Council and other tripartite bodies.

The influence of trade unions is reflected in the fact that in a 1997 poll for Barbados's "10 national heroes", five came from the trade union movement. These included Grantley Adams, first president of the BWU and later Prime Minister, Sir Hugh Springer, first BWU general secretary and later Governor, and Sir Frank Walcott, general secretary of the BWU from 1948-91.

3 Trade Union Centre

Barbados Workers' Union (BWU)

Address. Solidarity House, Harmony Hall, PO Box 172, St. Michael, Bridgetown

Phone. +1246 426 3492

Fax. +1246 436 6496

E-mail. bwu@caribsurf.com

Website. www.bwu-bb.org

Leadership. David Giles (president general); LeRoy Trotman (general secretary).

Membership. 25,000

History and character. The BWU, a general union, was registered in Oct. 1941, and was a direct descendant of the Barbados Progressive League formed after the 1937 disturbances. In its early years it recruited mainly from among ships' carpenters, foundry and port workers and sugar factory employees, but it absorbed a clerks' union in the 1950s and thereafter developed a significant white-collar element. Frank L. Walcott became general secretary in 1948 and held this post until 1991.

The BWU from the first participated actively in politics, its first president being Grantley Adams, the founder of the Barbados Labour Party (in 1938) and Prime Minister of Barbados from 1954–58 and of the short-lived West Indies Federation from 1958–62, while the first BWU general secretary was Sir Hugh Springer, later the Governor General of Barbados.

A split developed in the early 1960s when the union leadership broke with the Barbados Labour Party and transferred support to the more left-wing Democratic Labour Party, led by Errol Barrow (which took power in 1961 and held it continuously until 1976). Grantley Adams led a breakaway group called the Barbados Progressive Union of Workers in 1963 (although this soon folded). The BWU was recognized as the bargaining agent for a wide range of occupations in 1966.

The BWU runs a labour college (opened in 1974), which receives a government subsidy and provides training in industrial relations and union affairs, and there is also an associated BWU Cooperative Credit Union.

There are no affiliated unions. The BWU recruits members in all occupational fields, and negotiates directly with companies on behalf of the different sectors of its membership. A principal issue for the BWU currently is that of contract work, where workers who are in effect employees are put on individual contracts.

LeRoy Trotman, general secretary since 1991, is a former president of the ICFTU.

Publication. The Unionist

International affiliations. The BWU is affiliated to several of the international trade secretariats (UNI; IFBWW; IUF; ITF) and the Caribbean Congress of Labour (CCL, which has its headquarters in Barbados). It says it has "close fraternal links" with the ICFTU and the CTUC (the ICFTU lists it as in affiliation, as does the CTUC).

4 Other Trade Union Organization

National Union of Public Workers (NUPW)

Address. PO Box 174, Dalkeith House, Dalkeith Road, St. Michael, Bridgetown

Phone. +1246 426 1764

Fax. +1246 436 1795

E-mail. nupwbarbados@sunbeach.net

Leadership. Joseph E. Goddard (general secretary)

Membership. 8,000. The NUPW recruits predominantly in the public sector.

History and character. Founded in January 1944 and registered as a Trade Union in 1964; name changed in 1971 from Barbados Civil Service Association (BACSA) to National Union of Public Workers. Its political orientation is broadly social democratic. The union's objective is to ensure the complete organization of all persons employed by the government of Barbados and to bargain effectively on their behalf. The NUPW negotiates collective agreements, represents members in grievance cases, provides certain health benefits and a group medical insurance scheme, and has an educational arm (the Public Workers' Academy). It is affiliated to the CTUC, the Caribbean Congress of Labour and the international trade secretariats UNI and PSI.

Publications. Annual report; newsletter

Belarus

Capital: Minsk
Population: 10.37 m. (2000 est.)

1 Political and Economic Background

Belarus is a former Soviet republic that declared its independence in Aug. 1991. Although an integrated component of the Soviet Union prior to that time it had held a seat at the United Nations since 1945. Since July 1994, when he won the country's first presidential election campaigning on an anti-corruption and anti-privatization ticket, Alexander Lukashenko has presided over an authoritarian regime in which he has consolidated power in his own hands and a number of political opponents have disappeared. He remained in power after July 20, 1999, the date of expiry of his presidential term, under the authority of a constitutional referendum in 1996 whose legality was widely disputed. The Party of Communists of Belarus is the largest party in the legislature. Belarus has retained a closer relationship with Russia than have any of the other former Soviet republics, formally signing a treaty of union in Jan. 2000.

During the early 1990s Belarus experienced industrial

collapse, shortages of consumer goods, and hyper-inflation, and the privatization programme was beset by allegations of corruption. Lukashenko has largely reverted to the old command type economy, re-imposing state controls over prices (leading to shortages) and increased state regulation of the private sector, while subsidizing indebted state enterprises. The majority of workers are employed in the state industrial and agricultural sectors.

GDP (purchasing power parity) $55.2bn. (1999 est.); GDP per capita (purchasing power parity) $5,300 (1999 est.).

2 Trade Unionism

Belarus (as the Belarus Soviet Socialist Republic) ratified ILO Conventions No. 87 (Freedom of Association and Protection of the Right to Organize, 1948) and No. 98 (Right to Organize and Collective Bargaining, 1949) in 1956.

Independent trade unionism emerged in the Belarus Free Trade Union or Free Trade Union of Belarus (SPB, sometimes referred to as the SFB), which was founded in 1991. The Belarus branch of the former Soviet All-Union Central Council of Trade Unions, the official trade union structure, was re-constituted as the Federation of Trade Unions of Belarus (FPB). According to the FPB it represents 4.4 million members (including pensioners) and 92% of the work force is organized. The official unions retain a strong position through their control of areas of social welfare, such as pensions, and dominate centralized bargaining. As with other re-organized Soviet unions it generally accommodated to the new regime, but the decline of living standards has led to increasing tensions and some FPB leaders have said they have been subject to threats by government. In Oct. 1999 the Ministry of Justice refused to register the Belarussian Independent Association of Industrial Trade Unions (BIAITU), comprising three official unions with 340,000 members, that had taken positions critical of the government. The Minsk city authorities subsequently refused to allow a demonstration against the Justice Ministry's ruling.

Under the Constitution all workers, except security and military personnel, may join and form unions of their own choosing, engage in collective bargaining and strike. However, the membership of independent unions is small and activists are subject to considerable harassment and intimidation. Union members have been arrested for activities including distributing literature and holding unauthorized meetings, refused permission to enter work places and forced out of their jobs. Enterprises have refused to recognize and negotiate with the independent unions.

Strikes are prohibited in areas where work stoppages endanger "life and health". An order by the Cabinet of Ministers of March 28, 1995, defined these areas to include transport, radio and television, telecommunications, the petroleum and chemical industries and the food industry. A strike on the Minsk metro in Aug. 1995 led to police raids on the offices of the SPB and the associated Belarussian Congress of Democratic Trade Unions (BKDP). Registration of the SPB (as also the local organization of Minsk metro workers) was suspended by a presidential decree (No. 336) of Aug. 21, 1995 preventing it from functioning; its offices in enterprises were closed, its bank account frozen and payroll deductions to pay union dues ended. The FPB was given the task of participating in drawing up new trade union legislation. In Sept. 1995, SPB officials were reportedly prevented from leaving the country to meet with representatives of the Polish union Solidarity. On Nov.8, 1995, the Constitutional Court ruled that the administrative suspension of the SPB was in breach of ILO Convention No. 87 and national laws. In Dec. 1995 the government told the ILO that as a result of the Court's decision, the SPB had been allowed to resume its activities, but Decree 336 was not revoked and the threat of its implementation was used to harass the union thereafter. In May 1996 a high-level Solidarity delegation was expelled from the country after meeting with SPB repre-

sentatives and SPB leader Gennady Bykov and others were summonsed for holding an illegal gathering when workers met the Solidarity delegation.

In Dec. 1997 the BKDP was registered and the SPB re-registered. The BKDP encompasses four leading independent unions and is reported to have approximately 15,000 members.

Under a decree signed by Lukashenko in Jan. 1999 all trade unions, as well as organizations such as political parties, were subject to compulsory re-registration, with the threat of dissolution for those organizations not approved. In July 1999 Lukashenko signed a decree which sought to move workers to individual rather than collective contacts. The FPB and independent unions joined in staging a demonstration against this decree and falling living standards on Sept. 30, 1999. In 2000 there was extensive interference by the government in the affairs of the unions, including elections, although in Oct. 2000 Prime Minister Vladimir Yermoshin told the FPB congress that it had been a mistake to encourage companies to form "yellow" unions in an effort to split the unions.

3 Trade Union Centres

Belarus Free Trade Union (SPB)

Address. 24 Zakharova Street, Minsk 220030

Phone. +375 17 284 31 82

Fax. +375 17 284 59 94

E-mail. spb@user.unibel.by

Website. www.praca.by (reports both SPB and FPB) activities

Leadership. Gennady Bykov (president)

History and character. Founded in 1991, but its registration was suspended by presidential decree in Aug. 1995 for two years. It has faced continuing harassment and interference by the government since that time including efforts to install pro-government officials in leadership positions in its affiliates.

Federation of Trade Unions of Belarus (FPB)

Fax. + 375 17 210 43 37

Website. www.praca.by (reports both SPB and FPB activities)

Leadership. Vladimir Goncharik (president)

History and Character. The descendant of the Soviet era official unions, the FPB has come into increasing conflict with the Lukashenko government over falling living standards and inferference in union affairs. In Jan. 2001 the Justice Ministry warned the FPB that it was not allowed to put forward its leader, V. Goncharik, as a candidate in the national presidential elections due in 2001.

Belgium

Capital: Brussels
Population: 10.24 m. (2000 est.)

1 Political and Economic Background

Belgium is a constitutional monarchy and a member of the European Union. A division exists between the majority Flemish (Dutch)-speaking population of the north (Flanders) and the (generally poorer) French-speaking south (Wallonia), with Brussels a bilingual island within Flanders; there is a small German-speaking community in the east.

A process of regionalization that started in 1970 and was marked by considerable tension culminated in the adoption of a new federal structure in 1993. Under this Belgium became a federation of three regions, Flanders, Wallonia and Brussels, each with its own government and legislature, and three communities (Flemish, French and German) for educational and cultural purposes. The regions have considerable powers in the social and economic fields.

At federal level the national divisions are reflected in the composition of the legislature with the Flemish and Walloon communities having their separate parties for each ideological stream. The (Flemish) Christian People's Party (CVP) has normally been the strongest single party in recent decades, providing the Prime Minister in coalition governments which have included coalitions with the Liberals in 1981–88, the Socialists and the People's Union (VU) in 1988–91 and the Socialists in 1992–99. Following elections in June 1999, however, the CVP has been in opposition for the first time since 1958. There is a coalition government of six parties, comprising the Flemish and Walloon socialist, liberal and green parties, with the Prime Minister, Guy Verhofstadt coming from the Flemish Liberals (VLD).

Belgium has a generally prosperous economy based on services and a wide range of industries, and Brussels is the leading administrative centre for the institutions of the European Union. However, linguistic division is exacerbated by the fact that the north in general is more prosperous and has a more modern entrepreneurial and technology-based economy. During the 1980s, the old industrial sectors such as coal mining and iron and steel, which were heavily concentrated in Wallonia, suffered a severe decline and this contributed to the atmosphere of crisis that led to the constituional re-basing of the country as a looser federation. Unemployment is a continuing problem and Belgium also has a significantly lower rate of participation in the work force (57%) than neighbours such as the Netherlands (67%) and Germany (62%), let alone the US and Japan (74%). This reflects factors such as early retirement and Belgium's regime of high taxes and generous social provision and the incom-ing Liberal-led government in 1999 introduced measures to reduce employers' social contributions to try to assist job creation.

GDP (purchasing power parity) $243.4bn. (1999 est.); GDP per capita (purchasing power parity) $23,900 (1999 est.).

2 Trade Unionism

Belgium ratified ILO Convention No.87 (Freedom of Association and Protection of the Right to Organize, 1948) in 1951 and Convention No.98 (Right to Organize and Collective Bargaining, 1949) in 1953.

Trade unions in Belgium have a long history, with origins in the guilds of craftsmen that survived through the industrial revolution and provided a basis for the development of nineteenth-century craft unionism. They have traditionally been divided on linguistic, political and religious grounds. The two principal centres (as they have been since the end of World War II) are the Confederation of Christian Unions (CSC/ACV) and the (socialist) General Federation of Belgian Labour (FGTB/ABVV). Reflecting the balance of forces in political life, in Belgium it is the Christian rather than the socialist centre that has traditionally been the larger and the CSC/ACV, which has about 1.5 million members, has long been the WCL's leading affiliate in western Europe. The FGTB/ABVV has a membership of something over one million. For many years these two trade union centres (accounting for about 90 per cent of union members) kept apart, a habit reinforced by their political links (the CSC/ACV with the Christian Democrats, the FGTB with the Socialists) and poor personal relations between their leaders, but relations have improved since the late 1980s. The third significant centre is the General Confederation of Liberal Trade Unions of Belgium (CGSLB/ACLVB), which has 217,000 members.

The relative strength of the main centres has not greatly changed in recent times. A measure of comparative strength is provided by the social elections that took place in enterprises in May 2000 for works councils (conseils d'enterprise, CE), which remain valid for four years. The CSC took 52% of the votes, the FGTB took 33% and the CGSLB 10%, with the balance being made up by the small Confédération Nationale des Cadres (CNC), with 2%, and by independents. Union density has fallen since the early 1980s as a result of a shedding of jobs in heavy industry where the unions were strong, but at 60% union density is the highest in any developed country outside Scandinavia.

The unions' strength is reflected in their role in the process of "concertation" or social and economic partnership, a partnership that in turn reinforces the position of the unions. The foundations of the state-backed system of social partnership were laid during reconstruction after World War II and despite periods of difficulty this has remained well entrenched. The social partners meet in the bilateral National Labour Council (Conseil National du Travail, CNT/Nationaler Arbeitsraad, NA), established in 1952, which has been described by the government as a "social Parliament". The CNT provides advice and recommendations to the government and Parliament on social and employment-related issues. The CNT also provides the central representative organizations of employers and unions with a forum for negotiation of a two-yearly private sector framework bargaining agreement that gives the context for sectoral and plant-level negotiations. Likewise only unions affiliated to trade union centres represented on the CNT can participate in the public sector general bargaining committees.

The ILO Committee of Experts on the Application of Conventions and Recommendations has for many years criticized the preferential status the CNT gives those centres considered "most representative" by the government, to the detriment of independent unions. The criteria used by the government are not formally defined but include representative status (numerical strength and nationwide organization), organizational stability, and the ability to ensure respect for the agreements signed by members. The government also takes into account the fact that as the CNT works on the basis of unanimity it needs to be constructed on a basis that encourages consensus. It remains the case that only the Christian, socialist, and liberal trade union confederations are permitted to participate in the CNT. Representation is not strictly proportional to membership strength: there are 12 seats reserved on the CNT for the unions (the same number as for the employers' organizations), with 6 representatives from the FGTB, five from the CSC, and one from the CGSLB. It cannot be doubted, however, that the present system in use in Belgium has proved satisfactory to the great majority of Belgian trade unions. The unions are generally resistant to concepts of "de-regulating" Belgian society by reducing centralized bargaining and allowing more flexibility relating to specific circumstances.

The unions also participate in other state-sponsored institutions, including (at trade union centre level) the tripartite Central Economic Council (Conseil Central de l'Economie, CCE/CRB), set up in 1948, which has a consultative role on issues relating to the state of the economy as a whole, and the High Council on Preventive Measures and Protection at Work, which deals with health and safety. The unions carry out the role of paying unemployment benefits on behalf of the state.

Strikes are permitted, including in essential services, other than in the case of seamen, the armed forces and magistrates. In 1993 the main centres united to call the first general strike for 58 years in opposition to a government austerity package. Although it did not prevent introduction of the measures, its impact was consider-able -especially in Wallonia. The practice is not to prosecute strikers who fail to observe pre-strike procedures in collective bargaining agreements. Employers have sought to use the civil courts to obtain back-to-work orders but the legal position is ambiguous and courts sometimes say that labour conflicts are not within their jurisdiction.

3 Trade Union Centres

Centrale Générale des Syndicats Libéraux de Belgique (CGSLB)
Algemene Centrale der Liberale Vakbonden (ACLVB)
General Confederation of Liberal Trade Unions of Belgium

Address. Koning Albertlaan 95, B-9000 Gent

Phone. +32 9 222 5751

Fax +32 9 221 0474

E-mail. aclvb@aclvb.be *or* cgslb@cgslb.be

Website. www.aclvb.be (French/Dutch)

Leadership. Guy Haaze (national president)

Membership. 217,435

History and Character. The CGSLB, the smallest of the three Belgian centres, traces its origins back to the nineteenth century and adopted its present name in 1939. Its structure has changed little since that time other than adapting to national decentralization by creating regional organizations in 1989. It has links with the Belgian liberal parties although without political affiliation. It affiliates local and regional unions directly without occupationally based union structure.

The CGSLB is represented on the CNT and CCE. It argues for more flexibility than is provided by the system of two-yearly collective agreements and greater worker participation in the negotiating process.

The CGSLB complains that it has been denied affiliation to ETUC, which has a monopoly in representing union views in some EU bodies, in an "arbitrary fashion". It is instead affiliated to the European Confederation of Independent Trade Unions (CESI).

Publications. *Vrijuit* (Dutch)/*Librement* (French), (monthly)

International affiliations. TUAC; CESI

Confédération des Syndicats Chrétiens (CSC)
Algemeen Christelijk Vakverbond (ACV)
Confederation of Christian Trade Unions

Address. Chaussée de Haacht 579, 1031 Brussels

Phone. +32 2 246 3111

Fax. +32 2 246 3010

E-mail. acv@acv-csc.be

Website. www.acv-csc.be (French/Dutch; English under construction)

Leadership. Luc Cortebeek (president); Josly Piette (secretary general)

Membership. 1.5m.

History and character. The CSC/ACV is the larger of the two main Belgian centres. It is particularly strong in (Dutch-speaking) Flanders where its one million members outnumber those of the FGTB 2:1, whereas the FGTB and CSC have a similar level of support in Wallonia. The CSC is the leading European affiliate of the WCL and Willy Peirens, the CSC's former president (until 1999) was WCL president 1989–97.

The CSC has a long history. In 1886 the Christian Weavers of Ghent established the Ligue Antisocialiste des Ouvriers du Coton, the germ from which the CSC grew, in opposition to the first International developed from 1864 by Karl Marx. Thereafter Christian trade unions grew in a somewhat haphazard way, often in connection with the development of cooperatives, mutual savings banks and workers' improvement and self-help bodies. In Flanders, the model for Christian syndicalism was taken from the Medieval craft guilds. By 1901 there were 62 Christian associations with 11,000 members.

In 1904 the Sécretariat Général des Unions Professionelles Chrétiens de Belgique was formed, and between 1904 and 1908 professional "federations", with nearly 40,000 members, were created covering a wide range of trades and industries. In 1909 the Confédération Nationale des Syndicats Chrétiens et Libres was formed, with separate organizations for Dutch-speaking Flanders and French-speaking Wallonia, as part of the Ligue Démocratique Belge. In 1912 the organizations for Flanders and Wallonia were fused, and the confederation held its first convention autonomously from the Ligue Démocratique Belge. In 1923 the present name was adopted. All normal trade union activity ended after the German occupation of Belgium in 1940, but the CSC office resumed its work on the day Brussels was liberated (Sept. 4, 1944). During the 1970s a greater regional devolution of powers was carried out by the CSC, in parallel with the broader political process whereby increasing regional autonomy was granted to the three regions of Brussels, Flanders and Wallonia. The CSC established regional executives in 1974, and in 1978 special committees for the three regions were established at national headquarters.

The CSC/ACV is built on two pillars, the regional structure of 22 regional federations with 150 local secretariats, and its 17 "centrales professionnelles" (sectoral unions).

During the recession of the early 1980s the CSC called for work-sharing programmes to be adopted, but the employers proved unwilling to follow this lead in any significant way. The unions also faced challenges to the right to strike and exercise union powers, and to social security benefits. In the late 1980s, under the leadership of Willy Peirens, the CSC developed a much closer relationship with the socialist centre, the FGTB.

The CSC has no formal organizational ties to any political party, and since 1945 CSC officials have not taken political office, other than at the minor local level. Officially, the Christian Workers' Movements (MOC/ACW) give political expression to CSC policies; however, the MOC (in Wallonia and Brussels) has since 1972 been a pluralistic movement (with elected candidates belonging to different political parties). On the Flemish side, the ACW looks to the Christian Democratic Christelijke Volkspartij (CVP) for the implementation of its policies. A number of politicians have emerged through the CSC route, among them former CVP prime ministers Wilfred Martens, in office most of the period 1979–92, and his successor Jean-Luc Dehaene (1992–99).

In the late 1990s the main priorities of the CSC/ACV have included defending jobs and social security and campaigning for a fairer tax system.

CSC/ACV has an associated International Institute of Workers' Education.

International affiliations. WCL; ETUC; TUAC

Affiliated unions.

1. Bâtiment et Industrie (Building and Industry)
Address. rue de Trèves 31, 1040 Brussels
Phone. +32 2 285 02 11
Fax. +32 2 230 74 43
E-mail. cctbb@acv-csc.be
Leadership. Jacquy Jackers (president); Raymond Jongen (secretary general)
Membership. 285,000.
History and character. Formed in 1998 from the merger of the former Wood and Building Workers' Union with the union for miscellaneous industries.

2. Métal (Métal-CSC) (Metalworkers)
Address. rue de Heembeeck 127, 1120 Brussels
Phone. +32 2 244 99 11
Fax. +32 2 241 99 00
E-mail. ccmb@cav-csc.be
Leadership. Tony Janssen (president); Marc de Wilde (secretary general)
Membership. 230,000

3. Centrale Chrétienne des Mines, de l'Energie, de la Chimie et du Cuir (CCMECC-CSC) (Mines, Energy, Chemicals and Leather)
Address. Avenue d'Auderghem 26-32, 1040 Brussels
Phone. +32 2 238 73 32
Fax. +32 2 280 03 97
Leadership. Alfons Van Genechten (president); Michel André (secretary general)
Membership. 60,000

4. Central Chrétienne des Travailleurs du Textile et du Vêtement (Textiles and Clothing)
Address. Koning Albertlaan 27, 9000 Gent
Phone. +32 9 222 57 01
Fax. +32 9 220 45 59
E-mail. csctextile@acv-csc.be
Leadership. Jacques Jouret (president)
Membership. 90,595

5. Centrale Chrétienne des Ouvriers du Transport et des Ouvriers Diamantaires (CVD) (Transport and Diamonds)
Phone. +32 3 206 95 00

E-mail. cvd@acv-csc.be
Membership. 34,000

6. Centrale Chrétienne de l'Alimentation et des Services (CCAS, Food and Services)
Address. Rue des Chartreux 70, 1000 Brussels
Phone. +32 2 500 28 99
E-mail. ccvd-ccas@acv-csc.be
Leadership. Eric Delecluyse (president)
Membership. 192,000

7. Centrale Nationale des Employés et Cadres (CNE)
Address. Rue du Page 69-75, 1050 Brussels
Phone. +32 2 538 91 44
Website. www.cne-gnc.be
Membership. Organizes French- and German-speaking salaried staff and managers in the private sector.

8. Landelijke Bedienden Centrale-Nationaal Verbond Kaderpersonneel (LBC/NVK)
Address. Sudermanstraat 5, 2000 Antwerpen
Phone. +32 3 220 8711
Fax. +32 3 231 6664
E-mail. vakbond@lbc-nvk.be
Website. www.lbc-nvk.be
Leadership. Jef de Pauw (president); Jozef Mampuys (general secretary)
Membership. 250,000
Publications. Ons Recht (monthly)

9. Sports (Sporta-as)
Address. Rue de la Loi 121, 1040 Brussels
Phone. +32 2 237 34 64
Fax. +32 2 237 36 00
E-mail. sporta@acv-csc.be
Leadership. Marcel Van Mol (national secretary)

10. Centrale Chrétienne des Communications et de la Culture (SCCC) (Posts, Telecommunications, Railways, Shipping, Radio and TV etc.)
Address. Galerie Agora, rue Marché aux Herbes 105, BP 38/40, 1000 Brussels
Phone. +32 2 549 08 00
Fax. +32 2 512 85 91
E-mail. sccc@acv-csc.be
Leadership. Michel Bovy (president)
Membership. 53,000

11. Centrale Chrétienne des Services Publics (CSC-CCSP) (Public Services)
Address. Avenue d'Auderghem 26, 1040 Brussels
Phone. +32 2 238 72 11
Fax. +32 2 230 45 62
E-mail. ccsp@acv-csc.be
Leadership. Luc Hamelinck (president)
Membership. 125,000

12. Centrale Chrétienne du personnel de l'Enseignement technique (CCPET-CSC) (Technical Education)
Address. Rue de la Victoire 16, 1060 Brussels
Phone. +32 2 542 09 00
Fax. +32 2 542 09 08
E-mail. ccpet-uceo@acv-csc.be
Leadership. Prosper Boulangé (secretary general)
Membership. 8,500

13. Centrale Chrétienne des Professeurs de l'Enseignement moyen et normal libre (CEMNL) (Teachers in Secondary Education and Teacher Training)
Address. Rue de la Victoire 16, 1060 Brussels
Phone. +32 2 238 73 23
Fax. +32 2 238 73 23
E-mail. cemnl@acv-csc.be
Leadership. Willem Miler (president)
Membership. 9,000

14. Fédération des Instituteurs Chrétiens (FIC)
Address. Rue de la Victoire 16, 1060 Brussels
Phone. +32 2 539 00 01
Fax. +32 2 534 13 36
Website. www.fic.be
Leadership. Régis Dohogne (secretary general)
Membership. 16,000

15. Union Chrétienne des membres du Personnel de l'Enseignement officiel (UCEO-CSC)
Address. Rue de la Victoire 16, 1060 Brussels
Phone. +32 2 542 09 00
Fax. +32 2 542 09 08
E-mail. ccpet-uceo@acv-csc.be
Leadership. Prosper Boulangé (secretary general)
Membership. 3,500. Represents French and German speakers.

16. Christelijke Onderwijs Centrale (COC)
Address. Oudergemselaan 26, 1040 Brussels
Phone. +32 2 238 72 68
Fax. +32 2 230 38 83
E-mail. coc@acv-csc.be
Leadership. Hubert Buys (president)
Membership. 40,000

17. Christelijk Onderwijzers Verbond (COV) (Teachers' Union)
Address. Koningstraat 203, 1210 Brussels
Phone. +32 2 227 41 11
Fax. +32 2 219 47 61
E-mail. cov@acv-csc.be
Leadership. Guy Bourdeaud'hui (general president)
Membership. 39,000

Fédération Générale du Travail de Belgique (FGTB)
Algemeen Belgisch Vakverbond (ABVV)
General Federation of Belgian Labour

Address. Rue Haute 42, 1000 Brussels

Phone. +32 2 506 8211

Fax. +32 2 506 8229

E-mail. paul.gruseling@fgtb.be

Website. www.abvv.be (Dutch, French, English, German)

Leadership. Michel Nollet (president); Mia De Vits (secretary general)

Membership. 1,186,638

History and character. The FGTB traces its history back to a Trade Union Committee established by the Belgian Workers' Party (POB) in 1898. It became the Belgian Trade Union Confederation in 1937, and in 1945 took its present name, uniting a number of trade union federations on the basis of a statement of principle declaring its political independence.

Following an Extraordinary Congress of May 1978, the FGTB statutes provided for three inter-regional organizations covering Flanders, Brussels and Wallonia which correspond to the country's regional authorities. The FGTB's core strength is in the French-speaking heavy-industry region of Wallonia, where it has comparable support to the CSC, whereas it is much weaker than the CSC in Dutch-speaking Flanders. It has 21 regional organizations and interregional offices for Flanders, Brussels and Wallonia.

The FGTB emphasizes that it continues to adhere to socialist principles. In practical terms its current concerns include combating unemployment (its top priority); enhancing social dialogue; developing quality employment; lowering working hours; protecting public services and advancing social equality. It is also concerned at the "democratic deficit" in the EU, which it sees as leading to a gulf between people and politicians reflected in the rise of right-wing populist parties. It participates in the National Labour Council (CNT) and the Central Economic Council (CCE). The FGTB complains of efforts to undermine social partnership embodied in the CNT and CCE and that the CCE increasingly focuses on competitiveness to the exclusion of other issues.

There is a wide range of associated research, training, educational and social organizations attached to the FGTB.

Publications. Syndicats; Die Nieuwe Werker. Also makes radio and television programmes.

International affiliations. ICFTU; ETUC; TUAC

Affiliated unions. There are seven sectoral affiliates as follows:

1. Centrale Générale

Address. Rue Haute 26–28, 1000 Brussels
Phone. +32 2 549 0549
Fax. +32 2 514 1691
Membership. 299,232. Represents blue-collar workers in a wide variety of sectors including construction, mining, chemicals, forestry, security, cleaning companies and agriculture. Absorbed the mineworkers' union in 1994.

2. La Centrale du Métal

Address. Rue Jacques Jordaens 17, 1000 Brussels

Phone. +32 2 627 7411
Fax. +32 2 627 7490
Membership. 180,232. Blue-collar workers in metal, electricity, steel making and similar.

3. La Centrale du Textile, Vêtement, Diamant (Textiles, Clothing, Diamonds)

Address. Opvoedingsstraat 143, 9000 Gent
Phone. +32 9 242 86 86
Fax. +32 9 242 86 96
E-mail. abwtkd.fgtbtvd@glo.be
Leadership. Donald Wittevrongel (president)
Membership. 55,000

4. Union Belge des Ouvriers du Transport (UBOT) (Transport)

Address. Paardenmarkt 66, 2000 Antwerp
Phone. +32 3 224 31 11
Fax. +32 3 234 01 49
Membership. 26,796

5. La Centrale de l'Alimentation-Horeca-Services (Food, Hotels, Restaurants, Catering)

Address. rue des Alexiens 18, 1000 Brussels
Phone. +32 2 512 97 00
Fax. +32 2 512 53 68
Membership. 78,745

6. Syndicat des Employés, Techniciens et Cadres de Belgique (SETCa) (White-collar, Technical and Management Staffs)

Address. Rue Haute 42, 1000 Brussels
Phone. +32 2 512 5250
Fax. +32 2 511 0508
Website. www.setca.fgtb.be
Leadership. Christian Roland (president)
Membership. 250,000. Members are white-collar workers, technical staff and managers in the private sector. SETCa has also absorbed the former small Syndicat du Livre, representing white and blue-collar employees in the printing business, press and media.

7. Centrale Générale des Services Publics (Public Services)

Address. Place Fontainas 9–11, 1000 Brussels
Phone. +32 2 508 58 11
Fax. +32 2 508 59 02
Membership. 279,759. Represents all public servants and workers in public enterprises including central, state and local government, public education, cultural institutions, posts and telecoms and public transport.

Belize

Capital: Belmopan
Population: 249,000 (2000 est.)

1 Political and Economic Background

Belize (known until 1973 as British Honduras) became independent in 1981 as a full member of the Commonwealth. In the most recent elections, in Aug. 1998, the centrist People's United Party defeated the conservative United Democratic Party, which had been in government since 1993.

Belize's main economic activities are agriculture, fisheries and forestry, with sugar, citrus products, fisheries products and bananas being major sources of export revenue. However, agricultural output is liable to severe disruption through disease, drought, flooding and hurricanes and its value is subject to commodity price fluctuations, with prices generally depressed in the late 1990s. Clothing (mainly for export) is also an expanding industry, as is tourism.

GDP (purchasing power parity) $740m. (1999 est.); GDP per capita (purchasing power parity) $3,100 (1999 est.).

2 Trade Unionism

Following labour unrest in the 1930s the British authorities legalized trade unionism in 1941, the first registered union being the British Honduras Trade Union (1943). Belize ratified ILO Conventions No.87 (Freedom of Association and Protection of the Right to Organize, 1948) and No.98 (Right to Organize and Collective Bargaining, 1949) in 1983. About 11% of the workforce, including most civil service employees, are in unions. Union activities are free from administrative interference by the government. Unions tend to have alliances to one or other of the main political parties.

Employers are not required to recognize unions for collective bargaining purposes, but bargaining occurs in some sectors. Disputes may be referred to the Labour Commissioner for (non-binding, but usually accepted) guidance.

3 Trade Union Centre

National Trade Union Congress of Belize (NTUCB)
Address. PO Box 2359, Belize City Centre, Belize City
Phone. +501 2 71 596
Fax. +501 2 72 864
E-mail. ntucb@btl.net
Leadership. Eduardo Melendez (president); Antonio González (general secretary)
International affiliations. ICFTU; CTUC

4 Other Trade Union Organization

Christian Workers' Union (CWU)
Address. 83, George & Dean, I Canal Street, PO Box 533, Belize City
Phone. +501 72 150
Leadership. James McFoy (president); Antonio González (secretary general)
History and character. This organization was founded in 1963 and is a small general workers' union.
International affiliations. WCL

Benin

Capital: Porto Novo
Population: 6.40 m. (1999 est.)

1 Political and Economic Background

Benin (named Dahomey until 1975) became a self-governing republic within the French Community in 1958 and gained full independence in 1960. The current President, Mathieu Kérékou, originally came to power in a military coup in 1972, proclaiming the creation of a socialist society with Marxism-Leninism as its revolutionary philosophy and the Benin People's Revolutionary Party (PRPB) as sole legal party.

Following intense social conflict, with students and civil servants prominent, the Party renounced Marxism-Leninism in 1989 and Benin ceased to be a People's Republic. In 1991 multi-party elections were held which resulted in Kérékou being replaced by Nicephore Soglo. With increasing unrest, in 1994 Soglo began to rule by decree, but the 1995 legislative elections returned a majority for parties opposed to him. In 1996 Kérékou was elected president, in elections generally considered fair, but March 1999 legislative elections resulted in a majority for opposition groups led by Soglo's Benin Renaissance Party.

The nationalization-driven economic policies of the 1970s were dismantled from the middle of the 1980s and state owned enterprises such as oil and cement have been privatized. In practice, the majority of domestic trade had remained in the private sector. Agriculture (largely subsistence) represents the dominant factor in Benin's economy. Fewer than 100,000 of the population are categorized as employed (nearly half of these being engaged in the community, social and personal services).

GDP (purchasing power parity) $8.1bn. (1999 est.); GDP per capita (purchasing power parity) $1,300 (1999 est.).

2 Trade Unionism

Benin ratified ILO Convention No.87 (Freedom of Association and Protection of the Right to Organize, 1948) in 1960 and Convention No.98 (Right to Organize and Collective Bargaining, 1949) in 1968.

Several trade union centres, with different international affiliations, existed after independence but in 1974 Kérékou established a single centre, the Union Nationale des Syndicats des Travailleurs (UNSTB). The UNSTB survived under political pluralism but is now rivaled by its fellow ICFTU affiliate the Autonomous Trade Unions Centre (CSA) which is about half its size. 1993 merger talks proved unfruitful but relations between the two centres are generally good. The WCL has an affiliated centre, the CGTB. In early 2000, representatives of the ICFTU and WCL centres, together with two other centres, COSI and CSTB, attended a ceremony to mark the laying of the foundations of a new Workers' House in Cotonou.

Up to 75% of employees in the small formal sector are in unions, with public sector occupations most organized. In practice, unions generally operate freely, although on a small scale. The law prohibits anti-union discrimination and provides for private sector collective bargaining, although pay is set administratively in the public sector. There were strikes in the 1990s by civil servants and other groups affected by IMF-backed structural adjustment programmes, and teachers' strikes in 1999 over pay, conditions and the government's plans for merit-based promotion. A new labour code, drawn up after consultation with the unions and in force from Jan. 1999 was judged generally neutral in impact. There is a tripartite Economic and Social Council, set up in 1994.

3 Trade Union Centres

Central des Syndicats Autonomes du Bénin (CSA)

Address. 1 blvd. St. Michel, Bourse du Travail, 04 BP 1115, Cotonou

Phone. +229 303 182

Fax. +229 300 448

E-mail. csabenin@beninweb.org

Membership. 20,000

History and character: The origins of the CSA lie in concern that the former state-sponsored UNSTB would be unable to establish itself as genuinely independent of political parties. After the establishment of political pluralism there were merger talks between the UNSTB and the CSA and they continue to cooperate over industrial matters. The CSA membership opposed a merger, recalling the role of the UNSTB as sole officially sanctioned centre in the 1970s and 1980s.

International affiliation. ICFTU

Confédération Générale des Travailleurs du Bénin (CGTB)

Address. BP 06-2449 PK 3, Route de Porto-Novo, Cotonou

Phone. +229 33 50 07

Fax. +229 30 44 63

E-mail. cgtbpdd@bow.intnet.bj

Leadership. Pascal D. Todjinou (secretary general)

International affiliation. WCL

Union Nationale des Syndicats des Travailleurs du Bénin (UNSTB)

Address. BP 69, Cotonou

Phone. +229 30 36 13

Fax. +229 30 36 13

Membership. About 40,000

History and character. All pre-existing unions and federations were absorbed into this organization in 1974. The UNSTB became a designated mass organization of the PRPB, and there were no unions outside it. Several federations threatened to secede in 1989 following its failure to back industrial action, notably by civil servants. The following year it declared its intention to become independent of the party and a special assembly dismissed Romain Vilon Ouezo (the general secretary since its inception, a member of the PRPB Politburo and vice-president of the Permanent Committee of the National Assembly).

International affiliation. ICFTU. The UNSTB left the WFTU in 1990.

Bhutan

Capital: Thimphu
Population: 2.0 m. (2000 est.)

1 Political and Economic Background

Bhutan is a monarchy, in which power is shared between the hereditary King, a partly elected National Assembly (whose role was increased in 1998), a Council of Ministers, a Royal Advisory Council, and the Buddhist priesthood. There are no political parties. Some 100,000 ethnic (Hindu) Nepalis are in UNHCR camps in Nepal having fled Bhutan in the face of the "one nation, one people" policy adopted in the late 1980s.

Bhutan's economy is almost entirely dependent upon agriculture (mostly at subsistence level) and forestry, which account for 92 per cent of the active workforce. To complement traditional handicrafts and carpet weaving, a number of industrial estates have been established to encourage small-scale enterprises, but there has been little inward investment. Foreign nationals, especially from Nepal and India, carry out much non-agricultural work, and there is little indigenous skilled labour.

GDP (purchasing power parity) $2.1bn. (1999 est.); GDP per capita (purchasing power parity) $1,060 (1999 est.).

2 Trade Unionism

Bhutan is not a member of the ILO. Trade unionism is not permitted and does not appear to exist.

There is no Ministry of Labour in Bhutan. There is no collective bargaining. Wages, terms and conditions outside those of the Royal Civil Service are fixed by the Government, which requires workers and employers to have a contractual agreement in writing. The structure of wages is monitored.

Bolivia

Capital: La Paz
Population: 8.15 m. (2000 est.)

1 Political and Economic Background

Bolivia claimed independence from Spain in 1925 but then experienced almost continuous political instability, with no less than 189 military coups. Since 1982, however, there has been an elected civilian government although the society remains generally unstable. Following elections in June 1997, a coalition government was formed, with the President being Hugo Banzer Suárez of the National Democratic Action (AND) party.

The historical mainstay of the Bolivian economy is tin, but the majority of the workforce is engaged in subsistence agriculture and the country is one of the least developed and poorest in Latin America. In the 1980s Bolivia experienced hyper-inflation, with inflation in 1985 at 23,000 per cent. A stabilization plan introduced in 1985 returned the economy to relative normality but failed to alleviate poverty. The workforce suffered successive pay freezes under an IMF/World Bank pro-gramme intended to cut the enormous national debt; major enterprises closed down and unemployment reached 25 per cent of the workforce. During the 1990s successive governments have sought to liberalize the economy and many state enterprises have been privatized. Overall living standards remain low, with a poorly diversified economy and widespread under-employment.

GDP (purchasing power parity) $24.2bn. (1999 est.); GDP per capita (purchasing power parity) $3,000 (1999 est.).

2 Trade Unionism

Significant labour organization began early in the twentieth century. The (1921) first congress of Bolivian workers saw violent conflicts between anarchist and Marxist factions. Thereafter the key centre was the Bolivian Workers' Central (Central Obrera Boliviana – COB), strongly influenced by its most powerful industrial affiliate, the mineworkers' union Federación de Sindicatos de Trabajadores Mineros de Bolivia

(FSTMB). The FSTMB was founded in 1944, and in the April 1952 MNR revolution that overthrew military rule, the tin miners served as an armed militia. After this the FSTMB led in building the COB, with Juan Lechín Oquendo (the FSTMB executive secretary from its foundation until 1986) becoming COB executive secretary. Lechín became Minister of Mines in the Estenssoro government, presiding over the nationalization of the tin mining industry as Comibol. After this the FSTMB and the COB played a major part in sustaining MNR rule and in 1960 Lechín was elected Vice-President of Bolivia.

In 1964, however, Lechín was expelled from the MNR for opposing government plans to rationalize the loss-making Comibol by removing the union veto over management decisions, cutting the workforce, and expelling Communists from the FSTMB leadership. The resultant unrest split the MNR, destabilized the government, and opened the way to the 1964 coup. Juan Lechín was deported, precipitating a general strike and several days of heavy fighting between miners and industrial workers and the armed forces in which there were numerous casualties. Further serious disorders occurred in mining areas later the same year, with at least 30 deaths officially reported. In 1967 tin miners in Oruro, Huanini and Siglo Veinte, in sympathy with guerrillas led by Ernesto (Che) Guevara (who was captured and killed in October 1967), proclaimed the region 'a free territory' and 21 miners were killed during the suppression of the insurrection. From 1969 successive civilian and military governments failed to achieve political stability, and militant and at times insurrectionist tactics remained a feature of the COB and the FSTMB, despite the extended periods of exile imposed upon Lechín and other union leaders.

After 1974 individual unions were suppressed and the COB was likewise officially suspended from 1971 to 1978. A new military coup in 1979 was followed by a COB general strike and 200 deaths. After widespread resistance in La Paz and the mining areas to a new coup in 1980, the new regime again banned the COB and all trade union activity. Lechín and Simon Reyes, another leader of the FSTMB, were arrested and exiled.

The COB ban was lifted on the 1982 restoration of civilian rule but the organization rejected an invitation to participate in the government, and vigorously opposed its austerity measures. In 1983 the government granted majority representation on the Comibol board to the FSTMB, but rejected the COB programme. New austerity measures led to a COB general strike; from now on a pattern became established whereby the increasingly enfeebled government announced various austerity measures and then withdrew or sharply modified them in the face of strikes called by the COB.

New austerity measures approved by the IMF led to an estimated 27,000 miners losing their jobs between 1985 and 1988. In protest the COB organized a series of general strikes, to which the government responded with declarations of states of siege and temporary detention or internal exile. In Aug. 1986, some 5,000 miners marched on La Paz in a vain bid to prevent the government closing seven of the 24-state-owned mines and selling nine to miners' cooperatives. It was branded as insurrectionist and broken up by the army 60 km. from the capital.

A mass COB hunger strike of 1988 was estimated to have involved 4,000 workers, especially redundant miners, in protest against government social and economic policies. The President agreed to provide alternative stop-gap employment for unemployed miners.

Through the 1990s the COB sustained continual protests and industrial activity against privatization and other government policies, while in the mines, the FSTMB continued to oppose privatization or the introduction of joint ventures. In Mar. 1996 the COB called an indefinite general strike which was met by the declaration of a state of siege by the government; the two sides reached agreement to end the strikes at the end of April but the state of siege was not lifted until Oct. 1996.

On May 5, 1997, six COB leaders, including the executive secretary Edgar Ramírez, began a hunger strike saying the government refused to negotiate with them over demands for a living wage, and opposition to privatization and private pension funds. The hunger strike was timed to coincide with the run-up to national elections on June 1 and 70 other union leaders joined the hunger strike during May. It was finally called off on May 27 after agreement was reached with the government to set up working parties to examine the COB's demands.

Violence has continued to be a feature of industrial relations. In 1996, nine workers were killed during general strikes, while eight were killed in Dec. 1996 after the police and army intervened in a dispute at gold mines in the south. In Apr. 1998, amid a general strike called by the COB, deaths were reported in particular from the coca-growing region of Chapare, where tensions were exacerbated by government threats to eradicate the coca crop. Imprisonment and internal exile remain punishments meted out to strikers.

Bolivia ratified ILO Convention No.87 (Freedom of Association and Protection of the Right to Organize, 1948) in 1965 and Convention No.98 (Right to Organize and Collective Bargaining, 1949) in 1973, but has been held by the ILO to be substantially in breach of its obligations. Following an ILO visit in 1997 Bolivia said it would make substantial changes to protect workers against anti-union discrimination and end the authorities' powers to dissolve unions, but action was not forthcoming.

The labour code requires government permission to establish a union and that there may be only one union per enterprise. The authorities have extensive powers to supervise unions, which they may dissolve by administrative order. National Labour Court procedures for dealing with discrimination by employers against workers engaged in trade union activities are long drawn-out. Nonetheless, perhaps 30 percent of workers in the formal economy belong to trade unions.

Under the Labour Code, public employees (other than

in health, education and petroleum) are in theory not permitted to join trade unions, but in practice nearly all civilian government workers are organized.

Strikes are formally banned in the public sector. In the private sector workers may strike if 75% of the workforce vote in favour, although compulsory arbitration can be imposed. General and solidarity strikes are illegal. Nonetheless, as seen above, strikes on a large scale are common, and often heavily involve the public sector.

The 1996 Agrarian Reform Law extended national labour law protections to employed rural workers, but enforcement is problematic in this sector. This affects particularly the indigenous people who make up over 50 per cent of the population.

3 Trade Union Centre

Central Obrera Boliviana (COB)
Bolivian Workers' Central (Confederation)

Address. CP6552, Calle Sucre 916, La Paz

Leadership. Milton Gómez (secretary general)

History and character. The COB is the only Bolivian trade union centre. The history of the COB, as that of its principal affiliate, the Federación de Sindicatos de Trabajadores Mineros de Bolivia (FSTMB), is one in which insurrectionism, violent repression and considerable influence on the history of Bolivia, are intertwined (see above).

The COB remains highly politicized and it and its affiliates engage in constant opposition, strikes and demonstrations against various aspects of the government's efforts to implement "neo-liberal" policies. In

recent years its affiliated teachers' and coca growers' unions have shown particular militancy. The government has declared the objective of making Bolivia, one of the major producers of coca and cocaine products, a "zero coca" producer by 2002, but the COB has demanded an end to coca eradication programmes. Overall its influence has declined, however, with the privatization in the 1990s of state enterprises in which it was strongly represented. In the private sector, including privatized state industries, employers increasingly deal directly with their work force where bargaining occurs.

The COB appointed a new leadership in Dec. 1997 after a crisis triggered by the report of an independent commission accusing COB leaders of corruption, leading to the resignation of secretary general Edgar Ramírez.

The COB joined the WFTU in 1988.

International affiliations. WFTU

4 Other Trade Union Organization

Corriente de Renovación Independiente y Solidaridad Laboral (CRISOL)

Address. Final Calle Batallón Colorados No. 104, Casilla 7492, La Paz

Phone. +591 2 372 083

Fax. +591 2 358 898

E-mail. crisolbol@yahoo.com

Leadership. Luis Antezana (executive secretary); Francisco Figueroa (secretary general)

International affiliation. WCL

Bosnia-Herzegovina

Capital: Sarajevo
Population: 3.84 m. (2000 est.)

1 Political and Economic Background

The former Yugoslav republic of Bosnia-Herzegovina declared its independence in March 1992 following a referendum which had been boycotted by most of its Serbian minority, who feared separation from Serbia proper. Although Bosnia-Herzegovina (with a 44% Muslim population) quickly received international recognition as an independent state, a Bosnian Serb

Republic was declared within its territory by ethnic Serbs (31% of the population). The general war that followed also involved a separate conflict with the Croat population (17% of the whole). "Ethnic cleansing", primarily of Muslims, transformed the demographic balance of whole areas, and hundred of thousands fled abroad or to neighbouring former Yugoslav republics in the worst European conflict since World War II. In 1995 intensive military intervention by NATO against Serb forces provided the context for negotiations leading to the Dayton Agreement of Nov. 1995. Under this the integrity of a unified Bosnia-Herzegovina was maintained but the country for many purposes broke into two entities, one controlled by the Serbs (Republika Srpska) and the other by a Muslim–Croat federation. Stability is underpinned by the presence of a NATO-led Stabilization Force and a UN-appointed High Representative has responsibility for the civil implementation of the Agreement. Nationalist parties remain dominant in the two entities.

Bosnia's economic infrastructure was severely damaged by the 1992–95 war and reconstruction continues. Large-scale industrial enterprises have been damaged by the loss of the former Yugoslav market. Unemployment, under-employment and non-payment of wages are major problems; output remains well below pre-war levels and there is a heavy dependence on international aid and remittances from refugees abroad. There is a substantial informal sector.

GDP (purchasing power parity) $6.2bn. (1999 est.); GDP per capita (purchasing power parity) $1,770 (1998 est.).

2 Trade Unionism

Bosnia ratified ILO Conventions No.87 (Freedom of Association and Protection of the Right to Organize, 1948) and No.98 (Right to Organize and Collective Bargaining, 1949) in 1993.

Prior to the collapse of Yugoslavia in 1991–92, Bosnian trade unions were integrated into the overall Yugoslav trade union system and performed a wide range of social and economic functions. Trade union structures collapsed during the 1992–95 war. Since the 1995 Dayton Agreement trade unions have organized separately in the Serbian and Muslim–Croat entities. Croats have some independent organization in areas of the Federation where they are the majority, although they are generally represented by the federation union. There is no national unified labour legislation or legal framework for trade union recognition or collective bargaining.

Trade union activity is constrained by a range of factors. These include widespread unemployment (reported to affect 40% of the work force) and the collapsed state of industry. A 1999 ICFTU report noted that many owners of enterprises held their positions thanks to the ruling party and "woe betide those who protest". There is little collective bargaining. Strikes occur infrequently, mainly over non-payment of wages, and in practice many workers continue working for long periods without pay for lack of any alternative to the jobs they have.

The first post-war trade union demonstration since the war took place on Oct. 25, 1999, attended by a crowd variously estimated as 8,000 and 30,000. It was called by the Trade Union Confederation of Bosnia-Herzegovina and demands included payment of wage arrears, signing of collective agreements, and new labour legislation.

Botswana

Capital: Gaborone
Population: 1.58 m. (2000 est.)

1 Political and Economic Background

Botswana (until 1963 the British High Commission territory of Bechuanaland) became a fully independent member of the Commonwealth with republican status in 1966, and has a largely elected National Assembly together with a House of Chiefs. Politics since independence have been dominated by the Botswana Democratic Party, which again formed the majority in the National Assembly after elections in October 1999.

Diamond mining generated 38 per cent of GDP (and the bulk of government revenues) in 1999, but it and other mining represents only a relatively small source of employment; some 80 percent of the population are engaged in agriculture, mainly subsistence farming and cattle rearing. Export revenues and the strength of the main industries are liable to severe fluctuations, in the case of meat products because of the incidence of drought and of cattle disease, and in the case of mining because of the volatility of the world markets for diamonds and copper.

GDP (purchasing power parity) $5.7bn. (1999 est.); GDP per capita (purchasing power parity), $3,900 (1999 est.).

2 Trade Unionism

Although Botswana did not ratify ILO Conventions No.87 (Freedom of Association and Protection of the Right to Organize, 1948) and No.98 (Right to Organize and Collective Bargaining, 1949) until 1997, trade unions have been legal and active since before independence. Botswana's key statutes were passed in 1969: the Trade Union Act, the Trade Dispute Act, and the Regulation of Wages and Conditions of Employment Act.

The first trade union centre, the Bechuanaland Trade Union Congress, was formed in 1962 but lasted for three years only, constrained by the rural nature of the country's workforce and shallowness of support. A new attempt at a peak organization followed with the 1965 establishment of the Bechuanaland Federation of Labour, which began with four affiliates; by 1970 it had registered 13 affiliates under the legislation of 1969. The Botswana Federation of Trade Unions (BFTU) was formed in 1977 and is now the only trade union centre.

Trade union activity is limited in some sectors. Public servants and teachers may not belong to unions; they may form associations but these cannot negotiate wages. Agricultural and domestic workers are not covered by the Trade Unions Act and cannot belong to trade unions or bargain collectively. Only a small minority of the workforce are in organized industrial employment, and union members are mainly in the mineral sector, and to a lesser degree in railways and banking. The ICFTU has criticized regulations requiring elected union officials to work full-time in the industry the union represents, which it says limits union leaders' professionalism and effectiveness. The Minister of Labour must approve affiliation by unions to international organizations, and amalgamations and federations of unions. Unions are traditionally independent of the government and political parties.

In principle workers can go on strike, but owing to the complexity of pre-strike procedures, there has reportedly never been a legal strike. Collective bargaining may take place where unions have organized 25% of the workforce. There is one export processing zone, which is covered by national labour laws.

3 Trade Union Centre

Botswana Federation of Trade Unions (BFTU)

Address. PO Box 440, Gaborone

Phone. +267 3 352534

Fax. +267 3 352534

E-mail. bftu@info.bw

Leadership. Sandy Monyake (general secretary)

International affiliations. ICFTU; CTUC

Brazil

Capital: Brasilia
Population: 172.86 m. (2000 est.)

1 Political and Economic Background

Brazil is a federal republic. It was under military rule from 1964 to 1985, when a civilian government was formed under President José Sarney, although a process of liberalization had set in earlier in the decade with the staging of multi-party elections in 1982. In 1990 Sarney was succeeded by Fernando Collor de Mello of the National Reconstruction Party, the first Brazilian president to be elected by universal suffrage for 29 years. He had narrowly defeated the candidate of the Workers' Party (PT) Luís Inácio da Silva ("Lula") a leading figure in the trade union movement. Collor was impeached on corruption charges by the Chamber of Deputies in 1992, stripped of office, and replaced by Itamar Franco as interim president. The 1994 elections were comfortably won by Fernando Henrique Cardoso, founder of the Brazilian Social Democrats (PSDB), with 54.3% of the vote; Lula was again runner-up, with 27%. Cardoso was re-elected in Oct. 1998 and governs through a coalition including his own PSDB.

Brazil has a diversified industrial, agricultural and service economy. After rapid expansion in 1964–74 the economy was rocked by the oil price rises of the 1970s. Heavy external borrowing and IMF assistance became necessary, and by the mid-1980s external debt amounted to about US$100bn. Inflation was rampant and reached an annualized rate of 16,000 per cent. Following several crises, a 1988 agreement rescheduled the country's debt. Since that time Brazil has undergone successive national rescue plans aimed at controlling inflation while encouraging growth and privatizing state enterprises, which once accounted for about half industrial output. Most rescue plans have faced intense domestic opposition at the impact on living standards. While inflation fell from its worst levels, by 1993 it was back to close to 2,500 per cent annually. In mid-1994 the Plano Real was introduced and under it inflation dropped to 2% by 1998, and 4.9% in 1999. However, Brazil was severely affected by the knock-on effects of the Asian economic crisis; there was a flight of capital from the country from Aug. 1998, necessitating a $41.5bn. IMF support programme in Nov. 1998. In Jan. 1999 Brazil devalued its currency and declared it free floating, a move which had an adverse impact on its Mercosur trading partners. GDP growth was depressed to under 1% in 1999, although rising again in 2000.

The country is undergoing a process of technological catch-up, driven by forces such as telecoms privatization in 1998, the growth in services, and rising consumer expectations, and there is a gradual opening of its closed, authoritarian and paternalistic government and business structures. Brazil nonetheless remains characterized by extremely unequal distribution of wealth, with extreme affluence contrasting with problems of shanty town development, violent drug-related crime, and street children in the cities and a large class of landless peasants in the countryside. Social spending is reduced by heavy budget commitments to high public sector pensions and debt repayments.

GDP (purchasing power parity) $1.057 trillion (1999 est.); GDP per capita (purchasing power parity) $6,150 (1999 est.).

2 Trade Unionism

Brazil ratified ILO Convention No.98 (Right to Organize and Collective Bargaining, 1949) in 1952, but has not ratified Convention No.87 (Freedom of Association and Protection of the Right to Organize, 1948).

Labour organization in Brazil began in the first decade of the twentieth century. Two general confederations, the Confederación Nacional de Trabajo (CNT) and the communist-led Confederación General del Trabajo (CGT), were formed in the 1920s. Under the government of Getúlio Vargas (1930–45) unions were restructured on corporatist lines, with Mussolini's example in Italy as a model; strikes were prohibited, union structures absorbed into the state, and agricultural workers forbidden to organize. After 1946 greater freedom was allowed and the CGT reorganized, but attempts to create a unified national trade union centre were unsuccessful. Tight government control resumed after the 1964 military coup, with union affairs dominated by pro-government officials exercising authoritarian control. During the 1970s, although nominal rights to free collective bargaining and to strike existed, they were in practice largely negated by active government intervention in union affairs, and most strikes were declared illegal under the national security laws.

National reorganization of the labour movement began in 1981 with the first National Workers' Congress (CONCLAT). This brought together urban and rural workers and all ideological tendencies and reached agreement on the need for a unified national centre. After an initial failure there was success in Aug. 1983 when a CONCLAT attended by 5,000 delegates set up Brazil's first national trade union centre, the CUT.

Conservative and communist-led unions, including the main occupational federations, boycotted its formation, objecting to an arrangement whereby workers could organize to elect their own delegates if their unions refused to participate. These critics claimed that the CONCLAT would over-represent the liberal professions. The 'combatives' however, the main force behind the formation of the CUT, believed they had made sufficient concessions in acceding to participation by unrepresentative existing occupational federations and confederations, and decided to proceed.

The non-participants at the August congress staged their own in November, there creating a rival semi-permanent organization which took the name of the National Coordination of the Working Classes (Coordenação Nacional des Classes Trabalhadores, also known as CONCLAT). This body was officially not described as a trade union centre, but as a deliberative and executive body to prepare the way for the formation of such a centre. In the view of the CUT, this CONCLAT was dominated by accomodationist conservatives (pelegos) and communist machine bosses. Technically both the CUT and the CONCLAT were illegal, Brazilian labour law not permitting the formation of collective organizations of unions representing workers in different occupations, but the government tacitly acquiesced.

Following the return of civilian government prohibitions on national and regional inter-trade organizations were lifted, and in 1985, the CUT and the CONCLAT cooperated for the first time in a general strike. In 1986 CONCLAT was reformed as a permanent organization to be called the Central Geral dos Trabalhadores (CGT). Thereafter the CUT, and to a lesser extent the CGT, adopted a generally confrontational attitude towards successive governments, rejecting efforts to secure a social pact, and staging a succession of general strikes and other protests, which received declining support from their members. In 1991 a third centre, Força Sindical (FS) was created under the leadership of Luis Antônio Medeiros, who called for a "trade unionism that gets results" rather than what was seen as the sterile confrontational policies of the existing centres. The CUT, CGT and FS are today the leading Brazilian centres, and all are now affiliated to the ICFTU.

In the period of military rule there was high profile union resistance to the regime, and heavy handed suppression of their organizations by the state. Restoration of civilian rule was followed by numerous strikes, exacerbated by wage controls and other measures to deal with economic difficulties, which placed the repeal of authoritarian employment legislation in doubt. However, the 1988 constitution provided for the freedom of all workers to form autonomous trade unions and to strike. Labour laws adopted that year were regarded as the most fundamental reform for 40 years, providing for a broad right to strike, indemnity for workers dismissed without justification, the right of workers (including public servants) to form unions, and an end to control of unions by the Ministry of Labour. Since the late 1980s there has been a process of bedding in of new institutions and a general decline of authoritarian and populist tendencies. This has also been reflected in the positions taken by many unions.

Unions are funded by the "imposto sindical" (union tax), a compulsory levy equivalent to a day's pay, payable to the Ministry of Labour. The proceeds are divided between local, provincial and national unions according to their membership, with 20 per cent retained by the Labour Ministry (in theory to provide for unemployment benefits). Under the "unicidade" system only one union is in theory permitted for each occupational category in a given geographical area (although this is widely disregarded in practice). The unicidade is opposed by the unions as a relic of previous state control. In November 1998 the government proposed the abolition of the unicidade and the union tax, but this was not approved by Congress. About 12% of the work force is organized, with the unions main strength being in the Sao Paulo "ABC" industrial zone (the largest industrial area in the Southern hemisphere) and in public service areas. All workers may join unions except those in the police, armed forces and fire services.

The government may cancel collective agreements that are not consistent with its wage policy (although this power is not currently applied), and there are restrictions on collective bargaining for public servants. While all workers have a general right to strike (other than military, police and firemen), abuse of the right to strike is unlawful; such abuse includes not maintaining basic essential services or ignoring a labour court decision to end a strike. The courts have in recent years been less inclined to rule strikes "abusive".

Hundreds of landless rural workers and activists of the landless peasants' movement, the MST, have been killed during land disputes. The most celebrated victim of the gunmen was the leader of the CUT-affiliated Rubbertappers' Union and ecologist Chico Mendes. Chico Mendes had received a United Nations prize for making "an outstanding contribution to the life of our planet" for his work to protect the Amazonian forests from landowner depredation. He was shot dead in December 1988, and his convicted killers subsequently escaped. Occupations of unused land by the MST, and frequently violent evictions by landowners and police, are a continual feature of the Brazilian countryside.

Forced labour and debt bondage still persist in certain regions of Brazil. The government points to the difficulty of detecting such violations and enforcing labour laws in remote regions. The 1988 Brazilian Constitution categorically forbade the normal employment of any citizen under 14 but child labour remains a problem.

3 Trade Union Centres

Confederação Geral dos Trabalhadores (CGT)
General Confederation of Workers

Address. Rua Thomaz Gonzaga 50, 2° andar, Liberdade, Sao Paulo CEP 01506-020

Phone. +55 11 279 6577

Fax. +55 11 279 6452

E-mail. cgt@cgt.org.br

Website. www.cgt.org.br (Portuguese only)

Leadership. Antônio Carlos dos Reis (president); Francisco Canindé Pegado do Nascimento (secretary general)

Membership. 2.2 million

History and character. The CGT was founded on March 23, 1986, at the second national congress of the Clase de Trabajadora de Brasil (CTB), convened by the CONCLAT (see above). The CGT was created to give permanent form to the work of the CONCLAT, and was described as the successor to the previous CGT banned by the military government in 1964. In establishing the new organization, the congress rejected ILO Convention No.87 – adopted by President Dutra in 1948 but never ratified by the Brazilian Senate – which provides for full freedom and autonomy for trade unions, on the ground that "this divides the Brazilian trade union movement", a decision reflecting the basis of the new CGT in machine unionism of both the "yellow" and communist type.

It was resolved at the founding congress that the CGT would be independent and maintain fraternal relations with all three international organizations (i.e. ICFTU, WFTU and WCL). However, reflecting the changed shape of the international trade union movement in the wake of the collapse of Communism, it joined the ICFTU in 1991.

International affiliations. ICFTU

Central Única dos Trabalhadores (CUT)
Unitary Workers' Centre

Address. Rua Caetano Pinto 575, Sao Paulo, SP 03041-000

Phone. +55 11 242 9411

Fax. +55 11 242 9610

E-mail. cap@cut.org.br

Website. www.cut.org.br (Portuguese only)

Leadership. João Antonio Felício (president); Carlos Alberto Grana (secretary general)

Membership. 4,570,000

History and character. The CUT was created at a national workers' congress (CONCLAT) held in Aug. 1983, (i.e. after the return of civilian rule). The congress was boycotted by major conservative and communist-led unions, which subsequently formed their own organization (ultimately becoming the CGT).

Luís Inácio da Silva (Lula) was the leading figure in the creation of the CUT. He had emerged from within the Sao Paulo autêntico independent trade union movement in the late 1970s and gone on to found in 1980 the Workers' Party (Partido dos Trabalhadores, PT) in 1980 as the political voice of the "combative" wing of the labour movement. The PT and CUT developed in alliance in the late 1980s, the PT winning control of some city administrations and Lula running in successive national presidential elections with CUT support in 1990, 1994, and 1998.

The CUT is the most militant of the three centres, reflecting its membership base. The CUT's membership is reportedly split slightly less than one-third manufacturing workers, more than one-third public servants, and one-third farm workers. Its agenda is influenced by the struggle over privatization of public services and the prominence in Brazil of land issues.

In Jan. 1999, in the wake of the financial crisis and currency devaluation, the CUT declared that the "liberal model" of economic liberalization had failed in Brazil and called for a reversal of government policies.

Publication. Informacut

International affiliations. ICFTU

Força Sindical (FS)

Address. Palácio do Trabalhador, Rue Galvão Bueno 780, 13°andar, Sao Paulo SP 01506-000

Phone. +55 11 277 5877

Fax. +55 11 277 5877

E-mail. secgeral@fsindical.org.br

Leadership. Paulo Pereira da Silva (president)

Membership. 2.1 million

History and character. The FS was created in 1991 under the leadership of Luis Antônio Medeiros, formerly a leader within the CGT. Its slogan was "a trade unionism that gets results" and it advocated a new culture of dialogue as a way of moving on from the confrontational policies of the centres (CGT, CUT) created in the aftermath of the return to civilian rule. Two-thirds of its membership are in manufacturing industry. The FS favours a more open market economy, free from Brazil's traditional state corruption and paternalism, and more

equal distribution of wealth. It has generally supported the efforts of the Cardoso government since 1994 to get to grips with Brazil's underlying economic problems, but has criticized the government for lacking a social dimension to its economic reforms. The FS favours worker participation and co-determination. In Oct. 2000 the FS initiated a "40 day march" from Sao Paulo to Brasilia to demand an increase in the minimum wage.

International affiliation. ICFTU

4 Other Trade Union Organizations

Central Autónoma de Trabalhadores (CAT)

Address. Rua Castro Alves, 594, Aclimaçâo, Sao Paulo, SP 0153-2000

Phone. +55 11 277 4555

Fax. +55 11 277 3289

E-mail. cat@uol.com.br

Leadership. Laerte Teixeira Da Costa (president); Francisco Cardoso Filho (secretary general)

International affiliations. WCL

Confederaçâo Brasileira de Trabalhadores Cristâos (CBTC)

Address. Res. Areas Especiales, Lote 09, Caixa Postal 07925, CEP 70 649 970, Cruzeiro Velho, Brasilia D.F.

Phone. +55 61 233 0669

Fax. +55 61 361 8203

Leadership. Antonio Rodrigues da Silva Filho (president)

International affiliations. WCL (extraordinary member)

Brunei

Capital: Bandar Seri Begawan
Population: 336,000 (2000 est.)

1 Political and Economic Background

The Sultanate of Brunei, having been a British protectorate since 1888, was largely self-governing from 1959, and became fully independent in 1984. Since 1962, following an unsuccessful left-wing rebellion, a state of emergency has been in force under which the Sultan has

ruled by decree. Major responsibilities within the Cabinet are held by the Sultan, Sir Hassanal Bolkiah (as Prime Minister), and by other members of the royal family. There are no elections and no functioning political parties.

The Brunei economy is largely dependent on the production of petroleum and gas, and on oil refining and gas liquefaction. Together, these account for almost all of Brunei's exports and some three-quarters of gross domestic product; the state has participation in most oil and gas activities. Brunei has enjoyed a high standard of living owing to oil and gas revenues and the government has been able to subsidize food and housing and there is a well-developed system of welfare services and other social benefits. Most employment is for the government or relates to government contracts, while 40% of the work-force are foreigners coming in as temporary residents. Brunei's Economic Council believes that the current structure is unsustainable long-term and that Brunei must develop an independent and competitive private sector.

GDP (purchasing power parity) $5.6bn. (1999 est.); GDP per capita (purchasing power parity) $17,400 (1999 est.).

2 Trade Unionism

According to the law all workers except the military and police may join unions. Registered unions have legal status, and the government has not prevented registration of unions, but they are little developed. The US State Department reports that "there is little interest on the part of workers in forming trade unions", reflecting good wages and benefits and a cultural tradition that favours consensus. It says that of the three registered unions (all of them in the oil sector), one is "passive" and the other two "generally inactive". They represent less than 5% of the petroleum sector workforce. Unions may not affiliate with international federations. Collective bargaining is not generally practiced. Strikes are thought to be lawful under existing legislation but in practice do not occur. Brunei is not a member of the ILO.

Bulgaria

Capital: Sofia
Population: 7.80 m. (2000 est.)

1 Political and Economic Background

The Bulgarian Communist Party (BCP) came to power after World War II and then ruled according to the Soviet model until the disintegration of the regime in 1989-90. Since adoption of a multi-party system in 1990 the leading parties have been the Bulgarian Socialist Party (BSP), the successor to the Communist Party, and the Union of Democratic Forces (UDF). Since elections in Apr. 1997 the UDF has been the largest party in the legislature and holds most Cabinet positions.

Bulgaria has a significant base of industries in areas such as food processing, chemicals, metal and energy. While a high degree of state ownership remains, much of it of unprofitable enterprises, some 60% of economic activity is now in the private sector. More complete privatization has been held back by a variety of difficulties including union opposition. The post-1997 UDF government has tried to introduce structural reforms including liberalization of agri-cultural polices, reform of social insurance, and enhanced enforcement of laws, and has received IMF support. GDP contracted in 1996–97 but there has since been growth of 3.5% in 1998 and 2.5% in 1999, with triple digit inflation in 1996-97 reduced to only 1% by 1998 and 6% in 1999.

GDP (purchasing power parity) $34.9bn. (1999 est.); GDP per capita (purchasing power parity) $4,300 (1998 est.).

2 Trade Unionism

Bulgarian trade unions first appeared in the 1880s, and the General Workers' Trade Union Association was formed in 1904. After the Communist Party consoli-dated its ruling position from 1944, unions were incor-porated into the structure of the state and organized through the Central Council of Trade Unions (CCTU). Bulgaria ratified ILO Convention No.87 (Freedom of Association and Protection of the Right to Organize, 1948) and Convention No.98 (Right to Organize and Collective Bargaining, 1949) in 1959, although a single state-controlled trade union structure was in place at that time.

The 1991 Constitution, adopted after Bulgaria embraced multi-party democracy, guarantees the right of all workers to form or join trade unions of their own choosing. However, the unionized proportion of the work force (estimated at between 30 and 50%) is falling with the decline of large state enterprises and the devel-opment of small and medium-sized enterprises in the private sector.

There are two main trade union centres, the KNSB and Podkrepa, both affiliates of the ICFTU. In Dec. 1989, faced with de facto trade union pluralism the CCTU emulated the Communist Party, dismissed its leadership and changed its name to the Confederation of Independent Trade Unions of Bulgaria (KNSB, or CITUB). In February 1990 the old CCTU statutes were completely overhauled, and later in the year the KNSB withdrew from the WFTU. After its reincarnation

KNSB adhered firmly to a nonpartisan stance, insisting that industrial and not political priorities should determine its actions.

Podkrepa (Support) was formed by intellectuals in Feb. 1989. Its president, Konstantin Trentchev, was imprisoned with several other activists in June, but its statutes and programme were published in September, and it was involved in widespread strikes in 1989–90 that contributed to the disintegration of the Communist regime. It was closely associated with the Union of Democratic Forces (UDF), a coalition of diverse groups that provided the main political challenge to Communist rule. In the first multi-party elections in June 1990 (narrowly won by the BSP), Podkrepa sponsored UDF candidates while KNSB stayed neutral. In Oct. 1990 further elections resulted in the UDF forming the government. Thereafter the alliance between Podkrepa and the UDF dissolved and Podkrepa developed as a politically independent organization.

During 1992 these two main centres of Bulgarian trade unionism drew closer together as they developed a common distaste for the UDF government. In April both walked out of talks with the UDF government on price liberalization, declaring that a change of administration was needed and in the autumn reached an agreement on how to distribute the assets of the former CCTU.

In Jan. 1991 government and both sides of industry agreed a six-month agreement on social peace. Signatories included KNSB, Podkrepa, the National Union of Private Producers (Vazrazhdahe), the Union for Economic Incentive, the Union of Production Cooperatives, the Central Cooperative Union, and Bulgarian Economic Chamber. Subsequently a tripartite National Council for Social Partnership (NCSP) was established, and during 1991 it considered a range of social issues such as pensions provision and privatization. This first experiment in tripartism lapsed in Nov. 1991 following the election of the UDF administration.

Thereafter the non-party Berov "government of experts", in office 1992–94, created the National Council for Tripartite Co-operation (NCTC) and a wide network of branch commissions for negotiations at national and industry levels. The NCTC from 1992 became a forum for national incomes policy, and in 1993 broadened its responsibility to consideration of legal drafts across a wide range. In 1997 the incoming UDF government, inheriting a position of economic recession and hyper-inflation, effectively excluded the unions from discussion of adoption of an IMF structural adjustment programme, although tripartism resumed thereafter. The ICFTU *Annual Survey of Trade Union Rights* for 1999 noted that for several years there had been problems with the co-option of unrepresentative unions, often linked to political parties, onto the NCTC. In March 1998 the government initiated a census of trade union members that showed that only the KNSB and Podkrepa satisfied the criteria for being nationally representative and were thus qualified to participate in national-level tripartite bodies.

Both the KNSB and Podkrepa are affiliated to the ICFTU. In Feb. 1999 a WCL delegation visited two organizations wishing to affiliate to the WCL, the Association of Democratic Syndicates (ADS) and the National Trade Union Promyana. Both had been excluded from the NCTC. In Oct. 1999 Promyana was affiliated to the WCL.

The 1992 labour code provides for collective bargaining. According to the unions, while collective bargaining is practiced it is undermined by employers not honouring agreements and by the lack of means of enforcing agreements. The labour code also provides a right to strike, but strikes are not allowed in electricity, communications and health, and "political" strikes are unlawful. Under 1990 legislation a majority of workers in an enterprise must vote for strike action for it to be lawful. Public sector workers prevented from striking have used go-slows as an alternative. Strike action to oppose government policies in areas such as privatization and tax increases have been a feature of post-1989 Bulgaria. Strikes, go-slows, and demonstrations generally take place without government interference. Protests by blocking roads to protest against wage arrears were reported in 1999. In Nov. 1997 the KNSB and Podkrepa said they had a list of 246, mainly foreign-owned, enterprises that were taking advantage of Bulgaria's economic difficulties to violate the labour code. Violations were said to be most common in regions of high unemployment. There are long delays in remedying grievances through the labour courts.

A working group on revision of the labour code to bring it into conformity with international standards began work in May 1999. It comprised government officials, representatives of the Bulgarian Business Chamber, Podkrepa, and the KNSB, with representatives of the Bulgarian Investors Business Association (foreign investors) participating as non-members. In a statement issued May 10, 2000 Podkrepa criticized the apparent wish of the government to distance itself from enforcement of labour legislation and leave matters to employers in the absence of representative employers' associations able to bind their members.

3 Trade Union Centres

Confederation of Independent Trade Unions of Bulgaria (KNSB/CITUB)

Address. 1 Macedonia Square, 1040 Sofia

Phone. +359 2 870406

Fax. +359 2 9885969

Leadership. Dr. Jeliazko Hristov (president)

History and character. The KNSB's origins lie in the Central Council of Trade Unions (CCTU), which was established following the 1944 coup which led to the consolidation of power by the Bulgarian Communist Party. Until the 1980s no unions were permitted outside the CCTU structure and it was closely controlled by the ruling party. Since the end of the Communist regime it has sought to transform itself from an official single trade union structure to a new independent organization in a pluralist context.

The 5th (Nov. 1989) extended CCTU plenum repudiated the "conciliatory and yielding" posture of the official unions and acknowledged a widespread view that the confidence of working people could be regained only if the unions became uncompromising defenders of their interests. In a founding resolution the Bulgarian trade unions were now proclaimed independent of political organizations, and a month later the 6th extended plenum removed the entire collective leadership headed by Petur Dyulgerov and installed a new team led by Krastyo Petkov.

During Jan. 1990, a consultative CCTU ballot revealed substantial support for diversity of forms of property, opposition to the participation of political parties, and support for the newly independent unions entering the forthcoming elections in their own right. Petkov's position was legitimized at the 11th extraordinary congress of Feb. 17–18, 1990, which elected him unopposed as chairman and launched the Confederation of Independent Trade Unions of Bulgaria (KNSB). The extraordinary congress then became the constituent congress of KNSB and invited federations and unions to affiliate or leave it in freedom. Contacts were opened with the ETUC; WFTU affiliation lapsed. KNSB developed a critical view of the BSP (the reformed Communist Party) and stayed officially neutral during the June 1990 elections. At its third congress, KNSB approved a compromise resolution on the property and assets of the former state unions, currently in government hands, that amounted to renouncing its claims on the bulk of them.

"The transition to a market economy", the KNSB concluded in 1993, had so far "proved to be beneficial only for a thin layer of old and new profiteers". It called for faster structural reform including privatization, but insisted that this should proceed by agreement.

International affiliations. ICFTU; ETUC

Confederation of Labour Podkrepa (Support)

Address. 2 Angel Kantchef Street, 1000 Sofia

Phone. +359 2 981 4551

Fax. +359 2 981 2928

E-mail. koseva@bulinfo.net

Leadership. Dr Konstantin Trentchev (president)

History and character. Founded by a group of intellectuals in Feb. 1989, it immediately applied to the regime for official registration, declaring its aims to be the defence of members' interests and opposition to arbitrariness and encroachments by unscrupulous firms and state enterprises. Despite the imprisonment of several leaders, Podkrepa published its statutes and programme in September. At its first (March 1990) Congress it claimed 70,000 members and half a million two years later.

Podkrepa was a founder member of the coalition of opposition forces known as Sayuz na Demokratichni Sili (Union of Democratic Forces, UDF) its largest adherent and a powerful advocate of free market policies. It spon-

sored several candidates of the UDF in the first multiparty elections in June 1990. These were narrowly won by the (former communists) of the BSP. Podkrepa remained involved in industrial unrest through a prolonged period of political chaos when formation of a stable government became impossible. The UDF itself became involved in government for the first time in Dec. 1990, although it fragmented as did its relationship with Podkrepa.

Podkrepa's subsequent evolution showed a deteriorating relationship with the UDF government. In Aug. 1992 Konstantin Trentchev was arrested and charged with incitement to destroy public property in connection with an attack on the Sofia headquarters of the Bulgarian Communist Party. The Podkrepa secretary Svilen Marinov was arrested one day after Trentchev. Podkrepa also faced internal difficulties as in Jan. 1993 some Podkrepa branches broke away, a number of them becoming prominent founders of a new Community of Free Trade Union Organizations. Podkrepa's rival KNSB was also rebuilding itself and despite a partial rapprochement with KNSB, Podkrepa continued to regard its rival as a "communist trade union" that had not changed its totalitarian character. It declined an invitation to participate in the Oct. 1993 KNSB Congress.

In Jan. 1997 Podkrepa joined UDF-led demonstrations opposing the BSP-led government and calling for elections. As a result of elections in Apr. 1997, the UDF returned to power but relations with the UDF again quickly deteriorated. Following Podkrepa involvement in a Sofia transport workers' strike in July, the UDF daily newspaper accused Trentchev of having ties to the former Communist nomenklatura. Podkrepa has complained of the corruption and ineffectiveness of the privatization process. At the 2000 congress Trentchev accused the UDF government of corruption and responsibility for the country's economic difficulties, while acknowledging Podkrepa's role in putting it in power in the first place, and complained that social dialogue had ceased. In May 2000 Podkrepa issued a statement on planned changes to the labour code. It said that its guiding principles in this area were: strengthening the role of collective bargaining and tripartism; consolidating the protective function of the labour code; expanding worker participation in management (including requiring employers to inform the trade unions on the main issues concerning the activities of the enterprise); and bringing the labour code into line with international standards.

International affiliations. ICFTU (since 1991); ETUC

4 Other Trade Union Organization

NTU Promyana

Address. Graf Ignatiev str. 10A, 1000 Sofia

Phone. +359 2 986 3209

Fax. +359 2 986 6605

Leadership. Pancho Mutafchiev (president)

International affiliation. WCL

Burkina Faso

Capital: Ouagadougou
Population: 11.95 m. (2000 est.)

1 Political and Economic Background

Burkina Faso (named Upper Volta until 1984) became a self-governing republic within the French Community in 1958 and gained full independence in 1960. A 1966 military coup was followed by alternating periods of military and civilian rule. Blaise Compaoré took power as leader of a "Popular Front" in a military coup in 1987 and then went on to be elected president at the end of military rule in 1991 and again in 1998. The legislature is dominated by his Congress for Democracy and Progress.

Burkina has a backward economy, in which 85 per cent of the population is engaged in subsistence farming or nomadic herding. The West African area within which Burkina Faso lies has been subject to long periods of drought, and this, together with widespread disease, has sharply reduced agricultural output. Moreover, poor infrastructure facilities make the transportation of produce difficult. These are limited mineral resources, while manufacturing (mainly textiles and the processing of tobacco and food products) accounts for only about 10 per cent of total gross domestic product. Burkina Faso has a large trade deficit and is heavily dependent on multilateral and bilateral sources of finance. In 1991 it initiated an austere IMF structural adjustment plan, and like 13 of the 14 countries in the African franc zone Burkina participated in the 1994 devaluation of the CFA franc. A large proportion of the male workforce has seasonal employment in neighbouring countries.

GDP (purchasing power parity) $12.4bn. (1999 est.); GDP per capita (purchasing power parity) $1,100 (1999 est.).

2 Trade Unionism

Burkina Faso (as Upper Volta) ratified ILO Convention No. 87 (Freedom of Association and Protection of the Right to Organize, 1948) in 1960 and Convention No.98 (Right to Organize and Collective Bargaining, 1949) in 1962.

Unions in Burkina Faso (then Upper Volta) date from 1947, when the Union Syndicale des Travailleurs Voltaïques (USTV) was established; by 1978 six centres were in existence. Although having only a few thousand members, the unions were significantly involved in Burkina Faso's turbulent politics. In 1966 the Yameogo regime was brought down by army intervention following a general strike. President Lamizana was likewise deposed in a 1980 coup after several weeks of strikes and protests led by teachers and supported by the four main federations. The successor military regime of Colonel Zerbo banned the right to strike in 1981, describing it as "a luxury which our economy cannot allow in the difficult world situation". There were further coups in Nov. 1982 and Aug. 1983, following which the National Revolutionary Council (NRC) government eased restrictions on unions and militants dismissed under Zerbo were permitted to apply for their former jobs.

Relations between the NRC regime and the unions deteriorated following the 1985 arrest and detention of some 20 union leaders who had signed a declaration protesting against the introduction of economic austerity measures. Union discontent – particularly among the teachers – contributed to the 1987 coup in which NRC leader Thomas Sankara was overthrown, killed and replaced by his erstwhile friend and colleague Capt. (now President) Blaise Compaoré. Relations with the unions improved thereafter, pay and conditions were reviewed and more than 1,000 dismissed teachers were reinstated.

Most workers, including those in the public sector, are permitted to join unions, although their scale is limited by the small size of the formal economy. The unions operate without major restrictions. There are several confederations, including two (the CSB and ONSL) affiliated to the ICFTU and one (the CNTB) affiliated to the WCL.

Collective bargaining exists in the small formal economy and is backed up by labour tribunals. The right to strike is frequently exercised and generally respected by the government. Strikes are staged for both economic and political causes and sometimes have considerable political impact. In 1999 several general strikes were staged by unions involved in the Collective of Mass Organizations and Political Parties as part of a campaign to force exposure of the circumstances surrounding the Dec. 1998 death, apparently at the hands of members of the presidential guard, of an investigative reporter Norbert Zongo. There were also strikes by power workers over the police killing of a worker at the national electricity company SONABEL.

3 Trade Union Centres

Confédération Nationale des Travailleurs du Burkina (CNTB)
National Confederation of Workers of Burkina
Address. BP 445, Ouagadougou
Phone. +226 31 23 95
Fax. +226 31 08 50
Leadership. Laurent Ouedraogo (secretary general)
International affiliation. WCL

Confédération Syndicale Burkinabe (CSB)
Trade Union Confederation of Burkina

Address. Bourse du Travail 01, BP 1469, Ouagadougou

Phone. +226 36 23 62

Fax. +226 36 23 62

International affiliations. ICFTU

Organisation Nationale des Syndicats Libres (ONSL)
National Organization of Free Trade Unions

Address. BP 99, Ouagadougou

Membership. 6,000

History and character. ONSL was founded in 1960 and was formerly known as the Organisation Voltaïque des Syndicats Libres (OVSL). In the 1990s it increased its influence through agitation against the social impact of structural adjustment.

International affiliations. ICFTU

Burundi

Capital: Bujumbura
Population: 6.05 m. (2000 est.)

1 Political and Economic Background

Burundi (formerly part of the Belgian-administered Ruanda–Urundi UN trust territory) achieved full independence in 1962 as a kingdom, but following two successive coups in 1966 was declared a republic. Tribal antagonism between the Tutsi and the majority Hutu led to serious internal unrest between 1969 and 1972 and confirmation of Tutsi dominance. The Tutsi-dominated Party of the Union for National Progress (UPRONA, originally created in 1958) was formally recognized as sole political party in the 1974 Constitution and retained this position after a 1987 coup which brought the Military Committee of National Salvation (MCNS), headed by Maj. Pierre Buyoya, to power.

In the early 1990s Burundi, as many other countries in Africa, sought to move from a one-party state to a measure of pluralism and UPRONA also moved a number of Hutus into leadership positions. In 1993, presidential elections resulted in the defeat of UPRONA's candidate, Buyoya, by the candidate of the Burundi Front for Democracy, Melchior Ndadaye, a Hutu, who however appointed a number of UPRONA members to his government in an attempt to maintain stability. In October 1993 Ndadaye was killed in an unsuccessful coup attempt by dissident Hutu army officers, and this precipitated a period of inter-ethnic violence and political confusion. In July 1996 Buyoya returned to power in a coup and in 1998 signed a new constitution embracing power-sharing between Hutus and Tutsis, under which he also became president.

The Burundi economy is based almost exclusively on agriculture (largely subsistence), which accounts for 90 per cent of the labour force, and is also conditioned by the country's landlocked position, its high density of population and its paucity of natural resources. The principal cash crop is coffee (which accounts for some 80-90 per cent of export revenue but whose international markets and prices are subject to wide fluctuations). The small manufacturing sector is based mainly on the processing of agricultural products. Since 1993 the fragile economy has been further damaged by ethnic violence, which has led to the death or displacement of more than 1 million people.

GDP (purchasing power parity) $4.2bn. (1999 est.); GDP per capita (purchasing power parity) $730 (1999 est.).

2 Trade Unionism

Burundi ratified ILO Conventions No.87 (Freedom of Association and Protection of the Right to Organize, 1948) and No.98 (Right to Organize and Collective Bargaining, 1949) in 1993 and 1997 respectively.

The small scale of the formal economy and interethnic violence have limited the development of trade unionism. All previously existing unions were absorbed into the (Tutsi-dominated) Union des Travailleurs du Burundi (UTB) in 1967, this being closely linked to UPRONA. Another organization, the Fédération des Syndicats Chrétiens Ouvriers et Paysans du Burundi (FSCOPB), founded in 1958 and associated with the Belgian Confédération des Syndicats Chrétiens (CSC), had been closely linked with the Hutu tribe, and many of its members were killed in conflicts with the Tutsi.

There are no affiliates of the ICFTU or WCL. The US State Department reports that most trade unionists are civil servants in the urban areas and that Tutsis dominate both the formal economy and the unions. There are two confederations, the Confederation of Free Unions of Burundi (CSB) and the Confederation of Burundi Unions (COSEBU).

Cambodia

Capital: Phnom Penh
Population: 12.21 m. (2000 est.)

1 Political and Economic Background

The Kingdom of Cambodia became independent from France in 1953. In the 1960s it became affected by spill-over from the war in Vietnam. Prince Sihanouk was deposed by a pro-US regime in 1970. In 1975 the Chinese-backed Khmers Rouges under Pol Pot, preaching a form of virulently anti-Vietnamese communist agrarian fundamentalism, gained control of the country after a civil war and established Democratic Kampuchea (DK). Sihanouk was head of state until Apr. 1976 before being removed. Under the Khmers Rouges millions were forced out of the cities and in one of the worst examples of state terror of the century perhaps two million died. In 1979, the Pol Pot regime was driven out of Phnom Penh by Vietnamese-backed communist rebels, who went on to establish single party rule in a renamed People's Republic of Kampuchea (PRK). Fighting continued throughout the 1980s, with Russia and Vietnam backing the PRK government and China arming the Khmers Rouges, which also allied with Prince Sihanouk. In 1989 the country was renamed Cambodia as Vietnamese forces began to withdraw. Under the 1991 Paris Accords, Prince Sihanouk returned as head of state in 1993 and a coalition government was formed, with two joint Prime Ministers. One of these, Hun Sen, subsequently consolidated power in his own hands in a July 1997 palace coup, becoming sole Prime Minister the following year. Following elections in July 1998, there is a coalition government between the Cambodia People's Party and the United National Front for an Independent, Neutral, Peaceful and Cooperative Cambodia (FUNCINPEC).

Pol Pot refused to participate in the 1993 settlement and continued to fight in the jungle. However, the Chinese cut off aid in 1996, Pol Pot died in Apr. 1998, the military leader Ta Mok was captured in Mar. 1999, and in 1998-99 most remaining Khmers Rouges forces surrendered, were captured or dispersed. 1999 was considered the first peaceful year in Cambodia for three decades.

The country's infrastructure, industrial sector and financial institutions were destroyed in the 1970s. The PRK government directed an economy of three sectors: state, cooperative and family (private), and inaugurated Cambodia's first five-year plan in 1985, with "export and thrift" as the primary economic guidelines. But Cambodia was heavily dependent on aid from the Soviet Union and Vietnam, and in 1991 Soviet aid was cut by 80 per cent. As some kind of normalization was established, IMF credits were granted to Cambodia in 1994. The IMF again suspended its Cambodia programme after the 1997 coup, but resumed loans in Oct. 1999. In recent years Cambodia has shown progress in rebuilding the economy, but the infrastructure is poor, and virtually non-existent in rural areas, and the government has identified problems of bureaucratic restrictions and corruption. 80 per cent of the labour force is engaged in agriculture.

GDP (purchasing power parity) $8.2bn. (1999 est.); GDP per capita (purchasing power parity) $710 (1999 est.).

2 Trade Unionism

Cambodia became a member of the ILO in 1969 and ratified Conventions No.87 (Freedom of Association and Protection of the Right to Organize, 1948) and No.98 (Right to Organize and Collective Bargaining, 1949) in 1999.

Under the Vietnamese-backed People's Republic of Kampuchea (PRK) government, the Kampuchean Federation of Trade Unions (KFTU) was established in 1979. This was chaired by a member of the politburo of the ruling KPRP party and was the sole union centre. It was active in the 1980s and (as the Cambodian Federation of Trade Unions) is still recorded as a WFTU affiliate although no longer in existence.

Under the 1997 labour code workers in the private sector may form unions and bargain collectively. Most urban workers are, however, employed in small-scale enterprises, or are self-employed skilled workers or unskilled day labourers and most unions have been formed in the fast growing, mainly foreign-owned garment industry. Unions are not allowed in the public sector. Unions complain that there is little machinery for enforcing worker protections in the labour code and that inspectors are commonly excluded from factories.

By 1999 the government had registered 77 unions and four labour federations under the 1997 code. However, union organizers complained of delays in granting registration. The code says that union officers must not have a criminal conviction, and this was interpreted to mean that executive members must obtain police certificates of good conduct certified by the Justice Ministry. The ICFTU stated that "the certificates are time-consuming and costly to obtain ... there are reports that the only way to get the ID card is to give a substantial bribe to the police". A Free Trade Union of Workers of the Kingdom of Cambodia (FTUWKC) was formed in 1997 and registered in Dec. 1998, after the government relaxed registration procedures.

The ICFTU says that government-sponsored unions have been set up in enterprises where independent trade unions are active, while government officials have interfered in union elections. Anti-union discrimination is prohibited by the labour code but this is not enforced. Illegal dismissals in some cases have led to union members being reinstated.

Although the 1997 code provides for collective bargaining, in practice the unions are too weak for this to be a reality and only a few such agreements exist. The garment sector has been the main focus for strikes, most of them illegal, and sometimes ending in violence.

3 Trade Union Centre

There is no recognized trade union centre.

4 Other Trade Union Organization

Free Trade Union of Workers of the Kingdom of Cambodia (FTUWKC)

Leadership. Te Moc (president)

History and character. The FTUWKC was organized in Dec. 1996 and registration was conceded by the government in Dec. 1998. The FTUKWC has recruited in garment factories and in Feb. 1998 led a demonstration outside the US Embassy calling for the ending of Cambodia's trading privileges until labour conditions in the garment trade were improved. Later that year, the government said that it would monitor conditions in the garment sector and cancel licenses of employers in violation. Its second congress was held in Mar. 1999, the majority of delegates being women workers in the garment industry. It received a WCL visit on Sept. 1999. Further information on FTUWKC may be found at www.cleanclothes.org

Cameroon

Capital: Yaoundé
Population: 15.42 m. (2000 est.)

1 Political and Economic Background

The Republic of Cameroon acquired its present name in 1984 and comprises the former territories of the Federal Republic of Cameroon, created in 1961 from the trusteeship of French Cameroon (independent since 1960) and the British trusteeship of Southern Cameroons. Until 1990 the sole legal party (holding all the seats in the unicameral National Assembly) was the Rassemblement Démocratique du Peuple Camérounais (RDPC), established in 1985 to replace the Union Nationale Camérounaise. The RDPC won disputed multi-party

elections in 1992 and again in 1997. The elected President, Paul Biya, has held the position since 1982.

Agriculture represents the major sector of the economy, accounting for more than 40% of gross domestic product, but the industrial sector accounts for a further quarter. Industries include petroleum production and refining and food processing. During the 1990s the government followed IMF and World Bank programmes intended to encourage investment and increase efficiency, but with mixed success and uncertain commitment, with problems of bureaucratic inertia and corruption. State industries have been progressively privatized.

GDP (purchasing power parity) $31.5bn. (1999 est.); GDP per capita (purchasing power parity) $2,000 (1999 est.).

2 Trade Unionism

Cameroon ratified ILO Convention No.87 (Freedom of Association and Protection of the Right to Organize, 1948) in 1960 and Convention No.98 (Right to Organize and Collective Bargaining, 1949) in 1962.

Unions developed on the French model, with divisions along political lines, and at the beginning of the 1960s there were about 100 unions and several competing centres. The number of unions fell rapidly during the 1960s and in 1971 four survivors dissolved into a sole centre (Syndicat Central Unique), later known as the National Union of Cameroon Workers (Union Nationale des Travailleurs du Caméroun, UNTC), and thereafter as the Organization of Cameroon Workers' Unions (Organisation des Syndicats des Travailleurs Camérounais, OSTC). Before 1991 workers were restricted to joining unions affiliated to the sole trade union centre.

At a 1991 congress the OSTC resolved on complete restructuring and a further change of name to the Confederation of Cameroon Trade Unions (CSTC). In 1992 a new labour code provided for workers to have freedom to form and join unions of their own choosing. During 1993 the government introduced cuts in public sector salaries; in the case of teachers and doctors the reduction was almost half. The CSTC responded with strikes. This marked the beginning of a deteriorating relationship between it and the ruling party. Since 1993 there has been continual interference in the affairs of the CSTC by the government and the government also backed the creation of a rival organization, the USLC.

Trade unions must be registered and in recent years, the government has refused registration to some public sector unions, particularly those of teachers. Collective bargaining is provided for under the 1992 labour code but no collective bargaining negotiations have taken place in recent years. There is a right to strike (but not for civil servants) and strikes and strike threats are not uncommon. Some provisions of the labour code do not apply in export processing zones (EPZs) and the unions say that they are denied access to EPZ enterprises.

3 Trade Union Centres

Confédération Syndical des Travailleurs du Cameroun (CSTC)
Confederation of Cameroon Trade Unions (CCTU)

Address. BP 414, Yaoundé

Phone. +237 22 33 15

Fax. +237 23 52 54

Leadership. Benoit Essiga (president)

History and character. The CSTC, under different names, functioned as the trade union arm of the ruling RDPC until the relative liberalization of the early 1990s when it declared its independence of political parties. Thereafter relations with the RDPC deteriorated. In 1994 and early 1995 the CSTC suffered extreme forms of government interference in its internal affairs. The freedom of movement of its general secretary Louis Sombes was restricted and a new leadership imposed. Ministry supervision of CSTC affairs was instituted. Only in January 1995 were Sombes supporters able to force an extraordinary congress and secure his re-election. According to the ICFTU, the government was behind the formation of a rival centre, the USLC, in 1995 and engineered a split in the CSTC itself in 1997, when the Minister of Labour ruled that neither faction could be recognized. In Apr. 1998 a congress held under ILO auspices resulted in the election of a reform slate led by Benoit Essiga, but the government refused to recognize the new leadership.

International affiliation. ICFTU; CTUC

Union des Syndicats Libres du Cameroun (USLC)
Union of Free Trade Unions of Cameroon

Address. BP 13.306, Yaoundé

Phone. +237 20 66 54

Fax. +237 23 41 96

Leadership. Amado Sadjo (president); André Jules Mousseni (secretary general)

History and character. The USLC was created as a rival national centre to the ICFTU-affiliated CSTC in 1995, according to the ICFTU with government encouragement. Its secretary general, André Jules Mousseni, is a former deputy secretary general of the CSTC who took over as CSTC secretary general in 1994 when Louis Sombes was deposed by the government, before Sombes was restored by the membership in Jan. 1995.

International affiliation. WCL

Canada

Capital: Ottawa
Population: 31.3 m. (2000 est.)

GDP (purchasing power parity) $722.3bn. (1999 est.); GDP per capita (purchasing power parity) $23,300 (1999 est.).

1 Political and Economic Background

Canada comprises ten provinces and three territories. At the federal level in the period from the 1960s to the early 1990s there were two main national parties, the Liberals (who held office for nearly all the period from 1963-84) and the Progressive Conservatives, who most recently were in government from 1984–93. The third (minority) party at federal level was the social democratic New Democratic Party (NDP). Since then, however, while the Liberals have won three national elections in succession (in 1993, 1997 and 2000) under Prime Minister Jean Chrétien, the conservative vote has fragmented, the NDP has declined, and voting patterns have polarized very sharply on a regional basis. In the most recent elections, in Nov. 2000, the Liberals won 173 of the seats in the 301-member House of Commons. However, while the Progressive Conservatives slumped to only 12 seats nationally, a new more right-wing conservative formation, the Canadian Alliance, became the second largest party with 66 seats by virtue of winning 60 of the 73 seats in the three western provinces of British Columbia, Alberta and Saskatchewan. The Liberals won only eight seats in those three provinces. In the two populous eastern states of Ontario and Quebec, in contrast, the Liberals won all but 3 of the 103 seats in Ontario while in Quebec the Liberals and the separatist Bloc Québécois (BQ), won 37 seats each with only one seat going to another party (the Progressive Conservatives). The regional tensions, between western and eastern Canada, and between French-speaking Quebec (where a 1995 referendum only narrowly rejected a call for outright independence) and the rest of the country, have become the most fundamental problem facing Canada.

Canada is one of the Group of Seven (G-7) leading industrialized countries. Its economy is closely integrated with that of the United States, its major trading partner, and this relationship has intensified further as a result of the 1989 US–Canada Fair Trade Agreement (FTA) and the North American Free Trade Agreement (NAFTA) of 1994. Since 1980 most jobs created in Canada have been in the service sector: 75% of the labour force is now in services, 16% is in manufacturing, 5% construction and only 3% in the agricultural sector. Real growth rates have averaged 3% per annum since 1993, following a severe recession in the period 1990-92. Unemployment declined to 7.6% by 1999 from 11.2% in 1993. The Liberal government is now using budget surpluses to cut the high public debt and since taking office in 1993 has sought to reduce subsidies, control government spending and carry out privatization.

2 Trade Unionism

Although initially inspired by the British labour movement, Canada's unions later emulated the United States model. These two influences, together with the diversity of the Canadian provinces, partly explain the complexity of Canadian trade unionism. Trade unionism has deep roots in Canadian society, especially in the Atlantic states, and union density is the highest in the Americas.

Canada ratified ILO Convention No. 87 (Freedom of Association and Protection of the Right to Organize, 1948) in 1972 but it has not ratified Convention No.98 (Right to Organize and Collective Bargaining, 1949). In 1982 the Canadian constitution had appended to it a Charter of Rights which included freedom of association among its basic freedoms. The legal framework is complicated by the existence of separate industrial jurisdictions for each of the country's 10 provinces, and in recent years unions have found sharp divergences in their standing under the law in different parts of the country. The industrial relations policies followed by the provinces in the direct public sector and in public enterprises are markedly different from each other and from the federal pattern. Changes of administration can and do have a marked effect.

Virtually all workers in both the public and private sectors (but not members of the armed forces) may form and join unions of their own choosing and anti-union discrimination is prohibited by law. There are, however, some limitations on freedom of association. In Alberta academics in higher education do not have freedom of association. There are restrictions on freedom of association in agriculture and horticulture in several provinces. Union density has been in the 30–33% range for the last 25 years and Canada avoided the sharp decline in density experienced in most western industrialized countries in the 1980s. There are regional differences in density, with the highest levels in the eastern provinces of Newfoundland (39%) and Quebec (37%) and the lowest (22%) in the western province of Alberta.

The public sector is the most organized, with some three-quarters of employees in unions, and the public sector now represents slightly more than half of all union membership although accounting for less than 25% of jobs. The trade union movement from the 1970s into the 1990s maintained its overall strength by adding women members in the public sector to replace men in declining manufacturing industries. However, this substitution is now virtually exhausted and with virtually all job creation now taking place in private sector services, where unionization rates are the lowest, the unions face the challenge of recruiting in these areas to sustain their position into the future.

The national centre is the ICFTU-affiliated Canadian Labour Congress (CLC), formed in 1956, which has a membership of 2.3 million. There are no other nationwide centres. The Confederation of Canadian Unions (CCU), which says it is rank-and-file based, has only 7,000 members. There are, however, alternative centres based on French-speaking Quebec, the largest of which, the Confédération des Syndicats Nationaux (CSN), has some 232,000 members. There are also important unions in areas such as teaching and the health service without affiliation either to a Canadian or American centre.

There has been a continuing process of merger and rationalization of craft-based unions. The two largest unions are both in the public sector. The Canadian Union of Public Employees (CUPE) has 475,000 members and the National Union of Public and General Employees (NUPGE) has 325,000. Both increased their membership during the 1990s, especially CUPE. The largest private sector union is the Canadian Auto Workers' (CAW), with 230,000 members. All three are affiliated to the CLC. The most important independent union not linked to the CLC or other trade union centre is the 245,000-strong Canadian Teachers' Federation.

With so many Canadian plants owned by firms based in the United States and significant integration of the US and Canadian economies, there is a long-standing close relationship between US and Canadian unions. Although the majority of union members are in national (i.e. Canadian-based) unions there are also many unions constituted as Canadian branches of international (i.e. US-based unions). In some respects these relationships have deepened in response to developments such as the North American Free Trade Agreement (NAFTA) and common concerns such as globalization. However, at the organizational level, there has been a contrary trend, towards greater Canadian autonomy, encouraged by the deep problems US unions faced with falling memberships in the 1980s, when the Canadian unions were generally sustaining their position far better. The CAW left the (United States) United Auto Workers in 1985, after 50 years' affiliation following years of disagreement over the Canadians' demand for full national control of wage bargaining, strike authorization and staff appointments. The schism followed breakaways from the United Paperworkers' International Union in 1974, and the Oil, Chemical and Atomic Workers' Union in 1980 as well as ruptures in international links between woodworkers and food workers. The Teamsters' Union, expelled from the CLC in 1960 for "poaching" union members, was readmitted to the CLC in 1992 on a basis that emphasized the autonomy of the Canadian branch, which had been re-named Teamsters Canada.

The pattern of industrial relations legislation is complex and varied having its origins in a voluntarist British approach overlaid with a restrictive framework of rights and obligations which, for example, prohibit strikes in certain essential services, impose rules on balloting and registration and can result in large fines. The main feature of Canada's industrial relations system is its decentralization. Nearly all agreements are concluded between a single employer and a single union. Thus collective bargaining in the private sector is a localized process based on the single establishment and the single firm. Negotiations are rarely conducted across provincial boundaries or on an industry-wide basis. This does not mean a low incidence of collective bargaining: around half the workforce (public and private) is covered by agreements, including many non-unionized employees. Indeed the effect of decentralization is a proliferation of arrangements: as many as 10,000 collective agreements may be concluded in a single year, with an overwhelming majority of them being made between a single employer and a single union.

Throughout the 1980s and 1990s there was conflict at both federal and provincial levels over the scope of collective bargaining, especially in the public sector, with frequent complaints by unions to the ILO. In 1992 the ILO reprimanded the federal government and those of Manitoba, New Brunswick, Newfoundland and Nova Scotia for restricting Convention No.98 by imposing a wage freeze on public sector employees. Restrictive legislation at the federal level and in Manitoba, New Brunswick, Nova Scotia and Prince Edward Island expired in 1997. There are limitations on the scope of public sector bargaining in some provinces and at the federal level civil servants must negotiate in 100 separate units. In the private sector, most agricultural and domestic workers are excluded from collective bargaining and in other sectors the unions complain that provincial governments have done little to support collective bargaining rights where employers are hostile. In the most populous province, Ontario, legislation adopted by the incoming Conservative administration in 1995, and reversing 1993 legislation, excluded agricultural workers, domestic workers, architects, dentists, land surveyors, lawyers and doctors from the legal framework protecting trade union rights with the result that existing collective bargaining agreements were nullified.

There is a general right to strike and strikers are protected from retaliation by employers. Strikes are relatively frequent. The number of strikes tended to fall through the 1990s but remained at a higher level than in the UK and a much higher level than the USA. However, the right to strike has limitations. There has been persistent controversy at the federal level and in most provinces over the denial of the right to strike to workers in "essential services" and the definition of what essential services are. In Alberta, the right to strike is denied to hospital employees such as kitchen staff, porters and gardeners and the ILO has disputed that these are essential services. It has likewise criticized the prohibition of strikes in non-essential sectors such as agriculture and horticulture, as in Ontario, and railways and ports, by the federal government. In March 1993 a grain-handlers' strike was ended by a federal back-to-work order, but the the ILO Committee on Freedom of Association concluded that grain handling was not an essential service and recommended that the government refrain in future from using such powers where the service in question is not essential. In 1997 union opposition was successful in persuading the provincial government of Ontario to withdraw proposed legislation that would have banned strikes by public-sector employees for a two-year period.

The unions have filed a series of cases under the North American Agreement on Labour Cooperation (NAALC), part of NAFTA, which commits governments to uphold existing labour legislation in areas such as freedom of association, collective bargaining and the right to strike. The agreement was designed to prevent member countries from gaining unfair competitive advantage through labour violations. However, early cases concerning dismissal of workers for union organizing activities did not result in reinstatements.

3 Trade Union Centre

Canadian Labour Congress (CLC)
Congrès du Travail du Canada (CTC)

Address. 2841 Riverside Drive, Ottawa K1V 8X7

Phone. +1 613 521 3400

Fax. +1 613 521 8949

E-mail. communications@clc-ctc.ca

Website. www.clc-ctc.ca

Leadership. Kenneth V. Georgetti (president); Nancy Riche (secretary-treasurer)

Membership. 2.3 million

History and character. The CLC was formed in 1956 by merger of the Trades and Labour Congress (TLC) with the Canadian Congress of Labour (CCL). The TLC represented mainly craft unions and the CCL mainly industrial unions, in both cases with their affiliates having international headquarters predominantly in the United States.

The CLC is the only national trade union centre. However in Quebec there are three significant provincial centres outside the CLC, and overall the CLC includes only some 53% of the unionized work force. It has members in all areas of the economy, but its two largest unions, the 475,000-member Canadian Union of Public Employees (CUPE) and the 325,000-member National Union of Public and General Employees (NUPGE) are both based in the public sector. The overall shape of CLC membership has shifted over the last two decades, with the decline of manufacturing jobs and a great increase in women members in the public sector, with little net effect on total CLC membership, which was 2.2 million in the mid-1980s.

The largest private sector affiliate is the Canadian Auto Workers' (CAW), which recruits in a wide range of sectors. During 2000, however, the CAW was accused of "raiding" the membership of another CLC affiliate, the Service Employees' International Union (SEIU) and faced disciplinary sanctions.

The CLC supports the New Democratic Party (NDP), which it helped to found in 1961, and its policies tend to correspond closely to the social democratic outlook of that organization. Nancy Riche, the CCL secretary-treasurer, is Associate President, Labour, of the NDP. This alliance has been similar in some respects to that between the trade union centres and the social democratic parties in countries such as the UK (TUC and Labour Party) and Germany (DGB and SPD), or that in the USA between the AFL-CIO and the Democrats. However, whereas in these other countries the alliance has been with one of the two leading parties of government, the CLC's alliance with the NDP has been more peripheral in impact. Since its foundation the NDP has not succeeded in displacing the Liberal Party of Canada as the principal anti-conservative party at the federal level, and it took only 13 seats (of the total of 301) in elections to the House of Commons in Nov.2000, representing further decline from the 17 seats won in 1997. It has never seriously challenged to become the party of national government. It has, however, had somewhat more success at the provincial level, holding power in the most populous province of Ontario from 1990–95, as well as being in government for periods in the 1990s in several other provinces. At provincial level, periods of NDP government have been marked by enactment of pro-union legislation, sometimes reversed (as in Ontario in 1995) when power was lost.

The CLC has little direct involvement in collective bargaining, which is highly decentralized. It organizes boycotts of "unfair" employers, sometimes in association with US unions. At national level it has a strong focus on political lobbying. The CLC's current concerns include pension rights, defending public services, fairness in taxation, achieving full collective bargaining, organizing the growing services sector, and combating inequality and discrimination in the workplace and society. It also reflects the general Canadian interest in global and developing world issues. In 1999 the CLC led a labour delegation protesting at the World Trade Organization conference in Seattle, calling for mechanisms to ensure workers' rights and labour standards to be brought into the world trade system.

The ruling body is the national convention, held every three years (most recently in May 1999, when Ken Georgetti was elected president). Between conventions the ruling body is the 42-member executive council. Its structure includes 12 provincial and territorial federations and 125 district labour councils. The CLC is predominantly English-speaking, but the Francophone minority in Canada is recognized by the simultaneous publication of all documents in both languages. A Women's Bureau was established in 1972.

Publications. Outfront, Labour on Trade, The Economy, Faxpress, occasional research papers. (Accesible via website)

International affiliations. ICFTU, TUAC, CTUC

Affiliated Unions. CLC affiliates include provincial federations of labour, Canadian branches of US-based international unions, and Canadian occupationally based unions. The following list provides details on some of the more prominent affiliates. Further information on international unions based in the US can be found in the US country section.

1. Canadian Auto Workers (CAW)

Address. 205 Placer Court, North York, Ontario, M2H 3H9
Phone. +1 416 497 4110
Fax. +1 416 495 6559
E-mail. caw@caw.ca
Website. www.caw.ca
Leadership. Basil "Buzz" Hargrove (national president); Jim O'Neill (national secretary-treasurer)
Membership. 230,000
History and character. The CAW is the largest private sector union in Canada. Its membership is diverse (only 90,000 members are employed in the auto sector) and it is the leading Canadian union in fisheries, aerospace, electronics, auto and auto parts, speciality vehicles and shipbuilding. In 2000 it was put under sanctions by the CLC after charges of raiding the membership of another CLC union.
Publications. Contact newsletter, accessible via website

2. Canadian Federation of Nurses' Unions (CFNU)

Address. 2841 Prom. Riverside Drive, Ottawa, Ontario K1V 8X7
Phone. +1 613 526 4661
Fax. +1 613 526 1023
E-mail. cfnu@nursesunions.ca
Website. www.nursesunions.ca
Leadership. Debra McPherson (acting president)
History and character. Founded in 1981 and reorganized in 1999 as the national affiliating body for nurses to the CLC.

3. Canadian Union of Postal Workers (CUPW)

Address. 377 Bank Street, Ottawa, Ontario K2P 1Y3
Phone. +1 613 236 7238
Fax. +1 613 563 7861
E-mail. bpausche@cupw-sttp.org
Website. www.cupw-sttp.org
Leadership. Dale Clark (national president); Lynn Bue (1st vice-president)
Membership. 45,000
Publications. CUPW in the News; Bulletins (Accessible via website)

4. Canadian Union of Public Employees (CUPE)

Address. 21 Florence Street, Ottawa, Ontario K2P OW6
Phone. +1 613 237 1590
Fax. +1 613 237 5508
E-mail. cupemail@cupe.ca
Website. www.cupe.ca
Leadership. Judy Darcy (national president); Geraldine McGuire (national secretary-treasurer)
Membership. 475,000 in 2,156 locals
History and character. CUPE is Canada's largest and fastest-growing union, active in health care, education, local government, social services, libraries, utilities, transport and emergency services. More than half its members are women and about 25 per cent work part-time. A particular focus for the union is opposition to the privatization of public services.

Publications. Organize (magazine*); CUPE News Service.* Content accessible via website.

5. Communications, Energy and Paperworkers' Union of Canada (CEP)

Address. 350 Albert Street, Suite 1900, Ottawa, Ontario K1R 1A4
E-mail. info@cep.ca
Website. www.cep.ca
Leadership. Brian Payne (national president); André Foucault (national secretary-treasurer)
Membership. 150,000
History and character. Formed in 1992 by the amalgamation of the Canadian Paperworkers' Union, the Communications and Electrical Workers' of Canada, and the Energy and Chemical Workers' Union. It has members in a wide range of sectors including pulp and paper, telephone companies, oil, gas, chemicals, mining, media, printing, hotel workers and computer programmers. Internationally it is affiliated to the ICEM, UNI and IMF international trade secretariats.

6. International Association of Machinists and Aerospace Workers (IAMAW)

For general entry for the international union, see under USA
Canadian office:
Address. 15 Gervais Drive, Suite 707, North York, Ontario M3C 1Y8
Phone. +416 386 1789
Fax. +1 416 386 0210
E-mail. info@iamaw.ca
Website. www.iamaw.ca
Leadership. Dave Ritchie (general vice-president for Canada)
Membership. 50,000 (Canada)

7. Industrial, Wood and Allied Workers of Canada (IWA)

Address. 500-1285 West Pender Street, Vancouver, British Columbia, V63 4B2
Phone. +1 604 683 1117
Fax. +1 604 688 6416
E-mail. national@iwa.ca
Website. www.iwa.ca
Leadership. Dave Haggard (national president); Neil Menard (1st vice-president)
Membership. 55,000
Publications. Lumberworker (content accessible via website)

8. National Union of Public and General Employees (NUPGE)

Address. 15 Auriga Drive, Nepean, Ontario K2E 1B7
Phone. +1 613 228 9800
Fax. +1 613 228 9801
E-mail. national@nupge.ca
Website. www.nupge.ca
Leadership. James Clancy (national president); Larry Brown (national secretary-treasurer)
Membership. 325,000
History and character. NUPGE, Canada's second largest union (after the Canadian Union of Public Employees, CUPE), is itself a federation of 14 independent member unions, these being mainly unions of public employees at the provincial level. Its membership includes 30,000 private sector members. Internationally it is affiliated to PSI.
Publications. A wide range of publications, accessible via website

9. Public Service Alliance of Canada (PSAC)
Address. 233 Gilmour Street, Ottawa, Ontario K2P 0P1
Phone. +1 613 560 4200
Fax. +1 613 236 1654
E-mail. org@psac.org
Website. www.psac.com
Leadership. Nycole Turmel (national president); John Gordon (national executive vice-president)
Membership. 137,000
Publications. Alliance (magazine); *Union Update* (bulletin); other bulletins on specific topics. Content accessible via website.

10. Service Employees' International Union (SEIU)
For general entry for the international union, see under USA
Canadian office:
Address. 810–75 The Donway West, Toronto, M3C 2E9
Phone. +1 416 447 2311
Fax. +1 416 447 2428
Website. www.seiu.ca
Leadership. Sharleen Stewart (international vice-president, Canada)

11. Teamsters Canada
Address. 2540 Daniel Johnson Boulevard, Laval, Quebec, H7T 2S3
Phone. +1 450 682 5521
Fax. +1 450 681 2244
Website. www.teamsters-canada.org
  Leadership. Louis Lacroix (president)
Membership. 100,000
History and character. This is the Canadian affiliate of the US-based International Brotherhood of Teamsters (IBT). Expelled from the CLC in 1960 following disputes about demarcation boundaries with other affiliates, the Teamsters continued to organize in Canada. In 1976 the Canadian Conference of Teamsters was established within the IBT. In 1992 greater autonomy was granted to the Canadian branch, which was re-named Teamsters Canada, and in 1993 re-affiliation to the CLC was agreed.
   Members cover a wide variety of occupations beyond transport workers, with 17 trade divisions including aeronautics, bakeries and laundries, construction and building materials, port side industry and warehousing.
Publications. Teamsters Canada (quarterly magazine*)*

12. United Food and Commercial Workers International Union (UFCW)
See also entry for the International Union under the United States
Canadian office:
Address. 300–61 International Boulevard, Rexdale, Ontario, M9W 6K4
Phone. +1 416 675 1104
Fax. +1 416 675 6919
E-mail. info@ufcw.ca
Website. www.ufcw.ca
Leadership. Michael J. Fraser (Canadian director)
Membership. 205,000 (Canada)

Provincial federations of labour.
These affiliate directly to the CCL. The leading federations are:

1. Alberta Federation of Labour
Address. 350, 10451–170 Street, Edmonton, Alberta T5P 4T2
Phone. +1 780 483 3021
Fax. +1 780 484 5928

E-mail. afl@telusplanet.net
Website. www.afl.org
Leadership. Audrey Cormack (president); Les Steel (secretary-treasurer)
Membership. 107,000

2. British Columbia Federation of Labour
Address. 200–5118 Joyce Street, Vancouver, B.C. V5G 1H1
Phone. +1 604 430 1421
Fax. +1 604 430 5917
E-mail. bcfed@bcfed.com
Website. www.bcfed.com
Leadership. Jim Sinclair (president); Angela Schirer (secretary-treasurer)

3. Manitoba Federation of Labour
Address. 101-275 Broadway, Winnipeg, Manitoba R3C 4M6
Phone. +1 204 947 1400
E-mail. mbfedlab@mfl.mb.ca
Website. www.mfl.mb.ca
Leadership. Rob Hillard (president); Peter Olfert (treasurer)

4. Ontario Federation of Labour
Address. 15 Gervais Drive, Suite 202, Toronto, Ontario M3C 1Y8
Phone. +1 416 441 2731
Fax. +1 416 441 1893
E-mail. info@ofl-fto.on.ca
Website. www.ofl-fto.on.ca
Leadership. Irene Harris (executive vice-president); Ethel LaValley (secretary-treasurer)
Membership. 650,000

5. New Brunswick Federation of Labour
Address. 96 Norwood Avenue, Moncton, New Brunswick, E1C 6L9
Phone. +1 506 857 2125
Fax. +1 506 383 1597
E-mail. fttnbfl@nbnet.nb.ca
Website. www.intellis.net/fttnbfl
Leadership. Blair Doucet (president); Maurice Clavette (secretary-treasurer)
Membership. 32,000

6. Quebec Federation of Labour
Address. 545 boulevard Crémazie Est, 17e étage, Montreal, H2M 2V1
Phone. +1 514 383 8000
Fax. +1 514 383 8001
Website. www.ftq.qc.ca (French only)

7. Saskatchewan Federation of Labour
Address. 220-2445 13th Avenue, Regina, Saskatchewan, S4P 0W1
Phone. +1 306 525 0197
Fax. +1 306 525 8960
E-mail. info@sfl.sk.ca
Website. www.sfl.sk.ca
Leadership. Barbara Byers (president)
Membership. 80,000

4 Other Trade Union Organizations

Canadian Teachers' Federation (CTF)
Address. 110 Argyle Avenue, Ottawa, Ontario K2P 1B4

Phone. +1 613 232 1886

E-mail. info@ctf-fce.ca

Website. www.ctf-fce.ca

Leadership. Marilies Rettig (president); David Eaton (secretary general)

Membership. 245,000 in 14 provincial/territorial member organizations

Centrale des Syndicats Démocratiques (CSD)

Address. 801, 4e rue, Quebec City, Quebec GIJ 2T7

Phone. +1 418 529 2956

Fax. +1 418 529 6323

E-mail. csdmtl@globetrotter.qc.ca

Leadership. François Vaudreuil (president)

Membership. 60,000

History and character. The CSD was founded in 1972 following a rift in the Confédération des Syndicats Nationaux *(see below)* over organizational and ideological issues. CSD is non-partisan and practices direct democracy. It affiliated to the WCL in 2000.

International affiliation. WCL

Centrale des syndicats du Québec (CSQ)

Address. 9405 rue Sherbrooke Est, Montreal, Quebec H1L 6P3

Phone. +1 514 356 8888

Fax. +1 514 356 999

Website. www.csq.qc.net (French only)

Leadership. Monique Richard (president)

Membership. 140,000 members in 14 unions and federations. Members are primarily in public sector areas such as health and education.

Christian Labour Association of Canada (CLAC)

Address. 5920 Mississauga Drive, Mississauga, Ontario L4W 1N6

Phone. +1 905 670 7383

Fax. +1 905 670 8416

E-mail. headoffice@clac.ca

Leadership. Ed Grootenboer (executive director)

History and character. CLAC is a confederation that represents workers in more than 500 enterprises across English-speaking Canada and has expanded its membership in the 1990s. Its main strengths are in wood and building, health care, services and transport.

International affiliation. WCL

Confédération des Syndicats Nationaux (CSN)

Address. 1601 ave De Lorimier, Montreal, Quebec H2K 4M5

Phone. +1 514 598 2098

Fax. +1 514 598 2052

E-mail. intcsn@csn.qc.ca

Website. www.csn.qc.ca (French only)

Leadership. Marc Laviolette (president); Lise Poulin (secretary-general)

Membership. 232,000

History and character. The CSN originated in 1921 as the Confédération des Travailleurs Catholiques du Canada (CTCC, Confederation of Catholic Workers of Canada). The two main influences in the subsequent development of the CTCC were the efforts of the Catholic clergy to create confessional unions, and the nationalist resistance within the union movement to the attempt of the American Federation of Labour to control Canadian trade unionism. Membership in the organization – which was at that time concentrated mostly in the textile, clothing, pulp and paper, and metalworking industries, and the retail trades – had reached 94,000 by 1960, when the CTCC became officially secular and changed its name to the CSN. The CSN's membership more than doubled from 1960 to 1970 with the unionization of the public sector in Quebec. There was a split in 1972, with more conservative unions opposing the confrontation between the CSN and the Quebec government, and breaking away to form the CSD (see above). Membership fell to 160,000 in 1976, but then grew to reach 250,000 by 1990 and is now reported at 232,000.

Although the CSN has a Canada-wide charter, the vast majority of members in its 2,174 affiliated unions (syndicats) are in the (mainly French-speaking) province of Quebec. There are also some unions in Ontario and New Brunswick. The CSN membership constitutes one-quarter of the unionized workforce of Quebec. About 80% of the women members of CSN are in public services, while 80% of the men are in the private sector. The local unions are affiliated to regional councils and industrial federations. The CSN has 29 regional offices in Quebec and 650 employees.

The CSN is independent of political parties and in its relationships with other sectors of the Canadian labour movement, although it has worked with other unions on common campaigns. Since 1990 it has campaigned for the independence of Quebec from Canada and opposed trade liberalization within NAFTA, which exposes Quebec's industrial base to lower-cost competition. Its international relations are primarily with francophone countries and Latin America. It was affiliated to the WCL from 1946–86, but is now affiliated to the ICFTU.

Publication. Nouvelles-CSN

International affiliation. ICFTU

Cape Verde

Capital: Cidade de Praia
Population: 401,000 (2000 est.)

1 Political and Economic Background

Cape Verde achieved independence from Portugal in 1975 and had a one-party system under what became the African Party for the Independence of Cape Verde (PAICV) until moving to a multi-party system after 1990. In 1991 the newly formed Movement for Democracy (MPD), which had been set up by exiles in Lisbon calling for a multi-party democracy and a free enterprise economy, defeated the PAICV in elections to the National Assembly and the MPD's presidential candidate António Mascarenhas Monteiro was also elected. Monteiro was re-elected in 1996 and the MPD continues to hold a majority in the National Assembly.

Cape Verde has few natural resources. Some three-quarters of the population are dependent upon subsistence agriculture, but prolonged periods of drought have necessitated the import of over 90 per cent of food requirements, a large proportion of it under aid programmes. Much of the rural workforce is under-employed. Together with foreign aid, a major contribution to the economy is made from remittances from nationals working or residing abroad (who are estimated to number nearly 1,000,000). Fish processing and canning provide a limited amount of employment.

In 1992 the National Assembly approved privatization of most of the public sector, and the government has sought to attract foreign investment.

GDP (purchasing power parity) $618m. (1998 est.); GDP per capita (purchasing power parity) $1,500 (1998 est.).

2 Trade Unionism

There appears to have been no organized trade union activity before independence from Portugal. The UNTC-CS was created as the trade union arm of the ruling PAICV in the 1970s, but its legal monopoly was broken by the 1991 PAICV electoral defeat. The 1992 Constitution provides that workers shall have the right to join unions free of government control and a 1991 legislative decree provides protection against discrimination on the grounds of union activity. The UNTC-CS accepted pluralism and is now a member of the ICFTU. It is the main centre and has about 16,000 members, but there is now also a Council of Free Labour Unions.

Cape Verde ratified ILO Convention No.87 (Freedom of Association and Protection of the Right to Organize, 1948) in 1999. It ratified Convention No.98 (Right to Organize and Collective Bargaining, 1949) in 1979, but little collective bargaining takes place. There is a constitutional right to strike, which the government generally respects, but the government has on occasion made use of requisition orders to force strikers back to work, as in the case of disputes in 1997 involving workers at the ENACOL petrol company and in 1999 when seafarers struck against restructuring and proposed privatization of the national maritime company CNN.

3 Trade Union Centre

Uniao Nacional dos Trabalhadores de Cabo Verde – Central Sindical (UNTC-CS)
Trade Unions of Cape Verde Unity Centre

Address. CP 123, Praia, São Taigo

Phone. +238 61 43 05

Fax. +238 61 36 29

Membership. 16,000

History and character. In 1976 the organizing Commission of Cape Verde Unions was formed as a complement to the Guinea-Bissau National Union of Workers (UNTG). Two years later the UNTC-CS was established as the arm of the ruling PAICV. It is no longer controlled by the PAICV.

In Dec. 1991 the government confiscated the 1st May social centre which had been built for the UNTC-CS by international trade union donors. The government handed over the property to a breakaway faction. In Nov. 1998, however, the courts ruled the building belonged to the UNTC-CS as internationally recognized.

International affiliation. ICFTU

Central African Republic

Capital: Bangui
Population: 3.51 m. (2000 est.)

1 Political and Economic Background

The French territory of Ubangui-Shari became a self-governing republic within the French Community in 1958 as the Central African Republic and gained full independence in 1960. Col. Jean-Bedel Bokassa took power in 1966 (under him the country being renamed the Central African Empire from 1977 until his overthrow in 1979). Gen. André Kolingba came to power in 1981, and from 1986 there was a semi-civilian government with power exercised through Kolingba's Rassemblement Démocratique Centrafricain as the sole legal party. In April 1991, Kolingba, in line with many other African states at that time, announced a move to multi-party democracy but efforts to involve other parties in constitutional change repeatedly failed. In 1992 Bangui was hit by strikes supporting a sovereign national conference to set the country's constitution. When elections were finally held in 1993, the winner was Ange-Félix Patassé (a one-time Prime Minister under Bokassa, who had denounced Bokassa after being exiled by him) and the Central African People's Liberation Party (MLPC). In Dec. 1994 a referendum approved constitutional changes enhancing the power of the president. There were army mutinies in 1996 and 1997 and a UN mission was sent in 1998 to monitor implementation of a National Reconciliation Pact. Elections in Dec. 1998 resulted in political deadlock, until defections of five independents and one opposition member enabled parties headed by Patassé's Central African People's Liberation Party to form a government. Patassé was re-elected President in Sept. 1999.

The economy is based on subsistence agriculture, although the diamond industry accounts for more than half of exports. This is a poor landlocked country with little infrastructure and few workers with modern skills, while the economy also suffered disruption from military rebellions and unrest in the late 1990s.

GDP (purchasing power parity) $5.8bn. (1999 est.); GDP per capita (purchasing power parity) $1,700 (1999 est.).

2 Trade Unionism

Several labour federations were in existence at the time of independence in 1960, and the Central African Republic ratified ILO Convention No.87 (Freedom of Association and Protection of the Right to Organize, 1948) in 1960 and Convention No.98 (Right to Organize and Collective Bargaining, 1949) in 1964.

In the 1970s the ICFTU-affiliated General Union of Workers of Central Africa (Union Générale des Travailleurs du Centrafrique, UGTC), with its affiliated occupational federations, was the sole permitted organization. In 1973, and again in 1977, UGTC general secretaries were dismissed for participating in anti-government activities. President Dacko suspended the right to strike in 1980 and in 1981 dissolved the UGTC after it attempted to break the ban. He announced the formation of a new body, the National Confederation of Central African Workers (CNTC) but all union activities were suspended after a military coup that September. The CNTC resumed functioning but suffered harassment by the state. The last days of the Kolingba regime were marked by further repression, and in 1993 CNTC headquarters were surrounded by troops at the start of a planned civil service strike.

The 1995 Constitution provides for trade union pluralism and freedom of association. Several union federations have been formed, but the small scale of the formal economy has limited trade unionism, and most union members are public servants. The principal organization is the ICFTU-affiliated Union Syndicale des Travailleurs de Centrafrique (USTC), which has about 15,000 members. It has difficult relations with the government, with salary arrears averaging a year for government employees a source of tension. Trade unions are banned from holding meetings of a political nature and union officials must be employed full-time in the industry the union represents. Collective bargaining is not specifically authorized by the labour code and where bargaining occurs the government generally becomes involved. There is a right to strike in both private and public sectors, subject to conciliation and arbitration procedures, and teachers have staged lengthy strikes over the issue of pay arrears. In the last few months of 2000 there was a series of strikes by civil servants over unpaid salaries, contributing to the atmosphere of anti-government unrest and demonstrations.

3 Trade Union Centre

Union Syndicale des Travailleurs de Centrafrique (USTC)
Union of Central African Workers
Address. BP 1390, Bangui
Phone. +236 61 60 15
Fax. +236 61 60 15
Leadership. Théophile Sonny-Colé (secretary-general)
Membership. 15,000
History and character. In the late 1990s relations between the USTC and the government were strained by

factors including pay arrears for civil servants and the government's refusal to negotiate a social pact, and there were frequent strikes. Security forces ransacked the USTC headquarters and telephone lines were cut off. Following the December 1998 elections (see above) the USTC called for the formation of a representative government and organized protests against the defections in the National Assembly which had allowed the MLPC to form a government. Following these protests, in Jan. 1999 USTC general secretary, Théophile Sonny-Colé, was detained and beaten, apparently by members of the presidential guard, before being released after international pressure.

International affiliation. ICFTU

4 Other Trade Union Organizations

Confédération Nationale des Travailleurs de Centrafrique (CNTC)
National Confederation of Central African Workers
Address. BP 2141, Bangui

Phone. +236 61 24 51

Fax. +236 61 56 29

Leadership. Jean-Richard Sandos Oualanga (secretary general)

International affiliation. WCL

Confédération Syndicale des Travailleurs de Centrafrique (CSTC)
Address. BP 386 KM 5, Bangui

Phone. +236 50 25 36

Fax. +236 61 56 29

Leadership. Kpokol Sabin (secretary general)

International affiliation. WCL (affiliated 1999)

Chad

Capital: N'Djaména
Population: 8.42 m. (2000 est.)

1 Political and Economic Background

Chad became a self-governing republic within the French Community in 1958 and achieved full independence in 1960. A 1975 army coup inaugurated a prolonged period of internal dissent and secessionist attempts, punctuated by brief truces. Fighting broke out in 1983 in the north between government and Libyan-backed forces but President Habré's forces gradually consolidated their hold over major parts of the centre and south. Following the overthrow of Habré by (Colonel) Idriss Déby in a 1990 rebellion, eight political parties were legalized in 1992, but assassinations and union repression continued. The pluralist momentum then slowed fostering fears that Déby was seeking to install an authoritarian regime. In 1993 a Sovereign National Conference – organized by a tripartite commission – met and inaugurated an intended 12-month transition to democracy, but clashes continued. Finally in April 1995 a transitional government took office entrusted with overseeing preparations for elections.

Déby was elected President in 1996 and his Patriotic Salvation Movement (MPS) became the dominant force in the legislature following elections to a new National Assembly in 1997; both sets of elections were reportedly marked by ballot rigging. A further military rebellion, led by a former Defence Minister and based in the northwest, broke out in Oct. 1998. In Feb. 2000, Habré was indicted on charges of torture, and put under house arrest, in Senegal, where he had been in exile since 1990.

The economy of Chad has been disrupted by civil conflict for decades, its difficulties compounded by both drought and torrential rains. The income of 90 per cent of the population comes from agriculture (largely subsistence, together with livestock rearing and nomadic herding) and fishing in the richly stocked Lake Chad. Industry is based mainly on processing agricultural products. There is a heavy dependence on external aid and assistance from international donors has been directed mainly at improving the agricultural sector. Structural adjustment programmes in the 1990s have involved privatization and public sector wage cuts, which have provoked industrial action.

GDP (purchasing power parity) $7.6bn. (1999 est.); GDP per capita (purchasing power parity) $1,000 (1999 est.).

2 Trade Unionism

Chad ratified ILO Convention No.87 (Freedom of Association and Protection of the Right to Organize, 1948) in 1960 and Convention No.98 (Right to Organize and Collective Bargaining, 1949) in 1961.

French unions maintained branches in Chad until independence in 1960. Between then and 1988 there were two trade union centres, the Trade Union Confederation of Chad (CST) and the National Union of Workers of Chad (UNATRAT) which reflected tribal and geographical cleavages. A great deal of their energy was absorbed by rivalry and eventually a decision was taken to establish a national negotiating team to achieve unity. In 1988 the Habré-backed National Union of Chadian Trade Unions (UNST) was launched under a new general secretary, but it was dissolved two years later when Déby took power. Under the new regime the trade union movement split: UNST dissidents formed a new centre, the WCL-affiliated Free Confederation of Chadian Workers (CLTT) while loyalists staged a 1991 general strike to force reinstatement of their organization. The authorities agreed provided there was a change of name and the Chad Trade Union Confederation (UST) was born. It is Chad's ICFTU affiliate and the main trade union organization in the country. There are today several other federations and unions in existence, including the CLTT, and some unions are reported to have close ties to government officials. However, as Chad's economy is based on subsistence agriculture, with a small formal economy, the unions operate on a modest scale. The private sector is small scale and much of it informal and unions mostly represent employees in the state sector.

Strikes were illegal after 1975 and public employees barred from union membership after 1976. Unions were also prohibited from engaging in political activity and, while collective bargaining was permitted, collective agreements required government approval. In 1996 a new labour law substantially liberalized restrictions on trade union activities. It ended the 1975 ban on strikes and a 1976 ban on public servants forming or joining trade unions. It also ended the prohibition on trade unions engaging in political activity. The requirement for government approval of collective bargaining agreements was also ended, although the Ministry of Labour retained the right to comment on agreements and ask for re-negotiation. The requirement remained that authorization for the formation of associations is required from the Ministry of the Interior. This provision has been used on occasions in respect of trade unions.

3 Trade Union Centres

Confédération Libre des Travailleurs du Tchad (CLTT)
Free Confederation of Chadian Workers

Address. BP 553, Avenue Charles de Gaulle, N'Djamena

Phone. +235 51 76 11

Fax. +235 52 44 56

Leadership. Brahim Bakass (president)

History and character. The CLTT was founded early in 1991 by dissidents from the defunct national centre UNST, and became for the government an alternative rallying point to the reformed UST.

International affiliation. WCL

Union des Syndicats du Tchad (UST)

Address. BP 1143, N'Djamena

Phone. +235 51 42 75

Fax. +235 52 29 05

Membership. 25,000

History and character. The UST's origins lie in the National Union of Chadian Workers (UNST) formed by a 1988 merger of the tribally and geographically divided CST and UNATRAT. Its chief objectives included the building of a trade union culture in Chad and the extension of membership into a large part of the public sector. The UNST was dissolved in 1990 but its adherents re-established it ten months later under its present name.

The UST was legally recognized in 1992. That year it led a series of battles with the government over its economic adjustment programme; the security forces occupied its headquarters and ICFTU officials were denied visas to enter the country. In October all UST activities were temporarily suspended on the grounds that they were political. Despite this its influence was sufficiently great for it to have a place in the machinery overseeing the introduction of democracy. Secretary-general Djibrine Assali was made second vice-president of the Sovereign National Conference and elected to its supervisory council. In 1993 and 1994 the UST was to the fore in organizing industrial agitation against non-payment of wages and for the maintenance of living standards. This brought it into further conflict with the government. In 1995 the UST warned of the possibility of electoral fraud during the period of transition to democracy and it was suspended following its call for a boycott of the presidential elections in 1996. Its largest affiliate, the teachers' union, was reported to have broken away in 1998.

International affiliation. ICFTU

Chile

Capital: Santiago
Population: 15.15 m. (2000 est.)

1 Political and Economic Background

Chile was ruled by a military junta led by General Augusto Pinochet from the time of his violent overthrow of the Allende government in 1973 until 1981. In that year Pinochet became President for an eight-year term under a new constitution. Among other provisions this constitution formally prohibited Marxist and totalitarian groups. The 1980s brought growing opposition which eventually forced a relaxation of control; political parties were in 1984 partially freed and in 1987 allowed to register. In a 1988 plebiscite a majority voted against Pinochet remaining in office for a further eight years upon the expiry of his term in 1990. Elections in Dec.1989 resulted in the election as president of the Christian Democrat Patricio Aylwin Azócar at the head of a coalition of centre-left parties, the Coalition of Parties for Democracy (Concertación de los Partidos por la Democracia, CPD). Aylwin presided over municipal elections, the first for 21 years, in 1992, and inaugurated constitutional amendments to reassert the primacy of the presidency over the armed forces and to correct a right-wing bias in the electoral system. Pinochet remained Commander-in-Chief of the Armed Forces, but both Aylwin and Eduardo Frei (another Christian Democrat, who succeeded him as president in 1993, also as the candidate of the CPD) took incremental steps to subordinate the military to the civil power.

In Jan. 2000 Ricardo Lagos (a Socialist, and former ally of Allende), became the third CPD candidate in succession to be elected President, in a narrow victory over the right-winger Joaquín Lavin. The Christian Democrats remained the largest single group in the new Lagos cabinet and the incoming government's programme was seen as broadly consistent with that of the previous administration. Pinochet was arrested in London in October 1998 pending possible extradition to Spain, but was allowed to return to Chile in 2000.

The military after 1973 reversed the socialist policies of the preceding administration, including the return to private ownership of many of the enterprises nationalized under Allende, the encouragement of foreign investment, the dismantling of import barriers and the adoption of a fully free market economic system. In the 1990s civilian governments continued to pursue free market policies while trying to shift the emphasis of government intervention to social spending. Real growth averaged more than 7% per annum in the period 1991–97. Like other South American countries, however, Chile was affected by the 1997–98 financial crisis originating in Asia and in 1999 the economy contracted

by 1 per cent, although showing recovery in 2000. Inflation has been under control in recent years and in 1999 (at 3.4%) was the lowest for 60 years. There is a traditional dependence on relatively few economic sectors, such as copper mining, fishing and forestry.

GDP (purchasing power parity) $185.1bn. (1999 est.); GDP per capita (purchasing power parity) $12,400 (1999 est.).

2 Trade Unionism

Chile ratified both ILO Convention No.87 (Freedom of Association and Protection of the Right to Organize, 1948) and No.98 (Right to Organize and Collective Bargaining, 1949) in 1999.

The first Chilean union centre, the Federation of Chilean Workers (Federación Obrera de Chile, FOCH) was formed in 1909. Legalized trade unionism and collective bargaining developed in the 1930s under the Popular Front government, and in 1936 the Confederación de Trabajadores de Chile (CTCH) was created; this, however, broke into socialist and communist factions during the 1940s. A reunified centre, the Central Unica de Trabajadores de Chile (Central Union of Workers, CUT), was created in 1953, its membership including Christian democrats, socialists and communists.

In 1970 the CUT strongly backed Allende's election, and several CUT leaders became ministers. However, industrial unrest in the copper mines and strikes by lorry owners and other small businessmen destabilized the Allende government, paving the way for the 1973 coup, following which the CUT was banned. Strikes were declared illegal, collective bargaining suspended and some unions disbanded. Numerous trade unionists were executed, imprisoned or exiled, and the government intervened actively in the surviving unions by controlling their assets or appointing their officers. The 1980 Pinochet labour code made trade union affiliation and the payment of union dues voluntary; allowed collective bargaining but restricted the bargaining arena to the individual workplace; stipulated that a strike could be called only if approved by a secret ballot and after compulsory arbitration; and limited strikes to a maximum period of 60 days, the employer having the right to declare a lock-out and hire other labour after 30 days. Strikes were prohibited in any sector connected with national security, public services, "the normal supply of the market" or the "public interest". The essential elements of these decrees were entrenched in the 1981 constitution.

Union resistance to Pinochet regime was more open from 1981. In 1982 Tuscapel Jimenez, leader of the public employees' union, was found murdered shortly after announcing plans to establish a broad-based trade union front to oppose the government's economic policies. In 1983 the copper workers' union, the CTC, led a day of national protest, which led to widespread arrests of trade unionists and others. After this 60 CTC and other union leaders formed a coalition of labour groups opposed to the regime known as the National Workers' Command (CNT) to campaign for the reestablishment of democracy and the "free exercise of labour rights". This immediately initiated a long series of days of protest, leading to violence and mass arrests. The CNT embraced both left-wing and Christian Democratic elements, and although officially illegal established itself as the effective trade union voice in the country.

After disturbances during two days of CNT protest in 1985 union leaders were arrested and charged with violations of the national security law. Rodolfo Seguel (the copper workers' leader) and CNT general secretary Arturo Marínez were imprisoned but later released after further CNT protests in which four people died, and a hunger strike.

A CNT attempt in 1986 to hold its first national convention was prevented by the government, but thereafter, in an effort to improve the effectiveness of trade union opposition, the CNT worked towards the creation of a pluralistic single trade union confederation. Its efforts bore some fruit with the formation of the CUT in 1988. By 1990 there were three (technically illegal) national union centres in Chile, CUT – the largest with about 450,000 members, the Democratic Workers' Centre (CDT) and the Chilean Workers' Central (CTCh). The CTCh was led by figures closely associated with Pinochet.

Under President Aylwin (who took office in March 1990) the Pinochet labour code was amended in 1991 to permit the formation (without official approval), of central union organizations, enabling the CUT to achieve legal status in Apr. 1992. The legislation also allowed trade union centres to affiliate to international trade union organizations, and the CUT went on to affiliate to the ICFTU. The new government also brought a resumption of tripartite dialogue.

Unions now operate independently of the state, although there are considerable ties with political parties. There are legal prohibitions against discrimination by employers against union members. Union density is estimated at about 12%. Public employees associations are not registered as unions with the Ministry of Labour, but some are nonetheless of significant size. Among these are the National Public Employees' Association (ANEF) with perhaps 50,000 members, the Teachers' Association with 90,000, and the Public Health Workers with 20,000. The CUT has a number of public sector associations affiliated. Members of the police and armed forces may not join such associations.

Industry-wide collective bargaining is rare, with bargaining normally at the enterprise level. The majority of private sector workers are covered by individual employment contracts rather than collective bargaining. Workers in sectors such as agriculture, construction, mining, ports, fishing and entertainment are treated as temporary workers and have limited rights to bargain collectively, though they may form unions. Disputes may be referred to the Ministry of Labour for arbitration. In the private sector there is a right to strike, but workers at 30 companies providing essential services such as water and electricity may not go on strike and are subject to compulsory arbitration. Employee associations in the public sector do not have collective bargaining rights, and strikes are also not permitted in the public sector, although in practice groups such as teachers and health workers have gone on strike.

3 Trade Union Centres

Central Autónoma de Trabajadores (CAT)

Phone. +56 2 698 7318

Fax. +56 2 695 3388

Address. Calle Sazie 1761, Santiago 6510480

E-mail. catchile@entelchile.net

Leadership. Osvaldo Herbach Alvarez (president); Enrique Aravena (secretary general)

International affiliation. WCL

Central Unitaria de Trabajadores (CUT)
Unified Workers' Centre

Address. Av. Libertador Bernardo O'Higgins 1346, Santiago

Phone. +56 2 695 8053

Fax. +56 2 695 7308

E-mail. cutchile@unete.com

History and character. The modern CUT was formed in 1988 by disparate worker organizations in an effort to create a unified centre. The CUT backed Aylwin's candidature in 1989. It is Chile's largest centre with more than half of the country's trade unionists. It affiliated to the ICFTU in 1994.

Manuel Bustos, who was president of the CUT from its foundation until 1996, died on Sept. 26, 1999. He had suffered prolonged detention by the authorities for union activities in the 1980s but on his death the Chilean government called three days of mourning and gave a state funeral. He had been elected to the national legislature for the Christian Democrats in 1990.

International affiliation. ICFTU

China

Capital: Beijing
Population: 1.26bn. (2000 est.)

1 Political and Economic Background

The People's Republic of China was formally established in 1949 with the final defeat on the mainland of the Nationalist forces of Chiang Kai-shek by the Communist forces led by Mao Tse-tung (Mao Zedong). Under the 1982 constitution China is defined as "a socialist state under the people's democratic dictatorship led by the working class and based on the alliance of the workers and peasants". The sole and ruling political party is the Communist Party of China (CPC).

Under Mao, China pursued a series of initiatives including the "Great Leap Forward" of the late 1950s and the "Cultural Revolution" of the mid-1960s which provided the context for wholesale political purges allied with the implementation of fundamentalist communist economic policies that brought widespread famine and destitution. These campaigns alternated with periods when more pragmatic policies were followed. In the final years before Mao's death in 1976 a power struggle set in between radicals, who became known as the "gang of four", and moderates including Deng Xiaoping (purged during the Cultural Revolution and again in 1976 as a "capitalist roader"). By the beginning of the 1980s Deng had established control, denounced the excesses of the Great Leap Forward and the Cultural Revolution and set China on a course which emphasized the progressive loosening of centralized command economy policies while retaining the tight grip on power of the CPC. During the 1980s the commune system was ended, free markets for farm products were developed, and state businesses began to pay orthodox taxes instead of transferring their entire profits to the government. Central product allocation was reduced and (within limits) private businesses permitted. Certain coastal regions (the Special Export Zones – SEZs) were allowed economic autonomy and to develop cautious trading relations with neighbouring capitalist states. Finally, trade in privately-owned land was legalized.

During the 1990s, in the wake of the collapse of communist regimes in most of the rest of the world and the crushing of the democracy movement in Tiananmen Square in June 1989, the CPC retained power through a continuation and development of this broad policy, first under Deng and then his successor Jiang Zemin. The process of reforming state enterprises and encouraging the private sector intensified over the decade.

China is now committed to what it calls a "socialist market economy" or "socialism with Chinese characteristics". In this the state retains control of large and medium-sized state-owned enterprises (SOEs) in key industries; smaller SOEs are privatized (although there is official hesitation at the rate at which this is to be done); and foreign investment is encouraged, with restrictions. Inefficient state-owned enterprises are being closed. According to Chinese officials in 1997, the state would ultimately retain control over only 3,000 of the 370,000 SOEs. The policy creates tensions in terms of rising unemployment and accusations of favouritism and corruption in privatization and has had serious implications for the system of social welfare, which was enterprise-based. The policy of winding up inefficient enterprises has been moderated by the impact on employment and social stability, and the central government is also unable to ensure uniform implementation of its policies in all areas of the country.

Agriculture employs at least half the labour force of 700 million, but China has developed industries across a wide range of sectors. The importance of the private sector has been accelerating rapidly in the 1990s. In general, the coastal strip and the south-east of the country are the most economically advanced and since 1997 China has also regained sovereignty over Hong Kong, giving it a world-ranking commercial centre with developed relations with the West. While precise division between public and private is impossible because of the diversity of forms of ownership in China, the World Bank's International Finance Corp., estimated that in 1998 private businesses generated 33% of China's GDP compared with 37% from the state sector. While per capita incomes are still low, output has quadrupled in the past two decades and the size of China's population is such that total GDP is now second only to that of the USA. From a 1992 peak of 14.2%, annual growth in GDP then declined year on year to 7.1% by 1999, but was expected to rise in 2000.

GDP (purchasing power parity) $4.8 trillion (1999 est.); GDP per capita (purchasing power parity) $3,800 (1999 est.).

2 Trade Unionism

China has a single trade union system organized through the All-China Federation of Trade Unions (ACFTU).

Trade unions developed in the first quarter of the twentieth century in harness with the nationalist and revolutionary politics of the Kuomintang (KMT), and by 1927 an All-China General Labour Federation (founded 1925) claimed 3 million members. Following the establishment in 1927 of KMT rule under Chiang Kai-shek in Shanghai, however, many trade unionists were executed, and thenceforth the unions were restricted, with national and general federations prohibited, and government-sponsored "yellow" unions installed. The Red Army under Mao Zedong, which took power in

1949, was peasant-based, but in 1948 the Communist Party (CPC) organized the ACFTU which functioned for 18 years as sole trade union centre. It was abolished in 1966 during the Cultural Revolution, but restored in 1978 (after Mao's death in 1976) when the excesses of that era were denounced as the product of a conspiracy by the so-called "gang of four" radicals.

China has not ratified ILO Convention No.87 (Freedom of Association and Protection of the Right to Organize, 1948). It resumed participation in the work of the ILO in 1983, and the ACFTU says that "since 1983, the Chinese trade unions have actively urged the Chinese government and departments concerned to draw up plans for ratification and application of international labour conventions". Convention No. 87, however, is clearly in conflict with the position enjoyed by the ACFTU. Under the 1992 Trade Union Law (Art. 12) the ACFTU is designated as the "unified national organization" of trade unions and no provision is made for the existence of unions outside its structure. The organizational principle is defined as that of "democratic centralism" (Article 11), whereby a "trade union organization at a higher level shall exercise leadership over a trade union organization at a lower level."

The Trade Union Law defines the objectives of unions in detail.

Article 8 states that:

"Trade unions shall mobilize and educate the workers and staff members to approach their work with the attitude of masters of the country, to safeguard the property of the state and the enterprise and to observe labour discipline ... Trade unions shall organize the workers and staff members in launching socialist labour emulation drives, encouraging mass rationalization proposals, and promoting technological innovations and technical cooperation, so as to raise labour productivity and economic returns and develop the social productive forces."

Article 9 states that:

"Trade unions shall educate the workers and staff members in patriotism, collectivism and socialism... and raise their qualities in all aspects: ideological and ethical as well as scientific, cultural, technical and professional, so as to turn them into well-educated and self-disciplined labourers with lofty ideals and moral integrity."

The ACFTU stands at the apex of a pyramid comprising 16 national industrial unions, 31 federations of trade unions of provinces, autonomous regions and municipalities, and 586,00 trade union primary organizations. In general unions accept the "dual leadership" of local federations and higher-level industrial unions, although in railways, civil aviation, posts and telecommunications the industrial union is dominant. Unions are financed by a payroll tax: 2% of the total wages fund of the enterprise, plus 0.5% of each member's pay, is transferred by employers to the unions, 60% staying with the local union and 40% going to higher levels. The funds support the operation of tens of thousands of union-run facilities such as workers' schools, "halls of culture", sports complexes, hotels, restaurants, sanatoriums, etc.

The 1992 Trade Union Act lowered the threshold for trade union organization at a workplace from 200 to 25, this opening up the burgeoning urban cooperative, service and joint venture sectors to organization. The ACFTU says that 53,000 trade unions have been formed in overseas-funded enterprises, 23,000 in private enterprises and "the rate of union membership has kept rising". However, trade unions do not exist in all enterprises, particularly in smaller privately-owned firms, in rural areas, and in the special economic zones. While the great majority (above 90%) of workers in the state sector are unionized, in 1991 the ACFTU complained that a rate of 20% in foreign firms was too low: in February 1994 it launched a drive to raise membership in this sector. By the end of the 1990s there were some 5.5 million members in foreign-owned firms (31% of the workforce in that sector) and 1.7 m. in private domestically-owned firms (12% of the workforce). The inability of the trade unions to achieve a powerful presence in the new enterprises, which represent the more dynamic part of the economy, may long term be eroding the ACFTU's pivotal role in the Chinese political system.

The ICFTU says that these unions are "either under the control of the Communist Party, or the factory directors, who often simultaneously hold union office. Both employees and management are members of trade unions. Many of them are turned into cultural or social clubs, and often workers are unaware of their existence. In nearly all cases, local union committee members are Communist Party or higher-level union ACFTU appointees. Committee sessions can be regarded as formalities for reaffirming party or enterprise plans".

Workers' congresses exist within enterprises as a form of democratic control, with powers to "appraise and supervise" the managers, and to suggest their reward or even removal. The Trade Union Act (Article 30) says that the trade union committee of an enterprise is the "working body" of the "workers' congress", tasked with the implementation of its decisions. According to the ACFTU the workers' congress system has been set up in almost all state-owned enterprises in large and medium-sized cities and in 1997 the system resulted in 156,000 managers being rewarded and promoted, and 27,000 being removed from their posts. The events of 1989 had the effect of extending the role of the workers' congresses, but the trend of economic reform has been to emphasize the right of managers to make decisions and overcome obstacles to radical restructuring. In many enterprises the workers' congress is effectively moribund.

China has not ratified ILO Convention No.98 (Right to Organize and Collective Bargaining, 1949). In 1994 China adopted its first labour law (in force from 1995), providing a framework for bargaining at the enterprise level, and covering all types of enterprises. The law provides for both individual contracts (which may be negotiated with the assistance of the trade union) and collective contracts. Collective contracts can cover matters relating to remuneration, working hours, holidays, occupational safety and health, insurance and welfare and are to be negotiated through the trade unions and submitted to the workers' congress. Labour disputes and arbitration committees (LDACs) are established. It was reported at the 13th (1998) ACFTU congress that 240,000 enterprises had signed collective contracts, covering 60m. workers. However, many private companies do not have contracts and it also seems that many enterprises ignore the labour law, and the authorities commonly turn a blind eye to this.

The 1982 Constitution withdrew the nominal right to strike provided by the 1975 Constitution. Resolution of disputes is to be through legal and administrative channels where arbitration breaks down. In the first six months of 1999 LDACs dealt with 55,000 cases (58% up on 1998), with 80% of cases coming from the economically dynamic maritime provinces. Many cases arise because workers in private companies commonly do not have any sort of contract and the extent of meaningful collective bargaining is doubtful. However, enterprises regularly ignore adverse decisions from the committees.

Despite the non-existence of a right to strike, and the lack of approval of the official unions, wildcat strikes do occur. Typical causes of strikes are working conditions (exposure to toxic chemicals and other major hazards are common in China), non-payment of wages, excessive hours and harsh management discipline. Strikes have increased continuously since the early 1990s and in 1997, according to official figure, there were 71,000 strikes.

Efforts to create independent trade unions featured in the brief reform movement of 1989. The Workers' Autonomous Federations (WAFs) were founded in May, and represented the first major attempt to set up autonomous unions since 1949. The WAFs seem to have had particular success in Shanghai; there and elsewhere they focused on income discrepancies, poor working conditions, the lack of democracy at the workplace, the lack of involvement in policy-making, and the deterioration of living standards.

On June 2, 1989, the ACFTU called for the crushing of the independent unions. On June 4 troops put down demonstrations in Tiananmen Square. However the first secretary and vice-president of the ACFTU, Zhu Hou Ze, was regarded as having favoured the reform movement and this led to his dismissal in Dec. 1989; he was replaced by Yu Hon-Gen, former president of the National Coal Corporation. The leader of the Beijing Federation, Gou Hai Feng, expressed similar views and was arrested in August, charged with having set fire to a bus. On June 14, the Public Security Bureau declared WAFs illegal. A number of their members were posted on wanted lists and some are believed to have been sentenced to death. On June 16 delegates to the UN Special Session on Prevention of Discrimination and Protection of Minorities heard of 13 workers executed for 'counter-revolutionary crimes' and 67 arrested for their involvement in WAFs.

Around the time of the first anniversary of the Tiananmen Square events the authorities released several hundred prisoners incarcerated since June 1989. It was thought however that none of the WAF leaders was among them and also that the official position that only 45 of these were still held might be an underestimate. In 1999 the ICFTU reported that many activists involved with the WAFs were still in prison, psychiatric hospitals run by the Public Security Bureau, or forced labour camps. Others involved with the movement had been deported.

In 1992 an underground Free Labour Union of China was formed but its leaders were quickly arrested and imprisoned for "organizing and leading a counter-revolutionary group". They became known as the "Beijing 16". Since that time there have been recurrent efforts by individuals or small groups of dissidents to organize unions, or circulate petitions calling for free unions. Those involved have generally been imprisoned on criminal charges or subjected to "re-education through labour", a form of administrative detention which dispenses with the need for a trial. The treatment of those subjected to "re-education through labour" is said to be commonly worse than in the criminal justice system, with torture used.

These essentially individualistic acts by isolated dissidents have not represented a challenge to the existing trade union structure. However, the restructuring of the economy has led to the development of wider forms of industrial unrest, focused on living standards and working conditions, rather than broader political aspirations. The Chinese government itself reports that 11.9 million workers lost their jobs as a result of restructuring in 1997–99, 6.5 million of these remaining out of work. In Jan. 2000, the Minister of Labour and Social Security said that up to 12 million workers in state-owned enterprises (SOEs) were likely to lose their jobs in the coming year. Traditionally, workers have depended on the enterprise for a wide range of benefits, such as health care and housing. As many SOEs are effectively bankrupt, there are many cases of workers going unpaid for extended periods, laid-off workers not getting subsistence allowances, and pensioners not receiving their pensions. Enterprises have reportedly covered losses by diverting money from pension funds and embezzlement by senior managers is said to be not uncommon. While the enterprise-based system has broken down, an adequate state back-up system has not yet been constructed in its place. The Public Security Bureau reported 60,000 large demonstrations across the country in 1999, and was expecting this figure to rise to 100,000 in 2000. Laid-off workers, and workers owed back pay, have in many places laid virtual siege to government offices or blocked roads and railroads until dispersed by the police.

The approach adopted in dealing with such unrest has varied by locality. In some instances, the authorities have sought to find solutions to grievances; in others, demonstrations have been broken up by riot police or the army and leaders detained. There are reports that some activists have been subjected to administrative detention merely for taking up causes before labour disputes and arbitration committees. According to the ICFTU: "in some large plants, work committees, comprising officials from local ACFTU branches, the local labour bureau authorities and the Public Security Bureau (PSB), have been set up to monitor and pre-empt worker action. Many medium and large enterprises have detention facilities and security officials can detain and sentence protesting workers to three years in a labour camp".

In general branch unions have avoided giving support to any form of militancy such as work stoppages or go-slows and normally work to prevent such actions developing. However, according to the *China Labour Bulletin*, at "local plant level branch chairpersons are being laid off along with other workers, and more often than not it is the local party secretary who takes up the vacant union position". The history of past purges of union officials who fell out of step with official policy is a deterrent to local unions adopting positions unacceptable to higher bodies.

The official unions have been seeking to define a role that is in alignment with official policy while also helping to mitigate the impact of restructuring. The unions have opened more than 2,000 employment agencies and set up more than 6,000 vocational training organizations where 2.2 m. workers have been re-trained. They also have set up service businesses and market places and run a "warmth" programme to assist needy families. The unions are involved in efforts to reform the social security, employment, housing and medical insurance systems.

3 Trade Union Centre

All-China Federation of Trade Unions (ACFTU)

Address. 10 Fuxingmenwai Street, Beijing 100865

Phone. +86 10 685 92730

Fax. +86 10 685 62031

E-mail. acftuild@public3.bta.net.cn

Website. www.acftu.org.cn

Leadership. Wei Jianxing (chairman); Zhang Junjiu (first secretary of secretariat).

Membership. 103 million

History and character. The ACFTU is the largest national trade union organization in the world, reporting 586,000 primary trade union organizations and 103 million members. There are no legal trade unions outside the ACFTU. It describes itself as a "mass organization of the working class formed voluntarily by the Chinese workers and staff members". The overwhelming majority of workers in state enterprises are in unions, but significant numbers of workers in the private sector and foreign-owned or joint venture enterprises are not organized. The ACFTU does not organize China's peasant masses (half the 700 million workforce) although it has some 5 million members who are rural workers in township and village enterprises.

The first All-China Labour Congress was held in 1922, and the All-China General Labour Federation was founded at the second such conference held in 1925 (the ACFTU officially dates its origin to May 1, 1925). In 1948 this was reformed in areas controlled by the Communist Party of China (CPC) under its present name, and was extended to other areas of the country after the CPC took power throughout the country (except Taiwan) in 1949.

The ACFTU was (and remains) organized on the Soviet model on the principle of democratic centralism, i.e. that lower level bodies must be guided by higher levels. Until 1966 it and its associated unions were active at workplace level, principally in the areas of education, labour safety, welfare and propaganda. In 1966, however, Mao launched the Cultural Revolution to eliminate those accused of "bourgeois tendencies". Trade unions were replaced by workplace revolutionary committees and the ACFTU was itself dissolved in Dec. 1966. Trade unions were denounced as counter-revolutionary in purpose and methods. Following the death of Mao in 1976, however, the "gang of four" radicals were arrested and many of the policies adopted in the late 1960s reversed.

The ACFTU held its first congress since 1957 in Oct. 1978 and its newspaper, *The Workers' Daily,* which had been suppressed in 1966, resumed publication in the same month. In a statement to the congress, ACFTU chairman Ni Zhifu recalled that: "In December 1966 the office building (of the ACFTU) was occupied by force and *The Workers' Daily* was closed and sealed, at the personal instigation of Jiang Qing (Mao's widow and one of the gang of four) . . . Many trade unions at the provincial, municipal and autonomous regional levels, as well as basic-level trade unions, were battered and crushed. Their office buildings were occupied by force, properties divided and files lost". The first union to resume its activities, after 12 years' suspension, was the All-China Federation of Railway Workers' Unions, which began its national congress at the end of Oct. 1978.

The ACFTU was affected by the reform movement of the late 1980s that culminated in the crushing of the occupation of Tiananmen Square in June 1989. In 1988 Zhu Hou Ze was appointed as ACFTU 1st secretary. Zhu had been dismissed as head of the party propaganda department in Feb. 1987 because he was associated with the policies of the then party leader Hu Yaobang, who had failed to stop student demonstrations. As ACFTU 1st secretary Zhu probably encouraged moves to invigorate workers' congresses and to make unions more responsive to the welfare concerns of workers. He also appears not to have prevented members from participating in the reform and democracy movements of 1989. In December of that year he was replaced by Yu Hon-Gen, former president of the National Coal Corporation.

The 1992 Trade Union Law confirmed the ACFTU's role as the sole national organization of trade unions and defined the role of the unions as an instrument of official policy. This role was re-emphasized in the ACFTU's revised constitution of 1993. ACFTU chairman Wei Jianxing is a member of the CPC Politburo and there is a close mesh between union and party at all levels.

The 13th (five-yearly) congress of the ACFTU was held in Oct. 1998. Its theme was "holding high the great banner of Deng Xiaoping's theory" and mobilizing the workers "for the attainment of our nation's magnificent trans-century objectives". The congress "work report" on activities since the previous (12th) congress in 1993, delivered by the then first secretary Zhang Dinghua, declared that: "the trade unions at all levels have earnestly implemented the spirit of the 14th and 15th national congresses of the party [held in 1992 and 1997] ... and gone all out to make new contributions to the socialist modernization drive". The trade unions were operating "under the guidance of Deng Xiaoping's theory and the basic line of the party" in the "process of developing a socialist market economy".

At the same time the report recognized that the unions had shown "shortcomings and deficiencies" in "protecting workers' legitimate rights and interests and maintaining ties with the masses of workers". The report said that the organization, working methods and competence of trade unions and their officials were "incompatible with the needs of a socialist market economy". Trade unions needed to urge all enterprises to sign collective agreements and standardize individual contracts in the light of collective agreements, while the system of workers' congresses needed to be further developed.

The ACFTU has also shown awareness (as has the CPC) of the problems of social dislocation caused by economic reforms, unemployment, widespread non-payment of benefits and dissatisfaction as privatization is seen to make well-connected individuals wealthy at the expense of those who had built up the enterprises through their labour. The ACFTU is emphasizing its role in assisting workers to find new jobs, in providing retraining and organizing consumer cooperatives, and in organizing social benefits. Its "warmth project" provides assistance to needy workers in loss-making enterprises.

The ACFTU has a consultative role in drafting and revising laws, at national and local level, affecting labour and social welfare.

The ACFTU has not participated in the WFTU as an affiliate since the 1960s and has no other international affiliations. It nonetheless puts great emphasis on establishing bilateral relations with other unions (the international department having 60 staff), and says that it maintains relations with 400 trade unions in 130 countries. An ICFTU delegation, headed by general secretary Bill Jordan, visited China in Feb. 2000 and met ACFTU chairman Wei Jianxing. However, at least one international trade secretariat, the IUF, opposes all contact with the ACFTU.

Supreme authority is vested in a national congress held every five years (last in 1998). Between congresses authority resides with the executive committee (currently comprising 258 members elected by the congress), which elects the chairman, vice-chairmen and members of the presidium. When the executive committee is not in session, the presidium (which has 37 members) exercises the functions and powers of the executive committee. The secretariat is set up under the presidium and attends to day-to-day affairs. There is also an auditing commission of 41 members, elected by the congress. There are eight attached institutions: the Chinese Workers' Centre for International Exchange; the Chinese Workers' Technical Association; the China Labour College; the Chinese Workers' Centre for Audio-Visual Education; the Chinese Workers' Travel Service; the Chinese Workers' Publishing House; the Workers' Daily; and the ACFTU Cultural Troupe.

There are 31 trade union federations for the provinces, autonomous regions and municipalities. In parallel are 16 national industrial unions: Railway Workers' Trade Union; Civil Aviation Workers' Trade Union; Seamen's Trade Union; Road Transport Workers' Trade Union; Postal and Telecommunications Workers' Trade Union; Machinery and Metallurgical Workers' Trade Union; Petroleum, Chemical and Pharmaceutical Workers' Trade Union; Coal Miners' and Geological Workers' Trade Union; Water Conservancy and Electrical Power Workers' Trade Union; Textile Workers' Trade Union; Light Industry Workers' Trade Union; Construction and Building Workers' Trade Union; Agricultural and Forestry Workers' Trade Union; Financial and Commercial Workers' Trade Union; Educational Workers' Trade Union; and Banking Workers' Union.

Publications. The Workers' Daily.

International affiliations. None.

SPECIAL ADMINISTRATIVE REGIONS OF CHINA

Hong Kong

Population: 7.12 m. (2000 est.)

1 Political and Economic Background

Hong Kong reverted from British to Chinese rule, as a Special Administrative Region (HKSAR), on July 1, 1997. China's policy towards Hong Kong has been defined by the term "one country, two systems", indicating that it would not attempt to bring Hong Kong into conformity with mainland China but would seek to exercise sovereignty within the context of Hong Kong's different political, economic and judicial framework. The period since 1997 has largely been characterized by continuity from the period of British rule.

After a transitional period following the handover to China, in which there was a Provisional Legislative Council, the first elections to the Legislative Council under Chinese rule were held on May 24, 1998. Candidates of the opposition Democratic Party and allies won 13 of the 20 directly-elected seats, while the pro-Beijing Democratic Alliance for the Betterment of Hong Kong won only five. However, the legislature as a whole, where the majority of the 60 seats were reserved for specific groups, remained controlled by forces allied to Beijing or business groups favouring stable relations with Beijing. The administration is headed by a chief executive, appointed by the Chinese government.

Hong Kong is a key Asian manufacturing, financial and trading centre, with a buoyant free market economy. It represents a major economic asset and stepping-stone to international markets for China, which since 1997 has not sought to impose economic models and policies prevailing elsewhere in the country. Hong Kong enjoyed high growth rates throughout the 1980s and 1990s, but was badly hit by the Asian economic crisis of 1997–98, with unemployment at over 8% in 1999 at its highest for 25 years. However, after recession in early 1999, growth in GDP for the year as a whole was 3% and growth surged in 2000, with a full year forecast of over 10% and with unemployment falling.

GDP (purchasing power parity) $158.2bn. (1999 est.); GDP per capita (purchasing power parity) $23,100 (1999 est.).

2 Trade Unionism

Trade unionism first appeared early in the twentieth century, although unions did not achieve legal status until 1948. For many years Hong Kong trade unionism was clearly divided between the ICFTU-affiliated Hong Kong and Kowloon Trade Union Council (HKTUC) and the Hong Kong Federation of Trade Unions (HKFTU), each founded in the aftermath of legalization. The HKTUC was allied to the (Taiwanese) Chinese Federation of Labour. The larger HKFTU was oriented to Beijing. In addition many small unions operated independently of these centres. Both the HKTUC and the HKFTU continue in the aftermath of the reversion to Chinese rule in 1997. The HKTUC, however, has progressively declined as the relevance of its pro-Taiwanese orientation has disappeared, while the HKFTU is seen as closely aligned to the wishes of the Hong Kong authorities.

The final years of British rule also saw the emergence of a third centre, the Confederation of Trade Unions of Hong Kong (HKCTU), an ICFTU affiliate, and this has become the main focus of trade unionism independent of the HKFTU. The HKCTU sought to expand the rights available to free trade unions in the last years of British colonial rule in preparation for the handover to China.

Under British rule Hong Kong was not a member of the ILO in its own right and the UK made declarations on its behalf concerning the various conventions, including ILO conventions No.87 (Freedom of Association and Protection of the Right to Organize, 1948) and No.98 (Right to Organize and Collective Bargaining, 1949). Under the terms of agreement for the transfer of Hong Kong from British to Chinese rule, China was to continue to apply these conventions.

Under the Basic Law of the SAR (in effect, Hong Kong's constitution), the right to join unions is protected. However, as under British rule, there are no rights in respect of union recognition and collective bargaining, or institutional framework for these. Employers generally refuse to recognize unions and in practice less than one per cent of workers are covered by collective agreements. While there is a right to strike, the right is not protected in law, and employers can dismiss striking employees for breach of their contracts without compensation.

In the last days of British rule, Lee Cheuk-yan, the general secretary of the HKCTU, who was also a member of the Legislative Council, introduced a private member's bill which incorporated three ordinances designed to bring Hong Kong into compliance with ILO standards. The measure provided for unions to have rights to be recognized for collective bargaining or consultation, for workers dismissed for trade union activities to be reinstated, and to end the ban on the use of union funds for political purposes. The ordinances were passed at the last sitting of the Council under British rule in June 1997, but immediately suspended when the Chinese took control the following month. In Oct. 1997 the new Provisional Legislative Council overturned the main provisions of the new legislation, effectively returning the situation to what it had been in the period before June 1997. In Nov. 1998 the ILO Committee on Freedom of Association supported a complaint filed by the HKCTU against the government and called on the Hong Kong authorities to strengthen protections for trade unions and regretted the repeal of the collective bargaining legislation. The government indicated that it did not feel further action was necessary, and the HKFTU likewise declined to support the HKCTU on this issue.

In 1999 Lee Cheuk-yan again sought to introduce collective bargaining legislation in the Legislative Council, to which he had been elected in the first elections in May 1998. However, in July 1999 the president of the Legislative Council ruled the move inadmissible on the ground that bills relating to public expenditure, political structure and government operation could not be introduced as private members' bills unless approved by the chief executive. The government said that the measures proposed by Lee would add HK$40 million to its budget.

Since 1997 there has been some tightening of restrictions on freedom of association and right of assembly, but trade unionists have remained able to strike and stage demonstrations. In May 1999, in the face of government moves to restructure the civil service, civil servants staged a one-day "sick-out" and a protest rally organized by the Hong Kong Federation of Civil Service Unions and the HKCTU attracted 20,000. Strikes are not common, however, there being only three small strikes in 1999, and most individual employment contracts make striking a breach of contract that can lead to dismissal. There has been no interference with the international affiliation of the HKCTU to the ICFTU.

The trade unions are represented in the Legislative Council. In the first elections to the new 60-member body, held on May 24, 1998, nine trade unionists were elected: three from the HKCTU (including its general secretary, Lee Cheuk-yan and its chair, Lau Chin-shek); four from the HKFTU, including two of its vice-chairs; one from the Federation of Labour Unions (an HKCTU affiliate which adopted independent positions); and one from the non-aligned Association of Nursing Staff.

An estimated 22% of employees are in unions, with large numbers of small unions.

3 Trade Union Centres

Hong Kong Confederation of Trade Unions (HKCTU)

Address. 19th Floor, Wing Wong Commercial Building, 557–559 Nathan Road, Kowloon

Phone. +852 2770 8668

Fax. +852 2770 7388

E-mail. hkctu@hkctu.org.hk

Website. www.hkctu.org.hk

Leadership. Lee Cheuk-yan (general secretary); Lau Chin-shek (chair)

Membership. 145,000

History and character. Established in response to the Tiananmen Square events and the approach of transfer of sovereignty to China. In 1990 the HKCTU set itself the target of overtaking the pro-Beijing HKFTU and establishing a strong base before transfer to China. Despite steady growth, it did not reach that goal and attributes the continued success of the HKFTU in retaining members to the range of services the HKFTU is able to provide members.

The HKCTU describes its foundation as being the struggle for the rights of workers to organize independent and democratic trade unions and engage in collective bargaining with employers. Its general secretary, Lee Cheuk-yan, who is a member of the SAR's Legislative Council has promoted legislation to this end (see above). In April 1999, Lee Cheuk-yan also sought unsuccessfully to introduce minimum wage legislation in the Legislative Council.

The HKCTU identifies with opposition politics but not with one group. In the first elections to the new Legislative Council, in May 1998, general secretary Lee Cheuk-yan was elected on the Frontier platform, while chair Lau Chin-shek was elected on the Democratic Party platform.

Publications. *Turning Point* (in English, quarterly bulletin); *Hong Kong Labour Express* (monthly, in English). Content accessible via website.

International affiliation. ICFTU

Hong Kong Federation of Trade Unions (HKFTU)

Leadership. Cheng Yiu Tong (chairman)

Membership. 200,000

History and character. The HKFTU was founded in 1948 and in the British colonial period was oriented to Beijing. Following the handover of the teritory to China in 1997 the HKFTU affirmed its support for the new HKSAR government and its policy of "one country, two systems". It opposed the rival HKCTU's submission of a complaint to the ILO as an attempt to "internationalize the internal affairs" of the HKSAR. The rival HKCTU characterizes the HKFTU as an in instrument of the alliance between the authorities and the business oligarchies, but concedes that it has retained the affiliation of more workers, which is attributed to the HKFTU's substantial resources which allow it to run supermarkets, travel agencies, discount stores and health clinics at below-market rates.

Hong Kong and Kowloon Trades Union Council (HKTUC)

Address. Rex Building, 3rd Floor, 650-652 Nathan Road, Mongkok, Kowloon

Phone. +852 2384 5150

Fax. +852 2770 5396

Leadership. Tong Woon Fai (president); Liew Nan Kiem (general secretary)

History and character. Historically aligned with the Taiwanese Chinese Federation of Labour. It has declined in the face of the growth of the HKCTU in the 1990s.

International affiliation. ICFTU

4 Other Trade Union Organization
Joint Organization of Unions – Hong Kong

Address. Foundation for Asian Development, 104 Johnston Road, 2F, Wangchai

Phone. +852 892 0669

Fax. +852 289 18581

E-mail. fadltd@netnavigator.com

Leadership. Lam Wah-hui

International affiliation. WCL

Macau

Population: 446,000 (2000 est.)

1 Political and Economic Background

Macau, comprising a small peninsula in the south of the People's Republic of China and three neighbouring islands, was under Portuguese administration from the sixteenth century. It reverted to China as a Special Administrative Region in 1999. Under Portuguese rule it did not develop as a major commercial centre in the manner of Hong Kong, and its economy is based on tourism, including gambling (which represents an estimated 40% of GDP), and textiles.

GDP (purchasing power parity) $7.65bn. (1999 est.); GDP per capita (purchasing power parity) $17,500 (1999 est.).

2 Trade Unionism

Under the Portuguese constitution basic trade union rights were extended to Macau. However, there has been relatively little development and most unions are politically allied to Beijing and concentrate on welfare, social and cultural activities. Under the Basic Law, as with Hong Kong, China guaranteed that international labour conventions previously applied under Portuguese rule would remain in force. There has been little development of collective bargaining. There is a legal right to strike but protections against retribution are lacking and there were no strikes in 1999.

Colombia

Capital: Bogota
Population: 39.69 m. (2000 est.)

1 Political and Economic Background

Since the end of the Rojas dictatorship in 1957, the presidency of Colombia has alternated between the Liberal (PL) and Conservative parties, with the Cabinet being effectively bipartisan. President Barco Vargas (1986–90) formed a single party government, but his PL successors Gaviria Barco and Ernesto Samper Pizano returned the country to coalition rule; Samper was re-elected in 1994. Elections in 1998 resulted in the election of Andres Pastrana Arango, an independent conservative, as President. His Cabinet comprises members of the Conservative-led Great Alliance for Change coalition, which has a majority in the House of Representatives.

In 1991 a new constitution which contained significant labour provisions came into force with consensual backing from the political parties.

Drug trafficking and guerrilla warfare have for years scarred the political and the economic life of Columbia, which has also suffered a series of assassinations of political and trade union figures. Left-wing insurgents, notably the Colombia Revolutionary Armed Forces (FARC) and National Liberation Army (ELN), as well as right-wing death squads, are still active despite repeated attempts at national reconciliation by successive governments.

The economy has been adversely affected by the lack of stability and low investor confidence and the government has been forced to implement austerity measures while depending on foreign aid. The economy is also vulnerable to price fluctuations of coffee, oil and other export commodities. In 1999 GDP declined by 5% and unemployment rose to 20%.

GDP (purchasing power parity) $245.1bn. (1999 est.); GDP per capita (purchasing power parity) $6,200 (1999 est.).

2 Trade Unionism

Trade union organization appeared in the first decade of the twentieth century and unions were first legalized by the Liberal government in 1930. Colombia ratified ILO conventions No.87 (Freedom of Association and Protection of the Right to Organize, 1948) and No.98 (Right to Organize and Collective Bargaining, 1949), in 1976, and in 1977 unions became independent legal bodies, formally ending their direct political ties. About 6–7% of the workforce is unionized, with 89% of union members working in the public sector. In the private sector most union members belong to single enterprise

unions but the unions are generally weak and little collective bargaining takes place.

There have been constant splits and re-organizations of Colombian trade union centres over the decades. There are now three main centres, which between them have the affiliation of most of the 2,500 registered unions. The longest established centre, although itself affected by breakaways at different times, is the Confederación de Trabajadores de Colombia (CTC), which dates from the 1930s, is affiliated to the ICFTU, and traditionally is close to the Liberal Party. The Confederación General de Trabajadores Democráticos (CGTD), is politically independent and affiliated to the WCL. It was formed in 1992. The centre-left Central Unitaria de Trabajadores (CUT) was founded in 1986 and is the largest centre, with 45–50% of all unions affiliated to it.

Colombia is probably the most dangerous country in the world for trade unionists; it is certainly the most dangerous of those countries in which free trade unionism is protected by law. This bleak reality undercuts all formal legal protections.

The history of violence is a long one. A 1928 strike at the US-owned United Fruit company resulted in 'the massacre of the banana workers' when several hundred were killed by the army. In 1977 the then four leading confederations joined in a general strike in which about 18 people were killed in clashes with the security forces. By the 1980s "disappearances" and assassinations of political and union leaders by paramilitary groups were endemic. Violence continued throughout the 1990s. Large numbers of trade unionists fell victim to gun squads in the run-up to the 1990 presidential elections. In May the vice-president of the CTC was killed and the toll approached 1,000 for the three-year period to end-1990. After initial promise, the term of office of President Gaviria saw a large number of murders. The ICFTU *Survey of Violations of Trade Union Rights* found that 46 Colombian trade unionists had been murdered in 1993 and another 33 forced into hiding. The head office of the oil workers' union USO was bombed in Feb. 1993. While some of the killings were linked to drug barons and landowners, unions charged the security forces of complicity in some instances.

The ICFTU further estimated that there were 253 trade unionists murdered in 1996 and 156 in 1997. The teachers' union FECODE said that 61 teachers were killed in 1997 while four had disappeared. Many hundreds of trade unionists had left their homes because of death threats. Many of the murders were linked to industrial disputes, and were reportedly rarely investigated. Most of these deaths were attributed to paramilitaries with fewer reports of attacks by the security forces and guerrilla groups.

In Mar. 2000 the ICFTU reported that between 2,500

and 3,200 trade unionists had been killed since 1987, by paramilitary forces (sometimes with the complicity of the regular army), drug traffickers or far-left guerrillas. Among those killed in 1998–99 were CUT 1st vice-president Jorge Ortega Garcia (Oct. 20, 1998) and César Herrera Torreglosa, general secretary of the agricultural workers' union SINTRAINAGRO (Dec. 13, 1999). Rank-and-file union members particularly affected in this period were members of teachers' unions, agricultural workers and miners, while another centre of violence has been the oil-refining town of Barrancabermeja, the base of the oil workers' union, the USO. Arrests or convictions of those responsible for such murders are virtually unknown. Army and intelligence sources have sought in some instances to link union activists to guerrilla groups and lists of activists, effectively death lists, are reported to circulate.

In May 1998 the ILO, documenting more than 300 killings of trade unionists since 1995, criticized the government for having failed to provide evidence of arrests or convictions in a single case. In Nov. 1999 the government undertook to cooperate with the unions to end acts of anti-union terror, and the Labour Minister agreed to call on the ILO to despatch a "direct contacts mission" to evaluate how violence could be curbed. The CUT, CTC and CGTD have taken a number of joint initiatives in favour of peace and reconciliation.

Colombia's employment standards are laid down in the 1991 Constitution and the labour code, the latter regulating the right of association, organization of unions, federations and confederations, collective bargaining agreements, the right to strike and other union rights.

The ICFTU has noted the following restrictions on trade union activity: the labour code prohibits more than one union in any workplace; officers of unions must belong to the relevant trade or occupation; the authorities may supervise and intervene in the internal affairs of unions; industrial and branch unions must have 50% of workers in membership to bargain collectively; federations and confederations may not conduct collective bargaining; some public employees may not bargain collectively; the right to strike is restricted in many public services; and confederations and federations may not call strikes. Trade unions complain that legal measures brought in to combat terrorism, such as the introduction of witnesses with hidden identities, have also been used against trade union activists. In the period from 1996 the government made proposals to amend the labour laws to reduce the restrictions on trade unions but these measures have not been acted on by Congress.

The centres cooperate with each other. In Feb. 1997 they organized a public sector strike after the government declared a state of economic emergency. The oil workers' union the USO also threatened to shut down the state-run oil industry to oppose what it saw as a proposed creeping privatization. After a week, the government agreed wage increases and to set up a joint commission with the unions to study privatization plans, to review the criminal penalties being applied against trade union activists, and to set up a Commission for the Protection of Workers' Human Rights. The government also said it would promote a bill on collective bargaining in the public sector. In March, the constitutional court ruled that the economic state of emergency was unjustified.

The centres staged a general strike in Sept. 1998 to protest against the impact of structural adjustment programmes on wages and jobs. They also staged a strike, mainly in the public sector, Aug. 31–Sept. 1, 1999, in support of a 41-point economic and social recovery programme. The government agreed to hold discussions and not to penalize civil servants who had taken part in the strike.

3 Trade Union Centres

Confederación General de Trabajadores Democráticos (CGTD)
General Confederation of Democratic Workers

Address. Calle 39 A, n° 14–48, Apartado Aéreo 5415, Santafe de Bogota

Phone. +57 1 288 1560

Fax. +57 1 573 4026

E-mail. cgtd@col1.telecom.com.co

Leadership. Mario de J. Valderrama (president); Julio Roberto Gomez Esguerra (secretary general)

History and character. The CGTD was created in 1992 by fusion of the former WCL affiliate, the CGT, and the CTDC. The latter had itself been established in 1988 by the merger of the former leftist Trade Union Confederation of Colombian Workers (CSTC) and the Union of Workers of Colombia (UTC) together with a faction of the CTC. The CGTD is described as having a mix of Maoist and social Christian influences, reflecting the forces brought together at its creation. About 30% of Colombian unions are affiliated to it.

The WCL reported in 1998 that in the previous eight years, 27 leaders of the CGTD had been assassinated.

International affiliation. WCL

Confederación de Trabajadores de Colombia (CTC)
Confederation of Workers of Colombia

Address. Calle 39, No. 26A–23, Barrio de la Soledad, Bogota

Phone. +57 1 268 2084

Fax. +57 1 268 8576

E-mail. ctc@colnodo.apc.org

History and character. The CTC dates back to the 1930s and is traditionally allied to the moderate free-enterprise Liberal party. A former president, José Raquel Mercado, was assassinated by the revolutionary leftist M-19 movement in 1976. The CTC affiliates about 12–15% of Colombian unions.

International affiliation. ICFTU

Central Unitaria de Trabajadores (CUT)
Central Union of Workers

Leadership. Luis Eduardo Garzon (president); Hector Fajardo (secretary general)

History and character. The centre-left CUT, created in 1986 by affiliates of pre-existing centres, is the leading union centre in Colombia, representing some 45–50% of Colombia's unions. The CUT has been a regular target for terrorist attack: nearly 800 of its members were mur-

dered between 1987 and 1992 alone. Its 1st Vice-President, Jorge Ortega Garcia was shot dead at home on Oct. 20, 1998, during a national strike called over privatization and austerity measures. He had fled abroad for periods on several occasions during the previous few years because of death threats. CUT president Luis Eduardo Garzon was the winner of the 2000 AFL–CIO human rights award in recognition of his and the CUT's continuing role in the search for peace and reconciliation in Colombia.

Comoros

Capital: Moroni
Population: 578,000 (2000 est.)

1 Political and Economic Background

The Federal Islamic Republic of Comoros, a former French overseas territory accorded internal self-government in 1961, declared itself independent in 1975. (Mayotte, one of the four islands in the archipelago, voted in 1976 to remain within the French Republic). Since then it has experienced regular coups and insurrections, most recently in April 1999 when army commander Col. Assoumani Azali took power in a bloodless coup.

In Aug. 1997 separatists on the island of Anjouan, who had been demanding the return of French rule (to the embarrassment of France) declared independence, and troops were sent to put down the rebellion, sustaining dozens of fatalities. Secessionists remained in control of the island under their self-styled President Abdallah Ibrahim. In April 1999 representatives of Anjouan refused to sign an agreement, brokered by the Organization of African Unity, for the creation of a new federal "Union of Comoran Islands" and amid the resultant unrest Col. Azali, the Army Chief of Staff, took power in Moroni and suspended the constitution. In a referendum in Jan. 2000 Anjouan voted against incorporation in the proposed Union, which Azali was committed to implementing.

Agriculture occupies more than 80 per cent of the workforce, although there is high unemployment and rural under-employment and Comoros is not self-sufficient in food. Most of this activity is on a subsistence

basis with production seriously affected by erosion and drought, and markets for the few agricultural and agriculture-based exports are liable to wide fluctuations. The Comoros' economy has been severely disrupted by domestic upheavals and natural disasters and the country depends heavily on assistance from France and from Arab states in the Gulf area, and on agreements with the EU. Unemployment is estimated at 20 per cent.

GDP (purchasing power parity) $410 m. (1998 est.); GDP per capita (purchasing power parity) $725 (1998 est.).

2 Trade Unionism

The Comoros ratified ILO Conventions No.87 (Freedom of Association and Protection of the Right to Organize, 1948) and No.98 (Right to Organize and Collective Bargaining, 1949) in 1978. The economy is based on subsistence agriculture and fishing and very small-scale commerce and there are only some 7,000 employees in the formal economy, the majority of them working for the government. Unions of teachers, civil servants and dock workers exist.

There is no development of collective bargaining. Public sector strikes occur from time to time over non-payment of wages. In Jan. 1997 a strike over wage arrears for public servants was declared illegal after the government said it could not pay arrears in full, and leaders of the teachers and health workers were briefly detained. In Aug. 1997 all political and trade union demonstrations were banned, the government citing the activity of secessionists on Anjouan as justification.

Congo, Democratic Republic of (formerly Zaire)

Capital: Kinshasa
Population: 51.96 m. (2000 est.)

1 Political and Economic Background

Following a military coup in 1965, Congo became a one-party state ruled by President Marshal Mobutu Sese Seko, leader of the Mouvement Populaire de la Révolution (MPR). It was renamed as Zaire in 1971 in accordance with Mobutu's Africanization programme. From 1990 other political parties were allowed. A transitional administration, the High Council of the Republic (HCR) was elected in 1992 but came into conflict with Mobutu. After a lengthy period of confusion with at one point two rival cabinets coexisting, an election date of July 1995 was set. In May 1995 however, the elections were indefinitely postponed.

Mobutu was overthrown in May 1997 by the forces of Laurent Kabila, leader of the Alliance of Democratic Forces for the Liberation of Congo–Zaire, and died later that year in Morocco. On taking power Kabila announced that he would become President and that the country would be renamed as the Democratic Republic of Congo (DROC). Widespread massacres of ethnic Tutsis were reported. All political party activity and demonstrations were banned, but presidential and legislative elections were promised for April 1999. No elections were held, however and Kabila himself faced serious military rebellion with the forces of several African countries fighting on different sides. He was assassinated in Jan. 2001.

The DROC's weak economy has deteriorated since the 1980s and it is one of the world's poorest countries. It has been affected by huge influxes of refugees from several African states (including, in 1994, perhaps one million fleeing from Rwanda and Burundi), and in the late 1990s military conflict (exacerbated by foreign intervention) within its own borders. Foreign-owned businesses have scaled back their activity. Lack of infrastructure, corruption and the absence of a reliable legal and policy framework for business, are factors that have discouraged investment.

GDP (purchasing power parity) $35.7bn. (1999 est.); GDP per capita (purchasing power parity) $710 (1999 est.).

2 Trade Unionism

The DROC ratified ILO Convention No. 98 (Right to Organize and Collective Bargaining, 1949) in 1969, but has not ratified Convention No. 87 (Freedom of Association and Protection of the Right to Organize, 1948).

The trade unions were consolidated into the Union Nationale des Travailleurs du Zaire (UNTZa) in 1967 under the auspices of the ruling party. Thereafter it operated as the sole union centre. It was able to adopt more independence from the ruling party by the late 1980s. Following Mobutu's 1990 decision to allow freedom of association, as part of a move to political liberalization, some 80 new union organizations were founded: in the view of the ICFTU, only four were representative.

The ICFTU reported that by 1997 there were at least 199 trade unions although this was "largely because the authorities, politicians, employers and others were behind the creation and registration of a number of in-house unions and other unrepresentative and phantom unions, particularly in the public sector and state enterprises".

Following the seizure of power by Kabila in 1997, UNTZa was renamed as the Union Nationale des Travailleurs du Congo (UNTC). This remains the leading federation. However, the position of the trade unions has been undermined by the collapse of large parts of the formal economy and the shortage of regularly paid jobs. Collective bargaining scarcely exists in practice. Unions mainly represent public sector employees. There have been strikes under Kabila by civil servants, university administrators, health workers and other public sector workers over unpaid wages, with government action varying between giving concessions and arresting and imprisoning union leaders.

3 Trade Union Centres

Confédération Syndicale du Congo (CSC)

Address. BP 3107, Kinshasa

Phone. +243 12 20 953

Fax. +243 12 20 953

E-mail. kiko@ic.cd

Leadership. Fernand Kikongi (president)

History and character. This is the second largest confederation in the DROC. Its president, Fernand Kikongi, is also the president of the WCL (elected Dec. 1997). Kikongi told the 2nd CSC congress, held in Kinshasa in July 1999, that the trade unions had to find ways to assist in national reconstruction in the face of economic collapse, instability, closure of enterprises and malnutrition.

International affiliation. WCL

Confédération Démocratique du Travail (CDT)

Address. 5 ème Rue n.211 Limette, BP 10897, Kinshasa 1

Phone. +243 880 4573

History and character. Emerged as third largest union centre under pluralism, with 139 seats gained in the 1994 trade union elections. Affiliated to the ICFTU in 1994.

International affiliation. ICFTU

Union Nationale des Travailleurs du Congo (UNTC)
National Union of Congolese Workers

Address. Zone de la Gombe, BP 8814, Avenue Mutombo, Katshi 5, Kinshasa 1

Phone. +243 12 22 148

History and character. Founded 1967. Formerly known as Union Nationale des Travailleurs du Zaïre (UNTZa), once the single union centre of Zaire. It launched a contributory national health insurance scheme (UPM) in 1986, and thereafter a number of education, health, rural cooperative, agricultural, banking and other projects. It began to move away from the regime in the late 1980s with protests against the steady decline in the purchasing power of Zairean workers, which it attributed to "currency depreciation and abuse perpetrated under the guise of economic liberalism". In 1990 UNTZa was able to break away from the ruling party and expelled its general secretary Kombo Ntonga Booke, who was a member of the party central committee.

Of the three centres it remained closest to the regime, and in Zaire's first free pluralist trade union elections since 1967, it comfortably held first place with 1,126 seats. The UNTZa affiliated to the ICFTU in 1994; it remained the strongest trade union centre, comfortably winning the second (1994) "social" trade union elections by securing 1,324 seats, ahead of the 1,196 gained by its nearest rival the WCL-affiliated Confédération Syndicale du Zaire (CSZa). In 1997, after the fall of Mobutu and renaming of the country, UNTZa was renamed the UNTC.

International affiliation. ICFTU

Congo, Republic of

Capital: Brazzaville
Population: 2.83 m. (2000 est.)

1 Political and Economic Background

The Republic of Congo became a self-governing republic within the French Community in 1958 and achieved full independence in 1960. After some years of disturbed political conditions, a military coup took place in 1968, and in the following year a nominally Marxist regime was established under the Parti Congolais du Travail (PCT) as the sole political party. The country was renamed the People's Republic of the Congo in 1970 but reverted to its original name in 1991 after the PCT abandoned Marxism–Leninism.

A 1992 referendum approved a new multi-party constitution, and the country's first democratic elections followed the same year. Pascal Lissouba, leader of the Pan-African Union for Social Democracy (UPADS) was elected president, defeating the incumbent Denis Sassou-Nguesso of the PCT, who had been President since 1979. Further presidential elections scheduled for July 1997 were postponed because of internal unrest.

In Oct. 1997, after four months' fighting, "Cobra" militias backing Sassou-Nguesso (who was also supported militarily by the government of Angola) overthrew Lissouba, who went into exile in France. There have been no elections since the takeover of power by Sassou-Nguesso and the country is also affected by continuing military conflicts.

Agriculture, much of it at subsistence level but also including cash crops such as coffee, cocoa sugar and palm oil, provides a livelihood for much of the population. However the country is also an oil producer and the development of this sector in the 1970s and 1980s funded development as oil became the main contributor to government revenues. From the late 1960s the main sectors of the economy were progressively nationalized. As the country moved away from one-party rule, however, it embraced market principles and received external support for restructuring, although this has been disrupted by civil war and instability.

GDP (purchasing power parity) $4.15bn. (1999 est.); GDP per capita (purchasing power parity) $1,530 (1999 est.).

2 Trade Unionism

Congo ratified ILO Convention No.87 (Freedom of Association and Protection of the Right to Organize, 1948) in 1960, but did not ratify Convention No.98 (Right to Organize and Collective Bargaining, 1949) until 1999.

Trade unionism developed under the French but under

one party rule was coordinated by the Confédération Syndicale Congolaise (CSC). The CSC was designated by name in a decree as the sole trade union and benefited from compulsory check-off from the pay of all workers, which was introduced in 1973. However, the move to pluralism in the early 1990s was reflected in the CSC assuming independence from the ruling party and the emergence of alternative centres.

The current labour code provides for the free formation of trade unions. The formal waged sector is small but most employees in it are in unions. Collective bargaining is practiced and there is a legal right to strike, subject to giving a period of notice and non-binding arbitration procedures. A leading recent cause of strikes has been salary arrears for public servants.

In addition to the CSC, there are now two ICFTU affiliates: the Confédération des Syndicats Libres Autonomes du Congo (COSYLAC), and the Confédération Syndicale des Travailleurs du Congo (CSTC). There is also a WCL affiliate, the Confédération Africaine des Travailleurs Croyants (CATC).

3 Trade Union Centres

Confédération Africaine des Travailleurs Croyants (CATC)

Address. BP 624, 23 avenue Monseigneur Augouard-Quartier du Méridien, Brazzaville

Phone. +242 81 19 20

Fax. +242 81 18 28

Leadership. M'Villa-Biyaoula Fulgence (president); Mafoua Alain-David (permanent secretary)

International affiliation. WCL

Confédération Syndicale Congolaise (CSC)
Congolese Trade Union Confederation

History and character. The CSC was formed in 1964. CSC secretary-general Bokamba Yangouma was a member of the PCT political bureau under one-party rule. However, a strong independence movement gathered in CSC, leading to threats of secession on the part of some federations. The CSC responded with a general strike for its independence from the PCT in Sept. 1990, and this marked the opening of a period of greater freedom of political action.

International affiliation. WFTU

Confédération Syndicale des Travailleurs du Congo (CSTC)

Address. BP 14743, Brazzaville

International affiliation. ICFTU

Confédération des Syndicats Libres Autonomes du Congo (COSYLAC)

Address. BP 14861, Brazzaville

Phone. +242 83 42 70

Fax. +242 82 42 65

International affiliation. ICFTU

Costa Rica

Capital: San José
Population: 3.71 m. (2000 est.)

1 Political and Economic Background

Following a brief but bitter civil war in 1948 the dominant party, normally forming the government, was the social democratic National Liberation Party (PLN). In its earlier periods of office the PLN undertook a major programme of reform, including the dissolution of the army, a programme of nationalization (especially of the banks) and the establishment of a developed system of social security. In 1990, the PNL administration of President Arias was succeeded by a conservative government led by the Social Christian Unity Party (PUSC) of Rafael Calderón. Four years later the PLN returned to power under President José María Figueres but the most recent elections, in Feb. 1998, resulted in the election as President of the PUSC candidate Miguel Angel Rodríguez, the PUSC also winning the largest number of seats in the Legislative Assembly.

Costa Rica has a mixed economy including tourism, electronics and commercial agriculture (with the main export crops being coffee and bananas). Prices and levels of demand for coffee and bananas are liable to severe fluctuations in the international markets. Moreover, requirements for labour on the coffee estates vary seasonally so that there is frequent widespread rural under-employment.

The PUSC administration from 1990 pursued drastic IMF-backed "shock measures" but these met considerable opposition from public sector trade unions. Through the 1990s successive governments have been attempting to strengthen the private sector economy while retaining social measures, but this policy has been undermined by continuing government deficits and generally high inflation. In 1998 PUSC presidential candidate Rodríguez won a narrow victory on a platform that promised to deliver 6% per annum growth, attract foreign capital and privatize state companies. Political resistance subsequently slowed his programme but in Mar. 2000 the Legislative Assembly voted to end the state's monopoly in the electricity and telecommunications sectors. Growth in GDP was 7% in 1999, with inflation dropping to 11%.

GDP (purchasing power parity) $26bn. (1999 est.); GDP per capita (purchasing power parity) $7,100 (1999 est.).

2 Trade Unionism

The first artisans' union was recorded in 1905, and the growth of trade unionism (including the appearance of the first trade union centres) was fostered by favourable labour legislation introduced by the 1940–43 government of President Rafael Calderon Guardia. The 1949 Constitution guaranteed basic workers' rights, including a minimum wage and limitations on hours of work, and the rights to lock out and to strike (except in public services) were guaranteed. Costa Rica ratified ILO Conventions No.87 (Freedom of Association and Protection of the Right to Organize, 1948) and No.98 (Right to Organize and Collective Bargaining, 1949) in 1960.

Three of the then six national union centres – the Democratic Workers' Union (CATD), the Costa Rican Confederation of Democratic Workers (CCTD) and the National Confederation of Workers (CNT), all of social democratic persuasion – confederated in Aug. 1991 to form the 90,000 member Rerum Novarum (CTRN) with ICFTU affiliation. This is the largest centre. The WCL's affiliate is the CMTC and the WFTU also claims a number of affiliates. There are also independent unions not affiliated to any of the centres.

For years the unions faced a powerful rival in the Catholic-inspired Solidarismo movement, which by 1990 claimed members in some 1,200 associations, apparently ahead of the unions. The associations were affiliated either to the Solidarista Union (SURSUM) or to the Pope John XXIII School and sought harmonious relations between employers and employees. Members also gained practical benefits such as credit unions in return for renouncing the right to strike, and in 1990 established their own bank, financed by the American agency USAID.

Article 273 of the former (1943) labour code, required only five people to form a Solidarismo association whereas the figure for unions was 20. The Solidarist Act of 1984 granted the associations special legal status. The six national union centres were vehemently opposed to Solidarismo, arguing that employer preference was intended to eliminate independent unionism, as had actually occurred in the banana plantations. In 1989 Solidarismo employees at Tres Rios textiles did hold a brief and successful strike to gain greater control over their association, and there were other manifestations of discontent, but their associations continued to be the subject of repeated ICFTU complaints.

Business interests prevented modernization of the 1943 labour code in the 1980s, but in 1989 President Arias's Minister of Labour announced an agreement with the unions on new draft regulations which would promote union development by giving activists protection against dismissal. Its introduction into law was however blocked by fierce opposition from employers and Solidarismo. The same year the ICFTU submitted a complaint to the ILO about government efforts to promote Solidarismo, which it saw as a barrier to an independent trade union movement.

Finally in Oct. 1993 the legislature unanimously adopted a new labour code, much of which addressed problems identified by the ILO Committee of Experts. Among these was a reduction in the threshold membership of unions to 12 (a provision which removed the advantage enjoyed by Solidarismo); the banning of Solidarismo from collective bargaining; a series of protections against unfair dismissal, especially of union activists; and an end to workplace offences punishable by fine.

In its 1999 *Annual Survey of Trade Union Rights*, however, the ICFTU said that in the view of the unions the 1993 changes to the labour code had proved a "dead letter". Specific grievances included that:

1. Although the legal advantages of Solidarismo associations have been removed, employers still continue to set up such associations and the Labour Ministry to register them. In 1996, for example, only ten collective agreements were signed with trade unions while 45 agreements were reached with solidarist associations.

2. In the private sector it was "virtually impossible" to form trade unions because of hostility by employers and the reluctance of the government to enforce labour legislation. This was especially a problem in the nine export processing zones (EPZs) and on the banana plantations where trade unionists were dismissed and blacklisted. The ICFTU said the Labour Ministry takes 2–3 years to hear complaints, and in the case of the plantations and EPZs invariably found against the unions.

The trade unions have found it easier to organize in the public sector, where protections have been greater. Although 15% of the work force overall is unionized, most union members are in the public sector. There are restrictions on the right to strike in the public sector, although such strikes have occurred, usually of short duration. In Feb. 1998 the Supreme Court ruled that public sector workers, except those in essential positions, had the right to strike, and in practice the government had not enforced penalties against public sector strikers. The position of the unions in the public sector has been eroded to some degree during the 1990s by the impact of privatization, a process during which many public sector union leaders also lost their jobs. In Sept. 2000 the ICFTU complained that the courts were now undermining long-standing collective bargaining agreements in state industries such as the oil industry.

Strikes are banned in a wide range of sectors. These include insurance, banks, oil and related industries, electricity, water; communications; rail, maritime and air transport; ports; agricultural producers of seeds, fertilizers and insecticides; the cement industry; education; health care; sugar cane and coffee plantations, stock raising and forestry. Only two strikes were legal out of a total of 398 during in the period 1996–97.

Particular controversy has surrounded conditions in the banana sector, where unions have been particularly opposed by employers, and where there have been allegations of unsafe use of pesticides. In 1997 revelations about the conditions in the plantations by the SITRAP banana workers' union received international notice and led to threats by government ministers to prosecute the union for treason. In Dec. 1997, after international pressure, Del Monte signed an agreement allowing the SITRAP banana workers the right to organize in the industry. In Apr. 1999 the ICFTU filed a complaint with the ILO alleging violations of trade union rights by the banana exporting company Cobasur against the SITRASUR banana workers' union.

3 Trade Union Centres

Central del Movimiento de Trabajadores Costarricenses (CMTC)

Address. Apartado Postal No.4137–1000, Calle 20, Av. 3–5, Casa No.321, 'Continguo a la Iglesia La Medalla Milagrosa', San José

Phone. +506 221 7701

Fax. +506 222 6519

Leadership. Dennys Cabezas (president); José Angel Obando (secretary-general)

History and character. The Central de Trabajadores Costarricenses (CTC) was created by the regional organization of Christian unions, CLASC, as the Federation of Christian Workers and Peasants of Costa Rica (FOCC) in 1964, becoming the CTC in 1972 and the CMTC in the 1990s.

International affiliations. WCL

Confederación Costarricense de Trabajadores (Rerum Novarum) (CTRN)
Costa Rican Confederation of Workers (Rerum Novarum)

Address. Avenida 15 Calles 35–37, Casa 3540, Barrio Escalante, San José

Phone. +506 283 2647

Fax. +506 283 4244

E-mail. ctrnovan@sol.racsa.co.cr

History and character. The CTRN was formed in 1991, with 90,000 members, by the merger of three pre-existing broadly social democratic centres.

International affiliation. ICFTU

Côte d'Ivoire

Capital: Yamoussoukro
Population: 15.98 m. (2000 est.)

1 Political and Economic Background

Côte d'Ivoire (Ivory Coast) became a self-governing republic within the French Community in 1958 and gained full independence in 1960. From independence power was held by the Parti Démocratique de la Côte d'Ivoire (PDCI) led by Félix Houphouët-Boigny, the only legal political party. The PDCI's aim was to consolidate the country's independence on the basis of a free-enterprise economy, in cooperation with other West African states, and the maintenance of good relations with France. Until recent times it has been relatively stable politically by African standards.

Reflecting developments in many African states at that time Houphouët-Boigny in May 1990 endorsed a change to multi-partyism. The PDCI won multi-party elections

later that year but the move to multi-partyism exposed ethnic divisions, particularly between the mainly Muslim North and the Christian South. Houphouët-Boigny died in 1993 and was succeeded by the president of the Assembly Henri Konan-Bédié (a southerner), who successfully resisted (with French backing) an attempted northern-led coup. The PDCI easily won further (disputed) elections in 1995. Konan-Bédié was overthrown in a bloodless coup on Dec. 24, 1999 and replaced by a military junta led by Gen. Robert Guei, who said he would end corruption and hold elections by October 2000. Presidential elections were held as promised, with Laurent Gbagbo of the Popular Front (PFI) party apparently winning, after other leading contenders had been barred from standing. However, on Oct. 24 Guei declared himself the winner after he dissolved the National Electoral Commission and arrested its members. This resulted in widespread demonstrations, joined by troops, forcing the collapse of the Guei regime, and Laurent Gbagbo assumed the presidency.

Côte d'Ivoire's economy, one of the largest in Africa, is based on agriculture, with cocoa (of which it is the world's largest producer) and coffee being major cash crops. There is a large immigrant agricultural work force from neighbouring Burkina Faso, which has become the target for political attacks. There is also a manufacturing sector. In the 1980s, as revenues from export commodities declined, corrective public expenditure cuts provoked outbreaks of civil and industrial unrest. The state divested itself of many commercial enterprises in which it had a stake and increased the role of the private sector as part of a structural adjustment programme. Nevertheless, by 1992 Côte d'Ivoire was one of the most heavily indebted countries in Africa and under new pressure to introduce unpopular measures including the imposition of substantial pay cuts. That year's IMF-approved restructuring plan proposed to cut back the number of civil servants from 105,000 to 85,000. 1994 brought a 50% devaluation of the CFA franc and a boost for exports which contributed to the first year of growth in the 1990s. From 1996–99 growth averaged 5% per annum, but in 2000 GDP declined with cocoa prices depressed and with continuing unrest and abortive army mutinies in the wake of the coup. The country remains heavily indebted and international donor programmes have been limited or ended because of corruption. In May 2000 it became the second country (after Ecuador) to default on Brady bond repayments.

GDP (purchasing power parity) $25.7bn. (1999 est.); GDP per capita (purchasing power parity) $1,600 (1999 est.)

2 Trade Unionism

Trade unions developed under French rule and at independence in 1960 there were three national trade union centres. Côte d'Ivoire ratified ILO Convention No.87 (Freedom of Association and Protection of the Right to Organize, 1948) in 1960 and Convention No.98 (Right to Organize and Collective Bargaining, 1949) in 1961. In 1962, however, a single union system was organized through the Union Générale des Travailleurs de Côte d' Ivoire (UGTCI) under the leadership of the ruling PDCI. There was industrial unrest in the 1980s, mainly involving white-collar public sector employees such as teachers, as the country sought to deal with its high debt. The government response included dismissals, fines, conscription and threats of imprisonment. In 1990 the UGTCI recorded its intention to protect itself against "rebellious affiliates which had aligned themselves with the protesters and strikers". In 1991, however, several UGTCI affiliates broke away and a greater degree of pluralism was established, in line with the broader political changes in the country (as much of Africa) at that time. The UGTCI remained close to the government and other unions said they faced discriminatory treatment. The WCL affiliate Dignité emerged in the 1990s as the most active union outside the UGTCI.

All employees except the armed forces and police are legally entitled to join unions. Collective bargaining agreements exist in bigger enterprises and parts of the civil service. There is a right to strike although lengthy negotiation procedures mean strikes are often illegal. The UGCTI has rarely called strikes.

3 Trade Union Centres

Centrale des Syndicats Libres de Côte d'Ivoire (Dignité)

Address. BP 2031, Abidjan 03

Phone. +225 2037 74 89

Fax. +225 2037 85 01

E-mail. dignite@aviso.ci

Leadership. Basile Mahan Gahé (secretary-general)

History and character. Dignité emerged in the early 1990s. Members at the state agro-industrial company Ihro La Mé were sacked in 1993 for organizing union elections. A major dispute erupted at the plant which cost 15 lives in the months to come and culminated in the arrests of four Dignité leaders including the secretary-general in 1994. In June 1995, 618 Ihro La Mé workers and their families were reported living in the jungle after eviction from their houses by the army. Dignité members at the port of Abidjan also experienced repression: they were dismissed and replaced by new employees. After a protest march in Feb. 1998, police reportedly damaged the Dignité headquarters and surrounded it for a week. In Feb. 1999 police occupied Dignité headquarters to prevent a protest march called following the dismissal of trade unionists.

International affiliation. WCL

Union Générale des Travailleurs de Côte d' Ivoire (UGTCI)

Address. Bourse du Travail Avenue 1, Rue Barrée à Treichville 05, BP 1203, Abidjan 05

Phone. +225 24 16 95

Fax. +225 24 08 03

History and character. The UGTCI was formed in 1962 by merger of the four existing trade union centres and for many years, as the close ally of the ruling PDCI, was the sole centre.

International affiliations. ICFTU

Croatia

Capital: Zagreb
Population: 4.28 m. (2000 est.)

1 Political and Economic Background

Croatia was formerly a constituent republic of Yugoslavia. In May 1990, Franjo Tudjman became president after multi-party elections as the leader of the nationalist Croatian Democratic Union (HDZ). In May 1991 the HDZ government won a 94% referendum majority in favour of independence and declared secession from Yugoslavia in June. Military conflict broke out with Yugoslavia, primarily in areas of Croatia with a large ethnic Serb population, and this did not finally cease until 1995, although the government achieved control over most of the country, as well as international recognition, within the first few months. Tudjman remained in office until his death on Dec. 10, 1999, with the HDZ exercising a dominant and in respects authoritarian role in political life. However, elections in Jan. 2000 resulted in victory for an opposition coalition led by the Social Democratic Party and the Croatian Social Liberal Party, while Stipe Mesic of the Croatian People's Party became President.

Croatia was among the most prosperous republics of former Yugoslavia with a diverse economic base. Its progress to a market economy since independence has been fitful, with a significant private sector established but many major enterprises still in state hands or with the state having a stake. Many companies are considered insolvent without being bankrupted. The process of privatization has been criticized as benefiting allies of the ruling HDZ. As in other former Yugoslav republics, there are major problems of inter-enterprise debt (put at 18% of GDP), wage arrears, unemployment (estimated at 19% in 1999) and under-employment.

GDP (purchasing power parity) $23.9bn. (1999 est.); GDP per capita (purchasing power parity) $5,100 (1999 est.).

2 Trade Unionism

Croatia ratified ratified ILO Conventions No. 87 (Freedom of Association and Protection of the Right to Organize, 1948) and No. 98 (Right to Organize and Collective Bargaining, 1949) in 1991, following its declaration of independence.

Under communism the Union of Trade Unions of Croatia was affiliated to the Yugoslav national centre. The first completely independent union was the Trade Union of Railroad Engineers of Croatia, founded in Nov. 1989, which was quickly followed by several others. These and other dissident unions participated in the eighth congress of the former official body on May 11, 1990, and the inaugural congress of the Union of Autonomous Trade Unions of Croatia (SSSH) was held on the two following days.

This congress was dominated by conflict between communists and HDZ supporters. Although a reformed constitution and autonomous orientation were adopted, a communist president, Josip Klisovic, was elected. In reaction to this a congress of the Confederation of Independent Trade Unions of Croatia (CITUC) was held in June by unions defecting from SSSH and some of the new unions which had stayed aloof. A number of unions opposed to the SSSH leadership had stayed within its ranks and at an extraordinary session of the national council replaced the president with a working council pending the holding of elections. When these were held at a Jan. 1991 meeting of the council Dragutin Lesar was elected president. Meanwhile, in Dec. 1990 the Croatian Association of Trade Unions (HUS) had been formed under the sponsorship of the ruling HDZ.

All workers are entitled to form or join unions of their own choosing and an estimated 64% of the employed work force is unionized. There are now one major (SSSH) and four minor confederations (including CITUC and HUS) designated as representative under the 1999 Act on Trade Union Representativity as well as a number of independent unions. The SSSH represents about two-thirds of the organized workforce.

In May 1993 an agreement, brokered by the European Trade Union Confederation (ETUC), united the (then three) contending national centres over the principles that should govern the distribution of the assets of the former state unions. Demands were laid on the Croatian government to restore these assets. In Jan. 1998 the government announced it would take title to the assets until an agreement could be reached and approved by Parliament. In response to a request by the ILO, the government then gave the confederations more time and in July 1999 the five confederations signed an agreement on the division. The unions believed the government might be planning to confiscate assets permanently.

Conventional industrial relations began to emerge even before the war, beginning in June 1991, that established the country's independence, and throughout 1991 sectoral agreements were signed, principally by one union centre, the SSSH. The agreements were however frequently vulnerable to government intervention. At the height of the war emergency the three leading centres, SSSH, HUS and CITUC, signed an agreement with the government about cooperation and activity in circumstances of war (the War Agreement), although they later withdrew in protest against government employment policy. Threats of combined industrial action by those three national centres succeeded in Oct.1992 in forcing withdrawal of a government decree suspending the application of collective agreements and imposing wage controls.

The labour code provides a framework for collective bargaining contracts and protection of the right to strike. Collective bargaining is practiced, although implementation is undermined by high unemployment (19% in 1999) and the poor finances of some enterprises, with significant numbers of employees suffering wage arrears. There is no adequate mechanism for enforcement of collective contracts where employers ignore their provisions. There is no system of labour courts and there is a huge backlog of employment-related cases in the civil courts.

The right to strike is embodied in the constitution and retaliation against workers engaged in legal strikes is unlawful. Strikes are legal only after mediation has failed; arbitration can be used only where both parties consent. There are significant restrictions on the right to strike. Workers may only strike at the end of a contract period unless provided otherwise in the contract. In 1996 the Supreme Court ruled that strikes over wage arrears are unlawful, yet this is a major cause of discontent, with an estimated 10% of the working population experiencing wage arrears in 1999. The alternative, legal action, is endlessly protracted and ineffective. Those taking part in illegal strikes may be dismissed, and the union held liable for damages, although in practice no strikes were declared to be illegal during the course of 1999. The right to strike is restricted in the public sector and state sector employers have reportedly used coercion and intimidation to discourage strikes in some instances.

In Aug. 1993 the first meeting of a tripartite Economic and Social Council (GSV) was held. Under the 1995 labour code works council elections were to be held to determine which unions have "most representative" status for purposes of involvement on the GSV. Such elections were held for the first time in 1996, with the SSSH winning the great majority of seats, but there was controversy about the criteria for establishing representative status and the work of the GSV lapsed. It resumed in July 1999 after the Act on Trade Union Representativity defined the basis for representation.

3 Trade Union Centre

Savez Samostalnih Sindikata Hrvatske (SSSH)
Union of Autonomous Trade Unions of Croatia
(UATUC)

Address. Kresimirov trg 2, 10000 Zagreb

Phone. +385 1 465 5026 (international department)

Fax. +385 1 465 5011 (international department)

E-mail. sssh@sssh.hr

Website. www.sssh.hr (Croatian; English)

Leadership. Davor Juric (president)

Membership. 350,000 in 22 branch unions

History and character. The SSSH was formed in May 1990 by dissident independent unions founded under communism in the former Yugoslavia as well as former official unions. It suffered almost immediate defections from unions unprepared to accept its initial communist leadership but subsequently established its position as the leading Croatian trade union centre. It represents about 66% of the organized workforce. It has been accepted internationally as the principal voice of Croatian trade unionism; it affiliated to the ICFTU in 1996 and has had observer status with ETUC since 1998.

The SSSH supported the opposition coalition in the election campaign that led to the defeat of the ruling HDZ in elections in Jan. 2000. It favours Croatia's candidacy for EU membership, and in a declaration in Nov. 2000 called on the government to involve the trade unions in the accession process, to ratify the European Convention on Human Rights and European Social Charter, and to implement the European works council directive in multinational firms.

The SSSH has established an Industrial Democracy Centre to undertake trade union education activities.

Publications. Sindikalna akcija

International affiliation. ICFTU. Has observer status with ETUC

Cuba

Capital: Havana
Population: 11.14 m. (2000 est.)

1 Political and Economic Background

Revolutionary forces led by Fidel Castro overthrew the

Batista regime at the beginning of 1959. A Marxist–Leninist programme was proclaimed in 1961, and four years later the existing leading political organization became the Communist Party of Cuba. This remains the sole legal political party and politically the Cuban system remains substantially unreconstructed in the wake of the collapse of Communism in Europe. However, despite continuing US sanctions, Cuba was successful in reducing its diplomatic isolation in the late 1990s.

For decades, the Soviet Union heavily subsidized Cuba for geopolitical reasons. The 1990 withdrawal of subsidies worth \$4bn–\$6bn. per annum had serious implications for Cuba, which had in effect relied on subsidies to offset the failure of its domestic state-directed economy. The Cuban government announced in 1995 that GDP had declined by 35% between 1989–93. In 1994 agricultural markets were liberalized to some degree and the state has also sought to reduce subsidies to unprofitable enterprises. Cuba has reported growth since 1994 but living standards are considered depressed relative to the 1980s. An estimated 76% of the workforce remain employed in the state sector. The leading exports are sugar and tobacco and there has been an increase in tourism.

GDP (purchasing power parity) \$18.6bn. (1999 est.); GDP per capita (purchasing power parity) \$1,700 (1999 est.).

2 Trade Unionism

Trade unions first appeared in Cuba in 1865 in the tobacco and printing industries. The first workers' congress was held in 1898. The Confederation of Workers of Cuba (Confederación de Trabajadores de Cuba, CTC) was formed in 1939 and was thereafter the only important trade union centre, transformed rather than abolished following the 1959 revolution.

Cuba ratified ILO Conventions No.87 (Freedom of Association and Protection of the Right to Organize, 1948) and No. 98 (Right to Organize and Collective Bargaining, 1949) in 1952. In practice, however, free collective bargaining ceased in 1959 and the right to strike two years later. Strikes are banned under the constitution and do not occur.

The CTC (now the Central de Trabajadores de Cuba) has been the sole trade union centre since the assumption of power by Castro, and performs managerial as well as trade union functions.

There have been some attempts to set up independent trade unions in the 1990s but these have not met with success and have been in effect small dissident groups. The authorities have refused to grant legal status and activists have been arrested and imprisoned.

The ICFTU has sought to press the cause of independent trade unions within Cuba. The WCL affiliates an organization in exile (Solidaridad de Trabajadore Cubanos), based in Venezuela. A WCL delegation was refused entry to the country in Jan. 1999.

3 Trade Union Centre

Central de Trabajadores de Cuba (CTC)
Workers' Central Union of Cuba

Address. Calle San Carolos y Peñalver, Municipio Centro-Habana, Prov. Ciudad Habana.

History and character. The CTC traces its origins to the Confederación de Trabajadores de Cuba of 1939, an organization that became Cuba's only centre of consequence but whose history was marked by violent internal feuds. Important CTC elements sought accommodation with the Batista regime, and several, including the secretary-general Eusebio Mujal, followed him into exile. Under Castro, the CTC received its present name, and disaffiliated from the ICFTU to become the principal supporter of the communist-dominated World Federation of Trade Unions (WFTU) in the Americas. In 1960 the new secretary-general, David Salvador, was deposed and imprisoned, and at the next national congress only one list of candidates was presented. The 1966 congress defined the unions' role as one of supervising increases in output and efficiency, expansion of social facilities, and application of wage scales and production quotas.

The CTC retained its monopoly status through the 1990s, reflecting the insulation of Cuba from the changes affecting trade unions in most former Soviet bloc states. Its rules prescribe adherence to the policies of the ruling party.

International affiliation. WFTU

4 Other Trade Union Organization

Organization in exile

Solidaridad de Trabajadores Cubanos (STC)
Cuban Workers' Solidarity

Address. Apartado 50, Zona Postal 1204, San Antonio de los Altos, Estado Miranda, Caracas, Venezuela

Phone. +58 2 235 77 09

Fax. +58 2 237 71 71

E-mail. stc@webstc.com

Leadership. Heriberto Fernández (secretary-general)

International affiliation. WCL

Cyprus

Capital: Nicosia
Population: 758,000 (2000 est.)

1 Political and Economic Background

Cyprus achieved independence from the UK in 1960 under a constitution based on power-sharing between the majority Greek and minority Turkish communities. A period of inter-communal conflict was followed by Turkish military intervention in 1974 that confirmed the de facto partition of the island. In 1983 the Turkish-controlled part of the island was proclaimed the Turkish Republic of Northern Cyprus (TRNC), although this has not been internationally recognized other than by Turkey. No substantial progress has since been made in reconciling the two communities.

In (Greek Cypriot-controlled) Cyprus the government is formed by the conservative Democratic Rally (DISY), the party of President Glafcos Clerides. In the TRNC the leading political party since partition has been the National Unity Party (UBP) of Rauf Denktash, the President of the TRNC since its proclamation.

The Greek Cypriot portion of the island is relatively prosperous with a service-based economy including tourism. In the northern Turkish enclave, which has about one-fifth of the total population, the economy has tended to stagnate since partition and per capita GDP is only one-third that of the Greek area. Foreign investment in the TRNC has been restricted by its lack of international recognition and it depends mainly on agriculture, government jobs and aid from Turkey.

Greek Cypriot area: GDP (purchasing power parity) $9bn. (1998 est.); GDP per capita (purchasing power parity) $15,400 (1998 est.).

Turkish Cypriot area: GDP (purchasing power parity) $820 m. (1998 est.); GDP per capita (purchasing power parity) $5,000 (1998 est.).

2 Trade Unionism

Cyprus ratified ILO Conventions No. 87 (Freedom of Association and Protection of the Right to Organize, 1948) and No.98 (Right to Organize and Collective Bargaining, 1949) in 1966.

The British colonial authorities repressed the underground trade union movement in the 1930s, primarily because of its associations with nationalist and communist politics; however, unions not considered to be a security risk were permitted in 1937 and there was rapid growth thereafter.

Different trade unions operate in the Turkish and Greek parts of the island. Cyprus is highly unionized.

All workers, other than those in the police and military, may join unions and in the Greek area the police may join associations with collective bargaining rights. In the Greek area some 70% of the work force are in unions. In the Turkish sector an estimated 50–60% of private sector workers, and all public sector workers, are unionized. Unions in the TRNC say that some employers have set up company unions and that the authorities have sponsored public sector unions in opposition to the independent unions.

The trade union movement is fragmented with many small unions and no dominant centre. The principal Greek centres are the Pancyprian Federation of Labour (PEO), affiliated to the WFTU, and the Cyprus Workers' Confederation (SEK), affiliated to the ICFTU. In the Turkish sector, the principal centre is the ICFTU-affiliated Cyprus Turkish Trade Unions Federation (Turk-Sen). The WFTU also records an affiliate, Dev-Is (Revolutionary Trade Unions Federation).

In 1985, SEK and Turk-Sen reached an agreement under ICFTU auspices providing for reciprocal visits and closer cooperation on union issues. During the 1990s the unions from both the Greek and Turkish sides have issued a number of common statements endorsing the principle of the reunification of the island as a federal republic based on UN resolutions, with unitary employment and social standards.

Collective bargaining is widely practiced. All workers have the right to strike, other than in essential services, although in the Turkish portion employers have the right to recruit replacement labour during strikes. In the Greek sector, the government's Industrial Relations Service mediates some 280 cases annually, more than 90% of which are resolved without strike action. In the Turkish sector, because of high inflation, a tripartite commission reviews wages several times a year and makes cost of living adjustments.

3 Trade Union Centres

Greek Cypriot area

Demokratiki Ergatiki Omospondia Kyprou (DEOK)
Democratic Labour Federation of Cyprus

Address. 40 Byron Av., 1096 Nicosia

Phone. +357 2 67 6506

Fax. +357 2 67 0494

E-mail. deok@cytanet.com.cy

Leadership. Diomides Diomidous (general secretary)

Membership. 7,000 in four affiliated unions

History and character. Founded in 1962 after a split in the SEK. Was recognized by the government in

November 1998 as a social partner in consultative and tripartite national bodies and boards.

Publication. Greek-language newspaper, every two weeks

International affiliation. WCL; CTUC

Pankypria Ergatiki Omospondia (PEO)
Pancyprian Federation of Labour

Address. PO Box 1885, 31–35 Archermos Street, 1514 Nicosia

Phone. +357 2 34 9400

Fax. +357 2 34 9382

E-mail. peo@cytanet.com.cy

Website. www.cytanet.com.cy/peo (English/Greek)

Leadership. Pambis Kyritsis (general secretary)

Membership. 66,000

History and character. The PEO was founded in 1941. There are 9 affiliated occupational unions. It is, with SEK, one of the two main Greek Cypriot centres. The PEO has favoured reconciliation of the two communities in a non-aligned de-militarized federal state.

Publication. Ergatiko Vema

International affiliation. WFTU; CTUC

Pancyprian Public Servants' Trade Union (PASYDY)

Address. Dem. Severis Ave. 3, Nicosia 1066

Phone. +357 2 662 337

Fax. +357 2 665 199

E-mail. pasydy@spidernet.co.cy

Leadership. Glafkos Hadjipetrou (general secretary)

Membership. 14,000, representing 90% of white-collar central government employees.

Publication. Dimossios I Pallilos ("Public Servant") (fortnightly newspaper)

Synomospondia Ergaton Kyprou (SEK)
Cyprus Workers' Confederation

Address. PO Box 25018, 1306 Nicosia

Phone. +357 2 84 9849

Fax. +357 2 84 9850

E-mail. sek@sek.org.cy.net

Leadership. Demetris Kittenis (general secretary)

Membership. 64,000

History and character. Founded in Oct. 1944. In its early years the SEK faced bitter opposition both from the communist-controlled unions and, because of its support for self-determination for Greek Cypriots, from the colonial government. In 1949 SEK delegates took part in the founding conference of the ICFTU. Many of its leaders were arrested, imprisoned or killed during the struggle for independence in the late 1950s, seriously weakening the organization, but recovery took place in the 1960s. The SEK's political orientation is social democratic, but it supports no political party. It comprises seven federations organizing workers on the basis of occupation.

Publication. Ergatiki Phoni (Workers' Voice) (weekly newspaper)

International affiliations. ICFTU; ETUC; CTUC

Turkish Cypriot area

Cyprus Turkish Trade Unions Federation (Turk-Sen)

Address. 7–7A Sht Mehmet R. Huseyin Sokak, PO Box 829, Lefkosa–KKTC, Mersin 10, Turkey

Phone. +357 392 22 72444

Fax +357 392 22 87831

Leadership. Onder Konuloglu (president); Arslan Bicakli (general secretary); Nihad Elmas (international secretary)

Membership. 5,011

International affiliations. ICFTU; ETUC

Czech Republic

Capital: Prague
Population: 10.27 m. (2000 est.)

1 Political and Economic Background

The Communist Party became the dominant, and by 1948, the sole, political force in Czechoslovakia after the Red Army took control of the country in the latter stages of World War II. A brief liberalization of the regime under Alexander Dubcek in the "Prague Spring" of 1968 was crushed by military force by the Soviet Union and its allies and the Communist Party leadership purged. An underground dissident movement continued and, following the fall of the Berlin Wall in 1989, mass protest led by the Civic Forum alliance led to the rapid collapse of the regime in the so-called "velvet revolution". In Dec. 1989, dissident leader Vaclav Havel became President and the Communist Party issued an apology for its past actions.

In June 1992 elections resulted in victory for the neo-liberal Civic Democratic Party (ODS) in the Czech lands and for the nationalist Movement for a Democratic Slovakia (RZDS) in Slovakia. Two months later they concluded a dissolution agreement and on Jan. 1, 1993 two separate and independent states were peacefully established. In the Czech Republic the government has been led by the left-of-centre Czech Social Democratic Party (CSSD) following elections in June 1998 and the break-up of the former centre-right coalition.

The Czech Republic has made one of the most successful transitions of a Communist state to a free market economy. After 1989 successive governments steered towards economic liberalization. By Nov. 1991 some 10 per cent of the country's small enterprises had been sold to private bidders in a programme of "little privatization". The sale of 4,000 large enterprises began in 1992, despite difficulties caused by maladministration of sale vouchers, and by the end of 1993 the private sector was responsible for more than half of GDP. The separation of Slovakia in 1993 in general left the Czech Republic with the more dynamic sectors of the economy whereas decaying heavy industries were concentrated in Slovakia. In 1997, however, the country faced a financial crisis that resulted in austerity measures and in 1998–99 experienced recession with unemployment rising to 9% (from 3% in the mid-1990s) as restructuring of inefficient enterprises continued. A modest recovery was under way by 2000 with strong foreign direct investment although there was continuing concern over the precarious situation of some enterprises and banks.

GDP (purchasing power parity) $120.8bn. (1999 est.); GDP per capita (purchasing power parity) $11,700 (1999 est.).

2 Trade Unionism

A highly developed but fragmented pattern of trade unionism existed in Czechoslovakia before World War II. Unions were dissolved during the war, but competing Christian, social democratic and communist unions were reestablished in 1944. Once the Communist Party finally consolidated its complete authority in 1948 the Central Council of Trade Unions (URO) became the sole trade union centre, organizing the Revolutionary Trade Union Movement (ROH). In the 1968 "Prague Spring", the Dubcek government radically reorganized the unions, allowing them to assert their independence and acknowledging an ultimate right to strike. As late as March 1969 the URO congress showed defiance of the Soviet-led occupation of August 1968 and reaffirmed these reforms but dissent was suppressed soon after.

Thereafter the unions corresponded to the conventional Soviet bloc model for almost 20 years. Where disputes occurred they were generally settled by trade union branch arbitration commissions which were convened with considerable frequency: in 1987 almost 5,000 commissions dealt with some 36,000 disputes. In the last days of communism the URO helped draft a new labour code, described by chairman Miroslav Zavadil as a "legal document guaranteeing the social certainties of the working people and contributing to the intensification of discipline and to the more flexible deployment of the labour force". Structural amendments to the URO statutes were approved at a special national conference in September 1988.

Yet when, a year later, change came, the involvement of the unions was tardy. Industrial dissidents formed "Strike Readiness Committees" which spread rapidly across the country. By Dec. 1989 they were thought to have mobilized more than 5 million workers and an Association of Committees (ASC) was formed. Faced with this competition the URO crumbled despite an attempt to build a new identity. Zavadil resigned on Nov. 26 and his successor Karel Henes offered the ASC negotiations. He announced that the URO had severed its connections with the Communist Party and its plant-based party cells dissolved. It was re-launched as the Action Committee on Dec. 11, but in practice its fate had been determined by defections to the ASC. Negotiations were broken off and the Action Committee was never in a position to re-establish itself.

Although opposed in principle to the URO, the ASC firmly opposed fragmentation. Its approach decisively ensured trade union unity despite the emergence of some small independent centres. Early in 1990 each enterprise in Czechoslovakia organized elections (many under ASC supervision) and sent delegates to a national congress at which the Confederation of Czechoslovakian Trade Unions (CSKOS) was founded.

On its establishment, CSKOS declined to affiliate to the WFTU and quickly demonstrated its independence with the threat of a general strike to force the government to consult it on new union rights and social security regulations. CSKOS had 5.5 million members on the eve of foundation of the Czech Republic. This represented an apparent loss of more than one quarter from the URO, but the earlier figure reflected the involuntary membership of the URO.

The new structure of trade unionism evolved in step with nationalism and was thus fated not to last. CSKOS rested on two subordinate national bodies. Growing Czech and Slovak nationalism forced a rule change just three months into the life of the new organization (see below) and in May 1991 the Slovak Confederation threatened a general strike against the dismissal of the Slovak prime minister and his replacement by a Christian Democrat.

CSKOS doubted the advantages to either nation of splitting into two separate states. A memorandum it submitted to the government in the summer of 1992 forecast economic hardship and an explosion of the black market and disputed the assumption that the Czech part of the country could expect easy expansion once economically separate from Slovakia. The Sept. 1992 general council blamed the impending division of Czechoslovakia on mistakes committed by the old regime. In speeches to the ICFTU and the ETUC on Oct. 9 its president Richard Falbr expressed the determination of CSKOS to stay united, but within a month the Czech–Moravian Chamber of Trade Unions (CMKOS) had to be founded in acknowledgment of the new national realities with Falbr himself as president.

Under the reformed Czechoslovak state the point of origin for the constitutional status of trade unions and employers bodies was the Charter of Fundamental Rights and Liberties in the constitutional law of Jan. 9, 1991. It lists trade union rights and freedoms to be protected by the constitutional court (a new court was established by the Czech Republic in June 1993). The basic legal document specifically shaping employment practice is the labour code. International pacts on human rights and basic freedoms that have been ratified by the Republics take precedence over the law. These include ILO Conventions No. 87 (Freedom of Association and Protection of the Right to Organize, 1948) and No. 98 (Right to Organize and Collective Bargaining, 1949), ratified in 1993. In March 1992, Czechoslovakia became the first East European country to sign the European Convention on Human Rights.

Most workers remain in unions affiliated to CMKOS, although total union membership has been falling, partly reflecting restructuring of older industries. CMKOS is politically independent.

In Oct. 1990 the social partners in Czechoslovakia established a Council of Economic and Social Accord. This tripartite body had the responsibility of discussing all drafted legislative regulations, bills and legal standards prior to their submission to the government and to Parliament. In the Czech Republic a tripartite Economic and Social Council continued in being. However, tripartism, under which the country was largely strike free from the revolution to 1994, fell into abeyance in the mid-1990s as the centre-right government of Vaclav Klaus ignored the unions. In 1997, there was considerable industrial unrest as the government introduced austerity measures to combat a financial crisis involving bank closures and currency devaluation. Average real wages had only just returned to pre-1989 levels in 1996 and there was widespread disenchantment at the economic crisis. This culminated in a demonstration, described as the largest since 1989, in Prague on Nov. 8, 1997 at which CMKOS leader Richard Falbr said the problem was not economic liberalization but the way it had been implemented, and called for the resignation of the government. Later that month Klaus was forced out of office in connection with a past privatization scandal, paving the way for the election of a Social Democratic-led government in June 1998. In the late 1990s CMKOS was involved in drafting of a new labour code for consideration in 2000.

Employers and government have opposed industry-wide bargaining and in the private sector collective bargaining typically occurs at the enterprise level. In the state sector wages and conditions are regulated by law. According to CMKOS the number of workers covered by collective agreements is falling. Strikes are lawful only after mediation efforts have failed. In 1999 there were demonstrations in Prague against the problem of wage arrears in some manufacturing enterprises.

While ICFTU-affiliated CMKOS is overwhelmingly dominant, the WFTU claims a Czech affiliate, the Trade Union Congress of Bohemia, Moravia and Silesia (OSCMS) while the Christian Labour Coalicion (KOK) is affiliated to the WCL. Minority unions have the right to engage fully in collective bargaining and KOK successfully opposed moves by CMKOS to persuade Parliament to change this.

3 Trade Union Centre

Czech–Moravian Confederation of Trade Unions (CMKOS)

Address. Winstona Churchilla 2, 113 59 Prague 3

Phone. +420 2 2446 1111

Fax. +420 2 2422 6163

E-mail. mocmkos@mbox.vol.cz

Website. www.cmkos.cz (Czech only)

Leadership. Richard Falbr (president)

Membership. 1.3 million

History and character. The Czechoslovak Confederation of Trade Unions (CSKOS) was founded in March 1990, in the aftermath of the "velvet revolution" of late 1989, at a national congress whose delegates were chosen at nationwide enterprise elections. It inherited the assets of the former communist trade union structure, the Central Council of Trade Unions (URO). In Apr. 1990 a Confederation of Trade Unions was established for each nation, the Czech–Moravian Chamber (CMK-CSKOS) and the Confederation of Trade Unions of the Slovak Republic (KOZ SR), and in June the name of the organization was changed to the Czech and Slovak Confederation of Trade Unions. From this point on, as separatist tendencies grew, the new organization sought to avoid a split along nationalist lines. As late as July 1992 a comprehensive CSKOS memorandum foretold dire economic and political consequences should the separation of the Czech and Slovak lands be carried through; within a few weeks however, trade unionists on both sides were forced to start preparations for the inevitable. CMKOS was formed in Nov. 1992 in advance of the foundation of the Czech Republic. In May 1998, at the second congress, the name was changed from the Czech–Moravian Chamber of Trade Unions to the Czech–Moravian Confederation of Trade Unions (both CMKOS).

CMKOS is similar in orientation to CSKOS, which defined itself as an independent voluntary grouping of republic and other associations of individual unions and of self-standing unions. Its prime objectives were to achieve unity through trade union solidarity and common interests; to defend the rights and legitimate interests of affiliates; and to represent them in international non-sectoral organizations and in tripartite and collective bargaining activities. It is currently particularly concerned with representing its members and workers generally in the national process of preparation for accession to the European Union.

The CMKOS is not affiliated with any political party. The CMKOS president, Richard Falbr, is an independent member of the Czech Senate, elected with the support of the Czech Social Democratic Party (CSSD, the party leading the government since elections in June 1998) and a member of its Senate group.

CMKOS affiliated 40 unions at the time of formation of the Czech Republic; this total has now fallen to 30 with the merger of smaller unions.

Publications. Sondy (weekly), *Pohledy* (quarterly)

International affiliations. ICFTU; ETUC; TUAC

4 Other Trade Union Organization

Krestanska Odborova Koalice (KOK)
Christian Labour Confederation

Address. Senovazne nam. 24, 110 00 Prague

Phone. +420 2 241 02 450

Fax. +420 2 241 02 450

E-mail. kokanton@telecom.cz

Leadership. Anton Alois (president)

International affiliation. WCL

Denmark

Capital: Copenhagen
Population: 5.34 m. (2000 est.)

1 Political and Economic Background

Denmark is a constitutional monarchy and a member state of the European Union. Other than the period of Nazi occupation in World War II, the Social Democratic Party (SD) was the most significant force in Danish politics from the 1930s (when it laid the foundations of the welfare state) until the early 1980s, usually forming the government in coalition with other parties. From 1982–93 Prime Minister Poul Schlüter of the Conservative People's Party (KFP), led centre-right coalition governments. Since Jan. 1993, the SD has again led a series of coalition governments, with its leader Poul Nyrup Rasmussen as Prime Minister.

Denmark has a developed economy, with modern industrial, service and commercial agricultural sectors. Denmark lacks major global corporations, in contrast to neighbouring Sweden, but has a reputation for efficiency in its predominantly small and medium-sized enterprises. It has a large public sector workforce, an extensive welfare system and high taxation. Unemployment levels fell from over 12% in 1993 to 5.5% by the end of the decade, partly as a result of stricter job availability criteria but also reflecting a period of sustained growth. Denmark did not adopt the common European currency (euro) at its launch in Jan. 1999 and a referendum on its

adoption on Sept. 28, 2000 resulted in a vote to stay outside the eurozone.

GDP (purchasing power parity) $127.7bn. (1999 est.); GDP per capita (purchasing power parity) $23,800 (1999 est.).

2 Trade Unionism

Denmark ratified ILO Convention No.87 (Freedom of Association and Protection of the Right to Organize, 1948) in 1951 and Convention No.98 (Right to Organize and Collective Bargaining, 1949) in 1955.

Unions developed in the nineteenth century, and the Landsorganisationen i Danmark (LO, the Danish Confederation of Trade Unions) was founded in 1898. In 1899 – following a major dispute – the LO and the Confederation of Danish Employers (DA) reached a basic agreement on the right to organize and industrial partnership which formed the bedrock for subsequent trade union growth and industrial relations. The unions also administer unemployment insurance schemes directly on behalf of the government.

There are three centres representing employees. Unlike in many countries, these are not the result of political fragmentation, but are rather (as in other Scandinavian countries) based on the level of educational qualifications of their members. In broad terms, the largest centre, the LO, with 1.5 million members, represents skilled and unskilled workers, in all areas of the economy. The second-largest centre, the Salaried Employees' and Civil Servants' Confederation (FTF), with 400,000 members, represents those with an intermediate level of qualifications (particularly primary teachers, nurses and bank workers), while the smallest, the Danish Confederation of Professional Associations (AC), with 226,000 members, represents graduates. All three are affiliated to the ICFTU. Relations between these centres are generally good, but it is the LO that is the dominant voice of Danish trade unionism. The unions have retained a strong organizational base through the 1980s and 1990s, a period when unions in many other countries have lost ground in the face of the decline of traditional industries and deregulation, and in some sectors 95% or more of workers are unionized. Overall union density is 80%.

A factor in the enduring strength of the unions has been the Danish system of industrial relations. Under this unions and employers have taken primary responsibility for negotiating stable agreements which have underpinned the development of a free market economy in alliance with a secure system of employment rights and social provision. The Danish system is characterized by reliance on agreement rather than on legislation. The political system, in which governments are commonly formed by weak or minority coalitions and legislation adopted by consensus, and the centrist orientation of much of the electorate, has also meant that the national consensus in favour of the welfare state, high taxation (among the highest in the world) and the value of responsible trade unionism has survived the worldwide movement to neo-liberalism relatively unscathed.

The DA/LO General Agreement lays down principles of cooperation between the two sides at sectoral and enterprise level. Under it there are no strikes or lockouts while an agreement is in force. With some 80% of Danish workers in unions and about half of all employers members of an employers' association, agreements are strong. The DA and LO act as coordinators in the two-yearly or four-yearly negotiations but are not themselves parties to the final agreements. There are several hundred agreements detailing wages and conditions in industry and these are supplemented by local or plant agreements. The Agreement also provides for lawful notice of industrial action by either side, for rules governing unfair dismissals and for regulations governing shop steward representation. If the parties cannot agree, the Official Conciliator intervenes, with power to postpone industrial action. Where a dispute occurs nonetheless, arbitration may occur under rules of 1908 governing the conduct of disputes: these provide for renewed efforts by the DA and the LO and then for arbitration, and finally for reference to the Industrial Court.

Wage indexation, long a feature of collective agreements, was suspended during 1983–87. The 1987 Central Wage Agreement that followed suspension lasted four years, but clamour for a return to decentralized bargaining grew. The 1989 establishment of sectoral negotiating groups in most manual and some white-collar trades (on a pattern already established in engineering) was a partial response and set a pattern into the 1990s for more decentralized bargaining. In the public sector, negotiations continue to begin at the centre followed by decentralized negotiations in individual sectors. The bargaining process itself inhibits strikes and the number of working days lost each year through strike action is typically very low. In Apr. 1998, however, Denmark experienced the worst industrial action since 1985 after union members voted to reject a two-year wage agreement negotiated between the LO and DA. In the 2000 collective bargaining round it was agreed to extend the previous two-year period for which agreements applied to four years.

By Jan. 2000 some 25% of companies had employee representatives on their boards and the unions are working to increase that proportion.

3 Trade Union Centres

Akademikernes Centralorganisation (AC)
Danish Confederation of Professional Associations

Address. Nørre Voldgade 29, DK-1358 Copenhagen K

Phone. +45 3369 4040

Fax. +45 3393 8540

E-mail. ac@ac.dk

Website. www.ac.dk (Danish; English section)

Leadership. Svend M. Christensen (president); Martin Teilmann (general secretary)

Membership. 226,000 (includes self-employed and students)

History and character. The AC was founded in 1972 and has 22 affiliated organizations representing graduates. The AC has no party political affiliations. Its main purpose is to safeguard the salary and employment terms of its members and it engages in collective bargaining in both the public and private sectors on behalf of its member organizations. As a social partner it is engaged in councils and committees across a range of social and economic issues. It cooperates with the LO and FTF in dealings at European and international levels and represents both the LO and FTF as the Danish member of the steering committee of EUROCADRES (the Council of European Professional and Managerial Staff).

International affiliations. ICFTU; TUAC; ETUC; NFS; EUROCADRES

Affiliates. The following affiliates each have more than 10,000 members:

1. Danish Medical Association
Address. Trondhjemsgade 9, DK-2100 Copenhagen Ø
Phone. +45 35 44 85 00
Fax. +45 35 44 85 03
Website. www.dadl.dk
Membership. 19,244

2. Association of Danish Lawyers and Economists
Address. Gothersgade 133, PO Box 2126, DK-1015 Copenhagen K
Phone. +45 33 95 97 00
Fax. +45 33 95 99 99
Website. www.djoef.dk
Membership. 32,259

3. Danish Association of Masters and PhDs
Address. Magistrenes Hus, Lyngbyvej 32F, DK-2100 Copenhagen Ø
Phone. +45 39 15 30 45
Fax. +45 39 15 30 55
Website. www.magister.dk
Membership. 22,308

4. Danish Association of Business Language Graduates
Address. Skindergade 45–47, PO Box 2246, DK-1019 Copenhagen K
Phone. +45 33 91 98 00
Fax. +45 33 91 68 18
Membership. 10,368

5. Danish Association of Graduates in Economics and Business Administration
Address. Søtorvet 5, DK-1012 Copenhagen K
Phone. +45 33 14 14 46
Fax. +45 33 14 11 49
Membership. 13,317

6. National Union of Danish Upper Secondary Teachers
Address. Magistrenes Hus, Lyngbyvej 32F, DK-2100 Copenhagen Ø
Phone. +45 39 15 30 60
Fax. +45 39 15 30 60
Membership. 11,538

7. Danish Union of Engineers
Address. Domus Technica, Ved Stranden 18, DK-1780 Copenhagen V
Phone. +45 33 15 65 65
Fax. +45 33 93 46 22
Website. www.ingenioeren.dk/ida

Funktionærernes og Tjenestemændenes Fællesråd (FTF)
Salaried Employees' and Civil Servants' Confederation

Address. Niels Hemmingsens Gade 12, Postbox 1169, 1010 Copenhagen
Phone. +45 33 36 88 00
Fax. +45 33 36 88 80
E-mail. ftf@ftf.dk
Website. www.ftf.dk (Danish; English section)
Leadership. Anker Christoffersen (president)
Membership. 400,000

History and character. The FTF was founded in 1952 by 11 non-LO white-collar organizations. Among their concerns were the failure of staff salaries to keep pace with wage increases awarded to manual workers, and a desire for politically neutral leadership (i.e. unlike that of the socialist inclined LO). The LO and FTF achieved a working relationship by 1973, after the LO had earlier regarded the new organization with some hostility. The FTF is independent of any political party.

The FTF now affiliates 100 independent unions, the largest of which are the teachers' union, the nurses' union, the pre-school teachers' union and the financial services union. More than 95% of Danish nurses, teachers and bank employees are unionized. 75% of FTF members are in the public sector, with most members in the private sector being in banks and insurance companies.

The FTF has representation on more than 150 committees and councils dealing with health, safety, professional education, consumer issues and social problems. With the LO it administers the Danish Trade union Council for International Development Cooperation.

International affiliations. ETUC; TUAC; ICFTU; NFS

Affiliated unions. The following are the largest of the FTF's 100 affiliated unions.

1. Danish Pre-School Teachers' Union (BUPL)
Address. Blegdamsvej 124, 2100 Copenhagen
Phone. +45 35 46 50 00
E-mail. bupl@bupl.dk
Website. www.bupl.dk (Danish only)
Membership. 58,000

2. Danish Union of Teachers (DLF)
Address. Vandkunsten 12, 1467 Copenhagen K
Phone. +45 33 69 63 00
Fax. +45 33 69 63 33
E-mail. dlf@dlf.org
Website. www.dlf.org (Danish; English section)
Leadership. Hans Ole Laerer (head of secretariat)
Membership. 80,000 (60,000 active)
History and character. The DLF is the only union organizing primary and lower secondary education and 97% of teachers in this category are DLF members. Internationally it is affiliated to Education International and the European Trade Union Committee for Education.
Publication. Folkeskolen

3. Danish Nurses' Union (DSR)
Address. Vimmelskaftet 38, Postbox 1084, 1008 Copenhagen
Phone. +45 33 15 15 55
Fax. +45 33 15 24 55
E-mail. dsr@dansk-sygeplejeraad.dk
Website. www.dansk-sygeplejeraad.dk (Danish only)
Leadership. Connie Kruckow (chairman)
Membership. 70,000

4. Danish Financial Services Union (FINANSFORBUNDET)
Address. Langebrogade 5, 1411 Copenhagen K
Phone. +45 32 96 46 00
Fax. +45 32 96 12 25
E-mail. finansforbundet@finansforbundet.dk
Membership. 50,000, constituting 90% of employees in this sector.

Landsorganisationen i Danmark (LO)
Danish Confederation of Trade Unions

Address. Rosenørns Allé 12, 1634 Copenhagen V

Phone. +45 35 24 60 00

Fax. +45 35 24 63 00

E-mail. lo@lo.dk

Website. www.lo.dk (Danish; English summary)

Membership. 1.5 million

History and character. The LO was founded in 1898 in an attempt to coordinate the nascent Danish labour organizations. The following year it reached the first collective agreement with the Danish employers, this forming the basis for the future development of the Danish industrial relations system which emphasizes direct agreement between highly organized union and employer groups. It is also historically linked to the Social Democratic Party, the leading Danish party for much of the period from the 1930s, although the old organic relationship, whereby LO members sat on the party's governing bodies, and vice versa, has ended.

The LO is Denmark's main trade union centre, representing in particular unskilled and semi-skilled workers and industrial crafts. Within traditional areas of employment it dominates, with density sometimes as high as 95 per cent. Approximately one-third of its membership is in the public sector, one-third is in companies affiliated to the Danish Employers' Confederation, and one-third is in other private companies. Membership is almost exactly equally divided between men and women.

Rationalization of the union structure along industrial lines has been discussed for many years but has faced considerable resistance from unions based on traditional crafts or distinctive occupational categories. The number of affiliated unions is now 22, compared with 26 in 1993 and 30 in 1989, but many of the unions are quite small. To help coordination the LO has set up seven cartels uniting unions for different industrial sectors (building, construction and wood; industrial; trade; transport and services; municipal employees; state employees; graphical industry and media). These cartels have varying relationships with their member unions.

The LO constitution guarantees the sovereignty of member unions. The role of the LO is to provide coordination to union activities, develop and advocate policies at the national level and propose and coordinate guidelines for collective bargaining. The agreement negotiated between the LO and the employers' confederation normally provides the framework for negotiations at the sectoral level. While collective bargaining remains a pivotal aspect for the LO, increasingly it is focusing on legislative policy in areas such as taxation, social conditions and employment. The LO is active at the EU level (and has a Brussels office). Like most business organizations and political leaders it urged a vote in favour of Danish adoption of the common European currency in a national referendum on Sept. 28, 2000. However, divisions in the union movement were reflected in a tied vote on the issue on the executive of the LO's third biggest affiliate, the public employees' union, following opinion polls showing a majority of public sector workers opposed adoption of the common currency. In the event the referendum resulted in a decision not to adopt the currency. Notwithstanding its support for the euro, reflecting the strength of Euroscepticism in Denmark, the LO is opposed to any development of a "United States of Europe".

The congress of the LO – convened every four years – is its highest authority and lays down objectives and policies. The 50-strong General Council, on which all the affiliates are represented, is responsible for updating activities and objectives in the years between Congresses. A 15-member Executive Board, elected by Congress, implements policy and has authority between General Council meetings. The Secretariat, elected by the Congress and led by the President, is responsible for day-to-day affairs.

The LO runs three labour colleges and its unions are actively involved in the Workers' Educational Association (AOF). The training system (FIU), aimed mainly at shop stewards, involves 40,000 annually. Internationally it runs the Danish Trade Union Council for International Development Cooperation, in association with the FTF, and has a particular interest in the Baltic region and central and eastern Europe.

Publications. Danish Labour News (quarterly, English)

International affiliations. ICFTU; ETUC; TUAC; NFS

Affiliated unions. There are 22 member organizations, as follows:

1. Artist Forbund (dancers, artists)
Address. Vendersgade 24, 1363 Copenhagen K
Phone. +45 3332 6677
Fax. +45 3333 7330
E-mail. artisten@artisten.dk
Leadership. Nick Olander (president)

2. Blik- og Rørarbejderforbundet i Danmark (National Union of Plumbers)
Address. Immerkaer 42, 2650 Hvidovre
Phone. +45 3638 3638
Fax. +45 3638 3639
E-mail. forbund@blikroer.dk
Leadership. Per Frederiksen (president)
*Membership.*10,000

3. Bryggeriarbejderforbundet
Address. Artillerivej 40, Bygning 9B 3.Sal, 2300 Copenhagen S
Phone. +45 3296 0484
Fax. +45 3296 0565
E-mail. lc@bryggerne.dk
Leadership. Lone Christensen (president)

4. Dansk El-Forbund (National Union of Electricians)
Address. Vodroffsvej 26, 1900 Frederiksberg
Phone. +45 3329 7000
Fax. +45 3329 7070
*E-mail.*def@def.dk

Leadership. Erik Andersson (president)
Membership. 25,500

5. Forbundet af Offentligt Ansatte (National Union of Public Employees)
Address. Staunings Plads 1–3, Postboks 11, 1790 Copenhagen V
Phone. +45 3343 4600
Fax. +45 3313 4042
E-mail. foa@foa.dk
Website. www.foa.dk (Danish only)
Leadership. Poul Winckler (president)
Membership. 183,000

6. Dansk Frisør og Kosmetiker Forbund (hairdressers and beauticians)
Address. Lersø Parkallé 21, 2100 Copenhagen Ø
Phone. +45 3583 1880
Fax. +45 3582 1462
E-mail. dfk@dfk.dk
Leadership. Poul Monggaard (president)
Membership. 5,000

7. Funktionaerforbund, Dansk Serviceforbund (National Union of Workers in Service Trades)
Address. Upsalagade 20, 2100 Copenhagen Ø
Phone. +45 7015 0400
Fax. +45 7015 0402
E-mail. dff@funktionaerforbundet.dk
Leadership. Karsten Hansen (president)
Membership. 21,000

8. Handels- og Kontorfunktionaerernes Forbund i Danmark (HK) (National Union of Commercial and Clerical Employees)
Address. H.C. Andersens Boulevard 50, Postboks 268, 1780 Copenhagen V
Phone. +45 3330 4343
Fax. +45 3330 4099
E-mail. hk@hk.dk
Website. www.hk.dk (Danish; English summary)
Leadership. John Dahl (president)
Membership. 370,000
History and character. The HK was founded in 1900 and joined the LO in 1932. It is the largest LO affiliate and the largest union in Denmark. More than 75% of its members, who have clerical, administrative and technical jobs in both the private and public sectors, are women. The majority of its members are covered by collective agreements.

9. Haerens Konstabel- og Korporal Forening (HKKF) (National Union of Enlisted Military Personnel in the Army)
Address. Kronprinsengade 8, 1114 Copenhagen K
Phone. +45 3393 6522
Fax. +45 3393 6523
E-mail. hkkf@hkkf.dk
Leadership. Svend-Erik Larsen (president)
Membership. 4,300

10. Dansk Jernbaneforbund (National Union of Railwaymen)
Address. Svanemøllevej 65, 2900 Hellerup
Phone. +45 3940 1166
Fax. +45 3940 1771

E-mail. djf@dj.dk
Leadership. Kurt Christiansen
Membership. 7,000

11. Kvindeligt Arbejderforbund i Danmark (National Union of Women Workers)
Address. Applesbys Plads 5, 1411 Copenhagen K
Phone. +45 3283 8383
Fax. +45 3283 8667
E-mail. sf@kad.dk
Website. www.kad.dk (Danish; English summary)
Leadership. Lillian Knudsen president)
Membership. 90,000
History and character. Founded in 1885 and believed to be the only union in the world exclusively for women. Its members are mainly unskilled, divided equally between industry and the services sector. In industry, half the members work in iron and metal and one-quarter in food and catering. In services they are mainly employed as cleaners, but other occupations include care workers and laundry workers. The union primarily functions as a conventional trade union on the lines of other LO affiliates but it also has a specific involvement in campaigning on women's issues.

12. Malerforbundet I Danmark (National Union of Painters)
Address. Lersø Park Allé 109 st., 2100 Copenhagen Ø
Phone. +45 3916 7900
Fax. +45 3916 7910
E-mail. maler@maler.dk
Leadership. Jørn Erik Nielsen (president)
Membership. 10,600

13. Dansk Metalarbejderforbund (National Union of Metalworkers)
Address. Nyropsgade 38, Postboks 308, 1780 Copenhagen V
Phone. +45 3363 2000
Fax. +45 3363 2100
E-mail. metal@danskmetal.dk
Leadership. Max Baehring (president)
Membership. 117,000

14. Naerings- og Nydelsesmiddelarbejder Forbundet (Danish Food and Allied Workers' Union, NNF)
Address. C.F.Richs Vej 103, DK-2000 Frederiksberg
Phone. +45 3818 7272
Fax. +45 3818 7223
E-mail. nnf@nnf.dk
Website. www.nnf.dk
Leadership. Henry Holt Jochumsen (president)
Membership. 41,250

15. Dansk Postforbund (National Union of Postal Workers)
Address. Vodroffsvej 13A, DK-1900 Frederiksberg
Phone. +45 3321 4124
Fax. +45 3321 0642
E-mail. dpf@postforbundet.dk
Leadership. Jan Svendsen
Membership. 11,500
Publications. Posthornet

16. Paedagogisk Medhjaelper Forbund (National Union of Nursery and Childcare Assistants)
Address. St. Kongensgade 79, 1017 Copenhagen K

Phone. +45 3311 0343
Fax. +45 3311 3136
E-mail. pmf@pmf.dk
Leadership. Jakob Bang (president)
Membership. 30,000

17. RestaurationsBranchens Forbund (hotel, restaurants, catering and tourism workers)
Address. Thoravej 29–33, 2400 Copenhagen NV
Phone. +45 3833 8900
Fax. +45 3833 6791
Leadership. Preben Rasmussen (president)
Membership. 24,500

18. Socialpaedagogernes Landsforbund (National Federation of Social Educators)
Address. Brolaeggerstraede 9, 1211 Copenhagen K
Phone. +45 3396 2800
Fax. +45 3396 2996
E-mail. sl@sl-dk.dk
Leadership. Kirsten Nissen (president)
Membership. 22,500

19. Specialarbejderforbundet i Danmark (SID, Danish General Workers' Union)
Address. Kampmannsgade 4, Postboks 392, 1790 Copenhagen V
Phone. +45 3314 2140
Fax. +45 3397 2460
E-mail. sid@sid.dk

Website. www.sid.dk (Danish only)
Leadership. Poul Erik Skov Christensen (president)
Membership. 338,375 in 298 local branches
Publications. Fagbladet

20. Teknisk Landsforbund
Address. Nørre Voldgade 12, 1358 Copenhagen K
Phone. +45 3312 2200
Fax. +45 3311 4272
E-mail. tl@tl.dk
Leadership. Eske Pedersen (president)
Membership. 33,000

21. Telekommunikationsforbundet
Address. Rolfsvej 37, 2000 Frederiksberg
Phone. +45 3815 5500
Fax. +45 3815 5510
E-mail. tkf@tkf.dk
Leadership. Bo Stenør Larsen
Membership. 12,000

22. Forbundet Trae- Industri-Byg I Danmark (wood and furniture industries)
Address. Mimersgade 41, 2200 Copenhagen N
Phone. +45 3531 9599
Fax. +45 3531 9450
E-mail. tib@tib.dk
Leadership. Arne Johansen (president)
Membership. 68,000

Djibouti

Capital: Djibouti
Population: 451,000 (2000 est.)

1 Political and Economic Background

Djibouti, formerly the French Territory of the Afars and Issas, became independent in 1977 following a referendum and was ruled by President Hassan Gouled Aptidon from independence until succeeded by his nephew, Ismael Omar Guelleh, who was elected in April 1999. Tension between the majority Issas (of Somali ethnic origin) and the Afars (of Ethiopian ethnic origin) resulted in an armed insurgency by the Afars, organized as the Front for the Restoration of Unity and Democracy (FRUD), until an agreement at the end of 1994 under which the Afars were given representation in government. After 1981 only the President's Popular Rally for Progress party, supported mainly by the Issas, was permitted to present candidates until 1992. Elections to the Chamber of Deputies in Dec. 1997 (the most recent) resulted in all the

seats being won by an alliance of the ruling Popular Rally for Progress party with former FRUD rebels.

Djibouti has few natural resources, little arable land and hardly any industry. Unusually for an African country, some four-fifths of the population lives in urban areas. The country depends to a large extent on foreign aid. A free trade zone has been created to encourage the establishment of new industries and there is an entrepot trade based on the strategic position of the seaport, the airport and the railway link to the Ethiopian capital of Addis Ababa. Unemployment is estimated as high as 40–50% and per capita consumption fell 35% in the seven years through to 1999.

GDP (purchasing power parity) $550m. (1999 est.); GDP per capita (purchasing power parity) $1,200 (1999 est.).

2 Trade Unionism

Djibouti ratified ILO Conventions No.87 (Freedom of Association and Protection of the Right to Organize,

1948) and No.98 (Right to Organize and Collective Bargaining, 1949) in 1978.

Trade unions developed under French rule. Following independence until 1992 control by the government over individual unions was exercised through the single state-organized peak association, the General Union of Djibouti Workers (UGTD). However a new national centre, the ICFTU-affiliated Union of Djibouti Workers (UDT), was formed in 1992 in the face of official discouragement. Since 1995 the UGTD and UDT have formed a confederation.

In 1995 the UGTD and UDT joined in protests against austerity measures introduced as part of an IMF/World Bank structural adjustment programme. This led to the dismissal of the leadership of both centres and a series of actions against the unions. In 1995 the government sponsored the creation of a "Djibouti Labour Congress" (CODJITRA), led by Ministry of Labour officials, and in May 1996 security forces closed the UGTD-UDT headquarters, which was not restored to the UGTD-UDT until 1998.

Industrial action arising from non-payment of wages led to dismissals of teachers' union leaders in 1997 and hundreds of teachers were sent to a detention camp at Nagad. The lawyer representing trade unions was suspended in 1997 and no other lawyer could be found to take the brief. In Jan. 1998, the government told an ILO delegation that it would restore the UGTD-UDT's premises and open a dialogue with the unions, but it subsequently backtracked on this undertaking and did not attend the ILO conference later that year. Also in 1998, hospital workers were sent to the Nagad camp after industrial action.

In July 1999 the government sponsored a meeting to elect a new set of leaders of the UDT and UGTD. According to the ICFTU, "the only people who were invited to the meeting were diplomats, civil servants and

French military observers. Legitimate union members only discovered that the meeting had taken place when they saw it on television."

Despite the continuing attacks, the UDT and UGTD are reported to have increased their support in recent years and to represent 70% of workers in the formal economy. There is a formal right to collective bargaining but this scarcely exists in practice.

3 Trade Union Centres

Union Djiboutienne du Travail (UDT)
Union of Djibouti Workers

Address. BP 2767, Djibouti

Phone. +253 357 942

Fax. +253 355 084

Leadership. Ahmed Djama Egueh (president); Aden Mohamed Abdou (general secretary)

History and character. Founded in 1992, the UDT achieved government recognition in 1993 and since 1995 has acted in confederation with the UGTD in the face of continual government harassment. It joined the ICFTU in 1994.

International affiliations. ICFTU

Union Générale des Travailleurs de Djibouti (UGTD)
General Union of Djibouti Workers

Leadership. Kamil Diraneth Hared (general secretary)

History and character. Functioned as the official union arm of the ruling party, but has been in serious conflict with the government from 1995, since when it has acted in confederation with the UDT, sharing its headquarters.

Dominica

Capital: Roseau
Population: 72,000 (2000 est.)

1 Political and Economic Background

Dominica, formerly a West Indies Associated State, became a fully independent member of the Commonwealth in 1978 as a republic. The three major political parties are the conservative Dominica Freedom

Party (DFP), and two centre-left parties, the United Workers' Party (UWP) and the Dominica Labour Party (DLP). The most recent elections, in Jan. 2000, resulted in the UWP losing power and the formation of a coalition government of the DFP and DLP, with Roosevelt (Rosie) Douglas of the DLP becoming Prime Minister.

Agriculture, primarily banana production, employs 40 per cent of the workforce and the government has sought to diversify the economy in view of the vulnerability of banana exports (typically representing half of all exports) to price fluctuations and natural disasters such as hurricanes.

GDP (purchasing power parity) $225m. (1998 est.); GDP per capita (purchasing power parity) $3,400 (1998 est.).

2 Trade Unionism

Dominica ratified ILO Conventions No.87 (Freedom of Association and Protection of the Right to Organize, 1948) and No.98 (Right to Organize and Collective Bargaining, 1949) in 1983. All workers have the right to form unions, collective bargaining is practiced in non-agricultural sectors (including the public sector), there is a right to strike and there is also recourse to mediation and arbitration by government. However, unions are very small in scale and represent less than 10% of the workforce.

There is no trade union centre: the Dominica Trade Union fulfilled this role in the 1950s, but was subsequently weakened by the defection of some of its members to non-affiliated organizations. Relations between the various organizations were poor during the 1960s and early 1970s, but have since improved. The unions now operate under a loose umbrella, the Joint Unions Steering Committee.

3 Trade Union Centre

There is no trade union centre.

4 Other Trade Union Organizations

Dominica Amalgamated Workers' Union (DAWU)
Address. PO Box 137, 40 Kennedy Avenue, Roseau
Phone. +1767 448 3048
Fax. +1767 448 5787
Leadership. Fedeline Moulon (general secretary)
International affiliations. CTUC; WCL

Dominica Public Service Union
Address. PO Box 182, Roseau

Phone. +1767 448 2101
Fax. +1767 448 8060
E-mail. des@cwdom.dm
Leadership. Thomas Letang (general secretary)
History and character. This is the successor to the Dominica Civil Service Association (DCSA), which was originally founded as a staff association in 1938 and became a trade union in 1961. It is the major public service union in Dominica.
International affiliations. CTUC

Dominica Trade Union (DTU)
Address. 70–71 Queen Mary Street, Roseau
Phone. +1767 449 8139
Leadership. Leo B. Nicholas (general secretary)
History and character. Founded in 1945, the DTU was at its peak in its earliest years, having over 8,000 members from a wide occupational spectrum in the 1945-50 period. Until the 1960s it remained the only union in Dominica, but the labour movement fragmented thereafter and the DTU declined and had only a few hundred members by the 1990s. Its one-time political influence (when successive First Ministers were DTU members) has ended.
International affiliations. CTUC; ICFTU

National Workers' Union
Address. 69 Queen Mary Street, PO Box 387, Roseau
Phone. + 1 767 448 465
Fax. +1 767 448 1934
International affiliations. WCL

Waterfront and Allied Workers' Union (WAWU)
Address. 43 Hillsborough Street, Roseau
Phone. +1 767 448 2343
Fax. +1 767 448 0086
E-mail. wawu@cwdom.dm
Leadership. Louis Benoit (president); Catherine Valerie-Solomon (secretary/treasurer)
Membership. Over 1,000
International affiliations. ICFTU; CTUC

Dominican Republic

Capital: Santo Domingo
Population: 8.44 m. (2000 est.)

1 Political and Economic Background

Thirty years of authoritarian rule by Generalissimo Rafael Trujillo ended in 1961 with his assassination, which was followed by some years of confusion, civil war, and United States military intervention in 1965. Joaquín Balaguer of the anti-Marxist Social Christian Reform Party (PRSC), or Reformist Party, was elected President in 1966 (having previously held that office under Trujillo) and then held that office until 1978 and then again from 1986 until 1996, when Leonel Fernández of the centrist Dominican Liberation Party (PLD) was elected. He was succeeded as President following elections in May 2000 by Rafael Hipólito Domínguez, whose left-of-centre Dominican Revolutionary Party (PRD) had previously won a majority in both houses of the National Congress in 1998 elections.

The economy of the Dominican Republic is dominated by agriculture. Although sugar has traditionally been the principal crop, output varies because of climatic and international market factors. Manufacturing industry mainly centres on processing of agricultural products, while tourism is a major and growing earner of foreign exchange. There has been extensive development of export processing zones.

In Jan. 1995 President Balaguer announced the termination of subsidies to 33 state-owned companies, but declined to privatize them. After his election in 1996, Fernández launched a major programme of economic measures, including devaluation, raised sales taxes, income tax cuts, and privatization although some measures were stalled in the legislature. The economy grew by more than 7% in 1998 and 8% in 1999.

GDP (purchasing power parity) $43.7bn. (1999 est.); GDP per capita (purchasing power parity) $5,400 (1999 est.).

2 Trade Unionism

Workers' organizations developed in the 1920s and a Dominican Confederation of Workers (Confederación Dominicana de Trabajadores, CDT) was formed in 1930. Trujillo's assumption of power later that year, however, led to the dissolution of the CDT; some unions nevertheless continued to exist, and Trujillo also sponsored his own trade union centre, the CTD. This expired after his assassination in 1961 and was replaced by independent rival centres, including affiliates of the regional organizations of the three world centres. The trade union movement has traditionally been divided along ideological lines. The three largest centres are the ICFTU-affiliated CNTD and CTU, and the WCL affiliate the CASC. The WFTU also reports an affiliate and some unions are unaffiliated to any centre. The 1992 labour code permits workers to form trade unions with as few as 20 members: they may be enterprise unions, or sectoral unions and they have the right to federate or confederate. The various trade union centres tend to be unstable with frequent breakaways and ruptures. Overall, although all employees except police and military are legally free to form unions, less than 10% of the workforce is in unions and collective bargaining is not widely practiced. Strikes are legal subject to the support of an absolute majority of the workforce and a number of pre-strike procedures. Recent strikes have involved nurses, doctors, professors and teachers.

Although the Dominican Republic ratified ILO Conventions No.87 (Freedom of Association and Protection of the Right to Organize, 1948) in 1956 and No.98 (Right to Organize and Collective Bargaining, 1949) in 1953, the 1951 Trujillo labour code remained in force until 1992. International pressure over reported violations of human and civil rights culminated in a United States decision to remove the Dominican Republic from its Generalised System of Preferences effective from June 1992. In response a new labour code was adopted that relaxed restrictions on unions. The code established permissive procedures for the registration of unions and banned employers from dismissing employees for union activities. It gave public employees in non-essential industries the right to strike; withdrew the previous prohibition against general strikes; and ended the 48-hour maximum duration limit on strikes. Under the code collective agreements could be concluded at the enterprise or sector level. In Jan. 1993 new labour courts established by the code began to function. Ostensibly the code applied to all workers in the private sector, even those in the export processing zones, despite the opposition of ADOZONAS, their employers' association.

In its 1999 *Annual Survey of Trade Union Rights* the ICFTU said that while the 1992 labour code had brought many improvements, there were still significant problems:

1. In the 40 export processing zones (EPZs), where 200,000 were employed (mainly women garment workers), employers commonly ignored the labour laws and the government had been unable or unwilling to apply them. Collective agreements were virtually unknown in the EPZs. A tripartite commission was established in 1993 to resolve disputes over non-implementation of the labour code in the zones, but had been ineffective.

2. A union must represent 50% of the workers in an enterprise before it can be recognized for collective bargaining purposes, and employers commonly got rid of activists before this figure is achieved.

3. Union activity in the sugar plantations has been curtailed and Haitians employed as sugar cane cutters work in conditions of virtual slavery.

4. The labour court system was ineffective and the judiciary "weak and corrupt".

3 Trade Union Centres

Confederación Autónoma Sindical Clasista (CASC)

Address. Juan Erazo 39, Apartado Correos 309, Santo Domingo, D.N.

Phone. +1809 687 8533

Fax. +1809 686 8602

Leadership. Gabriel Del Río Doñé (secretary-general)

International affiliation. WCL

Confederación Nacional de Trabajadores Dominicanos (CNTD)

Address. C/José de Jesús Ravelo 56, Esquina Juan Erezo, Sector Villa Juana, Santo Domingo, D.N.

Phone. +1809 221 2117

Fax. +1809 682 0195

History and character. The CNTD (like the leftist CUT) originated in the United Workers' Front for Autonomous Trade Unions (FOUPSA) founded in 1961; when FOUPSA split the more right-wing faction in 1962 took the name National Confederation of Free Workers (CONATRAL). CONATRAL adopted a neutral position at the time of the US-led intervention in 1965 and received the assistance of the US-backed American Institute for Free Labour Development (AIFLD). The CONATRAL in turn became the CNTD in 1971. In 1988 it absorbed the membership of the Unión General de Trabajadores Dominicanos (UGTD). In 1991–92 the CNTD was a key organizer of the pressure which induced the Balaguer regime to rescind and replace the Trujillo labour code.

International affiliation. ICFTU

Confederación de Trabajadores Unitaria (CTU)

Address. Tunti Caceres No.222, Santo Domingo, D.N.

Phone. +1809 562 3392

Fax. + 1809 562 3245

Leadership. Nelsida Altagracia Marmolejos (president); Jacinto de los Santos (secretary-general)

History and character. Formed by the 1991 merger of four confederations, the CTM, the CTC, the CTI, and the CUT. Claims to be the largest centre in the country and may indeed rival the CNTD.

International affiliation. Many of the constituent unions formerly had affiliations to the WFTU, but the CTU is now ICFTU affiliated.

Ecuador

Capital: Quito
Population: 12.92 m. (2000 est.)

1 Political and Economic Background

Ecuador has been a separate republic since 1830 and has had prolonged periods of political instability, with the military as a major factor in political life. This pattern continued in the 1990s. Successive governments proved unable to implement programmes backed by international funders involving privatization and structural reforms. In 1996 Abdal Bucaram Ortíz of the Ecuadorean Roldosist Party (PRE) was elected on a populist platform which had as its slogan, "vote for the madman, vote for the clown". In office, however, he attempted to press ahead with the previous govern-

ment's austerity and privatization measures, leading to massive price rises and widespread protests led by unions and Indian groups (one-third of the country's population, and disproportionately the poorest, being highland Indians), organized as the Patriotic Front. He was also accused of embezzlement of government funds and amid mounting chaos was declared "mentally incapacitated" by Congress and deposed in Feb. 1997. After a brief interlude with multiple claimants to the presidency, Congress voted in its Speaker to serve as President for an interim term of 18 months.

In July 1998 Jamil Mahuad of the centre-right Popular Democracy Party (DP) was elected President but his period in office was marked by a deepening political and economic crisis as he attempted to implement recovery measures while appeasing intense domestic opposition of the sort that had toppled Bucaram. During 1999,

Ecuador, which owed $16 billion, defaulted on interest payments to its international creditors, who indicated that they would not provide further bail-outs without structural reform; banks collapsed and accounts were frozen; and hyper-inflation set in as there was run on the national currency, the sucre. There were repeated strikes and protests. On Jan. 6, 2000 Mahuad declared a state of emergency, following a week in which the sucre had lost 35% of its value, and ahead of a general strike planned for Jan. 15. On Jan. 9 he further announced the "dollarization" of the economy, i.e. that the sucre would be replaced by the US dollar as the national currency. On Jan. 18 thousands of Indians mobilized by the Confederation of Indian Nationalities of Ecuador (CONAIE), protesting against poverty, corruption and dollarization, occupied the Congress and other government buildings, and were joined by elements of the Army. On Jan. 21 Mahuad was ousted and replaced by a three-man junta comprising an army colonel, the CONAIE president and a former president of the Supreme Court, before the armed forces commander in turn dissolved the junta and secured the succession to the presidency of the Vice-President, Gustavo Noboa.

Noboa subsequently went ahead with plans for the replacement of the sucre by the dollar, Congress approving this in March. He also announced an increase in the minimum wage to help offset the impact of dollarization, but planned to press ahead with reforms of the labour market and the opening up of the oil, electricity and telecoms sectors to foreign investment. Extensive funding by international agencies was expected to help Ecuador deal with the impact of dollarization and cope with its economic crisis.

GDP (purchasing power parity) $54.5bn. (1999 est.); GDP per capita (purchasing power parity) $4,300 (1999 est.).

2 Trade Unionism

Workers' associations developed during the 1920s, with the right to join trade unions recognized in the 1928 Constitution, and the three main trade union centres – CEDOC, CTE and CEOSL – were formed in 1938, 1944 and 1962 respectively. CEOSL is affiliated to the ICFTU, CEDOC to the WCL and the CTE to the WFTU. The centres are politically independent.

Notwithstanding their different international alignments, the different centres have a history of working together and have been a factor in blocking changes sought by successive governments to reduce budget deficits and dependence on foreign loans. In 1971 they set up a loose coordinating organization, the United Workers' Front (Frente Unitario de Trabajadores, FUT). In the 1990s FUT has coordinated a series of general strikes to protest against government attempts at economic reform and austerity measures. The unions, in association with Indian groups and other organizations, were actively involved in the strikes and protests that led to the deposing of President Bucaram in Feb. 1997.

The FUT called further strikes and protests through 1997–99. Some of these resulted in violence: five people were reported killed in clashes in a general strike in Oct. 1998. In March and again in July 1999 President Mahuad declared a state of emergency in the face of strikes and protests demanding an end to plans to privatize state-owned telephone and electric companies, a moratorium on repayments on foreign debts, and unfreezing of bank accounts. Mahuad partly capitulated to these protests, but his announcement of plans to abandon the sucre and dollarize the economy led to his fall in a coup staged against the background of popular insurrection in Jan. 2000.

Despite its general instability, Ecuador has not seen widespread death squad-type activity against trade unionists.

Ecuador ratified ILO Convention No.98 (Right to Organize and Collective Bargaining, 1949) in 1959 and No.87 (Freedom of Association and Protection of the Right to Organize, 1948) in 1967. The labour code guarantees (private sector) workers the right to join trade unions of their own choosing. However, the majority of the workforce works on the land, in the informal economy, or in small enterprises, and only about 12% of workers, mainly in larger enterprises and the public sector, are in unions. While the majority of public servants are formally prohibited from setting up trade unions and from striking, in practice unions of such employees do exist, are dealt with by the government for collective bargaining purposes, and go on strike. The two largest individual unions are reported to be the teachers' union and the union of social security workers, both affiliated to the far-left Democratic Popular Movement (MPD, which won only two seats in the last elections to Congress in 1998). Unions are not legally permitted to participate in the activities of political or religious parties. In addition the right to bargain collectively is reserved exclusively to works' councils, and may not be asserted by federations or confederations.

3 Trade Union Centres

Central Ecuatoriana de Organizaciones Clasistas (CEDOC)

Address. Calle Rio de Janeiro 407 y Juan Larrea, CP 3207, Quito

Phone. +593 2 231269

Fax. +593 2 528142

Leadership. Fernando Ibarra (president); Bolívar Pozo Guerra (secretary-general)

History and character. The CEDOC was established in 1938, with the assistance of the Roman Catholic Church, as the Ecuadorean Confederation of Catholic Workers. It affiliated to the International Federation of Christian Trade Unions (IFCTU, the predecessor of the World Confederation of Labour, WCL) in 1952, and to the regional organization of the WCL, CLAT, on its formation in 1954. In 1972 the organization adopted its current name, reflecting the loosening of earlier ties with the Church. The CEDOC assists members by providing or organizing a range of services, including legal aid, social and cultural clubs, neighbourhood committees, cooperatives, credit unions, and local workers' education institutes. Its orientation is humanistic, and it has no political affiliation.

International affiliation. WCL

Confederación Ecuatoriana de Organizaciones Sindicales Libres (CEOSL)
Ecuador Confederation of Free Trade Union Organizations

Address. Casilla Postal 1373, Quito

Phone. +593 2 522 511

Fax. +593 2 500 836

E-mail. ceosl@hoy.net

Leadership. José Chávez Chávez (president)

History and character. CEOSL was founded in 1962 and is probably the largest centre in Ecuador. It participates in the United Workers' Command (FUT) grouping of national centres and has been an active participant in successive strikes and other protests in the late 1990s that have contributed to the toppling of two Presidents (see above). CEOSL leader Chávez was detained on Jan. 15, 2000, under the State of Emergency declared by President Mahuad, and accused of subversion for his role in the crisis engulfing in the country, but released on Jan. 19.

International affiliation. ICFTU

Egypt

Capital: Cairo
Population: 68.36 m. (2000 est.)

1 Political and Economic Background

Egypt was declared a republic in 1953 and ruled thereafter by a series of presidents with strong executive powers, currently Hosni Mubarak, who was re-elected unopposed to a fourth term in Sept. 1999. Mubarak's National Democratic Party (NDP) has won every election since it was set up in 1978.

The government has faced persistent problems with terrorist activity by Islamic fundamentalists (one faction of which assassinated Mubarak's predecessor as President, Anwar Sadat, in 1981) and emergency legislation in force since 1981 has restricted a range of civil liberties, with phases of mass arrests. There are an estimated 12,000 political detainees. Religious-based political parties are nominally banned but the fundamentalist Muslim Brotherhood is the main source of opposition to the government. Following elections in Oct. 2000, however, 17 members of the Muslim Brotherhood were allowed to take seats in parliament for the first time in a decade, constituting the largest opposition bloc.

Large parts of the economy were nationalized in the 1950s and early 1960s and the public sector still accounted in the early 1980s for about three-quarters of industrial production. In 1991 Egypt agreed a programme of far-reaching economic reforms with the IMF and the World Bank under which Egypt was to make

progress to a market economy, cut subsidies and control its budget deficits. Under this Egypt benefited from major debt relief, but the pace of structural reforms, including privatization, has been slow. While key sectors of the economy remain under state control, the private sector consists mainly of small employers. There is a large informal sector.

GDP (purchasing power parity) $200bn. (1999 est.); GDP per capita (purchasing power parity) $3,000 (1999 est.).

2 Trade Unionism

The first trade union appeared in 1899 and thereafter unions tended to develop in association with contending political factions. Legal recognition was given to trade unions in 1942 and the Egyptian Trade Union Federation (ETUF) was established under Nasser in 1957 as a centre for all existing unions. Also in 1957 Egypt ratified ILO Convention No.87 (Freedom of Association and Protection of the Right to Organize 1948), having ratified Convention No.98 (Right to Organize and Collective Bargaining, 1949) in 1954. In principle, most workers in both the public and private sectors may join unions. However, the main membership of unions is in the public sector.

While perhaps the largest trade union centre in the Arab world, ETUF is a legally prescribed monopoly single trade union structure. All unions are required to belong to it and there is a close integration between

ETUF and the ruling party. The government has claimed that the single-trade-union structure reflects the historical unity of the Egyptian trade union movement.

Collective bargaining is permitted in the private sector, but unions there are weak and the scale of enterprises mostly small. Unions may negotiate collective bargaining contracts in the public enterprises, but there is no obligation on the employers' side to negotiate and in practice wages and conditions are generally set administratively. Under the system inherited from Nasser, public sector workers have traditionally enjoyed considerable job security.

Strikes are regarded as a form of disorder not a contractual dispute, and hence are illegal. In practice the ETUF prefers to resolve disputes through the courts rather than by industrial action. However wildcat strikes (usually short-lived and sometimes broken up by the security forces) took place in the late 1990s over issues such as privatization, cuts in wages and benefits at loss-making state enterprises, failure to pay annual bonuses, and compulsory early retirement. Nearly all these strikes were in the public sector or at privatized state enterprises.

Formal sector non-agricultural employment is predominantly male. Women work on the land or in the informal sector. There is use of child labour in agriculture and in areas such as brick-making, carpet-making and textiles.

3 Trade Union Centre

Egyptian Trade Union Federation (ETUF)

Address. 90 El Galaa Street, Cairo

Membership. 2.5 million

History and character. The ETUF was founded in 1957 as the unifying body for 1,300 separate unions (now reduced to 23). It is the sole permitted trade union centre, a position that it favours. It has close links with government and the ruling party.

Some ETUF officials are members of the legislative People's National Assembly or the Consultative Council (Majlis ash-Shoura) and represent workers' interests in those forums. However, public disagreements between the ETUF and the government are rare. The ETUF affiliates to the ICATU and OATUU.

El Salvador

Capital: San Salvador
Population: 6.12 m. (2000 est.)

1 Political and Economic Background

El Salvador became fully independent from Spain in 1839. Throughout its history, the military has tended to rule directly or be an important factor in political life. José Napoleón Duarte, the founder of the Christian Democratic Party (PDC), was elected President in 1972 but then forced to flee following a military coup. He returned in 1979, after the collapse of the military regime, and was appointed President by the civilian-military junta. During a prolonged period of unrest marked by violent guerrilla activity led by the Farabundo Martí National Liberation Front (FMLN) and activities by right-wing death squads, the PDC maintained its grip on power until it lost control of the legislature in elections in 1988. In 1989 the right-wing National Republican Alliance (ARENA) candidate Alfredo Cristiani was elected President to the great concern of the unions which suffered assassinations of leaders and attacks on their premises throughout the year. Cristiani implemented a liberal economic programme and opened talks with the insurgent FMLN guerrillas, which had launched major military offensives in 1990. In Jan. 1992, by which time more than 75,000 people had died, the government and the FMLN signed a peace agreement and the FMLN later than year reorganized itself as a political party. Cristiani was succeeded as president in 1994 by Armando Calderón Sol, and in 1999 by Francisco Flores, also both of ARENA. In March 2000 legislative elections resulted in the FMLN taking more votes than ARENA for the first time, although ARENA retained control of the National Assembly in coalition with other parties.

El Salvador's dominant economic activity is agriculture and its exports are dominated by coffee and textiles. Its trade deficits are offset by remittances from the large numbers of Salvadorans living abroad and by external aid. It has pursued privatization and lowered tariff barriers and eliminated capital controls. Despite the end of civil war, and 5% per annum average economic growth since that time, the country remains poor. It adopted the dollar as its currency at the start of 2001, the third Latin

American country to do so, in an effort to build confidence with foreign investors.

GDP (purchasing power parity) $18.1bn. (1999 est.); GDP per capita (purchasing power parity) $3,100 (1999 est.).

2 Trade Unionism

The first trade union federation was formed in 1922 and a degree of trade union activity persisted throughout the period of military rule. Centres affiliated to the ICFTU, WCL and WFTU appeared from 1958–65. The history of El Salvador's unions is bound up with politics, with divisions on ideological lines, fluid structures and transient alliances and reorganizations. Coordinating centres appear from time to time. During the civil conflict of the 1980s there were sharp differences between the unions about government policy. The centres listed below are those affiliated to the ICFTU and WCL; there is now no WFTU affiliate.

El Salvador has ratified neither ILO Convention No.87 (Freedom of Association and Protection of the Right to Organize, 1948) nor No.98 (Right to Organize and Collective Bargaining, 1949). The personal security of trade unionists was for many years threatened by the prevalence of terrorism and political assassination. Perhaps 10,000 trade unionists lost their lives during the period of greatest unrest.

Unions and collective bargaining are lawful in the private sector and under the 1994 labor code trade union rights were extended to workers in agriculture. There are legal protections against discrimination based on union activities. Trade unions are nominally banned in most of the public sector, although workers may form associations that do, in practice, carry out collective bargaining and go on strike and public sector associations are among the most powerful unions. There has been a series of public sector strikes over privatization in recent years. There are about 150 unions and public employee associations. The labour code nominally bars political activities by trade unions although this is ignored in practice.

Particular concern has attached in recent years to conditions in the export processing zones (EPZs), where 90,000 (mostly young women) are employed. General labour laws in principle apply in the zones. In 1996, following international controversy over conditions, including the imposition of codes of conduct by some US retailers on their suppliers, legislation was adopted applying sanctions, such as loss of tax concessions, against EPZ companies breaking the labour laws.

However, employers have ensured that unions have been largely excluded from the zones.

3 Trade Union Centres

Central Autónoma de Trabajadores Salvadoreños (CATS)

Address. Av. Bernal 568, Urb. Yumuri, San Salvador

Phone. +503 260 4616

Fax. +503 260 4717

E-mail. cats@cyt.net

Leadership. William Huezo (secretary general)

History and character. This influential centrist organization was formed in 1966 and was first known as UNOC and later as the Consejo Sindical Salvadoreño (CONSISAL) and then Central de Trabajadores Salvadoreños (CTS). The CTS as a Christian Democrat organization was a supporter of the 1980s government of President Duarte, but by 1988 was criticizing it for its failure to end the civil war and prosecute those responsible for political assassinations, and had joined the opposition alliance, the UNTS.

International affiliation. WCL

Central de Trabajadores Democráticos (CTD)

Address. Bulevar Dr. Hector Silva 165, Colonia Médica, San Salvador

Phone. +503 225 4130

Fax. +503 225 4130

History and character. The CTD was formed in the mid-1980s with the backing of the AFL-CIO in the United States.

International affiliation. ICFTU

Federación Nacional Sindical de Trabajadores Salvadoreños (FENASTRAS)

Address. 10a Ave. Norte, No. 120, San Salvador

Phone. +503 22 0141

Fax. +503 22 2849

Leadership. Juan José Huezo (general secretary)

Membership. 36,000

History and character. FENASTRAS was formed in 1975. It was a particular target for attacks, including killings and torture, during the 1980s civil war and its headquarters was bombed in Oct. 1989. It was a member of the opposition UNTS alliance, founded in 1986, which developed links with the FMLN.

International affiliation. ICFTU

Equatorial Guinea

Capital: Malabo
Population: 474,000 (2000 est.)

1 Political and Economic Background

The former Spanish overseas provinces of Fernando Pó
and Río Muni achieved autonomy in 1963 and independence in 1968. Over the next 10 years the Macías
Nguema regime banned all existing parties and merged
them into the sole National (Workers') Party; large numbers of refugees and foreign workers left the country;
competent administration effectively collapsed; and
accusations were made of gross violations of human and
civil rights. In 1979 Obiang Nguema seized power in a
coup, and he has remained in power since then, exercising control through a ruling clique of family and clan
members. His Democratic Party of Equatorial Guinea
controls the National Assembly, while President Obiang
was himself most recently elected in Feb. 1996 winning
99% of the vote in a contest described by international
observers as "a farce". Security forces operate to suppress dissent with impunity.

Subsistence farming is the main livelihood for most
workers, and since independence production of the main
cash crops of cocoa and coffee has declined drastically
because of mismanagement. However, since the mid-
1990s there have been significant revenues from oil
exploitation and this has fueled economic growth, with
15% growth in real GDP in 1999.

GDP (purchasing power parity) $960 m. (1999 est.);
GDP per capita (purchasing power parity) $2,000 (1999
est.).

2 Trade Unionism

Equatorial Guinea has been a member of the
International Labour Organization since 1981 but has
ratified neither ILO Convention No.87 (Freedom of
Association and Protection of the Right to Organize,
1948) nor Convention No.98 (Right to Organize and
Collective Bargaining, 1949).

No unions are reported to exist, collective bargaining
does not take place and strikes are illegal. The oil industry is the major source of private sector formal employment and international oil companies until 1999
recruited local workers exclusively through a government-controlled agency that screened applicants to prevent opponents of the regime from getting jobs.
Government officials and their families reportedly own
most other private businesses.

Eritrea

Capital: Asmara
Population: 4.14 m. (2000 est.)

1 Political and Economic Background

Eritrea is a former Italian colony that established de facto
independence from Ethiopia in 1991 after 30 years of
insurgency and, after a referendum, declared independence in May 1993. The ruling People's Front for
Democracy and Justice (PFDJ) was established in 1994 on
the basis of the Eritrean People's Liberation Front (EPLF)
which had led the struggle for independence. There have
been no elections to the National Assembly, which is controlled by the PFDJ and appoints the President. Further
border conflict with Ethiopia resumed in 1998.

Eritrea is a poor country with little infrastructure and
few skilled workers. 80% of the population are engaged
in subsistence farming and herding, but there is also a
little light industry. The government wishes to develop a
market economy but there has been little foreign investment to date.

GDP (purchasing power parity) $2.9bn. (1999 est.);
GDP per capita (purchasing power parity) $750 (1999
est.).

2 Trade Unionism

Eritrea ratified ILO Conventions No.87 (Freedom of
Association and Protection of the Right to Organize,
1948) and No.98 (Right to Organize and Collective

Bargaining, 1949) in 2000. Since securing independence, the government has said it favours a free and independent trade union movement and there are no legal restrictions on the formation of unions.

Factory-based unions were established in Eritrea in 1948. In 1952 the first congress was held of the National Union of Eritrean Workers for Independence (NUEWI) but this was speedily repressed by the Ethiopian regime, which banned all unions in Nov. 1953. Trade unions had an essentially political character during the struggle for independence, and sent delegates to the first congress of the EPLF in 1977. The founding congress of the National Union of Eritrean Workers (NUEW) was convened in liberated areas in 1979. Because of its integration in the liberation movement, the NUEW (now the National Confederation of Eritrean Workers) gained considerable influence in the ruling party. Many figures in the EPLF leadership were recruited from the ranks of the unions.

Phone. +291 1 11 61 87

Fax. +291 1 12 66 06

Membership. 23,000

History and character. The NCEW was founded (as the National Union of Eritrean Workers) in Nov. 1979 in the liberated areas, but traced its origins to the National Union of Eritrean Workers for Independence set up in the 1950s. It held further congresses in 1983 and 1988 but during the war for independence essentially functioned as part of the EPLF. It was active in the Eritrean diaspora. The Dec. 1992 congress – the first after independence – approved a labour code issued by the provisional government but expressed concern that the country was being pushed by international financial interests into privatization. The NCEW is now reported to be independent of the government and the PFDJ. It comprises 129 unions and five federations.

International affiliation. ICFTU

3 Trade Union Centre

National Confederation of Eritrean Workers (NCEW)

Address. PO Box 1188, Asmara

Estonia

Capital: Tallinn
Population: 1.43 m. (2000 est.)

1 Political and Economic Background

Estonia, absorbed into the USSR in 1940, achieved its independence with the dissolution of the Soviet Union in 1991. Following elections in Mar. 1999 there is a centre-right coalition government led by Prime Minister Lennart Meri of the Pro Patria party. There is a multiplicity of small parties. There is a remaining 29% ethnic Russian population, many originally resettled from Russia under Soviet rule, who complain of discrimination.

The immediate effect of the loss of former Soviet markets after 1991 was severe. In the two years 1991-93 the Russian share of Estonian exports fell from over 90 to 38 per cent, with Finland becoming the major trading partner. In Aug. 1993 privatization began in earnest with

the creation of the Privatization Agency and much of the former state sector has now been privatized. During the transition to a market economy many jobs were lost in large-scale industry, notably in textiles, engineering and oil shale processing but the services sector grew in importance. In 1999 Estonia was badly hit by the effects of the 1998 Russian financial crisis. Estonia has applied for admission to the European Union.

GDP (purchasing power parity) $7.9bn. (1999 est.); GDP per capita (purchasing power parity) $5,600 (1999 est.).

2 Trade Unionism

The 1992 Constitution provides the right to join unions and Estonia ratified ILO Conventions No.87 (Freedom of Association and Protection of the Right to Organize, 1948) and No.98 (Right to Organize and Collective Bargaining, 1949) in 1994.

Estonia's national centre remains the Association (formerly the Central Organization) of Estonian Trade Unions (EAKL), which as early as Dec. 1989 severed its links with the AUCCTU of the USSR. Its membership fell rapidly from the 800,000 claimed under Communism once membership became voluntary and this decline was accelerated by the break up of large enterprises and privatization. Membership by 1999 was put at only 65,000.

EAKL is the national centre and ICFTU affiliate, but does not enjoy undivided support as breakaway unions have formed other federations. The Organization of Employee Unions (TALO) split from the EAKL in 1993 and has 45,000 members, and a separate union of food processing and rural workers was established in 1997. However, a Finnish trade union report in 1998 concluded that unions were unpopular in Estonia, and that only 10–20% of the work force remained in unions (a recent estimate suggests the figure is 12%, the lowest in the Baltic region). The Finnish trade unions have been attempting to help the Estonian unions in areas such as creating effective membership registers and training in bargaining and other skills.

A law regulating collective bargaining was passed in 1993. The unions' lack of influence is also reflected in the fact that although EAKL has concluded framework agreements with employers, collective bargaining is not highly developed and few enterprise-level agreements have been signed. In the mid-1990s EAKL reported that few workers clearly understood the difference between management and labour for bargaining purposes. In addition payment of part of wages "under the counter" was widespread and stood in the way of transparent contracts.

There is a legal right to strike and retribution against strikers is unlawful. The first tripartite agreement was signed in Apr. 1993 but tripartism is very little developed, hindered in part by the lack of representative employers' organizations.

The 1996 Non-Profit Associations Act gave the authorities the power to dissolve unions and imposed a range of restrictions on unions' internal procedures. Unions were required to register under the Act by Mar. 1, 1999.

3 Trade Union Centre

Association of Estonian Trade Unions (EAKL)

Address. 4 Rävala Boulevard, 10143 Tallinn

Phone. +372 6 612383

Fax. +372 6 612542

E-mail. eakl@eakl.ee

Leadership. Kadi Pärnits (chairman)

Membership. 65,000.

History and character. As the Central Organization of Estonian Trade Unions this was the official centre under Soviet rule, but it disaffiliated from the AUCCTU in 1989 and began to change its function the following year by voluntarily yielding control of social security and sickness payments to the state. This signaled its intention to achieve a voluntary membership, and in the ensuing years the number of members fell heavily. Whereas the AUCCTU had claimed to represent 800,000 members in Estonia (i.e. effectively the entire work force) EAKL's reported membership fell to 500,000 by 1992 and 330,000 by 1993. It is now estimated at 65,000.

While supporting privatization EAKL complained that enterprises were being sold off cheaply, without consultation, and to the detriment of the employment rights of those who work in them.

The EAKL was involved in the development of the post-Soviet labour code, which prohibits anti-union discrimination. It participates with employers and government in setting the minimum wage.

EAKL is broadly supportive of Estonia's application, lodged in 1998, to join the EU, although this is reportedly viewed with suspicion by much of the work force. At the 3rd congress in April 2000, Kadi Pärnits was elected chairman in succession to Raivo Paavo, who was to concentrate on his role as a member of the parliament. Pärnits had previously been responsible for legal affairs and particularly involved with issues surrounding harmonization of Estonian legislation with that of the EU.

International affiliation. ICFTU

Ethiopia

Capital: Addis Ababa
Population: 64.12 m. (2000 est.)

1 Political and Economic Background

Emperor Haile Selassie was deposed in 1974 and

Ethiopia became a socialist state under military rule; all major sectors of the economy rapidly entered state ownership, including the land, which hitherto had been held largely on a feudal basis. Under Lt.-Col. Mengistu Haile Mariam, head of state 1977–91, the (Marxist) Workers' Party of Ethiopia (WPE) became the country's sole political party. During the Mengistu era, Ethiopia received considerable economic assistance from the USSR and military help from Cuba in its efforts to combat secessionist movements in Eritrea, Tigre and the Ogaden. By early 1991, large areas were under rebel control and Eritrea had established de facto independence. Mengistu fled and the Ethiopian People's Revolutionary Democratic Front (EPRDF) took power under President Meles Zenawi.

Ethiopia's economy is largely agricultural and pastoral, and has suffered not only from the internal upheavals of the Eritrean war but also from prolonged periods of almost total drought and widespread famine; both of these factors have led to mass migrations (and also removals of population). International prices for commodity exports have been low, and the level of exports has been sharply reduced by climatic conditions, disruption and disease. Some 80% of the workforce is engaged in the agriculture sector. Much of the country's previous modest manufacturing capacity lay in Eritrea, now lost. The poverty of the country has been exacerbated by heavy expenditure on continuing border conflict with Eritrea.

GDP (purchasing power parity) $33.3bn. (1999 est.); GDP per capita (purchasing power parity) $560 (1999 est.).

2 Trade Unionism

The first clandestine trade unions were formed after 1947, and the basis of a trade union centre known as the Ethiopian Labour Union (ELU) was formed in 1954. After liberalization in 1962, the ELU was reorganized as the Confederation of Ethiopian Labour Unions (CELU), linked to the ICFTU. Ethiopia ratified ILO Conventions No.87 (Freedom of Association and Protection of the Right to Organize, 1948) and No. 98 (Right to Organize and Collective Bargaining, 1949) in 1963.

Following the installation of a Marxist military regime, the CELU was abolished in 1975 and reformed in 1977 as the All-Ethiopian Trade Union (AETU) and in 1986 as the Ethiopian Trade Union (ETU). The role and tasks of the ETU were embodied in law. Unions were legally obliged to spread knowledge of the development plans of the government and Marxist–Leninist theories among the workers, and to implement the decisions and directives of the authorities. It affiliated to the communist-dominated WFTU. Following the fall of Mengistu, the seventh (1993) congress of the ETU renamed itself as the Confederation of European Trade Unions (CETU) and proclaimed its complete independence. This began a deterioration of relations with the authorities and the government closed CETU down in 1994 and then restructured it in 1997.

There is a constitutional right for most workers to join unions and legal protection against discrimination by employers against union members. However, only a small proportion of the total workforce is employed in the formal waged economy and the total of union members is estimated at about 300,000. Teachers, public officials and medical personnel may not join trade unions and there has been particular conflict in teaching. Unions may also not engage in political activity. The Ethiopian Teachers' Association (ETA) president, Dr. Taye Woldesemayat, was arrested in May 1996 and subsequently accused of conspiracy against government officials and inciting an armed uprising. He has been detained since then and in June 1999 was sentenced to 15 years' imprisonment. In May 1997 police shot dead a member of the ETA executive council while seeking to arrest him on terrorism charges. The government has taken control of ETA offices, detained its officials, and transferred its assets to a faction supporting the government. There has also been government interference in the affairs of other unions, with instances of union leaders fleeing the country.

Collective bargaining exists in the small unionized sector. Collective bargaining agreements are conditional on their approval by the Ministry of Labour, which must verify that such agreements conform to the basic policies of the government. There is a legal right to strike, subject to conciliation and arbitration procedures. However, there were no strikes in 1999 and there is reported to be scepticism among unions as to the willingness of the government and courts to respect and enforce the law. Strikes are prohibited in a range of essential services.

3 Trade Union Centre

Confederation of Ethiopian Trade Unions (CETU)

Membership. Formerly reported as 120,000 but believed to have declined because of government harassment.

History and character. The Confederation of Ethiopian Labour Unions (CELU) was founded in 1963 and developed with the assistance of western unions. Following the fall of Haile Selassie in 1974, the new Marxist military regime first purged the CELU leadership and then after sporadic strikes and disturbances dissolved CELU in Nov. 1975 and in Jan. 1977 set up a new All-Ethiopian Trade Union (AETU). AETU's first leader, Ato Tewodros Bekele, was killed a month later, one of many victims of Ethiopia's power struggles, and his successor Temesgen Madebo shared his fate later the same year.

At its third (1986) congress the AETU changed its name to the Ethiopian Trade Union (ETU). Following the change of regime, and in line with reform trends at that time evident in much of Africa, the seventh (1993) congress (which transformed the organization into the Confederation of Ethiopian Trade Unions) proclaimed the complete independence and autonomy of the trade unions. It adopted positions critical of the government's economic policies.

From this point the CETU began to find itself the subject of hostile state attention. During 1994 it was excluded from its head office, its registration canceled, and its accounts were frozen. There were raids on its property and its leadership was eventually driven into exile in Kenya. The lock-out continued in defiance of rulings in the CETU's favour by the Court of Appeal.

In Apr. 1997 CETU was restructured, reportedly with government involvement; its registration was restored and headquarters and bank accounts re-opened. Its

former president Dawi Ibrahim and two executive council members fled the country saying their lives were in danger.

International affiliation. WFTU

Federated States of Micronesia

Capital: Paliki (Pohnpei Island)
Population: 133,000 (2000 est.)

1 Political and Economic Background

The UN trusteeship of these islands ended in 1990 and they are now an independent state in a compact of free association with the United States. There is a parliamentary system of government but no formal political parties.

These are remote and scattered islands with little infrastructure. There is subsistence farming and fishing and the economy depends on US financial assistance.

GDP (purchasing power parity) $240m. (1997 est.); GDP per capita (purchasing power parity) $2,000 (1997 est.).

2 Trade Unionism

There is a general constitutional right to form associations but no trade unions have been formed. The government is the main formal employer, and sets wages administratively. Micronesia is not a member of the ILO.

Fiji

Population: 832,000 (2000 est.)
Capital: Suva

1 Political and Economic Background

Fiji became a fully independent member of the Commonwealth on independence from the UK in 1970. Its post-independence politics have been dominated by tensions between the indigenous (Melanesian-Polynesian) Fijian population, comprising 51% of the population, and the Indo–Fijians, 42% of the population. Traditionally, the Indo–Fijians have dominated the private business sector, while the indigenous population have dominated the government and armed forces.

From independence until Apr. 1987, the Alliance

Party, representing the indigenous population, was in power. A new government was then formed by parties drawing mainly on support from those of Indian descent. This precipitated military intervention led by the army commander, Sitiveni Rabuka, and power was restored to representatives of the indigenous population. In 1990 a new constitution was framed with the intention of giving indigenous Fijians a built-in majority in the legislature through reservation of seats on an ethnic basis.

Rabuka's Fijian Political Party (FPP) won the 1992 general election, the first since the 1987 coup, and he was re-elected in 1994 despite splits within his coalition. In 1997 a new constitution was adopted, based on the recommendations of the Reeves Commission, which ended the provisions of the 1990 constitution entrenching the legislative dominance of the indigenous population. This allowed Fiji to be re-admitted to the Commonwealth, of which it had ceased to be a member after the 1987 coup. In elections in May 1999, the ethnic Indian Fijian Labour Party (FLP), won 37 of the 71 seats in the House of Representatives, and its leader Mahendra Chaudhry became Prime Minister. On May 19, 2000, George Speight, a businessman, and his supporters seized the Parliament and took the Prime Minister and 30 MPs hostage. Martial law was declared on May 26 but the military showed no inclination to release the legislators, while military decrees were issued to remove Indo-Fijians from the public services. After 55 days Chaudhry and other remaining hostages were released from Parliament, but Chaudhry was deposed as Prime Minister by the military and an interim government appointed that included individuals with links to the coup plotters. Speight was given immunity from prosecution although clashes subsequently occurred between sections of the military and Speight supporters and he was arrested on July 27. The new Prime Minister, Laisenia Qarase, said that a new constitution would be adopted in 2001 under which fresh elections would be held in 2002. It was predicted that a new constitution would reserve the position of Prime Minister for indigenous Fijians.

Agriculture dominates the Fijian economy, with sugar as the principal cash and export crop. There is also a small manufacturing sector and a tourist industry, although this has been affected by political instability.

GDP (purchasing power parity) $5.9bn. (1999 est.); GDP per capita (purchasing power parity) $7,300 (1999 est.).

2 Trade Unionism

Fiji ratified ILO Convention No.98 (Right to Organize and Collective Bargaining, 1949) in 1974 but has not ratified Convention No.87 (Freedom of Association and Protection of the Right to Organize, 1948).

Union activity developed following the Industrial Associations Ordinance of 1942, but was affected by racial divisions between Fijians, Indians and Europeans. When racially based unionism declined in the 1960s the Fiji Trades Union Congress (FTUC) emerged as the dominant central organization. Its main base of support remained in the ethnically Indian population, however. Other than for restrictions in the government sector, most workers enjoyed the right to form and join unions of their own choosing.

In 1985 the Fiji Labour Party (FLP) was created as a multi-racial party (although it drew most of its support from the Indian community) with the FTUC as the prime mover. After elections in Apr. 1987 the FLP formed the government in alliance with the National Federation Party (NFP), but this was almost immediately overthrown in a military coup.

After the 1987 coup union rights were severely curtailed provoking international protests from ICFTU affiliates in Australia and New Zealand. The military

regime opened negotiations with the ICFTU-affiliated FTUC and gave assurances that rights would soon be restored; Australian and New Zealand unions dropped a threatened air traffic ban, and an ICFTU delegation visited Fiji the following year. But unions continued to suffer legal adversity, detentions of leaders and an arson attack on the FTUC head office. In 1988 the then FTUC national secretary, Mahendra Chaudhry, was arrested and interrogated by police, accused of attempted arms shipments. A further ICFTU visit produced another report critical of the government's failure to recognize the FTUC or to re-establish the country's Tripartite Forum. Continued representations from the FTUC itself for re-establishment of formal industrial relations institutions were made without effect, and the government proceeded towards the establishment of racially based unions.

In 1992 Chaudhry was brought before a Fijian court, charged with holding dual trade union office, an offence against 1991 legislation which also banned industrial associations (formed mainly among indigenous Fijian workers) from participating in disputes and introduced mechanisms to facilitate the formation of employer-sponsored unions. The case against Chaudhry – who held office in two FTUC affiliates as well as his national post- was adjourned on technical grounds.

The 1997 constitution (formally in effect from July 27, 1998) eased restrictions on the unions and reversed legalized discrimination against Indo-Fijians. As a result of elections in May 1999, Chaudhry, as leader of the ethnic Indian Fijian Labour Party (FLP), became Prime Minister. However, Chaudhry was taken hostage in May 2000 and then deposed by the military (see above), and the 1997 constitution was overturned and a constitutional review commission set up dominated by indigenous Fijians.

Historically most workers have been generally free to join unions and an estimated 55% of the formally employed work force is unionized, with heavy organization of the major foreign exchange earning sectors, sugar and tourism. There is a legal requirement on employers to recognize a union where it has recruited more than half the workforce. In practice unions are usually successful in preventing discrimination against workers for union activities, although the law does not require that workers dismissed for union activities must be reinstated.

While some unions remain ethnically based, both Indo-Fijians and ethnic Fijians hold leadership roles, and the FTUC has also sought to emphasize its multi-ethnic base. However, unions have also been formed outside the FTUC fold, primarily recruiting the indigenous population.

The right to bargain collectively is recognized. Restrictions were imposed in the years after the 1987 coup, but were lifted after 1992. Most collective bargaining takes place at the enterprise level. However, in Apr. 1998 the government introduced an order limiting wage increases to 3% for 1998–99, regardless of provisions in collective agreements. While national labour laws apply in the export processing zones, the unions have had little success in organizing workers or achieving collective contracts in the zones. Strikes are generally legal, but industrial associations, to which many indigenous Fijians belong, may not strike.

3 Trade Union Centre

Fiji Trades Union Congress (FTUC)

Address. 32 Des Voeux Road, PO Box 1418, Suva

Phone. +679 315377

Fax. +679 300306

E-mail. ftucl@is.com.fj

Leadership. Felix Anthony (national secretary)

History and character. The FTUC was founded in 1952 as the Fiji Industrial Workers' Congress, with sugar workers' unions its main affiliates. Under its present name from 1966, the FTUC steadily broadened its base among Fijian unions. It is the only Fijian trade union centre.

In 1985 it launched the Fiji Labour Party (FLP) to challenge government policy (the FTUC having previously been politically unaffiliated). Although the FLP was nominally separate, FTUC treasurer Robert Kumar became FLP treasurer also; Mahendra Chaudhry, then FTUC assistant national secretary, became FLP assistant secretary-general. FTUC vice-president Krishna Dutt became the party's secretary-general and Public Service Association president, Timori Bavadra, its president. The FLP allied with the opposition National Federation Party (NFP), and in 1987 this coalition came to power.

Bavadra became Prime Minister and senior FTUC officials also joined the government, but their success was brief for the government was overthrown after a month in a military coup led by Lt.-Gen. Sitiveni Rabuka.

Although civilian government was restored the FTUC operated thereafter for some years under severe constraint. Its offices were burned down and a number of union leaders were imprisoned. The FTUC still continued to function, however, criticizing restrictions on collective bargaining, deregulation, the creation of free trade zones, and the government objective of registering racially based unions.

In 1997 the FTUC warmly greeted the new constitution, which reversed legalized discrimination against Indo-Fijians and eased restrictions on unions. In May 1999, former leader of the FTUC and the then general secretary of the Fiji Public Service Association, Mahendra Chaudhry, became Prime Minister. Following the May 2000 seizure of Chaudhry and other parliamentarians by supporters of George Speight, the FTUC allied itself with the main employers' association, religious, community and other civic groups to try to find a solution that did not result in reversal of the gains of the 1997 constitution. FTUC leader Felix Anthony was briefly detained by the military. Following the replacement of Chaudhry as Prime Minister the FTUC called for the return of the 1997 constitution and condemned the establishment of a constitutional review commission dominated by indigenous Fijians and with a minority of Indo-Fijians allegedly motivated by "financial greed".

International affiliations. ICFTU; CTUC

Finland

Capital: Helsinki
Population: 5.17 m. (2000 est.)

1 Political and Economic Background

Finland became independent from Russia in 1917. For a quarter century from 1966 to 1991, the Finnish Social Democratic Party (SSDP) led a series of centre-left governments. In 1991 a centre-right coalition came to office, headed by the Centre Party (KESK). In 1995, however, elections restored the SSDP's position and its leader Paavo Lipponenen became Prime Minister of a five-party "rainbow coalition" government also including

conservative, liberal, left-wing and green parties. This coalition was confirmed in office as a result of elections in March 1999. Finland joined the European Union in 1995.

Since World War II Finland's primarily rural economy has diversified into a wide range of industries and services that have greatly raised living standards. Its industries include wood, metal, engineering, telecommunications and electronics. The collapse of the USSR, Finland's major export market, led to a period of major economic difficulties in the early 1990s. The centre-right government sought to improve Finland's competitiveness by austerity policies but drastic measures including currency devaluation and tough national agreements with the unions did not bring quick success. By the end of 1993, the country's longest-ever recession had seen GDP decline by around 15% and unemployment reached 20% the following year. There has been marked recovery since that point, with unemployment down to 10% by 1999. In Sept. 2000 rankings by the World Economic Forum put Finland in first place, ahead of the US and Germany, in a "current competitiveness" league table which focuses on ability to compete in world markets and general business environment including government policies, infrastructure and skills. Finland was the only Scandinavian country to adopt the European single currency at its launch in Jan. 1999.

GDP (purchasing power parity) $108.6bn. (1999 est.); GDP per capita (purchasing power parity) $21,000 (1999 est.).

2 Trade Unionism

The Congress of Trade Unions in Finland (SAJ) was formed by the SDDP in 1907 with 18 affiliates and 25,000 members. This Marxist-led organization was dissolved by the government in 1930 but reorganized the same year (purged of communist influence) as the Confederation of Finnish Trade Unions (SAK). Thereafter the unions were constrained by world economic depression, right-wing political influences and, finally, war. After 1945 they recovered but in 1959-60 split between the SAK and a new rival Finnish Trade Union Federation (SAJ). A decade later the SAJ and the SAK reunited as the Central Organization of Finnish Trade Unions (also known as SAK); membership of the united centre rose from 560,000 to over one million by 1980.

Finland is one of the most highly unionized countries in the world, with around 85% of the working population in unions (which also have pensioners in their membership totals). There are three trade union centres, with a correlation between educational qualifications and affiliation to the different centres (as in other Scandinavian countries). SAK, with close to 1,070,000 members, is the largest organization and although its membership its diverse it represents in particular manual and semi-skilled workers and trades. STTK, the Confederation of Salaried Employee Organizations, represents primarily white-collar and technical employees and reports 643,000 members. Its membership doubled in the early 1990s with the collapse of the rival Confederation of Salaried Employees of Finland (TVK). AKAVA, the smallest of the three, with 360,000 members, is an organization representing mainly graduate professionals and many of its affiliates may be characterized as professional associations. All three centres have larger memberships than in the 1980s (in the case of SAK, only marginally so) reflecting the continued strength of unions in Finland despite underlying changes such as the shift to services that have weakened unions in many countries. In Finland union membership rose even in the severe recession of the early 1990s.

The three centres have had a cooperation agreement between them since 1978 and all three are affiliated to the ICFTU. The SAK and STTK in particular cooperate in areas such as education, lobbying and solidarity work. Reflecting the importance of the social dimension of the European Union, the three centres have joint representation in Brussels.

Finland ratified ILO Convention No.87 (Freedom of Association and Protection of the Right to Organize, 1948) in 1950 and Convention No.98 (Right to Organize and Collective Bargaining, 1949) in 1951. The pattern of industrial relations is influenced by the institutional strength of the unions and a highly developed system of tripartism and national collective agreements. The foundation stone for this system is seen as having been laid at the height of the "winter war" with the Soviet Union in the so-called "January betrothal" of 1940, when as an expression of national unity the Central Organization of Finnish Employers (STK), with government support, accepted SAK as a negotiating partner. Since the 1960s, the union centres and employers' organizations (with government participation) have typically negotiated incomes policy agreements covering a wide range of aspects of working conditions including salaries and benefits, working hours, unemployment benefits, social security provisions, pensions and taxation. Framework agreements negotiated at the centre are mirrored in sectoral and enterprise agreements. Industrial action during the lifetime of these agreements has tended to be uncommon. Employers have recently been calling for a ban on sympathy strikes.

There is a close involvement of the unions in politics. 118 of the 200-member Parliament elected in March 1999 are union members. Of these 63 belong to AKAVA, 36 to SAK and 19 to the STTK. Union members are found in a range of political parties and there is no cross-party union lobby. In terms of representing union issues, those from SAK are typically the most active and those from AKAVA the least. The strongest ties are between SAK and the Social Democrats, although there is also a minority SAK involvement with the Left Alliance. Paavo Lipponen, the Social Democratic Prime Minister, is a member of a SAK union. Unions commonly provide financial or other support to political candidates.

3 Trade Union Centres

AVAKA (Confederation of Unions for Academic Professionals in Finland)

Address. Rautatieläisenkatu 6, FIN-00520 Helsinki

Phone. +358 9 141 822

Fax. +358 9 142 595

E-mail. tarja.paajonen@akava.fi

Website. www.akava.fi (in Finnish, Swedish and English)

Leadership. Risto Piekka (president)

Membership. 360,000 (includes 58,000 students represented by AKAVA's student council) in 32 affiliates.

History and character. AKAVA was founded in 1950 and represents employees with university-level, professional or other high-level training. It represents 80% of employees in the areas it serves and the majority of members work in the public sector, with slightly more than 50% being women. Its seeks to safeguard the economic and professional position of its members and is involved in research, policy negotiations and lobbying. It provides collective bargaining for its members, at national and regional levels, although a few member unions undertake their own collective bargaining.

AKAVA's affiliates function as both trade unions and professional associations, with an emphasis on education and training. AKAVA seeks to ensure that members enjoy a status and income level in keeping with their training, experience and special skills. It supports the preservation of the welfare state while emphasizing the need for taxation policy to provide an incentive to work and provide employment.

AKAVA is active at the international and especially the European level, with a special interest in EURO-CADRES, the European Council of Professional and Managerial Staff.

Publications. AKAVA News

International affiliations. NFS; ETUC: EURO-CADRES: ICFTU; TUAC

Affiliates. AKAVA has some 32 affiliates, the largest of which include:

1. Trade Union of Education in Finland
Address. Rautatieläisenkatu 6, FIN-00520 Helsinki
Phone. +358 9 150 271
Fax. +358 9 145 821

2. Finnish Association of Graduate Engineers
Address. Ratavartijankatu 2, FIN-00520 Helsinki
Phone. +358 9 229 121
Fax. +358 9 2291 2922

3. Union of Professional Engineers in Finland
Address. Ratavartijankatu 2, FIN-00520 Helsinki
Phone. +358 9 476 770
Fax. +358 9 143 971

4. Finnish Association of Graduates in Economics and Business Administration
Address. Ratavartijankatu 2, FIN-00520 Helsinki
Phone. +358 9 476 777
Fax. +358 9 476 7677

5. Finnish Medical Association
Address. PL 49 (Mäkelänkatu 2)
Phone. +358 9 393 091
Fax. +358 9 393 0794

Suomen Ammattiliittojen Keskusjärjestö (SAK)
Central Organization of Finnish Trade Unions

Address. PO Box 157, FIN-00531 Helsinki
Phone. +358 9 77 211

Fax. +358 9 772 1447
E-mail. sak@sak.fi
Website. www.sak.fi (in English, German, French, Spanish, Swedish and Finnish)
Leadership. Lauri Ihalainen (president)
Membership. 1,073,873

History and character. The SAK traces its history back to 1907 (see above). Under Finland's system of centralized agreements on wages and conditions it has enjoyed substantial economic and political influence. Its central role has, however, been affected in recent years by the growing importance of unaffiliated white-collar unions.

Although it is politically independent the SAK majority has traditionally been associated with the Social Democrats (SSDP), with a minority supporting the Left Alliance. However, a growing number of members define themselves as politically non-aligned.

SAK negotiates framework agreements with the employers, these setting the context for sectoral negotiations involving its member unions. It formulates policy and acts as a lobby and advocate for labour to government and (increasingly) at EU level.

SAK has 26 affiliated unions in both private and public sectors. Some of these represent very small constituencies, such as the Finnish Social Democratic Journalists' Union with 334 members. In general there has been a reluctance to create unions representing a multiplicity of occupational groups. The biggest member union is the 210,500-member Municipal Workers' Union, but in 1998 four private sector service unions, of which the largest are the Union of Commercial Employees and the Hotel and Restaurant Workers, began negotiations with a view to merging in 2001. This would create a super-union of similar size to the Municipal Employees. Local SAK organizations – of which there are some 150 – unite all the branches of different affiliates within particular localities, typically at the municipality level.

At international level SAK participates in development work and has a particular interest in the ex-Soviet Baltic states. SAK and all 26 of its affiliates (together with three member unions from the white-collar confederation STTK) are members of SASK, the Trade Union Solidarity Centre of Finland, which provides development assistance to Third World countries.

Publications. Publications in Finnish and Swedish; regular articles in English accessible via website.

International affiliations. ICFTU; ETUC; TUAC; NFS
Affiliates. The following SAK affiliates each have more than 30,000 members, listed in order of size (Dec. 31, 1999).

1 Municipal Workers' Union (KTV)
Address. PO Box 101, 00531 Helsinki
Phone. +358 9 77031
Fax. +3658 9 7703 397
Membership. 210,500

2 Metalworkers' Union (Metalli)
Address. PO Box 107, 00531 Helsinki
Phone. +358 9 77071

Fax. +358 9 7707 277
Membership. 167,392

3 Union of Commercial Employees
Address. PO Box 54, 00531 Helsinki
Phone. +358 9 775 71
Fax. +358 9 7011 119
Membership. 131,086

4 Construction Trade Union
Address. PO Box 307, 00531 Helsinki
Phone. +358 9 770 21
Fax. +358 9 7702 241
Membership. 76,592

5 Finnish Transport Workers' Union (AKT)
Address. PO Box 313, 00531 Helsinki
Phone. +358 9 613 110
Fax. +358 9 739 287
Membership. 50,722

6 Wood and Allied Workers' Union (PUU)
Address. PO Box 318, 00531 Helsinki
Phone. +358 9 615 161
Fax. +358 9 761 160
Membership. 50,419

7 Paperworkers' Union
Address. PO Box 326, 00531 Helsinki
Phone. +358 9 708 91
Fax. +358 9 7012 279
Membership. 49,353

8 Hotel and Restaurant Workers' Union (HRHL)
Address. PO Box 327, 00531 Helsinki
Phone. +358 9 77 561
Fax. +358 9 7756 223
Membership. 48,243

9 Finnish Food Workers' Union (SEL)
Address. PO Box 213, 00531 Helsinki
Phone. +358 9 393 881
Fax. +358 9 712 059
Membership. 42,542

10 Chemical Workers' Union (KEMIA)
Address. PO Box 324, 00531 Helsinki
Phone. +358 9 773 971
Fax. +358 9 7538 040
Membership. 34,555

STTK (Finnish Confederation of Salaried Employees)

Address. Pohjoisranta 4A, PO Box 248, 00171 Helsinki

Phone. +358 9 131 521

Fax. +358 9 652 367

E-mail. anttila@stk.fi

Website. www.sttk.fi (in Finnish, Swedish and English)

Membership. 643,300 in 26 affiliated unions.

History and character. The STTK is the second largest

centre and the leading voice of salaried employees in Finland. The rival Confederation of Salaried Employees of Finland (TVK), which dated back to 1922 and was considered second in importance to the SAK, collapsed into bankruptcy in the early 1990s, resulting in STTK doubling its membership. Members are in both the private and public sectors.

The rate of unionization of salaried employees has been increasing since the 1960s and now stands at 80%. Some 67% of STTK's members are women and the STTK emphasizes the concept of equal pay for work of equal value. STTK negotiates framework collective agreements and its member unions negotiate at sectoral level. STTK favours an activist government role in supporting employment and training and supports experiments with new models of sharing working time.

In common with other Scandinavian unions, STTK participates in a wide range of international forums, and EU-level industry committees are important to its affiliates.

International affiliations. NFS; ETUC; TUAC; ICFTU
Affiliates. Leading affiliated unions include:

Union of Health and Social Care Services (TEHY)
Address. Asemamiehenkatu 4, 00520 Helsinki
Phone. +358 9 1552 700
Fax. +358 9 148 3038
E-mail. etunimi.sukunimi@tehy.fi
Website. www.tehy.fi (Finnish; English section)
Membership. 121,000

Federation of Municipal Officers (KVL)
Address. Asemamiehenkatu 4, 00520 Helsinki
Phone. +358 9 155 231
Fax. +358 9 155 2333
E-mail. etunimi.sukunimi@kvl.fi
Website. www.kvl.fi (Finnish; English section)
Membership. 73,500

Union of Technical Employees (TL)
Address. Selkämerenkuja 1A, PL 183, 00181 Helsinki
Phone. +358 9 172 731
Fax. +358 9 1727 3330
E-mail. etunimi.sukunimi@teknliitto.fi
Website. www.teknliitto.fi (Finnish only)
Membership. 72,000

Finnish Union of Practical Nurses (SuPer)
Address. Ratamestarinkatu 12, 00520 Helsinki
Phone. +358 9 2727 9171
Fax. +358 9 2727 9120
E-mail. etunimi.sukunimi@superliitto.fi
Website. www.superliitto.fi (Finnish; English section)
Membership. 60,000

Union of Salaried Employees in Industry (STL)
Address. Asemamiehenkatu 4, 00520 Helsinki
Fax. +358 9 148 1930
E-mail. etunimi.sukunimi@stl.fi
Website. www.stl.fi (Finnish; English section)
Membership. 45,000

France

Capital: Paris
Population: 59.3 m. (2000 est.)

1 Political and Economic Background

France has a parliamentary system in which the directly elected President, who is elected for a seven-year term, has considerable executive powers. In 1995, Jacques Chirac, of the conservative Rally for the Republic party, became President, bringing to an end the 14-year presidency of Socialist François Mitterand. In 1997 elections to the National Assembly (lower House), conversely, the Socialist Party emerged as the largest single party, and left-leaning parties in an overall majority, ending a four-year period of centre-right governments and bringing a new period of "co-habitation" with a conservative President in office and a Socialist-led government.

Among the major initiatives taken by the new Socialist-led government was the introduction of a 35-hour week, legislated for in 1998 and in force in companies of 20 or more employees from Feb. 1, 2000. The Socialist Party has abandoned its former commitment to nationalization and presents its position as bridging the gap between the relatively pro-free market "third way" of the incumbent British Labour government and the "social market orientation" of parties such as the German SPD.

The economy is diverse and largely market-based. The state continues to have majority ownership of companies in a range of key industries such as electricity, gas, aircraft manufacture, railways and telecommunications, although there is an ongoing process of selling off state holdings in enterprises. There is a large public sector and one-quarter of all salaried employees work for the state. GDP grew 3.2% in 1998 and 2.8% in 1999, and in 1999 420,000 new jobs were created, mainly in the services sector. However, France has relatively high structural unemployment, which still stood at nearly 10% in 2000 after falling from a peak of 12.6% in 1997. A major element in recent job creation has been temporary work though employment agencies. France is a member of the EU and joined the single European currency zone on its creation at the start of 1999.

GDP (purchasing power parity) $1.373 trillion (1999 est.); GDP per capita (purchasing power parity) $23,300 (1999 est.).

2 Trade Unionism

France ratified ILO Conventions No.87 (Freedom of Association and Protection of the Right to Organize, 1948) and No.98 (Right to Organize and Collective Bargaining, 1949) in 1951.

Trade union organizations were given legal recognition in 1884 and the oldest confederation still in existence, the Confédération Générale du Travail (CGT), was founded in 1895. The CGT was dominated by socialist, anarcho-syndicalist and communist factions and in 1919 unions influenced by social Catholicism founded the Confédération Française des Travailleurs Chrétiens (CFTC). The CGT was weakened in the inter-war period by the creation of the breakaway Confédération Générale du Travail Unitaire (CGTU), in which communists took control, in 1921; the CGTU rejoined the CGT in 1936 but the majority of its adherents were expelled in 1939 following the Nazi-Soviet pact. Existing union centres were dissolved by the Vichy government under the Nazi occupation in 1940, but in 1943 the underground leaders of the CGT and CGTU agreed to the formation of a united centre. The CFTC, however, refused after the war to accept a merger with the CGT, which in turn was split again in 1947 by the formation of the CGT-Force Ouvrière (FO), which went on to join the anti-Soviet ICFTU. The CFTC in its turn broke into two in 1964, a minority faction retaining the old name and the majority reorganizing as the (secular) Confédération Française Démocratique du Travail (CFDT). These four centres, together with the Confédération Générale des Cadres (CGC, now known as the CFE-CGC), were officially designated as "nationally representative" in 1966, this designation being favoured by the government as simplifying the process of dealing with the unions. Unions affiliated to a recognized centre enjoyed the benefits of being able to conclude collective bargaining agreements or form an enterprise branch union without having to prove representative status in the workplace or industry concerned. However, this formula also tended to exacerbate the fragmentation of the labour movement as it conflicted with the idea of a sole bargaining agent.

The process that completed with the 1964 CFDT split left the pattern that broadly prevails today. The same five centres have been regarded as "nationally representative" since the 1960s. Like Italy, and unlike Britain, Germany or the USA, France has not had a single dominant trade union centre accepted as speaking for the organized labour movement. The two ICFTU affiliates, the CFDT and the CGT-FO, do not together represent a clear majority force in the labour movement in the way that the ICFTU affiliates do in most other Western nations. Also like Italy, the main lines of division have been based on ideology and, in some respects, religion, although this factor has declined noticeably since the 1980s. Only in the 1990s, with the collapse of Communism in Europe, has the antagonism between the traditionally orthodox Communist-led CGT and the politically heterogeneous but vehemently anti-Stalinist CGT-FO begun to recede. The CFDT was closely

Results of the industrial tribunal elections of December 1997:

	Industry	Commerce	Agriculture	Miscellaneous	Management	Totals
Votes	4,193,055	4,465,452	553,244	3,704,831	1,742,189	14,658,771
% abstentions	52.3	72.4	68.2	71.7	66.4	65.6
CGT	40.7	32.8	23.8	30.3	16.2	33.1
CFDT	22.3	24.2	32.9	27.7	31.5	25.3
CGT-FO	21.3	23.3	21.6	21.6	10.4	20.6
CFTC	6.3	7.4	7.5	8.7	9.9	7.5
CFE-CGC	3.7	3.9	5.6	3.5	21.9	5.9
Main Confederations -total	**94.2**	**91.6**	**91.4**	**91.8**	**89.9**	**92.4**
Unsa	0.08	0.5	5.7	0.6	2.1	0.7
CSL	4.2	4.9	1.1	4.4	3.4	4.2
Groupe des Dix	0.05	0.6	0.6	0.3	0.4	0.3
Others	1.4	2.9	1.1	2.9	4.2	2.3

associated with the Socialists into the mid-1980s, though it now has taken a more neutral stance. The CFTC, which affiliates to the WCL, is essentially religious-based in inspiration. While competition between the centres is still considerable, and they commonly take positions and sign agreements in opposition to each other, in fluctuating coalitions, there has been a general convergence in recent years. Pressure from the broader society for the unions to justify their role has contributed to this as has a comparatively greater degree of political consensus.

Every five years (most recently in 1997) all private sector employees (and, separately, all private employers) take part in the election of more than 14,000 councillors to local industrial tribunals or conciliation boards, (conseils de prud'hommes), with the responsibility of adjudicating individual employment disputes. The prud'homme tribunals are organized into a series of sections for industry, commerce, agriculture, miscellaneous and management. The unions compete actively for support in these elections because they are widely interpreted as measuring support for the different confederations and also because they offer an opportunity to raise their profile in areas of union weakness such as small business and service industries.

The 1997 elections confirmed that the CGT, with one-third of the votes, remained the leading force as it had been consistently since 1979 when the industrial tribunal electoral system was established. However, since 1979 the CGT share of the vote had declined from 42.4% to 33.1%, with all the other centres making small gains. The CGT is based especially in traditional industries and is weakest among management. The CDFT is broad-based and in the 1997 industrial tribunal elections for the first time beat the specialist management confederation the CFE-CGC into second place in the vote for the management staffs electoral college. The turnout in industrial tribunal elections has been falling progressively since 1979 (to 34.5% in 1997).

The Confédération Française Nationale du Travail

(CFNT), set up as a trade union wing of the extreme right-wing National Front (FN) had no impact in the elections overall, but locally did better in towns where the FN has electoral support. The other confederations organized legal appeals to challenge the status of the CFNT as a bona fide trade union organization.

All enterprises of more than 50 employees are obliged to have works councils (comités d'enterprise), with responsibilities predominantly in the welfare, health and safety, and social areas. The CFDT in contrast to the industrial tribunal elections did fractionally better than the CGT in works council elections. Between 1981 and 1991 the CGT's share of the vote in works council elections fell from 32% to 20.4%, but then stabilized. The results of works council elections also illustrate the significance of representation by non-unionized workers, this figure (29.9%) having risen from a level of 22% in the mid-1980s.

Results of 1997 elections to comités d'enterprise (% of votes):

CFDT	20.8
CGT	20.4
CGT-FO	12.1
CFE-GCC	6.4
CFTC	5.1
Other unions	6.2
Non-unionized	29.9

Union density, having stood at 24% in 1975, fell to only 9% by the end of the 1990s, the lowest in the European Union. In the private sector only 6% of employees are paid-up union members, and trade unionism has virtually no presence in wide swathes of the economy, especially small and medium sized enterprises and the expanding service sector. With their strength concentrated in the public sector and in state-owned enterprises, the unions have been strongly resistant to privatization and efforts to cut back the bureaucracy, and have enjoyed considerable success in this. Although the precipitous fall in union membership from the late 1970s to early 1990s has now ended, and indeed the CFDT has increased membership slightly, France's current buoyant economy is being driven forward by an expansion of "new economy" IT-related innovation, the service sector, and the growth of informal working patterns, none of which are helping the trade unions. The French unions have generally been slow in the development of services to individual members seen in most industrialized countries.

The two largest centres, the CFDT and CGT, have a combined membership (1.41 million) which is only half that of the biggest individual German union, IG Metall. Historically, indeed, French unions have been inclined to exaggerate their membership figures to hide their low levels. Membership slumped across the board from the late 1970s as old economy jobs were lost and unemployment increased and the unions failed to compensate by building their position in newer areas of the economy.

The union movement in France has nonetheless had an influence greater than membership statistics alone might suggest. Strike action, although no longer as frequent as in the 1970s, occurs on a wider scale than in most leading industrialized countries and is intensified in its effects by occurring particularly in critical public services such as public transport, education and health care, where the unions are strongest. While the other centres are often characterized as "pragmatic" and "moderate" compared with the CGT, the CGT-FO and CFDT have also involved themselves in strikes and demonstrations with some frequency. At the same time France's relatively fragile political establishment has often buckled in the face of concerted action by relatively small but militant groups, whether from organized labour, independent lorry drivers or small farmers.

The French industrial relation system has tended to buttress the position of the trade union centres. The unions are generally weak at the enterprise level, and indeed the main employers' organization (Mouvement des enterprises de France, MEDEF, until 1998 known as the Conseil National du Patronat Français, CNPF) is campaigning for collective bargaining to be devolved to this level in part for that very reason. The system of devolved bargaining, which many French unions disparage as the "Anglo-Saxon system", depends on strong workplace unionism and to some extent on the willingness of employers to recognize unions as negotiating partners; it also runs independently of direct government intervention. The French system tends to rely on the state to drive forward collective bargaining and the whole process of social partnership.

This pattern is reinforced by the system whereby trade unions are designated as "representative" and therefore empowered to negotiate on behalf of the workers in an industry, without needing in practice to demonstrate representativeness in any objective way. Notionally, representative status is accorded on the basis of criteria including membership, independence from employers, dues paid, experience and stability and even patriotism in World War II. However, the

same five centres (CGT, CGT-FO, CFDT, CFTC, CFE-CGC) have been the only ones recognized as nationally representative since the 1960s. While these undoubtedly remain the major centres, their representativeness relative to the workforce as a whole, including those not in unions, is clearly questionable. Unions affiliated to any of these centres are automatically accorded recognition as representative at sectoral or enterprise level, regardless of their real strength, and this gives them a range of benefits including allowing them to negotiate sector-level and enterprise agreements, organize work place elections where their candidates have a monopoly in the first round of voting, and appoint union delegates in companies. The system has the effect of artificially strengthening the hand of the unions, by giving them a role in enterprises even when they have little real membership, while also discriminating against independent unions. In collective bargaining the "single signature" rule means that one or more "representative" union may in principle bind all workers in a particular sector or company to an agreement even if it or they only represents a minority of the workforce. One consequence is that while only 6% of French private sector workers are in unions, 90% are covered by collective bargaining agreements. Other representative unions may oppose such agreements through the courts, provided they have won at least 50% of the votes of those registered to vote (i.e. normally, a substantial majority of those who actually did vote) in the most recent works council elections. However, individual or fluctuating coalitions of unions commonly reach agreements that other unions refuse to sign. As such agreements (short of legal challenge) are binding on all in any case, a union can refuse to sign, whether out of disagreement or for factional reasons, in a relatively casual way. At work place level, the unions not uncommonly, in view of the question of legitimacy of agreements reached under this system, make use of referenda or consultations to measure support for proposed agreements.

In Oct. 1997 the newly elected Socialist-led government announced plans to introduce the 35-hour week. The main employers' organization, MEDEF, thenceforth froze inter-sectoral collective bargaining in protest. However, the process of negotiating the detailed implementation of the new law (which took effect in Feb. 2000) stimulated intensive bargaining at sectoral and company level. In so doing it triggered considerable debate about the issue of representative status. The small confederations, UNSA and the Groupe des Dix, which do not enjoy representative status, have called for changes to the rules. The biggest confederations, the CGT and the CFDT, have indicated a willingness to show flexibility on the issue. However, the weaker confederations which do enjoy representative status, the CGT-FO, CFTC and CFE-CGC, have rejected any changes to the rules for the time being.

Trade union delegates do not exist in many smaller companies. In 1995, the CFDT, CFE-CGC and CFTC (but not the CGT and CGT-FO) reached agreement with

MEDEF to introduce a system of "mandating". The agreement was renewed in 1999. Under this (where a sectoral agreement to this effect exists) a union may mandate employees to conclude collective agreements, or elected staff representatives may reach agreements, subject to approval by sectoral union-employer committee. The move was viewed with suspicion by the CGT and FO as eroding the monopoly position of the unions in bargaining, while its adherents saw it as a means of extending collective bargaining mechanisms into a wider range of work places. The pattern of early sectoral agreements was that these were introduced mainly in agriculture and service areas with many small employers, while the CFDT and CFTC were most involved in mandating (although both the CGT and FO, despite not signing the inter-sectoral agreement, participated to some degree). However, actual impact at work place level was modest, partly because of the opposition of many employers. The 1998 legislation on the 35-hour week also made it possible for mandating to take place without a prior sectoral agreement, but only in respect of negotiation of working hours. All the centres, except the small CFTC, require that a candidate for mandating must already be a member of the union. However, as in collective bargaining generally, the application of mandating does not embody any clear criteria of representativeness at the work place level.

The small size of their memberships has also created issues in terms of the financing of unions because membership dues are insufficient to finance operations and the other sources of financing are often not transparent. Among the practices that were the subject of government and newspaper reports and public debate in 1999–2000 were the payment of union officers through the payroll of publicly funded social welfare agencies and pension funds jointly managed by unions and employers. In Jan. 2000 the *Le Monde* newspaper, citing a confidential government watchdog report, said that in 1995-98 the five nationally representative unions received (apparently with the approval of MEDEF) more than 34 million francs in salaries for union officials from the CRI compulsory complementary pension fund, which they jointly administer with the employers. This was in addition to a generous system of funding of union expenses. In response to criticism the CGT said that reform of the system was needed but that "the social functions fulfilled by the unions justify the existence of a transparent and fair system of public financial support in parallel to funding through union member dues". All the main union centres acknowledge that they cannot function without funding beyond that provided by union dues, but in public statements have begun to recognize the need for more transparency in this. The CFE-CGC has called for a system of direct state funding based on election results. In contrast, reflecting its historical antagonism to statist involvement in union affairs, the CGT-FO opposes public funding of unions as weakening the independence of the unions in respect of the state. In some cases, the unions as part of collective agreements have negotiated

forms of additional funding from employers as a contribution to "social dialogue". Thus an agreement in June 2000 between Renault and four of the five centres provided for the company to give funding to all unions achieving at least 5% of the vote in works council elections.

Collective bargaining at the end of the 1990s and into 2000 was dominated by the issue of working hours, job creation and job flexibility, within the context of the 35-hour week legislation. In some sectors, such as banking, resolution of these issues was accompanied by industrial action. Pay restraint characterized much bargaining in the late 1990s, in part influenced by France's relatively high and persistent unemployment, and also by the focus on working hours and job creation engendered by the 35-hour legislation. However, after peaking in 1997, unemployment has since decreased and skill shortages have developed in some areas, leading to increasing pay demands. Strikes remain a feature of French industrial relations, but have shown long-term decline since the early 1980s recession.

France has a range of institutions in which the unions are represented. The social protection institutions managing social security funds (for health, pensions and family allowances), supplementary pension funds and unemployment insurance are jointly managed by the employers and the five representative union centres. However, while the system is somewhat similar to that in Germany, in Germany the employers and unions normally find consensus and so secure independent management of these funds, whereas in France, lack of such agreement has led to regular state intervention. In Nov. 2000, in a continuing campaign against the compulsory 35-hour week, MEDEF threatened to end participation in administration of social funds at the end of the year.

The Economic and Social Council (Conseil économique et social, CES), founded in 1947, is a consultative assembly, with the right to be consulted on all aspects of economic and social policy. Its 231 members include representatives of labour, state companies, private companies, agriculture and other interests. It includes 68 union representatives (17 each from the CFDT, CGT and CGT-FO; 7 from the CFE-CGC; 6 from the CFTC; 3 from UNSA and 1 from the FSU). However, its influence has been negated by lack of consensus on key issues and it has been consulted with decreased frequency by government over the last few years.

In Nov. 1999 the employers' organization MEDEF issued a statement criticizing the "constant attempts of the law and the government to dominate the social partners" and called for a "new social constitution" to define the role of the social partners. This call became the subject of discussion with the unions in 2000. The CFDT called for the social partners to have a major role in the development of social policy, as sought at the EU level, although the issue of the representative status of French unions was inevitably an issue in seeking such a goal.

3 Trade Union Centres

Confédération Française Démocratique du Travail (CFDT)
French Democratic Confederation of Labour

Address. 47–49 avenue Simon Bolivar, 75950 Paris Cedex 19

Phone. +33 1 42 03 80 00

Fax. +33 1 42 03 81 44

E-mail. international@cfdt.fr

Website. www.cfdt.fr (French only)

Leadership. Nicole Notat (secretary-general)

Membership. 765,990

History and character. The CFDT was formed in 1964 by the majority faction of the Confédération Française des Travailleurs Chrétiens (CFTC), the minority retaining the previous name (for origins of the rift, see entry for CFTC). The founders of the CFDT sought to restrict the religious influence within the federation and to reshape it as a democratic socialist centre. It played a significant role in the industrial unrest of 1968, leading to a period of greater politicization. After 1978 however there came a period (under the leadership of Edmond Maire) of – "resyndicalization" – i.e. emphasizing closely defined trade union issues -with the emphasis on union adaptation to economic change. The CFDT joined the ICFTU in 1979. Under Jean Kaspar, Maire's successor as secretary-general, the CFDT sought to unite all centres except the CGT. In 1992 Nicole Notat, former national secretary, became the CFDT's first woman leader.

The CFDT had a membership of close to 1 million in 1980 but then suffered considerable losses of members in the 1980s, as was true of other confederations. However, it says that after 10 years of renewed growth its membership recovered to 756,990 by 1999. It came second to the CGT in industrial tribunal elections in 1997 but was fractionally ahead in works council elections and its reported membership is slightly higher than that of the CGT.

The CFDT emphasizes the importance of participation of its members in the democratic process; favours constructive dialogue with government and employers; seeks to combat social exclusion; and supports a trade unionism based firmly in the workplace. It emphasizes its independence of the state, the churches, and of political parties. The CFDT was closely associated with the Socialist Party until 1988, after which it abandoned a reference to socialism in its Statutes, and in the 1997 elections it did not officially endorse any party, although its policies were in many respects similar to those of the Socialists. Its focus since the end of the 1970s on achieving negotiated settlements has helped it grow relative to the traditionally more militant and protest-oriented CGT.

The CFDT experienced some factional conflict in the 1990s. Widespread strike action in public services against proposed social security reforms in Dec. 1995 saw the CFDT divided, with a minority actively supporting the strikes. This minority claimed it was the inheritor of an earlier tradition, prevalent in the 1970s, emphasizing broad political objectives and the achievement of socialism. In early 1996 the minority organized itself as the "United We Stand" faction. "United We Stand" also identified itself with the unemployed people's movement that developed in 1997 and took part in many occupations of public buildings. Other dissidents broke away to join the independent union Solidaires, Unitaires et Démocratiques (SUD). However, at the 1999 congress the report on activities of the secretary-general, Nicole Notat, was approved by 73% of the votes cast, reportedly the highest margin since 1979 and the United We Stand faction suspended active opposition.

The CFDT has improved its relations with the CGT, traditionally the most militant of the centres, which had fractured after an accord on unity of action ruptured at the end of the 1970s. This convergence partly reflected movement towards the centre-ground from the CGT, and partly the emphasis on unions' finding common ground in detailed negotiations on implementation sector by sector of the 35-hour week, but it also was a response to the demands of the opposition faction within the CFDT.

The CFDT, as one of the five confederations designated as nationally representative, benefits from the privileges such status confers, including the right for its affiliated unions to enter into collective bargaining agreements with a presumption that they are representative regardless of their actual membership in a particular sector or enterprise. However, the CFDT has taken the initiative (and in so doing attracted the opposition of the other centres, except the CGT) in arguing that reform is needed to improve the legitimacy of the unions in view of their low membership. The CFDT has called for the system to be revised so that "representativeness" would be more objectively determined at work place level by ballots. It also argues that the current system means that employers can usually find a minority union to sign an agreement, however unsatisfactory it is to the majority, and this is then binding on all.

In response to public controversy over the extent of funding of unions from the resources of jointly-managed social funds and other non-union sources, in July 2000 the CFDT disclosed that of its 220 million franc budget in 1999, 159 million came from the CFDT's own resources, of which 104 million was membership dues from its affiliated unions.

The CFDT structure comprises 1500 unions in the private and public sector; 18 professional federations and 3 confederal unions; and 22 regional unions comprising 95 departmental unions or similar. The professional federations, grouping unions in the same sector of the economy, provide co-ordination to collective bargaining; the inter-professional regional unions serve especially to support solidarity among workers and combat social exclusion.

The Institut Belleville is the CFDT's organ for international trade union cooperation.

Publications. CFDT Magazine (monthly, for members); *La Revue* (monthly, debates and ideas); *CFDT en direct* (monthly newsletter); *Social actualité* (monthly); *Action juridique* (two-monthly; *Syndicalisme* (for activists). Content accessible via website.

International affiliations. ICFTU; ETUC; TUAC. The CFDT left the WCL in 1978 and then joined the ICFTU.

Affiliates. The 18 CFDT professional federations and three confederal unions are based at 47–49 avenue Simon Bolivar, 75950 Paris Cedex 19, other than where shown below. Their e-mail and website addresses are as follows:

1. Fédération des banques et sociétés fiancières
Phone. +33 1 44 52 71 20
E-mail. banques@cfdt.fr
Website. www.cfdt-banques.fr

2. Fédération chimie énergie (FCE)
Phone. +33 1 44 84 86 00
E-mail. fce@cfdt.fr
Website. www.fce.cfdt.fr

3. Fédération communication et culture (FTILAC)
Phone. +33 1 42 52 52 70
E-mail. ftilac@cfdt.fr

4. Fédération des établissements et arsenaux de l'état (FEAE)
Phone. +33 1 44 52 55 33
E-mail. feae@cfdt.fr

5. Fédération des finances et affaires économiques
Phone. +33 1 53 72 73 00
E-mail. finances@cfdt.fr
Website. www.digiplace.com/cfdt-finances

6. Fédération formation et enseignement privés (FEP)
Phone. +33 1 40 18 53 53
E-mail. fep@cfdt.fr

7. Fédération générale agroalimentaire (FGA)
Phone. +33 1 53 38 12 12
E-mail. fga@cfdt.fr

8. Fédération générale de la métallurgie et des mines (FGMM)
Phone. +33 1 44 52 20 20
E-mail. fgmm@cfdt.fr

9. Fédération générale des transports-équipements (FGTE)
Phone. +33 1 44 84 29 50
E-mail. fgte@cfdt.fr

10. Fédération de l'habillement, du cuir et textile (HACUITEX)
Phone. +33 1 44 52 71 10
E-mail. hacuitex@cfdt.fr

11. Fédération nationale construction bois (FNCB)
Phone. +33 1 53 72 87 20

E-mail. fncb@cfdt.fr
Website. www.cfdt-construction-bois.fr

12. Fédération nationale INTERCO
Phone. +33 1 40 40 85 50
E-mail. interco@cfdt.fr
Website. www.interco-cfdt.fr

13. Fédération unifiée des postes et des telecoms (FUPT)
Phone. +33 1 44 84 30 30
E-mail. fupt@cfdt.fr

14. Fédération protection sociale, travail, emploi (PSTE)
Phone. +33 1 40 18 77 72
E-mail. pste@cfdt.fr

15. Fédération des services
Address. +33 1 48 10 65 90
E-mail. services@cfdt.fr

16. Fédération des services de santé et services sociaux
Phone. +33 1 40 40 85 00
E-mail. santesociaux@cfdt.fr
Website. www.fed-cfdt-sante-sociaux.org

17. Fédération des syndicats généraux de l'éducation nationale (SGEN)
Phone. +33 1 40 03 37 00
E-mail. sgen@cfdt.fr
Website. www.sgen-cfdt.org

18. Union confédérale des cadres (UCC)
Phone. +33 1 53 38 95 70
E-mail. ucc@cfdt.fr
Website. www.ucc-cfdt.fr

19. Union confédérale des retraités (UCR)
Phone. +33 1 44 52 12 90
E-mail. union-retraites@cfdt.fr

20. Union des fédérations des fonctions publiques et assimilés (UFFA)
Phone. +33 1 42 02 44 70
E-mail. uffa@cfdt.fr

21. Fédération justice
Phone. +33 1 42 38 64 10
E-mail. justice@cfdt.fr

Confédération Française des Travailleurs Chrétiens (CFTC)
French Confederation of Christian Workers

Address. 13 rue des Ecluses – Saint Martin, 75483 Paris, Cedex 10

Phone. +33 1 44 52 49 00

Fax. +33 1 44 52 49 18

E-mail. communication@cftc.fr

Website. www.cftc.fr (French only)

Leadership. Alain Deleu (president); Jacques Voisin (secretary-general)

History and character. Unions influenced by social Catholicism developed from the mid-1880s, and the CFTC itself was formed in Nov. 1919 at a constituent congress of 321 unions with nearly 100,000 members. The CFTC participated the same year in the establishment of the International Federation of Christian Trade Unions, the predecessor of the WCL. The CFTC, like the CGT, recruited many new members in 1936 and lost fewer of them in the rest of the decade. The Vichy government dissolved the CFTC in 1940 and thereafter it supported the Council of the Resistance. Open activity resumed in Aug. 1944 when the underground leaders of the CFTC and the CGT formed an inter-confederal committee of understanding, but the CFTC rejected CGT proposals for a merger after the war.

In its early period the CFTC was fundamentally Catholic in emphasis, but after World War II a fraction known as the *minoritaires*, grouped around the journal *Réconstruction,* pressed to release the federation from the religious strait-jacket to permit it to challenge the CGT and the FO. In 1947 the CFTC began the process of weakening its links with the Catholic Church by abolishing a constitutional provision whereby its activities were to be based on the papal encyclical Rerum Novarum. By 1964 the reformers were in the majority, and a special congress voted to change the name of the organization to the Confédération Française Démocratique du Travail (CFDT – see separate entry). A minority, composed largely of miners' and white-collar unions, consequently separated themselves, retaining the previous name as the CFTC.

The CFTC today maintains its social Christian orientation, emphasizing as fundamental the primacy of the individual and the inalienable rights (and duties) of each individual; the defence of the family; the rejection of the class struggle; the development of contractual relations between free and independent organizations; and the rejection of the politicization of trade unions. Nevertheless the organization does not require religious adherence of its members. It takes a particular interest in similarly-oriented unions affiliated to the WCL in the developing world. It regards its commitment to the WCL as having primacy over its membership in ETUC, although that position has been a source of controversy within the CFTC.

The CFTC, although considered "nationally representative" in the French system, is much weaker than the main three nationally representative general trade union centres (CGT, CFDT and CGT-FO). Indeed its share of the overall vote in the most recent (1997) industrial tribunal elections, 7.5%, was only slightly ahead of the CFE-CGC, which represents only managerial and professional staff. In work place elections it had only 5% of the vote, but it has greater support in some regions, such as Alsace, Lorraine and the Nord-Pas-de-Calais and in sectors such as private education, health, social services and metalworking. It has capitalised on the recent development of mandating in enterprises without union delegates, mandating more employees to September 1999 than any centre other than the CFDT.

Publications. La Vie à Défendre (monthly magazine)

International affiliations. WCL; ETUC

Confederation Française de L'Encadrement CGC (CFE-CGC)
French Confederation of Professional and Managerial Staff

Address. 30 rue de Oramont, 75002 Paris

E-mail. presse@cfecgc.fr

Website. www.cfecgc.org (French only)

Leadership. Jean-Luc Cazettes (president); Jean-Louis Walter (secretary-general)

Membership. 193,000.

History and character. Founded in 1944 as the Confédération Générale des Cadres (CGC), taking its present name in 1981. The CFE-CGC is one of the five confederations (with the CGT, CGT-FO, CFDT and CFTC) considered "nationally representative", although it is the only one not recruiting across the workforce. Its members are managers, professional and technical employees.

The CFE-CGC has traditionally had a pragmatic orientation and has emphasized that its members are the driving force of economic progress and have a unique role in constructing new forms of economic citizenship and in facilitating the partnership of labour and capital. It viewed the decline of trade unions in France, as many other countries, in the latter part of the twentieth century as reflecting a failure of the unions to adapt to changes in the structure and expectations of the workforce. However, the CFE-CGC also experienced this decline, its membership falling from 398,000 in 1976 to 181,000 by 1991 before stabilizing and then increasing marginally to 193,000 by the end of the decade.

In the 1997 industrial tribunal (conseils de prud'hommes) elections the CFE-CGC lost its customary first place in the vote for the managerial and professional staff electoral college, taking only 22% of the vote compared with 31.5% for the CFDT. Following this in 1998 the CFE-CGC announced plans to intensify and broaden its recruitment efforts, including among self-employed professionals, and to reform its "highly centralized and hierarchical" structures to increase accessibility and grass-roots involvement.

International affiliation. TUAC

Confédération Générale du Travail (CGT)
General Confederation of Labour

Address. 263 rue de Paris, 93516 Paris, Montreuil Cedex

Phone. +33 1 48 18 81 28

Fax. +33 1 48 18 84 43

E-mail. internat@cgt.fr

Website. www.cgt.fr (French only)

Leadership. Bernard Thibault (secretary-general)

Membership. 650,000

History and character. The CGT was founded at Limoges in 1895 and from the beginning was affected by ideological divisions between socialists, syndicalists and others. Before 1914 it campaigned against militarism but during the First World War the CGT secretary, Léon Jouhaux, served as a "commissioner of the nation", mobilizing it behind the war effort. Membership, which had been only 400,000 among a six million industrial workforce grew rapidly to 2.5 million by 1920, but tensions generated by conflicting responses to the example of the Russian Revolution led to expulsions of members of the revolutionary minority, and the formation in 1921 of the Confédération Générale du Travail Unitaire (CGTU). The CGTU, and the French Communist Party (PCF, formed 1920) to which it was linked, subsequently engaged in a bitter ideological struggle with the CGT. In 1936, during the Popular Front era, the CGTU was readmitted to the CGT and the unified organization led a wave of strikes that stimulated a massive surge in membership. By the end of 1936 the CGT was four to five million strong, only to decline to a quarter of this figure by 1939 in increasingly unfavourable political conditions.

Rapid shifts in PCF policy on the eve of World War II led to its adherents being purged from the CGT, and they pursued a policy of sabotaging war production before the fall of France. After the German invasion of the Soviet Union in June 1941, however, the PCF became a major factor in the Resistance. The CGT had been liquidated by Vichy in Nov. 1940 but some leaders were recruited into a new official labour organization, including René Bélin, who became Minister of Labour responsible for the implementation of a corporatist Labour Charter. In May 1943 the communists were readmitted to the (clandestine) CGT, with three of the eight seats on the executive board.

In Sept. 1945, in step with a surge of post-war support for the PCF (which participated in the post-war De Gaulle government) Benoît Frachon, a communist, was appointed a co-equal CGT secretary-general with Jouhaux, and during 1946–47 the communists achieved control of most of the CGT apparatus. Communist policies stressed the demands of economic recovery, including a wages standstill backed by the CGT, and confrontation between the different wings of the CGT was initially avoided. Membership in 1946 stood at more than 5 million. However, the onset of the Cold War, the removal of PCF ministers from the government and the party's switch to a strategy of industrial confrontation in 1947 precipitated the break-up of the CGT, the socialist minority led by Jouhaux forming the CGT-Force Ouvrière (see separate entry). Many non-communists remained loyal to the CGT however, and it remained the premier union centre throughout the post-War period. Into the 1970s the CGT still claimed 2.25 million members.

Membership of the CGT began to fall steadily from the late 1970s. A CGT official said in 1985 that at least 700,000 members had been lost in the previous seven years. All the main French trade union centres lost membership during this period, but the disproportionately large losses of the CGT were variously attributed to factors such as the decay of heavy industries in which it was strong, unemployment, its image of ideological and bureaucratic inflexibility and adherence to the PCF sometimes at the expense of union issues, and its failure to respond to social and economic modernization and to recognize the importance of organizing white-collar employees in the small business sector.

During the 1990s the position of the CGT has stabilized to some degree. It remains the strongest centre in traditional industrial sectors, and in the industrial tribunal elections of 1997 (the most recent) it retained first place, with 33.2% of the votes, an almost identical position to 1992. It is relatively weak in the more dynamic sectors of the economy, however, and now has a smaller membership than the CFDT.

Difficulties arose from PCF participation in the left government of the early 1980s; following the PCF withdrawal from office the CGT opposed aspects of government policy, isolating the socialist minority (although the return of the Right to power in 1986 permitted a reconvergence of views within the CGT). The collapse of the Soviet Union and the end of the Cold War had serious repercussions for the CGT. A CGT representative held the post of secretary-general of the (communist-dominated) World Federation of Trade Unions continuously from 1947 until in 1978 the CGT failed to offer a candidate, criticizing the insuffficient autonomy of the trade unions of the Soviet bloc countries. The CGT remained within the WFTU, however, as its most prominent affiliate in the western world. It was not until 1994, five years after the general collapse of communism in Eastern Europe, that the CGT severed its ties to the WFTU. In 1999, 25 years after it first applied for membership, the CGT was admitted to the European Trade Union Confederation (ETUC), its application approved by all member organizations except the CGT-FO.

The CGT under secretary-general Louis Viannet (who was succeeded by his favoured successor, Bernard Thibault, in 1999) began to moderate its tradition of militancy in favour of a modernized approach seeking dialogue and negotiation. Viannet termed this a policy of "moving from a trade unionism of protest to a trade unionism of proposals". This shift in emphasis reflects an awareness of a need to change in view of the CGT's dwindling strength and its lack of impact or relevance in wide areas of the economy, especially its more dynamic sectors, as it stood out against virtually every aspect of labour market reform. The CGT nonetheless remains far more inclined to embrace industrial action than most other western European centres: its new secretary-general Bernard Thibault, formerly secretary general of the CGT rail workers' federation, came to prominence as a leader of the Dec. 1995 strike movement against the welfare reform policies of the conservative government of Alain Juppé. The CGT, through its unemployed committees, was also the centre most involved in supporting and working with the locally-based unemployed associations that were particularly active, and staged many occupations of government offices, in 1997–98.

Traditionally the CGT followed the communist line of opposing the development of what has become the European Union. Only in the latter part of the 1990s did it come to a grudging acceptance of the EU, a factor that assisted its admission to ETUC.

While relations between the different centres and their affiliates tend to fluctuate from one issue to another, and historic frictions still exist between the CGT and the FO, the CGT has noticeably improved its relations with the CFDT, which is now the CGT's equal, or even exceeds it, in membership and influence. The intense negotiations with employers in all sectors in 1998–2000 on implementation of the 35-hour week put a premium on the unions finding unity of purpose, although this has was not always achieved in practice.

International affiliation. ETUC (since 1999)

Confederation Générale du Travail – Force Ouvrière (CGT-FO)
General Confederation of Labour – Workers' Strength

Address. 141 Avenue du Maine, 75680 Paris, Cedex 14

Phone. +33 1 40 52 82 00

Fax. +33 1 40 52 82 02

E-mail. mblondel@force-ouvriere.fr

Website. www.force-ouvriere.fr (French only)

Leadership. Marc Blondel (secretary-general)

Membership. About 300,000

History and character. The CGT-Force Ouvrière was formed in 1948, with the secession from the CGT of a large number of trade unionists opposed to the communist methods and policies of the CGT. At the time of the breakaway the CGT had an estimated 5 million members. The new group was led by Léon Jouhaux, who had been secretary-general of the CGT from 1909 to 1946 until compelled to accept a division of his authority, as co-secretary, with the communist Benoît Frachon, himself a former official of the communist CGTU. The immediate cause of the secession was a wave of communist-led strikes and violent disturbances in November–December 1947, viewed by the FO as a co-ordinated attempt to threaten the stability of the new post-war French Republic, which was governed by a centre-left alliance of popular republicans and socialists. A further source of division between the CGT and the FO was the issue of US economic aid to Europe: the CGT executive (in accordance with Soviet policy) denounced the Marshall Plan as "a war machine of American imperialists against the liberty and independence of other nations", but the FO favoured acceptance of such aid. Most of the strength of the new FO was in the white-collar and public services sectors.

Perhaps the main reason for the secession of nearly one million CGT members to form the CGT-FO was the belief that the policies of the CGT were controlled not by the members themselves but by the French Communist Party. Indeed, the CGT-FO retains the title CGT in its name because it claims that it remains true to the fundamental democratic principles that characterized the CGT from its original 1906 Charter of Amiens. This ideological tension between the CGT and CGT-FO has declined in the 1990s with the end of the Cold War and the re-positioning of the CGT, but a degree of friction remains. In general, relations between the CFDT and CGT are much better than those between the CGT and the FO.

The FO, despite being the sole ICFTU-affiliated centre in France for three decades, failed to achieve the dominant status enjoyed by ICFTU affiliates in most other western industrial countries. This partly reflected the continued (if declining) strength of the CGT, but was also in part a result of the existence of the CFDT as a major democratic socialist alternative (the CFDT itself also affiliating to the ICFTU in 1979).

The FO emphasizes that it stands independent of any political party or religion and in practice has sought to avoid being associated with any party, in contrast to the one-time close identification of the CGT with the Communists and the CFDT with the Socialists. It has traditionally included diverse political elements and became a target for entryism by far-left groups such as the Trotskyist Workers' Party (Parti des Travailleurs, PT), activity facilitated by the relatively small size of the FO. Internal political conflicts in the 1990s culminated in an unsuccessful challenge to the leadership of Marc Blondel (secretary-general since 1989) at the 1996 congress (the 18th), following which his opponent Jacques Mairé and some other regional and sectoral leaders defected to the Union National des Syndictas Autonomes (UNSA). However, the 19th congress, in March 2000 demonstrated a restoration of unity and Blondel was re-elected with 97% of the vote.

While the Communist-led CGT opposed the development of the EU, the FO was an enthusiastic advocate of the European project. In the 1990s their positions have come closer together, the CGT embracing a grudging acceptance of the EU and the FO's enthusiasm cooling somewhat. While the FO at the industrial level remains less militant than the CGT and more committed to dialogue and negotiation it also regularly backs strike action and protests as part of fluctuating alliances with other centres. In 1995 it participated alongside the CGT in a wave of protests against welfare reforms proposed by the conservative government of Alain Juppé. However, the CGT-FO has remained sceptical of the CGT and in late 1998 Blondel said of the CGT's growing rapport with the CFDT that "their close relationship will last no longer than it takes to dance a tango". In 1999 the FO stood alone in opposing the CGT's admission to ETUC, 25 years after it first applied.

The FO has traditionally opposed "corporatism". In the 1980s it declined (unlike the CFDT and CGT) to participate in the socialist government elected in 1981 believing that "it is not possible to be the ruler and the ruled at the same time", and rejected that government's policy of "social compromise". Blondel has emphasized that the union movement should be independent and cannot "be lawmaker, joint lawmaker, manager or joint manager of private or state capitalist interests".

Publications. *Force Ouvrière* (content accessible via website)

International affiliations. ICFTU; ETUC; TUAC

Affiliated unions. The FO structure comprises 27 professional federations, grouping unions in the different sectors of the economy.

1. Action Sociale
Address. 7 Passage Tenaille, 75680 Paris Cedex 14
Phone. +33 1 40 52 85 80
Fax. +33 1 40 52 85 79
Leadership. Michel Pinaud (secretary-general)

2. Administration Generale de l'Etat
Address. 46 rue des Petites Ecuries, 75010 Paris
Phone. +33 1 42 46 40 19
Fax. +33 1 42 46 19 57
Leadership. Francis Lamarque (secretary-general)

3. FGTA Agriculture, Alimentation et Tabacs (agriculture, food and tobacco)
Address. 7 Passage Tenaille, 75680 Paris Cedex 14
Phone. +33 1 40 52 85 10
Fax. +33 1 40 52 85 12
E-mail. fgtafo@lemel.fr
Leadership. Rafael Nedzynski (secretary-general)

4. Bâtiment-Travaux Publics, Bois, Céramique, Papier Carton -Matériaux de Construction (building and allied trades)
Address. 170 Avenue Pannentier, 75010 Paris
Phone. +33 1 42 01 30 00
Fax. +33 1 42 39 50 44
Leadership. Michel Daudigny (secretary-general)

5. Cheminots (railwaymen's federation)
Address. 61 rue de la Chapelle, 75018 Paris
Phone. +33 1 55 26 94 00
Fax. +33 1 55 26 94 01
Leadership. Eric Falempin (secretary-general)

6. Coiffure, Esthetique et Parfumier (hairdressers and beauticians)
Address. 3 rue de la Croix Blanche, 18350 Nerondes
Phone. +33 2 48 78 89 32
Fax. +33 2 48 74 81 26
Leadership. Michel Bourlon (secretary-general)

7. Cuirs, Textiles-Habillement (leather and textiles)
Address. 7 Passage Tenaille, 75680 Paris Cedex 14
Phone. +33 1 40 52 83 00
Fax. +33 1 40 52 82 99
Leadership. Jean-Claude Humez (secretary-general)

8. Enseignement, Culture et Formation Professionelle (education, culture, professional development)
Address. 7 Passage Tenaille, 75680 Paris Cedex 14
Phone. +33 1 40 52 85 30
Fax. +33 1 40 52 85 35
Leadership. François Chantron (secretary-general)

9. Employés et Cadres (white collar staff)
Address. 28 rue des Petits Hôtels, 75010 Paris
Phone. +33 1 48 01 91 91
Fax. +33 1 48 01 91 92
Leadership. Rose Boutaric (secretary-general)

10. Energie, Electrique et Gaz (energy, electricity, gas)
Address. 60 rue Vergniaud, 75640 Paris, Cedex 13
Phone. +33 1 44 16 86 20
Fax. +33 1 44 16 86 32
E-mail. fo.fneg@wanaddo.fr
Leadership. Gabriel Gaudy (secretary-general)

11. Finances
Address. 46 rue des Petites Ecuries, 75010 Paris
Phone. 1 33 1 42 46 75 20
Fax. +33 1 47 70 23 92
Leadership. Jacky Leseuer (secretary-general)

12. Fonctionnaires (civil servants)
Address. 46 rue des Petites Ecuries
Phone. +33 1 44 83 65 55
Fax. +33 1 42 46 97 80
Leadership. Roland Gaillard (secretary-general)

13. Fédéchimie CGTFO (chemical industries)
Address. 60 rue Vergniaud, 75640 Paris, Cedex 13
Phone. +33 1 45 80 14 90
Fax. +33 1 45 80 08 03
E-mail. fedechimiecgtfo@wanadoo.fr
Leadership. Michel Decayeux (secretary-general)

14. Livre (publishing/print trades)
Address. 7 Passage Tenaille, 75680 Paris Cedex 14
Phone. +33 1 40 52 85 00
Fax. +33 1 40 52 85 01
Leadership. Maurice Rossat (secretary-general)

15. Métaux (metalworkers)
Address. 9 rue Baudoin, 75013 Paris
Phone. +33 1 53 94 54 00
Fax. +33 1 45 83 78 87
Leadership. Michel Huc (secretary-general)

16. Mineurs, Miniers et Similaires (miners and related)
Address. 7 Passage Tenaille, 75680 Paris Cedex 14
Phone. +33 1 40 52 85 50
Fax. +33 1 40 52 85 48
Leadership. Bernard Fraysse (secretary-general)

17. Défense, Industries de l'Armament et Secteurs Assimilés (defence)
Address. 46 rue des Petites Ecuries, 75010 Paris
Phone. +33 1 42 46 00 05
Fax. +33 1 45 23 12 89
Leadership. Albert Sparfel (secretary-general)

18. Personnel des Services des Départements et des Régions
Address. 46 rue des Petites Ecuries, 75010 Paris
Phone. +33 1 42 46 50 52
Fax. +33 1 47 70 26 06
Leadership. Michèle Simonnin (secretary-general)

19. Pharmacie
Address. 7 Passage Tenaille, 75680 Paris Cedex 14

Phone. +33 1 40 52 85 60
Fax. +33 1 40 52 85 61
Leadership. Gilbert Lebrument (secretary-general)

20. Police
Address. 6 rue Albert-Bayet, 75013 Paris
Phone. +33 1 45 82 28 08
Fax. +33 1 45 82 64 24
Leadership. Jean-Jacques Penin (secretary-general)

21. PTT (post, telegraphs, telephones)
Address. 60 rue Vergniaud, 75640 Paris, Cedex 13
Phone. +33 1 40 78 31 50
Fax. +33 1 40 78 30 58
Website. www.fo-ptt.com
Leadership. Jacques Lemercier (secretary-general)

22. Services Publics et de Santé (public services and health)
Address. 153–55 rue de Rome, 75017 Paris
Phone. +33 1 44 01 06 00
Fax. +33 1 42 27 21 40
Website. www.fo-sante.com
Leadership. Camille Ordronneau (secretary-general)

23. Spectacle-Presse-Audiovisuel (entertainment, press and broadcasting)
Address. 2 rue de la Michodière, 75002 Paris
Phone. +33 1 47 42 35 86
Fax. +33 1 47 42 39 45
Leadership. Bertrand Blanc (secretary-general)

24. Transports
Address. 7 Passage Tenaille, 75680 Paris Cedex 14
Phone. +33 1 40 52 85 45
Fax. +33 1 40 52 85 09
Leadership. Roger Poletti (secretary-general)

25. L'équipement des transports et des services
Address. 46 rue des Petites Ecuries, 75010 Paris
Phone. +33 1 42 46 36 63
Fax. +33 1 48 24 38 32
Leadership. Yves Veyrier (secretary-general)

26. Union des cadres et Ingénieurs (managers and technicians)
Address. 2 rue de la Michodière, 75002 Paris
Phone. +33 1 47 42 39 69
Fax. +33 1 47 42 03 53
Leadership. Hubert Bouchet (secretary-general)

27. Voyageurs-Représentants-Placiers (sales representatives)
Address. 6–8 rue Albert-Bayet, 75013 Paris
Phone. +33 1 45 82 28 28
Fax. +33 1 45 70 93 69
Leadership. Michel Bouteleux (secretary-general)

4 Other Trade Union Organizations

Confédération des Syndicats Libres (CSL)
Confederation of Free Trade Unions

Address. 37 rue Lucien Sampaix, 75010 Paris
Phone. +33 1 55 26 12 12

Fax. +33 1 55 26 12 00
E-mail. csl@ifrance.com
Website. www.ifrance.com (French only)
History and character. A small conservative-inclined organization, founded in 1959 and formerly known as the Confédération Française du Travail. It describes its orientation as "neither red nor yellow" but as the "colour of the tricolour", patriotic, independent of political and religious affiliations, and opposed to the class struggle. It was in sixth place in the 1997 industrial tribunal elections, with just over 4% of the vote, having strengthened its position over the preceding decade.

Fédération Syndicale Unitaire (FSU)

Address. 3/5 Rue de Metz, 75010 Paris

Phone. +33 1 44 79 90 30

Fax. +33 1 48 01 02 52

Website. www.fsu.fr (French only)

History and character. Founded in 1993, this is now the largest union in the central government civil service, reflecting its leadership position among teachers, who represent half of civil servants employed by central government. It has strongly resisted government efforts to reform the education system.

Union Nationale des Syndicats Autonomes (UNSA)
National Federation of Independent Unions

Address. 48 rue La Bruyère, 75009 Paris

Phone. +33 1 40 16 78 00

Fax. +33 1 40 16 78 12

Website. www.unsa.org (French only)

History and character. The UNSA was founded in 1993 as an alliance of independent unions, mainly from the civil service sector. Most prominent among these was the National Education Federation (FEN), historically the biggest teaching union, although it has now lost this position to the FSU. It was also joined by dissidents from the FO. UNSA has yet to achieve official recognition alongside the CGT, FO, CFDT, CFTC and CFE-CGC as nationally representative.

UNSA has built a close relationship with the CFDT. In May 1999 its admission to membership of the European Trade Union Confederation (ETUC) was approved (with the support of the other French members except the CGT-FO) on the basis of a partnership agreement with the CFDT whereby the two would form one delegation and speak with one voice. UNSA is also strongly in favour of changing the rules on representative status, to prevent affiliates of the the big five nationally representative centres having the automatic right to conclude collective agreements in work places where they are a minority. It has welcomed the initiative of the CFDT in proposing reform of this system to require majority approval for agreements and thereby improve the legitimacy of the unions.

International affiliation. ETUC

Union Syndicale – Groupe des Dix
Address. 80/82 rue de Montreuil, 75011 Paris
Phone. +33 1 43 73 91 94
Fax. +33 1 43 73 91 95

E-mail. g10@ifrance.com
Website. www.g10.ras.eu.org
History and character. It is based mainly in the public sector and includes the SUD (Solidaires, Unitaires, Démocratiques faction that broke away from the CFDT).

FRENCH OVERSEAS POSSESSIONS

In the French overseas departments (French Guiana, Guadeloupe, Martinique and Reunion), overseas territorial collectivities (Mayotte, St Pierre and Miquelon), and overseas territories (French Polynesia, French Southern and Antarctic Territories, New Caledonia and Wallis and Futuna Islands), the metropolitan French trade union confederations generally maintain local branches.

Gabon

Capital: Libreville
Population: 1.21 m. (2000 est.)

1 Political and Economic Background

Gabon became a self-governing republic within the French Community in 1958 and gained full independence in 1960. Albert-Bernard (Omar) Bongo succeeded to the presidency in 1967, and in the following year a one-party system of government was formally established with the newly created Gabonese Democratic Party (PDG) as the sole permitted party.

In 1990, opposition parties were legalized. Seven gained representation in the National Assembly following phased elections that autumn though the PDG retained a majority. A new coalition government of the PDG and five other parties was still dominated by the PDG with three-quarters of the positions. Progress towards pluralism was slow and free elections for the presidency were not held until 1993 when Omar Bongo was narrowly returned for his fourth term. However

opposition candidates refused to accept the result, alleging fraud, and established a rival High Council of the Republic (later High Council of the Resistance) which had trade union support. There was fighting between government and opposition forces early in 1994 and unrest and political divisions continued during the year. In September 1994 a settlement between government and opposition was negotiated in Paris and under this agreement (approved by referendum in 1995) the opposition took a number of posts in the government. The most recent elections to the National Assembly (in 1996) again gave the PDG a majority, while Bongo retained the presidency in presidential elections in Dec. 1998.

Gabon has one of the highest per capita incomes in Africa, with its relative wealth being based largely upon its (depleting) petroleum resources. Oil accounts for 50% of GDP. It also has valuable resources of timber and minerals. The oil price increases of the 1970s fueled heavy spending in Gabon and the country became heavily indebted in the 1980s as oil prices fell, pushing it into a series of debt rescheduling arrangements and austerity measures leading to political tensions. There is substantial immigration of workers from poorer west African countries, who work in the informal and service sectors. The state dominates some sectors of the economy, including the key export sectors of oil and timber, although some basic services have been privatized. While Gabon has a significant modern sector, 60% of the labour force work in agriculture, much of it at subsistence level.

GDP (purchasing power parity) $7.9bn. (1999 est.); GDP per capita (purchasing power parity) $6,500 (1999 est.).

2 Trade Unionism

Under French rule a pluralistic system of trade unionism developed on the French model. As an independent state, Gabon ratified ILO Convention No.87 (Freedom of Association and Protection of the Right to Organize, 1948) in 1960 and Convention No.98 (Right to Organize and Collective Bargaining, 1949) in 1961, but a single-trade-union structure was imposed in 1969 under the Gabonese Trade Union Confederation (COSYGA). Under legislation of 1980 employers were required to deduct a mandatory trade union solidarity tax from the pay of all workers for the benefit of COSYGA.

COSYGA remained the sole trade union centre until 1991, when it lost this status in parallel with the development of a measure of political pluralism. In summer 1991 the new independent Gabonese Confederation of Free Trade Unions (CGSL) was formed. The compulsory payroll tax in favour of COSYGA was ended in 1992 and COSYGA itself also adopted a more independent position, joining the CGSL in strikes and protests against aspects of government policy in the mid-1990s.

A revised labour code adopted in 1994 provided increased protection of trade union rights. All workers are legally free to join trade unions and most private sector workers in the formal economy are reported to be unionized. Leading unions represents teachers, civil servants, transport workers, and communications workers.

Under the labour code collective bargaining is to take place on an industry-wide rather than enterprise basis. There is a right to strike subject to pre-strike arbitration procedures. In the public sector, the right to strike is limited where there is risk to public safety.

3 Trade Union Centres

Confédération Syndicale Gabonaise (COSYGA)
Gabonese Trade Union Confederation

Address. BP 14017, Libreville

Phone. +241 72 14 98

Fax. +241 70 07 04

Leadership. Martin Allini (secretary-general)

History and character. A single union centre, the Fédération Syndicale Gabonaise (FESYGA), was created in 1969 by the amalgamation of the three main existing centres as an organ of the ruling PDG. It changed its name to COSYGA at its 1978 congress. Its founding statutes affirmed '"responsible participation" in economic and social development of the country, and it launched various production and consumer cooperatives, and ventures in workers' education. After 1991, however, COSYGA evolved into a more independent organization. COSYGA affiliated to WCL after being visited by a WCL delegation in Sept. 1994. It is considered to be broadly aligned with the government but critical on issues where it sees the government acting against worker interests.

International affiliation. WCL

Confédération Gabonaise des Syndicats Libres Gabonese (CGSL)
Gabonese Confederation of Free Trade Unions

Address. BP 8067, Libreville

Phone. +241 77 37 82

Fax. +241 74 45 25

International affiliation. ICFTU

Gambia

Capital: Banjul
Population: 1.37 m. (2000 est.)

1 Political and Economic Background

Gambia became independent as a full member of the Commonwealth in 1965 and a republic in 1970. From independence until 1994 the ruling party was the People's Progressive Party (PPP).

The PPP won 25 of the 36 directly elected seats in the 1992 legislative elections and in presidential elections, held simultaneously, Sir Dawda Jawara of the PPP was elected to his fifth consecutive term. In July 1994, however, Jawara was overthrown in a bloodless military coup led by Capt. Yahya Jammeh. The new regime withstood attempts to overthrow it later in the year and in 1995. A new civilian constitution was endorsed in a referendum on Aug. 8, 1996, but the PPP and other significant opposition parties were banned. In Sept. 1996 Jammeh was elected President and in Jan. 1997 legislative elections resulted in victory for his Patriotic Alliance for Reorientation and Reconstruction.

Gambia has few resources and much of the population is engaged in subsistence agriculture. The small manufacturing sector is based mainly on processing agricultural products, notably groundnuts, and there is also a tourism industry.

GDP (purchasing power parity) $1.4bn. (1999 est.); GDP per capita (purchasing power parity) $1,030 (1999 est.).

2 Trade Unionism

The Gambia has ratified neither ILO Convention No.87 (Freedom of Association and Protection of the Right to Organize, 1948) nor No.98 (Right to Organize and Collective Bargaining, 1949).

There is, however, a history of trade unionism. The Gambia Labour Congress had its origins in 1929 and participated in the founding congress of the WFTU in 1945. It was affiliated to the People's Progressive Party banned after the 1994 coup. The two principal centres now are the Gambian Workers' Confederation (affiliated to the WCL) and the Gambia Workers' Union (affiliated to the ICFTU), both of which are recognized by the government.

Under the 1990 Labour Act all employees except civil servants have a legal right to join unions and bargain collectively. Under it employee contacts may not prohibit union membership. There are an estimated 30,000 union members. Strikes are lawful subject to notice periods and the courts may ban strikes that are considered politically motivated. In practice, strikes rarely occur.

3 Trade Union Centres

Gambian Workers' Confederation (GWC)

Address. Trade Union House, 31 Leman Street, PO Box 698, Banjul

Phone. +220 223 080

Fax. +220 227 214

Leadership. Pa Moudou K.B. Faal (secretary-general)

History and character. Pa Faal was arrested by the National Investigation Agency in Dec. 1996 and again in Apr. 1997, when he planned to travel abroad.

International affiliation. WCL

Gambia Workers' Union (GWU)

Address. 12 Clarkson Street, PO Box 979, Banjul

Phone. +220 28 17 7

International affiliation. ICFTU

Georgia

Capital: Tbilisi
Population: 5.02 m. (2000 est.)

1 Political and Economic Background

Georgia is a former republic of the USSR that became independent in 1991. It has experienced considerable conflict since that time. Its first post-independence leader, Zviad Gamsakhurdia, was deposed in Jan. 1992 in a military coup that resulted in former Soviet Foreign Minister Eduard Shevardnadze coming to power as chairman of the governing military council. Shevardnadze was elected President in 1995 and re-elected in Apr. 2000, and the Citizens' Union of Georgia party he founded in 1993 has a majority in Parliament. The central government has no control of the breakaway region of Abkhazia, from which both the army and the majority ethnic Georgian population were driven out in 1993, or of much of South Ossetia, and Russian peace-keeping forces are present in both those regions. There are an estimated 283,000 internally displaced persons.

The Georgian economy was badly damaged by the loss of former Soviet markets followed by civil conflict in 1992–93 surrounding the overthrow of Gamsakhurdia and the Abkhaz revolt. Under Shevardnadze and with backing from the IMF (which it joined in May 1992) it has sought to develop a market economy and achieved healthy growth from 1993, although affected by the Russian crisis of 1998. Economic activities include commercial agriculture, tourism and mining, with a small industrial sector.

GDP (purchasing power parity) $11.7bn. (1999 est.); GDP per capita (purchasing power parity) $2,300 (1999 est.).

2 Trade Unionism

The national centre is the Georgian Trade Union Amalgamation (GTUA), founded in 1990, when the Georgian unions seceded from the Soviet AUCCTU. It faced major attacks on its independence in 1991–92, but has since established itself as generally free from government interference. Georgia ratified ILO Convention No. 87 (Freedom of Association and Protection of the Right to Organize, 1948) in 1999 and No. 98 (Right to Organize and Collective Bargaining, 1949) in 1997. The right to form and join trade unions is provided by the 1995 Constitution and the 1997 Law on Trade Unions. A Law on Collective Bargaining was enacted in 1997.

On Jan. 31, 1999 President Shevardnadze signed a decree ordering all governmental agencies to consult and negotiate with unions, but this appears to have been disregarded. The GTUA supported a series of public sector strikes in 1999 over the issue of non-payment of wages.

3 Trade Union Centre

Georgian Trade Union Amalgamation (GTUA)

Address. Shartava Street 7, 380122 Tbilisi

Phone. +995 32 934087

E-mail. gtua@geo.net.ge

Leadership. Irakli Tugushi (president)

Membership. Claims 850,000 in 33 sectoral unions but dues-paying membership believed much lower.

History and character. The GTUA (also referred to as Amalgamated Trade Unions of Georgia, ATUG) is the successor to the Confederation of Independent Trade Unions of Georgia (CITUG), which was founded in 1990, when the Georgian unions seceded from the Soviet AUCCTU.

The CITUG did not fare well under independence. It supported the democratic opposition to the dictatorial rule of former president Gamsakhurdia. In Aug. 1991, it was abolished along with all its branch unions at an extraordinary congress convened on the president's orders and packed with his delegates. The congress established in its place a single trade union centre and most of its property was confiscated by the state. In opposition to this move the CITUG unions in the medical, cooperative, transport and communications sectors began to meet in secret but their efforts were overtaken by the fall of Gamsakhurdia in Jan. 1992.

Following Gamasakhurdia's overthrow it resisted efforts by the Military Council to bring it under control and its present structure was created in 1992 and most property returned. In 1998–99, however, it was still trying to get back union property transferred to the state in 1991–92. Its claim was contested by the CITUG president at that time, who had subsequently set up the Free Trade Union of Georgia, claiming the GTUA was not the legitimate successor to the CITUG.

The US State Department Human Rights report for 1999 says that the GTUA has no affiliation with the government and receives no government funding.

International affiliation. Affiliated to the ICFTU in Nov. 2000

Germany

Capital: Berlin
Population: 82.8 m. (2000 est.)

1 Political and Economic Background

Following World War II Germany was partitioned by the Allied forces, the US, British and French zones of occupation becoming the Federal Republic of Germany (FRG, West Germany) and the Russian zone becoming the German Democratic Republic (GDR, East Germany). In 1990, following the collapse of the GDR, the two Germanys were united on the basis of the West German political, social and economic order. Post-unification Germany is a federal republic in which there are 16 states (länder), each of which enjoys substantial powers in the economic and social fields.

From 1949 to 1966 the Christian Democratic Union (CDU) and its Bavarian counterpart, the Christian Social Union (CSU), dominated the federal government in West Germany, although the (liberal) Free Democratic Party (FDP) participated until 1956 and again from 1961; other smaller parties were also within the government until 1960. Since 1966 there have been successively coalitions of the CDU, CSU and Social Democratic Party (SPD) – the "grand coalition" – from 1966 to 1969; of the SPD and FDP from 1969 to 1982; and of the CDU, CSU and FDP from 1982 to 1998. In elections to the lower house (Bundestag) in Sept. 1998, however, the SPD emerged as the largest party and the SPD's Gerhard Schröder succeeded the CDU's Helmut Kohl as Chancellor, heading a coalition government in which the SPD was joined by the Greens (the so-called "red-green coalition"). Following setbacks in elections at state level in September–October 1999, the SPD-led federal government was left commanding only 26 out of 69 votes in the Bundesrat (the upper legislative house representing the states). A mixed pattern of political control exists at state level.

Germany has the largest economy in Europe and is noted especially for the scale, strength and diversity of its manufacturing sector. It is traditionally the motor economy of the EU but Germany has faced an immense task in privatizing, integrating and modernizing the former East German command economy against a background where East Germans had high expectations of sharing immediately in West German prosperity. Unemployment in the East, peaking at over 20%, was twice that in the West in the late 1990s and transfer payments to the East were still running at $100bn. per annum. The costs of integration have been a major contributor to Germany's persistent deficits. At the same time Germany has been reluctant to reduce its generous social welfare provision or undertake radical deregulation of its economy and labour practices, and in the view of critics this has contributed to a problem of persistent structural unemployment in both West and East. Unemployment showed a falling trend in 2000, however.

GDP (purchasing power parity) $1.864 trillion (1999 est.); GDP per capita (purchasing power parity) $22,700 (1999 est.).

2 Trade Unionism

West Germany ratified ILO Convention No.87 (Freedom of Association and Protection of the Right to Organize, 1948) in 1957 and Convention No.98 (Right to Organize and Collective Bargaining, 1949) in 1956. These ratifications apply to united Germany.

Trade unionism developed as Imperial Germany industrialized. Despite various restrictions, by 1914 there were 2.5 million members of social democratic unions, 340,000 members of Christian unions and 105,000 in liberal or "yellow" Hirsch-Duncker unions. The unions were again a powerful industrial and political factor in the Weimar Republic after World War I, but were abolished and coordinated into the German Labour Front (Deutsche Arbeitsfront) after Hitler came to power in 1933.

From 1945 unions in the West were reorganized on the principle of one union per industry, and were subsequently coordinated by the German Trade Union Federation (DGB). West German trade unionism avoided altogether the division on political lines seen in other western European countries such as France and Italy. Likewise, although there was a religious-based centre, the CGB, this lacked the scale and influence of such centres in Belgium or the Netherlands. The conventional distinction between blue-collar and white-collar workers, crystallized into separate trade union structures in Scandinavian countries, existed to some degree in Germany, and was reflected in the existence of the German Salaried Employees' Union (DAG) and the German Civil Servants' Federation (DBB), but the DGB and its affiliates were structured as inclusive of all occupational and educational groups.

In the GDR unions affiliated to the Free German Trade Union Confederation (Freier Deutscher Gewerkchaftsbund – FDGB) and were organized on the Soviet model. At its peak the FDGB claimed a membership of 9.6 million unionists, pensioners, students and others, comprising "97.7 per cent of all production workers, office employees, intellectuals and professional people", according to official claims. This figure exceeded union membership in the much larger West German state.

The approach of unification stimulated reorganization at the FDGB where a number of leaders rapidly fell into disgrace. It still claimed 8.6 million members at the start of 1990, but an extraordinary congress converted it into a confederation, a step that freed the 16 industrial unions to formulate their own statutes. Despite this they were slow to change, notwithstanding increasing competition from the powerful and proximate DGB as well as newly emerging independent unions. That autumn the presidents of the FDGB's affiliates concluded it was not viable and it dissolved at the end of 1990. Most constituent unions soon shared its fate. By April 1991, 3 million former FDGB members had joined a DGB affiliated union and unionism in the new länder proceeded thenceforth within the expanding structures of the West German unions.

The DGB faced a major challenge in establishing an efficient structure in the new länder. While some affiliates moved swiftly to capitalize on the membership opportunities presented there – IG Metall which already claimed to be the largest union in the Western world quickly put its claim beyond doubt – they also collided with different expectations of unions among prospective recruits. There were early indications that prospective union members in the East continued to regard the creation of job opportunities as a union responsibility whereas the newly-arrived DGB affiliates regarded their priorities as the negotiation of better wages and conditions. The process of absorption of members of the defunct organizations was completed by 1992 but was only a partial success: much of the formal membership of the defunct unions was lost. In the absence of pluralism GDR union density ran at around 90%, but it fell in the new eastern länder of united Germany to 50%.

The immediate result of unification was that the membership of the former West German trade unions, which had been fairly stable during the 1980s, swelled dramatically. Thereafter, trade union density in the country as a whole fell rapidly year-on-year from 40.6% in 1991 (13,749,000 union members) to only 32.2% (10,278,000) by 1998. Furthermore the union membership included rising proportions of unemployed and retirees, so that in reality only one in four of the active working population was in a union by the end of the 1990s. Membership of the DGB itself, having risen from 7.9 million in 1990 to 11.8 million in 1991 then fell by 30% to 8.3 million in 1998. Those not adversely affected were the Christian CGB, whose membership had not increased as a result of unification and remained stable at just over 300,000 throughout the 1990s, and the civil service confederation the DBB, which managed to increase its membership somewhat as a result of recruitment in the east German public sector.

To a considerable degree the fall in total union membership reflected a continuing shake-out in east Germany. DGB membership fell by an average 11.7% per annum 1991–98 in the east, compared with only 2.1% per annum in the west. The east German economy remains much weaker than that of the west, with wholesale closures of old economy industries and unemployment reaching over 20% by the late 1990s.

At the same time the unions are concerned at their declining position quite apart from the special factors created by unification. By the end of 1997, nearly 19% of DGB members were pensioners, and the proportion of members under the age of 25 had fallen sharply. Like unions throughout much of the western world (except Scandinavia) the DGB was struggling to make an organizational impact in growing private sector services to match its dominant position in traditional blue-collar old economy industries. In 1997 while 60% of career public servants and 43% of blue-collar workers were union members, only 20% of white-collar workers were in unions. The German unions have not been able to replicate the success of Scandinavian unions in the 1990s in organizing previously weak areas such as private service businesses and women workers in lower paid jobs. They have struggled to keep pace with the increase in part-time working and growth of temporary work managed by temporary work agencies. Their memberships tend to reflect the structure of the economy as it was a generation ago rather than as it is today. Complicating their position further, the established demarcation lines between unions have been eroded by the development of new sectors, especially in services, and unions have found themselves competing with each other to organize in difficult environments.

One result of contracting union memberships has been the merger of DGB unions, all of which – except the Police Union – experienced significant membership falls during the 1990s. Mergers of DGB unions in 1996-99 resulted in the number of affiliates falling from 16 to 11. The DAG white-collar confederation saw relatively little gain from unification and its membership fell from 585,000 in 1991 to 480,000 in 1998, lower than it had been in the 1980s in West Germany alone. In Oct. 1997, it and five DGB service sector affiliates (the ÖTV, DPG, HBV and IG Medien, as well as the teachers' union GEW, which later withdrew) announced plans to form a super-union, the largest (non-official) union in the world, Ver.di. (United Service Sector Union). In the autumn of 2000 special congresses of the DAG, DPG, HBV and IG Medien voted overwhelmingly in favour of completing the merger in 2001. However, an ÖTV congress failed to produce sufficient support and the union deferred a final decision to an extraordinary congress in March 2001 when an 80% majority would be needed to proceed.

Overall the five organizations participating in the proposed formation of Ver.di had lost 26% of their membership in the period 1991–98. According to the merger programme agreed in 1999 the "future of German trade unionism will be decided in the service sector" because of structural changes in the economy. Ver.di would have a decentralized structure, allowing a degree of separate identity to the different sectors it represented, but would seek to coordinate their strength to work for a service sector dominated by "public benefit" rather than profit.

As a consequence of the environment in which the unions were restructured after World War II, union policies have generally been pragmatic and cautious in character, and intended to assist the rebuilding of the economy while stabilizing the institutions of democracy. Radical and authoritarian political currents have been absent at all levels in the leadership to a marked degree. The unions' status in society and numerical strength benefited from the perception that they had contributed to the re-building of the German economy after World War II, and the anti-union political currents that affected many western countries in the 1980s were not pronounced in Germany. Management generally accepted unions as a co-determining factor in the running of industry, an acceptance institutionalized in labour representation on company boards and in company decision-making. While at any one time a majority of the DGB leadership is likely to be of an SPD orientation, care is always taken to ensure that there are CDU members in the elected leadership as well, an orientation which corresponds to that of a number of individual unions. Both major political parties maintained support organizations for their union members, the loosely structured AfA for the SPD and the autonomous CDA for the CDU.

To a considerable degree the unions have retained their role and position in unified Germany. However, that role is under some pressure. During the 1980s the trade unions maintained their membership at stable levels (the DGB membership of 7.88 million in 1980 rising fractionally to 7.94m. in 1990) at a time when union memberships in most other western countries were falling sharply. Despite a conservative CDU-led government being in office for 16 years from 1982, little was done to match the moves to encourage labour market flexibility seen in the UK. However, in the 1990s, the German model has come under strain. Unemployment by the end of the decade was the highest since World War II and employers complained that Germany's high labour costs and social security system were making Germany increasingly uncompetitive in world markets. The SPD has likewise moved towards a politics of the "new centre" akin to Britain's "third way" in which new emphasis is put on creating a framework for individual enterprise.

While the basic structure of the old (West) German collective bargaining system, which was formalized through the Collective Agreements Act of 1949, remains in place, it has come under pressure as a result of these changes. Under the established collective bargaining system, most bargaining has occurred at regional level by industry sector, although bargaining also occurs at national and company levels, with patterns varying between industries. Agreements bind the signatory parties. Customarily, the terms of agreements have been applied to all employees whether or not union members. In addition, at the request of either unions or employers, the terms of agreements covering 50% of employees can be extended by the Minister of Labour to cover employees of companies that are not signatories through an association. In general, under the "favourability principle" deviations from agreements at company level have only been allowed to the benefit of the employees. There is a "duty of peace", based on labour

court decisions, on both parties not to engage in strikes or lock-outs during the term of an agreement. Furthermore, an agreement remains in effect even after its date of expiry if a new agreement has not been reached. While strike action is not uncommonly threatened during the negotiation process, industrial conflict in practice has been relatively unusual. Employers and unions have generally worked to achieve compromise and strikes are in any case normally called only after approval by at least 75% of the union membership in a special ballot.

While this system shows enduring strength, and has been rigidly enforced by the labour court system, fault lines have begun to appear. In part this is a result of the unification of Germany. In the east, where unemployment exceeded 20% in the late 1990s (compared with just over 10% in the west), there is considerable divergence from the general German model. Real wages in the east, including benefits and bonuses, remain generally below those in the west. For example, a public sector agreement covering 3.1 million employees, reached by the DGB public sector unions, DAG and DBB with employers in June 2000, called for east German pay levels to be raised to 90% of those in the west by 2002. The unions had sought pay parity as living costs were similar in east and west but the employers rejected this on the grounds that there had been no improvement in productivity in the east. In the private sector, IG Metall agreements have included equal pay for east and west since the mid-1990s but workers in the east have fewer benefits and longer hours. This represents less a form of discrimination than a recognition of the continuing comparative inefficiency of the work force in the east and the parlous state of many of its companies.

In 1993, in the first agreement of its kind, IG Metall signed a collective agreement for the east German metalworking industry which included a "hardship clause", allowing companies with severe difficulties to pay less than the collectively agreed rates for a period of time. The scheme was jointly administered by IG Metall and the employers, who had agreed to application of the hardship clause in 100 cases by 1997. This agreement, while providing an escape clause for weak companies, nonetheless also reinforced the principle that trade unions and employer associations should supervise and approve such exemptions, rather than leaving this as a matter for the individual enterprises. However, increasing numbers of east German employers are not members of employer associations and are not bound by sectoral collective agreements.

While the east remains a special case, employers throughout Germany have called for more flexibility in reaching company-level agreements that take account of the needs of individual companies to survive and grow. The view of employers is that wage costs and inflexibility are damaging German competitiveness. In newer sectors, such as IT, the unions have found it hard to achieve blanket sectoral agreements. New start companies and companies spun off from established businesses are resistant to being bound by such agreements, preferring (as do some employees) company-level or individual contracts. Avoidance of blanket agreements has been a stimulus to outsourcing. The coverage of the centralized bargaining system has shrunk. Where once 90% of all employees were covered by centrally negotiated rates (even though the union density ratio in West Germany was always lower), by 1997 the proportion of west German private sector employees covered by industry-level agreements had fallen to 65%, and in the east the proportion was only 49%. Only 9% of west German and 14% of east German enterprises were covered by company agreements. While large employers continue in general to participate in industry collective bargaining, many small and medium-sized companies do not.

Increasingly, companies are seeking to achieve agreements at enterprise level that significantly modify sectoral agreements by agreeing so-called "opening clauses" with unions that modify the terms of agreements to fit the position of their companies. In other cases, employers are ignoring collective agreements. This process is reinforced by the fact that although two-thirds of German employees are still covered by agreements reached between unions and employer associations, an increasing minority of employers are not members of the employer associations that sign sectoral agreements.

Under the Collective Agreements Act, agreements may be reached only with trade unions. However, Germany also has a parallel system of works councils, these having a right to be informed, consulted and to participate in company decisions so as to encourage cooperation and partnership between the two sides of industry. These councils are elected every four years. In 1998 works council elections, 62% of councillors and 73% of council chairs, were DGB members. However, non-union candidates have been increasingly successful in these elections and in 1998 one in three councillors and one in five chairs were non-union.

Under the 1952 legislation that regulated the establishment of works councils, they specifically are excluded from dealing with "remuneration and other conditions of employment that have been fixed, or are normally fixed, by collective agreement". However, there has been a trend towards employers reaching "employment pacts" with works councils, whereby employees agree concessions on wages and hours in return for job guarantees and thereby undercut collective sectoral agreements. Some employers have also called for changes to the Works Constitution Act (as has the opposition FDP) to allow works councils to conclude collective agreements.

The employers' associations have generally been cautious about calling for major overhaul of the collective bargaining system. However, in Feb. 2000 the leaders of the four main employers' and business associations (the Confederation of German Employers' Associations, BDA; the Confederation of German Industries, BDI; the German Association of Chambers of Commerce, DIHT;

and the Central Association of German Crafts, ZHD) jointly called for changes to the Collective Agreement Act. They sought a redefinition of the favourability principle to allow worse conditions to be agreed at company level, through works councils, arguing that employees are themselves constrained from agreeing remedial action to save an ailing firm. The changes sought by the employers' associations were nonetheless much less sweeping than those proposed by the opposition FDP and other critics of the system, such as the OECD, who see its rigidities as a contributory factor to Germany's high structural unemployment. The leading employers' association, the BDA, has said it wants to see reform but still preserve the basic structure of branch-level sectoral bargaining. To some degree, the existence and status of the employers' associations themselves are tied up with the continuance of the existing bargaining system.

By the late 1990s (usually tripartite) regional Alliances for Employment had been formed in most of the länder. At the federal level the CDU-FDP government attempted to set up a similar Alliance in Jan. 1996, with the target of cutting unemployment in half by 2000, but this quickly collapsed when the unions withdrew in protest at government policies. A 1997 initiative focused on the problems of the east also faltered. Following the election of an SDP-led government, in Dec. 1998 a new tripartite "Alliance for Jobs" (Bündnis für Arbeit), chaired by Chancellor Gerhard Schröder, was created. However, while the Alliance could agree on general aspirations to promote employment, in practice unanimity on concrete actions has proved more difficult to achieve. In 2000 average union pay demands were for a 5.5% increase, leading employers to question the unions' commitment to job creation in seeking pay increases beyond gains in productivity (actual pay awards ultimately ran at half this level). Union proposals to increase jobs by cutting hours or by investing more in infrastructure or environmental projects have been rejected by employers as simply increasing business costs and the public deficit. The employers call for structural reform to improve flexibility and reduce regulations, reductions in the burden of social security contributions and taxes on business, and cuts in unemployment benefits to encourage people back to work. The SDP-led government, while repealing some CDU legislation, has also underlined that the days of deficit spending as a way to generate employment are over and that Germany needs to liberalize its working practices to remain competitive. In Sept. 2000, IG Medien became the first DGB affiliate to withdraw support from the Alliance for Jobs, saying it had become a means of restraining pay claims rather than creating employment.

One of the favourite panaceas of the unions for job creation, as in France, has been cutting working hours. In the metal industry the 35-hour week was introduced in 1995, but in most sectors working hours are longer, particularly in the east. Where reductions of working hours are agreed they generally involve increased working time flexibility and employers are hostile to any across-the-board reduction, such as has been legislated for in France.

A general right to strike is included in the national Constitution (Basic Law) although the law has been largely shaped by judgments in the courts. To be lawful a strike must be conducted by a union, taken as a last resort, and be in pursuit of an objective that may be regulated by a collective agreement: thus wildcat and protest and solidarity strikes are not legal. Career public servants ("beamte"), who enjoy special protection against dismissal may organize collectively (as in the DBB) but may not strike. Their pay is determined administratively but customarily has been linked to the levels agreed for other public sector workers.

In addition to the works council system, in larger firms there is "co-determination", which allows employee representatives to join the Supervisory Board of firms with more than 2,000 employees in numbers equal to those representing stockholders; firms below this size have one-third labour representation on the Supervisory Board. In the coal and steel industries, under the 1951 Coal, Iron and Steel Industry Co-Determination Act, there is parity on supervisory boards, but this now affects only 400,000 employees. The system of co-determination runs in parallel to and separately from that of collective bargaining through unions, and because most contentious issues are dealt with through collective bargaining, the practice of co-determination has tended to be characterized by a high level of cooperation between employers and employees. However, supervisory board co-determination is declining, with less than a quarter of private sector employees covered by co-determination by the mid-1990s, compared with 30% a decade earlier. In addition, the number of employees covered by works councils has been declining so that more than 60% of private sector employees are no longer covered by any form of co-determination. Fewer than 10% of companies with less than 20 employees have a works council. The unions argue that in addition to securing better representation for employees' interest, co-determination is also beneficial in providing ways for employers and workers to discuss and resolve issues relating to efficient working practices, skills development and quality that improve flexibility and competitiveness. Critics have maintained that it is another aspect of inflexibility in the German system, limiting the right and responsibility of managers to manage.

In the late 1990s alliances of the unemployed existed in many parts of German, although these had not reached the same level of activity as in France, partly because of the high level of welfare benefits for the German unemployed. Most German trade unions organize the unemployed.

3 Trade Union Centre

Deutscher Gewerkschaftsbund (DGB)
German Trade Union Federation

Address. Burgstrasse 29-30, D-10178 Berlin

Phone. +49 30 24060 211 (press office)

Fax. +49 30 24060 324 (press office)

E-mail. info@bundesvorstand.deb.de

Website. www.dgb.de (German, with sections in English, French and Spanish)

Leadership. Dieter Schulte (president); Ursula Engelen-Kefer (vice-president)

Membership. 8.3 million

History and character. The General German Federation of Trade Unions (Allgemeiner Deutscher Gewerkschaftsbund – ADGB) was founded in 1868 by delegates representing 142,000 workers. Bismarck's Anti-Socialist Law of 1878 sharply curtailed union activity, but when this law expired in 1890 a new and overwhelmingly social democratic confederation, the General Kommission der Gewerkschaften (General Commission of Trade Unions), was formed. After World War I this was in turn succeeded by a re-born ADGB, set up in 1919 and the largest confederation in the Weimar period. The ADGB, in common with other trade union organizations, was abolished after the accession to power of Hitler in 1933, when the unions were co-ordinated into the Labour Front (Deutsche Arbeitsfront – DAF).

Following the surrender and Allied occupation of Germany in 1945, trade unions were at first permitted only on a land (state) or zonal basis, and in April 1947 the Deutscher Gewerkschaftsbund (DGB) was set up in the British zone (which included the Ruhr). After initial resistance from the French military government, the three occupying powers agreed to the establishment of a tri-zonal federation. At a 1949 Munich conference a tri-zonal DGB was formed by 101 unions representing over 4.8 million members. Workers in the Soviet zone were by this time organized in an entirely separate body, the FDGB, and the constitution of the DGB provided that only unions operating within the territory of the new West German Federal Republic would be admitted to membership (although it also operated in West Berlin).

Among the principles adopted at the founding convention were: (i) the participation of organized labour in economic planning; (ii) the nationalization of key industries such as mining, iron and steel, large chemical, and power industries and major credit banks; (iii) freedom for unions to engage in collective bargaining with employers. The evolution of federal public policy after 1949 led for some years to strained relations between the (Christian Democratic) coalition government and the DGB, and the ultimate enactment of legislation providing a framework for modified forms of co-determination, while the issue of nationalization waned in significance. Historically, the DGB has been associated with the main outlines of policy of the Social Democratic Party (SPD), although it is politically unaffiliated.

Sixteen industrial federations were created on the industrial union principle, which united all workers at a plant in the same union. These federations are autonomous and bargain separately (the DGB as an umbrella organization neither negotiates nor concludes collective bargaining agreements), but must accept the DGB constitution. They have no direct religious or political affiliations. The DGB's role is to co-ordinate joint demands and broad campaigns for its affiliates and represent the union movement as a whole. It also provides information and advice to unions at company level and to works councils. The form of organization adopted in the 1940s reflected a compromise between those advocating a highly centralized structure, with coordinated industrial sector unions, and those who advocated a central organization on the model of the British TUC, where the individual unions are freely associated bodies with total autonomy. In practice the larger unions, such as IG Metall, enjoy a degree of autonomy, arising from their industrial strength, virtually comparable with that of the major British unions.

The DGB is entitled to equal representation in the executive bodies for the self-regulation of social insurance funds (health, accident and pension funds) as well as the Federal Office of Employment. Its representatives also sit on a range of other public bodies.

The DGB has an executive board (of which the president is a member) elected by a delegate congress every four years (most recently in 1998). A federal executive committee is formed by the executive board and the presidents of the 11 member unions. However the highest decision-making body between conventions is the federal council, which is composed of the executive committee, the presidents of the regions of the DGB and representatives of the DGB's affiliates.

During the 1980s, while union centres throughout the western world experienced losses in membership, the position of the DGB remained stable. Membership of 7.88 million in 1980 was little changed at 7.94 million in 1990. The DGB faced particular challenges following the unification of Germany, absorbing the unionized workforce in the former East Germany (see section on Trade Unionism above). Most DGB affiliates recorded large membership gains as they absorbed members from the new länder only to lose numbers under the impact of the recession and shake-out in inefficient industries in the east from 1991 onwards. This was exacerbated by losses in west Germany caused by structural changes in the economy. DGB membership surged to 11.8 million in 1991 only to fall back to 8.3 million by 1998. While the loss of members was most extreme in the east, where membership fell by an average 11.7% per annum in the period 1991–98, there was also decline in the west, averaging 2.1% per annum in the same period. The only affiliate not to suffer heavy losses after 1991 was the Police Union (GdP).

One consequence of falling membership was the merger of affiliates. In the late 1990s the number of DGB affiliates was reduced from 16 to 11. In 1996 the horticulture, agriculture and forestry union (Gewerkschaft Gartenbau-, Land- und Forstwirtschaft, GGLF) merged with the building and construction union IG Bau-Steine-Erden (IG BSE) to form IG Bauen-

Agrar-Umwelt (IGBAU). In 1997 three affiliates merged to form Industriegewerkschaft Bergbau, Chemie, Energie (IGBCE) (mining, chemicals and energy), while the textile and clothing workers' union Gewerkschaft Textil-Bekleidung and wood and plastics union Gewerkschaft Holz und Kunststoff were absorbed into IG Metall in 1998–99.

The number of affiliates is set to fall to eight during 2001 subject to completion of a proposed merger of four DGB unions, together with the currently independent DAG, to form the DGB-affiliated Ver.di (Vereinigte Dienstleistungsgewerkschaft), which would be larger than IG Metall. The unions involved are the Public Services, Transport and Traffic Union (ÖTV), the Media union (IG Medien), the Commerce, Banking and Insurance union (HBV) and the Postal Workers' union (DPG). Between them these unions had lost in the range between 23% (DPG) and 36% (HBV) of their members in the period 1991–98. The objectives are to rationalize the unions' cost base in view of declining memberships, avoid demarcation conflicts and create the scale and resources to organize service areas that are currently little unionized. The participating unions said that the new organization would be decentralized, retaining separate decision making and collective bargaining for its different sectors, and would not be a centralized "super-union". In the autumn of 2000 special congresses of all unions planning to form Ver.di voted in favour of the merger, except the ÖTV (the largest), in which significant minority dissent had developed and where a final decision would not be taken until March 2001.

Further rationalization of affiliates is considered likely. An increasing problem is that the historic demarcation lines between DGB affiliates have been confused by the rapid development of new sectors. In telecommunications, IG Metall, IG BCE and Ver.di unions have all signed collective agreements.

In Nov. 1996 an extraordinary reform congress meeting at Dresden agreed a new basic programme (grundsatzprogramm). The programme was widely interpreted as marking the formal abandonment by the DGB of its historical demand for nationalization of key industries, in favour of a social market economy. Its key themes included:

1. Concern that radical market deregulation would undermine the functioning of the collective bargaining system. The trade unions had a "fundamental interest in the existence of well-functioning employers' associations" which could conclude and enforce collective agreements, and the spread of individual contracts was undermining this.
2. Concern that such "market radicalism" would in turn undermine the consensual nature of the state. "The trade unions will not accept a market economy which dispenses with the social state framework rooted in the constitution."
3. Fears of the impact of globalization on German workers with their relatively high costs: the DGB pressed for cooperation between the ILO and WTO

on the implementation of core labour standards to prevent countries with unregulated labour markets from achieving competitive advantage.

4. Awareness of the challenges to the union structure posed by the rise of non-traditional employment: home-working, self-employment, individual contracts, part-time working, temporary agency work, fixed term contracts, and the informal economy. Such forms of labour were difficult to reconcile with the traditional forms of collective bargaining and standard conditions of employment, and those involved in such employment were outside union structures. This was reflected in the membership of the unions. The unions also had to be increasingly aware of the needs of those not in the working economy at all, such as the unemployed, pensioners and the prematurely retired. A "more open" union culture was required, with more attention paid to small workplaces.

5. Emphasis on finding at the European level a coordinated Europe-wide collective bargaining policy, an executive accountable to the European Parliament, and a strengthening of the European Trade Union Confederation (ETUC).

6. The extension of co-determination in the workplace, including expanding the role of works councils to smaller enterprises.

While arguing for the extension of the role of works councils co-determination, in areas such as work organization and job protection, the DGB has also sought the further involvement of trade unions in steering works council activities. It is concerned at the trend for works councils to reach agreements with employers that modify or undermine collective bargaining agreements reached with unions. The DGB has also called for more regulation of temporary work agencies and measures to ensure temporary workers have the same terms and conditions as regular employees.

In 1997 the DGB launched an "Action Programme for Employment and Social Justice". This emphasized job creation and advocated a basket of policies including reducing overtime, encouraging part-retirement, introducing a 35-hour week, increasing vocational training and an active employment policy to assist the long-term employed get back to work.

The DGB was founded on the principle that it should be a unified union, not exclusively representative of any party or political tendency. However, it has an historic majority identification with the SDP, just as the employers' associations have a majority identification with the conservative parties. Between 75 and 85% of DGB officials are estimated to be members of the SDP, and three-quarters of SDP members of the Bundestag are members of DGB-affiliated unions. The only prominent CDU supporter in the DGB at the time of the 1998 elections was the leader of the Police Union (GdP). While the DGB did not officially endorse any party in the 1998 elections, its electoral platform focused on the failures of the CDU-FDP government to stop the rise in unemployment and called in many respects for policies similar to those advocated by the SDP. Walter Riester, the vice-president of IG Metall, went on to become Minister of Labour in the incoming SDP-led government.

At the same time, tensions have arisen over what some in the DGB seen as the pro-business "new middle" ("neue mitte") policies of the new government. While union leaderships have made some moves towards accepting the need for greater flexibility, there is a continuing basic unease about policies that emphasize the primacy of the market and encouragement of entrepreneurship. Within the SDP there has also been a current of opinion seeking more distance (on the model of the Labour Party and the British TUC) between the party and the unions. This is reinforced by the fact that the DGB, with declining membership, and little representation in many dynamic sectors of the economy, can no longer speak with assurance as the voice of labour. The unions saw as a setback the resignation of Oskar Lafontaine, a socialist traditionalist, as party leader and Finance Minister in March 1999.

The DGB, faced with falling membership dues and escalating costs for its retired employees, was forced in 1998 to cut pension rates for new retirees, a mirror of the problems facing German society as a whole as a result of an aging population. However, government proposals in 2000 to tackle the mounting burden of pension costs, with state pension levels currently running at 70% of average earnings and wholly funded by the current working population, attracted union criticism. In Dec. 2000 it was reported that the government had reached agreement with union leaders on a new package of pension proposals after the government made a series of concessions.

In Aug. 2000 the DGB issued a joint statement with the Confederation of German Employers' Associations (BDA) on promoting initiatives to combat xenophobia and neo-Nazi extremism in the work place. This had emerged as a problem especially in the east.

International affiliations. ICFTU; ETUC; TUAC

Affiliated unions. There are now 11 industrially based affiliates. In order of size, based on their percentage of total DGB membership as of 31 December, 1998, these are: IG Metall (33.4%), ÖTV (19.0%), IGBCE (11.5%), IGBAU (7.4%), HBV (5.7%), DPG (5.7%), GdED (4.2%), GEW (3.4%), NGG (3.4%), GdP (2.3%), IG Medien (2.2%). (A 12th union then in existence, the GHK, had 1.8%)

1. IG Bauen-Agrar-Umwelt (IGBAU) (construction, agriculture and environment)

Address. Olof-Palme-Strasse 19, Frankfurt-am-Main 60439
Phone. +49 69 95737 0
Fax. +49 69 95737 109
E-mail. international@igbau.de
Website. www.igbau.de (German only)
Leadership. Klaus Wiesehuegel (president). Wiesehuegel is an SPD member of the Bundestag.
Membership. 580,000
History and character. Formed by the 1996 merger of the horticulture, agriculture and forestry union (Gewerkschaft

Gartenbau-, Land- und Forstwirtschaft, GGLF) and the building and construction union IG Bau-Steine-Erden (IG BSE).
Publications. Grundstein/Der Säemann (monthly magazine to all members); *Fundamente* (quarterly). A range of information services can be accessed via the website (German only)

2. Industriegewerkschaft Bergbau, Chemie, Energie (IGBCE) (mining, chemicals and energy)

Address. Königsworther Platz 6, Hannover 30167
Phone. +49 511 7631 0
Fax. +49 511 7631 713
E-mail. (European department) abt.europa@igbce.de
Website. www.igbce.de
Leadership. Hubertus Schmoldt (president)
Membership. 672,770
History and character. The IGBCE held its founding congress in Oct. 1997 and was the result of the merger of the merger of three previous DGB affiliates, IG Bergbau and Energie (mining and energy), IG Chemie-Papier-Keramik (chemicals, paper and ceramics) and the much smaller Gewerkschaft Leder (leatherworkers). Hubertus Schmoldt, formerly president of IG Chemie, became president of the new union. Internationally it is affiliated to the European Mine, Chemical and Energy Workers Federation (EMCEF) and the International Federation of Chemical, Energy, Mine and General Workers' Unions (ICEM).
Publications. Magazin (monthly); *Umschau* (bi-monthly)

3. TRANSNET Gewerkschaft GdED

Address. Weilburger Strasse 24, Frankfurt 60326
Phone. +49 69 7536 212
Fax. +49 69 7536 222
E-mail. (press office) presse@gded.de
Website. www.gded.de (German only)
Leadership. Norbert Hansen (president)
Membership. 340,000
History and character. The new name was adopted in May 2000 by the Gewerkschaft der Eisenbahner Deutschlands (railway workers' union, GdED) to reflect better the broadening of its membership to include workers in other transport, services, and telecommunications. In addition to recruiting in the telecoms field GdED is also looking to gain members in passenger transport areas dominated by the ÖTV.

Norbert Hansen, GdED president, is also president of the European Transport Workers' Federation (ETF) and the union emphasizes international cooperation between unions in the transport field. It is also a member of the ITF. In Feb. 1998 a federal labour court ruled that GdED must recognize an association of its own employees for bargaining purposes. It had refused to negotiate other than with the works council and claimed that its employees could not form a separate union as they were already members of GdED.

4. Gewerkschaft Erziehung und Wissenschaft (GEW) (education and science)

Address. Reifenberger Str. 21, Frankfurt 60489
Phone. +49 69 78973 0
Fax. +49 69 78973 201
E-mail. info@gew.de
Website. www.gew.de (German only)
Leadership. Eva-Maria Stange (president), Norbert Hocke (vice-president)
Membership. 280,000
History and character. In May 1997, Dieter Wunder became the first president of a DGB affiliate to be voted out of office,

being succeeded by Eva-Maria Stange, the first woman to lead the union and the first leader of a DGB affiliate from the former East Germany. She had previously been a member of the East German GUE teachers' union, which was absorbed into the GEW after unification. 44% of the GEW's membership (i.e. a disproportionately large number) were reported to be in east Germany.

In Oct. 1997 GEW was one of five DGB affiliates that announced their intention to merge (together with the independent DAG) to form a new super-union, Ver.di. In July 1998, however, GEW withdrew from merger discussions. Concern had developed that the 289,000 members of GEW would lose identity and distinctive representation in a super-union of more than 3 million members.
Publications. Members' magazine (monthly), *Erziehung und Wissenschaft*

5. Gewerkschaft Handel, Banken und Versicherungen (HBV) (commerce, banking and insurance)

Address. Kanzlerstr. 8, Düsseldorf 40472
Phone. +49 211 9040 0
Fax. +49 211 9040 888
E-mail. info@hbv.org
Website. www.hbv.org (German only)
Leadership. Margaret Mönig-Raane (president)
Membership. 480,000
History and character. The decision of the HBV is to merge into the service sector super union Ver.di in 2001 was endorsed by a 78% vote at an extraordinary congress in Nov. 2000.

6. IG Medien – Druck und Papier, Publizistik and Kunst (media- printing and paper, advertising and arts)

Address. Friedrichstrasse 15, Stuttgart 70174
Phone. +49 711 2018
Fax. +49 711 2018 199
E-mail. igmedien-hv-werneke@link-do.soli.de
Leadership. Detlef Hensche (president)
Membership. 197,300
History and character. IG Medien is due to merge into the proposed super-union Ver.di in 2001.
Publications. Druck und Papier; Forum; Menschen Machen Medien; Kunst und Kultur

7. IG Metall (IGM) (metalworkers)

Address. Lyoner Str. 32, Frankfurt 60528
Phone. +49 69 6693 2667 (international dept.)
Fax. +49 69 6693 2843
Website. www.igmetall.de (German; English section)
Leadership. Klaus Zwickel (president)
Membership. 2.8 million
History and character. Prior to German unification in 1990 IG Metall, with one-third of the total DGB membership, was the largest union in the Western world and the spearhead of the DGB. It united workers on the industrial union principle throughout metal manufacturing, metal processing and engineering.

In a membership drive in 1990–91 IG Metall spent some DM 30 million to build a base in former East Germany. Some 150 IG Metall officials were sent to the East to organize a ballot for employees there on joining the union. This was largely successful and IG Metall's membership rose by some 945,000 between the end of 1989 and end of 1991, to 3.62 million.

In June 1991 IG Metall marked its centenary with celebrations in Frankfurt which were attended by Chancellor Kohl and Jacques Delors, President of the European Commission. Kohl urged the unions to play the same role in uniting Germany as they had in building the Federal Republic.

Franz Steinkühler (IG Metall president since 1986) was at that time Germany's most prominent union leader. He was re-elected to a third term as president with a 90 per cent majority at the 1992 delegate conference, but his career was abruptly halted when he announced his resignation in May, following revelations that while a member of the supervisory board of Daimler-Benz (D-B), he had made DM 64,000 by speculating in the shares of Mercedes Holdings, a D-B subsidiary. In 1993, at an extraordinary congress, IG Metall elected Klaus Zwickel as Steinkühler's successor with Walter Riester as his deputy.

IG Metall's membership had fallen to 2.66 million by the end of 1997, a drop of 27% (960,000) since 1991 and taking membership levels to below 1989 (pre-unification) levels. The drop was most precipitous in the east, 64% of the 999,000 members in the east at the end of 1991 disappearing by the end of 1997, but membership had also fallen significantly (12.6%) in the west. Furthermore, the proportion of members who were unemployed or retired had risen to 33% from 28% in 1992. According to estimates, IG Metall's active membership of 1,784,000 in 1997 represented only 31% of workers in the metalworking and steel industries, which had a work force of 5.4 million. The loss of members was attributed to the impact of restructuring (especially in the east), rising unemployment and the growing diversification of metal industry employers into areas such as telecommunications and IT, eroding IG Metall's organizational area.

In 1998–99 IG Metall absorbed two other DGB unions, Gewerkschaft Textil-Bekleidung (GTB, textile and clothing), which joined with effect from June 1998, and Gewerkschaft Holz und Kunststoff (GHK, wood and plastics), which joined at the end of 1999. The textiles and clothing sector had been severely reduced by cheaper international competition, and of the 300,000 jobs in this sector in east Germany before unification only 24,000 were left by the late 1990s. The GTB had lost 43% of its members since 1991. GHK had likewise been badly affected by loss of members, losing 33% in the period 1991–96.

IG Metall has been the leading force on the issue of working hours reduction. In the 1980s it led a determined fight to achieve a shorter working week, at one point (in 1984) mounting a sustained national strike which seriously affected the German reputation for industrial relations peace. Although its success at that time was a qualified one, the union finally won its point in 1990 when the employers conceded the introduction of a 35-hour week by 1995, although hours remained longer in the east. In Apr. 1997 IG Metall president Klaus Zwickel proposed a general working time reduction to 32 hours and a 4-day week by 1999. The metalworking employers' association Gesamtmetall, in contrast, believes the introduction of the 35-hour week was an error that has damaged German competitiveness.

Walter Riester, Minister of Labour in the SDP-led government, was IG Metall vice-president before taking up office. In Oct. 1999 he announced agreement in principle with IG Metall on the idea of retirement at 60 (rather than the current 65) with no loss of pension rights, the additional costs to be paid for from a new collective bargaining fund. Gesamtmetall rejected the idea and said that in view of demographic trends the need in the future would be for longer working hours.

IG Metall is the leading individual member of the International Metalworkers' Federation trade secretariat.

Publications. Metall (monthly magazine)

8. Gewerkschaft Nahrung-Genuss-Gaststätten (NGG) (food, beverages, catering)
Address. Haubachstr. 76, Hamburg 22765
Phone. +49 40 38013 0
Fax. +49 40 3892637
E-mail. hauptverwaltung@ngg.net
Website. www.gewerkschaft-ngg.de (German only)
Leadership. Franz-Josef Möllenberg (president)
Membership. 280,000

9. Gewerkschaft Öffentliche Dienste, Transport und Verkehr (ÖTV) (public services and transport workers)
Address. Theodor-Heuss-Str. 2, Stuttgart 70174
Phone. +49 711 2097 0
Fax. +49 711 2097 462
Website. www.oetv.de (German only)
Leadership. Frank Bsirske (president)
Membership. 1.5 million
History and character. The ÖTV is the DGB's second largest affiliate. It was the largest of the unions involved in planning the creation of a service sector super-union, to be known as Ver.di, in 2001. In Nov. 2000, however, the executive's plans to merge the union into Ver.di were approved by only 65% of delegates at a special ÖTV congress. This lukewarm support led to the resignation of ÖTV president Herbert Mai, whose successor, Frank Bsirske, said he would seek further negotiations on the proposed structure of Ver.di. A final decision would be taken in March 2000 when 80% backing would be needed for the merger to go ahead.

10. Gewerkschaft der Polizei (GdP) (police)
Address. Forststr. 3a, Hilden 40721
Phone. +49 211 7104 0
Fax. +49 211 7104 138
E-mail. gdp-bund-hilden@gdp-online.de
Website. www.gdp.org (German only)
Leadership. Norbert Spinrath (president)
Membership. 193,000

11. Deutsche Postgewerkschaft (DPG) (postal workers)
Address. Rhonestr. 2, Frankfurt 60528
Phone. +49 69 6695 0
Fax. +49 69 6666 941
E-mail. internet@dpg.org
Website. www.dpg-hv.de (German; English section)
Leadership. Kurt van Haaren (president)
Membership. 451,000
History and character. A special congress voted overwhelmingly in Nov. 2000 to join the proposed new service sector super-union Ver.di in 2001.

4 Other Trade Union Organizations

Christlicher Gewerkschaftsbund Deutschlands (CGB)
German Christian Workers' Union

Address. Konstantinstrasse 13, 53179 Bonn
Phone. +49 228 3570 62
Fax. +49 228 3570 83
E-mail. cgbbonn@t-online.de

Website. www.dhv-cgb.de (German only)

Membership. 300,000

History and character. The CGB, which was founded in 1959, is of a social Christian orientation, although the churches have generally not actively supported religious-based unionism since World War II. It is a general confederation with members spread across the blue and white-collar sectors and the public service.

The CGB was little affected by unification, gaining only a few thousand new members in former East Germany, giving it 311,000 members in 1991. Conversely, it was also little affected by the general loss of trade union memberships in the east after 1991 and its membership remained little changed through the 1990s. There has been persistent conflict between its mining affiliate and IG Metall.

International affiliations. CESI

Deutsche Angestellten-Gewerkschaft (DAG)
German Union of Commercial, Clerical and Technical Employees/German Salaried Employees' Union

Address. Johannes-Brahms Platz 1, D-20355 Hamburg

Phone. +49 40 349 1501

Fax. +49 40 491 5400

Website. www.dag.de (German only)

Leadership. Roland Issen (president)

Membership. 480,000

History and character. The DAG, which began organizing in 1945, was formed on a national basis in April 1949, after the formative DGB decided that white-collar staff should be organized in industrial unions, on the one plant, one union, basis, rather than given separate representation. The DAG took a position independent of the state, political parties, religious communities and other institutions and aspired to unite all salaried employees.

During the 1990s the DAG drew closer to the DGB. At the same time its membership, briefly increased by unification (to 584,000 in 1991), fell back to below the levels they had been at in the former West Germany.

In Oct. 1997 the DAG began a process that was intended to result in its merger in 2001 with DGB affiliates to create a super-union Ver.di (see DGB entry). An extraordinary DAG congress in Nov. 2000 voted 99% in favour of joining Ver.di.

In Jan. 2000 DAG reached a banking sector agreement that was opposed by the DGB's Commerce, Banking and Insurance Union (HBV), with which DAG was due to merge in Ver.di. HBV subsequently accepted the agreement and to avoid further conflict the two unions then formed a joint bargaining commission to negotiate an insurance sector agreement in May 2000.

International affiliation. ETUC

Deutscher Beamtenbund (DBB)
German Civil Servants' Federation

Address. Peter-Hensen Strasse 5–7, D-53175 Bonn

Phone. +49 228 8110

Fax. +49 228 811 171

E-mail. post@dbb.de

Website. www.dbb.de (German; English summary)

Leadership. Erhard Geyer (president)

Membership. 1.2 million

History and character. The DBB traces its origins back to 1918: it was dissolved by the Nazis in 1933 and recreated in 1950. It represents both white-collar and wage-earning public employees, as well as civil servant status employees, and by law must be involved in the formulation of legislation and regulations relating to civil service matters. The DBB undertakes to defend and promote the social, legal and professional interests of its members and those of its affiliated organizations. It is politically independent.

Members include teachers, policemen, employees and civil servants of the armed forces, railway and post office officials, employees in the justice system, and social services staff. They work in the public sector and the privatized services sector. There are 37 member unions and state associations in all 16 of the länder. Unlike most trade union organizations, the DBB did not suffer membership losses in the 1990s.

"Beamte", or career public servants (in 1995 constituting 1.9 million of 5.4 million public sector employees), have traditionally enjoyed guaranteed lifetime employment in exchange for a duty of loyalty, which includes a prohibition on taking strike action. The 1997 Act on Civil Service Law Reform took some steps towards making performance rather than seniority the key to promotion and remuneration and reforming pension schemes. The DBB opposed the reforms saying they were aimed at cutting costs rather than introducing modern management methods. In the summer of 1997 it organized demonstrations (along with DGB public sector affiliates, including the GEW teachers' union, most of whose members are classified as career public servants) against the new law.

Organs of the DBB include the DBB-Tarifunion, which represents employees on wages and salaries issues; the DBB-Frauen, representing the 320,000 women members; and DBB-Jugend (youth).

The DBB has permanent contacts with government. It has a legal claim to involvement in the formulation of general legislation and regulations governing public service matters. It provides a social service and has an education programme and college (BISOWE).

Publications. *DBB-Magazin; Europa-Nachrichten; DBB-Aktuell.*

International affiliations. CESI; CIF

Ghana

Capital: Accra
Population: 19.53 m. (2000 est.)

1 Political and Economic Background

Ghana became an independent member of the Commonwealth in 1957 and a republic in 1960 under the leadership of the socialist Kwame Nkrumah. Nkrumah was overthrown in 1966 and there was then a succession of mainly military administrations until Flt.-Lt. Jerry Rawlings seized power temporarily in 1979, and then permanently in 1981. A civilian constitution was approved in a referendum in Apr. 1992 and Rawlings was elected President later that year as the candidate of his National Democratic Congress party. He was re-elected four years later and according to the constitution was obliged to stand down as President by the end of 2000. He did so and elections in Dec. 2000 resulted in the election of John Kufuor, of the opposition centre-right New Patriotic Party (NPP), a development seen as indicating greater political stability and the consolidation of pluralism in the country. Rawlings' National Democratic Congress party has a comfortable majority in Parliament.

Ghana's foreign exchange generating resources include gold, timber and cocoa. Under Rawlings since the mid-1980s Ghana has moved away from state economic control and encouraged the private sector. During the 1990s Ghana enjoyed annual average GDP growth above 4% and international donors such as the IMF and the World Bank backed the government's economic liberalization programme. However, Ghana has remained reliant on international assistance and austerity measure have led to periodic outbreaks of discontent. Some 60% of the working population are engaged in subsistence agriculture. Incoming President Kufuor said he would push ahead with free market reforms and cut wasteful subsidies.

GDP (purchasing power parity) $35.5bn. (1999 est.); GDP per capita (purchasing power parity) $1,900 (1999 est.).

2 Trade Unionism

Ghanaian trade unionism has a long history stretching back before World War II, by which time there were a number of well-established unions. Provision for the registration of trade unions was made under British rule in 1941, and the organized labour movement subsequently became linked to the political movement for independence. The TUC was the sole central organization from its creation in 1945 but has been reorganized on a number of occasions in response to political devel-

opments. More recently WCL affiliates have formed their own federation.

The foundation statute governing employment relations in Ghana is the Industrial Relations Act 1958. Ghana ratified ILO Convention No.87 (Freedom of' Association and Protection of the Right to Organize, 1948) in 1965 and Convention No.98 (Right to Organize and Collective Bargaining, 1949) in 1959.

The 1981 revolution formally provided for free collective bargaining in both the private sector and in the state-owned enterprises (SOEs). National strikes are rare. Most open disputes are at company level and occasionally they may lead to government intervention. The ICFTU has complained of the wide discretionary powers given the Registrar of Trade Unions to refuse to register unions and of lengthy pre-strike procedures which mean that there has been no legal strike since independence.

3 Trade Union Centre

Trades Union Congress of Ghana (TUC)

Address. Hall of Trade Unions, PO Box 701, Accra

Phone. +233 21 22 65 55

Fax. +233 21 66 71 61

E-mail. tuc@ncs.com.ngh

History and character. The TUC of Ghana was founded in 1945 as the Gold Coast Trades Union Congress. It became closely linked to Nkrumah's Convention People's Party and was reorganized following the Nkrumah's fall in 1966. It was dissolved in 1971 and reorganized again in 1972. Following the 1981 Rawlings' coup the TUC secretary-general Alhaji A. M. Issifu was forced to resign and a radical faction supporting the new regime announced that all senior officials of member unions had been dismissed. The union movement remained in turmoil in 1982–84, as workers' defence committees vied with the radicalized unions for the representation of Ghana's workers. However, following a 1984 reorganization of defence committees, the labour movement was restored to its former structure. The TUC committed itself to the new government's basic goals, but criticized aspects of government policy. The TUC's principal concern was to maintain living standards in the face of price liberalization under the economic recovery programme.

The TUC was actively involved in the move to greater democracy in the early 1990s and had ten members of the Consultative Assembly that wrote the new civilian Ghanaian constitution adopted in a referendum in April 1992. It subsequently opposed government austerity measures and called for "circumspection" in the privatization process. In 2000 the TUC was consulted in the drafting of a proposed new labour code.

The TUC comprises 17 affiliated national unions. There is an associated Ghana labour college, founded in 1967.

International affiliation. ICFTU

4 Other Trade Union Organization

Ghana Federation of Labour (GFL)

Address. PO Box 1582, Tema

Phone. +233 22 30 44 29

Fax. +233 22 20 62 51

Leadership. Abraham Koomson (general secretary)

International affiliations. WCL (affiliated 1999)

Greece

Capital: Athens
Population: 10.6 m. (2000 est.)

1 Political and Economic Background

The military took power in Greece in 1967 and ruled until 1974. Since then the dominant political parties have been the Pan-Hellenic Socialist Movement (PASOK) and conservative New Democracy (ND), both of which were founded in 1974. Under the ND Greece joined the EU in 1981. The ND was in government from 1974–81 and again from 1990–93, while PASOK held power 1981–90 and has formed the government since Oct. 1993, gaining a very narrow victory over the ND at elections in Apr. 2000. PASOK has largely abandoned its left-wing rhetoric of the 1980s and instead professes a social democratic identity supportive of Greek membership in the EU and NATO.

Greece has a relatively small industrial base and services, including tourism, shipping, trade, and banking, predominate. There is a significant informal economy and many small enterprises. At the start of the 1980s, PASOK pursued an expansionist policy, relaxing fiscal and income controls and espousing socialization of industry. Mounting economic difficulties gradually forced a reversal, and from 1987 PASOK began to liberalize the economy, a policy continued by ND after 1990 and PASOK again since 1993. A driving force for Greece in recent years has been the need to achieve qualifying criteria to join the European Monetary Union. Greece failed in 1998 to meet any of the criteria needed to participate in the single European currency from the start in 1999, but joined with effect from the beginning of 2001. The double-digit inflation of the 1980s and

early 1990s has been brought under control, and since 1995 Greece has enjoyed growth above the EU average, although remaining the poorest EU country. Governments have had less success in tackling issues of deregulation, flexibility and privatization, where there is considerable resistance from unions, professional groups, political institutions and public opinion. The public debt (driven up by social security programmes and government takeovers of failing enterprises) although falling remains high (at 105% of GDP in 1999) and the state sector still accounts for 45% of GDP. EU funding is a significant factor in assisting economic restructuring.

GDP (purchasing power parity) $149.2bn. (1999 est.); GDP per capita (purchasing power parity) $13,900 (1999 est.).

2 Trade Unionism

The first unions were formed at the end of the nineteenth century and the GSEE (General Confederation of Greek Labour) was founded in 1918. Greece ratified ILO Conventions No.87 (Freedom of Association and Protection of the Right to Organize, 1948) and No.98 (Right to Organize and Collective Bargaining, 1949) in 1962. Trade union rights were severely curtailed under the rule of the military junta from 1967 to 1974 but restored under the 1975 Constitution.

All workers other than those in the armed forces may join unions and union density is estimated at about 26%, compared with 30% at the start of the 1990s. However, 20 workers are needed to form an enterprise union, which excludes many of Greece's large number of small and medium-sized enterprises. Anti-union discrimination is illegal and the courts have reinstated workers dismissed for organizing unions. Under 1982 legislation there is a prescribed three level structure of trade unions, primary (local or enterprise-level), secondary (regional or sectoral) and tertiary (national centres), these forming a pyramid. At the apex are the GSEE, which represents both private and public sector workers, and ADEDY, which represents civil servants.

Most union funding comes me not from dues but from a state body, the Workers' Welfare Foundation (literally, the Workers' Hearth, OEE), whose board comprises representatives of employers, government and the unions. The OEE was established in 1931 with the goal of elevating the economic, spiritual and intellectual condition of the workers. Its main role, however, has been to fund unions, on criteria that were described in a 1998 report by the GSEE's research arm, INE-GSEE, as being "regarded as neither impartial nor objective". The OEE's funds come mainly from compulsory contributions paid by all employers and employees, whether or not members of unions.

The unions are politicized and politically divided, a condition encouraged by a tradition of political interference. In the 1985–89 period the GSEE virtually disintegrated over its relations with the PASOK government. Both the GSEE and ADEDY remained arenas for political battles. PASOK supporters organize in the PASKE faction, New Democracy supporters in DAKE and the Communists in EAK.

Before the 1990s Greek industrial relations oscillated between turbulent disputes and compulsory arbitration by the Ministry of Labour. However, a 1990 law on free collective bargaining marked the withdrawal of the state from regulation of incomes, repealing a statute of 1955 and thus ending the long-standing system of compulsory arbitration. This law was the first explicit acknowledgment of the principle of voluntary negotiation. While still providing for voluntary arbitration it now put mediation centre-stage through the good offices of a national Mediation and Arbitration Service (OMED). The 1990 Act also introduced two new types of agreement to supplement the already existing national collective agreements and occupational agreements. These were sectoral agreements (which, like occupational agreements may be concluded at the national, regional or city level), and enterprise agreements. Under the terms of the Act national agreements apply automatically to all employees without further Ministry of Labour intervention while more limited agreements have legal standing provided they improve on the minimum laid down in the national agreements. During the 1990s there has been a steady increase in the number of collective bargaining agreements concluded directly between employers and unions and a corresponding decrease in the number of arbitration decisions reached through OMED. The GSEE draws up a framework National General Collective Agreement (most recently in May 2000 covering 2000/2001) with the central employers' organizations.

There are no restrictions on private sector collective bargaining but there are restrictions in the civil service, although this has been balanced by the substantial entrenched power of the Civil Servants' Confederation, ADEDY. The courts sometimes declare strikes illegal, for reason such as lack of sufficient notice, but active enforcement of such rulings is not usual. Skeleton staffing must be maintained a in range of basic services, such as electricity, postal services, transport and banking, during strike action.

There is a tradition of strikes directed against broad aspects of government policy. These strikes tend to affect mainly the public sector. In the late 1990s this has been reflected in action against government policies of privatization, deregulation and budgetary control designed to bring Greece into line with its EU partners and pave the way for Greece's accession to the eurozone in Jan. 2001. The Greek public sector is large, accounting for 45% of GDP, and generally considered inefficient by observers. However, union density is 75% in the public sector, compared with 25% or less in the private, and the unions have been resistant to government privatization plans. The unions also argue that, as Greece's unit labour costs are the lowest in the EU outside Portugal, a solution to Greece's lack of competitiveness cannot be found by attacking living standards but lies in areas such as the quality of training. In 1996–98 there were numerous strikes, including a series of brief general strikes called by the GSEE and ADEDY, against government policies. Of 30 strikes in 1998, 22 were in the public sector. There was comparatively little industrial unrest and no general strikes in 1999, however. One of the principal concerns of the unions is that, while Greece's double-digit inflation of the early 1990s (when real wages fell sharply) has been ended (inflation being 2.5% in 1999), and real wages have again risen (15% from 1995–99), unemployment at nearly 11% in 1999 was the highest in recent decades. The unions have called for active measures to combat unemployment and improve unemployment benefits.

The PASOK government has sought to extend the concept of social partnership, a relatively undeveloped concept in Greece, in implementation of its policies. On Nov. 10, 1997, the GSEE, ADEDY, Federation of Greek Industries (SEV) and the National Confederation of Greek Commerce (ESEE) signed a "Confidence Pact" with the government outlining broad objectives in dealing with issues such as labour relations, improving competitiveness and social protection. However, the Pact was limited because of its avoidance of a range of contentious issues and the GSEE only endorsed it on a split basis, subsequently withdrawing from some aspects of social dialogue.

Greek trade unionism remains heavily male dominated. Women make up 30% of the (formal) work force but in 1998 only 6% (133 of 2067) of elected members of union administrative boards/ executive committees. Similarly, only 20 of the 520 delegates to the 1998 GSEE congress were women.

3 Trade Union Centres

General Confederation of Greek Labour (GSEE)

Address. Odos 28, Octovriou 69, Athens 104

Phone. +30 1 8834 611

Fax. +30 1 822 9802

Membership. About 500,000

History and character. The GSEE held its founding congress in 1918. Following the eighth congress in 1946 the government deposed the elected executive and imposed one in its favour, and the GSEE thenceforth remained subject to government intervention. Following the end of the military dictatorship in 1974 the GSEE retained a semi-official character and was opposed by a significant proportion of the labour force organized in independent unions which were unrecognized by the government and did not receive funding from the Ministry of Labour. A congress (the 22nd) broadly representative of the organized labour movement was held for the first time since military rule in Dec. 1983, and elected a governing council with a PASOK majority and a large communist minority. From 1986–89 there was an internal struggle between supporters of the PASOK government and others, and Communists and others boycotted the 23rd (1986) and 24th (1988 congresses). The government was accused of direct interference in the confederation's affairs. The boycotted 1988 Congress elected only members of PASKE (the faction supporting PASOK) to its administration and in 1989 the courts installed a new administration representing all five factions.

Factionalism remains institutionalized in the GSEE. PASOK supporters in PASKE remain the leading element but New Democracy (which was unrepresented in the 1980s, when the GSEE was split between PASOK and a strong Communist element) is now a factor. The 29th Congress, held in March 1998, elected a 45-member administrative board (to remain in office for three years) comprising 22 seats for PASKE (which lost its absolute majority), 10 for DAKE (the New Democracy faction), 10 for EAK (the faction of the Communist Party, KKE), and three for "Autonomous Intervention", the faction of the Coalition of the Left and Progress (Synaspismos). In Feb. 1999 the factional division was reflected when the administrative board voted 23 to 22 not to participate in the process of social dialogue on tax reform. A statement put out by the majority, without PASKE participation, said the process of social dialogue following the signing of a tripartite Confidence Pact in Nov. 1997 had been "bankrupt, perfunctory and unacceptable".

GSEE policy reflects a compromise between these different currents. While participating in dialogue with the government, the GSEE in 1996-98 also led a series of (brief) general strikes against aspects of PASOK government policy (privatization and restructuring of state enterprises, taxation, increased labour flexibility in state enterprises, social policies). These stoppages have mainly affected public sector areas such as transport, state banks and hospitals. Key issues for the GSEE currently include unemployment (in the late 1990s the highest since World War II), resistance to labour market deregulation, the demand for tax reform, and implementation of the 35-hour week. In July 2000, the government invited the GSEE to participate in bilateral talks, in parallel to talks it would have with the employers, on issues such as unemployment, anti-inflation policies, use of EU resources, competitiveness, development of entrepreneurship and social exclusion.

The GSEE negotiates a National General Collective Agreement (every two years) with the employers, which serves as a framework for sectoral and enterprise agreements.

Attached to the GSEE is the Institute of Labour (INE/GSEE-ADEDI) which was set up in 1990 to carry out research and to plan and implement trade union education and training and vocational training.

International affiliations. ICFTU; ETUC; TUAC

4 Other Trade Union Organization

Civil Servants' Confederation (ADEDY)

Address. 2 Psilla Street, 10557 Athens

Leadership. G. Koutsoukos (president)

Membership. 280,000 in 60 federations

History and character. ADEDY is the umbrella organization for civil servants. Like the GSEE it is divided into factions allied to political parties. The public service is highly organized, with 90% unionization.

In 1999 civil servants for the first time were able to bargain collectively over terms and conditions, excluding pay and pensions. Prior to this, although ADEDY lacked the formal right to engage in collective bargaining, and conditions were set by government, in practice it was consulted informally. Public sector workers outside the civil service are represented by GSEE unions. Although these have had full collective bargaining rights, their weaker bargaining power has meant that agreements reached in consultation with ADEDY have tended to be applied across the board.

ADEDY has regularly led brief strikes in recent years (often with the GSEE) on issues such as pay, taxation and privatization.

International affiliation. ETUC

Grenada

Capital: St George's
Population: 89,000 (2000 est.)

GDP (purchasing power parity) $360 m. (1999 est.); GDP per capita (purchasing power parity) $3,700 (1999 est.).

1 Political and Economic Background

Grenada (a former West Indies associated state) became an independent member of the Commonwealth in 1974. In 1979 Maurice Bishop's left-wing New Jewel Movement staged a coup and formed a People's Revolutionary government. Parliament was dissolved and the Constitution suspended and close diplomatic and economic links were established with Cuba and countries of the Soviet bloc, while relations with the United States deteriorated. Factional conflict within the government led to Bishop's murder in Oct. 1983 and a Commonwealth Caribbean force together with some 2,000 US troops landed on the islands and imposed order, following which an interim advisory council was appointed and the 1974 Constitution restored. 1984 elections to the House of Representatives were won overwhelmingly by the New National Party (NNP) which also accordingly secured a large majority in the nominated Senate. The last foreign military personnel were withdrawn in 1985.

The centrist National Democratic Congress held office from 1990–95, but in 1995 was defeated at the polls by Keith Mitchell's conservative New National Party (NNP). In Jan. 1999 the NNP won a landslide victory in a general election, taking all 15 seats in the House of Representatives.

Grenada's economy is agriculturally based, and there is only a limited manufacturing sector. Tourism is the major foreign exchange earner. Growth averaged 6% per annum 1998–99 but there is significant unemployment.

2 Trade Unionism

Grenada ratified ILO Convention No.98 (Right to Organize and Collective Bargaining, 1949) in 1979 and Convention No.87 (Freedom of Association and Protection of the Right to Organize, 1948) in 1994. All workers may join trade unions, which are well established and estimated to represent about 35% of the workforce. Legislation provides protection against anti-union discrimination and employers must recognize a union where it has majority support. There is a right to strike and there are mechanisms for resolving disputes through the Labour Commissioner and arbitration tribunals.

3 Trade Union Centre

Grenada Trades Union Council (GTUC)

Address. PO Box 411, Tanteen, St George's

Phone. +1809 440 3733

Fax. +1809 440 6615

E-mail. gtuc@caribsurf.com

Leadership. Ray Roberts (general secretary)

History and character. The GTUC was founded and registered in 1955. It is the island's only centre and has all significant unions in membership. It receives a government subsidy to assist its work.

International affiliations. ICFTU; CTUC

Guatemala

Capital: Guatemala City
Population: 12.64 m. (2000 est.)

1 Political and Economic Background

Guatemala has suffered from persistent military inter-

ventions in government, instability and civil strife. In Dec. 1996 thirty years of war between left-wing guerrillas and the Army came to an end with the signing of a peace accord between the government of President Alvaro Arzú of the centre-right National Advancement Party (PAN) and the Guatemalan National Revolutionary Movement (UNRG), which subsequently reorganized itself as a political organization. In Feb. 1999 a report by the independent Historical Clarification Commission attributed 90% of crimes in the war, in which up to 200,000 died, to the Army. The first elections held since the peace accord, in November–December 1999, resulted in the conservative Guatemalan Republican Front (FRG), gaining control of the legislature and the presidency.

Agriculture employs more than half of the workforce (in some cases at subsistence level) and accounts for 2/3 of exports, although there is also a manufacturing sector based largely on the processing of agricultural products and clothing assembly. In the 1990s governments have sought to follow economic liberalization policies.

GDP (purchasing power parity) $47.9bn. (1999 est.); GDP per capita (purchasing power parity) $3,900 (1999 est.).

2 Trade Unionism

Trade unionism developed in a period of reformist civilian government prior to a military coup in 1954. In 1952 Guatemala ratified ILO Convention No.87 (Freedom of Association and Protection of the Right to Organize, 1948) and No.98 (Right to Organize and Collective Bargaining, 1949). Thereafter the unions were held back by tactics of repression (including the assassination of union leaders by death squads), blacklisting and corruption, as well as more formal legal restrictions.

Under the labour code unions may not participate in party politics, while the right to strike is generally limited and denied to agricultural workers at harvest time and to workers in essential public services (with heavy penalties prescribed for violators). These constraints are less significant in practice than the general climate of fear and violence in which industrial and political relations have historically been conducted. The disappearance and assassination of trade unionists have been the subjects of complaints to the ILO by the world centres and several damning reports. Murders, torture and intimidation continued into the 1990s, though not on the scale of the late 1980s when 2,000 trade unionists were thought to have been murdered in one year. The WCL reported in late 1998 that: "the hopes that the (Dec. 1996) peace treaty had brought about have not come true" and that systematic violence continued.

Unions currently complain particularly about conditions in the export processing zones (EPZs, or maquiladoras) and the banana plantations. According to the ICFTU's 1999 *Annual Survey of Trade Union Rights,* although the government (in response to international pressure) in 1996 introduced the threat of sanctions against employers in the EPZs who flouted labour laws, in practice these are not applied. The ICFTU reported that employers in the EPZs blacklist activists and have largely excluded the unions while the labour inspection system is inefficient and corrupt. There has been considerable anti-union violence in the banana plantations. In 1999 a bitter dispute developed between the SITRABI banana workers' union and a Del Monte subsidiary. However, the International Union of Food and Agricultural Workers (IUF) in March 2000 signed an agreement with Del Monte which established a framework for local negotiations and Del Monte agreed to respect minimu labour standards.

The Solidarismo movement of Costa Rica is also present in Guatemala. There are reported to be some 4000 solidarist associations with 170,000 members. According to the unions some employers have sponsored the formation of such associations as an alternative to trade unions.

There are centres affiliated to each of the international confederations. The Confederation of United Unions of Guatemala (CUSG) is the largest and is affiliated to the ICFTU. The Union Guatemalteca de Trabajadores (UGT) is a loose coordinating body for the confederations. In Sept. 1997 this called on the people of Guatemala to step up the struggle against "violence, impunity, corruption, insecurity, cost of living, clearance sales of public property, ignoring of peace agreements".

All employees other than members of the armed forces enjoy freedom of association under the constitution and the labour code. In formal terms the labour code provides protection for trade union activities and prohibits anti-union discrimination, and the government has also moved in the 1990s to simplify its procedures for registering a union to give it legal status. However, the history of violence and repression, the hostility of employers and the military, the lack of protection through the labour courts, and poverty and widespread unemployment have had the result that, according to the Ministry of Labour, only 2% of the 3.5 million workforce are in unions. The unions have most strength in the public sector, where strikes are also common. The practice of collective bargaining is limited by the general weakness of the unions and employer resistance and most unionized workers are not covered by collective agreements.

3 Trade Union Centres

Confederación de Unidad Sindical de Guatemala (CUSG)

Address. 12 Calle "A", 0-37 Zona 1, Guatemala City

Phone. +502 232 8154

Fax. +502 232 8154

E-mail. cusg@guate.net

History and character. Founded in 1983, with social democratic orientation.

International affiliation. ICFTU

Central General de Trabajadores de Guatemala (CGTG)

Address. 3ra Avda. 12-22, Zona 1, Guatemala City

Phone. +502 232 1010

Fax. +502 251 3212

E-mail. cgtg@guate.net

Leadership. José Pinzón (secretary-general)

History and character. Is descended from the Central Nacional de Trabajadores (CNT), which operated clan-destinely after the disappearance of 21 of its leaders arrested on June 21, 1980. Eight CGTG leaders were murdered between 1992–98 and none of the cases has been solved.

International affiliation. WCL

Guinea

Capital: Conakry
Population: 7.47 m. (2000 est.)

1 Political and Economic Background

Guinea became fully independent from France in 1958. For over 25 years the government was dominated by President Sekou Touré, as leader of the socialist and nationalist Parti Démocratique de Guinée (PDG, which was constituted as the sole legal political party). Upon his death in 1984, a military coup took place, a military-civilian administration was set up under Lansana Conté at the head of a Military Committee of National Recovery, the Constitution was suspended and the PDG and the unicameral National Assembly were dissolved. Under Sekou Touré official policy was applied with considerable severity but in the early 1980s, there was some relaxation while the international isolation into which Guinea had withdrawn was exchanged for a policy of "positive neutrality".

During 1990 the military drew up a draft constitution which was approved by popular referendum in December. Until 1995 a Transitional Committee for National Recovery served as a legislature. In 1992 the first political parties were registered. Conté was elected President in 1993 and in 1995 his Party of Unity and Progress likewise won elections to the National Assembly. Conté was re-elected in Dec. 1998.

Guinea has considerable resources (including 25% of word bauxite reserves) and 80% of export earnings come from mining, especially bauxite, gold and diamonds. However, 85% of the population is engaged in subsistence agriculture. Under Sekou Touré the economy was almost wholly socialized and private trade was largely prohibited in 1975. After his fall the government sold off state enterprises and sought to liberalize the economy with IMF support.

GDP (purchasing power parity) $9.26bn. (1999 est.); GDP per capita (purchasing power parity) $1,200 (1999 est.).

2 Trade Unionism

Following independence in 1958 Guinea ratified ILO Conventions No.87 (Freedom of Association and Protection of the Right to Organize, 1948) and No.98 (Right to Organize and Collective Bargaining, 1949) in 1959.

From 1958 Sekou Touré combined the position of President with leadership of the sole union centre, the Confédération Nationale des Travailleurs de Guinée (CNTG). After his death, the new regime announced that free unions would be permitted. The CNTG continues to exist, is still the largest centre, and is still considered close to the state. There are now two ICFTU-affiliated rivals, the Organisation Nationale des Syndicats Libres de Guinée (ONSLG) and the Union Syndicale des Travailleurs de Guinée (USTG). The USTG faced repression in 1994, including arrests of leading figures and an attempt on the life of its president. It has agitated against the impact of economic restructuring on employment.

There is a constitutional right to form unions for all workers except members of the armed forces and protection against discrimination based on union membership. However, most of the work force is engaged in subsistence agriculture and unions mainly represent civil servants, employees of the national utilities and workers in foreign-owned companies. There is a right to strike, subject to a notice period, but binding arbitration can be imposed in essential services, including public transport and communications.

3 Trade Union Centres

Confédération Nationale des Travailleurs de Guinée (CNTG)

Address. Bourse du Travail, Corniche Sud 004, BP 237, Conakry

Phone. +224 415 044

Fax. +224 415 044

Leadership. Dr Mohamed Samba Kébé (secretary-general)

History and character. Sekou Touré became leader of the Guinea branch of the French Confédération Générale du Travail (CGT) in 1948, by which time he had also founded the Parti Démocratique de Guinée (PDG), which demanded independence from France. When Touré became the first President of independent Guinea in 1958 his union (renamed as the Confédération Nationale des Travailleurs de Guinée – CNTG – in 1956) became the sole trade union organization and was integrated into the structure of the PDG (the sole legal party).

Following Touré's death in 1984 and the consequent military coup, the CNTG's new leader, Samba Kébé, stated that the trade union movement was now "free and had good relations with the Military Committee of National Recovery" and a 1986 ordinance affirmed the legal independence of the organization from the state. In 1993, however, the ILO criticized the government for involving itself in the affairs of the CNTG to block the efforts of reformers and the ICFTU stated in 1999 that the CNTG remains indirectly funded by the state. The CNTG is now affiliated to the WCL. It remains the largest trade union centre in Guinea.

International affiliation. WCL

Organisation Nationale des Syndicats Libres de Guinée (ONSLG)

Address. BP 4033, Conakry

Phone. +224 41 52 17

Fax. +224 41 52 17

International affiliation. ICFTU

Union Générale des Travailleurs de Guinée (UGTG)

Address. BP 5522, Conakry

Phone. +224 453 076

Leadership. Mamadou Mara (president)

International affiliation. WCL

Union Syndicale des Travailleurs de Guinée (USTG)

Address. BP 1514 Conakry

Phone. +224 41 1741

Fax. +224 41 2565

International affiliation. ICFTU

Guinea-Bissau

Capital: Bissau
Population: 1.29 m. (2000 est.)

1 Political and Economic Background

Guinea-Bissau became formally independent of Portugal in 1974 (its independence having been proclaimed unilaterally in 1973). Initially the governments of both Guinea-Bissau and Cape Verde (the latter independent from 1975) were formed by the African Party for the Independence of Guinea and Cape Verde (PAIGC) with a view at that stage to the eventual integration of the two countries. A new constitution, adopted in May 1984, defined Guinea-Bissau as an anti-colonialist and anti-imperialist republic with a policy of national revolutionary democracy. The PAIGC, as the sole and ruling party, was described as the leading political force in society and in the state.

In 1989 João Vieira, the President since 1980, was elected unopposed but pressure mounted for the estab-

lishment of democracy. In 1991 the ruling PAIGC approved a plan to introduce a multi-party system but the country's first free elections were not held until July 1994. They brought an overwhelming victory to the PAIGC, while in presidential elections Vieira won a narrow victory over Koumba Yalla of the Social Renewal Party (PRS). In June 1998 Vieira faced a military rebellion in 1998 led by Ansumane Mané; this led to an agreement introducing various constitutional reforms, but in May 1999 Vieira was removed from power in a coup. In elections to the National People's Assembly in Nov. 1999 the PAIGC lost power for the first time since independence, with PRS beoming the leading party. In Jan. 2000 PRS leader Koumba Yalla was elected President.

Guinea-Bissau is a poor country with low life expectancy and most of the work force dependent on subsistence farming and fishing. The limited infrastrucuture was badly damaged by fighting in 1998. The country is heavily in debt.

GDP (purchasing power parity) $1.1bn. (1999 est.); GDP per capita (purchasing power parity) $900 (1999 est.).

2 Trade Unionism

After independence, Guinea-Bissau ratified ILO Convention No.98 (Right to Organize and Collective Bargaining, 1949) in 1977 but it has not ratified Convention No. 87 (Freedom of Association and Protection of the Right to Organize, 1948). Trade union activities were severely restricted under Portuguese colonial rule. After independence the União Nacional dos Trabalhadores da Guiné became sole centre, with close ties to the ruling PAIGC party. Under the constitution workers may form and join unions of their own choosing. However, most of the work force is engaged in subsistence agriculture and there is only a small formal economy in which unions operate, with most union members working for the government or parastatals. There are reported to be 11 functioning unions, seven of which are affiliated to the UNTG. Formal collective bargaining does not exist to any degree. There is a legal right to strike, subject to a notice period.

3 Trade Union Centre

**União Nacional dos Trabalhadores da Guiné (UNTG)
National Union of Workers of Guinea-Bissau**

Address. Caixa Postal 98, Avenida Osvaldi Vievra No. 13, Bissau

Phone. +245 20 10 36

Fax. +245 20 18 50

E-mail. untgdis@sol.gtelecom.gw

Leadership. Desejado Lima da Costa (secretary-general)

History and character. The UNTG when in exile was affiliated to the ICFTU, but after independence transferred its affiliation to the WFTU. As an arm of the ruling party before 1991, it emphasized the need to mobilize the workers to achieve greater productivity and overcome problems of backwardness. It has now re-affiliated to the ICFTU. In the 1990s it retained close relations with the PAIDG.

International affiliation. ICFTU

Guyana

**Capital: Georgetown
Population: 697,000 (2000 est.)**

1 Political and Economic Background

Guyana (formerly British Guiana) became a fully independent member of the Commonwealth in 1966 and a republic in 1970.

The principal division in Guyanan politics is racial. The People's Progressive Party (PPP) was founded as a left-wing anti-colonial party by Cheddi Jagan in 1950 but came to be supported almost exclusively by the Indian-descended community (49% of the population). Jagan won elections and held office under colonial rule, but following independence power was held continuously until 1992 by the People's National Congress Party (PNC), with its base in the African-descended community (32% of the population).

The PPP was in its early years heavily communist-influenced, but in Oct. 1992 Jagan was elected president as a democratic socialist. Jagan died in March 1997 and in elections in Dec. 1997 his widow, Janet Jagan, was declared the winner in the face of claims by the PNC that the vote had been rigged (similar claims against the PNC had been a feature of its years in office). The PPP also won a majority in the legislature. Through several months in 1998 there were repeated disturbances and attacks on Indian-owned businesses which the PPP said were being organized by the opposition (which boycotted the National Assembly) to destabilize the government. In June 1998, however, a CARICOM inquiry concluded that there had been no fraud.

In the 1970s the ruling PNC adopted a strongly left-wing position influenced by Marxism–Leninism. The 1980 constitution declared a socialist society and three-quarters of the economy was socialized. From 1987, however, under Desmond Hoyte, the PNC shifted to free market policies and Jagan was elected in 1992 on a platform that promised to continue this policy to attract foreign investment. Prior to 1998 Guyana had enjoyed six consecutive years of growth at 5% p.a., but political unrest contributed to negative growth in 1998. Agriculture is the principal productive sector and sugar the main export crop. The bauxite sector is also a principal export earner.

GDP (purchasing power parity) $1.86bn. (1999 est.); GDP per capita (purchasing power parity) $2,500 (1999 est.).

2 Trade Unionism

Unions have existed since the establishment of the British Guiana Labour Union (BGLU) by Hubert Critchlow in 1922. The Guyana Trades Union Congress (GTUC or TUC) was founded in 1941. Guyana ratified ILO Convention No.87 (Freedom of Association and Protection of the Right to Organize, 1948) in 1967 and Convention No.98 (Right to Organize and Collective Bargaining, 1949) in 1966. The constitution protects trade union rights and legislation passed by the PPP government since 1992 has included the Trade Union Recognition Act, in effect from 1999, which requires employers to recognize a union where it enjoys majority support. About 34% of the workforce is unionized with most union members working in the public sector and state-owned enterprises.

The unions have been divided in their allegiances between the PNC and the PPP, with the division (as of the two political parties) largely on racial lines. The Guyana Agricultural and General Workers' Union (GAWU), the biggest union in Guyana, is close to the PPP and has had a difficult relationship with the ICFTU-affiliated Guyana Trades Union Congress (GTUC), where the influence of PNC supporters is strong. For many years, the GAWU stood outside the GTUC, calling itself a suspended member, and was the leading member of a Federation of Independent Trade Unions in Guyana (FITUG) set up in opposition to the GTUC in 1988 by unaffiliated or PPP-supporting unions.

The GAWU subsequently rejoined the GTUC. In April–June 1999, however, a nine-week public service pay strike (ultimately referred to arbitration) was led by the Guyana Public Service Union (GPSU), whose president, Patrick Yarde, also headed the GTUC. GTUC support to the strike led the GAWU to suspend its membership in the GTUC. The GAWU argued that the strike was politically inspired by supporters of the opposition PNC and had led to intimidation of workers, attacks on police, denial of medical treatment to Indian patients, attacks on Indian businesses, and lost jobs.

Collective bargaining exists in both in the public and private sectors and under the Trade Union Recognition Act employers must bargain with unions enjoying majority support. The centralized bargaining position formerly allotted to the GTUC under a 1984 Act was ended in 1993 (i.e. after the PNC lost power). The state's involvement in Guyanese industrial relations arose from its position as employer of nearly half the nation's workforce, and was shaped in part by close links between the ruling PNC and the GTUC. Before 1992, when the PPP was in opposition, strikes were often led by the Guyana Agricultural & General Workers' Union (GAWU). Retaliatory measures by employers against strikers are restricted by the Trade Union Recognition Act.

3 Trade Union Centre

Guyana Trades Union Congress (GTUC)

Address. Critchlow Labour College, Woolford Avenue, Non Pareil Park, Georgetown

Phone. +592 2 61493

Fax. +592 2 70254

E-mail. gtuc@guyana.net

Leadership. Lincoln Lewis (general secretary)

History and character. The GTUC originated in 1941 as the British Guiana Trades Union Council. While in power the PNC government (while disavowing an intention to control the GTUC) generally retained a dominant influence in it, allegedly in part by the creation of small PNC-controlled unions which made exaggerated membership claims to secure a disproportionate representation at GTUC congresses. There has been persistent conflict between the GTUC and the pro-PPP Guyana Agricultural and General Workers' Union (GAWU), the leading individual union in Guyana. The GAWU suspended its affiliation again in May 1999, GAWU leader Komal Chand stating that "the TUC cannot earn the respect of all the workers when it continues to facilitate paper unions and allows affiliated unions to register with greater numbers of members than they represent at the workplaces".

The GTUC's former role in centralized collective bargaining was ended in 1993. It comprises 22 afffiliated unions.

International affiliations. ICFTU; CTUC

4 Other Trade Union Organizations

Guyana Agricultural and General Workers' Union (GAWU)

Address. 104–106 Regent Street, Lacytown, Georgetown

Phone. +592 2 72091

Fax. +592 2 72093

E-mail. gawu@networksgy.com

Membership. 21,000

Leadership. Komal Chand (president); Seepaul Narine (general secretary)

History and character. The GAWU is the biggest union in Guyana. It was founded in 1946 as the Guiana Industrial Workers' Union but lapsed in the 1950s when the country's constitution was suspended by the colonial power. It was resurrected as the Guyana Sugar Workers' Union in 1961, then renamed in 1962 as the Guyana Agricultural Workers' Union and finally took its present name later in the decade. Its membership is predominantly of Asian descent.

The GAWU is affiliated to the PPP and says that from 1964–92, while the PNC was in government and had the support of many of the unions, Guyana declined from being among the most prosperous economies in the Caribbean to the level of Haiti.

Having rejoined the Guyana Trades Union Congress (GTUC), GAWU in May 1999 again suspended its membership after the GTUC executive council recommended its affiliates to take part in a 3-day general strike to support striking public sector workers. The

GAWU maintained that grievance procedures had not been exhausted, that the pay demands were unreasonable in view of the difficult economic situation, and that the strike was politically motivated by a section in the GTUC allied to the opposition PNC.

Publication. Combat

International affiliation. WFTU; IUF

National Workers' Union (NWU)

Address. PO Box 12 12213, Bourda, Georgetown

Phone. +592 2 72091

Fax. +592 2 70322

Leadership. Rohan Jahessar (president)

International affiliation. WCL

Haiti

Capital: Port-au-Prince
Population: 6.87 m. (2000 est.)

GDP per capita (purchasing power parity) $1340 (1999 est.).

1 Political and Economic Background

Haiti was ruled from 1957 to 1986 by the authoritarian and repressive Duvalier family, after which there was civil turmoil and military intervention. Jean-Bertrand Aristide was elected President in 1990; he was deposed by the army the following year and then restored by US intervention in Sept. 1994. Since then the political situation has remained unstable. Legislative elections held in Apr. 1997 (in which Aristide's Lavalas party won majorities in both houses of the National Assembly) were in June 1999 declared invalid by the Provisional Electoral Council. Further, disputed, elections in 2000 resulted in victory for Lavalas and Aristide's election as President. There are regular political killings. The armed forces have been demobilized and replaced by the Haitian National Police.

Under "Papa Doc" and "Baby Doc" Duvalier Haiti became the poorest country in the Western Hemisphere, known for the prevalence of voodoo cults and endemic violence. 75% of the population still live in abject poverty. There are acute shortages of skilled labour and massive unemployment and under-employment. 70% of the population is dependent on agriculture, which is mainly subsistence farming, and there has been little job creation in the formal economy since 1995. There is a small industrial sector including the assembly of electronic and other goods for the export market (principally the USA, which accounts for over half of Haiti's exports).

GDP (purchasing power parity) $9.2bn. (1999 est.);

2 Trade Unionism

Several trade union centres functioned in the period from 1946–57, but following the assumption of power by François "Papa Doc" Duvalier in 1957, unions were either eliminated or brought under government control. The ICFTU-affiliated Union National d'Ouvriers d'Haiti (UNOH), the principal centre before 1957, functioned in exile for a time but then lapsed. Haiti ratified ILO Convention No.98 (Right to Organize and Collective Bargaining, 1949) in 1957, shortly before Duvalier came to power, and Convention No.87 (Freedom of Association and Protection of the Right to Organize, 1948) in 1979.

During Aristide's brief period in office in 1990–91, the unions enjoyed some assistance from the administration. But after his overthrow union operations were effectively nullified by repression and a great number of leading figures killed or driven underground or into exile. Even after the 1994 restoration there were continued attacks and even murders of trade unionists, albeit far fewer in number.

Figures for union membership in Haiti are unreliable. According to the US State Department Human Rights Report for 1999 there are six principal labour federations, representing about 5% of the work force, with most union members in the Port-au-Prince area, state enterprises, the civil service, and assembly sector. Unions were reportedly generally free to operate although there is little enforcement of laws protecting rights of association under the constitution and labour code. Collective bargaining does not exist.

Honduras

Capital: Tegucigalpa
Population: 6.25 m. (2000 est.)

1 Political and Economic Background

Honduras has had a number of military regimes but since 1981 has experienced civilian administration, with the military nonetheless remaining an important factor in politics. In 1993 the centrist Liberal Party of Honduras (PLH) won back power from the conservative National Party of Honduras (PNH), and the PLH secured a further victory in presidential and congressional elections in Nov. 1997. The government has sought to reduce the independent power of the military: in 1997, the (Roman Catholic) Archbishop of Tegucigalpa became head of the national police force on an interim basis during its transition from military to civilian control, while the post of Commander-in-Chief of the Armed Forces was abolished. It was reported that a planned coup by a section of the Army in July 1999 had been thwarted.

Honduras is a poor and heavily indebted country. The economy is largely agricultural, with bananas, coffee, timber and sugar as leading exports. There is vulnerability to hurricane damage and fluctuations in commodity prices. There is also a substantial export processing sector. Both the main parties, the PLH and PNH, campaigned on free market platforms in the 1997 elections.

GDP (purchasing power parity) $14.1bn. (1999 est.); GDP per capita (purchasing power parity) $2,050 (1999 est.).

2 Trade Unionism

Widespread strikes and unrest in 1954 forced the US-owned United Fruit Company to negotiate with its employees. In 1955 the government extended legal recognition and the right to strike to trade unions, and Honduras ratified ILO Conventions No.87 (Freedom of Association and Protection of the Right to Organize, 1948) and No.98 (Right to Organize and Collective Bargaining, 1949) in 1956. Thereafter trade unionism remained alive in Honduras despite the assassination of many union activists (especially in peasant unions), the use of blacklisting, intimidation and corruption by employers, and waves of organized repression. There was a general improvement in the human rights situation in Honduras in the late 1990s.

Unions operate free of government control but represent only an estimated 14% of the workforce. Much of the population works on the land and peasant organizations affiliate to the unions. Attempts have been made by employers to introduce a solidarismo movement in Honduras, on the Costa Rican model, though only with limited success.

Only one union may be formed per enterprise and some agricultural workers are excluded from labour code protections. While the labour code provides formal protection against victimization by employers for union activities, harassment or dismissal of union organizers nonetheless occurs. The courts may compel employers to re-hire workers dismissed for union activities but such rulings are not common. Collective bargaining exists in companies where unions are established. Public sector strikes are banned, other than in state-owned enterprises, although strikes by public sector workers in areas such as health and education do in practice occur. Federations and confederations may not legally call strikes.

There has been international criticism of conditions in the export processing zones (EPZs, or maquiladoras), where 90,000 are employed, and US companies imposed controls on suppliers after unfavourable publicity in 1996. South Korean and Taiwanese-owned firms have been particularly criticized. However, a significant minority of plants in the EPZs have agreed to recognize unions after the employers' association adopted a voluntary code in 1997 recognizing the right to organize. Controversy has also surrounded practices in the banana plantations, where the unions allege the indiscriminate use of dangerous pesticides. The unions are highly critical of the labour inspection scheme.

3 Trade Union Centres

Central General de Trabajadores (CGT)

Address. Apartado Postal 1236, Tegucigalpa DC

Phone +504 225 25 09

Fax. +504 225 25 06

Leadership. Felícito Avila (secretary-general)

History and character. The CGT is traditionally closely linked to the National Party of Honduras (PNH), which was most recently in office from 1989 to 1993. Its membership, previously reported as 65,000, includes organizations of peasants and shanty dwellers.

International affiliation. WCL

Confederación de Trabajadores de Honduras (CTH) Honduras Workers' Confederation

Address. Apartado Postal 720, Tegucigalpa

Phone. +504 238 7859

Fax. +504 237 4243

History and character. The CTH is the largest union centre in Honduras and was founded in 1964.

International affiliation. ICFTU

Hungary

Capital: Budapest
Population: 10.14 m. (2000 est.)

1 Political and Economic Background

Following World War II Hungary was under communist control for more than four decades until it became one of the first Soviet bloc countries to break free. Political change and liberal economic reforms accelerated from the mid-1980s and in Feb. 1989 the ruling Hungarian Socialist Workers' Party conceded political pluralism. In Oct. 1989 the Hungarian Republic was declared in succession to the former People's Republic. Power has changed hands at successive elections since the introduction of multi-partyism. Elections in May 1990 resulted in the formation of a government by the centre-right Hungarian Democratic Forum (MDF). In May 1994 elections, the reformed former communists of the Hungarian Socialist Party (MSzP) became the largest party and formed a coalition government with the liberal Alliance of Free Democrats (SzDSz). Most recently, elections in May 1998 resulted in the MSzP taking second place to the centre-right Federation of Young Democrats–Hungarian Civic Party (FIDESz–MPP), and FIDESz–MPP now leads a coalition government headed by Prime Minister Viktor Orban and including the Independent Smallholders' Party (FKGP) and the MDF.

Prior to 1989 the Hungarian economy was predominantly under state ownership. Hungary's post-communist transition has been among the most successful of any country, with continuity between different governments, after overcoming the initial shock that resulted in falling living standards in the early 1990s. It has largely completed its privatization programme and 80% of GDP is now generated by the private sector. It joined the OECD in 1996 and is currently negotiating accession to the EU. In recent years it has enjoyed economic growth (put at 4.1% in 1999) and a generally stable social and economic environment.

GDP (purchasing power parity) $79.4bn. (1999 est.); GDP per capita (purchasing power parity) $7,800 (1999 est.).

2 Trade Unionism

The first Hungarian unions were founded in the 1860s under the Austro-Hungarian Empire and a Central Trade Union Council (formed by the Social Democratic Party) was put on a permanent basis in 1899. Under the Horthy regime (1920–44) independent unionism was curbed or banned but under communist rule the Council became the Central Council of Hungarian Trade Unions (SZOT). For 40 years SZOT was Hungary's official and inclusive centre, though challenged briefly in 1956 when independent workers' councils emerged to stage a general strike against military intervention by the USSR. Hungary ratified ILO Conventions No.87 (Freedom of Association and Protection of the Right of Organize, 1948) and No.98 (Right to Organize and Collective Bargaining, 1949) in 1957, i.e. shortly after the suppression of the independent workers' councils formed outside the single trade union structure. Hungary's pre-1989 constitution did not formally prohibit the formation of other trade unions outside this structure, provided they undertook to protect and construct socialist society.

Organizational change in SZOT – aimed at separating the centre from the state – anticipated the fall of communism by about a year. In March 1990, SZOT was dissolved with two-thirds of its affiliates forming a new centre the Confederation of Hungarian Trade Unions (MSzOSz). Although it quickly lost about half of its members MSzOSz became and remained the principal centre. In 1993 it reported a membership of 1,370,000, of whom almost two-thirds were wage-earners, but active membership is now under 500,000. Initially MSzOSz inherited all the substantial assets of SZOT, estimated at 4.5 billion forints, but under pressure of legislation the centres agreed a division among themselves and MSzOSz retained only 40 per cent. The trade union press was also the subject of an amicable settlement, with the daily *Népszava* (Voice of the People) becoming the joint property of all unions.

MSzOSz is now affiliated to the ICFTU, which also has two other smaller Hungarian affiliates. These are the Autonomous Trade Union Confederation (ASzSz) and the Democratic Confederation of Free Trade Unions (LIGA). The WCL's affiliate is the MOSz (National Federation of Workers' Councils) and there is no WFTU affiliate. Public service unions have also formed the Forum for the Cooperation of Trade Unions (SzEF). Some unions do not affiliate to any of these centres. In general, the different centres have tended to have positive relations with each other.

The 1992 labour code recast the legal framework of trade unions and industrial relations and provided for trade union pluralism and collective bargaining. Among the issues it covered were wages and taxes, union elections, the administration of unemployment benefit, and the distribution of the assets of the former communist unions. It also provided for the establishment of works councils in any enterprise employing more than 50 workers. When elections to works councils were held in 1993, MSzOSz showed a clear lead with 53% of the vote, followed by LIGA with 17% and MOSz with 15%.

Union density overall is about 30% and has not changed greatly following the initial impact of the changes in 1989–90. Some large-scale industrial enterprises, such as chemicals, electricity and the railways are almost completely unionized, but unions are weak in small enterprises and emergent private sector services. Some employers actively discriminate against union organizers and the unions complain of lack of redress because of ambiguities in the law and backlogs of cases in the labour courts. Some foreign-owned companies have set up company unions. The unions believe that the government favours lax enforcement of labour regulations to encourage foreign investment.

The 1992 labour code provides for collective bargaining at the industry or enterprise level. About 50% of workers are covered by collective agreements, struck mostly at workplace level, but many private sector employers actively resist collective bargaining. The detailed content of collective bargaining agreements has commonly been shrinking in recent years, and often includes little more than the basic terms guaranteed by the labour code. Public servants may negotiate working conditions, but Parliament must approve salary increases. In 1999 the government proposed to give works councils the right to conclude collective bargaining agreements, which was interpreted by the unions as a threat to their position. Employees except the military and police officers have the right to strike, though strikes have been fairly uncommon in the post-communist period.

The unions have generally supported the process of political and economic reconstruction, including associated job losses in inefficient industries, under which Hungary has become a market economy and one of the most successful and stable of the post-communist societies, with a high likelihood of early admission to the EU. However, the centre-right government elected in 1998 has been accused of moving away from tripartism and seeking to weaken the position of the unions. The tripartite Interest Reconciliation Council (IRC), on which the trade union centres were all represented, provided a framework for agreement on the minimum wage, wage recommendations and broader socio-economic issues. However, arguing that it wished to end corporatism, the government in 1999 abolished this and set up alternative structures, such as the National Labour Affairs Council (OMT) which the unions say provide forums for airing opinions but are disregarded by government. One consequence is that there was no tripartite agreement for 2000 on a general wage recommendation, although the unions and employers made a bilateral recommendation. The government has also abolished the Ministry of Labour, which was established in 1990 to monitor employment, wages and wage policy, labour legislation, vocational training, and labour safety regulation and to represent the government in tripartite structures. The functions of the Ministry have been split between the Economics Ministry and newly created Ministry of Social and Family Affairs (the latter being given employment issues and responsibility for drafting labour-related legislation).

3 Trade Union Centres

Autonóm Szakszervezetek Szövetsége (ASzSz)
Autonomous Trade Union Confederation

Address. Benczúr út. 45, 1046 Budapest

Phone. +36 1 342 1774

Fax. +36 1 342 9975

E-mail. autonom@euroweb.hu

International affiliations. ICFTU; ETUC

Független Szakszervezetek Demokratikus Ligája (LIGA, or FSzDL)
LIGA Democratic Confederation of Free Trade Unions

Address. Thokoly út. 156, 1146 Budapest

Phone. +36 1 251 2300

Fax. +36 1 251 2288

Leadership. Istvàn Gaskó (president)

Membership. 98,000. Leading affiliates represent railway workers, metalworkers, teachers, transport and construction workers.

History and character. LIGA was the first non-communist union confederation in Hungary. It was founded early in 1989 to break communist control and, though it failed to gain majority status after this it emerged as a strong minority and second to MSzOSz in the works councils elections of 1993. It was seen as close to the liberal Alliance of Free Democrats (SzDSz). It is one of the ICFTU's three Hungarian affiliates.

Publications. Liga Harsona

International affiliations. ICFTU, ETUC, TUAC

Magyar Szakszervezetek Országos Szövetsége (MSzOSz)
National Confederation of Hungarian Trade Unions

Address. Dózsa György út. 84/b, 1068 Budapest

Phone. +36 1 478 5266 (international department)

Fax. +36 1 342 1799 (international department)

E-mail. kgyorgy@mszosz.hu

Website. www.mszoz.hu (Hungarian; English section)

Leadership. Dr. László Sandor (president)

Membership. 465.000 active members and 250,000 pensioners and apprentices, in 43 affiliated unions.

History and character. MSzOSz was formed out of the former official communist centre SZOT, which was the only national centre until 1988. Radical changes in organization, policy and personnel began that year and anticipated the impact of the collapse of the Berlin Wall in 1989. The Dec. 1988 congress ended the dependence of SZOT on the party, redefined its principal objective as safeguarding the interests of the employed, and determined to convene a transformation congress. In March 1990 SZOT was dissolved and MSzOSz founded with the support of about two-thirds of SZOT affiliates.

From that point on MSzOSz focused on advocacy of agreements on behalf of wage-earners in the fairly hostile atmosphere of the early 1990s. The other centres were sharply critical of the way it had inherited SZOT's assets, and a law of July 1991 would have divided these on the basis of electoral support in a special poll. However, MSzOSz reached an agreement with other centres in Sept. 1992 by which it retained 40%. The works council elections of 1993 confirmed and legitimized the premier position of MSzOSz, with it taking over half of all votes. In 1993 its ICFTU affiliation figure was 1,368,500, but membership is now about half this.

MSzOSz, despite being the leading single centre, has not been able to achieve unequivocal national leadership, partly because of its descent from the communist-era SZOT and partly because of its closeness to the reformed communist Hungarian Socialist Party (MSzP).

MSzOSz's orientation is broadly social democratic although it comprises a spectrum of views. It supports Hungary's proposed accession to the EU, currently being negotiated, and called for ratification of the European Social Charter (ratified by Hungary in 1999) and a programme of "social stabilization" alongside financial and economic stabilization to meet EU standards. This would include comprehensive reform in areas such as social security, pensions, health insurance, taxation and health and safety. MSzOSz calls for a 38-hour week within four years and active measures to combat Hungary's problems of unemployment (8.8% in 1999) and underemployment, Hungary having a rate of participation in the work force (53%) well below the EU average (over 60%), and less than half the EU average in older age groups most affected by the restructuring of the Hungarian economy. It also wishes to see the European Trade Union Confederation (ETUC) develop as an effective pan-European voice for labour.

MSzOSz says that it has contributed positively as a social partner to the successful restructuring of the Hungarian economy in the 1990s. It is critical of what it sees as the movement of the centre-right government elected in 1998 away from tripartism and accuses it of abandoning social dialogue, as in the 1999 abolition of the Council for Interest Conciliation.

International affiliations. ICFTU; ETUC; TUAC

Munkástanácsok Országos Szövetsége (MOSz)
National Federation of Workers' Councils (NFWC)

Address. Tárogáto út. 2-4, 1021 Budapest

Phone. +36 1 275 1445

Fax. +36 1 394 2802

E-mail. mosz.int.dept@pronet.hu

Leadership. Imre Palkovics (president); Imre Nagy (vice-president)

Membership. 56,000

History and character. Workers' Councils emerged in 1989 as they had during the events of 1956. In the context of trade union pluralism MOSz has sought to provide an alternative, sympathetic to Christian democratic values.

International affiliation. WCL; ETUC

Szakszervezetek Együttmüködési Fóruma (SzEF)
Forum for the Cooperation of Trade Unions

Address. Puskin út. 4, 1088 Budapest

Phone. +36 1 338 26 51

Fax. +36 1 318 73 60

E-mail. szef@mail.matavnet.hu

Website. www.szef.westel.hu (Hungarian; English section)

Leadership. Dr. Endre Szabó (president)

Membership. Reports 274,000 active members and 172,000 retired.

History and character. SzEF represents mainly white-collar workers in public education, social services and health care, cultural institutes, state and local government, and the legal system. It was founded in June 1990 by a loose alliance of 30 organizations as a standing consultative forum. In response to deteriorating conditions in the public service it was re-launched as a professional organization at the first SzEF congress in May 1995. It joined the ETUC in 1998 and held its second congress in 1999. It is independent of political parties.

International affiliations. ETUC

Iceland

Capital: Reykjavik
Population: 276,000 (2000 est.)

1 Political and Economic Background

Iceland was a Danish possession until 1944, although with home rule from 1874. Since independence the leading party has usually been the liberal-conservative Independence Party (IP), which has led coalition governments with a range of other parties. Following elections in May 1999, in which the IP remained the largest party, it has been in coalition with the centrist Progressive Party. The IP's David Oddsson has been Prime Minister since 1991.

Iceland's economy has a heavy dependence on fishing and fishing products, which generate the bulk of export earnings although providing only 12% of jobs. Fish stocks in the North Atlantic are in decline and Iceland has ongoing disputes with various nations over fishing rights, while fear of loss of control of fisheries is a leading reason for Iceland not wishing to join the EU. The economy is diversifying into areas including financial services, tourism, software development and biotechnology. There has been a gradual process of privatization since the early 1990s, with the largest privatization, of Iceland Telecom, scheduled for 2001. Iceland has a high standard of living with a developed welfare state, low unemployment, even income distribution and a high level of social cohesion.

GDP (purchasing power parity) $6.06bn. (1998 est.); GDP per capita (purchasing power parity) $22,400 (1998 est.).

2 Trade Unionism

Iceland ratified ILO Convention No.87 (Freedom of Association and Protection of the Right to Organize, 1948) in 1950 and Convention No.98 (Right to Organize and Collective Bargaining, 1949) in 1952. The labour laws were revised in 1996, with the objective of bringing them into compliance with the European Convention for the Protection of Human Rights and Fundamental Freedoms.

Iceland's workforce of 150,000 is highly organized, with union density estimated at 80%. The law prohibits acts of antiunion discrimination and employers may be required to reinstate workers dismissed for union activities. There are two trade union centres, both affiliated to the ICFTU. The larger is the Icelandic Federation of Labour (ASÍ), to which about 73,000 workers are affiliated including a high proportion of private sector employees. The other centre is the Confederation of State and Municipal Employees of Iceland (BSRB),

which has 18,000 members in the public sector. The unions are politically independent.

Prior to 1988 the ASÍ and the Confederation of Icelandic Employers (CIE) usually made a national framework agreement to be followed by federation level bargaining. This pattern broke down and the government intervened with a ban on strikes and a wage freeze, leading the ASÍ to file a complaint with the ILO Committee on Freedom of Association in 1991. In 1995 the Committee asked the government "to refrain in future from having recourse to such measures of legislative intervention". In recent years, the government has played almost no role in private-sector collective bargaining.

Most workers have the right to strike. Public sector workers have had the right to strike since 1986, although with a requirement to maintain services essential to health and safety. There were no strikes in 1999.

3 Trade Union Centres

Althydusamband Íslands (ASÍ)
Icelandic Federation of Labour

Address. PO Box 8720, Reykjavik 128

Phone. +354 581 3044

Fax. +354 568 0093

E-mail. skrifst@asi.is

Website. www.asi.is (Icelandic only; English to be added)

Leadership. Gretar Thorsteinsson (president); Ari Skulason (general secretary)

Membership. 73,000

History and character. The ASÍ was established on a permanent basis in 1916. The federation was organizationally part of the Social Democratic Party until 1940, when it became (as it remains) an independent trade union federation without political ties. It affiliates close to half the Icelandic work force. Public sector workers are organized separately in the BSRB.

Originally individual trade unions were direct members of the ASI; after about 1950, however, unions in a number of sectors organized their own national federations, and now have indirect membership in the ASÍ through those federations. Only a few unions remain directly affiliated to the ASÍ. The federation is financed mainly by pro rata contributions from the member unions, but receives limited government funding to support some of its cultural, educational and other activities.

The ASÍ established a Workers' Educational Association in 1969, and it also has its own art gallery and travel bureau, and a share in a cooperative trade union bank.

Publications. Vinnan (6 times per year)

International affiliations. ETUC; ICFTU; TUAC; NFS

Bandalag Starfsmanna Rikis og Baeja (BSRB)
Confederation of State and Municipal Employees of
Iceland

Address. Grettisgata 89, 105 Reykjavik

Phone. +354 562 6688

Fax. +354 562 9106

E-mail. bsrb@bsrb.is

Website. www.bsrb.is (Icelandic, summary in English)

Leadership. Ogmundur Jonasson (chairman)

Membership. 18,000

History and character. Founded in 1942, the BSRB represents 35 unions of public service employees. Two-thirds of its members are women.

The BSRB provides support for collective bargaining by its member unions. A particular concern is the privatization of public services. The BSRB says that while it is not categorically opposed to privatization per se, it has opposed "privatization for the sake of privatization", which it says was carried out through the 1990s and is now planned for telecommunications and the postal service.

Publications. BSRB-Tidindi

International affiliations. ICFTU, ETUC, NFS, PSI

India

Capital: New Delhi
Population: 1.014bn. (2000 est.)

1 Political and Economic Background

India gained independence from the United Kingdom in 1947, when the sub-continent was divided into the new states of India and Pakistan. The Union of India, comprising 25 self-governing states and seven union territories, is under its constitution (with amendments which came into force in 1977) "a sovereign socialist secular democratic republic". The legislative field is divided between the Union and the states, the former possessing exclusive powers to make laws on foreign affairs, defence, citizenship and trade with other countries. Central legislative power is vested in Parliament, consisting of the President (who appoints a Prime Minister and a Council of Ministers), the indirectly-elected Council of States (Rajya Sabha, the upper house) and the directly elected House of the People (Lok Sabha).

The Indian National Congress–Congress (I) party, which has a broadly socialist and secularist orientation, has been the governing party for most of the period since it led India to independence in 1947, although it has suffered various splits. It first went into opposition after elections in 1977, having tried to rule through widely detested emergency powers from 1975. It regained power in 1980 and then held office until 1996, other than for a period in 1989–91. Successive Congress Prime Ministers, Indira Gandhi and her son Rajiv, were assassinated, in 1984 and 1991 respectively.

In the general elections of Apr.–May 1996, Congress-I was heavily defeated, winning only 136 of the 534 seats declared. The Hindu-based BJP party, with 161 seats, emerged as the largest single party but there has since been a series of weak coalition governments. Following elections in Sept.–Oct. 1999, the BJP remained the largest party in the Lok Sabha and leads a multi-party coalition National Democratic Alliance government, headed by BJP Prime Minister Atal Bihari Vajpayee. Varying coalitions hold the state governments.

India's population is 80% Hindu and tensions between the majority and the 14% Muslim minority have been a recurrent theme, although the BJP in government has moderated its earlier Hindu fundamentalism. A 1999 report by Human Rights Watch said that oppression of India's 160 million Dalits ("untouchables") had increased dramatically in the 1990s. There are separatist movements active in various parts of the country, notably Kashmir.

The dominant economic activity in India is peasant cultivation, which accounts for two-thirds of the labour force, although agriculture represents only 25% of GDP. India also has a diversity of industries, ranging from traditional areas such as textiles, chemicals, food processing, steel, cement and machinery, to important new sectors in pharmaceuticals and information technology. There is a vast informal economy and the population growth rate (adding 15–20 million per year) is a major downward drag on per capita income growth. India has had some success in attracting inward investment but onerous regulations have been a deterrent and it suffers from poor infrastructure in areas such as power, telecommunications and transport. India has 246 public sector enterprises, which include steel plants, airlines, chemical and mining companies, and hotels, and there has been no concerted campaign to privatize these in the face of entrenched opposition, although a department of disinvestment was set up in 1999 with the stated object of accelerating sell-offs. Both the bureaucracy and the unions have strongly resisted privatization. However, India's fiscal deficit in 1999 was 10% of GDP and the IMF warned India in June 2000 that, "downscaling of the public sector is the need of the hour".

In the 1990s governments have sought to move away from central planning and introduce free market reforms, but these have been held back by the weakness of successive coalition governments and the entrenched Indian tradition of bureaucratic regulation. India began to open export processing zones (EPZs) in the 1980s but only a handful survive. In Apr. 2000 it was reported that India is planning to create special economic zones on the Chinese model to improve its export performance.

GDP (purchasing power parity) $1.805 trillion (1999 est.); GDP per capita (purchasing power parity) $1,800 (1999 est.).

2 Trade Unionism

India has ratified neither ILO Convention No.87 (Freedom of Association and Protection of the Right to Organize, 1948) nor No. 98 (Right to Organize and Collective Bargaining, 1949). However, freedom of association has existed since the Trade Union Act of 1926 and collective bargaining and the right to strike both exist, although these have been increasingly restricted.

Illiteracy, caste and religious animosities inhibited the early development of trade unions. Development was also restricted because unions tended, at least until World War I, almost always to recruit members from a narrow labour aristocracy. The seasonal and migratory nature of much industrial labour, as well as the control of workers through company housing, also contributed to a relatively weak trade union movement. In 1920, however, the All-India Trade Union Congress (AITUC) was formed; this remained the principal centre until after independence in 1947 when it became the focus of intense conflict between nationalists and communists. This stemmed from differences that had surfaced during the World War II when the Communist Party chose, against nationalist opinion, to support Britain's war effort. Having done so, its members were able not only to escape imprisonment, unlike their nationalist colleagues, but also effectively to gain control of the AITUC. The wartime split led the ruling Congress Party in 1947 to favour and sponsor the creation of a rival Indian National Trade Union Congress (INTUC).

There is no one clearly dominant trade union centre. INTUC has generally been considered the largest in recent decades, and still claims to have 6 million members. Its close relationship with the Congress Party was undoubtedly a major factor in its favour for most of the period since independence, and it has likewise declined in influence as the Congress's power has waned. Conversely, the Bharatiya Mazdoor Sangh (BMS), with links to the BJP, has benefited from the rise of that party and the movement it represents. In 1996, official figures of the "verified memberships" of the different centres indicated that the BMS had overhauled INTUC. While the BMS's rivals challenged the validity of the figures, it is clear that the BMS has emerged as a major player. The third largest centre is the Hind Mazdoor Sabha (HMS) claiming five million members and founded by socialists opposed to government domination of INTUC. It has a strong industrial base and, like INTUC, is affiliated to the ICFTU. The All-India Trades Union Congress (AITUC) was the national centre until independence when Congress inspired the foundation of the INTUC: AITUC is linked to the Communist Party of India (CPI) and has a WFTU affiliation. The Centre of Indian Trade Unions (CITU) is linked to the Communist Party of India–Marxist (CPI(M)), with particular strength in West Bengal and Kerala.

The total number and membership of trade unions is uncertain and contentious and it is common for unions to exaggerate membership figures. Official "verified membership" figures are always disputed, partly because verification has significance for determining representation on public bodies. The high level of politicization, the lack of a sound mass base in many sectors, the looseness of ties between local and central unions, and the lack of adequate financial resources have reduced the organizational cohesion of the unions. Furthermore, there is no institutionalized system for the recognition of a union, which in effect depends on union strength in a given plant and the attitude of the employer. Total union membership is estimated as being approximately of the order of 13–15 million. As a percentage of the entire active workforce of 400 million, the unionized proportion is very small. However, whereas most Indians work on the land or in the informal sector, most union members are in the much smaller formal sector of the economy, which accounts for only about 30 million jobs. Unions are also concentrated in key industries and service sectors, such as railways, telecommunications, airlines and banks, and so have an influence disproportionate to their numerical strength. This has been amplified by their close alliances with political parties. Other than some traditional strongholds such as the jute industry, the unions are strongest in India's extensive public sector industries, which is reflected in the particular opposition of unions to privatization. Many new private sector enterprises are resistant to recognizing unions, which employers see as difficult to deal with, resistant to change and highly political.

Nearly all agricultural workers (except in tea and other plantations), as well as domestic and casual workers, are unorganized. It is estimated that the range of legal protections of workers' rights are effective or meaningful only in respect of the 30 million workers in the formal industrial sector, compared with a total workforce of some 400 million. The influence of organized labour is further weakened by the high levels of unemployment and under-employment and availability of non-union casual labour. In general, organized workers constitute a comparative elite, and the unions have overall done little to ameliorate the plight of the non-union masses in sweatshops, the informal economy and on the land.

The plight of rural workers in particular is, however, now being taken up more vigorously not only by well-established organizations like INTUC, but also by bodies like the Confederation of Indian Rural Workers' Unions (Hind Keth Mazdoor Sabha – HKMS) which is affiliated to the HMS. The Confederation has appealed for rural poverty and unemployment to be relieved not so much by aid and food hand-outs, but by the creation of job opportunities for the needy through a programme of extensive public works. Many workers on the land face seasonal unemployment and destitution.

While the different centres sometimes have found common ground (notably in resisting, with some success, proposals to amend the labour laws), they are generally divided by political alignments. The INTUC and AITUC both supported the Emergency declared from 1975–77 (despite the suspension of trade union rights and ban on strikes), in line with the position of the political parties with which they were associated, i.e. the Congress Party and the Communist Party of India (CPI). In 1994 the communist centres, AITUC and CITU, together with the socialist HMS and a number of industrial and public service federations, farmers' and agricultural workers' organizations, women's and youth and students' movements, convened the National Platform of Mass Organizations (NPMO). The immediate impetus behind formation of the platform was opposition to the (Congress Party) government's decision to sign the 1994 GATT agreement. This culminated in a general strike, claimed to be the biggest ever in India, on Sept. 29, 1994. The participating organizations claimed the backing of 25 million, with total stoppages in West Bengal, Kerala, Tripura, Tamil Nadu and Bihar, 85% of all coal miners on strike, and a complete shut-down of banking and insurance. Some four million public sector employees also participated. Following the 1998 election of a BJP-led government committed to pushing ahead with reform and privatization of the state sector, including the closure of some particularly unsuccessful enterprises, the NPMO called a one-day national strike on Dec 11, 1998. Organizers claimed the strike was the biggest since independence and it was supported by 56 unions, most of them affiliates of the communist-linked centres, together with most opposition parties (except Congress) and even two of the governing coalition parties. The strike was most successful where it enjoyed the support of state governments, in West Bengal, Kerala and Tripura, all ruled by the Communist-led Left Front, and in Bihar and Tamil Nadu, where regional opposition parties held power. Neither the BMS nor INTUC participated, reflecting their political alignments and the commitment of Congress and BJP to the reform process.

The BJP party (in power in coalition since 1998) has moderated some of its earlier Hindu fundamentalist rhetoric but there are substantial concerns remaining. In Mar. 2000 the BJP-led government, under pressure from Congress-I and also several of the BJP's own coalition partners, reluctantly ordered the government of Gujarat to restore a ban on civil servants being members of the semi-secret fundamentalist organization Rashtriya Swayamsevak Sangh (RSS, Organization of National Volunteers). This has close links to both the BJP and the BMS.

Bonded labour was outlawed in 1976 but there are still widespread reports of its existence, especially on the land. Bonded labourers are bound to work for their creditor until a debt is settled; the effect of a low rate of pay and high interest rates is such that bonded status is commonly life-long or even hereditary. The problem of child labour appears to be equally intractable. Urban child employment tends mostly to be concentrated in hotels and restaurants, building construction sites, automobile workshops, and fireworks and match factories, and children are also widely used as domestic servants. In rural areas children are used in agriculture, herd tending and the hand loom industry. Children are also bonded.

Official and unofficial strikes and demonstrations, often of a highly political nature, are frequent. Many strikes revolve around issues of parity of pay, promotional opportunities and status. There have also been strikes through the 1990s over austerity measures, threats to public sector jobs and terms and conditions, and planned privatization. General strikes are not uncommon but are often localized in effect and confined to a few sectors. However, union militancy has been one factor in the slow progress in reducing the Indian public sector as governments have tended to back down in the face of labour militancy.

The BJP-led government of Prime Minister A.B. Vajpayee was re-elected in the autumn of 1999 on a platform that included reforming India's highly inefficient state-run sector. In Jan. 2000 it faced concerted strikes by power workers in Uttar Pradesh and by dockers nationwide, seen as challenging government plans for eventual privatization. In the power strike, about 4,000 of the 90,000 strikers were sacked, and the main leaders jailed, although reinstatement was offered as part of the compromise settlement.

Employer-union attitudes are commonly adversarial, and the government frequently acts as mediator, a role encouraged historically by the close association of many unions (notably those of INTUC) with the governing Congress Party. Likewise the ideology of the Congress Party, the dominant party for most of the period since independence, has favoured tripartism, which is embedded in the industrial relations system.

3 Trade Union Centres

All-India Trade Union Congress (AITUC)

Address. 24 Canning Lane, New Delhi 110001

Phone. +91 11 338 7320

Fax. +91 11 338 6427

E-mail. aitucong@bol.net.in

Leadership. K.L. Mahendra (secretary-general)

History and character. The AITUC was founded in 1920 and was the primary trade union centre until independence in 1947 and the formation of the Congress Party-linked INTUC. Since then it has been closely linked to the Communist Party of India (CPI). Its traditional strongholds are Karnataka, Andhra Pradesh, Bihar, Gujarat, Delhi, and Punjab. It participates in the National Platform of Mass Organizations which has opposed the efforts of the Congress Party and BJP-led governments in the 1990s to reform public sector enterprises and liberalize the economy. Globally it is one of the most prominent members of the WFTU.

International affiliations. WFTU; CTUC

Bharatiya Mazdoor Sangh (BMS)

Address. Ram Naresh Bhavan, Tilak Gali, Paharganj Ganj, New Delhi 110 055

Leadership. Harshubaih Dubey (general secretary)

History and character. The BMS was founded in July 1955. BMS goals and objectives are inspired by the basic tenets of a Hindu Nationalist socio-cultural organization, the Rashtriya Swayamsevak Sangh, which is also the mother organization of the BJP political party, now in government. The BMS constitution specifically bars politicians and the BMS itself avoids direct political alignments or affiliations. However, the BMS has grown steadily in influence in association with the BJP following that party's establishment as a breakaway from the Janata party in 1980. Its rise paralleled that of the BJP, which went from obscurity in the early 1980s to being the third largest party at the 1989 elections, to second in 1991 and then 1st in elections in 1996, 1998 and 1999. By the mid-1990s, according to official figures for "verified memberships" the BMS was the largest centre, and although this was strongly disputed by its rivals, its rise had clearly been remarkable.

The BMS opposed the New Economic Policy launched by the Congress party in 1991 on the grounds that economic self-reliance would be undermined; that economic sovereignty would be jeopardized; that there would be adverse effects upon employment and inflation, and that the changes were being rushed through under dictation from the World Bank and the IMF. As an alternative the BMS suggested patronizing indigenous consumer goods; publication by manufacturers of their production costs; introduction of new technology on a selective basis "where suitable to the Indian condition"; and (ultimately) evolution of an indigenous economic system.

The formation of a BJP-led government at national level in 1998 has inevitably influenced the BMS's positions to some degree. The BJP by this point had become strongly committed to achieving the New Economic Policy goals that had largely gone unfulfilled by the Congress party. The BMS has, however, criticized the new government for adopting the Congress programme of economic liberalization, while not endorsing the sort of full-scale protests mobilized by some of the other centres. Recent BMS campaigns have included opposition to opening up the insurance sector to the market and against the lifting of restrictions on agricultural imports under World Trade Organization rules.

International affiliations. None

Centre of Indian Trade Unions (CITU)

Address. 15 Talkatora Road, New Delhi 110001

Phone. +91 11 371 4071

Fax. +91 11 335 5856

E-mail. citu@nda.vsnl.net.in

Leadership. M. K. Pandhe (general secretary)

Membership. 2.8m. (1997)

History and character. CITU was formed in 1970. CITU reported that many of its members and officials were driven from their homes or killed in attacks by Congress supporters and other factions in the early and mid-1970s. CITU is closely linked to the Communist Party of India (Marxist), whose power base is in West Bengal, Kerala and Tripura, in all of which communist-led Left Front governments held office in the late 1990s. In 1998 there were reports that a large number of CITU members were defecting to the Communist Party of India-affiliated AITUC amid friction between the Communist Party of India and Communist Party of India (Marxist), the main components of the Left Front coalition ruling West Bengal. The CITU participates in the National Platform of Mass Organizations, which has opposed the efforts of the Congress Party and BJP-led governments in the 1990s to reform public sector enterprises and liberalize the economy.

International affiliations. CTUC

Hind Mazdoor Sabha (HMS)
Indian Labour Organization

Address. (Delhi office) 120 Babar Road, New Delhi 110001

Phone. +91 11 331 5519

Fax. +91 11 373 6037

E-mail. hms@nde.vsnl.com

Website. http://members.rediff.com/hms (English)

Leadership. A.Subramaniam (president)

Membership. 5.02 million

History and character. The HMS was founded on Dec. 29, 1948, in rejection of the communist domination of the AITUC and the control of the INTUC by the Congress Party. It defines its ideals as "secularism, socialism, democracy, free trade unionism and nationalism". It is independent of government, employers and political parties and says it is the only major centre in India not linked to a political party. It has been, however, seen as close to the socialist Janata Dal party.

Its position was one of extreme difficulty during the

Emergency from 1975–77 when the HMS leadership was divided over the issue of acquiescence in the suspension of trade union rights.

The HMS believes in "the overall development of its members", and many of its affiliates run schools, holiday homes, education centres, community halls, and medical and family planning facilities. It has been undertaking a massive workers' education programme and has its own education and research institute, the Maniben Kara Institute, at Bombay, and a Rural Workers' Institute at Talegaon in Maharshtra state. Its Rural Workers' Federation not only organizes rural workers but also assists them in establishing self-employment programmes.

The HMS identifies the New Economic Policy of the 1990s, unemployment, privatization, and the ever increasing mass of unorganized casual and contract workers as among the principal problems facing the Indian trade union movement. It believes the new world trade order will produce joblessness in many domestic industries. It favours an extension of workers' participation in industrial management, a concept that has had little practical result in India despite numerous experiments since 1947.

The HMS has 2,300 affiliated trade unions, organized into 16 industrial federations. Major unions are the railway trade unions throughout India, transport and dock workers' unions in the 10 major ports, Air India employees, plantations, coal, textiles, steel, engineering, forestry, chemicals, seafarers and electricity. About 15% of its membership are women and it is seeking to increase that proportion.

Publications. *HMS Bulletin* (monthly, in English and Hindi)

International affiliations. ICFTU; CTUC

Indian National Trade Union Congress (INTUC)

Address. Shramik Kendra, 4 Bhai Veer Singh Marg, New Delhi 110011

Phone. +91 11 374 7767

Fax. +91 11 336 4244

Website. http://members.rediff.com/intuc

Leadership. Sanjeeva Reddy (president); S. Mookherjee (general secretary)

Membership. 6 million

History and character. INTUC was founded on May 3, 1947, inspired by Gandhian principles, and claims to be the largest trade union centre in India. It is closely linked to the Congress Party and this has allowed it to stay at the centre of trade union affairs and be influential in all industrial relations legislation for most of India's post-independence history.

INTUC says that unlike "the Western trade union movement, whose main concern is the conditions of employment", or the "Eastern trade unions' highly regimented attitude and approach", Gandhi's concept of the movement, on which the INTUC's policies and programmes are based, puts more emphasis on "human considerations". It defines its aim as being to foster a society that is free from hindrances to the development of the human personality and progressively eliminates exploitation and inequality. It defines itself as being "in the vanguard of India's march towards her cherished goal of establishing a secular and socialist democracy" and favours "national ownership and control" of industry.

INTUC is calling for greater protection for the unorganized mass of rural workers, many of them dependent on seasonal employment, and the creation of a system of unemployment benefit.

International affiliations. ICFTU; CTUC

4 Other Trade Union Organization

Confederation of Free Trade Unions of India (CFTUI)

Address. PO Box 7194, Kurla, Bombay 400070

Phone. +91 22 823 10 74

Fax. +91 22 624 05 78

Leadership. Ashok Trivedi (president); Mujeeb Ahmed (general secretary)

History and character. The CFTUI is the former BATU India, a WCL affiliate that acted as an organizing centre and promoter of union education in the sub-continent. In 1994 BATU India resolved to transform itself into the CFTUI in order to consolidate its ranks and build up solidarity. It held its first ordinary congress in Apr. 1999 and became a full member of WCL the same year.

International affiliation. WCL

Indonesia

Capital: Jakarta
Population: 224.8 m. (2000 est.)

1 Political and Economic Background

Indonesian independence was recognized by the Netherlands in 1949. Some 88% of the population is Muslim, making it the most populous predominantly Muslim country in the world. From 1966–98, President Suharto ruled through his New Order regime. From 1971 the government-sponsored Golkar ("Joint Secretariat of Functional Groups") held an absolute majority of seats in the legislature.

For much of Suharto's period of rule, the Indonesian economy grew rapidly, growth exceeding 6% per annum for a quarter of a century. However, the impact of the late 1997 Asian economic crisis on Indonesia was severe. The domestic currency collapsed, GDP contracted by 14% in 1998, and there were massive outflows of capital and rampant inflation. Although Suharto was re-elected in March 1998, widespread unemployment, the return home of laid-off migrant workers from other Asian countries, and cuts on subsidies on prices of fuel, electricity and transport, led to strikes and riots in May 1998 in which 1200 people were killed. Suharto resigned on May 21 and was succeeded by his Vice-President, B.J. Habibie.

Legislative elections in June 1999 resulted in defeat for Golkar and victory for an alliance of the National Awakening Party (PKB), the Democratic Party for Struggle (PDI-P) and the National Mandate Party (PAN). In Oct. 1999 the People's Consultative Assembly elected Abdurrahman Wahid, leader of the PKB and a liberal Muslim cleric, as President, although the Vice-President, Megawati Sukarnoputri of the PDI-P, emerged as an increasingly dominant force.

In Aug. 1999 the people of East Timor (annexed by Indonesia in 1976) voted for independence and the resultant campaign of terror by paramilitaries, abetted by the Army, to prevent this happening provoked worldwide condemnation by the trade union movement. All Indonesian trade union centres, including the semi-official SPSI, supported Timorese independence. On Sept. 20, 1999 Australian-led international peace-keepers were deployed and East Timor is now under a UN Transitional Administration. The military retains a strong position in Indonesian politics, but in Feb. 2000 President Wahid suspended Lt.-Gen. Wiranto, commander of the armed forces during the East Timor conflict, from his position as Coordinating Minister for Politics and Security. Thousands of lives were lost in 1999–2000 in the provice of Aceh, where separatists confront the military, and in inter-communal violence between Christians and Muslims in the Moluccas. Mob violence against Chinese-owned businesses at the time of the fall of Suharto is estimated to have led to the withdrawal of $20bn. from the economy by Chinese business interests.

Some 45% of the labour force are engaged in agriculture but Indonesia also has a range of industries including petroleum, textiles and mining and exploitation of rubber and wood resources. The 2000–2001 budget envisages covering the deficit by receipts from privatization rather than external borrowing.

GDP (purchasing power parity) $610bn. (1999 est.); GDP per capita (purchasing power parity) $2,800 (1999 est.).

2 Trade Unionism

Indonesia ratified ILO Convention No.98 (Right to Organize and Collective Bargaining, 1949) in 1957 and Convention No.87 (Freedom of Association and Protection of the Right to Organize, 1948) in 1998.

The first Indonesian federation, Persatuan Pergerakan Kaum Buruh (United Workers' Movement) was formed in 1919, but lasted only two years; union activities continued, however, and were heavily influenced by nationalist and communist politics, until suppressed under the Japanese occupation in World War II. The Barisan Buruh Indonesia (Indonesian Workers' Front – BBI) was established in 1945 as a united trade union centre, but this almost immediately fragmented. Some unions were actively involved in communist agitation and insurgency in the 1950s and 1960s and these were suppressed after an attempted coup in 1965.

The Suharto regime's official ideology was the philosophy of Pancasila, which stressed the objectives of national unity and consensus. Under 1985 legislation Pancasila was "the sole ideological foundation" of all mass organizations: they could have no concept of the strike, because "strike action represents force from one side upon the other". In practice this ideology was used to curb the development of independent trade unionism.

In 1973 the All-Indonesian Labour Federation (FBSI) was created under government auspices as a central coordinating body; the existing trade union centres remained in existence, however. In 1985 the FBSI was reorganized as the All-Indonesia Union of Workers (SPSI) and its affiliated industrial unions brought under tighter central control. In 1990 they were reorganized again, this time into 13 industrial sectors. The SPSI, the sole legally registered trade union centre, was unsuccessful in its efforts to gain international recognition and affiliation to the ICFTU and was criticized as an instrument of the government and for the level of involvement of former military officers in its leadership both centrally and locally.

Civil servants were coordinated in a separate association, the Indonesian Corps of Civil Servants (KORPRI), set up by the government in 1971 and chaired by the Minister of Internal Affairs. KORPRI was seen as a mechanism of the ruling GOLKAR party. Other than the SPSI, the sole recognized trade union was the Indonesian Teachers' Association (PGRI), which was registered in 1990 and claimed 1.3 million members. Although restricted in its activities, this body participated in international teaching organizations.

In Apr. 1994 the ILO governing body censured Indonesia for violations of trade union rights including suppression of independent unions, intimidatory use of the military, and restrictions on collective bargaining and strike action. However, efforts continued to develop trade unions outside government control. Of these the most successful in the 1990s was the Prosperous Labour Union of Indonesia (SBSI), formed in 1992 to fight for workers' welfare and uphold employment law. The SBSI experienced heavy state repression and its leader, Muchtar Pakpahan, was imprisoned after riots in 1994.

Collective bargaining was protected in law under Suharto, but many difficulties existed in practice and rules favoured the monopoly position of the SPSI as a bargaining agent. A 1994 decree said that unions independent of the SPSI could be set up and negotiate collective agreements in enterprises where at least half the workforce agreed to the establishment of the union. However, if an independent enterprise union wished to join a federation it could only join one affiliated to the SPSI. Around 1,200 non-SPSI enterprise-level unions had been formed by the end of 1997, according to government figures. Representatives of the Manpower Department or security forces were reported commonly to involve themselves in collective bargaining, and agreements were often ignored by employers or proved unenforceable. Employers enjoyed broad freedoms to dismiss workers for trade union activities without redress and employers' representatives themselves took leadership posts in the SPSI at regional and national levels. At enterprise level, employers were sometimes able to control SPSI unions but this was not always the case and the formation of SPSI enterprise unions was sometimes resisted by employers. Normally, however, the agreement of employers was necessary to allow an enterprise-level SPSI union to function.

Although nominally legal in private enterprises not deemed vital to the national interest, legal strikes were difficult to stage and most industrial action tended to be short-lived unofficial actions that not uncommonly ended in violent clashes with the police or military. Although SPSI enterprise-level unions staged strikes over issues such as non-payment of the minimum wage, such actions were not supported by the SPSI centrally or through its industrial federations. Industrial actions increased steadily during the 1990s, with the level of officially recorded strikes rising from 19 in 1989 to 350 by 1996. In Jan. 1994 the government repealed a decree that permitted military intervention in disputes, but in practice this was not observed, and the ICFTU calculated that there were 23 cases of army intervention in strikes in the two months after the decree was rescinded. Under a 1996 decree the army was permitted to intervene "particularly in cases pertaining to strikes, work contracts, dismissals and changes in status or ownership of a company".

New labour legislation passed in Sept. 1997, and which had been due to come into force in Oct. 1998, still maintained the SPSI monopoly, said that collective agreements could be made only at plant level and only by registered trade unions, and maintained broad restrictions on strikes.

After Suharto's resignation the incoming government of President Habibie announced from May 26–June 2, 1998, a series of major changes affecting trade unions.

1. Workers were to be free to set up independent trade unions provided their establishment was consistent with Pancasila.
2. The military would not intervene henceforth in industrial disputes.
3. The SPSI monopoly as the sole legal trade union centre was ended and its affiliated unions required to re-register. Several new confederations were announced in the aftermath of this.
4. The government said it would recognize the SBSI, which could legally register its member unions. Its leader Muchtar Pakpahan was released from prison.
5. The government ratified ILO Convention No. 87 on Freedom of Association and the Right to Organize.
6. It was announced that it would no longer be compulsory for civil servants to be a member of KORPRI, although this was not to be given trade union freedoms.

In Sept. 1998 the government announced postponement of the entry into force of the 1997 labour law, and that it would be amended after consultations as it was not consistent with ILO Convention No. 87. It was also announced that public service employees would be allowed to organize trade unions and during 1999 the requirement for workers in state-owned enterprises and civil servants to belong to KORPRI was ended. However, compulsory membership of the teachers' union was retained. In Sept. 1999 a government decree removed the requirement that unions must have Pancasila as their guiding principle.

Notwithstanding the considerable liberalization in the treatment of trade union activity following Suharto's fall, industrial disputes have continued to escalate into clashes between strikers and the military. The military remains a potent force in Indonesian society not always within the control of the government. In addition the SBSI has continued to experience resistance from employers to registering unions at enterprise level. The ICFTU has four Indonesian affiliates, GASBIINDO, GOBSI, KBIM and SARBUMUSI, but these have had little influence or presence. The SBSI is affiliated to the WCL.

3 Trade Union Centres

GASBIINDO (Gabungan Serikat 2 Buruh Islam Indonesia)

Address. Jalan Taman Tanah, Abang III No. 12A, Tromol Pos 406/JKT, Jakarta Pusat

Phone. +62 21 34 57 82

International affiliation. ICFTU

GOBSI (Gerakan Organisasi Buruh Sjarikat Islam Indonesia)

Address. Jalan Taman Amir, Hamzah No. 2, PO Box 7520 Jatma, Jakarta 13075

Phone. +62 21 390 4101

International affiliation. ICFTU

KBIM (Kongres Buruh Islam Merdeka)

Address. Jalan Kramat Raya 45, Jakarta 10450

Phone. +62 21 35 3755

International affiliation. ICFTU

SARBUMUSI (Sarikat Buruh Muslimin Indonesia) Federation of Indonesian Muslim Trade Unions

Address. Jalan Kramat Raya No. 164, Jakarta 10430

Phone. +62 21 323 033

Fax. +62 21 421 8425

International affiliation. ICFTU

Serikat Buruh Sejahtera Indonesia (SBSI) Prosperous Labour Union of Indonesia

Address. Jl. Pemuda no. 289, Rawa Mangun, Jakarta 13220

Phone. +62 21 470 1101

Fax. +62 21 470 7416

E-mail. sbsi@pacific.net.id

Leadership. Muchtar Pakpahan (chairman)

History and character. The SBSI was founded in 1992 and grew rapidly through a high-profile campaign of enforcing employment legislation. From its inception the SBSI faced severe state repression including arrests and raids. Its national congress of July 1993 was broken up by soldiers only 40 minutes into the proceedings. In the first two years of its life the SBSI suffered the murder of three activists, the arrest of 250 and the dismissal of 2,500 from employment.

The SBSI called successfully for a general strike to achieve employment law enforcement in February 1994; it was blamed for riots in Medan (North Sumatra) in April and June, many local leaders were apprehended, and in September its leader, Muchtar Pakpahan, was arrested and sentenced to prison. Although the sentence was quashed by the Supreme Court in Sept. 1995, it was re-imposed in Oct. 1996 and he also subsequently faced charges arising out of July 1996 riots.

Failure of the authorities to grant official registration to the SBSI attracted condemnation by the WCL (to which it affiliated in June 1997) and the ICFTU. Repression intensified before presidential elections in March 1998, when Suharto was re-elected. The police closed the SBSI office in Jakarta until after the election.

Following the riots of May 1998 and Suharto's resignation, Muchtar Pakpahan was released from prison on May 26 and granted an amnesty. The SBSI was given official recognition and representatives of the SBSI were included in Indonesia's delegation to the annual ILO conference. Tensions between the SBSI, the government and the military continued however and troops surrounded the SBSI Jakarta office on July 24, 1998, following the threat by the SBSI to stage a demonstration demanding the resignation of President Habibie. In the event only a token march was held.

International affiliation. WCL

Iran

Capital: Tehran
Population: 65.62 m. (2000 est.)

1 Political and Economic Background

The Islamic Republic of Iran was proclaimed in 1979 after the overthrow of Shah Reza Pahlevi and is a theoc-
racy. The Ayatollah Ruhollah Khomeini, the country's "spiritual leader" from 1979, died in 1989 and was succeeded by Ayatollah Sayed Ali Khamenei. He has substantial authority over areas such as the military and the judiciary and is the most powerful political figure. The position of spiritual leader is held for life after selection by the Assembly of Experts, made up of clerics, who are elected from a list approved by the government. The

President since 1997 has been Mohammad Khatami, who is seen as a mildly reformist force. In elections to the legislature (Majlis) in Feb. 2000 candidates of the informal Islamic Iran Participation Front, supporters of President Khatami, won a majority.

Under the 1979 Constitution all large-scale industry, including oil, minerals, banking, foreign exchange, insurance, power generation, communications, aviation and road and rail transport, were put under public ownership. Oil is the major contributor to foreign exchange earnings. The private sector comprises mainly small-scale trading and services. Real per capita GDP more than doubled between 1960 and 1976 but then rose only 5% over the next 21 years of war, revolution and clerical rule.

GDP (purchasing power parity) $347.6bn. (1999 est.); GDP per capita (purchasing power parity) $5,300 (1999 est.).

2 Trade Unionism

Iran has ratified neither ILO Convention No.87 (Freedom of Association and Protection of the Right to Organize, 1948) nor No.98 (Right to Organize and Collective Bargaining, 1949).

Trade unions organized vigorously and openly after World War II until the Shah assumed full powers after the overthrow of the government of Dr. Mohammed Mussadeq in 1953. The Shah thereafter suppressed independent trade unions and promoted the government-controlled Workers' Organization of Iran (WOI), although unofficial strikes contributed to the instability of the regime in the late 1970s. After the fall of the Shah in 1979, independent trade unionism was vigorously suppressed. In the period up to 1983 many thousands of militants were arrested and detained.

After the elimination of independent organizations, the Biet Alomal, "the Workers' House", was founded in 1982. It is headed by the Minister of Labour and is the only permitted national labour organization. The Worker' House provides coordination to the Islamic labor councils, whose role and regulations are prescribed by the state. 1985 legislation provided for the establishment of an Islamic labour council, made up of representatives of the workers and one representative of management, in every enterprise or industrial, agricultural or services unit of more than 35 employees. The purpose of the councils was: (i) to encourage cooperation between workers to enhance productivity; (ii) to represent the problems of the workers to management and to cooperate with management in devising methods to improve working conditions; and (iii) to cooperate with the unit's Islamic association. In turn each council was to be consulted by management on issues affecting wages, working hours and conditions, and would appoint a (non-voting) delegate to represent it on the enterprise's board of directors. A tripartite body would be set up in every district, composed of representatives of the Islamic councils, enterprises and the Ministry of Labour and Social Affairs; these bodies would have powers to supervise and dissolve the labour councils and to rule on disputes between the councils and management. The councils serve as instruments of government control, although they have also proved able to represent workers in blocking layoffs.

In 1991 Iran adopted a new labour code which formally allows employers and employees to establish guilds or trade unions. In the case of employees the choice open to them is for an Islamic labour council, or a trade or guild union, or workers' representatives. Guild unions in Iran denote regional organizations that issue vocational licences and help members to find jobs. Their membership is open to the self-employed, as well as to the employed. All guilds must register with the Minister of Labour: if their statutes are approved they are entitled to set up provincial trade centres and a Supreme Centre of Trade Societies at national level. The code does not state explicitly whether independent unions will be permitted to function, but allows the authorities to appoint a representative to any union organization and in practice independent unions are not permitted. Efforts to form a national workers' organization in 1997 were broken up.

Under the labour code agreements may be made locally or centrally but in either case they are subject to approval by the Ministry of Labour and Social Affairs. Disputes are to be referred to a local tripartite Board of Inquiry and thereafter to a tripartite National Dispute Board. Following significant industrial unrest in 1991-93, new legislation banning strikes and demonstrations by workers was promulgated by the Majlis in Oct. 1993. Despite this, strikes still occur, and according to one estimate there were 181 protests and strikes by workers in the period from March 1998 to March 1999. A principal cause of strikes was unpaid wages. It was reported in Dec. 2000 that plans to liberalize the economy by cutting subsidies for state enterprises had been shelved in part because of fears of job losses and social unrest ahead of presidential elections in June 2001.

There are no affiliates of the ICFTU or WCL. The WFTU recognizes an exile group.

Iraq

Capital: Baghdad
Population: 22.68 m. (2000 est.)

1 Political and Economic Background

Iraq has been an independent state since 1932. The Republic of Iraq was declared in 1958 following the overthrow of the monarchy. Since 1979 power has been concentrated in the hands of Saddam Hussein, his family and close associates, controlling an extensive security apparatus. Saddam is President (his presidency being approved by a reported 99.6% of the electorate in a 1995 referendum), Prime Minister, Chairman of the Revolutionary Command Council and leader of the Ba'ath (Renaissance) Arab Socialist Party, the only legal party since the overthrow of a previous military regime in 1968. While Shia Muslims are the majority (60–65%) population, the Sunni Muslims are dominant.

Despite engaging in two catastrophic wars, first with Iran (1980–88) and then with a US-led coalition following his 1990 invasion of Kuwait, Saddam has retained power through ruthless eradication of rivals and the lack of any democratic alternative. However, Kurdish forces control parts of the north of the country, while there is continuing rebellion by Shias in the southern marshes. Iraq remains subject to UN sanctions following the Gulf War, although these have been moderated under an oil-for-food scheme introduced in 1996. The government controls all major industries, including the critical oil sector. The impact of two decades of war and sanctions on the economy has been immense.

GDP (purchasing power parity) $59.9bn. (1999 est.); GDP per capita (purchasing power parity) $2,700 (1999 est.).

2 Trade Unionism

The first trade unions formed in the 1920s were violently suppressed. At the end of World War II 16 unions were formed to cover workers in all sectors except the oil industry, but in the following decade these were broken up or severely curtailed. Following the overthrow of the monarchy in 1958 the first oil workers' union was formed and the General Federation of Trade Unions (GFTU) established. Since 1968 all unions have been organized in the GFTU and have been instruments of the Ba'ath Party. The GFTU is affiliated to the WFTU.

Repression of opposition trade unionists intensified after 1978, with many imprisoned or forced into exile. In 1979 the general secretary and the president of the GFTU were executed after being accused of conspiring against the security of the state. Conscription of labour occurred following the beginning of the war with Iran in 1980. In 1987 the Iraqi government passed a decree making all workers in the state sector civil servants without rights of association. The GFTU did not protest against the withdrawal of trade unions rights and was accused by the ICFTU of having cooperated in the conscription of troops during the war against Iran.

Iraq has not ratified ILO Convention No.87 (Freedom of Association and Protection of the Rights to Organize, 1948), but it ratified Convention No.98 (Right to Organize and Collective Bargaining, 1949) in 1962. However, there are no legislative protections for collective bargaining. In the state sector pay levels are set administratively, and in the relatively small formal private sector by the employer or by individual negotiation. The 1987 labour law restricts the right to strike and in practice strikes have not been reported for two decades.

Uday Hussein, Saddam's son, is head of the Iraqi Union of Journalists and in Sept. 1999 reportedly secured the dismissal of hundreds of members of the union for praising Saddam too faintly. Under the penal code prison sentences may be imposed on public employees guilty of breaches of "discipline", including leaving their job.

3 Trade Union Centre

General Federation of Trade Unions of Iraq (GFTU)

Address. PO Box 3049, Tahrirr Square, Rashid Street, Baghdad

Phone. + 964 1 887 0810

Fax. + 964 1 886 3820

Leadership. Fadhil Mahmoud Gharib (president); Jamil Salman Ahmed (vice-president)

Membership. 850,000 in 6 industrially-based trade unions and 18 local federations

History and character. Founded 1959. The GFTU is closely associated with the ruling Ba'ath Party and is the sole permitted trade union organization. It describes its objectives as being to build and defend the homeland; to protect the interests of the working masses; to increase production in the interest of national prosperity, and to work for an end to UN sanctions on Iraq.

Publication. Way Al-Ummal (Workers' Consciousness)

International affiliation. WFTU

Ireland

Capital: Dublin
Population: 3.80 m. (2000 est.)

1 Political and Economic Background

Ireland achieved independence from the United Kingdom in 1921. The leading political parties are the conservative-nationalist Fianna Fáil (FF) and the traditionally more liberal Christian Democratic Fine Gael (FG). The social democratic Labour Party has only ever had a minority position. Following elections in June 1997, FF returned to power under Prime Minister Bertie Ahern, leading a coalition including the small Progressive Democrats party.

Ireland has enjoyed an economic boom in the 1990s, encouraged by EU funding and inward investment by international companies. Annual growth rates have been the highest in the EU, with GDP increasing 8.4% in 1999, while inflation has remained low although seen as likely to rise as "overheating" in the economy became apparent. Although unemployment has been a continuing problem, the unemployment rate fell in 1999 to 5.5% the lowest in 30 years. Agriculture has declined in importance and industry and services now drive the economy. Ireland joined the single European currency at its launch on Jan. 1, 1999.

GDP (purchasing power parity) $73.7bn. (1999 est.); GDP per capita (purchasing power parity) $20,300 (1999 est.).

2 Trade Unionism

Ireland ratified ILO Conventions No.87 (Freedom of Association and Protection of the Right to Organize, 1948) and No.98 (Right to Organize and Collective Bargaining, 1949) in 1955. The constitution guarantees the right of citizens to form associations and unions, as well as the right not to join unions.

An Irish Trade Union Congress, the predecessor of the present Irish Congress of Trade Unions (ICTU) was founded in 1894, and unions developed strongly under British rule. The ICTU is Ireland's only national trade union centre. Some Irish unions also affiliate to the British Trades Union Congress (TUC); likewise, some unions in the British province of Northern Ireland affiliate to both the TUC and ITUC. The number of ICTU affiliates has gradually reduced through mergers, but there are still 63 member unions, some of them quite small. About half the work force is unionized.

Ireland faced major economic difficulties in the early- to mid-1980s. However, since 1987, Ireland has had a series of three-year tripartite partnership agreements providing a framework for the management of the economy, social change and wage increases. These have been the Programme for National Recovery (1987–90), the Programme for Economic and Social Progress (1990–93), the Programme for Competitiveness and Work (1994–97) and Partnership 2000 (1997–2000). In addition to covering a wide range of social and economic objectives these agreements have provided the framework for detailed collective bargaining. A 1998 public opinion survey undertaken for the ICTU found that 94% of the public believed that the unions' participation in these agreements had been successful, while the agreements are generally considered to have created an environment of economic stability and industrial peace that has encouraged foreign investment. The most recent agreement, called the Programme for Prosperity and Fairness, was approved by the unions in Apr. 2000.

The right to strike, in both private and public sectors, is protected by immunity from civil suits for trade unions. Police and military personnel may form associations but may not strike. The Industrial Relations Act of 1990 maintained immunities and permitted peaceful picketing, but did introduce a Code of Practice providing for voluntary arbitration in essential public services. The Act also established the Labour Relations Commission (LRC) with overall responsibility for promoting good industrial relations through conciliation and advisory services and the preparation of codes of practice. Disputes that can not be resolved directly between employers and unions are referred to the LRC, whose conciliation service resolves the majority of such cases. In the case of continued dispute, referral may be made to the Labour Court, an independent body with equal numbers nominated by the ICTU and the Irish Business and Employers' Confederation (IBEC). Although the Court's decisions are not binding they are normally respected.

A National Minimum Wage Act came into effect in 2000, providing what the ICTU says is the highest minimum in the EU. Prior to this there was no prescribed minimum wage other than in limited sectors (notably agricultural workers) where rates were set by Joint Labour Committees set up under the Labour Court.

3 Trade Union Centre

Irish Congress of Trade Unions (ICTU)

Address. 31–32 Parnell Square, Dublin 1

Phone. +353 1 889 7777

Fax. +353 1 887 2012

E-mail. congress@ictu.ie

Website. www.ictu.ie

Leadership. Peter Cassells (general secretary)

Membership. 734,842

History and character. The Irish Trade Union Congress was founded in 1894. This body split in two in 1945 with the formation of the breakaway Congress of Irish Unions (which rejected the inclusion of British-based unions), but was reunited under the present name in 1959. The principle of a united Irish trade union centre persisted through the period of British rule to the separation of the North from the rest of Ireland. The ICTU is politically non-aligned.

Reported membership has grown slightly during the 1990s, reflecting a broad public acceptance of the positive role of trade unions. The proportion of members who are women has been rising steadily and is now 44%.

The ICTU's role has been strengthened by the development of tripartism in recent years. Since 1987 the ICTU has participated in a series of three-year partnership agreements with employers and government. The latest of these, approved by the unions in Apr. 2000 and called the Programme for Prosperity and Fairness, covers a wide range of issues relating to international competitiveness, the distribution of the national wealth, enhancing social inclusion, and building a knowledge-based society. Detailed areas of the programme cover topics such as taxation, pensions, workplace relations and modernizing the public service, as well as providing a framework for wage bargaining in the next three years.

Reflecting the importance of the EU in Ireland's recent development, in 1994 the ICTU set up a specialist unit, the European Information Service.

Publications. Various, including biennial report.

International affiliations. ICFTU; ETUC; TUAC

Affiliated unions. There are 63 affiliated unions. The trans-national character of many of these unions reflects the complex historical entanglements of Ireland and the United Kingdom, the close economic relationship between the two countries and the ambiguous status of the British province of Northern Ireland. Just as unions based in Britain (i.e. the United Kingdom excluding Northern Ireland) have members in the Irish Republic, unions based in the Irish Republic have members in Northern Ireland, and there are even unions affiliated to the ICTU which have members only in Northern Ireland.

Of the ICTU's 63 affiliates, 26 are Irish branches of unions based in Britain, usually with members in both the Republic and Northern Ireland (although there are instances of British-based unions with members in Northern Ireland but not the Republic which are affiliated to the ICTU). Four are unions with members in both the Republic of Ireland and Northern Ireland but not in Britain; 30 are unions with members only in the Republic of Ireland; and 3 are unions based in Northern Ireland but without members in the Republic.

The following unions have in excess of 3,000 members in the Irish Republic. These include unions based in Britain with an Irish regional office in the Republic, or with an Irish regional office in Northern Ireland and a district office in the Republic (in which case the address given is that in the Republic), or unions operating only in the Republic.

1. Amalgamated Engineering and Electric Union
Head office – see entry under United Kingdom
Office in Republic of Ireland.
Address. 5 Whitefriars, Aungier Street, Dublin 2
Phone. +353 1 475 0129
Leadership. B. Fenelon (divisional organizer)
Membership in the Republic of Ireland. 11,192
Membership in Northern Ireland. 23,343

2. Amalgamated Transport and General Workers' Union
Head office – see entry under United Kingdom
Office in Republic of Ireland.
Address. 55–56 Middle Abbey Street, Dublin 1
Phone. +353 1 873 4577
Leadership. B. Kearney (district secretary)
Membership in the Republic of Ireland. 18,203
Membership in Northern Ireland. 29,048

3. Association of Secondary Teachers, Ireland
Address. *ASTI House, Winetavern Street, Dublin 8*
Phone. *+353 1 671 9144*
Fax. +353 1 671 9280
E-mail. info@asti.ie
Leadership. Charlie Lennon (general secretary)
Membership in the Republic of Ireland. 16,510
Membership in Northern Ireland. Nil

4. Building and Allied Trades Union
Address. Arus Hibernia, 13 Blessington Street, Dublin 7
Phone. +353 1 830 1911
Leadership. P. O'Shaughnessy (general secretary)
Membership in the Republic of Ireland. 9,030
Membership in Northern Ireland. Nil

5. Civil and Public Service Union
Address. 19/20 Adelaide Road, Dublin 2
Phone. +353 1 676 5394
Leadership. B. Horan (general secretary)
Membership in the Republic of Ireland. 12,003
Membership in Northern Ireland. Nil

6. Communication Workers' Union
Address. Aras Ghaibreil, 575 North Circular Road, Dublin 1
Phone. +353 1 836 6388
Leadership. C. Scanlon (general secretary)
Membership in the Republic of Ireland. 19,600
Membership in Northern Ireland. Nil

7. Graphical, Paper and Media Union
Head office – see entry under United Kingdom
Office in Republic of Ireland.
Address. Graphic House, 107 Clonskeagh Road, Dublin 6
Phone. +353 1 269 7788
Leadership. E.A.Kirkpatrick (Irish representative)
Membership in the Republic of Ireland. 4,811
Membership in Northern Ireland. 2,652

8. Irish Bank Officials' Association
Address. 93 St. Stephens Green, Dublin 2
Phone. +353 1 475 5908
Fax. +353 1 478 0567
E-mail. iboa@eircom.net

Leadership. Ciaran Ryan (general secretary)
Membership in the Republic of Ireland. 10,095
Membership in Northern Ireland. 5,540

9. Irish Medical Organisation
Address. 10 Fitzwilliam Place, Dublin 2
Phone. +353 1 676 7273
Leadership. G. McNeice (general secretary)
Membership in the Republic of Ireland. 4,252
Membership in Northern Ireland. Nil

10. Irish Municipal, Public and Civil Trade Union (IMPACT)
Address. Nerney's Court, Dublin 1
Phone. +353 1 817 1500
Fax. +353 1 817 1501
E-mail. rnolan@impact.ie
Leadership. Peter McLoone (general secretary)
Membership in the Republic of Ireland. 35,000
Membership in Northern Ireland. Nil

11. Irish National Teachers' Organisation
Address. 35 Parnell Square, Dublin 1
Phone. +353 1 872 2533
Leadership. J. O'Toole (general secretary)
Membership in the Republic of Ireland. 20,909
Membership in Northern Ireland. 6,135

12. Irish Nurses' Organisation
Address. 11 Fitzwilliam Place, Dublin 2
Phone. +353 1 676 0137
Fax. +353 1 661 0466
E-mail. ino@ino.ie
Leadership. Liam Doran (general secretary)
Membership in the Republic of Ireland. 24,816
Membership in Northern Ireland. Nil

13. MANDATE
Address. 9 Cavendish Row, Dublin 1
Phone. +353 1 874 6321
Leadership. O. Nulty (general secretary)
Membership in the Republic of Ireland. 37,089
Membership in Northern Ireland. Nil

14. Marine Port and General Workers' Union
Address. 14 Gardiner Place, Dublin 1
Phone. +353 1 872 6566
Leadership. M. Hayes (general secretary)
Membership in the Republic of Ireland. 3,004
Membership in Northern Ireland. Nil

15. Manufacturing, Science, Finance (MSF)
Head office – see entry under United Kingdom
Office in Republic of Ireland.

Address. 15 Merrion Square, Dublin 2
Phone. +353 1 676 1213
Leadership. J. Tierney (national secretary)
Membership in the Republic of Ireland. 21,000
Membership in Northern Ireland. 10,000

16. Operative Plasterers and Allied Trades Society of Ireland
Address. Arus Hibernia, 13 Blessington Street, Dublin 7
Phone. +353 1 830 4270
Leadership. N. Irwin (general secretary)
Membership in the Republic of Ireland. 3,000
Membership in Northern Ireland. Nil

17. Public Service Executive Union
Address. 30 Merrion Square, Dublin 2
Phone. +353 1 676 7271
Leadership. D. Murphy (general secretary)
Membership in the Republic of Ireland. 8,000
Membership in Northern Ireland. Nil

18. Services Industrial Professional Technical Union
Address. Liberty Hall, Dublin 1
Phone. +353 1 874 9731
Leadership. J. McDonnell (general secretary)
Membership in the Republic of Ireland. 190,501
Membership in Northern Ireland. 7,001

19. Teachers' Union of Ireland
Address. 73 Orwell Road, Rathgar, Dublin 6
Phone. +353 1 492 2588
Fax. +353 1 492 2953
E-mail. tui@tui.ie
Leadership. James Dorney (general secretary)
Membership in the Republic of Ireland. 10,338
Membership in Northern Ireland. Nil

20. Technical, Engineering and Electrical Union
Address. 5 Cavendish Row, Dublin 1
Phone. +353 1 872 2369
Fax. +353 1 874 7048
E-mail. teeu@teeu.ie
Leadership. Owen Wills (general secretary)
Membership in the Republic of Ireland. 28,628
Membership in Northern Ireland. Nil

21. Union of Construction, Allied Trades and Technicians
Head office – see entry under United Kingdom
Office in Republic of Ireland.
Address. 56 Parnell Square West, Dublin 1
Phone. +353 1 873 1599
Leadership. J. Moore (national secretary)
Membership in the Republic of Ireland. 10,832
Membership in Northern Ireland. 2,840

Israel

Capital: Jerusalem
Population: 5.84 m. (2000 est.)

1 Political and Economic Background

The state of Israel declared its independence in 1948, following the end of the British mandate to administer what was then Palestine. It consolidated its position and expanded its territory as a result of a series of wars with its Arab neighbours, in 1948, 1956, 1967 and 1973. In the mid-1990s it conceded a limited form of self-rule for Palestinians in the Gaza Strip and West Bank, territory taken in 1967. Talks on the long-term status of the Palestinian entity broke down under the (right-wing) Likud government of Benjamin Netanyahu, resumed following the election of a Labour government headed by Ehud Barak in May 1999, then were stalled following renewal of violence in the occupied territories in autumn 2000. Likud returned to power in Feb. 2001. There is persistent tension in Israeli politics over the degree to which Israel should exchange occupied territory, and allow full Palestinian autonomy, in exchange for the prospect of improved security.

Israel has a diversified modern economy, with important commercial agriculture and a high profile in technology-based innovation. Government has traditionally dominated the economy, although the private sector has become more vigorous. Immigrants from the Jewish diaspora built the country, and in the period 1989–98 Israel absorbed a further 750,000 Jewish immigrants from the former Soviet Union. There are significant disparities between the living standards of Jewish and Palestinian workers and a reliance on imported labour in sectors such as construction and agriculture. Employment is divided between the public sector (approximately 30%) the private sector (approximately 50%) and the sector owned by the main trade union centre Histadrut (20%). The private sector is dominant in manufacturing, the public sector in utilities and Histadrut in agriculture, transport and construction.

GDP (purchasing power parity) $105.4bn. (1999 est.); GDP per capita (purchasing power parity) $18,300 (1999 est.).

2 Trade Unionism

The Histadrut, the dominant labour organization in Israel, was formed in Palestine in 1920 as an expression of both trade union and Zionist aspirations, and played a major role in building the state of Israel. It served to provide a wide range of health, education and welfare services, and through the Hevrat Ovdim, Histadrut became a major owner of enterprises, generating 20% of GDP.

Histadrut dominates Israeli trade unionism, but there is also a much smaller National Labour Federation, the Zionist Histadrut Haovdim Haleumit. There are also a small number of independent individual unions, representing secondary teachers, doctors and university professors.

Histadrut historically has been close to the Labour Party. Political parties receive funding from the Histadrut budget in proportion to their representation on its elected governing bodies, and from its foundation in 1920 until 1994 Labour always had an absolute majority within the Histadrut. Relations with the Likud government of Benjamin Netanyahu (1996–99) were poor. In 1996–97 Histadrut led a series of nationwide public sector strikes against the Netanyahu government's policies on privatization and public sector pensions. In Dec. 1997 the government agreed to consult with Histadrut on restructuring plans and backed down on the pension issue.

Israel ratified ILO Conventions No.87 (Freedom of Association and Protection of the Right to Organize, 1948) and No.98 (Right to Organize and Collective Bargaining, 1949) in 1957. A wide range of labour laws, mostly passed in the 1950s, provides the framework for the regulation of hours, holidays, youth and women's employment, disputes, national insurance, etc. In general workers are free to join unions of their won choosing. However, Palestinians from the occupied territories (now with limited Palestinian self-rule) of the Gaza Strip and West Bank may not join trade unions operating in Israel, and unions based in the Gaza and West Bank may not operate in Israel. Non-resident workers in Israel are covered by collective agreements negotiated by Israeli unions.

Strikes are common, and in the late 1990s strikes over the impact of privatization on jobs and benefits were widespread. Where essential services are affected the government may ask the labour courts to impose back-to-work orders while negotiations continue, as happened particularly in the case of major public sector strikes organized by Histadrut in 1997.

3 Trade Union Centre

Histadrut
General Federation of Labour in Israel
Address. 93 Arlosoroff Street, 62098 Tel-Aviv
Phone. +972 3 692 1513
Fax. +972 3 692 1512
E-mail. histint@netvision.net.il

Website. www.histadrut.co.il (under construction, Dec. 2000)

Leadership. Amir Peretz (chairman)

Membership. 650,000. Membership has fallen from a previous height of 1.65 million. Histradut membership is open to all ethnic groups and three-quarters of Arab and Druze workers in Israel are members.

History and character. The Histadrut was founded in 1920 in Haifa by 4,400 (Jewish) members of different trades, who decided to create a single organization to represent all crafts and professions. As Jewish settlers came in increasing numbers to Palestine, the Histadrut took on a broad role in developing housing, social services, and education and in training workers and building the economy. At the same time it fostered the development of cooperative enterprises and settlements, creating an entire network of enterprises and communities, and as part of its work, oversaw the creation of trade unions. As well as its role as a trade union, Histadrut is the most important economic organization in Israel, involved a wide range of enterprises directly or in cooperation with private investors, although this role has been declining.

The Histadrut is not a federation of autonomous unions; a worker joins directly, and through this membership becomes a member of the appropriate trade union. The basic unit is the enterprise works committee, and all Histadrut members in each district elect the local Histadrut branch – the labour council. Each individual union is governed by a council elected by the union membership. Judicial control of the elected bodies is exercised by the court of honour, which at present is elected by the Histadrut council. Local courts, elected by local labour councils, hear claims by individual members or institutions relating to the affairs of the organization. However, these courts may not try criminal cases.

The Histadrut's trade union department represents 27 national trade unions. One responsibility of the department is to ensure Histadrut policies are implemented by the individual unions. All Histadrut members automatically have membership in the appropriate trade union. Within the various unions are works committees (at plant level) and local unions (members of the same trade in the same locality); these are linked to other trades through the local labour councils (multi-union local bodies). Each national union has a council, elected by secret ballot on party political lines, as its governing body; the council elects a national secretary, who represents the national union at Histadrut headquarters.

At local and enterprise level, candidates for office stand as individuals, but national elections are based on political slates. Political parties receive funding from the Histadrut budget in proportion to their representation on its elected governing bodies. From 1920–94 Labour always had an absolute majority, but in May 1994 former Labour Health Minister Haim Ramon's "New Life in the Histadrut" slate (backed by Mapam, the CRN and the Shas party) polled 46.2% and Labour only 32.82%. Ramon subsequently put together a coalition administration of Histadrut, with backing from the Labour list. In Dec. 1994, after the assassination of Prime Minister Yitzhak Rabin, Haim Ramon was appointed Minister of the Interior and resigned from his Histadrut post. Amir Peretz, M.K., was elected Histadrut chairman. In 1998 the coalition led by Peretz received 58.6% of the vote. This coalition includes members from a wide spectrum of political parties.

At the national level collective bargaining agreements are negotiated between the Histadrut executive committee and employers, and specific agreements between the national trade unions and employers in their industries. A high degree of wage standardization exists throughout the economy, and the wage policy set by the Histadrut executive committee is binding on the unions, no matter how strong their individual bargaining power.

Up to 1994, Histadrut's health insurance system (Kupat Holim) embraced 75% of the population, but a law effective from October introduced a new health tax payable by all citizens to fund nationwide health care. In effect this step broke the link between membership of the Histadrut and entitlement to health care, as each citizen now has the right to choose his or her preferred health scheme. While this shift coincided with the outlook of the new Histadrut leadership, it does pose a financial problem since health income subsidized some of the organization's other activities.

In conjunction with the Ministry of Labour and the trade unions, Histadrut operates a nationwide network of vocational training schools and apprenticeship classes. Mishlav (the Israel Institute for Education through Correspondence) offers day and evening classes at secondary school level. The Histadrut Department for Higher Education conducts university-level courses in management and the Culture and Education Centre conducts a wide range of activities, reaching the whole community, including the Arab and Druze populations.

The Histadrut pension funds deal with pensions and various other benefits such as holiday and compensation payments. Mish'an, established in 1931, provides loans for a variety of purposes, and operates old age homes and pensioners' clubs, and programmes for children and orphans. Dor le Dor provides financial aid for the elderly, and Lev Zahav offers them nursing services on behalf of the National Insurance Institute.

Every member of the Histadrut is simultaneously a member of Hevrat Ovdim (General Cooperative Association of Labour in Israel), which is in turn open only to members of Histadrut. It is an autonomous establishment acting as a holding company for the Histadrut's assets.

Every woman member of the Histadrut is a member of Na'amat (Working Women's Movement in Israel). It has its own governing bodies, the highest of which is the convention, elected every four years at the same time as the general Histadrut elections. Na'amat operates child care, nursery school, vocational training and adult education programmes. Na'amat also lobbies for legislation of specific interest to women.

Hano'ar Ha'oved Ve'halomed is the youth organization, with its own elective bodies. Its trade union department provides professional direction to youths serving apprenticeships and youths working in holiday jobs, while also supervising their conditions of employment, protecting their wages and protecting them from exploitation.

The Histadrut is represented on all government councils with labour and social welfare responsibilities, and in many cases the Minister of Labour is required to consult the Histadrut on the application of the laws. It is the recognized representative of workers in the labour courts.

In 1958 the Histadrut established the Afro-Asian Institute for Labour Studies to provide courses in trade union, economic and social matters for trade union and community activists from Africa and Asia. A parallel Latin American Centre was founded in 1962. At the end of 1990, the Eastern and Central European Foundation was set up for the purpose of offering labour education facilities to the trade union movements of the former Soviet bloc countries. These institutes were amalgamated in 1994, under the framework of Peoples – The International Institute for Solidarity and Development of the Histadrut.

International affiliations. ICFTU; TUAC

4 Other Trade Union Organization

Histadrut Haovdim Haleumit
National Labour Federation in Eretz-Israel (NLF)

Address. 23 Shprintzak Street, Tel-Aviv 64738

Phone. +972 3 695 8351

Fax. +972 3 696 1953

E-mail. hol@netvision.net.il

Leadership. Abraham Hirschson (chairman)

History and character. The National Labour Federation in Eretz-Israel was founded in Jerusalem in 1934, to unite those workers who believed in solving the country's social and economic problems on the basis of the teachings of Herzl, Nordau and Jabotinsky.

The NLF is committed to the principles of Zionism, and has as its banner the national flag. It believes in the separation of the functions of employers and trade unions, and in this respect stood in opposition to the Histadrut national trade union centre which also developed as a major employer in its own right. Like the Histadrut it was also a major provider of health care services (especially in the occupied territories). Although disclaiming political affiliations, it has been seen as sympathetic to Likud.

International affiliations. None

PALESTINE NATIONAL AUTHORITY

Population: Gaza 1.13 m.; West Bank 2.02 m. (2000 est.)

1 Political and Economic Background

Under a series of interim agreements in 1993-95 Israel has transferred limited powers of autonomy in the Gaza Strip and parts of the West Bank to a Palestine National Authority. Negotiations on a permanent settlement were stalled under the Netanyahu government from 1996–99, but resumed following the election of a Labour government in Israel in May 1999 before faltering amid renewed violence during 2000. Some 120,000 Palestinians from the occupied territories work legally or illegally in Israel and both the Gaza and West Bank economies are highly vulnerable to closures of the

Israeli borders at times of unrest. Living standards are much poorer than in Israel.

Gaza GDP (purchasing power parity) $1.17bn. (1999 est.); GDP per capita (purchasing power parity) $1,060 (1999 est.).

West Bank GDP (purchasing power parity) $3.3bn. (1999 est.); GDP per capita (purchasing power parity) $2,050 (1999 est.).

2 Trade Unionism

Following the 1967 Arab–Israeli war, when Israel occupied the West Bank and Gaza, many Palestinian unions were permanently closed on the West Bank and there was complete suppression in Gaza.

In 1989 the ICFTU Executive Board heard a report

from a fact-finding mission to the West Bank and urged Israel to lift restrictions on union activity there. It also called on the West Bank unions to rationalize and exhorted Histadrut to engage in dialogue with bona fide West Bank and Gaza union leaders. Histadrut responded with a policy shift at its 1990 convention, and in 1991 formed a Committee for Workers from the Occupied Territories under the leadership of its Arab Affairs Department.

In this period the Palestine General Federation of Trade Unions (PGFTU) consolidated its position as the representative centre, and by 1993 claimed 100,000 members. It held its first bilateral meeting with the Histadrut in Nov. 1993.

The Palestinian authorities have been drafting a Palestinian labour code. Pending its enactment, labour activity has been governed by a mix of former Jordanian law and Israeli military decrees (on the West Bank), and by Palestine Authority decisions in Gaza. Government is the largest provider of formal employment in the territories, but early drafts of the labour code included a ban on public servants joining unions, leading to opposition from the PGFTU. Unions must submit grievances prior to strike action to the Palestine Authority Labour Ministry. If the union strikes following arbitration, this is to be referred to the courts. There is no body of legislation in this area.

Unions in Jerusalem (regarded by Israel but not internationally as part of Israel proper) are formally prohibited from federating with West Bank unions, although this has not been enforced. In practice some Palestinian workers in Jerusalem belong simultaneously to unions affiliated with West Bank federations and to Histadrut. The estimated 120,000 Palestinians from the West Bank and Gaza who work in Israel or Jerusalem are not full members of Histadrut, but are required to contribute 1% of their wages to Histadrut. In 1996 it was agreed that half of this levy would be transferred to the PGFTU.

3 Trade Union Centre

Palestine General Federation of Trade Unions (PGFTU)

E-mail. pgftu@p-ol.com

Membership. The great majority of unions affiliate to the PGFTU and there has been extensive reorganization and consolidation of unions. An estimated 88,000 workers in the West Bank are members of the 12 PGFTU-affiliated unions, while there are 43,000 members in the eight PGFTU affiliates in Gaza. The PGFTU estimates that dues-paying members make up about 30% of all Palestinian workers. The PGFTU has applied for membership in the ICFTU.

Italy

Capital: Rome
Population: 57.6 m. (2000 est.)

1 Political and Economic Background

For nearly half a century following the end of World War II, the Italian political system was characterized by the instability of individual administrations set against the overall dominance of the Christian Democratic Party, which was continuously in government until 1992. In the early 1990s, however, the established party system disintegrated amid a torrent of scandals, mostly concerning illegal party financing and other corruption. The party establishments reacted by creating new party names and alliances, thus giving a new façade to Italian politics while maintaining underlining orientations.

In the most recent (1996) elections to the 630-member Chamber of Deputies (lower House), the Olive Tree Movement (broadly a coalition of centre-left parties),

with 284 seats, and the Freedom Alliance (an alliance of conservative parties), with 246 seats, emerged as the leading forces. The Olive Tree Movement formed a minority government under Romano Prodi of the liberal wing of the Christian democratic Italian Popular Party (PPI). Prodi's administration fell in October 1998 (Prodi in 1999 becoming President of the European Commission) and was replaced by a new somewhat more left-wing centre-left coalition under the Democratic Socialists' leader, Massimo D'Alema. After a further political crisis, D'Alema stood down in Apr. 2000 and a new, politically similar, coalition was formed under the non-party Giuliano Amato, the 58th republican government since World War II.

Italy has a diversified mainly private sector economy. The state still has a stake in a range of enterprises, but the reduction of the state's role in the economy was symbolized by the closure of the state holding company, Iri, in June 2000. There is a sharp disparity between living standards in the prosperous north and the backward south. In 1999 unemployment was 11.1% nationally but ranged from only 5.4% in the north to 21.1% in the south. The contrast has been reflected in the creation of a separatist northern party, the Lega Nord. Italy took systematic action in the 1990s to control its chronic problems of high inflation and public deficits in order to meet EU convergence criteria. This process was assisted by a series of tripartite social pacts emphasizing wage moderation and increasing labour flexibility. Italy joined the single European currency zone at its foundation in January 1999. Growth remained weak in the late 1990s, but GDP growth was expected to rise to 3% in 2000.

GDP (purchasing power parity) $1.212 trillion (1999 est.); GDP per capita (purchasing power parity) $21,400 (1999 est.).

2 Trade Unionism

Italy ratified ILO Conventions No.87 (Freedom of Association and Protection of the Right to Organize, 1948) and No. 98 (Right to Organize and Collective Bargaining, 1949) in 1958. Freedom of association has prevailed since the end of World War II.

The (socialist) Confederazione Generale di Lavora (CGL) and the (Catholic) Confederazione Italiana dei Lavoratori (CIL) were founded in the first decade of the twentieth century; both faced intense opposition from employers, with especially violent conflict in the agrarian sector where the unions recruited many agricultural labourers. During the period of political upheaval and labour unrest following the end of World War I, the claimed membership of the CGL increased to 2 million and that of the CIL to over one million. In 1925, under Mussolini, fascist unions were accorded monopoly representation and by 1927 all other unions had been abolished. In June 1944 (when Italy was effectively divided between German and Allied occupying forces), socialist, communist and Christian democrat trade unionists in the 'Pact of Rome' agreed on the formation of a unified national centre, the Italian General Confederation of Labour (Confederazione Generale Italiana del Lavoro – CGIL). Under the Pact, each of the three political tendencies was to have equal representation on the CGIL executive bodies. However, the CGIL progressively disintegrated and by 1950 a tripartite division had developed, with the CGIL dominated by communists, the Confederazione Italiana dei Sindacata Lavoratori (CISL) dominated by Christian democrats (but with some socialist influence) and the Unione Italiana del Lavoro (UIL), the smallest of the three, led by social democrats and republicans. These three remain the leading centres. The CGIL, CISL and the UIL are all now ICFTU affiliates, the CGIL having left the WFTU in 1978.

Italy's union centres have tended to be weak and under-funded, reflecting the relatively recent development of trade as opposed to class unionism, and the disunity of the labour movement. Local chambers of labour, linked directly to their respective trade union centres and uniting workers regardless of industry, have often been of more significance than industrially based unions. Competition between the centres has traditionally led to exaggeration of their membership figures (which are not independently certified). Low dues levels have been offset by fees received from the government as contractors providing social welfare assistance through the "patronati" arrangements. In the late 1990s, CGIL claimed more than 5.2 million, the CISL just over 4 million and the UIL over 1.7 million.

The memberships of all the confederations are greatly inflated, however, by the number of pensioners included. This is a vastly greater component of membership than in any other comparable country, reflecting the prevalence of early retirement in Italy. As of 1999, 55% of CGIL members, 50% of CISL members and 25% of UIL members were pensioners. These were organized in separate affiliates. In total the three confederations had 5.35 m. retired members included in their total membership of 11.037 m. (48.5% of the total). So large are the pensioners' unions within the confederations that each confederation has rules designed to limit the representation of its pensioners' unions in the decision-making bodies. Thus in the CGIL, any affiliate is limited to a ceiling of 25% of voting delegates in any such body; in practice, this affects only its pensioners' union, the Union of Italian Retired Workers (Sindacato Pensionati Italiani, Spi), which has 55% of the aggregate CGIL membership.

The pensioners' unions are active in providing a wide range of services to members and each has a non-profit mutual aid organization attached. They are also a substantial political force, the three confederal pensioners' unions adopting an annual common platform for negotiation with central and local government. The pensioners' unions are organized on a local and territorial basis so their organizational structure matches the structure of local government, assisting them in exerting influence. In the period 1993–97 the pensioners' unions reached some 2,000 collective agreements with municipal authorities. These covered issues such as reduced pensioner charges for utilities, local tax reductions, services such as home helps, health care and housing, and local leisure facilities. Pension issues have come to the fore in recent years because of the mounting burden of costs on the state. In 1995 the government adopted legislation aimed at a progressive raising of the retirement age, but retirement ages remain extremely low, giving rise to the phenomenon of the so-called "baby pensioners", especially in the public sector. A schedule adopted with the agreement of the three confederations in 1997 for white-collar workers provided only for the retirement age to be raised to 54 in the private sector by 1998 and in the public sector by 2000. The 1995 legislation also provided for the introduction of private pension funds to reduce the burden falling on the state.

The reported memberships of all three confederations were higher in the late 1990s than they had been in the early 1980s. From 1980–96 the combined membership of the three confederations rose by 1,636,492, or 18.2%, to a new record high of 10,642,287. However, the driver of this growth was the increase in pensioner numbers, pensioners making up 47.6% of members by 1996 compared with only 20% in 1980. The number of active workers in membership of the three confederations actually fell by 25.8% in the same period. Worst affected was CGIL, whose membership of active workers fell by 33.2%, while CISL lost 25.3%, and the UIL 6.4%. Overall, while the three confederations had 49% of the active workforce in membership in 1980, this had fallen to 36.6% by 1996.

The fall in active membership reflected in part the loss of jobs in manufacturing sectors, this especially affecting CGIL, traditionally the biggest force among blue-collar manufacturing workers. It also reflected the lack of success in recruiting in newer service industries and smaller enterprises, and among women, and workers in "irregular" forms of employment. The most unionized sectors are agriculture, public administration and manufacturing industry, in that order, while commerce and services generally are least organized.

Outside the main centres are numerous independent unions. Many of these reflect the interests of narrow occupational or professional groups who have felt neglected by the main confederations. Independent unionism flourished particularly in the 1980s as a result of the extreme compression of wage differentials that took place in the 1970s and into the early 1980s, which led to widespread dissatisfaction with the confederations' strategy of trying to flatten differentials. The proliferation of independent unions is particularly apparent in public sector areas, where there are some 700 trade unions, some of them with only a few dozen members. About 45% of public sector employees are unionized, with about two-thirds of these belonging to unions affiliated to the three main confederations. Leading autonomous unions include the Unione General del Lavoro (UGL), formerly known as CISNAL, and the Confederazione Italiana Sindacati Autonomi Lavoratori (CISAL). While these are weak overall, they have influence in particular sectors. In teaching, the autonomous unions Gilda and Cobas called a national teachers' strike and demonstration on Feb. 17, 2000, against new assessment procedures for performance related pay agreed by the three confederations. The protest was sufficiently well supported to cause the government to back down on implementation. In the loss-making Italian State Railways (FS) successive plans to tackle chronic problems of over-manning and inefficiency have been frustrated in part by minority autonomous unions that have been prepared to engage in disruption of services.

In the north, the Lega Nord, which has advocated the independence of "Padania" (the lands north of the Po), has also tried to set up its own trade union organization, the Sindacato Nazionale Padano (SinPa). According to Lega Nord's leader, Umberto Bossi, the three confederations had "robbed the northern workers". Although a mass organization drive for SinPa in 1997 was a conspicuous failure, it has had some success in plant-level

elections, calling for regional level collective bargaining to take account of the higher cost of living in the region.

The 1990s saw important changes in the development of social partnership in Italy. The Italian economy was previously characterized by deficit spending, high inflation, lack of consensual relationships between employers and unions, and direct state involvement in matters that in countries such as Germany were settled by collective bargaining between the two sides of industry. For 18 years from 1975 Italy had a system of wage indexation (the Scala Mobile) that by the 1990s had become a principal target for economic reformers as a driver of inflation not linked to productivity. It was finally abandoned in 1992. Thereafter there have been a series of national agreements extending the scope of social partnership. The process has involved achieving agreement between the social partners and government, with such agreements then embodied (sometimes in amended form) in legislation. In July 1993 a tripartite agreement was reached on incomes and employment policy, the structure of collective bargaining, and worker representation at company level. In Sept. 1996 the social partners entered into a Pact for Employment, this including provision for area (local and regional) pacts in order to promote jobs and investment in areas of high unemployment. These area agreements were to focus on planning for investment in infrastructure, increasing local level bargaining on work flexibility, and reducing bureaucracy. In 1997 legislation was adopted to increase flexibility, including the legalization of temporary work agencies. In Dec. 1998, a new social pact was agreed following the formation of the D'Alema government, this including measures such as further public investment, tax relief for companies, increased training schemes and action against irregular employment in the black economy. In July 2000, on the basis of the 1998 pact, the government said that it would use higher than expected tax receipts to reduce the tax burden on small and medium enterprises and on families, and help the poorest in society.

While negotiation and implementation of these various agreements has been accompanied by periodic threats of withdrawal by the various parties, the general willingness to seek convergence through discussion has represented a change in Italy's social and economic culture in which confrontational posturing has tended to be a tradition. Italy's over-riding need to achieve convergence with its EU partners in target areas such as inflation and size of the public deficit has been one factor. Another has been a growing willingness by the unions to accept that without greater flexibility, unemployment and regional under-development could not be tackled effectively. Most of the 450,000 new jobs created in 1998–99 were in areas such as part-time work, fixed-term contracts and temporary agency work. For the unions, the challenge has become to adapt to changing realities and build new positions. In the area of temporary work, the operation of temporary work agencies was legalized only in 1997, but in 1998 the temporary workers' organizations attached to the three confederations signed a collective agreement with the temporary workers' agencies association, Confiterim. In 1999 the parties reached agreement to extend the activities of agencies to low-skilled workers, agriculture and construction, the unions thereby agreeing to further flexibility but cementing a bargaining role in the process. The regulation of temporary work represented an advance for the unions on a situation in which a vast shadow economy of unregulated irregular work had grown up over which the unions had no influence.

The main employers' organization, Confindustria, has nonethless shown impatience with the pace of change, especially since its appointment of a new president, Antoni d'Amato, in May 2000. D'Amato has charged the unions with taking an "objectively conservative position" on issues such as welfare and pension reform and work flexibility. He has called for an "alliance for modernization" of the social partners and government to enable Italy to improve its lagging position in areas such as infrastructure, scientific research, innovation, job creation and growth rates.

One aspect of increased social partnership is that the trade union centres have shown more willingness in the 1990s to work together to find a coherent and unified voice for organized labour. This is not an entirely new process. From the 1960s, as the CGIL accepted the EEC and liberal Catholicism strengthened, relations between the CGIL and CISL improved. In 1972 CGIL, CISL and UIL jointly agreed that to achieve a unitary policy the confederations must be independent of the government and political parties, and they all accepted that union officials could not also be leaders of political parties, members of parliament, senators or town, provincial or regional councillors. A loose CGIL-CISL-UIL federation was then in place from 1972 until falling apart in disputes over the operation of the Scala Mobile in 1984.

Encouraged by the process of social partnership, by 1997, the leaders of all three centres were talking of merging their respective organizations into a unified centre by 2000. The merger project had lapsed by 1999, however, reflecting the fact that while the confederations have found common ground in many areas, they are divided in others, particularly the CGIL and CISL. Notwithstanding the decline of the old polarities in Italian politics, there are residual political differences, with the CISL seen as broadly sympathetic to the Partito Popolare Italiano (PPI), the heir to the Christian Democratic tradition, while the CGIL and UIL leaderships are close to the social democratic Democrats of the Left (Democratici di Sinistra, DS). These differences were reinforced in Oct. 1998 when the PPI left the government to go into opposition, with the subsequent formation of a new coalition government led by Massimo D'Alema of the DS.

The leaders of the confederations have also pointed to philosophical differences in that the more centralized CGIL adheres to a view of itself as the leader of a "labour movement", comprising both union and non-union workers, wile CISL sees itself as an association, stressing the role of union members in the individual workplace. CISL strongly favours worker representation on the board of companies, while CGIL opposes arguing that trade unions cannot represent the interests of both workers and employers.

The CGIL and CISL have also differed on the question of how far flexibility should be extended, the CGIL refusing to sign area agreements involving what it saw as too many concessions on this issue. The CISL has taken the view that the problems of areas of high unemployment (especially in the south where unemployment at the end of 1999, at 21.7%, was four times the level in the prosperous north of the country) can only be met by local agreements on setting wage levels below those in national agreements, but this view has been opposed by CGIL and the UIL.

Collective bargaining permeates the industrial relations system (often with direct political involvement) and tends to be wide-ranging. For example, the development of occupational pensions since 1997 came mainly though the establishment of sector-level large-scale schemes negotiated through collective bargaining. Under the 1993 tripartite agreement, private sector bargaining takes place at two levels. At national levels sectoral agreements are negotiated that must take into account the planned inflation rates agreed by the social partners and overall national competitiveness and set minimum rates of pay. These agreements may be supplemented by company-level or (particularly in the case of small enterprises) local area agreements that deal with specific local conditions and reflect performance and productivity. Traditionally the local level is the natural locus of Italian trade union activity more than is the enterprise and while sectoral agreements are widespread, only a minority of workplaces (mostly in large companies) are covered by company-level agreements. The principle applied by custom in collective bargaining is that an agreement applies to all workers in a bargaining unit, whether or not they are members of the signatory organizations. In the civil service pay and conditions are established by law, following negotiations with the trade unions, while such employees are immune from dismissal other than for disciplinary reasons. However, following an agreement with the unions in March 1997, nearly 3 million public employees, including state employees such as teachers and postal workers and employees of local authorities such as administrators and health workers, were removed from civil service status. Their bargaining arrangements were brought into line with the private sector, leaving only 800,000 employees (including the police and armed forces) with civil servant status. One consequence is that public sector managers may now be removed for inefficiency.

Traditionally Italian unions have been organized on clear sectoral lines but the development of new industries, and increasing diversification by firms out of their core sectors, has increasingly muddied these lines. In the telecommunications area, where multiple unions are operating, and there is no employers' association with bargaining rights, a collective agreement was negotiated directly by the three national centres with Confindustria in June 2000.

The 1993 agreement also led to the strengthening of private sector workplace representation by the establishment of a new structure, the unitary trade union representation body (Rappresentanze Sindacali Unitarie, RSU). The RSUs, which were extended to the public sector from 1997, have a dual function in that they not only carry out the role of participation and consultation typically seen in European works councils but also engage in collective bargaining as the representative of the trade unions. RSUs are made up of two-thirds delegates elected by all employees and one-third nominated by the trade unions that have signed the collective agreement in force in the company. The unions have traditionally been weak at the company level in the Italian system and the creation of the RSUs has been seen as consolidating their role and providing a more robust framework for industrial relations at this level. Elections to the RSUs also provide a benchmark for measuring the strength of the various unions. About 80 per cent of the votes have gone to candidates on lists presented by CGIL, CISL and UIL.

While conciliation and arbitration procedures exist, historically the adversarial nature of industrial relations has been such that the parties have tended to have recourse to other means of resolving disputes such as appeals to the courts, intervention by the state or resolution by conflict. Individual labour disputes run at extraordinary levels, with more than one million cases pending in the courts in 2000. There has traditionally been a virtually unrestricted right to strike, and this has been freely exercised. During the 1990s, however, the level of collective industrial disputes fell sharply from the level in the 1980s. Essential public services remained prone to disruption, often as a result of action by minority unions. This was despite 1990 legislation stipulating that providers of essential public services and unions must reach collective agreements on providing a guaranteed minimum service in the event of industrial action. Application of the 1990 law is supervised by an independent Guarantee Authority, but violations have been commonplace. In Apr. 2000 Parliament approved legislation extending the principle of self-limiting codes to other groups such as lawyers, taxi drivers and road haulage contractors, whose activities had caused disruption. The measure was welcomed by the main confederations but lawyers went on strike in protest.

3 Trade Union Centres
Confederazione Generale Italiana del Lavoro (CGIL)
Italian General Confederation of Labour

Address. Corso d'Italia 25, 00198 Rome

Phone. +39 6 84 761

Fax. +39 6 884 5683

Website. www.cgil.it (Italian only)

Leadership. Sergio Cofferati (secretary-general)

Membership. 5,231,360

History and character. The CGIL was formed by agreement between socialists, communists and Christian democrats in the "Pact of Rome" of June 1944 as a unified trade union centre. The CGIL at first functioned only in southern and central parts of Italy controlled by the Allies, but was accepted as nationally representative at a conference with the chambers of labour from the industrialized north in June 1945 after the surrender of German forces in that area. Under the Pact of Rome, socialists, communist and Christian democrats were to enjoy equal representation on the CGIL executive bodies. However, tensions between the different factions were encouraged after 1945 by the emergence of the Christian Democrats as the major political party and by the intensification of the ideological division of Europe, which was reflected in a campaign of strikes and violent unrest led by communists within the CGIL in 1947–48. By 1950 most socialists and Christian democrats had withdrawn from the CGIL (see CISL and UIL), and the confederation after that time was dominated by supporters of the Communist Party (PCI), although with a socialist minority, with close financial and other ties to the party.

The CGIL was for many years closely associated with the policies of the Soviet Union and its allies, but a modification of its position enabled the formation of the CGIL-CISL-UIL federation in 1972. In 1974, in step with the move to advocacy by the PCI of Eurocommunism, it downgraded its relationship with the WFTU, of which it had previously been the largest Western European affiliate, to that of associate, and withdrew altogether in 1978. In 1987 the CGIL called for union pluralism in Poland. The CGIL mainstream is now seen as broadly sympathetic to the policies of the Democrats of the Left (DS) party. The DS is descended organizationally but not ideologically from the Italian Communist Party (PCI) and is of social democratic orientation; the ideological descendants of the PCI are the Communist Refoundation Party (PRC), which also has support within CGIL. At the first congress of the DS, in Feb. 1997, Massimo D'Alema (the party leader) described CGIL secretary general Cofferati as being "closed and deaf" on the need for a radical overhaul the generous welfare and pension system. He warned that CGIL would be marginalized if it failed to adapt to social change.

CGIL membership rose from an average of 4.57 m. in the early 1980s to around 5.2 m in the early 1990s, since when it has remained fairly stable. However, the proportion of its membership that are pensioners has escalated, reaching 55% by 1999. In the period 1980–96 the number of CGIL members who were in the active work force fell by 33%. Traditionally CGIL's strength has been in manufacturing industry – where it has had about the same membership as the CISL and UIL combined – but this sector has declined and CGIL has had much less success in growing service sectors. While all three of the main centres have experienced this problem to some degree, the fall in membership among the actively employed has been most pronounced in the CGIL.

As in the other confederations, the pensioners are organized in their own union, which in the case of CGIL was founded as early as 1949. To offset the dominance of pensioner interests, the CGIL has rules that prevent any affiliate having more than 25% of the vote in decision-making bodies. The only affiliate affected by this is its pensioners' union (Sindacato pensionati italiani, SPI).

Of the three main centres the CGIL was the most reluctant to relinquish the Scala Mobile system of automatic wage indexation. When in July 1992 then secretary-general Bruno Trentin finally agreed to sign the tripartite agreement ending it, the resultant hostility led him to tender his resignation (subsequently rescinded).

During the 1990s relations with the other centres improved in step with the development of social partnership, as reflected in a series of tripartite agreements from 1993. In May 1997 the CGIL executive committee proposed the creation of a unified trade union centre by 2000, and the CISL and UIL also embraced this project. However, conflicts developed (in particular with CISL) over issues such as wage flexibility, where the CGIL proved unwilling to agree local area pacts that visualized lower wages to increase job creation, and over political alignments. CGIL secretary-general Sergio Cofferati told the May 1999 CISL assembly that it was no longer possible to continue with the merger project.

On May 20, 1999, Massimo D'Antona, the head of the juridicial council of CGIL and an adviser to the Minister of Labour, was assassinated by the Red Brigades terrorist organization. A Red Brigades statement called him the "political-operational pivot between the government and the confederal unions, the person who developed the political impact of the social pact and of the neo-corporatist strategy".

In May 1998 Sergio Cofferati said that the unions must press for uniform labour legislation across the EU and for European-level collective agreements, although this would take a decade or more to achieve.

International affiliations. ICFTU; ETUC; TUAC. The CGIL joined the ETUC in 1974 and in 1989 (with CISL and UIL support) became the first formerly communist-oriented West European union to enter the TUAC. The 1991 Congress resolved to seek entry into the ICFTU, and it joined the following year, again with the backing of the other two centres.

Confederazione Italiana Sindacati Lavoratori (CISL)
Italian Confederation of Workers' Trade Unions

Address. Via Po 21, 00198 Rome

Phone. +39 6 84731

Fax. +39 6 841 3782

E-mail. cisl@cisl.it

Website. www.cisl.it (Italian with English section)

Leadership. Sergio D'Antoni (secretary-general)

Membership. Reported 4,000,524 members in 1999, but of these 2,012,614 were pensioners.

History and character. CISL was founded in 1950 as a primarily Christian democratic split from the CGIL, and in its early years it received direct support from both the Roman Catholic Church and the AFL-CIO. It is one of the three main Italian confederations, all of which are affiliated to the ICFTU.

CISL has a diverse membership. It lags behind CGIL in manufacturing but is traditionally the leading confederation in the public sector. It is also the leading centre in representation of the self-employed. Like CGIL it has become increasingly an organization of pensioners, its pensioners' union (the Federazione nationale dei pensionati, FNP) representing 50% of total membership by 1999. To prevent sectional interests distorting policy, CISL rules limit any affiliate to 25% of the delegates at its congresses. Its membership in the active workforce fell by 25% from 1980–96.

CISL describes itself as non-partisan, non-ideological and non-denominational. Although many of its affiliates have a Catholic orientation, and many members are from the Christian democratic tradition, it also combined with CGIL and the UIL to oppose measures from Christian Democrat governments seen as inimical to its members. CISL was the first main union centre to adopt an incompatibility rule barring elected officers from running for political office. Thus Franco Marini, predecessor of D'Antoni in the office of secretary-general, resigned before taking up the position of Minister of Labour in 1991.

Following the electoral collapse of the Christian Democrats (the dominant party since World War II) amid corruption scandals in 1992–94, the party was re-launched as the Partito Popolare Italiano (PPI) in 1994. Participation by the PPI in the Prodi government of 1996–98 was a factor in encouraging CISL's positive engagement with government at that time. Conversely, since the PPI left the government in Oct. 1998 the CISL have had poorer relations with the succeeding coalitions led by the Democrats of the Left (DS). On Nov. 20, 1999, CISL organized an anti-government demonstration without the support of the other centres, criticizing the government on issue such as widening gap in employment between north and south and lack of action to reduce the tax burden on families. The CGIL and UIL are broadly sympathetic to the DS.

In May 1998 CISL secretary-general Sergio D'Antoni backed a strategy of creating a new alliance of Christian-oriented social, economic and political organizations, including the PPI, although CISL deputy secretary-general Raffaele Morese, expressed doubts about this initiative saying CISL should engage only in trade union, and not political, activities.

CISL says it seeks to protect not just the formally employed but those who have an irregular or marginal role in the labour market, including home workers, those in informal or undeclared employment, the unemployed, the disabled, the young and elderly. It advocates a strong regional policy to assist the economically backward southern region of the country. The CISL accepts that there needs to be much greater flexibility in wage policy and market regulation, and a different tax regime, for the south if jobs are to be created there. In contrast to the other centres, CISL sees flexibility as strengthening the unions, through increasing the role of local area and company bargaining.

CISL was the first of the major confederations to back the policy of "concertation", which led to a tripartite basis for economic reform, the defence of wages and jobs while containing inflation. It backed Italy's accession to the single European currency. It favours economic democracy and worker representation on company boards, an area where it disagrees with CGIL.

D'Amato said at the May 1999 CISL assembly that the goal was to cut the number of affiliated sectoral federations from 17 to 10.

CISL maintains several institutes and research centres. Prof. Enzo Tarantelli, then director of the CISL Research Institute, was murdered by Red Brigades terrorists in 1985.

International affiliations. ICFTU; ETUC; TUAC

Unione Italiana del Lavoro (UIL)
Italian Labour Union

Address. Via Lucullo 6, 00187 Rome

Phone. +39 647 531

Fax. +39 647 53 208

E-mail. info@uil.it

Website. www.uil.it (Italian with some information in English)

Leadership. Luigi Angeletti (general secretary)

Membership. 1,758,729

History and character. The UIL was founded in 1950 and named after an earlier organization which had split from the USI (Anarcho-Syndicalist Federation) in 1918 and opposed the fascists until banned under Mussolini. The UIL was created with predominantly republican and social democrat leadership, in opposition to the communist domination of the CGIL and the mainly Christian democratic control of CISL, and was expressly non-confessional. In the post-war ideological division of the trade union movement, the UIL was partly funded by the AFL-CIO. Subsequently it evolved to a left-wing reformist position which it still maintains.

The UIL describes itself as socialist, non-confessional and politically independent, and as being an advocate of full internal union democracy rather than adherence to ideological positions influenced by outside forces (i.e. in contrast, it argues, to the CGIL and CISL). It has, however, also called on occasions for unification of the various centres and backed the failed integration project launched in 1997. In recent years it has on occasions acted as a peacemaker between CISL and CGIL.

The UIL is the smallest of the three Italian centres. UIL membership includes a high proportion of pensioners, although at 25% in 1999 this was far less than the proportion of pensioners in the membership totals of the CGIL (55%) and CISL (50%). Similarly the proportion of members who are in the active workforce has declined less than that of the CGIL and CISL, falling 6% in the period 1980–96.

While nominally politically independent, and adhering to the self-imposed rule whereby union and political office cannot be held simultaneously, there are close ties to democratic socialist politics. UIL general secretary Giorgio Benvenuto stood down to become deputy finance minister early in 1992 and was then briefly leader of the Italian Socialist Party (PSI) in 1993. The UIL is now seen as close to the Democrats of the Left (DS), ideologically the successor to the PSI.

Pietro Larizza, who succeeded Benvenuto as UIL general secretary, was appointed president of the National Council for Economic Affairs and Labour (CNEL) in June 2000, and was succeeded by Luigi Angeletti.

UIL has created a variety of service organizations for members. These include ITAL (Institute for the Protection and Welfare of Workers; this operates both in Italy and in many countries to which Italians have emigrated); ENFAP (National Vocational Training Agency); UNIAT (National Union of Tenants); CREL (Centre for Economic and Labour Research); Instituto Progretto Sud (to develop cooperation with "the unions of the South", i.e. the Third World); ACPA (Citizens' Association for the Environment), and others.

The basic units are the branch workplace and regional unions. The UIL as a national confederation is formed by national unions of all categories and territorial, regional and provincial unions.

International affiliations. ICFTU; ETUC; TUAC

4 Other Trade Union Organizations

Confederazione del Comitati di Base (Cobas)
Address. Via Sannio 61, 00183 Rome

Phone. +39 6 772 50325

Fax. +39 6 772 06060

E-mail. internazionale@cobas.it

Website. www.cobas.it (Italian only)

History and character. Cobas originated in the late 1980s as rank-and-file movements dissatisfied with the leadership of the three main confederations. They comprised particularly skilled or professional groups that thought their interests were neglected by the confederations, and who rejected the partisan alignments of the confederations. Their main influence has been in public sector areas such as the state railways, essential services and the educational system. Their strength declined in the 1990s.

Confederazione Italiana Sindacati Autonomi Lavoratori (CISAL)
Italian Confederation of Free Workers' Unions
Address. Viale Giulio Cesare 21, 00192 Rome

Phone. +39 6 32 07941

Fax. +39 6 32 12521

E-mail. cisal@cisal.org

Website. www.cisal.org (Italian only)

Leadership. Giuseppe Carbone (general secretary)

History and character. CISAL was founded in 1957 and now associates 50 autonomous trade unions. CISAL has support mainly in schools and public administration. At its congress in Nov. 1999, it resolved to end the practice of signing "pirate agreements" with conditions inferior to those negotiated by the confederal unions, and to begin a process of reconciliation with the confederations, especially CISL.

International affiliations. European Confederation of Independent Trade Unions (CESI)

Unione Generale del Lavoro (UGL)
General Labour Union
Address. Via Margutta 19, 00187 Rome

Phone. +39 6 32 4821

Fax. +39 6 32 4822

Website. www.ugl.it (Italian only)

Leadership. Stefano Cetica (general secretary)

History and character. Founded in 1950, the UGL was known as the Confederazione Italiana dei Sindacati Nazionali dei Lavoratori (CISNAL) until 1996. Its links with right-wing politics made CISNAL's relationships with other trade union centres difficult. UGL says it is a union that emphasizes the centrality of the individual human being. Its structure includes 18 affiliated industrial federations. It affiliated to the WCL in Dec. 1997.

Publications. La Meta Sociale

International affiliations. WCL

Jamaica

Capital: Kingston
Population: 2.65 m. (2000 est.)

GDP (purchasing power parity) $8.8bn. (1999 est.); GDP per capita (purchasing power parity) $3,350 (1999 est.).

1 Political and Economic Background

The pro-Western Jamaica Labour Party (JLP) was founded in 1943 as the political wing of the Bustamante Industrial Trade Union. This formed the government from independence from the UK in 1962 to 1972, and again from 1980–89. In 1989 the People's National Party (PNP), previously in power from 1972–80 under Prime Minister Michael Manley, returned to office and has since won successive general elections in 1993 and 1997. During the 1970s the PNP took a radical left-wing course, opposing US policy and associating with Cuba, but in more recent years has adopted a centrist position. Manley retired in 1992 and was succeeded as Prime Minister by Percival Patterson.

The Jamaican economy is based principally upon sugar, bauxite and tourism. During the 1990s the PNP has applied policies of market liberalization and deregulation, ending most price controls and privatizing state enterprises. Jamaica continues to be affected by sluggish growth, however, and remains less prosperous than most of its neighbours in the English-speaking Caribbean.

2 Trade Unionism

Jamaica ratified ILO Conventions No.87 (Freedom of Association and Protection of the Right of Organize, 1948) and No.98 (Right to Organize and Collective Bargaining, 1949) in 1962, and there has been significant trade union activity since the 1940s.

The development of Jamaican trade unionism proceeded in harness with that of the country's political party system, with the Bustamante Industrial Trade Union (BITU), founded as a general union in 1938 by Alexander Bustamante, providing the basis for the creation of the Jamaica Labour Party in 1943. Similarly the National Workers' Union of Jamaica (NWU) was founded as an affiliate of the People's National Party (PNP) in 1952. Both the BITU and NWU were previously affiliated to the ICFTU, but ICFTU representation is now coordinated in the Jamaica Confederation of Trade Unions (JCTU).

The right to form unions and bargain collectively is regulated by the Labour Relations and Industrial

Disputes Act (LRIDA) of 1975 (as amended) which prohibits discrimination against workers for union membership. Unions operate freely and about 15% of the workforce is organized.

Collective bargaining is developed. Where agreement between management and unions cannot be reached issues may be referred for adjudication to the Ministry of Labour, and appeals against Ministry decisions may be made to the independent Industrial Disputes Tribunal (IDT). The IDT deals with some 35–40 cases per year.

The right to strike is prohibited under LRIDA in a range of "essential services" including banking, transport, the docks and oil refining, and the Labour Minister is empowered to refer all disputes to compulsory arbitration. "Essential services" has been interpreted to include areas such as bauxite mining and education, where compulsory arbitration has been imposed to end strikes.

The labour laws apply to the export processing zones (where about 10,000 are employed), but no unions have been established in the zones.

Jamaica has a number of bipartite and tripartite institutions including the Labour Advisory Council and the National Planning Council. Unions are consulted about industrial relations matters and assist in the development of social programmes.

3 Trade Union Centre

Jamaica Confederation of Trade Unions (JCTU)

Address. 1A Hope Boulevard, Kingston 6

Phone. +1876 927 2468

Fax. +1876 977 4575

E-mail. jctu@cwjamaica.com

Website. www.jctu.org (under construction Dec. 2000)

Leadership. Lloyd Goodleigh (general secretary)

Membership. Comprises 11 of Jamaica's major trade unions.

International affiliations. ICFTU; CTUC

Japan

Capital: Tokyo
Population: 126.5 m. (2000 est.)

1 Political and Economic Background

The Liberal Democratic Party (LDP) has been in office almost continuously since its formation in 1955. Although its position weakened in the early 1990s amid a series of scandals and splits, it has remained the largest party through a succession of unstable government coalitions and constant realignments and changes of name among the various other political parties. The LDP took 233 of the 500 seats in the most recent elections to the House of Representatives in June 2000 and dominates the ruling coalition, which includes two other parties, New Komeito and the New Conservative Party. The Prime Minister is Yoshiro Mori of the LDP.

Japan suffered catastrophic defeat in World War II. In the following decades it rebuilt its economy on the basis of intensive government-industry cooperation, a strong work ethic and the development of world-class export-oriented companies in sectors such as automobiles and electronics. In the late 1980s the soaring value of the yen led to a phase of speculative investment and an asset

price bubble that burst in the early 1990s to be followed by years of sluggish domestic demand, nil or negligible growth, deflation, commercial collapses and rising unemployment. Further recession in 1997–98 was followed by marginal growth (0.3%) in 1999, with full year growth recovering somewhat to a projected full year 1.6% for 2000. With business investment depressed by low profitability and lack of confidence and consumers not spending, the economy appeared incapable of generating any growth without a series a series of injections of government spending, these producing a mounting burden of public debt. In all from 1992–99 the government announced ten supplementary spending packages with a total value in excess of $1 trillion without producing any sustained growth. Much of this money reportedly went into "pork barrel" public works projects to aid political interests rather than supporting innovation and restructuring. Western interest in the "Japanese model" as a paradigm for success, at its peak in the late 1980s, has given way to the perception of Japan as a country unable to adapt to the transformation of world markets and rise of lower-cost competitors. It nonetheless remains the world's third largest economy, after those of the US and China, with a good living standard for most citizens.

GDP (purchasing power parity) $2.95 trillion (1999 est.); GDP per capita (purchasing power parity) $23,400 (1999 est.).

2 Trade Unionism

In the mid-1930s there were 420,000 trade union members and a Japan Confederation of Labour (Nihon-Rodei-Sodomei). By 1940, this confederation had been dissolved by the government, and until the defeat of Japan in World War II workers were mobilized in Sangyo Hokoku (Service to the State through Industry). Following World War II the Trade Union Law of December 1945 for the first time formally guaranteed workers the right to organize trade unions, and Article 28 of the 1946 Constitution guaranteed workers the right to organize, bargain collectively and to strike. Sodomei was re-established in 1945 but the trade union movement was divided by intense ideological conflict over the following decade against a background of appreciable industrial unrest and underwent a complex process of fragmentation.

As of the mid-1980s, there were two major centres, Sohyo (with 4.36 million members) and Domei (with 2.16 million members), while a third significant centre, Churitsuroren had 1.56 million members. These three accounted for 65% of organized labour. Domei alone was internationally affiliated (to the ICFTU). Churitsuroren and Domei were based overwhelmingly in the private sector, while 60% of Sohyo members were in the public sector. In the period 1987–89 the mainstream trade union movement underwent unification. In 1987 a new private sector trade union centre, Rengo, was formed by the affiliates of Domei and Churitsuroren and a number of the private sector affiliates from Sohyo. Then, in 1989, private sector Rengo and Sohyo merged to form the Japanese Trade Union Confederation (Rengo), which became the third largest national centre affiliated to the ICFTU.

As of 1998, according to Ministry of Labour figures, there were 12,093,000 union members. Of these 7,476,000 (62%) were in unions affiliated to Rengo. The only alternative trade union centre of any significance is Zenroren (National Confederation of Trade Unions), which according to the Ministry of Labour had 837,000 members, although Zenroren itself claimed 1,531,000. There is also a small third centre, Zenrokyo (National Trade Unions Council), which has only 270,000 members. There are some large independent unions, the biggest of which is Zenkensoren (National Federation of Construction Workers' Unions), with 715,000 members. In addition, unions federate in some important sectoral bodies, most notably the Japan Council of Metalworkers' Unions (IMF-JC), with 2,356,000 members.

The basic rights of private sector workers – comprising 82% of all organized workers – are guaranteed by the Trade Union Law of 1945 and the Labour Relations Adjustment Law, but public sector employees are covered by separate legislation. In addition Japan ratified ILO Conventions No.98 (Right to Organize and Collective Bargaining, 1949) in 1953 and No.87 (Freedom of Association and Protection of the Right to Organize, 1948) in 1965. Managers with direct authority in respect of hiring, firing, promotions and transfers are barred from joining unions under the Trade Union Law. With middle managers (who mostly have only shared or ambiguous involvement in hiring and firing) themselves now significantly affected by de-layering in big companies, and the unions anxious to find new sources of recruitment, the trade unions have pushed through collective bargaining to broaden the areas of supervisory personnel they may recruit. Public sector employees, other than police, fire fighters, prison employees, the Self Defence Forces and the Coast Guard, are permitted to organize and may not be discriminated against for so doing; such organizations may negotiate with the employer within limits but may not take industrial action. For many years controversy has surrounded the position of firefighters, as these are usually allowed to join unions in countries where the military and police are not; in 1995 the government agreed a consultation process with Rengo affiliate Jichiro for the firefighters, but they still may not to join unions.

The basic form of trade union organization in Japan is the single-enterprise union, which is either workplace- or enterprise- based, and which organizes all full time workers regardless of job classification. (A parallel system exists in the public sector, based on individual offices, corporations, etc.). Industrial federations and confederations – which are poorly funded relative to the enterprise unions – have negligible control over their affiliated enterprise unions, and the role of the industrial federations has often been peripheral. Their role is weakened by the fact that as multiple trade union centres existed into the 1980s there are commonly several industrial federations operating in any one sector. Their role has tended to increase somewhat in more recent years, however, as the industrial federations have become involved in such issues as the introduction of new technology and the problems of depressed areas and industries, and increasing job mobility may ultimately weaken the dominance of enterprise unionism.

Although industrial relations were commonly adversarial in the 1940s and 1950s, with a strong ideological element in trade unionism at that time, the character of enterprise unionism has come to reflect and reinforce that of modern Japanese industrial relations. This is characterized by a close relationship between the two sides of industry, involving a high degree of both formal and informal consultation in good faith. To a considerable degree, the view prevails that "the union exists because the company exists". Japan's consistently strong performance after World War II enabled large employers in effect to guarantee a job for life, and individuals entering the workforce typically made career plans involving a commitment to a particular firm rather than to type of occupation. Employers preferred to re-train workers in line with changes in technology and business focus, rather than lay them off and recruit new workers. Furthermore, as salary levels were rigidly tied to seniority, loyalty brought an increasing reward. The enterprise unions became enmeshed in the company to the degree that union chairmen were often given access to highly confidential information about the company's position and strategies. The process of consultation provided for a degree of flexibility in making decisions about working conditions that could reflect the enterprise's underlying condition. A pattern was created of union officers moving on to management positions within the same company, often switching roles on the same day. Large employers have adopted policies that have entrenched the position of the enterprise unions. The majority of large companies operate union shop agreements, with union membership for new workers becoming compulsory within a set period of joining the company. Where closed shops exist, the activism and commitment of members to the union is not tested by voluntary payment of contributions, and apathy is considered widespread with union dues seen as a tax on the job.

While the foundations of this system have been disturbed to some degree by Japan's persistent economic difficulties in the 1990s, and major corporations have initiated lay-offs and begun to link pay more to performance, the changes have not yet been fundamental. Both Rengo and Nikkeiren (the Japan Federation of Employers' Associations) remain wedded to a view of industrial relations that emphasizes the desirability of jobs for life and payment linked to length of service (basic salaries in large companies rising with age until 50). Surveys at the end of the 1990s indicated that more than half of Japanese corporations would prefer to retain the lifetime employment system if at all possible, regardless of short-term business results. Indeed, some research indicates that average length of service at one place of employment has actually increased in the 1990s.

One consequence of the enterprise union system is that it has excluded large sections of the workforce. The typical union member is in full-time work and employed by a major company or in the public sector. In 1999 some 57.2% of employees in private sector companies with more than 1,000 employees were union members. In contrast, a mere 1.4% of employees in companies of fewer than 99 employees were in unions. The enterprise union system is based on the existing major companies; it lacks the flexibility to deal effectively with new companies in emergent industries and with new forms of irregular work. The industrial federations are in most cases poorly resourced to undertake organizational activities and the enterprise unions are by definition more concerned with what happens in their own company rather than in the sector as a whole.

While trade union leadership nationally is aware of this problem and has set goals to broaden organizational work, this aspiration has had little impact. The total number of workers in unions has stagnated over the last two decades, standing at 12.47 million in 1981

and 11.83 million in 1999. However, with the expansion of the workforce this meant that density declined from 30.8% in 1981 to 22.2% by 1999. Furthermore, the unions lost members steadily in the late 1990s. Although density declined every single year 1981–99, union membership actually peaked at 12.7 million in 1994. After that it fell for five straight years thereafter, reflecting job losses in unionized sectors, and in 1999 falling below 12 million for the first time since 1973.

The process of wage bargaining is coordinated in the "shunto" or "Spring Labour Offensive" in which co-ordinated wage demands are presented to all employers each Spring. The agreements reached through the shunto affect wage determination for all workers, including those denied true collective bargaining rights and non-union workers. The shunto – which in effect coordinates what would be the otherwise limited bargaining power of Japanese enterprise unionism – was first employed on a significant scale (under Sohyo leadership) in the 1950s. It was encouraged thereafter by the rapid development of the Japanese economy and labour shortages, with Domei unions (which had initially opposed the practice) joining in the 1960s. Despite the militant format of the shunto, since the 1970s wage increases achieved through this process have generally trailed productivity gains and although most strikes occur around the time of the shunto the level of industrial disputes has been low since the 1970s. Simultaneously with negotiations in the private sector, settlements for labour in public corporations and national enterprises are reached through mediation by the Public Corporation and National Labour Relations Commission and are subsequently embodied in an arbitration award. In practice the Commission normally links public sector awards closely to those in the private sector. The same is true of awards for public service employees reached through the National Personnel Authority and for local public service awards made at municipality level.

Japan's protracted economic difficulties in the 1990s have put strains on the bargaining system. With the economy stagnant, wage increases in absolute terms have fallen to new low levels, in the range 2–3% each year 1995–2000, and falling to a record low of 2.06% for major private employers in 2000 (but against a background of a deflationary economy experiencing almost zero growth). Unemployment rose steadily from 2.9% in 1994 to 4.7% by 1999 and although these levels are not high by international standards, the phenomenon of radical restructuring and downsizing is a new one and has unsettled the unions, as have the growth in part-time and discretionary working. At the same time, employers have shown increasing dissatisfaction with the stranglehold of national norms and have begun to show increasing awareness of the interests of shareholders as opposed to employees. In Spring 2000, the five major companies in the steel sector, facing increasing competition among themselves for market share, for the first time put forward and agreed different basic wage increases rather than acting as a group. The development was seen as significant as this sector customarily sets trends for industry as a whole.

The number of days lost in industrial disputes declined steadily after the high inflation of the mid-1970s, and strikes are now rare. During 1998, for instance, only 105,000 working days were lost, with only 42,000 employees involved. Indeed, there has been a trend for unions to reallocate strike funds to cover shortfalls in general operating costs caused by falling memberships since the mid-1990s. The right to strike is guaranteed in the private sector, but employees in national and local government and the national enterprises (postal service, forestry service, government printing and the mint) are prohibited from striking. The right to strike is also restricted in the electric power and coal mining industries, the merchant marine and in the public utilities generally. Political and sympathetic strikes (which are rare) are generally considered unlawful, as are wildcat strikes, strikes involving sabotage or a threat to safe workplace practices, and strikes violating industrial peace clauses of existing collective bargaining agreements. Unions engaged in legitimate strikes are exempt from civil and criminal liabilities; where strike action is considered illegitimate, employers may seek to dismiss or discipline the strike leaders but rarely seek damages from the union, or to impose sanctions on those who merely followed the strike call. The Labour Relations Adjustment Law provides for conciliation, mediation and arbitration, which may be carried out through the Labour Relations Commission; this body (which is structured at both national and local levels) is tripartite in composition. In practice, however, most disputes are settled directly between employers and unions. A Public Corporation and National Enterprise Labour Relations Commission exists to adjust disputes in the national enterprises (where industrial action is prohibited), and this is supplemented by a Grievance Handling Joint Adjustment Council. Local public enterprises are excepted from certain areas of the Trade Union Law and Labour Relations Adjustment Law, but disputes in this field are adjusted by the Labour Relations Commission.

Japan has an ageing population. In Apr. 2000 Rengo and the employers' association Nikkeiren issued a joint statement calling on companies to make their operations more family friendly, by expanding child care and allowing more flexible working time arrangements. The ageing population is also putting pressure on the pensions system. The qualifying age for the basic state pension is to be raised in stages from 60, one year every three years from 2001, until it reaches 65 by 2013. In response to this, unions are seeking a raising of company retirement ages, which in major companies are currently nearly always set at 60, so that employees do not have to retire before they qualify for a state pension. This was a leading issue in the Spring 2000 shunto. Some companies have also warned that as a result of low interest rates and the ageing workforce, company pension scheme reserves would prove insufficient without further injections of funds.

3 Trade Union Centre

Rengo
Japanese Trade Union Confederation

Address. Sohyo Kaikan bldg., 3-2-11 Kanda Surugadai, Chiyoda-ku, Tokyo 101-0062

Phone. +81 3 5295 0550

Fax. +81 3 5295 0535

E-mail. jtuc-kokusai@mud.biglobe.ne.jp

Website. www.jtuc-rengo.org (Japanese; English)

Leadership. Etsuya Washio (president); Kiyoshi Sasamori (general secretary)

Membership. 7,476,000

History and character. Rengo was formed as a unified national trade union centre in 1989 by the merger of the former private sector Rengo (itself created in 1987, and based largely on the former Domei) and the public sector Sohyo. As of 1999, 63.3% of the Japanese unionized work force were in Rengo affiliated unions.

Domei and Sohyo had their origins in the complex restructuring and splits that affected the Japanese trade union movement for two decades after World War II. Sohyo originated in 1950 as a breakaway from a communist-dominated All-Japan Congress of Industrial Unions, which existed from 1946–58. Sohyo's initial intent to affiliate to the ICFTU changed in opposition to that organization's stance on the Korean War, the 1951 Japan-US Security Treaty and related issues. In the mid-1950s a faction within the leftist leadership of Sohyo emphasizing economic demands, rather than conflict with the USA, gained the ascendancy, and in 1956 Sohyo and other unions initiated the full shunto. Radical politics and class struggle ideology declined thereafter at Sohyo and by the 1980s it was emphasizing the modernization of industrial relations to take account of the changed realities of Japanese economic and political life. The drive to privatize the National Corporations, particularly the Japan National Railways which was split into a number of private companies in 1987, seems to have convinced most Sohyo public sector affiliates that it was necessary to ally with the more thriving private sector unions. Domei, whose membership was overwhelmingly in the private sector, was formed in the early 1960s and pursued polices based mainly on a contractual approach to industrial relations.

New Rengo had to reconcile the different political traditions of the former Domei and Sohyo. Throughout its history Sohyo was linked to the Japan Socialist Party (JSP, renamed the Socialist Democratic Party of Japan, SDJP, in 1991). The JSP, founded in 1945, was briefly involved in a coalition government in 1947–48 but then was in opposition for several decades, providing the principal opposition to the ruling LDP. Its party platform in the 1960s advocated non-alignment and a democratic transition from capitalism to socialism but by the 1980s the party was moving from its more leftist positions to a European socialist model. The party was heavily dependent on Sohyo support, having a much weaker membership base than socialist parties in western European countries. As of 1985, 65 of the 111 Socialist members of the House of Representatives and 29 of the 43 Socialist members of the House of Councillors were former officers of Sohyo or its member unions. Domei in contrast was the most important supporter of the small Democratic Socialist Party (DSP), which had originated as a right-wing breakaway in 1960 from the Socialist Party.

Rengo's founding president Akira Yamagishi was an advocate of building a centre-left challenge to the LDP, which had dominated Japanese politics since World War II, and sought a fusion of the SDPJ and the DSP. At the same time, many of the traditional party alliances of former Domei and Sohyo unions remained intact and relations between the two parties were poor. The absolute dominance of the LDP was indeed broken in elections in July 1993 elections when the LDP, although remaining the largest party, lost power to an opposition coalition which included the DSP and the SDPJ. However, Japanese politics had become highly unstable and fractious, with continuing political realignments and Rengo's own strategy fell victim to this. In Apr. 1994 the SDPJ left the coalition and in June 1994 a new government was formed with Tomiichi Murayama of the SDJP as Prime Minister but with the LDP as the dominant force and the SDPJ abandoning some of its historic policies. The Sept. 1994 decision of Rengo president Akira Yamagishi to stand down early on grounds of ill health was viewed as influenced by his disappointment at seeing his hopes for a DSP and SDPJ merger dashed by the SDPJ entering government, thus leaving the two parties opposed to each other. In addition, some union leaders believed Rengo was becoming too deeply embroiled in party politics, which would only result in a split, and should re-focus on economic issues. As a result of further political realignments, by the time of the 1998 elections to the House of Councillors (upper house) Rengo was giving its main support to the Democratic Party of Japan (DPJ), formed in 1997, but also supported other candidates opposed to the LDP and the Japan Communist Party. Following elections to the House of Representatives in June 2000 the DPJ remained the largest opposition party, increasing its total of seats from 95 to 127.

Organizationally, Rengo is built on a base of unions formed at the enterprise level, but enterprise unions are absent in many small companies, as well as often representing only full-time workers. From Rengo's foundation a goal was to expand the unionized sector beyond full-time employees in big corporations and the public sector so as to reach out to the large number of non-core part-time and irregular workers and to workers in small and medium-sized enterprises where unions rarely exist. In 1996 Rengo launched a project to recruit 1.1 million members over three years, setting up a regional union structure to which individual workers who were not in enterprise unions could affiliate directly. This initiative has also been taken up by some of its key industrial fed-

eration affiliates. However, these measures have thus far had little impact on the overall position and Rengo's membership declined from 7.88 million in the late 1980s to 7.48 million by 1998. To some degree this reflects a perception by employees in irregular work and smaller enterprises that trade unionism is irrelevant to their needs. It also reflects the fact that resources are concentrated at the enterprise union level and enterprise unions are concerned with the position in their own companies rather than broader organizational drives. With membership dues falling the trend has been for unions to cut staffing levels, with an impact on scale of operations. Likewise pursuit of a policy of equal opportunities for women has only had modest impact, only 6.5% of officers of Rengo affiliates being women as of 1998. In Japan not only are women responsible for most household duties, there is a strong perception, which affects all areas of society, that this burden precludes them from effectively exercising other responsibilities. Japanese unions, being enterprise based, customarily do not represent the unemployed. However, in Sept. 1999, Rengo affiliate Zensen (the Japanese Federation of Textile, Garment, Chemical, Mercantile, Food and Allied Industries Workers' Unions) said it would set up an organization specifically for the unemployed.

Japan's protracted economic difficulties in the 1990s, the historically unprecedented levels of unemployment, the mounting demands of employers for more labour flexibility, and the declining number of union members, have put Rengo on the defensive. General secretary Kiyoshi Sasamori told the 1999 congress that "job security is the life line of labour unions" and Rengo has concentrated on trying to defend established positions in areas such as automatic increases for seniority and jobs for life. It calls for increased government spending to stimulate the economy and increase jobs and criticized the 2000 budget for lack of emphasis on public works. Overtime (often unpaid) is widespread in Japan and Rengo has called for reduced overtime working to allow job-sharing and for tighter restrictions on dismissals. A 1996 Rengo survey showed that average annual hours worked per employee were 2,040 and it has campaigned to reduce this to 1,800 (government figures indicated that average hours worked fell from 1,919 in 1996 to 1,840 in 1999).

While there has been no wholesale repudiation of the established system by big corporations, some employers are more aggressively pursuing a policy of restructuring and cutting costs and calling for wages and conditions to more realistically reflect the position of individual companies. Kiyoshi Sasamori said in May 2000 that advocates of such changes "propose a shift to American-style management, which focuses on short-term profits and caters to shareholders – a shift from a far-sighted to a short-sighted system". The vital issues of deregulating markets and reforming the bureaucracy have to some degree divided the unions, however. Unions representing export-oriented sectors such as autos and electronics are not unsympathetic to the view that areas of the economy that are inward-looking with low productivity should be reformed, and there remains a fault line between the private and public sectors.

Rengo has encouraged unification and realignment of its affiliates, but this has been a slow process. There are 74 affiliated industry federations and some of these are very small, with only a few thousand members, lacking resources to organize effectively. Kiyoshi Sasamori has said that he wishes to see the Rengo affiliates at industry level reduced to about 20 in the coming years. However, in recent years there have been only two substantial mergers, those leading to the formation of CSG Rengo in 1996 and the 1999 merger of Zenkin Rengo and Kinzoku Kikai to form the Japanese Association of Metal, Machinery and Manufacturing Workers (JAM). The latter was the largest merger since the formation of Rengo and created its fifth largest affiliate, with 500,000 members.

Rengo has an associated think tank, the Research Institute for the Advancement of Living Standards (RIALS). Its Japan International Labour Foundation (JILAF) promotes international cooperation in the labour area. In 1995 Rengo set up the Institute of Labour Education and Culture (ILEC) which runs programmes and workshops.

Rengo participates in the tripartite Industry and Labour Round-Table Conference, set up in 1970. The focus of the Conference series in recent years has been mainly on structural change. It also takes part, as the representative of organized labour, on the Government-Labour-Management Council on Employment Problems, established in Sept. 1998.

International affiliations. ICFTU; TUAC

Affiliates. The following are the major Rengo affiliates, in order of size.

1. Jichiro (All-Japan Prefectural and Municipal Workers' Union)

Address. Jichiro Kaikan Bldg, 1 Rokuban-cho, Chiyoda-ku, Tokyo 102-8464
Phone. +81 3 3263 0263
Fax. +81 3 5210 7422
E-mail. info@jichiro.or.jp
Website. www.jichiro.or.jp (Japanese; English section)
Membership. 1,024,210
History and character. Founded in 1954, this is the largest Japanese trade union with 3,243 local unions and 47 prefectural headquarters. Its members are primarily employees of local government and enterprises established by local authorities, and its main concern is the impact of privatization and downsizing on job security and working conditions. Although 40% of members are women, 90% of elected officials are men and while Jichiro has adopted a programme to rectify the imbalance, this is proving difficult in practice. Jichiro runs a range of mutual aid programmes for members and has also established an Asia Children's Homes project, which has built homes in Vietnam, Laos and Cambodia. It is a member of Public Services International (PSI).

2. Jidosha Soren (Confederation of Japan Automobile Workers' Unions, JAW)

Address. c/o U-Life Center, 1-4-26 Kaigan, Minato-ku, Tokyo 105-0022

Phone. +81 3 3434 7641
Fax. +81 3 3434 7428
Website. www.jaw.or.jp (Japanese only)
Leadership. Tadayoshi Kusano (president)
Membership. 792,420
History and character. Founded in 1972, this is the largest Rengo private sector affiliate. It comprises 12 federations of enterprise-based unions.

3. Denki Rengo (Japanese Electrical, Electronic and Information Union)

Address. Kaikan Bldg, 1-10-3 Mita, Minato-ku, Tokyo 108-8326
Phone. +81 3 3455 6911
Fax.. +81 3 3452 5406
Website. www.jeiu.or.jp (Japanese; English section)
Leadership. Katsutoshi Suzuki (president)
Membership. 764,658

4. Zensen (Japanese Federation of Textile, Garment, Chemical, Mercantile, Food and Allied Industries Workers' Unions)

Address. Zensen Domei Kaikan Bldg, 4-8-16 Kudan-Minami, Chiyoda-ku, Tokyo 102-0074
Phone. +81 3 3288 3549
Fax. +81 3 3288 3728
E-mail. soumu@zensen.or.jp
Website. www.zensen.or.jp (Japanese only)
Membership. 577,362
History and character. Zensen was based in the textile industry but as this sector has declined it has diversified into new areas such as the computer industry.

5. Japan Association of Metal, Machinery and Manufacturing Workers (JAM)

Address. Yuai Kaikan Bldg, 2-20-12 Shiba, Minato-ku, Tokyo 105-0014
Phone. +81 3 3451 2141
Fax. +81 3 3452 0239
E-mail. zenkin@union.email.ne.jp
Website. www.jam-union.or.jp (Japanese only)
Membership. 500,000
History and character. JAM was formed in Sept. 1999 by the merger of two Rengo affiliates, Zenkin Rengo (Japanese Federation of Metal Industry Workers' Unions) and the smaller Kinzoku Kikai (National Metal and Machinery Workers' Union of Japan).

6. Seiho Roren (National Federation of Life Insurance Workers' Unions)

Address. Tanaka Building, 3-19-5 Yushima, Bunkyo-ku, Tokyo 113-0034
Phone. +81 3 3837 2031
Fax. +81 3 3837 2037
Membership. 407,973

7. Nikkyoso (Japan Teachers' Union)

Address. Nihon Kyoiku Kaikan Bldg, 2-6-2 Hitotsubashi, Chiyoda-ku, Tokyo 101-0003
Phone. +81 3 3265 2171
Fax. +81 3 3230 0172
E-mail. international@jtu-net.or.jp
Website. www.jtu-net.or.jp (Japanese; English section)
Leadership. Yuji Kawakami (president)
Membership. 380,000

8. Joho Roren (Japan Federation of Telecommunications, Electronic Information and Allied Workers)
Address. Zendentsu Rodo Kaikan Bldg, 3-6 Kanda Surugadai, Chiyoda-ku, Tokyo 101-0062
Phone. +81 3 3219 2231
Fax. +81 3 3253 3268
E-mail. info@joho.or.jp
Website. www.joho.or.jp (Japanese only)
Membership. 266,217

9. Denryoku Soren (Confederation of Electric Power Related Industry Workers' Unions of Japan)
Address. Tds Mita 3F, 2-7-13 Mita, Minato-ku, Tokyo 108-0073
Phone. +81 3 3454 0231
Fax. +81 3 3798 1470
Membership. 250,295

10. CSG Rengo
Address. Yuai-Kaikan Bldg, 20-12, Shiba 2-chome, Minato-ku, Tokyo 105
Phone. +81 3 3453 3801
Fax. +81 3 3454 2236
Membership. 237,474
History and character. CSG Rengo was formed in Oct. 1996 by merger of the Japanese Federation of Chemical and General Workers' Unions, the National Federation of General Workers' Unions and the Council of Chemical Workers' Unions. Its diverse membership is in areas including pharmaceuticals, cosmetics, chemicals, building materials, printing, hospitals, city gas, hotels, foodstuffs, commerce, distribution and transportation. Its initials CSG signify "Chemistry, Services and General".

11. Tekko Roren (Japan Federation of Steel Workers' Unions)
Address. 1S-Riverside Bldg, 1-23-4 Shinkawa, Chuo-ku, Tokyo 104-0033
Phone. +81 3 3555 0401
Fax. +81 3 3555 0407
Membership 193,472

12. Shitetsu Soren (General Federation of Private Railway and Bus Workers' Unions of Japan)
Address. Shitetsu Kaikan, 4-3-5 Takanawa, Minato-ku, Tokyo 108-0074
Phone. +81 3 3473 0166
Fax. +81 3 3447 3927
Membership. 184,716

13. Zentei (Japan Postal Workers' Union)
Address. Zentei Kaikan Bldg, 1-2-7 Koraku, Bunkyo-ku, Tokyo 112-8567
Phone. +81 3 3812 4261
Fax. +81 3 5684 7201
Website. www.zentei.or.jp (Japanese only)
Membership. 158,691

14. Unyu Roren (All Japan Federation of Transport Workers' Unions)
Address. Zennittsu Kasumigaseki Bldg, 3-3-3 Kasumigaseki, Chiyoda-ku, Tokyo 100-0013
Phone. +81 3 3503 2171
Fax. +81 3 3503 2176
Website. www.unyuroren.or.jp (Japanese only)

Membership. 138,883

15. Zosen Juki Roren (Japan Confederation of Shipbuilding and Engineering Workers' Unions)
Address. Yuai Kaikan Bldg, 2-20-12 Shiba, Minato-ku, Tokyo 105-0014
Phone. +81 3 3451 6783
Fax. +81 3 3451 6935
Membership. 133,407

16. Shogyo Roren (Japan Federation of Commercial Workers' Unions)
Address. 2-23-1 Yoyogi, Shibuya-ku, Tokyo 151-0053
Phone. +81 3 3370 4121
Fax. +81 3 3370 1640
Membership. 129,043

17. Shokuhin Rengo (Japan Federation of Food and Tobacco Workers' Unions)
Address. Hiroo Office Bldg 8F, 1-3-18 Hiroo, Shibuya-ku, Tokyo 150-0012
Phone. +81 3 3446 2082
Fax. +81 3 3446 6779
Website. www.airnet.ne.jp/jfu (Japanese only)
Membership. 116,747

18. Kotsu Roren (Japan Federation of Transport Workers' Unions)
Address. Yuai Kaikan Bldg, 2-20-12 Shiba, Minato-ku, Tokyo 105-0014
Phone. +81 3 3451 7243
Fax. +81 3 3454 7393
Membership. 103,307

19. Goka Roren (Japanese Federation of Synthetic Chemistry Workers' Unions)
Address. Senbai Bldg, 5-26-30 Shiba, Minato-ku, Tokyo 108-8389
Phone. +81 3 3452 5591
Fax. +81 3 3454 7464
Membership. 91,242

20. Zen Yusei (All Japan Postal Labour Union)
Address. Zenyusei Kaikan Bldg, 1-20-6 Sendagaya, Shibuya-ku, Tokyo 151-8502
Phone. +81 3 3478 7101
Fax. +81 3 5474 7085
E-mail. zenyusei@mrj.biglobe.ne.jp
Membership. 77,718

21. JR-Rengo (Japan Railway Trade Unions Confederation)
Address. Toko Bldg, 1-8-10 Nihonbashi Muro-machi, Chuo-ku, Tokyo 103-0022
Phone. +81 3 3270 4590
Fax. +81 3 3270 4429
Membership. 77,700

22. JR-Soren (Japan Confederation of Railway Workers' Unions)
Address. Meguro Satsuki Kaikan Bldg, 3-2-13 Nishi Gotanda, Shinagawa-ku, Tokyo 141-0031
Phone. +81 3 3491 7191
Fax. +81 3 3491 7192
Membership. 70,710

23. Nikkenkyo (Council of Japan Construction Industry Employees' Unions)

Address. Moriyama bldg, 1-31-16 Takadanobaba, Shinjuku-ku, Tokyo 169-0075

Phone. +81 3 5285 3870

Fax. +81 3 5285 3879

Membership. 70,152

24. Kagaku Soren (Japanese Federation of Chemical Workers' Unions)

Address. Kyodo Bldg, 2-4-10 Higashi-Shinbashi, Minato-ku, Tokyo 105-0021

Phone. +81 3 5401 2268

Fax. +81 3 5401 2263

Membership. 67,629

25. Gomu Rengo (Japanese Rubber Workers' Union Confederation)

Address. Gomu Sangyo Kaikan Bldg 2F, 2-3-3 Mejiro, Toshima-ku, Tokyo 171-0031

Phone. +81 3 3984 3343

Fax. +81 3 3984 5862

Membership. 62,307

26. Zenkoku Ippan (National Union of General Workers)

Address. Zosen Kaikan bldg 5fl., 3-5-6 Misaki-cho, Chiyoda-ku, Tokyo 101-0061

Phone. +81 3 3230 4071

Fax. +81 3 3230 4360

Membership. 60,096

27. Kamipa Rengo (Japanese Federation of Pulp and Paper Workers' Unions)

Address. Kami Pulp Rodo Kaikan bldg, 2-12-4 Kita-Aoyama, Minato-ku, Tokyo 107-0061

Phone. +81 3 3402 7656

Fax. +81 3 3402 7659

Membership. 52,957

28. Kaiin Kumiai (All Japan Seamen's Union)

Address. Kaiin Bldg, 7-15-26 Roppongi, Minato-ku, Tokyo 106-0032

Phone. +81 3 5410 8312

Fax. +81 3 5410 8339

E-mail. kaiin@jsu.or.jp

Website. www.jsu.or.jp (Japanese only)

Membership. 50,000

4 Other Trade Union Organizations

Japan Council of Metalworkers' Unions (IMF-JC)

Address. Santoku Yaesu Bldg., 2-6-21 Yaesu, Chuo-ku, Tokyo 104-0028

Phone. +81 3 3274 2461

Fax. +81 3 3274 2476

E-mail. imf-jc@mxi.mesh.ne.jp

Leadership. Teruhito Tokumoto (president); Yukuo Ajima (general secretary)

Membership. 2,470,000 in seven industrial unions. It is affiliated to the International Metalworkers' Federation.

Zenken Soren
National Federation of Construction Workers' Unions

Address. 2-7-15 Takadanobaba, Shinjuku-ku, Tokyo 169-8650

Phone. +81 3 3200 6221

Fax. +81 3 3209 0558

E-mail. zenkensoren@pop17.odn.ne.jp

Membership. 715,000. This is the largest Japanese independent union.

Zenrokyo
National Trade Union Council

Address. Kotsu bldg, 5-15-5 Shinbashi, Minato-ku, Tokyo 105-0004

Phone. +81 3 5403 1650

Fax. +81 35403 1653

Membership. 270,000

Zenroren
National Confederation of Trade Unions

Address. 6-19-23, Shinbashi, Minato-ku, Tokyo 105

Phone. +81 3 5472 5841

Fax. +81 3 5472 5845

E-mail. zenintel@po.iijnet.or.ip

Website. www.iijnet.or.jp/c-pro/union (Japanese and English)

Leadership. Yoji Kobayashi (president); Mitsuo Bannai (general secretary)

Membership. Zenroren claims 1,531,000 but the Ministry of Labour figure is 837,000. Zenroren says the difference is because the government figures "exclude local unions which are not affiliated to any national industrial unions, but to the prefectural federations under Zenroren, as well as pensioners' unions".

History and character. Zenroren was formed in 1989 as the self-described "national centre of militant trade unions" in opposition to "anti-communism and labour-capital collaboration" by the Rengo trade unions. Zenroren says it is independent of political parties, but it is closely aligned with the Japan Communist Party. Its programme has had a broadly political and anti-US flavour.

Zenroren has accused Rengo of undermining the "Spring struggle" (shunto) and of cooperating in corporate restructuring. Its key issues in 1999 included the struggle against unemployment, in which it sought to work with other unions and social forces; the demand for improved social security systems; and opposition to US–Japan military cooperation. It called for large wage increases and cuts in taxes on consumption to revive the economy.

In July 2000 a Zenroren delegation visited the ACFTU Chinese trade union centre and agreed on the establishment of friendly relations. The visit reflected the restoration of relations between the Japan Communist Party and the Communist Party of China.

Zenroren is composed of 28 national industrial unions and 46 prefectural federations.

Publications. English language newsletter on website.

International affiliations. None

Jordan

Capital: Amman
Population: 5.0 m. (2000 est.)

1 Political and Economic Background

The Hashemite Kingdom of Jordan is a monarchy in which King Hussein ruled from 1952 until his death in Feb. 1999, when he was succeeded by his son, Abdullah ibn al-Hussein. Independents loyal to the King dominate the legislature and the King enjoys a high degree of authority. Political parties have been legal since 1992.

Jordan has few natural resources. It benefited from substantial Arab aid in the 1970s and early 1980s oil boom but this support then declined. The Gulf War, in which Jordan sided with Saddam, led to large scale repatriation of its citizens and a surge of unemployment. It has made some efforts to implement IMF structural adjustment programmes, ending subsidies and price controls in some areas, but has continuing problems of low growth, public debt and unemployment, thought to be as high as 25–30%. Jordanians have a reluctance to do some jobs and there are 300,000 foreign workers. King Abdullah is seen as sympathetic to liberalizing the economy and encouraging foreign investment.

GDP (purchasing power parity) $16bn. (1999 est.); GDP per capita (purchasing power parity) $3,500 (1998 est.).

2 Trade Unionism

Jordan ratified ILO Convention No.98 (Right to Organize and Collective Bargaining, 1949) in 1968, but has not ratified Convention No.87 (Freedom of Association and Protection of the Right to Organize, 1948).

Workers in the private sector and in some state-owned companies (but not otherwise in the public sector) may join unions and an estimated 30% of the workforce are organized into 17 unions, all of which belong to the General Federation of Jordanian Trade Unions (GFJTU). Non-citizens may not join unions. Workers may file complaints of anti-union discrimination with the Labour Ministry, which can order their reinstatement.

Collective bargaining exists in the unionized sectors and there is a framework for mediation and arbitration, including referral to an industrial tribunal, whose decisions are legally binding. Strikes are illegal while these processes are underway, and in practice are rare, although threatened from time to time. Strikes in public sector enterprises are not permitted. During 1999, the Labour Ministry intervened in various disputes to find solutions where there had been a breakdown in discussions, leading to the reinstatement of workers who had struck illegally. Domestic servants and agricultural workers are not covered by the labour code.

3 Trade Union Centre

General Federation of Jordanian Trade Unions (GFJTU)

Address. PO Box 1065, Amman 11118

Phone. +962 6 567 5533

Fax. +962 6 568 7911

History and character. The GFJTU (formerly the Jordan Federation of Trade Unions – JFTU) has traditionally avoided political matters, focusing on workplace issues. The Government subsidizes and audits the GFJTU's salaries and activities. The federation now has 17 unions affiliated, having lost two following Jordan's withdrawal of administrative responsibility for the West Bank in 1988. Although affiliation is not compulsory, all Jordanian unions belong to it.

International affiliation. ICFTU

Kazakhstan

Capital: Astana
Population: 16.73 m. (2000 est.)

1 Political and Economic Background

Kazakhstan became an independent state upon the dissolution of the Soviet Union in Dec. 1991. It has been ruled since independence by President Nursultan Nazarbayev, who had also been the chairman of the Supreme Soviet in 1990–91. Nazarbayev has broad powers, which he has extended by decree. He was re-elected in Jan. 1999 with 82% of the vote, several potential candidates having been barred by decree from standing.

Kazakhstan has immense energy fossil fuel reserves and is rich in minerals. However, it has a legacy of traditional heavy industries, many of them redundant or obsolescent, from the Soviet period and the collapse of demand for its products with the end of the Soviet Union imposed severe difficulties. In 1992 Kazakhstan launched an ambitious programme to privatize state industries, but this had limited success; by mid-1994 the private share of the economy was not above 20 per cent. Negative growth rates, hyper-inflation and removal of price controls led to serious unrest in 1994. Kazakhstan was badly affected by the effects of the Asian and Russian economic crisis of 1997–98, together with falls in prices for oil, metals and grains, its major exports. In Feb. 2000 Nazarbayev said that the stalled privatization process would be re-launched.

GDP (purchasing power parity) $54.5bn. (1999 est.); GDP per capita (purchasing power parity) $3,200 (1999 est.).

2 Trade Unionism

The Federation of Trade Unions of the Republic of Kazakhstan coordinates the official trade unions. It claims to have 4 million members, which is believed to be a substantial over-estimate. It maintains friendly relations with the WFTU. An independent Confederation of Free Trade Unions of Kazakhstan (KSPK) has been formed, and this has led strikes over issues such as the non-payment of wages. Although the KSPK claims it has 250,000 members the actual number is thought to be much lower and most workers continue to be members of the official unions. At most enterprises an automatic check-off system continues to generate dues for the official unions.

There has been frequent industrial unrest since independence in mining areas. A 32-day strike in the Karaganda coal fields ended in June 1992 with an agreement that 15 per cent of output would be the property of the miners' collectives. Leaders of the strike broke away from the Miners' Union of Kazakhstan (an affiliate of the Federation of Trade Unions of the Republic of Kazakhstan) to form the Independent Miners' Union (IMU).

Many workers are owed back wages, and in 1999 many enterprises were paying their workers in scrip rather than cash, partly because their customers in the former Soviet Union were not paying cash. Wage arrears have been the leading cause of strikes, demonstrations, blockading of railways and even mass hunger strikes in factories. Protests have frequently been broken up by police action and those taking part in actions have been sentenced to prison.

Although workers are in theory free to join unions of their own choosing, the ICFTU says that there is "constant harassment" of independent unions, with intimidation, dismissals and prosecutions, and investigation and surveillance by KNB intelligence officers. A particularly contentions issue has been the receipt of financial support from overseas unions, which the government has banned. Numerous obstacles are put in the way of registering unions and in June 1998 a new national security law defined "unsanctioned gatherings, public meetings, marches, demonstrations, illegal picketing, and strikes" as a threat to national security.

Kazakhstan has ratified neither ILO Convention No.87 (Freedom of Association and Protection of the Right to Organize, 1948) nor Convention No.98 (Right to Organize and Collective Bargaining, 1949). A new labour law came into effect in Jan. 2000. This provides for a system of individual contracts, but with "optional" collective contracts.

3 Trade Union Centres

Confederation of Free Trade Unions of Kazakhstan (KSPK)

Leadership. Leonid Solomin (president)

History and character. Most independent unions belong to the KSPK, although its claimed membership of 250,000 is thought to be an exaggeration. The KSPK led demonstrations in 1996 following which Solomin was in 1997 investigated by the National Security Agency (KNB) on charges including violating a provision of the 1995 constitution that prevents unions from receiving funds from abroad, although the charges were eventually dropped. Other forms of harassment have continued. Despite this, the KSPK has been given representation on the tripartite Committee on Social Partnership and on other national working groups.

International affiliations. None

Federation of Trade Unions of the Republic of Kazakhstan

History and character. Organizes the official trade union system surviving from the Soviet period. Automatic deductions from wages in most enterprises provide revenue, and the majority of workers are still members.

Kenya

Capital: Nairobi
Population: 30.34 m. (2000 est.)

GDP per capita (purchasing power parity) $1,600 (1999 est.).

1 Political and Economic Background

Kenya achieved independence from the United Kingdom in 1963 and became a republic the following year. Daniel Arap Moi, leader of the Kenya African National Union (KANU), became Kenya's second President in 1978, in succession to Jomo Kenyatta, and has held the office ever since, being most recently re-elected in 1997. KANU was for many years the sole legal party until a multi-party system was conceded in principle in 1991: in practice opposition groupings found it hard to maintain legality. Throughout 1993 and 1994 opponents of the government faced heavy-handed suppression, and at one point one-quarter of the parliamentary opposition was in jail. Freedom of association and speech has eased since that time, although a level of harassment and intimidation of opposition groups persists. KANU remains the largest party in the National Assembly following elections in Dec. 1997.

Kenya's economy is primarily based on agriculture, which occupies 75–80% of the workforce. Export crops include tea and coffee. There is a manufacturing sector based on consumer goods and agricultural processing, and tourism. A privatization programme was initiated in 1991 but many key enterprises are still in state hands. International assistance has been restricted for several years because of doubts over government commitment to economic reform and the level of official corruption. In July 2000 the government won a renewal of IMF financial support with a pledge to push ahead with privatization and anti-corruption measures, with the state telecoms, railways and Mombassa container terminal key enterprises scheduled for privatization. Major problems include persistent inter-ethnic conflict, the HIV/AIDS epidemic now affecting 14% of the adult population, high crime levels, power shortages, GDP growth lagging population growth, widespread unemployment and under-employment, and localized drought and famine.

GDP (purchasing power parity) $45.1bn. (1999 est.);

2 Trade Unionism

Trade unions developed after World War II under British colonial labour legislation, and were closely linked to nationalist politics. The Central Organization of Trade Unions (COTU) was founded in 1965 and since then has been the sole trade union centre. There is one major union outside COTU, the Kenya National Union of Teachers (KNUT), which has about 260,000 members, more than 40% of the organized workforce. Unions must be registered with the government to have legal status.

Kenya ratified ILO Convention No.98 (Right to Organize and Collective Bargaining, 1949) in 1964 but has not ratified Convention No. 87 (Freedom of Association and Protection of the Right to Organize, 1948). In practice workers in the formal economy have the right to join unions of their choice although this is circumscribed in some sectors. Civil servants and professionals such as university academic staff, doctors and dentists may only belong to associations with no collective bargaining rights. In the export processing zones there is considerable resistance to the formation of unions although national labour laws largely apply. Workers in many small firms also face dismissal if they join unions. Overall, however, the trade union base in Kenya is relatively broad and established and COTU has affiliates in a wide range of industries, with new unions registered in several sectors in the 1990s. At the end of the decade there were 36 unions representing about 600,000 workers, comprising up to one-third of all workers in the formal sector. Under the Trade Disputes Act it is illegal to dismiss or discriminate against workers for trade union activities and although long delays occur in hearing cases workers affected have often been reinstated.

Collective bargaining is permitted by labour legislation and collective agreements must be registered with the Industrial Court. Most workers (including in essential services) have a legal right to strike after giving a period of notice. In practice, the government commonly involves itself by instituting mediation and referral to the Industrial Court and by declaring strikes illegal if this process breaks down. A strike by nurses in 1997-98 resulted in the nurses being dismissed and being required to re-apply for their jobs. In 1998 a strike by the teachers' unions KNUT was declared illegal and the government arrested teachers' leaders and broke up union meetings, bringing the strike to an end.

3 Trade Union Centre

Central Organization of Trade Unions (COTU)

Address. Solidarity Building, Digo Road, PO Box 13000, Nairobi

Phone. +254 2 76 13 75

Fax. +254 2 76 26 95

Membership. About 350,000

History and character. COTU was founded in 1965 in succession to the Kenya Federation of Labour and the African Workers' Congress, which were dissolved. The legislation establishing COTU gave the Kenyan President the right to dismiss the three leading officials of the centre.

During the early 1990s, in line with the movement to political liberalization then sweeping much of Africa, the COTU sought to establish its independence from the ruling KANU party, criticizing government policies and corruption. This led to a period of tension in which the government in 1993 actively interfered in COTU affairs to secure a more compliant leadership. COTU is now considered to be passive politically although some of its affiliates press for greater independence from the state, political reform and opposition to corruption.

The COTU affiliates 32 of the 36 registered unions, but does not include in membership the largest and most influential single union, the Kenya National Union of Teachers (KNUT). Some COTU unions are reported to have evolved on an ethnic basis.

International affiliation. ICFTU

Kiribati

Capital: Tarawa
Population: 92,000 (2000 est.)

1 Political and Economic Background

The Republic of Kiribati, formerly the Gilbert Islands, became an independent state within the Commonwealth in 1979. Teburoro Tito has been President since 1994, heading a non-party government. Kiribati has few resources and little infrastructure and 90% of the work force is occupied in fishing or subsistence farming. External aid (mainly from the UK and Japan) is a major component of the national income.

GDP (purchasing power parity) $74 m. (1999 est.); GDP per capita (purchasing power parity) $860 (1999 est.).

2 Trade Unionism

Kiribati is not a member of the ILO. Freedom of association is provided for by the (1979) Constitution and in practice the government has not interfered in the formation of trade unions. Despite the very small base of the formal sector economy, unions have developed and in 1982 a national centre was set up, the Kiribati Trade Union Congress (KTUC), which achieved affiliation to the ICFTU. Its 2,500 members are mostly in the public sector.

Collective bargaining is allowed under the Industrial Relations Code. In the public sector pay tends to be set administratively, although there is bargaining in some agencies and state-owned enterprises. Industrial relations are generally harmonious and although there is a legal right to strike, no strikes have been recorded since 1980.

3 Trade Union Centre

Kiribati Trade Union Congress (KTUC)

Address. PO Box 502, Tarawa

Phone. +686 26277

Fax. +686 25257

E-mail. kiosu@tskl.net.ki

Leadership. Tatoa Kaiteie

Membership. 2,500

History and character. Founded in 1982 by the seven

registered trade unions in Kiribati. All unions are affiliated to the KTUC. The KTUC has been active in promoting self-help and educational projects, with help from Japanese unions, the ICFTU regional organization APRO and other trade union sources.

International affiliation. ICFTU

North Korea

Capital: Pyongyang
Population: 21.69 m. (2000 est.)

GDP per capita (purchasing power parity) $1,000 (1999 est.)

1 Political and Economic Background

The Democratic People's Republic of Korea (North Korea) was established in 1948 in what had been the Soviet zone of occupied Korea. Political control is exercised by the communist Korean Workers' Party (KWP), which was led until his death in 1994 by President Kim Il Sung, the "Great Leader". Since 1994 the dominant figure has been his son, Kim Jong Il (the "Dear Leader"), as leader of the party (the position of President being effectively abolished in 1998 when Kim Il Sung was declared "Eternal President").

In 1991 North Korea joined the UN, a move from which it had recoiled previously on the grounds that it would lead to South Korean admission and affirmation of the division of the country. In the event the two countries joined simultaneously. Relations between the two states have improved recently.

North Korea has adhered rigidly to Stalinist-type central planning. Industry, like land, is nationalized, with production centred upon steel, cement, chemicals, military equipment and machine building rather than consumer products. North Korea has not recovered from the 1991 collapse of the Soviet Union, its biggest market and chief source of aid. Famine in the period 1994–98, caused by natural disasters and the failure of collectivized farms, cost hundreds of thousand of lives and North Korea was forced to accept foreign food aid.

GDP (purchasing power parity) $22.6bn. (1999 est.);

2 Trade Unionism

A single-trade-union system is in force, coordinated by the General Federation of Trade Unions of Korea (GFTUK), and unions function on the former Soviet model, with responsibility for mobilizing workers behind productivity goals and state targets, and for the provision of health, educational, cultural and welfare facilities. North Korea has remained one of the most closed societies on earth and no form of independent trade unionism has been tolerated. There is no collective bargaining or strikes.

By joining the UN North Korea became eligible to join the ILO but did not move beyond observer status.

3 Trade Union Centre

General Federation of Trade Unions of Korea (GFTUK)

Address. PO Box 333, Pyongyang

History and character. Founded on Nov. 30, 1945, the GFTUK is described as a political organization of the working masses. It conducts ideological education to ensure its members fully understand the ideas of Kim Il Sung and to enable them to contribute towards the socialist construction and management of the economy.

International affiliation. WFTU

South Korea

Capital: Seoul
Population: 47.47 m. (2000 est.)

1 Political and Economic Background

The Republic of Korea (South Korea) was established as an independent state in 1948 in what had been the post-World War II US occupied zone. The division of the country stood in the way of UN entry (simultaneously with North Korea) until 1991.

Korea's history post-independence was characterized by mainly authoritarian governments led or dominated by military figures, with episodes of civil unrest. In the mid-1980s a powerful pro-democracy movement gathered pace, leading to the adoption of a new constitution in 1987. Since then South Korea has had civilian rule. Kim Dae-jung was elected President in Dec. 1997, presiding over a coalition government led by his centre-left Millennium Democratic Party (MDP). The MDP won fewer seats than the conservative Grand National Party (GNP) in legislative elections in Apr. 2000. Political parties and allegiances tend to be fluid.

South Korea's economic rise has been one of the prime Asian success stories. It has taken the country from a backward low-income economy at independence to become a leading world player by the 1990s in industries such as automobiles, electronics, chemicals, shipbuilding and steel, with per capita GDP on a purchasing power parity basis 13 times that in North Korea. The South Korean model was based on close interlocks between government and industry, directed credits, and protectionism with a focus on labour productivity balanced by job security.

The Asian financial crisis of the late 1990s had a particularly severe impact on South Korea, however. The crisis exposed fundamental weaknesses in the financial sector and in Korea's system of closed markets and government intervention. Structural adjustment programmes required by the IMF as a condition of bail-outs began a move to more open markets. The crisis, though severe, proved brief as a 1998 contraction of GDP by 10.7% turned into growth of 10.9% in 1999.

GDP (purchasing power parity) $625.7bn. (1999 est.); GDP per capita (purchasing power parity) $13,300 (1999 est.).

2 Trade Unionism

The first Korean trade union was the Song-Jin Dockers' Union organized in May 1898, and unions began to develop after the annexation of Korea by Japan in 1910, becoming a centre of opposition to Japanese rule. Following the end of Japanese rule and the establishment of US military government in the south of Korea, a General Council of Korean Trade Unions was formed under communist control and this led general strikes in 1946 and 1947. In 1946 however the General Federation of Korean Trade Unions was created with US backing; it became a founder member of the ICFTU in 1949. Communist organizations were banned in 1947.

Following a 1961 military coup (which inaugurated the 18-year rule of General Park, assassinated in 1979), all labour organizations were dissolved and replaced by the Federation of Korean Trade Unions (FKTU). After industrial unrest in the late 1960s, trade union rights were restricted by a series of measures brought into force in the early 1970s. The government justified these measures as necessary to create a stable market for foreign investors and in the interest of national security.

Under the Trade Union Law of 1980 only one union was permitted in each enterprise; only enterprise-level unions could negotiate with employers, without any intervention by third parties (i.e. seriously weakening the role of industry-wide federations); and there were restrictions on the dues which unions could collect from their members. Disputes were to be settled directly between union and employer, under the authority of tripartite labour committees representing the interests of employers, workers and the government but whose members were nominated by the government. The immediate effect of this legislation was to reduce total union membership from 1,200,000 to 820,000.

The anti-government political activity of the 1980s was reflected in major strikes, which drew fierce repression by the state. In 1986 the Labour Minister dissolved 14 dissident unions in the Seoul-Inchon area, an anti-reform stance backed by FKTU. 1987 however inaugurated the "Great Workers' Struggle": it was the most disputatious year for a decade with 3,749 separate disputes, mostly for pay but also for the right to engage freely in trade union activities. Labour unrest on this scale challenged employers, government and the FKTU leadership. Despite the technical illegality of the strikes, the authorities tended to tolerate them, and perhaps half gained concessions on pay and conditions. A short-lived Committee for the Democratization of Trade Unions tried to make the FKTU more representative and replace its leadership. Such "democratic unions", which found support among white-collar financial workers, grew to number 300. They were the industrial counterpart of the country's wider dissident movement, in contrast with the majority of the so-called "company unions".

One result of the 1987 upheavals in Korean society was a great increase in trade union membership. The peak of membership was reached in 1989 when 1,932,000 people were in the unions, but the 1990s brought decline, and official figures recorded 1,803,400 organized workers at the end of 1991.

The Government only recognized as legitimate unions affiliated to the FKTU or the Korean Federation of Free Clerical and Financial Workers, despite the view of the courts that non-affiliation was not a sufficient reason to deny registration. This factor continued to compromise the FKTU's independent status, but it remained the largest national centre with a claimed membership of 1.44 million out of some 1.8 million organized workers. New unions founded after 1987 which stayed aloof from it formed 14 (later 17) regional councils and a number of industrial councils, but were prevented by law from forming an alternative centre. A total of 602 (with an initial membership approaching 200,000) formed such a centre nonetheless in 1990 under the title Korean Trade Union Congress (KTUC, or Chonnohyup) but it came under heavy repression. Also formed in 1990 was the, mainly white collar, Korea Congress of Independent Industrial Trade Union Federations (KCIIF, or Upjonghweui), which united with the KTUC in the National Workers' Rally.

There was severe repression of the non-FKTU unions in 1990 and 1991. In 18 months 848 trade unionists were arrested, of whom 615 were associated with the KTUC. There were also many raids on union offices. In Nov. 1991 the centre staged a commemorative rally on the anniversary of the death of Chun Tae Il, a textile worker who burned himself to death in 1970, and turned out the largest dissident labour protest in the country's history.

Korea became a member of the ILO in 1991, and the Ministry of Labour then began a systematic review of employment law in the light of ILO Conventions. It had previously claimed that Korean employment law satisfied 105 of the ILO's 115 Conventions. A Labour Reform Study Committee was set up, involving representatives of the FKTU and the employers' confederation, the KEF. This was supposed to report by 1994 but its report was kept secret amid charges that independent experts and public interest representatives had made recommendations unpalatable to both the KEF and FKTU. Even before ILO entry the KTUC and the KCIIF formed the National Workers' Joint Committee for Ratification of Basic ILO Conventions and Employment Law Reform. In 1992 this Committee lodged a freedom of association complaint against the government over its prohibition of more than one union per enterprise, the prohibition of third party interventions in disputes, and bans on unions for teachers and many public servants. In 1993 the ILO called on Korea to make fundamental reforms, but the government told the ILO that its employment laws had to be judged in the light of the country's "Confucian tradition" whereby family concepts and not adversarialism were the norm. Korea's admission to the OECD in 1996 was made conditional on it undertaking reforms in areas such as freedom of association. However, despite liberalization, Korea has still not ratified the basic ILO conventions on freedom of association and collective bargaining, Nos.87 and 98.

In 1993 the KTUC, KCIIF and unions based at Hyundai and Daewoo, came together to form the Korean Council of Trade Union Representatives (KCTU,

Chonnodae), which in turn in 1995 became the Korean Confederation of Trade Unions (KCTU, Minju Nachong). The KCTU adopted a position critical of the quasi-monopoly position enjoyed by the FKTU and campaigned to achieve recognition for itself and its affiliates. In Dec. 1996–Jan. 1997 it led strikes against government labour legislation. In the period 1997–99 significant improvements were made in the position of the trade unions. In 1997 the previous ban on third parties such as federations giving support to unions in disputes was ended, as was the prohibition against political activities by unions (although funding of political parties by unions remained unlawful). Teachers' unions belonging to the FKTU and KCTU were legalized from July 1999. On Nov. 23, 1999, the Ministry of Labour finally accorded legal recognition to the KCTU, which by this time had also achieved affiliation to the ICFTU alongside the FKTU. It is about half the size of the FKTU.

Despite the progress made since the mid-1980s, and especially in the late 1990s, barriers to free trade unionism remain in Korea. At the workplace level, only one union is permitted currently, although pluralism at this level is scheduled to be introduced by 2002. More than one million white-collar government employees may not form trade unions or bargain collectively, although since Jan. 1999 they may form workplace councils with limited rights. Strikes are prohibited in government agencies, state run enterprises and the defence industry and compulsory arbitration may be imposed (although this is not common) in a wide range of industries deemed to be in the "essential public interest", including public transport, utilities, public health, banking and telecommunications. While industrial conflict is not widespread, it not infrequently takes a violent turn with heavy police intervention and with arrest and imprisonment of strikers, often on charges of "obstruction of business". According to the KCTU, in June 1999 there were 61 individuals in prison for various forms of trade union activity, while the ICFTU complained in July 2000 that the government had "once more fully embarked on the path of repression and violence" in dealing with strikes and other trade union actions. The ICFTU believes that the position of trade unionists in Korea in respect of freedom of association is worse than in any other of the OECD group of industrial nations. Underlying trends in the economy have also proved detrimental to the unions. More than 50% of the work force is said to be in various forms of irregular work, such as subcontracting or in the informal economy and such workers are outside the protection of the Labour Standards Act. The enterprise-based system of unions is a weakness in situations where employers are hostile. Trade union density reached a peak of 19.8% in 1989, in the wake of the political upheaval, but since then has gradually declined, to a level of 12.6% by the end of the 1990s. Only 7% of women workers are organized.

The history of employer and government antagonism to independent trade unionism has historically gone hand-in-hand with a paternalist and protective employment system, particularly in large enterprises, somewhat akin to the Japanese model. The Asian crisis from 1997 subjected this system to unprecedented strain. The OECD urged Korea to adopt greater labour flexibility, backed up by an improved social welfare safety net, to assist economic reconstruction. Many small enterprises closed; for the first time major employers such as Hyundai, where lifetime employment had been taken for granted, initiated compulsory lay-offs after this was legalized in February 1998. Unemployment rose to 8.7 per cent in 1998 before falling in 1999. Workers were affected by casualization of employment and many workers lost their jobs without redundancy payments and with little or no social security. In 1998 wages fell for the first time since 1975. The crisis led to some increase in industrial militancy, but disputes remained at a relatively low level: only 146,000 workers were involved in industrial disputes in 1998 and efforts by the unions to mount demonstrations in 1998–99 against restructuring programmes were thinly attended. The unions became involved with the government and employers' confederation in the Tripartite Commission, which was set up to try to restore national confidence, but both the FKTU and KCTU withdrew claiming bad faith by the other parties. One result of the crisis, which was widely attributed to the opaque business practices of Korean financial institutions and conglomerates (chaebols) was that the unions are demanding greater transparency in business, including union participation in decision-making.

3 Trade Union Centres

Federation of Korean Trade Unions (FKTU, Nochong)

Address. 35, Yoido-dong, Youngdeungpo-ku, Seoul

Phone. +82 2 786 3970

Fax. +82 2 786 2864

E-mail. fktu@fktu.org

Website. www.fktu.org (Korean and English)

Membership. 1.1 million

History and character. The Korean Labour Federation for Independence Promotion (KLFIP) was established in 1946, and after the creation of the Republic of Korea in 1948 was re-named as the General Federation of Korean Trade Unions (GFKTU). This became one of the founding members of the ICFTU the following year. In 1961, following a military coup, all its affiliates were dissolved by military decree, and the FKTU was created in its place under the guidance of the military authorities. Until 1999 the FKTU remained the sole legal trade union centre in South Korea, while also maintaining its affiliation to the ICFTU. The FKTU was severely weakened under 1980 legislation which excluded it from direct involvement in industrial disputes and collective bargaining, leaving it only a generalized role of representing the interests of organized labour to government.

The role of the FKTU in the widespread movement for constitutional reform in 1985–87 is open to various interpretations. In its official publications, the FKTU places itself at the heart of the movement and outlines its support of the reforms gained. However, the federation's close ties to the Chun regime were most vividly demonstrated when it supported the President's 1987 decision to suspend talks on constitutional revisions. A number of "democratic unions" during the widespread labour unrest of 1987 derided what they perceived to be the FKTU's tendency to compromise too quickly. In an attempt to gain legitimacy amongst workers whose democratic aspirations had been raised by the 1988 constitutional reforms, the FKTU pledged to adopt a more political role. It established a political-education committee, called for an end to restraints on the political activities of unions, and decided to support pro-union candidates, whether from opposition parties or from the ruling Democratic Justice Party, in impending legislative elections. At a special convention of 1988 the FKTU elected a new reformist leadership pledged to increase its independence. However, independent trade unions, brought into being in the 1980s unrest, remained outside the FKTU fold and in 1993 created the KCTU, which was hostile to the FKTU's monopoly on legal status.

In 1995 the FKTU jointly created with the Ministry of Labour and employers' organization KEF, the Korea International Labor Foundation (KOILAF) to address the impact of globalization and inward investment on Korea's economy and society.

In the late 1990s crisis the FKTU initially participated in the Tripartite Commission with employers and government, set up to restore confidence and find solutions, but withdrew complaining that employers were arbitrarily laying off workers and that the government was pushing through restructuring programmes without reference to the needs of the workers. The FKTU demanded improved social safety nets for workers affected by unemployment and reduced working. However, FKTU efforts to mobilize workers, as in a general strike call in June 1999, met with a lukewarm response.

The FKTU has 24 affiliated industrial federations; 16 municipal and provincial offices; and 50 local offices. Affiliated bodies include the FKTU Research Institute and the FKTU Education Centre.

International affiliation. ICFTU

Korean Confederation of Trade Unions (KCTU, Minju Nochong)

Address. 5th floor, Daeyoung Bldg., 139 Youngdeungpo-2-ga, Youngdeungpo-ku, Seoul 150–032

Phone. +82 2 636 0165

Fax. +82 2 635 1134

E-mail. inter@kctu.org

Website. www.kctu.org (Korean and English)

Leadership. Dan Byung-ho (president); Lee Soo-ho (general secretary)

Membership. 573,490 in 1,226 individual unions (July 1999)

History and character. An Association for Korean Workers' Welfare and Benefits (AKWW) was formed in March 1984 by leaders of non-FKTU unions and enjoyed brief success in its campaigns until, in 1985, it was suppressed. This movement re-emerged as the Federation of Korean Democratic Workers (FKDW) at the end of the decade and shortly after became the Korea Trade Union Congress (KTUC, or Chonnohyup).

The KTUC was founded in January 1990 by 602 independent unions formed since 1987 and launched in defiance of legislation forbidding the establishment of an alternative centre. Its chairman was arrested in Feb. 1990 following the detention of 150 other union leaders. Over the next year-and-a-half its activists accounted for three-quarters of those arrested by the state. At the end of this period however the organization had consolidated its position by winning many workplace positions in the 1991 workplace elections, and by calling a highly successful demonstration in Seoul.

The Korean Congress of Independent Industrial Federations (KCIIF, Upjonghweui), also formed in 1990, was a loose coalition of white collar federations in finance, nursing, the media, construction, and the public sector, and also included the banned teachers' federation Chonkyojo. In June 1993 the KTUC and KCIIF, with some other unions, joined forces to create the Korean Council of Trade Union Representatives (KCTU, Chonnodae) as a single focal point for unions outside the FKTU monopoly structure. This in turn in Nov. 1995 became the Korean Confederation of Trade Unions (Minju Nochong), claiming a membership of 862 enter-prise unions and 418,000 members. Although trade union involvement in politics was banned, members of the Democratic Party assisted in the formation of the KCTU.

The KCTU's programme announced in March 1996 emphasized the need to end the prohibition of more than one union in an enterprise, which entrenched the monopoly position of the FKTU, an organization which, it said, had "submitted and yielded" to military repression in the 1980s and made "the union structure a supplementary mechanism of labour control". Other elements of the programme included securing trade union rights for 1.5 million public servants and also for teachers; an end to the ban on trade unions engaging in political activities; and an end to state interference in trade union affairs.

On Nov. 22, 1999, the KCTU finally achieved legal recognition. All its affiliated unions are now legalized.

Its policy objectives include: the repeal of repressive legislation such as the National Security Law; worker participation in the management of enterprises; increased involvement of women in the trade union movement, and gender equality; opposition to the extension of subcontracting and irregular employment; effective worker involvement in tripartite institutions such as the Labour Relations Commission and the Minimum Wage Review Committee; improvement in Korea's poor health and safety record; full rights for migrant workers; and opposition to monopolies and ologopolies in Korean economy and society. The KCTU wishes to develop the industrial union system to overcome the limitations of enterprise unionism.

International affiliation. ICFTU

Kuwait

Capital: Kuwait City
Population: 1.97 m. (2000 est.)

1 Political and Economic Background

Kuwait has been ruled by monarchs (Amirs) from the al-Sabah family for more than 200 years, and members of the family hold all the key government posts. Under the 1962 constitution there is a national assembly, but there are no political parties and the Amir has ruled by decree for periods, most recently 1986–92. Kuwait was invaded and occupied by Iraq in 1990, and its sovereignty restored by US led military action in 1991. Following this the ruling family said that the 1962 Constitution would be respected. Of the population of two million, nearly 1.2 million are foreigners.

The economy is based on oil, which generates 75% of government revenues and provides a high standard of living for native Kuwaitis. More than 90% of indigenous Kuwaitis work for the state, whereas foreigners constitute 98% of the private sector labour force and 80% of the total labour force.

GDP (purchasing power parity) $44.8bn. (1999 est.); GDP per capita (purchasing power parity) $22,500 (1999 est.).

2 Trade Unionism

Trade unions were first accorded legal recognition under legislation of 1964. By law, employers guilty of anti-union discrimination must reinstate victimized workers. There are 14 unions with a total of about 50,000 members; all the unions except the Bank Worker's Union and the Kuwait Airways Workers' Union, which together comprise approximately 4,500 workers, are affiliated to the national trade union centre, the Kuwait Trade Union Federation (KTUF). Nine of the KTUF's affiliates represents civil and public servants and three represent petrol and chemical sector employees. There are various restrictions on the right to join unions and their free operation, which the ILO has repeatedly found in violation of Convention No. 87 (Freedom of Association and Protection of the Right to Organize, 1948), which Kuwait ratified in 1961.

There are more than one million foreign workers (constituting 80% of the workforce), who may join a union only after five years' residence. Although this restriction is not always enforced, in practice only a few thousand foreign workers are in unions, representing 10% of the unionized sector. Furthermore, foreign workers may join unions only as non-voting members and union officials must be citizens. The government involves itself directly in union affairs, contributing up to 90% of most union budgets and retaining extensive powers of oversight. Unions are barred from engaging in political or religious activities and in principle may be dissolved for threatening "public order and morals" although this has not happened in practice. Only one trade union may be formed in any occupational area and the formation of more than one national centre is not permitted.

More than 90% of all working Kuwaitis are to be found in the civil service or elsewhere in the public sector. "Kuwaitization" (the displacement of foreign by indigenous employees) has progressed much further in the state sector than in the private sector, and the pace of change was hastened by the impact of the 1990–91 occupation by Iraq and subsequent Gulf War. Little more than one-third of pre-War foreign nationals on the government payroll were rehired. Despite numerous restrictions, however, Kuwaiti nationals were again in a minority in the population by the end of 1992.

Kuwait has not ratified ILO Convention No. 98 (Right to Organize and Collective Bargaining, 1949). In the government service there is no collective bargaining as such, but the government consults informally with the unions. Collective bargaining is allowed in the private sector, although restricted by the low level of unionization. There is a mechanism for mediation and arbitration. There are no legal protections for strikers and strikes are not common.

Domestic servants are not protected by labour legislation and foreign workers may not switch jobs without permission from their original sponsoring employer before they have been in the country for two years. Some foreign workers are in effect indentured servants.

3 Trade Union Centre

Kuwait Trade Union Federation (KTUF)

History and character. The KTUF was founded in 1968. It has 12 member unions, divided into two sectors (state and oil), with close to 50,000 members. It is the sole legal trade union centre.

In the 1980s it opposed US policy in the Middle East and offered support for the "peace initiatives" of the Soviet Union. Two former presidents of the KTUF, Nasser al Faraq and Mliehan al Harbi, were arrested and tortured by the Iraqi forces during the 1990–91 occupation. Both died within days of their release. Their successor Hayef al Agami escaped from Kuwait shortly after the invasion in Aug. 1990. The KTUF joined with the democratic opposition during the Gulf War to demand restoration of the 1962 Constitution, with guarantees of freedom of expression and women's equality. It also campaigned actively for the return of Kuwaitis detained in Iraq.

International affiliation. Reported as affiliated by the WFTU

Kyrgyzstan

Capital: Bishkek
Population: 4.69 m. (2000 est.)

1 Political and Economic Background

Kyrgyzstan declared its independence from the Soviet Union in Aug. 1991. Its President since that time has been Askar Akayev. Kyrgyzstan is a primarily agricultural country, producing cotton, wool and meat. It has introduced market reforms and much of the government's stake in enterprises has been sold off. It suffered economic decline following the break-up of the Soviet Union but has shown recovery since the mid-1990s.

GDP (purchasing power parity) $10.3bn. (1999 est.); GDP per capita (purchasing power parity) $2,300 (1999 est.).

2 Trade Unionism

Kyrgyzstan ratified ILO Conventions No.87 (Freedom of Association and Protection of the Right to Organize, 1948) and No. 98 (Right to Organize and Collective Bargaining, 1949) in 1992. The post-Soviet era labour law of 1992 provides for the right of all workers to belong to trade unions. The former official unions were reconstituted as the Federation of Trade Unions of the Kyrgyz Republic. The Federation has criticized aspects of government policy, especially privatization, although in general the unions carry out similar functions to those in the Soviet era. There are a number of smaller unions not affiliated to it. The right of unions to negotiate collectively is recognized by law. Occasional strikes have been reported and these have been tolerated.

Laos

Capital: Vientiane
Population: 5.5 m. (2000 est.)

GDP per capita (purchasing power parity) $1,300 (1999 est.).

1 Political and Economic Background

The Lao People's Democratic Republic was established in 1975 following the victory of the communist Pathet Lao forces. The country is ruled by the (communist) Lao People's Revolutionary Party (LPRP), and all the seats in the National Assembly are held by the LPRP or LPRP-approved candidates.

Some 80% of the population are engaged in subsistence agriculture, primarily the cultivation of rice. Laos suffers from limited infrastructure, and outside the principal towns there are few roads and no electricity. Although under communist political control, sine the mid-1980s Laos has encouraged the development of private enterprise and has enjoyed steady economic growth, averaging 8% per annum 1988–96, although then hit by spill over from the Asian financial crisis of 1997–98, which affected Thailand, its main market. The country has a reliance on foreign aid.

GDP (purchasing power parity) $7bn. (1999 est.);

2 Trade Unionism

Laos has been a member of the ILO since 1964, but has ratified neither Convention No.87 (Freedom of Association and Protection of the Right to Organize, 1948) nor Convention No.98 (Right to Organize and Collective Bargaining, 1949). A single trade union system prevails, organized through the Federation of Lao Trade Unions (FLTU), which is controlled by the ruling LPRP. The FLTU absorbed the few small pre-existing unions after the establishment of the present regime in 1975. No union may be formed outside the FLTU structure. The state is the main employer in the formal economy and the FLTU's 78,000 members are reported to be mainly public servants. There is no collective bargaining and in the state sector the government sets wages and conditions, although there are forms of consultation with the official unions. Strikes are not illegal but rarely occur. The FLTU is affiliated to the WFTU.

Latvia

Capital: Riga
Population: 2.4m. (2000 est.)

1 Political and Economic Background

Latvia was an independent state from 1920 until annexed by the USSR in 1940. It repudiated Soviet rule in May 1990 and its independence was recognized by the Soviet Union in Sept. 1991. The last Russian troops left in 1994. Since independence there has been a multiplicity of political parties, with no clear dominant party emerging: in the most recent elections to the 100-seat legislature, in Oct. 1998, six parties won between 8 and 24 seats each. There is a coalition government headed since May 2000 by Prime Minister Andris Berzins. Accession to the EU is a political priority.

The loss of former Soviet markets led to a decline in the contribution of industry to GDP from 38% to 28% between 1990 and 1997. The immediate impact of the collapse of the former planned economy was a sharp fall in GDP, with a further setback caused by a banking crisis in 1995, but there has been recovery since 1996. Services are now the main driver of growth and by 1997 the private sector contributed 60% of GDP. Planned privatization of remaining large enterprises in state hands in shipping, telecoms and energy has been slow to materialize.

GDP (purchasing power parity) $9.8bn. (1999 est.); GDP per capita (purchasing power parity) $4,200 (1999 est.).

2 Trade Unionism

All workers, except uniformed members of the military, may join trade unions. The Free Trade Union Confederation of Latvia (LBAS) is the only centre and is descended from the old Soviet era trade union structure. LBAS did not restructure itself until 1990. In 1991 the level of union density was as high as 77%, reflecting the compulsory nature of trade unionism in the past. It has fallen steadily with the decline of the state sector but is still estimated at 25–30%. This is twice the level of the other Baltic republics, Lithuania and Estonia. However,

this seems to reflect the slow process of change in Latvia rather than any organizational vigour in the union sector. Just as the opening up to the free market of larger enterprises has proceeded relatively slowly in Latvia, the trade union sector appears relatively ossified. The US State Department Human Rights report for 1999 said that, "in general the trade union movement is undeveloped and still in transition from the socialist to the free market model".

Latvia ratified ILO Conventions No. 87 (Freedom of Association and Protection of the Right to Organize, 1948) and No. 98 (Right to Organize and Collective Bargaining, 1949) in 1992. Laws on trade unions and collective bargaining were passed in 1991. There is legal protection against anti-union discrimination, although some new private sector enterprises effectively deter unionization. Unions are free to bargain collectively and strike, although there has been little industrial action in recent years.

3 Trade Union Centre

Free Trade Union Confederation of Latvia (LBAS)

Address. Bruninieku 29/31, 1001 Riga

Phone. +371 727 0351

Fax. +371 727 6649

E-mail. lbas@com.latnet.lv

Leadership. Juris Radzevics (president)

Membership. 200,000 in 26 branch unions

History and character. LBAS is the reformed Soviet era trade union structure, reorganized in 1990. It is politically independent.

International affiliation. ICFTU; observer status with ETUC

Lebanon

Capital: Beirut
Population: 3.58 m. (2000 est.)

1 Political and Economic Background

Lebanon became fully independent from France in 1944. It was formerly a regional commercial and financial centre but the economic infrastructure and political authority progressively decayed following the outbreak of civil war in 1975. The war, fought out by militias largely organized on religious lines, and with intervention by Lebanon's neighbours on the different sides, disrupted the fragile compromise on which the state had been established since the National Covenant of 1943. Under this compromise, the President was conventionally a Maronite Christian, the Prime Minister a Sunni Muslim, and the Speaker of the National Assembly a Shia Muslim.

Since the end of the war in 1991 considerable stability has been restored. Although Israel withdrew its troops from southern Lebanon in 2000, parts of the country are under military control by Syria (including parts of Beirut) or the Shia militants of Hizbollah. The economic infrastructure was progressively rebuilt during the 1990s. There is relatively little industry, with most of the private sector workforce in services.

GDP (purchasing power parity) $16.2bn. (1999 est.); GDP per capita (purchasing power parity) $4,500 (1999 est.).

2 Trade Unionism

Lebanon ratified ILO Convention No. 98 (Right to Organize and Collective Bargaining, 1949) in 1977 but has not ratified Convention No. 87 (Freedom of Association and Protection of the Right to Organize, 1948).

The first trade unions appeared under French rule. The labour movement tended to remain fractured on craft, religious or political lines as it came under pressure from the same forces that destroyed the country's unity. The unions lost members and in many respects ceased to function during the civil war. The labour movement remains fragmented and this is reflected in the fact that the ICFTU records no less than 13 affiliates for Lebanon, far more than for any other country. The closest to a trade union centre is the General Confederation of Lebanese Workers (CGTL), although this is not itself affiliated to the ICFTU.

There are an estimated 160 unions and associations, with some 375,000 members; about 200,000 workers are reported to be in the 22 organizations affiliated to the CGTL. Palestinian refugees may organize their own unions, but few of them are in unions. Government employees may not form unions or bargain collectively. The government must authorize the formation of unions and approve the results of all trade union elections, and unions may be dissolved administratively. Unions may not engage in political activities. There has been regular government interference in union elections and affairs, including those of the CGTL.

3 Trade Union Centre

Confédération Générale des Travailleurs du Liban (CGTL)
General Confederation of Lebanese Workers

Leadership. Elias Abu Rizk (president)

History and character. Founded 1958 and loosely confederates some 22 trade union organizations. In the years following the end of the civil war in 1991, the CGTL called a succession of strikes and protests on issues such as living standards, privatization, corruption and restrictions on civil liberties, attracting hostile attention from the government. In Apr. 1997, despite a campaign of government intimidation including seizure of CGTL premises, the CGTL president, Elias Abu Rizk, was re-elected. The government then recognized a breakaway faction and arrested Abu Rizk. In May 1998, however, the government withdrew its support for the breakaway faction, and recognized the re-election of Elias Abu Rizk in July.

Lesotho

Capital: Maseru
Population: 2.14 m. (2000 est.)

1 Political and Economic Background

Lesotho became an independent member of the Commonwealth in 1966 as a constitutional hereditary monarchy. In 1970 the Constitution was suspended by the Prime Minister, Chief Leabua Jonathan, and the power of the King eroded. His regime was in turn overthrown by a Military Council in 1986. Legislative and executive powers were returned to King Moshoeshoe II in conjunction with the Military Council. In 1990 the Military Council took effective power from the King and he went into exile, to be replaced by his son, Letsie III. In Mar. 1993 multi-party elections resulted in a landslide victory for the Basotho Congress Party (BCP). In August 1994 Letsie III dissolved the National Assembly and dismissed the BCP government, but national and international opposition forced him to restore the elected government and he abdicated in favour of his father. In 1996, however, King Moshoeshoe died, and Letsie returned to the throne. In elections to the National Assembly in May 1998 the Lesotho Congress of Democracy claimed to have won 79 of the 80 seats, but opposition parties disputed the result. This led to considerable unrest, widespread damage to property in the capital, mutiny in the army, and the intervention of South African troops to restore order in Sept. 1998 at the request of the government.

The country is economically dependent on South Africa, which surrounds it on all sides. Remittances from over 65,000 migrant Lesotho workers employed in the South African mines are a major source of foreign exchange, and constitute more than one-third of GDP. Domestically, much of the labour force is involved in subsistence agriculture. There is a small private sector in areas such as garment manufacturing.

GDP (purchasing power parity) $4.7bn. (1999 est.); GDP per capita (purchasing power parity) $2,240 (1999 est.).

2 Trade Unionism

Several unions existed prior to independence and Lesotho ratified ILO Conventions No. 87 (Freedom of Association and Protection of the Right to Organize, 1948) and No. 98 (Right to Organize and Collective Bargaining, 1949) in 1966. Other than civil servants, workers are by law permitted to join unions of their choosing. The trade union movement is weak and fragmented, however, with two small centres that are said to rarely cooperate with each other. In addition, according to the ICFTU, "there are multiple unions competitively organizing small numbers of workers in the same sector" and many employers obstruct union organization and blacklist activists. Union density is estimated at about 10% in the small formal sector. Many mineworkers working in South Africa are members of that country's National Union of Mineworkers but the NUM as a foreign organization may not carry out union activities in Lesotho.

Collective bargaining is poorly developed in most areas and employers often refuse to bargain. The complexity of pre-strike procedures and other restrictions are such that there has reportedly been no legal strike since independence. Strikes do occur, however, and in some cases the government has involved itself to secure the reinstatement of workers dismissed during illegal strikes and therefore denied the protection of the law. Strikes in several sectors led to intervention by the security forces in the mid-1990s and in Sept. 1996 15 members of the Construction and Allied Workers' Union of Lesotho (CAWULE) were shot dead by police during a dispute at the Butha Butha site of the Lesotho Highland Water Project. In 1997 teachers were banned from striking under a 1995 law designating teaching as an essential service.

3 Trade Union Centres

Congress of Lesotho Trade Unions
Address. PO Box 13282, Maseru 104
Phone. +266 322 035
Fax. +266 321 951
Leadership. Thabane Motlatsi (general secretary)
International affiliation. CTUC

Lesotho Trade Union Congress
Address. PO Box 727, Maseru 100
Phone. +266 312 768
Fax. +266 312 768
Leadership. Simon M. Jonathan (general secretary)
International affiliation. CTUC

Liberia

Capital: Monrovia
Population: 3.16 m. (2000 est.)

1 Political and Economic Background

Liberia, an independent state from 1847, was founded by freed black slaves from the USA, whose descendants dominated the government until 1980. President (then Master-Sergeant) Samuel K. Doe seized power in a bloody 1980 coup and ruled through the People's Redemption Council (PRC). A civil war broke out in 1989 and led to Doe's overthrow and death in 1990. Fighting continued, however, with internationally sponsored peace agreements collapsing until 1996. In 1997 elections were held resulting in a large majority in the legislature for the National Patriotic Front of Liberia and the election of its presidential candidate, Charles Taylor, who had launched the rebellion that led to the overthrow of Doe in 1990.

About 70% of the workforce are engaged in agriculture, largely at subsistence level. The country is also a source of primary commodities, notably iron ore, timber, rubber and diamonds, exploitation of which tends to be in the hands either of the state or of multinationals. Civil war in the 1990s caused widespread economic dislocation, capital flight, massive unemployment, and declining living standards. There are continuing problems of lack of infrastructure, inter-ethnic violence, and rampant corruption and extortion impeding legitimate business.

GDP (purchasing power parity) $2.85bn. (1999 est.); GDP per capita (purchasing power parity) $1,000 (1999 est.).

2 Trade Unionism

Liberia ratified ILO Conventions No. 87 (Freedom of Association and Protection of the Right to Organize, 1948) and No. 98 (Right to Organize and Collective Bargaining, 1949) in 1962. Trade unions have had legal status since 1963 but there has been only modest development and they have been subjected to numerous restrictions.

Before the civil war the main focus of trade union activity was in the plantations of the Firestone rubber company, by far the biggest employer in the country, which saw battles for union recognition. This closed its operations in Dec. 1989 as a result of the civil war,

resuming production in Feb. 1996. A strike in Sept. 1997 resulted in Firestone workers being wounded by security forces.

Civil conflict and economic collapse in the 1990s undermined the trade unions although there were some 32 functioning unions with a total of about 60,000 members (many of them unemployed) at the end of the decade. Most of the population is engaged in subsistence agriculture and in the towns there is wholesale unemployment and dependence on informal economic activity. There has been persistent government interference in union affairs especially in leadership struggles. The main union centre is the Liberian Federation of Labour Unions (LFLU), affiliated to the ICFTU, but WCL affiliates have also traditionally been active in Liberia. Under the constitution unions are barred from taking part in political activity. There is a nominal right of all workers, except civil servants, to engage in collective bargaining but this has little practical application. Teachers and Firestone plantation workers went on strike in 1999, the former over wage arrears, but strike action is otherwise rare against a background of wholesale unemployment.

3 Trade Union Centre

Liberian Federation of Labour Unions (LFLU)

Address. J.B. McGill Labor Center, Gardnersville Freeway, PO Box 415, Monrovia.

Phone. +231 223 483

Fax. +231 226 219

History and character. Formed in 1980 by amalgamation of the United Workers' Congress and the Liberia Federation of Trade Unions (the latter formed in 1977 by merger of the former Congress of Industrial Organizations and Labour Congress of Liberia, both of which had been founded in the 1950s).

International affiliation. ICFTU

4 Other Trade Union Organization

Federation of Organizations Affiliated to ODSTA/WCL

Address. PO Box 4436, Ashmun Street, Monrovia

Leadership. Levelaku B. Stanley (president)

International affiliation. WCL

Libya

Capital: Tripoli
Population: 5.12 m. (2000 est.)

GDP (purchasing power parity) $39.3bn. (1999 est.);
GDP per capita (purchasing power parity) $7,900 (1999 est.).

1 Political and Economic Background

The monarchy was overthrown in a military coup in 1969 led by Col. Moamer al Kadhafi, who has remained the ruler of the country as the "leader of the revolution" although holding no official position. There is a hierarchy of people's committees, which form an indirect electoral base for the General People's Congress, which functions as the legislature. Kadhafi's Arab Socialist Union is the sole permitted political party and there is no significant organized domestic opposition.

The economy is based on oil, which is government controlled. There has been some effort since 1992 to diversify and encourage the private sector but there is extensive state regulation and the majority of the work force are in the state sector. UN sanctions were suspended in 1999 and Libya has been seeking to encourage foreign investment.

2 Trade Unionism

Libya ratified ILO Convention No. 98 (Right to Organize and Collective Bargaining, 1949) in 1962 (i.e. under the monarchy) but has not ratified Convention No. 87 (Freedom of Association and Protection of the Right to Organize, 1948).

Independent trade unions are not permitted and a single-trade-union system is in force, organized by the General Federation of Producers' Trade Unions (GFPTU), created in 1972. This is closely associated with the regime and is affiliated internationally to the WFTU. No strikes have been reported for many years. According to the government workers may strike but do not need to because they control their enterprises.

Liechtenstein

Capital: Vaduz
Population: 32,000 (2000 est.)

1 Political and Economic Background

The Principality of Liechtenstein is a constitutional and hereditary monarchy. The government is formed by the Patriotic Union (VU) party and the opposition led by the (more conservative) Progressive Citizens' Party (FBP). Prior to 1997 these two parties were in coalition continuously from 1938.

Liechtenstein enjoys a high standard of living. Its industrial sector employs a substantial number of resident foreigners together with thousands who come to work daily from neighbouring Switzerland and Austria. The other major sector of the economy is financial services, Liechtenstein being a centre for offshore banking. There is virtually no unemployment.

GDP (purchasing power parity) $730m. (1998 est.); GDP per capita (purchasing power parity) $23,000 (1998 est.).

2 Trade Unionism

All workers, including foreign workers, are free to join unions. There is one trade union, the Liechtenstein Employees' Association (LANV). Collective bargaining agreements are usually based on agreements reached in Switzerland. There is a right to strike, other than in essential services, but there were no strikes in 1999. Liechtenstein is not a member of the International Labour Organization.

3 Trade Union Centre

Liechtensteiner Arbeitnehmer- Verband (LANV)
Liechtenstein Employees' Association

Address. Dorfstrasse 24, alte Weberei, Postfach 54, 9495 Triesen

Phone. +423 399 38 38

Fax. +423 399 38 39

Leadership. Alice Fehr-Heidegger (president)

History and character. The LANV is the only union and represents about 13% of the workforce.

International affiliation. WCL

Lithuania

Capital: Vilnius
Population: 3.62 m. (2000 est.)

1 Political and Economic Background

Lithuania, under Soviet rule from World War II, resumed de facto independence in 1990. Its independence was recognized by the USSR in Sept. 1991. The Lithuanian Reform Movement (Sajudis) led the drive for independence, and won elections in 1990, but in 1992, in the face of economic adversity, the electorate voted the reformed communists of the Lithuanian Democratic Labour Party (LDDP) into office. In 1996 elections resulted in the formation of a coalition government led by the conservative Homeland Union (TS) party, itself the successor to Sajudis.

The early 1990s were marked by deep economic difficulty in the aftermath of independence and the collapse of the Soviet planned economy, and disputes over the pace and nature of privatization. GDP grew strongly thereafter before declining in 1999 (with unemployment rising to a post-independence high of 10%) in the wake of the financial crisis of Aug. 1998 in Russia, Lithuania's leading trading partner. There is a continuing privatization programme against a background of significant remaining state control. Lithuania is seeking accession to the EU.

GDP (purchasing power parity) $17.3bn. (1999 est.); GDP per capita (purchasing power parity) $4,800 (1999 est.).

2 Trade Unionism

The 1992 Constitution and the 1991 Law on Trade Unions recognize the right to form and join trade unions. Lithuania ratified ILO Conventions No. 87 (Freedom of Association and Protection of the Right to Organize, 1948) and No. 98 (Right to Organize and Collective Bargaining, 1949) in 1994. The Law on Trade Unions formally extends this right to employees of the police and the armed forces, although the Collective Agreements Law of 1991 does not allow collective bargaining by government employees involved in law enforcement and security related work. According to the law, unions, in order to be registered, must have at least 30 founding members in large enterprises or have a membership of one-fifth of all employees in small enterprises. About 15% of the labour force are unionized.

Independent trade unionism began as early as 1988 with the formation of the Lithuanian Workers' Union (LDS). The LDS and the Lithuanian Trade Union Unification (LPSS) affiliated to the ICFTU in 1994. The official centre under communism was renamed after independence as the Confederation of Free Lithuanian Trade Unions. At that time it claimed a membership of 1.1 million. In 1993 this merged with other unions to form the Lithuanian Trade Union Centre (LTUC). There was a continuing dispute through the 1990s between the unions over the distribution of assets of the former official unions. According to the LDS, managers in some state enterprises discriminate against the independent unions in favour of the LTUC unions.

Collective bargaining is provided for under the Collective Agreements Law, although collective bargaining is not widespread. The government issues wage guidelines for the state sector. There is a legal right to strike, other than for public employees engaged in essential services. However, there are lengthy pre-strike procedures and a two-thirds majority in favour of action is required in a secret ballot.

In 1997 on the initiative of ETUC the joint National Integration Commission of Lithuanian Trade Unions was established. In Feb. 1999 the government, employers and trade unions signed a General Tripartite Agreement and working groups were set up to recommend amendments to labour laws.

3 Trade Union Centres

Lithuanian Federation of Labour (LDF)

Address. V. Mykolaicio-Putino 5-140, 2026 Vilnius

Phone. +370 2 312029

Fax. +370 2 227153

E-mail. ldf@takas.lt

Leadership. Kazimiras Kuzminskas (president); Regina Rekesiene (secretary)

International affiliation. WCL

Lithuanian Workers' Union (LDS/LWU)

Address. V. Mykolaicio-Putino 5, 2009 Vilnius

Phone. +370 2 621 743

Fax. +370 2 615 253

E-mail. ltds@takas.lt

Leadership. Aldona Balsiene (president)

Membership. 50,000

History and character. The LDS was founded in 1988 as a component of the Sajudis national movement. It supported the call for independence from the Soviet Union at a time when this was opposed by the official unions. It joined the ICFTU in 1994. It has close relations with the leading trade union centres in the Baltic region as well as with the US AFL-CIO, which has provided it with considerable assistance and supports its trade union education programmes. It participates in Lithuania's various tripartite structures. The LDS unites 10 industrial-occupational federations.

International affiliations. ICFTU; ETUC (observer status)

Lithuanian Trade Union Unification (LPSS)

Address. J. Jasinskio 9 –213, 2600 Vilnius

Phone. +370 2 61 0921

Fax. +370 2 61 9078

E-mail. lpss@takas.lt

Leadership. Algirdas Sysas (president); Grazina Gruzdien (vice-president); Ieva Svirskyt (international secretary)

Membership. 41,650

History and character. The Lithuanian Trade Union Unification was established in Feb. 1992 and comprises eleven branch unions. It seeks to represent and coordinate its member unions in relations with the government and employers' organizations and works with other organizations aiming to strengthen democracy and the basis of law in Lithuania. It is represented on all national tripartite councils and commissions. Its structure includes a Women's Council, Youth Centre, and Education Support Fund. The president of LPSS, Algirdas Sysas, is a member of the Seimas (Lithuanian Parliament).

International affiliations. It became a member of the ICFTU in 1994 and has had observer status with ETUC since 1998.

Luxembourg

Capital: Luxembourg -Ville
Population: 437,000 (2000 est.)

GDP per capita (purchasing power parity) $34,200 (1999 est.).

1 Political and Economic Background

Historically the strongest party has been the (Christian democratic) Christian Social Party (CSV). Since 1919 it has formed coalition governments with various other parties and the Prime Minister has almost continuously come from the CSV. From 1984 to 1999 the CSV ruled in coalition with the social democratic Luxembourg Socialist Workers' Party (LSAP). Following elections in June 1999, a new coalition was formed in which the CSV was joined by the liberal Democratic Party (DP). Luxembourg is a member of the EU and a base for a number of its institutions. It joined the single European currency at its launch on Jan. 1, 1999. 97% of the population are formally Roman Catholic.

The Luxembourg economy was traditionally based on iron and steel, but as that industry declined it has successfully developed a range of other industries and a major financial services sector. Economic growth has averaged 5% per annum since 1985. 83% of the work force are now employed in services and only 14% in industry. One-third of the labour force of some 230,000 is foreign, coming primarily from other EU countries. Living standards are high and unemployment negligible.

GDP (purchasing power parity) $14.7bn. (1999 est.);

2 Trade Unionism

Luxembourg ratified ILO Conventions No. 87 (Freedom of Association and Protection of the Right to Organize, 1948) and No. 98 (Right to Organize and Collective Bargaining, 1949) in 1958. The workforce is highly organized, with about 57% belonging to unions. There are two major trade union centres, the Luxembourg Confederation of Christian Trade Unions (LCGB) and the Luxembourg Confederation of Independent Trade Unions (OGB-L). The OGB-L also forms the core of the Luxembourg General Confederation of Labour (CGTL), an umbrella which is the affiliate of the ICFTU. The centres are independent politically, but there are traditional links between the LCGB and the Christian Social Party (CSV) and between the OGB-L and the social democratic Luxembourg Socialist Workers' Party (LSAP).

The trade union movement is fragmented and relations between unions can be fractious. Under the Luxembourg system, which is somewhat akin to that in Belgium, the designation of being "nationally representative" confers significant rights and discriminates against unions without this status. These rights include representation on the country's numerous and influential tripartite bodies, such as the National Conciliation Office and the Tripartite Coordination Committee. In addition, only "nationally representative" organizations, or their affiliates, can conclude legally enforceable collective bargaining agreements. The status of being "nationally representative" is ultimately determined by government on criteria that are not explicitly defined but depend on quantitative (number of members) and qualitative (stability) factors. "Social elections" are held (most recently in Oct. 1998) at which workers vote, inter alia, for members of employee committees/works councils and for the so-called "professional chambers". The chambers are consulted on all legislative matters relating to the interests of those whom they represent. Some 93,000 private sector white-collar workers elect representatives to the Chamber of Private Sector White-Collar Staff (Chambre des Employés Privés) while 101,000 blue-collar workers elect representatives to the Chamber of Labour (Chambre du Travail). In 1995 the government asked the tripartite Economic and Social Council for recommendations on reforming the criteria to determine nationally representative status, but the Council could not produce agreement.

There are currently only two union organizations considered "nationally representative" for both blue- and white-collar workers, the LCGB and the OGB-L, the two main trade union centres. In the most recent social elections (in Oct. 1998) these won 750 of the 1250 seats on works councils. However, many workers support unions not linked to these two. In elections for the Chamber of White-Collar Staff, the OGB-L took 12 seats and the LCGB nine, while the (independent) Luxembourg Association of Bank Staffs (ALEBA) took six, a newly formed Confédération des Employés Privés (CEP) took 3 and the Union des Employés Privés (UEP) took two. (The Fédération des Employés Privés (FEP), considered representative for private sector non-manual workers but which had lost membership rapidly in the previous few years, was barred from participating after its list of candidates was rejected by a supervisory body). In Apr. 1999 ALEBA and the UEP announced they had formed a new federation (Fédération Syndicale ALEBA-UEP), and ALEBA struck a collective bargaining agreement with the ABBL bank employers' organization in the name of both ALEBA and ALEBA-UEP. The Ministry of Labour refused to register this agreement (thereby making it invalid) on the ground that ALEBA was not nationally representative (even though it is considered the leading banking union). ALEBA complained to the ILO, arguing that the government was guilty of "interference in trade union affairs through the creation of monopolies that favour political unions" (i.e. the LGGB and OGB-L). In Mar. 2000 the ILO's Committee of Experts on Freedom of Association asked (as in the case of Belgium) for the government to review the criteria.

Collective bargaining is widely practiced and employers are obliged to bargain when asked to do so by a "representative" trade union. In the event of breakdown, there is mandatory conciliation procedure through the tripartite National Conciliation Office (Office National de Conciliation). A strike (or lock-out) may not be called until the chair of the Office says that all attempts at conciliation have failed. There was a public sector general strike in 1998 over the issue of civil service pension reform.

The Tripartite Coordination Committee (Comité de Coordination Tripartite), chaired by the Prime Minister, drew up a National Action Plan for Employment for 1998–99.

3 Trade Union Centres

Confédération Générale du Travail du Luxembourg (CGT-L)
Luxembourg General Confederation of Labour

Address. 60 Boulevard J.F. Kennedy, 4170 Esch/Alzette

Phone. +352 54 05 45

Fax. +352 54 16 20

E-mail. ogb-l@ogb-l.lu

Website. www.ogb-l.lu (French/German)

Leadership. John Castegnaro (president)

History and character. The CGT-L was founded in 1927 by the metal workers' union and the federation of railway workers. In 1978 the trade union Lëtzebuerger Aarbechterverband (the precursor of the present Confederation of Independent Trade Unions, OGB-L) took the initiative to form a united trade union movement based on the Austrian or West German model. The Christian trade unions in Luxembourg organized in the LCGB (see below) refused to become part of this new organization, as did some unions in the CGT-L. The outcome was that both the OGB-L and CGT-L continued in existence, with the CGT-L becoming a loose federation embracing the OGB-L, the National Federation of Railway Workers, Transport Workers and Officers (FNCTTFEL) and the Luxembourg Federation of Publishing and Printing Workers (FLTL).

The OGB-L is the dominant factor in the CGT-L, providing it with offices and services, and is the recognized trade union centre within Luxembourg. The CGT-L is a federal umbrella, which holds the affiliations to ICFTU and ETUC. John Castegarno is president of both the OGB-L and the CGT-L.

International affiliations. ICFTU; ETUC; TUAC

Lëtzeburger Chrëschtleche Gewerkschafts-Bond (LCGB)
Luxembourg Confederation of Christian Trade Unions

Address. 11 rue du Commerce, 1351 Luxembourg

Phone. + 352 49 94 24 1

Fax . +352 49 94 24 49

E-mail. lcgb@euromail.lu

Website. www.lcgb.lu (French/German)

Leadership. Robert Weber (president); Marc Spautz (secretary general)

Membership. 34,000

History and character. The LCGB was formally created in 1921, although it traces its origins back to the nineteenth century. Its orientation is social-Christian, and it gives no financial aid to political parties and is not involved in party politics. It provides a range of welfare and similar services and conducts collective bargaining. It comprises nine sectoral unions.

Publication. Soziale Fortschrëtt

International affiliations. WCL; ETUC; TUAC

Onofhängege Gewerkschaftsbond Lëtzebuerg (OGB-L)
Luxembourg Confederation of Independent Trade Unions

Address. 60 Boulevard J.F. Kennedy, 4170 Esch/Alzette

Phone. +352 54 05 45

Fax. +352 54 16 20

E-mail. ogb-l@ogb-l.lu

Website. www.ogb-l.lu (French/German)

Leadership. John Castegnaro (president); Jean-Claude Reding (secretary general)

History and character. The OGB-L was formed in January 1979 as the successor organization to LAV (Lëtzebuerger Aarbechterverband), founded in 1916. It is, with the Christian-influenced LCGB, one of the two Luxembourg trade union centres considered "nationally representative" for all private sector workers. It is the leading force within the CGT-L, which serves as a loose umbrella and holds the affiliations with the ICFTU and ETUC. The OCB-L comprises 15 occupationally based unions.

Publications. Aktuell/Actuel (monthly)

Macedonia

Capital: Skopje
Population: 2.04 m. (2000 est.)

1 Political and Economic Background

Macedonia, formerly a Yugoslav republic, became independent with the break-up of Yugoslavia in 1991. Its path to general international recognition was obstructed by Greek objections to the name Macedonia, and in 1993 it was admitted to the UN under the title "Former Yugoslav Republic of Macedonia".

Since elections in autumn 1998 there has been a coalition government led by the nationalist Internal Macedonian Revolutionary Party (IMRO), the party that led Macedonia to independence. The leading opposition party is the Social Democratic Union of Macedonia (SDSM), the reformed former ruling League of Communists of Macedonia.

Macedonia was the poorest Yugoslav republic and the collapse of the planned economy, loss of former markets as a consequence of the disintegration of Yugoslavia, and an economic blockade by Greece (maintained until 1995), led to several years of plummeting output in which GDP halved. There has been a recovery since 1996 although Macedonia was again affected by loss of access to markets in Serbia and elsewhere as a result of the 1999 Kosovo crisis, when refugees for a time inflated the population by one-sixth (most subsequently returning home). Most enterprises have now been privatized. Inflation of 200% in 1993 had been cut to 1% by 1999. Unemployment is high (estimated at 35% in 1999) with wage arrears also common.

GDP (purchasing power parity) $7.6bn. (1999 est.); GDP per capita (purchasing power parity) $3,800 (1999 est.).

2 Trade Unionism

Macedonia ratified ILO Conventions No. 87 (Freedom of Association and Protection of the Right to Organize, 1948) and No. 98 (Right to Organize and Collective Bargaining, 1949) in 1991, following independence. The Macedonian Federation of Trade Unions (SSM) is the principal centre in the country and is the successor to the former Yugoslav official trade union structure, whose assets it has retained. It has observer status with ETUC. The SSM participates in tripartite bodies as labour's representative. Independent unions are permitted and there is an Association of Independent and Autonomous Unions (UIASM), which has gained affiliation to the WCL. There is no ICFTU affiliate. There is no legislative framework for collective bargaining. There were numerous small-scale work stoppages in 1999, mostly over pay arrears and issues relating to privatization and management changes in the state sector.

Madagascar

Capital: Antananarivo
Population: 15.5 m. (2000 est.)

1 Political and Economic Background

Madagascar became fully independent from France in 1960. It was under military rule from 1972, with Didier Ratsiraka becoming President in 1975. Until 1990 parties only existed within the National Front for the Defence of the Revolution (FNDR). In 1993 multi-party elections were held which resulted in Ratsiraka losing power, but he was re-elected in 1996. His AREMA party also dominates the legislature, to which elections were held most recently in May 1998.

Most of the workforce is engaged in agriculture, much of it at subsistence level. The small manufacturing sector includes textiles and processing of agricultural products. Growth in GDP lagged behind the increase in population in the 1990s and there has been periodic discontent reflected in strikes and demonstrations over government policy and IMF sponsored austerity measures. By 1999 some 46 state companies, including major employers in sugar and oil, had been privatized.

GDP (purchasing power parity) \$11.5bn. (1999 est.); GDP per capita (purchasing power parity) \$780 (1999 est.).

2 Trade Unionism

Madagascar ratified ILO Convention No. 87 (Freedom of Association and Protection of the Right to Organize, 1948) in 1960 and Convention No. 98 (Right to Organize and Collective Bargaining, 1949) in 1998. Under the Ratsiraka regime from 1975 until the early 1990s independent trade unions were restricted in their activities and preference given to government-controlled bodies. The 1992 constitution and the 1995 labour code give workers, except those in essential services, the police and military, the right to form and join unions of their own choosing. However, the formal economy is small and the base of unions is narrow and they have little influence. Unions are strongest in the public sector. There are currently two WCL affiliates in Madagascar (SEKRIMA and USAM) and one centre affiliated to the ICFTU (FMM).

Collective bargaining is lawful but in practice is little used. There is a legal right to strike, with restrictions in essential services and subject to conciliation, mediation and arbitration procedures. In law union rights exist in the export processing zones. However, trade union rights are reported in practice to be denied to the 27,000 workers in the zones who are effectively unable to join unions or go on strike; in these zones, according to the ICFTU, the "authorities are unable, or unwilling, to enforce the labour law". J.C. Razafimandimby, the confederal secretary of the WCL affiliate SEKRIMA, said in Sept. 1999 that "wrongful dismissals of trade union leaders have become common practice, particularly in the Free Industrial Zones in which the employers take advantage of the high rate of unemployment in Madagascar".

3 Trade Union Centres

Fivondronamben'ny Mpiasa Malagasy (FMM)
Confederation of Malagasy Workers

Address. BP 846, Antananarivo 101

Phone. +261 22 205 20

History and character. Founded 1957 but largely lapsed into inactivity during the period of military rule. The 8th (1992) conference of the FMM was the first since 1981.

International affiliation. ICFTU

Sendika Kristianina Malagasy (SEKRIMA)
Christian Confederation of Malagasy Trade Unions

Address. BP 1035, Route de Majunta-Soarano, Antananarivo 101

Phone. +261 20 222 74 85

Fax. +261 20 222 74 85

Leadership. Jean Chrysostôme Razafimandimby (confederal secretary)

Membership. 7,000

History and character. Formed in 1938 as a section of the Catholic-inspired CFTC (France), the organization became the CCSM in 1956 and adopted the name SEKRIMA in 1964. From 100,000 members in the mid-1950s, it declined in importance during the 1960s under the first republic. It virtually ceased to exist after 1972, but it revived in the 1980s.

International affiliation. WCL

Union des Syndicats Autonomes de Madagascar (USAM)

Address. BP 1038, Lot III M 33, Andrefan' Ambohijanahary, Antanarivo 101

Phone. +261 20 222 74 85

Fax. +261 20 222 74 85

E-mail. usam@dts.mg

Leadership. Norbert Rakotomanana (president); Samuel A. Rabemanantsoa (secretary)

International affiliation. WCL

Malawi

Capital: Lilongwe
Population: 10.39 m. (2000 est.)

1 Political and Economic Background

The former British protectorate of Nyasaland, Malawi became a republic within the Commonwealth in 1966, two years after gaining independence from the UK. Dr Hastings Kamuzu Banda, Malawi's first Prime Minister under UK rule, became President in 1966 and his conservative and traditionalist Malawi Congress Party (MCP) was henceforth the sole legal party. All Malawi citizens were party members.

Resistance to the Banda regime culminated in the 1992 announcement that the imprisoned union leader Chakufwa Chihana would chair an interim committee of a new opposition group, the Alliance for Democracy (AFORD). In 1993 Malawians voted decisively for a multi-party system; after a turbulent period elections in May 1994 were won by the United Democratic Front (UDF) of Bakili Muluzi, who became President, with Chihana in third place. Chihana and other AFORD leaders joined Muluzi in government in September. In 1995 Banda was tried and acquitted on murder charges. The UDF remained the largest party following legislative elections in June 1999.

More than 80% of the labour force work on the land and tobacco, tea and sugar generate 78% of export earnings. Poor in natural resources, Malawi's small-scale industry is largely based on food processing. The country's landlocked position and poor access to potential markets have contributed to its low level of development and there is little inward investment.

GDP (purchasing power parity) $9.4bn. (1999 est.); GDP per capita (purchasing power parity) $940 (1999 est.).

2 Trade Unionism

Malawi ratified ILO Convention No. 98 (Right to Organize and Collective Bargaining, 1949) in 1965 but did not ratify Convention No. 87 (Freedom of Association and Protection of the Right to Organize, 1948) until 1999. Most workers, including civil servants (but excluding police and military personnel) may lawfully join unions and there are legal protections requiring reinstatement of employees dismissed for union activities. However, only 12% of the workforce are in the formal sector and unions represent only a small minority of formal sector employees. The unions report that some employers actively prevent union organization. The Malawi Congress of Trade Unions (MCTU) has been the only trade union centre since independence. A Congress of Malawi Trade Unions (COMATU) was also created in the late 1990s.

Under the 1996 Labour Relations Act (LRA) where a union represents 20% of the workforce in an enterprise, or 15% in a sector, it may engage in collective bargaining at that level and agreements are legally binding. The LRA provides for industrial councils to be set up as a forum for negotiation and dispute resolution where collective bargaining does not take place. The ICFTU says there is ambiguity in the interpretation of which strikes are legal; however, as the law requires a secret ballot prior to strike action, most that occur may be illegal. In 1997 a strike by the CSTU public servants' union led to the detention and alleged torture by police of a number of union activists before the resumption of negotiations led to the strike being called off. In 1998 the government responded to a general strike called by the MCTU against price rises by calling on employers to dismiss strikers. Strikes are not lawful in essential services. National labour law applies in the export processing zones. There are few functioning mechanisms for protecting workers' rights under the legislation.

3 Trade Union Centre

Malawi Congress of Trade Unions (MCTU)
Address. PO Box 1271, Lilongwe
Phone. +265 740 235
Fax. +265 740 235
Leadership. Francis Antonio (general secretary)
Membership. 45,000
History and character. The MCTU was founded on independence in 1964 in succession to the Nyasaland Trades Union Congress. It is also variously referred to as the Trades Union Congress of Malawi (TUCM) and the Malawi Trades Union Congress (MTUC). Its affiliation to the ICFTU was suspended in 1993-94 on the grounds of its compliant attitude to the Banda regime. By the late 1990s the MCTU faced increasing government interference in its affairs, including disruption of its meetings, as it called protests against price rises and working conditions. The government said that opposition politicians were using the MCTU as a vehicle to promote unrest.
International affiliation. ICFTU

4 Other Trade Union Organization

Congress of Malawi Trade Unions (COMATU)
Address. PO Box 30347, Chichiri, Blantyre 3
Phone. +265 670 088
Fax. +265 677 452
Leadership. Thomas Banda (interim president)
International affiliation. CTUC

Malaysia

Capital: Kuala Lumpur
Population: 21.79 m. (2000 est.)

GDP (purchasing power parity) $229.1bn. (1999 est.); GDP per capita (purchasing power parity) $10,700 (1999 est.).

1 Political and Economic Background

Malaysia gained independence from the United Kingdom in 1957. The major political force is the National Front, a coalition of parties representing the country's major ethnic groups (Malay, Chinese and Indian). The National Front has held power since its formation in 1973, when it superseded the Alliance Party, which had itself held power since independence. The leading party within the National Front is the United Malays National Organization (UMNO), which is based on the numerically dominant Malay population, and UMNO's leader Mahathir bin Mohamad has been Prime Minister since 1981. In the most recent elections, in Nov. 1999, the National Front won 148 of the 193 seats in the House of Representatives.

Malaysia has developed in recent decades from an economy based on primary commodities, with rubber, tin, palm oil and timber as its staples, to a diversified industrial economy. Manufacturing supplanted agriculture as the largest sector of the economy in 1985. In the 1990s growth averaged 8% per annum and the government proclaimed its Vision 2020 goal of raising Malaysia to the same level as developed western economies by the year 2020. Against that background, the impact of the 1997–98 Asian financial crisis, which led to a 7% contraction in GDP in 1998, had a particularly severe impact on confidence in Malaysia. Mahathir responded with a series of emotive statements claiming that foreigners were using the crisis to try to take over the Malaysian economy. Malaysia imports labour, and during the crisis, in Jan. 1998, the government ordered all employers to arrange for the deportation of foreign workers on temporary contracts, although Indonesian workers were exempted. The 1998 recession, though deep, proved short-lived however and in 1999 GDP grew 5%, led by a strong export sector.

Following a series of race riots, in 1971 Malaysia introduced the New Economic Policy with the aim of raising the economic status of the Malay majority (bumiputras) to that of the wealthier Chinese minority, an objective which has been the cornerstone of successive National Front governments. In 1991 the NEP (which had raised the bumiputra share of corporate activity to 20 per cent) was replaced by a more moderate National Development Policy (NDP) that was less prescriptive about patriation of assets. In 1998 the government announced there would be a relaxation of racial laws on the ownership of businesses.

2 Trade Unionism

Chinese hongs, or guilds, were predecessors of trade union organizations before World War II, and there was also some organization among immigrant Indian workers, under the influence of trade union developments in the subcontinent. After the War and defeat of Japan the Malayan Communist Party (MCP) formed the General Labour Union (GLU), later the Pan-Malayan Federation of Trade Unions (PMFTU). To counteract this influence the British encouraged the development of 'free' trade unions, and British trade unionists came to assist in the education of union officers. Following widespread industrial unrest from 1946–48, a State of Emergency was declared, the MCP was outlawed and the PMFTU was de-registered. The free trade unions formed the Malaysian Trades Union Congress (MTUC) in 1949.

The MTUC is the national trade union centre, reporting 198 affiliates with 482,991 members in 1999. Its centre of gravity has shifted with the emergence of the teachers' union as the largest affiliate in place of the plantation workers. The Congress of Unions of Employees in the Public and Civil Services (CUEPACS) affiliates unions organizing around 120,000 public sector staff members. For many years there were regular attempts made to merge these two organizations into a United Malaysian Labour Movement (UMLM) and harmonize representation at the ILO, but they were bedeviled by CUEPACS' fears over the loss of its identity and controversy over the leadership of the new organization. However, public sector unions affiliate to both the MTUC and CUEPACS. CUEPACS benefited directly from a 1990 decision of the government to allow quasi-governmental employees' organizations to affiliate to it.

Many trade unionists were arrested in 1987 under the Internal Security Act to "calm rising racial tension", among them Dr. V. David, then MTUC secretary-general and Transport Workers' leader, on his return from a US convention where he had criticized conditions in the free-trade zones and complained of the denial of trade union rights to young women workers in the electronics industry. He and two other union leaders spent a year in a political detention camp for 'rehabilitation'. David coupled his MTUC leadership with membership of the opposition in the National Assembly. When the AFL-CIO called (unsuccessfully) for Malaysia's preferences under the United States General System of Preferences to be suspended for disrespect of international union rights standards, Mahathir described this as 'an imperialist plot by the West to ruin Malaysia's economy'.

The oppositionist politics of the MTUC leadership at that time was the major factor leading a number of unions, including the National Union of Bank Employees, the National Union of Commercial Workers, the National Union of Petroleum and Chemical Workers, and several others, to launch a rival Malaysian Labour Organization (MLO) in 1989. The MLO's constitution stipulated that office bearers could not hold a position in any political party. Registered as a trade union in 1990, the MLO had about 135,000 members in 32 unions two years later. It was endorsed by the government as an alternative to the highly political MTUC: the MTUC counter-charged that the MLO was a political arm of the ruling party. The government certainly assisted the MLO (and enraged the MTUC) by naming it as an advisor to its 1992 ILO delegation and inviting it to join the National Labour Advisory Council (NLAC). MLO officials were also appointed to two of the four union places on the Employee Provident Fund, previously a preserve exclusively of the MTUC. After 1992, however, with less anti-government forces in control of the MTUC the rationale for the MLO declined and it merged back into the MTUC in 1996.

In 1995 there were officially recorded 502 unions with 701,334 members. This represented union density of only 8.6%, with density lowest in mining and construction and highest in electricity, gas and water. These figures comprised 364 in-house trade unions with 299,618 members and 138 national trade unions with 401,144 members. About 60% of union members are in unions affiliated to the MTUC. Under the 1959 Trade Unions Act unions are not allowed to organize outside their primary occupational area and this has limited the growth of sizable national unions: the teachers' union is the only one of the MTUC's affiliates to have more than 30,000 members. Total union membership has been growing slowly year-on-year.

Malaysia has not ratified ILO Convention No. 87 (Freedom of Association and Protection of the Right to Organize, 1948). The Department of Trade Union Affairs (headed by the Director General of Trade Union Affairs) is set up within the Ministry of Human Resources to enforce the Trade Unions Act, register trade unions and ensure that they "function in a healthy, democratic and responsible manner". The Director General must also give his approval for a union to affiliate internationally.

The right of association is limited by the Societies Act of 1966, under which any association (including trade unions) of seven or more members must register. The Trade Unions Act of 1959 as amended gives the Registrar of Trade Unions wide discretionary powers to deny recognition to new unions or to suspend existing unions. Peninsula-based unions may not have members from Sabah and Sarawak, and vice versa. If seven workers petition for a union the Registrar of Trade Unions has to consider their request; recognition by the employer is mandatory if wanted by a majority of employees. The Trade Unions Act restricts a union to representing workers in a "particular establishment,

trade, occupation or industry". This provision has been invoked on a number of occasions to force unions to disaffiliate members. General Electric, Hitachi and Mitsumi Electronics are among companies that have successfully called on the Director General of Trade Union Affairs to bar their employees from remaining as members of the MTUC-affiliated Electrical Industry Workers' Union. It is reported that employees of a furniture manufacturer were not allowed to join the Metal Industry Employees' Union because the company used both metal and wood for its products.

Employers are barred from penalizing workers for participating in lawful trade union activities. However, according to the ICFTU, many employers "go to extreme lengths to deny union recognition and evade collective bargaining. They often challenge government directives to accord union recognition and refuse to comply with Industrial Court awards to reinstate wrongfully dismissed workers." Some categories of workers are excluded from union membership. These include categories of workers defined as "confidential", "managerial and executive", defence forces and the police. Foreign workers (of whom a majority are in any case probably in the country illegally) are not allowed to join unions. Work permits issued to foreign workers stipulate that they may not join "associations". This is a particular factor in the plantations, where the government estimates that as much as 90% of the workforce in the plantations is foreign. The National Union of Plantation Workers (NUPW), traditionally the largest MTUC affiliate, saw its membership halved after 1980 under the impact of rising numbers of contract and undocumented workers who will not join a union. Unions do exist in the free trade zones, where national labour laws apply. The government has adopted a policy of officially discouraging the formation of a national unions in the large electronics sector, and the MTUC seems to have reluctantly accepted that it is better to have enterprise unions in that sector than none at all, although employers also reportedly have resisted the formation of enterprise unions.

A range of legislation not specifically aimed at trade unions, such as the Internal Security Act, allowing detention without trial, the Police Act, the Sedition Act, and the Printing Presses and Publications Act, are seen as inhibiting unions' political activities and freedom of expression. This is reinforced by the possibility of dissolution under the Societies Act. Unions are also prohibited from using funds for political purposes, which are defined in detail.

ILO Convention No. 98 (Right to Organize and Collective Bargaining, 1949) was ratified by Peninsula Malaysia in 1961 and by Sabah and Sarawak in 1964. Collective bargaining is widespread where unions are set up. There are restrictions on collective bargaining in the public sector under the Industrial Relations Act of 1967 and amendments, and in so-called "pioneer industries". The parties to a dispute must notify the Ministry of Human Resources and the Ministry's Industrial Relations Department may become involved in conciliation efforts. If these fail, the Ministry is empowered to refer the dispute to the Industrial Court. The tripartite Industrial Court has a record of making findings on the workers' side more often than not, although its procedures are slow.

For a strike to be legal it must first be approved by two-thirds of the workforce in a secret ballot. Unions may not strike over recognition issues. There are additional restrictions on strikes in "essential services". In practice, significant strikes are rare and brief, most being settled by conciliation with the assistance of the Ministry of Labour or in the Industrial Court. The government has powers to impose compulsory arbitration making strikes illegal and punishable by imprisonment.

The unions are represented on a wide range of advisory boards and official bodies, including the Industrial Court, the National Labour Advisory Council. The MTUC has eight representatives on the latter body, CUEPACS five, and the National Union of Plantation Workers, one.

3 Trade Union Centre

Malaysian Trades Union Congress (MTUC)

Address. 10-5 Jalan USJ 9/5T, Subang Jaya 47620

Phone. +60 3 724 2953

Fax. +60 3 724 3224

E-mail. mtuc@tm.net.my

Website. www.mtuc.org.my

Leadership. Zainal Rampak (president); G. Rajasekaran (secretary-general)

Membership. 482,991 in 198 affiliated unions

History and character. The MTUC, founded in 1949 by the 'free' trade unions, was initially known as the Malayan Trades Union Council; in 1958 it became the Malayan Trades Union Congress, and took its present name with the formation of Malaysia.

The former MTUC secretary-general, Dr V. David, was detained by the Malaysian government from Oct. 1987 until his conditional release in June 1988. David symbolized the strongly oppositionist stance of the MTUC at that time and at the 29th (1988) biennial delegates' conference, he and the president were re-elected. However, when the 1992 convention met it proved a triumph for a reform slate headed by G. Rajasekaran of the Metal Industry Employees' Union, which swept all incumbents except the president from their places. David's defeat ended 14 years as MTUC general secretary.

The MTUC says that its membership is 64% Malay, 16% Chinese, 17% Indian and 3% other; 59% are men and 41% women. It includes 50 public sector unions with 174,968 members and 148 private sector unions with 308,023 members. The largest member union is the National Union of the Teaching Profession, with 76,311 members, but many of its affiliates are small and the MTUC has called for an end to restrictions on unions organizing across trades. Some public sector affiliates (including the National Union of the Teaching Profession) are also affiliated to the public sector Congress of Unions of Employees in the Public and Civil Services (CUEPACS).

The MTUC has called for an end to the mass importation of foreign workers of the 1990s, which it says threatens wage levels. It calls for minimum wage regulations; the opportunity to organize freely in the free trade zones; an end to restrictions on collective bargaining in "pioneer" industries; retraining and re-employment programmes for laid-off workers; reform of restrictive trade union and internal security legislation; and revitalization of the conciliation system. It complains that the government ignores its nominees to tripartite bodies and that vacancies on the Industrial Court remain unfilled for months. It is opposed to privatization of essential services such as medicine, electrical supply, water, postal service and railways, and says that in Malaysia privatization is used for "political patronage" rather than economic reform.

The MTUC is not allied politically.

International affiliations. ICFTU; CTUC

4 Other Trade Union Organizations

Congress of Unions of Employees in the Public and Civil Services (CUEPACS)

Address. 1st Floor Wisma CUEPACS, Jalan Gajah, Off Jalan Yew Pudu, 55100 Kuala Lumpur

Phone. +60 3 985 6110

Fax. + 60 3 985 9457

Leadership. N. Siva Subramaniam (general secretary)

Membership. 120,000

International affiliation. CTUC

MKTR

Address. 434 Jalan Hose, 50460 Kuala Lumpur

Phone. +60 3 244 6161

Fax. +60 3 244 6213

E-mail. mktr@tm.net.my

International affiliation. WCL

Maldives

Capital: Malé
Population: 301,000 (2000 est.)

1 Political and Economic Background

Maldives was a British protectorate until 1965. President Maumoon Abdul Gayoom has been President since 1978, being re-elected four times, most recently (unopposed) in 1998. Although not illegal, political parties are discouraged and do not exist, candidates for the legislature (the Majlis) running as individuals.

Tourism and fishing are the leading sources of employment for the 64,000 workforce, with the majority of workers engaged outside the formal wage economy.

GDP (purchasing power parity) $540m. (1999 est.); GDP per capita (purchasing power parity) $1,800 (1999 est.).

2 Trade Unionism

While the formation of unions is not expressly prohibited, neither are there any protections in law for creating and joining unions. In practice, trade unions do not exist and there have been no recent reports of efforts to set up unions. Maldives is not a member of the ILO.

Mali

Population: 10.69 m. (2000 est.)
Capital: Bamako

1 Political and Economic Background

Mali was ruled by France until 1960. Following a coup in 1968 until 1991 Mali was a one-party unitary state with a mixed military–civilian government, but in that year the regime of General Moussa Traoré was overthrown. After a turbulent transitional period a constitutional referendum in Jan 1992 approved a multi-party system, and in March 1992 elections to the legislative assembly were won by the Malian Alliance for Democracy (ADEMA). In April 1992 ADEMA's leader Alpha Oumar Konare was elected president. A national peace pact with Tuareg rebels was signed the same month. In elections in 1997 Konare again won the presidency, in a poll boycotted by most opposition groups, and ADEMA retained control of the legislature after re-run elections in July–Aug. 1997 dogged by accusations of malpractice.

Mali is one of the world's poorest and least developed countries. Most of the workforce is engaged in subsistence farming, which is vulnerable to drought, and the country is heavily dependent on foreign aid. Ten per cent of the population are nomadic livestock-herders.

Cotton is the main cash crop. There is limited small-scale industry based mainly on food processing. The country is carrying out an IMF-backed structural adjustment programme and recorded 5% growth in 1999.

GDP (purchasing power parity) $8.5bn. (1999 est.); GDP per capita (purchasing power parity) $820 (1999 est.).

2 Trade Unionism

Mali ratified ILO Convention No. 87 (Freedom of Association and Protection of the Right to Organize, 1948) in 1960 and Convention No. 98 (Right to Organize and Collective Bargaining, 1949) in 1964. Branches of the metropolitan French confederations existed before independence in 1960, but trade union activity was subsequently coordinated in a single-trade-union system organized by the Union Nationale des Travailleurs du Mali (UNTM). The UNTM participated prominently in the movement to pluralism in 1991–92. The UNTM, which is now affiliated to the ICFTU, remains the national centre but a breakaway group, the Trade Union Confederation of Mali Workers (CSTM) was formed in 1997.

The 1992 Constitution and the labour code provide for freedom of association, other than for the military and police. The unions are well established in the small formal sector, including teachers, health workers and civil servants, and virtually all salaried employees are reported to be unionized. Bargaining occurs between unions, employers' organizations and the Ministry of Labour. There is a labour court for resolution of disputes. There is a constitutional right to strike, including for civil servants and other public sector workers, subject to notice periods and mediation procedures. The labour code prohibits retribution against strikers.

The ICFTU reported in 1999 that following the transition to multi-partyism and reforms of 1992 freedom of association and the right to bargain collectively "were generally respected for several years". In June 1996, however, three union general secretaries were among those arrested for involvement in a general strike called by the UNTM in protest at the government's refusal to enter into dialogue with it and the UNTM subsequently came under significant harassment.

3 Trade Union Centre

Union Nationale des Travailleurs du Mali (UNTM)
National Union of Workers of Mali

Address. Bourse du Travail, Boulevard de I'Indépendence, BP 169, Bamako

Phone. +223 22 36 99

Fax. +223 23 59 45

Membership. Reported as 130,000 prior to the 1997 split

History and character. Founded 1963. The UNTM under the regime of Gen. Moussa Traoré was closely supervised. In the late 1980s the UNTM nonetheless became involved in numerous protests over rising prices, delays in payment of public sector wages and privatization. In 1990 it called for the introduction of a multi-party system and UNTM industrial action was a major feature of the unrest that brought the downfall of the Traoré regime in March 1991.

In 1994 relations between the government and the UNTM deteriorated as a result of the devaluation of the CFA franc, about which it had not been consulted. The UNTM called a strike in June 1996 to protest at the lack of dialogue with the government. On Apr. 16, 1997, the UNTM headquarters were surrounded by troops after charges of fraud in national legislative elections had led to demonstrations. The constitutional court declared the elections invalid and the elections were re-run in July (with the ruling ADEMA party retaining power), and again troops surrounded the union headquarters amid further protests about electoral fraud. In August the government was reported to have funded the congress of a breakaway rival centre, the CSTM. In Oct. 1997 police occupied the UNTM headquarters and sealed the general secretary's office. The UNTM has, however, subsequently succeeded in maintaining its autonomy from the Government.

International affiliation. ICFTU

Malta

Capital: Valletta
Population: 392,000 (2000 est.)

1 Political and Economic Background

Malta became independent from the United Kingdom in 1964. The leading parties are the conservative Nationalist Party (NP) and the socialist Malta Labour Party, with the NP forming the government under Prime Minister Eddie Fenech Adami since Sept. 1998.

The economy is based on the export of manufactured goods, including electronics and textiles, freight transshipment and tourism. More than one-third of the workforce are in the public sector and fears of the impact of EU accession on public sector subsidies and economic controls are a factor in the opposition of the Labour

Party to the government's application for EU membership.

GDP (purchasing power parity) $5.3bn. (1999 est.); GDP per capita (purchasing power parity) $13,800 (1999 est.).

2 Trade Unionism

Malta ratified ILO Conventions No. 87 (Freedom of Association and Protection of the Right to Organize, 1948) and No. 98 (Right to Organize and Collective Bargaining, 1949) in 1965. Before World War II unions acted principally as beneficial guilds, but the General Workers' Union (GWU) was formed in 1943 as a full trade union, with early strength among the white-collar and skilled workers of the British naval dockyards. The Confederation of Malta Trade Unions (CMTU) was founded in 1959. The GWU (which is affiliated to the ICFTU) and the CMTU (a WCL affiliate) are the two trade union organizations recognized under the 1976 Industrial Relations Act as being representative at the national level. In total there are 35 registered trade unions, organizing 50% of the workforce. Anti-union discrimination by employers is prohibited under the 1976 Industrial Relations Act.

The GWU is closely linked to the Labour Party, being officially amalgamated with it for 14 years from May 1978. The CMTU does not have direct political links, though as a member of the WCL its orientation is essentially social Christian. From 1983 to 1986 the Labour administration excluded the CMTU from the official Maltese delegation to the ILO, although it continued to send unofficial participants.

Annual tripartite discussions provide a framework for industrial relations and income policy. There is a right to strike for all workers except uniformed military and the police. The responsible minister may under the Industrial Relations Act of 1976 compulsorily refer disputes to the tripartite Industrial Tribunal for binding settlement (i.e. in effect limiting the right to strike). Three disputes were referred to the Tribunal in 1999.

3 Trade Union Centres

Confederation of Malta Trade Unions (CMTU)

Address. 13/3 South Street, PO Box 467, Valletta CMR 01

Phone. +356 237313

Fax. +356 250146

Leadership. Charles Magro (general secretary)

Membership. 31,000

History and character. The CMTU was founded in 1959. It was known as the Malta Confederation of Trade Unions until 1978 when the Labour government, which had a close association with the rival GWU, prohibited by law the use of the word Malta in the name. After Labour lost power in 1987 the word Malta appeared again in the CMTU name. The CMTU makes no financial contributions to political parties and is politically non-aligned.

International affiliations. WCL; CTUC; ETUC

General Workers' Union (GWU)

Address. Workers' Memorial Building, South Street, Valletta VLT 11

Phone +356 244 451

Fax. +356 242 975

E-mail. gwu@maltanet.net

Leadership. Tony Zarb (general secretary)

Membership. 35,495 (approximately half of unionized workers)

History and character. The GWU was founded in 1943 and has a membership distributed throughout the major sectors of the economy. Politically it is identified with the Malta Labour Party, and its president and general secretary have in the past participated in Cabinet meetings. For 14 years from 1978 the two were statutorily fused, and though the fusion was dissolved they still share many common goals.

When the Nationalist Party took power in 1987, after 16 years of Labour government, the GWU engaged in a series of actions opposing its plans for management of the important para-statal sector, and especially privatization. Conflict reached a peak in 1988 when dry dock workers blockaded the main port by anchoring a tanker across the mouth of the breakwater, thus preventing a visit by four British warships. Later, arrests of union members for interrogation about the incident led to further demonstrations.

GWU opposition to current government policy extends to Malta's bid for EU membership, launched in 1990 but not yet successful. In this the GWU is allied with the Labour Party. There are particular concerns that EU accession would force an end to government subsidies to the dry dock, a GWU stronghold.

The ICFTU claimed that GWU general secretary Tony Zarb and president James Pearsall were "brutally attacked" by police in Aug. 1999 during an industrial dispute at Malta International Airport.

The GWU is a multi-industrial union at the national level and its blue and white-collar membership is grouped in sections organized on an industrial or professional basis. Each section has its own executive committee and is autonomous but must abide by GWU principles.

International affiliations. ICFTU, ETUC; CTUC

Marshall Islands

Capital: Majuro
Population: 68,000 (2000 est.)

1 Political and Economic Background

The Marshall Islands are a group of atolls in the central Pacific, an independent nation in a compact of free association with the United States. There is small-scale farming, a little tourism, and a heavy dependence on US financial support.

GDP (purchasing power parity) $105m. (1998 est.); GDP per capita (purchasing power parity) $1,670 (1998 est.).

2 Trade Unionism

The 1979 Constitution accords a general right of association, but no trade unions have been formed. There is no legislation concerning trade union organization, collective bargaining or strike action.

Mauritania

Capital: Nouakchott
Population: 2.67 m. (2000 est.)

1 Political and Economic Background

The Islamic Republic of Mauritania was constituted in 1960, nominally as a parliamentary democracy, in practice as a one party state. From 1978 until 1992 it was ruled by a Military Council of National Salvation, headed from 1984 by the Armed Forces Chief of Staff, Col. Moaouia Ould Sid'Ahmed Taya. In line with developments in much of Africa at that time, the early 1990s brought greater pluralism, reflected in a new Constitution in 1991. However, although other political parties have been legalized, Taya has remained in power and was most recently re-elected as President in 1997 with more than 90% of the vote, in an election boycotted by opposition parties. His Democratic and Social Republican party (PRDS) also has an overwhelming majority in the National Assembly following elections (marked by widespread fraud) in 1996.

The majority of the population depends on subsistence level agriculture and herding. Iron ore and fish products account for most export revenues. Recurrent drought and plagues of locusts since the 1970s have led to urbanization of much of the former farming and nomadic population and there is extensive urban unemployment and poverty. There is a reliance on foreign assistance.

Traditionally, slavery was common among the black

or mixed-race descendants of freed slaves (haratin) of the south. In 1980 Mauritania officially abolished slavery and in 1984 the UN recorded that it had virtually disappeared.

GDP (purchasing power parity) $4.9bn. (1999 est.); GDP per capita (purchasing power parity) $1,910 (1999 est.).

2 Trade Unionism

Mauritania ratified ILO Convention No. 87 (Freedom of Association and Protection of the Right to Organize, 1948) in 1961 but has not ratified Convention No. 98 (Right to Organize and Collective Bargaining, 1949). Before political pluralism was established in the early 1990s the Union of Mauritanian Workers (UTM) was the only permitted trade union organization. The UTM had close links with the regime and did not support the 1991 protests against it. However disagreements were increasingly open between the UTM secretary-general and leading affiliated federations such as the miners and fishermen. The 1991 Constitution provided for trade union pluralism, but the labour code legitimizing pluralism did not come into force until 1993. In practice the UTM's privileged position under law persisted until 1994, when an independent organization, the General Confederation of Mauritanian Workers (CGTM) finally achieved recognition after more than a year of litigation. The UTM is now reported by both the ICFTU and WCL as being an affiliate and the CGTM is affiliated to the ICFTU. According to the US State

Department Human Rights Report for 1999 the UTM is still regarded by many workers as closely allied with the government and ruling PRDS and has lost ground to both the CGTM and a third confederation, the Free Confederation of Mauritanian Workers (CLTM), which achieved recognition in 1998 and affiliated to the WCL in 2000.

Under the 1991 constitution all workers except police and armed forces may join unions of their own choosing. Most of the workforce is in the informal sector, but the great majority of workers in the formal waged economy are in unions. Agreements on wages and conditions are often negotiated on a tripartite basis between employers, unions and government. There is a constitutional right to strike but in some cases the authorities have intervened to prevent industrial action and although strikes occur they tend to be infrequent and short lived. There is also provision for binding arbitration to end disputes. The government provides financial assistance to the trade union confederations to assist them in their educational and training activities and the confederations are also represented on labour tribunals and consultative bodies.

3 Trade Union Centres

Confédération Générale des Travailleurs de Mauritanie (CGTM)
General Confederation of Mauritian Workers

Address. BP 6164, Bouakchott

Phone. +222 2 58057

Fax. +222 2 58057

History and character. Independent trade union formed in 1993 but banned until passage of the law on trade union pluralism in July. It achieved legal recognition in January 1994 after a lengthy legal process but continued to complain of pressure on members from the authorities to renounce membership. The CGTM is politically independent but tends to be associated with opposition groups.

International affiliation. ICFTU

Union des Travailleurs de Mauritanie (UTM)
Union of Mauritanian Workers

Address. BP 630, Bourse du Travail, Nouakchott

Phone. +222 2 51 681

Fax. +222 2 56 521

Leadership. Elyould Brahim (secretary-general)

History and character. Founded 1961 and traditionally associated with the ruling PRDS, having been the sole authorized trade union organization prior to the reforms of the early 1990s. It has lost ground to the two confederations formed since that time.

International affiliations. ICFTU; also reported by WCL

Mauritius

Capital: Port Louis
Population: 1.18 m. (2000 est.)

1 Political and Economic Background

The former British colony of Mauritius achieved independence in 1968. The British monarch remained head of state and represented by a Governor-General, who appointed the Prime Minister, and on his advice, Cabinet ministers, until 1992, when Mauritius became an independent republic within the Commonwealth.

From 1983 the Mauritian Socialist Movement of Sir Aneerood Jugnauth was the dominant partner in coalition governments until elections held in Dec. 1995 resulted in an alliance of the Labour Party and the leftist Mauritian Militant Movement winning every seat in the National Assembly. The two parties have maintained a coalition government since that time, with Navinchandra Ramgoolam,

the leader of the Labour Party, as Prime Minister. Mauritius is one of the most stable and open societies in Africa.

Mauritius has a diversified economy, with only 14% of the labour force in agriculture. Manufacturing for export (especially garments) based mainly in the export processing zones, sugar and tourism, and increasingly offshore financial services, are the pillars of the economy. The standard of living is one of the highest in Africa.

GDP (purchasing power parity) $12.3bn. (1999 est.); GDP per capita (purchasing power parity) $10,400 (1999 est.).

2 Trade Unionism

Mauritius ratified ILO Convention No. 98 (Right to Organize and Collective Bargaining, 1949) in 1969. It has not ratified Convention No. 87 (Freedom of

Association and Protection of the Right to Organize, 1948) but all workers except the police and security forces have the right to form and join trade unions.

The trade union movement is developed but fragmented with many small unions. In total there are some 335 unions with 125,000 members, representing 25% of the workforce. There is a tradition of diversity in labour federations, and there is no unified centre, although the Mauritius Labour Congress (MLC) is the most important organization. It is affiliated to the ICFTU. The WCL affiliate is the National Trade Unions Confederation.

There are some 92,000 workers in the export processing zones (EPZs), about 18% of the total labour force. National labour law broadly applies in these zones, but the unions complain that employers prevent union organizers from entering their plants and intimidate workers who wish to join unions. Unionization in the EPZs is put at 12.5%.

Collective bargaining is legally recognized, although there is reported to be very little collective bargaining in the EPZs. There is a legal right to strike but compulsory cooling-off periods and binding arbitration mean that most strikes are technically illegal. Industrial relations legislation of the mid-1990s empowers the Prime Minister to declare a strike illegal if he believes it "imperils the economy".

Demonstrations and marches are sometimes restricted. The WCL reported in July 1999 that leaders of its affiliate the FSCC had faced "brutal violence" from the Special Support Unit while assembling outside government buildings to present a letter to the government.

3 Trade Union Centres

Federation of Progressive Unions (FPU)

Address. Arcades Rond-Point, Rose-Hill

Phone. +230 464 3392

Fax. +230 464 3625

E-mail. fpumel@intnet.mu

Leadership. Rajesnarain Gutteea (general secretary)

Membership. 35,000

International affiliation. CTUC

Mauritius Labour Congress (MLC)

Address. 8 Louis Victor de la Faye Street, Port Louis

Phone. +230 2124343

Fax. +230 2088945

E-mail. lalmel@bow.intnet.mu

Leadership. J. Lollbeeharry (general secretary)

Membership. 67,000

History and character. The MLC was formed in 1963 as a result of a merger of the Mauritius Trades Union Congress and the Mauritius Confederation of Free Trade Unions. It is the largest trade union centre and includes unions covering all the main sectors of the economy: sugar, tea, transport, docks, aviation, banks, insurance, construction, textiles, public service, para-statals and local authorities.

International affiliations. ICFTU; CTUC

National Trade Unions Confederation (NTUC)

Address. c/o FCSU, Room 308, 3rd Floor, Jade Court, Jummah Mosque Street, Port Louis

Phone. +230 216 1977

Fax. +230 216 1475

International affiliation. WCL

Affiliates. The NTUC's principal affiliates are:

1. Federation of Civil Service Unions (FCSU/FSCC)
Address. Room 308, 3rd Floor, Jade Court, Jummah Mosque Street, Port Louis
Phone. +230 216 1977
Fax. +230 216 1475
E-mail. fcsu@intnet.mu
Leadership. Soondress Sawmynaden (general secretary)
Membership. 25,000

2. Organization of Artisans' Unity (OAU)
Address. 42 Sir William Newton Street, Port Louis
Phone. +230 212 4557
Fax. +230 208 2438
Leadership. Roy Ramchurn (general secretary)
Membership. 2,700
History and character. Traditionally based in the tea and sugar industries in rural areas. It has recently organized textile workers in the export processing zone and hotel and catering workers.

Mexico

Capital: Mexico City
Population: 100.3m. (2000 est.)

1 Political and Economic Background

The Institutional Revolutionary Party (PRI) formed the government continuously from 1929 until 2000. In the 1930s the party developed a huge network for social control and patronage, including labour and peasant unions and professional associations, and this system survived periods of discontent to keep the party in power. The political orientation of the PRI tended to depend largely on the faction represented by the presidential incumbent. In the 1990s, however, the position of the PRI eroded. President Carlos Salinas de Gortari fled into exile in 1995 in view of his unpopularity. In 1997 the PRI lost its overall majority in the Federal Chamber of Deputies (the lower house), although remaining the largest party. Then, in elections in July 2000, the PRI lost the presidency to Vicente Fox of the Alliance for Change (dominated by Fox's National Action Party, PAN) and suffered further erosion of its position in the legislature, with PAN narrowly becoming the largest party. The PRI remained in power in half the 32 states.

Parts of Mexico are affected by relatively low-level guerrilla insurgency, occasionally flaring into full-scale local revolt as in the 1993–94 rebellion led by the Zapatista National Liberation Army (EZLN) in the southern state of Chiapas.

Mexico has a diversified economy at widely varying levels of development including both subsistence peasant cultivation and modern assembly plants for electronic products. Most Mexican enterprises are small: 97 per cent employ fewer than four people. Privatization has been extensive, with the number of state enterprises reduced from 1,155 in 1982 to less than 200 by the end of the 1990s. The government is trying to further increase competition in the major sectors of the economy but this has been a slow process. There are great disparities of wealth within the country and widespread under-employment. Mexico had recurrent financial crises in the 1980s and 1990s and real wages have not yet recovered to the levels of before the last major crisis in 1994. Mexico joined the North American Free Trade Area (NAFTA) in 1994, since then doubling its trade with the US and Canada, and in March 2000 signed a free trade agreement with the European Union, the first Latin American country to do so.

GDP (purchasing power parity) $865.5bn. (1999 est.); GDP per capita (purchasing power parity) $8,500 (1999 est.).

2 Trade Unionism

Mexico ratified ILO Convention No. 87 (Freedom of Association and Protection of the Right to Organize, 1948) in 1950 but has not ratified Convention No. 98 (Right to Organize and Collective Bargaining, 1949). The Mexican constitution and federal labour law provide for the right of workers to form and join unions. Most unionized workers are to be found in the formal sector, which employs about 50% of the labour force. The public sector is particularly heavily organized, the unions are strong in industrial areas, and there are also many peasant organizations. There have traditionally been elements of corruption, racketeering and strong-arm methods in the Mexican union movement.

Since the 1930s, the dominant force has been the Confederación de Trabajadores de México (CTM), which is closely allied with the PRI, the party of government continuously from 1929 until the end of the century. Fidel Velásquez, "Don Fidel", as secretary-general of the CTM from 1941 until his death on June 21, 1997, aged 97, was regularly consulted by national presidents and was seen as able to deliver millions of votes to the PRI. In exchange the government entered into social and economic pacts with the CTM. Its support for successive government policies is probably a major factor explaining the historically low level of union unrest in Mexico. The CTM is affiliated to the ICFTU. The WCL, generally relatively strongly represented throughout South and Central America, does not have a current affiliate and has criticized the CTM's role as a "transmission belt" for the ruling party.

The CTM is the dominant factor in the loose Congress of Labour (Congreso del Trabajo, CT) which provides an umbrella for dozens of federations and independent unions. The CT was founded in 1966 to provide a unifying voice for labour, each organization having one vote, on the principle that only unanimous decisions would be binding. Many unions and federations outside the CTM such as the Revolutionary Confederation of Workers and Peasants (CROC) have also historically been allied to the PRI. Officials of pro-PRI unions have campaigned for and run as PRI candidates for political office and there has always been a strong group of union (and especially CTM) representatives in the PRI delegations in the legislature.

The recent decline of the PRI has encouraged the development of unions not linked to it. In July 1997 elections, the PRI lost its absolute majority in the Chamber of Deputies for the first time in nearly seven decades. The following month, 100 unions, saying they represented one million workers, announced they would unite in a new organization (the UNT) to challenge the

CTM and work with the opposition to alter federal labour laws.

While competitive unions have been allowed in the private sector, a legal trade union monopoly has existed in public administration. The single-union rule in the public sector was widely seen as one of the mechanisms by which the PRI had controlled the state apparatus for decades in alliance with the 1.8 million member Federation of Unions of Government Workers (FSTSE). On May 12, 1999, the Supreme Court ruled that under the constitution, municipal, state and federal employees were free to join unions other than those belonging to the FSTSE. However, the Supreme Court had made a similar ruling in 1996 in respect of the states of Jalisco and Oaxaca without this affecting practice.

To have legal status unions must be registered with the Federal Labor Secretariat (Secretaria del Trabajo y Prevision Social, STPS) or the appropriate conciliation and arbitration boards (JLCA). These bodies are reported to have refused registration on occasions to unions hostile to the government or major employers. In addition, as the composition of labour boards is tripartite, there have been cases of registration being refused to organizations hostile to unions represented on the boards. The registration requirement has tended to entrench the position of unions, such as those affiliated to the CTM, allied with the government. Independent unions denied registration cannot bargain or call strikes, and are excluded from tripartite organizations. Collective agreements also often include closed shop and exclusion clauses allowing unions to control hiring and force the sacking of workers expelled by the union.

There is a tradition of tripartite framework agreements and collective bargaining occurs at all levels. There is no official collective bargaining in the public sector though unions have bypassed official structures, transforming "general working conditions" discussions into actual collective bargaining agreements. Notice must be given of strike action. If a conciliation and arbitration board rules a strike illegal, employees must return immediately to work or face dismissal. Conversely, if a strike is ruled legal, the employer must close the plant and may not hire new replacement workers. In practice, although strike notices are common, actual strikes are not, although unofficial stoppages occur more frequently.

A major contributor to economic and employment growth is the maquiladora (sub-contract assembly) sector launched in 1966. By the late 1990s it had grown to provide employment to 900,000 in thousands of mainly US-owned plants close to the US border. The competitive advantage of the maquiladora sector is low cost labour for exported products. The firms exhibit a much greater growth rate than that shown by the Mexican economy as a whole. US unions have expressed their growing concern at the use of the maquiladora sector – which began as a zone to give work to migrants denied entry into the United States – to undercut domestic activity and labour standards. The ICFTU says that so-called "protection contracts" are widespread in the maquiladoras. Under these, sham unions are registered with their organizers paid to avert strikes and independent union organizing.

Following the victory of Vicente Fox and the PAN in the July 2000 election, the president elect was reported to be considering proposals including abolition of the closed shop, a ban on solidarity strikes, and limiting strike action to a maximum of 30 days.

3 Trade Union Centre

Confederación de Trabajadores de México (CTM) Confederation of Mexican Workers

Address. Vallarta No. 8 Col. Tabacalera CP 06030, Mexico, DF

Phone. +52 5 35 0658

Fax. +52 5 90 50966

E-mail. ctmrelaciones@netservice.com.mx

Leadership. Leonardo Rodríguez Alcaine (secretary-general)

Membership. Reports 5 million

History and character. The CTM is by far the largest and most influential Mexican centre, and has always been closely allied to the ruling PRI. It was formed in 1936, and soon became the dominant force in Mexican trade unionism, its power surviving a series of breakaways by factions critical of the relationship with the PRI. The dominant figure in the CTM for decades was Fidel Velázquez (Don Fidel), who was the secretary-general from 1941 until his death in 1997 and also exercised significant influence over parts of the labour movement outside the CTM. CTM officials have held numerous political offices, including seats in Congress and as state governors for the PRI. The CTM has played a key role in the development of the social security system and federal institutions in the field of social and economic welfare and in creating housing schemes for the low-paid. Its critics maintain that it is bureaucratic and has prevented the development of union democracy and effective plant and industry-level collective bargaining.

In the 1980s and 1990s the CTM entered into a series of tripartite pacts with government and employers aimed at controlling price and wage inflation and controlling public deficits. A series of financial crises triggered by problems including foreign debt, inflation and lack of investor confidence punctuated the agreement of such pacts. The pacts (which have now lapsed) produced episodes of tension between the CTM leadership and rank and file and CTM and government as one consequence was that real wages fell behind.

In the 2000 presidential election campaign (where it supported the defeated PRI candidate Francisco Labastida Ochoa) the CTM called for free collective bargaining without government interference, for pension contributions to be tax free, better protection of the consumer's right to fair prices, expansion of the social welfare system, a more equitable tax system aimed at financing improved public services and greater devolution to the regions.

International affiliation. ICFTU

Moldova

Capital: Kishinev
Population: 4.43 m. (2000 est.)

1 Political and Economic Background

Moldova declared independence from the Soviet Union in 1991. Following elections in March 1998, there is a non-communist majority in the legislature but the communists are the largest party. Formation of a stable government has proved difficult, and the government led by Prime Minister Dumitru Braghis since Dec. 1999 has a Cabinet comprised mainly of technocrats.

The Moldovan economy is primarily agricultural, with 40% of the labour force working in the farm sector. There is an ongoing land privatization programme and state-owned enterprises have been privatized through a voucher system. Like most former Soviet republics Moldova experienced deep recession in the early 1990s with loss of its former markets. Living standards are low, and there was a further recession in 1998–99 as a knock-on from the crisis in Russia, Moldova's major trading partner.

GDP (purchasing power parity) $10bn. (1998 est.); GDP per capita (purchasing power parity) $2,200 (1998 est.).

2 Trade Unionism

Moldova ratified ILO Conventions No. 87 (Freedom of Association and Protection of the Right to Organize, 1948) and No. 98 (Right to Organize and Collective Bargaining, 1949) in 1996. The constitution and other legislation provide for the formation of independent trade unions. However, the old Soviet period trade union structure, reformed as the General Federation of Trade Unions of Moldova (FGSRM), retains an effective monopoly. The Soviet pattern of near total union membership continues.

National minimum wage levels are set though tripartite negotiations, providing a framework for sectoral and enterprise-level collective bargaining. There is no right to strike for government employees or those in essential services. In other sectors, a strike is legal only if approved by two-thirds of the work force in a secret ballot. The leading cause of strikes is now wage arrears.

3 Trade Union Centre

Consiliul Federatei Generale A Sindicatelor Din Republica Moldova (FGSRM)
Council of the General Federation of Trade Unions of Moldova (GFTU)

Address. Rue 31 Aout 129, 277 012 Kishinev

Phone. +373 2 23 7418

Fax. +373 2 23 7689

E-mail. cfsind@cni.md

History and character. The FGSRM is the reformed trade union structure from the Soviet era and the only trade union centre in Moldova. It has retained the assets of the former structure, such as social and holiday facilities, and also has a continuing role in the administration of the state social insurance system. Virtually all workers are members of its affiliated unions. In 1999 the FGSRM was active in leading protests over the problem of wage arrears.

International affiliation. ICFTU

Monaco

Capital: Monaco Ville
Population: 32,000 (2000 est.)

1 Political and Economic Background

The Principality of Monaco is a hereditary monarchy in which the Prince (since 1949, Rainier III) appoints the government, with French involvement. There is a popularly elected 18-member National Council, but no system of political parties.

Economic activities include light manufacturing, tourism and financial services, and Monaco is a leading tax haven. Nationals of Monaco and foreign residents do not pay income tax, and taxation on company profits is low. Only 16% of the population are Monegasques, with a wide range of foreign residents.

GDP (purchasing power parity) $870m. (1999 est.); GDP per capita (purchasing power parity) $27,000 (1999 est.).

2 Trade Unionism

Freedom of association and the right to strike are guaranteed by the 1962 Constitution. Monaco is not a member of the International Labour Organization.

Trade unions participate in Monaco's consultative Tripartite Economic Council along with the Employers' Federation of Monaco. Anti-union discrimination is prohibited by law but union density is estimated at less than 10%. There is no ICFTU or WCL affiliate. Collective bargaining is practiced. Strikes rarely occur and are prohibited in the case of government employees.

Mongolia

Capital: Ulan Bator
Population: 2.65 m. (2000 est.)

1 Political and Economic Background

From 1924 until 1990 Mongolia was a one-party communist state ruled by the Mongolian People's Revolutionary Party (MPRP). In 1990 political pluralism was introduced, the MPRP retaining power in elections that year and in 1992. In 1996, the MPRP was heavily defeated by a coalition of opposition parties known as the Democratic Union, but the MPRP returned to power in a landslide victory in elections in July 2000.

Most of the labour force is engaged in herding and cultivating the land, with mining and processing of minerals the major form of industrial activity. Mongolia was badly affected by the loss of Soviet aid in 1990-91. From 1996, the Democratic Union pushed ahead with a programme to liberalize the economy and attract foreign investment, and although most larger enterprises remained under state control the private sector generated 70% of GDP at the end of the decade. The MPRP government elected in 2000 was seen as divided between traditional communists and those who believed in continuing free market reforms but at a moderate pace.

GDP (purchasing power parity) $6.1bn. (1999 est.); GDP per capita (purchasing power parity) $2,320 (1999 est.).

2 Trade Unionism

Mongolia ratified ILO Conventions No. 87 (Freedom of Association and Protection of the Right to Organize, 1948) and No. 98 (Right to Organize and Collective Bargaining, 1949) in 1969.

Trade unions were established in the 1920s after the communist Mongolian People's Revolutionary Party (MPRP) came to power, although there was little development until after World War II. Until 1990 the unions functioned in accordance with the Soviet bloc model: there were no organizations outside the single structure of the Central Council of Mongolian Trade Unions (CCMTU); the Council's constitution named the MPRP as the leader and guide of the working masses.

Following the end of the one-party state, Mongolia adopted a new constitution in 1992. Under this all workers may form or join union or professional organizations of their choosing. The CCMTU has transfigured itself into the Confederation of Mongolian Trade Unions, now affiliated to the ICFTU, and most union members are affiliated to this. There is also a newer Association of Free Trades Unions.

Union membership is reported to have fallen to 430,000 by 1999, representing less than half of the workforce. This reflects the impact of privatization and downsizing of state enterprises and the development of small non-union firms.

Collective bargaining is provided for and there is a right to strike, other than in essential services, which include police, utilities, and transportation workers. A new labour law took effect in 1999.

3 Trade Union Centre

Confederation of Mongolian Trade Unions (CMTU)
Address. Sukhbaataryn Talbai 3, Ulan Bator 11
Phone. +976 1 327 253

Fax. +976 1 322 128

E-mail. cmtu@magicnet.mn

Leadership. Shiilegiin Batbayar

History and character. The Central Council of Mongolian Trade Unions was formed under communist rule in 1927. At its 13th Congress in 1987 dissatisfaction began to be expressed at the way in which union reform was failing to keep pace with economic change. Delegates strongly criticized the centre for being too bureaucratic

and out of touch with the membership. In 1990, reformed as a federation (later a confederation) it held an extraordinary congress and adopted a new action programme and constitution. The following year its long-standing affiliation to the WFTU was suspended, and it later joined the ICFTU. It has eleven affiliated unions.

Publication. Khudulmur

International affiliations. ICFTU

Morocco

Capital: Rabat
Population: 30.12 m. (2000 est.)

GDP (purchasing power parity) $108bn. (1999 est.); GDP per capita (purchasing power parity) $3,600 (1999 est.).

1 Political and Economic Background

The Kingdom of Morocco was established in 1957 (the former French and Spanish protectorates having joined together as an independent sultanate the previous year). Under the 1992 constitution the powers of the monarch were reduced, although direct criticism of the monarchy is still not considered acceptable. King Hassan II was the monarch from 1961 until his death on July 23, 1999, when he was succeeded by his son, Mohammed VI.

Elections to a reformed legislature held in 1997 resulted in no individual party achieving dominance, eleven parties winning between 11 and 42 seats each in the lower house. In Feb. 1998 the King appointed Abderrahmane Youssoufi, the leader of the Socialist Union of Popular Forces (USFP) as Prime Minister in a coalition government dominated by opposition parties. The change of government was reflected in pledges to investigate the fate of hundreds of government opponents who had "disappeared" in the period from the 1960s to the 1980s. Youssoufi had himself been sentenced to death in absentia in the 1970s, before receiving a Royal pardon in 1980.

Unlike most Arab countries, Morocco is not a major oil producer, and its economy benefited from the slump in oil prices from the mid-1980s. It is the world's leading exporter of raw and refined phosphates. Agriculture (badly affected by drought in recent years) employs 50% of the work force and fluctuations in farm output because of drought make overall economic performance erratic. Other sectors include fishing, light manufacturing and tourism. Morocco has a mixed economy and launched a privatization programme in 1990. It has continuing problems with the level of its external debt and in attracting foreign investment.

2 Trade Unionism

Although Morocco ratified ILO Convention No. 98 (Right to Organize and Collective Bargaining, 1949) in 1957 it has never ratified Convention No. 87 (Freedom of Association and Protection of the Right to Organize, 1948). However, the right to form unions is enshrined in the constitution, which says that any group of eight workers may organize a union. Multiple unions exist within different enterprises. There is no law specifically prohibiting anti-union discrimination and union activists can be dismissed without effective sanctions, while some employers promote company unions.

There are three major centres, the UMT, the UGTM and the CDT. Accurate figures for their numerical strength are elusive due to double-counting and non-paying adherents, and estimates vary widely, but in total they have several hundred thousand members. There are also about a dozen smaller federations.

Although union density is only about 5 per cent, organized trade unionism arguably constitutes the strongest independent social force in Morocco. Under the 1992 constitution the upper house of the legislature, the Chamber of Councillors, has 270 members indirectly elected as representatives of local authorities, professional chambers and trade unions. In Dec. 1997 elections, the CDT took 11 seats, the UMT eight seats, and the UGTM took three seats, while five smaller union bodies took one seat each. The UMT has no political party affiliation, the CDT is affiliated with the Socialist Union of Popular Forces of the Prime Minister Abderrahmane Youssoufi, and the UGTM with the centrist Independence Party (Istiqlal).

According to the US State Department's Human Rights report for 1999: "Sometimes union officers are subject to government pressure. Union leadership does not always uphold the rights of members to select their own leaders. There has been no case of the rank and file voting out its current leadership and replacing it with another".

Collective bargaining exists in many industries, and also in some service and public sector areas, although for most employees collective bargaining does not occur. Disputes over non-implementation of agreements by employers are common. The Ministry of Labour provides conciliation services and unions have made increasing use of the courts in industrial disputes. While the right to strike exists in law and open disputes are not uncommon, government agencies tend to intervene in disputes on an ad hoc basis. In sectors where national security is deemed to be at stake, strikes are outlawed and in some cases union officials have been imprisoned. Despite government interference with the right to strike, stoppages including strikes and sit-ins, are frequent, though usually short-lived. The ICFTU 1999 Survey of Trade Union Rights reported that in the private sector "trade unionists are sacked, fined, and imprisoned for belonging to unions, carrying out union activities, and going on strike. Employers regularly collude with the police, who often use violence against striking workers. Criminal charges can be, and frequently are, brought against strikers for "withdrawing labour"... even the election of union leaders in an enterprise can result in management calling the police".

The unions have been affected by past waves of repression and "disappearances". Scores of trade unionists, many of them members of the UMT, were arrested during 1991. That year also, two of the UMT leaders thought missing since 1972, were discovered to have been in detention since that time. In 1992 the CDT leader Noubir Amaoui, made statements to the press critical of the monarchy and Morocco's political system, was tried and received a two-year prison sentence. Driss Laghnimi, regional secretary of the UGTM, was jailed soon after for making insulting remarks about King Hassan. They were not released until July 1993.

The change of government as a result of elections at the end of 1997, and the accession of a new King in July 1999, have been seen as improving respect for civil liberties, and 1999 was the fourth consecutive year without reports of "disappearances". However, the ICFTU in late 1999 reported that trade unionists continued to be arrested and imprisoned and in Sept. 1999 it lodged a complaint with the ILO. On Oct. 8, 1999, ICFTU general secretary Bill Jordan wrote to Prime Minster Youssoufi complaining of the detention of strikers under the penal code. Jordan observed that the continuation of this practice "is all the more incomprehensible, given that it clearly runs counter to the new, more open political and social climate announced recently". In Nov. 1999 the King dismissed the hard-line Interior Minister, Driss Basré, who was regarded as having been the driving force behind past abuses by the security forces.

Labour laws are enforced to some degree in the public sector and large enterprises (although in some cases the authorities lack the resources or the will to enforce laws where employers are resistant) but in small businesses and the informal sector breaches are common and child labour occurs. The custom of families adopting young girls and using as indentured domestic servants is socially accepted and unregulated.

3 Trade Union Centres

Confédération Démocratique du Travail (CDT)
Democratic Confederation of Labour

Address. 51 rue Abdallah Mediouni, BP 576, Casablanca

Leadership. Noubir El Amaoui (secretary-general)

History and character. The CDT was founded in Nov. 1978. A general strike called by the CDT in 1981, and attendant demonstrations, resulted in incidents in which dozens died in clashes with the security forces. During the 1980s the CDT built its influence mainly in the public sector. It criticized the government on issues such as corruption, emphasis on short-term prestige projects, lack of respect for trade union freedoms, the absence of a proper framework for collective bargaining, and dependence on external forces such as the International Monetary Fund. In 1991, the CDT opposed the participation of Moroccan troops in the Gulf War coalition. In 1992–93 secretary-general Amaoui was imprisoned after describing the government as 'a bunch of thieves with no future' but was released after widespread international protests.

The CDT is allied to the Union Socialiste des Forces Populaires (USFP), which is affiliated to the Socialist International. The party's leader, Abderrahmane Youssoufi, became Prime Minister in early 1998.

Union Générale des Travailleurs du Maroc (UGTM)
General Union of Moroccan Workers

Address. 9 rue du Rif, Angle Route de Médiouna, Casablanca

Phone. +212 2 28 78 71

Fax. +212 2 28 21 44

E-mail. ugtmaroc@iam.net.ma

Leadership. Abderrazzaq Afilal (secretary-general)

History and character. Founded in 1960, the UGTM is linked with the centrist Independence Party (Istiqlal). Istiqlal is represented in the coalition government formed by Youssoufi in 1998.

While the UGTM has public and private sector members, its traditional core strength is among agricultural workers. In the past it has been less militant than the other federations, but participated in the 1990s demands for reform. The UGTM opened a research and training centre in Rabat in 1998. The theme of the 8th congress, held in Nov. 1999, was "Participative Trade Unionism:

Our Way to Sustainable Growth and Development for Everyone".

International affiliation. WCL

Union Marocaine du Travail (UMT)
Moroccan Workers' Union

Address. 232 Avenue des Far, Casablanca

Phone. +212 2 30 0118

Fax. +212 2 30 78 54

Leadership. Mahjoub Ben Seddiq (secretary-general)

History and character. The UMT was founded in 1955 and is the oldest of the main Moroccan centres. It has members in both the public and private sectors. In 1960 it suffered the secession of the UGTM and three years later the UMT left the ICFTU after the formation of the All-African Trade Union Federation, (the predecessor to the OATUU), which opposed African centres having affiliations to non-African international organizations. However in 1990 it re-affiliated to the ICFTU after its secretary-general Mahjoub Ben Seddiq (Morocco's best-known trade unionist, who has led it since its inception) declared that the UMT could not afford to remain isolated from the world.

In 1991 the UMT discovered that long-missing leaders had been incarcerated in state jails for 20 years.

In July 1998, it reported that a total of 1,400 elected officials had been sacked for union activities in recent years, and that many faced criminal charges after calling strikes. In Oct. 1998, a UMT leader, Abdelhaz Rouissi, who has been missing since Oct. 1964, was pronounced officially dead, as part of the process whereby the Consultative Council of Human Rights sought to establish what had happened to those who had disappeared in the 1960s–1980s.

International affiliation. ICFTU

WESTERN SAHARA

Sovereignty over Western Sahara is disputed, with Morocco and the Polisario Front engaged in military conflict from 1975–91 prior to the intervention of a UN peacekeeping force. Moroccan trade unions exist in the Moroccan-controlled area of Western Sahara (which comprises most of the territory and all the population centres). There is a Polisario-sponsored labour front, the Sario Federation of Labour, but this has no active presence in Western Sahara. Most union members are employees of the Moroccan Government or state-owned organizations.

Mozambique

Capital: Maputo
Population: 19.1 m. (2000 est.)

1 Political and Economic Background

Mozambique achieved independence from Portugal in 1975 after more than a decade of guerrilla war against Portuguese colonial rule. A people's republic was declared, with Marxism–Leninism as the official ideology, and the Front for the Liberation of Mozambique (Frelimo) became the sole legal party. The regime continued to be opposed militarily by the anti-communist Mozambique National Resistance (Renamo). In 1989 Frelimo abandoned Marxism–Leninism and in 1990 a new constitution was adopted providing for a multi-party electoral system and a free market economy. In Oct. 1992 Frelimo and Renamo signed a peace accord, which was implemented by 1994. The first multi-party elections, in Oct. 1994, resulted in Frelimo taking 129 of

the 250 Assembly seats and Renamo 112, while the incumbent President, Joaquim Chissano of Frelimo, was elected. Chissano and Frelimo won again in presidential and legislative elections in Dec. 1999 (Frelimo taking 133 seats and Renamo 117) although Renamo disputed the validity of the results.

During the 1990s, and with the end of the civil war, Mozambique carried out market-oriented reforms, privatized many state enterprises, and encouraged foreign investment. It enjoyed growth rates in excess of 10 per cent per annum, giving it a reputation as one of the most economically successful African states in the period post-democratization. Nonetheless some 80% of the workforce is engaged in agriculture, much of it at subsistence level, the formal economy is still small and there is a continuing dependence on foreign aid.

GDP (purchasing power parity) $18.7bn. (1999 est.); GDP per capita (purchasing power parity) $1,000 (1999 est.).

2 Trade Unionism

Mozambique joined the ILO in 1976 and ratified Conventions No. 87 (Freedom of Association and Protection of the Right to Organize, 1948) and No. 98 (Right to Organize and Collective Bargaining, 1949) in 1996.

Trade union activities were closely circumscribed under Portuguese rule. In 1983 a single-trade-union system, the OTM, was created under the control of the ruling Frelimo party. With the adoption of pluralism, trade union rights were embodied in the 1990 constitution and 1991 labour law. Since then the OTM has remained the national trade union centre while emphasizing its independence from the state. It is now affiliated to the ICFTU. However, a number of independent unions have also established a Confederation of Free and Independent Unions of Mozambique (CONSILMO).

Labour legislation provides for collective bargaining and since 1991 the government has abandoned its former role of setting all wages administratively. The minimum wage is negotiated through the tripartite Consultative Commission on Labour, which includes representatives of both the OTM and CONSILMO. There is a constitutional right to strike other than for civil servants, the police, armed forces and workers engaged in essential services, which are defined to include areas such as health care, water, electricity and posts and telecommunications. The labour law prohibits retribution against strikers. Labour disputes are normally arbitrated through a system of workers' committees, however.

3 Trade Union Centre

Organização dos Trabalhadores de Moçambique (OTM)
Mozambique Workers' Organization

Address. Rua Manuel António de Sousa 36, Maputo

Phone. +258 1 42 8300

Fax. +258 1 42 1671

E-mail. otm@otm.uem.mz

Leadership. Joaquim Fanheiro (secretary-general)

Membership. 250,000

History and character. The OTM was created in 1983 following a decision of the ruling Frelimo party to create trade unions on the basis of the pre-existing production councils. The OTM's stated aims were "to develop socialist consciousness among the workers", to mobilize the workers to raise their productivity, to improve working conditions and to help to develop the country and combat famine and poverty. According to its original constitution the OTM was guided and led by Frelimo, but in 1990 the second congress declared its independence of all non-union bodies. This position has since been maintained, although critics in opposition unions say it is still close to Frelimo. In July 2000 the OTM called off a threatened general strike after the government agreed an increase in the minimum wage; had it gone ahead this would have been the first strike ever led by the OTM.

International affiliations. ICFTU; CTUC

Myanmar (Burma)

Capital: Rangoon
Population: 41.73 m. (2000 est.)

1 Political and Economic Background

Burma achieved independence from the United Kingdom in 1948. In 1962 the constitution was suspended and Gen. Ne Win took power at the head of a Revolutionary Council. In 1964 all political parties were banned except the government-controlled Burma Socialist Programme Party (BSPP). In 1988, amid mounting chaos, a new military regime took power, abolished all state organizations, renamed the country

Myanmar and set up a State Law and Order Restoration Council (SLORC) to rule the country. In 1990 elections were held for a new Constituent Assembly, but these resulted in victory for the opposition National League for Democracy, and the regime refused to allow the elected legislature to convene, the country remaining under military rule from that time. Some of those elected joined insurgent movements, which remain active in some areas. In 1997 the SLORC was replaced by a so-called State Peace and Development Council (SPDC). Political parties are not allowed.

Following the Ne Win coup, many of the major sectors of the economy -notably industry, transport, internal and external trade, communications and finance -were brought into public ownership and control. In the 1990s the government aimed to increase private sector activity and foreign investment, although state control remains dominant in key areas such as energy, heavy industry and the rice trade. 65% of the workforce are engaged in agriculture.

GDP (purchasing power parity) $59.4bn. (1999 est.); GDP per capita (purchasing power parity) $1,200 (1999 est.).

2 Trade Unionism

Trade unions first developed in the 1920s in reaction to the then widespread use of immigrant Indian and Chinese labour and union activities subsequently became closely linked to nationalist politics, with many strikes in the 1945–48 period. Following independence in 1948 (which led to the emigration of most non-Burmese workers), trade union rights granted in 1926 under British rule were incorporated in the constitution. In 1955 Burma ratified ILO Convention No. 87 (Freedom of Association and Protection of the Right to Organize, 1948). Unions were active both politically and industrially and although in 1961 the total membership of the 173, mainly one-shop, registered unions then in existence was put at only 64,000 of an urban labour force of one million, there were many unregistered unions.

In 1964, however, Gen. Ne Win abolished all trade unions. In 1968 Ne Win set up a new system for workers' representation, consisting of local workers' councils at factory and township level, and a central asi-ayone (union) presided over by the Minister of Labour and controlled by Burma Socialist Programme Party (BSPP) officials. The primary task of the workers' councils was to ensure labour discipline and explain government policies and targets.

During August and September 1988 a general strike was in force throughout Rangoon and other areas of Burma in support of demonstrators' demands for the installation of a democratically elected government. The Armed Forces took control of the country on Sept. 18 and ordered a return to work. The new regime dissolved the previous government-controlled union structure and passed a Law on the Formation of Associations and Organizations, effectively banning the formation of any labour organization without official approval. In 1998 the ILO Conference condemned the government for its continuing failure to observe Convention No. 87. In response the Foreign Ministry announced that it would "cease participation in activities connected with Convention 87". In addition to internal controls, the government requires that Burmese seamen working on foreign ships do not participate in any activities of the International Transport Workers' Federation (ITF).

A Federation of Trade Unions of Burma is reported to work underground, but its scale and effectiveness is unlikely to be great.

Burma has not ratified Convention No. 98 (Right to Organize and Collective Bargaining, 1949) and collective bargaining is not practiced. The Central Arbitration Board, set up to resolve labour disputes, has not functioned since 1988. In the public sector the government sets wages and in the private sector market forces generally apply. No strikes were reported in 1998 or 1999.

Burma's human rights violations and used of forced labour have attracted intense criticism from unions and human rights organizations. In 1989 the United States suspended Burma's eligibility for trade concessions under the Generalized System of Preferences (GSP) programme pending steps to afford its labor force internationally recognized worker rights. In 1997 Burma's trade benefits on its exports to the EU were canceled. In 1998 an ILO Commission of Inquiry found the regime guilty of "widespread and systematic" use of forced labour on a massive scale, including transportation of supplies for the military, and the building of roads, railways and bridges. In June 1999 the ILO Conference agreed to suspend Burma from receiving ILO technical assistance or attending ILO meetings due to its "flagrant and persistent failure to comply" with Convention 29 on forced labor. This move, seen as amounting to the de facto exclusion of Burma from the ILO, in was greeted by the ICFTU as "an unprecedented move in the annals of this agency". In response the government said it would "cease participation in activities connected with Convention 29." The use of forced labour is believed to have increased since 1997 when the regime required military commanders to become more self-sufficient logistically. Forced labour (including forced child labour) has also been used for the construction of civilian infrastructure such as roads, the reclamation of land for agriculture, and harvesting.

3 Trade Union Centre

There is no trade union centre.

4 Other Trade Union Organization

Federation of Trade Unions of Burma (FTUB)

E-mail. ftub@hotmail.com

Leadership. Maung Maung (general secretary)

History and character. Unions affiliated to the FTUB played a major role in the 1988 democracy movement. It now works underground inside Burma "to educate, organize and strengthen Burmese workers and other pro-democracy groups to assert their rights and push the military regime to enter substantive tripartite negotiations with the National League for Democracy and the leaders of Burma's ethnic peoples". Myo Aung Thant, a member of the FTUB executive committee was sentenced in 1998 to life imprisonment for labour organization activities inside Burma.

International affiliations. None, but has links with unions internationally.

Namibia

Capital: Windhoek
Population: 1.77 m. (2000 est.)

1 Political and Economic Background

Namibia became independent in 1990 following 75 years of South African rule and 23 years of guerrilla war. Under a constitution drawn up by all parties in the Constituent Assembly elected in 1989, Namibia has a liberal constitution with a limited executive presidency. The South West African People's Organization (SWAPO) won 41 of the 72 seats in the Constituent Assembly and its leader, Sam Nujoma, became the country's first President. In elections in Dec. 1999 SWAPO retained control of the legislature and Nujoma was re-elected President after the constitution had been amended to allow him to stand for a third term.

Extraction and processing of a wide range of minerals are the bedrock of the formal economy and give Namibia a relatively high GDP by African standards. However, 50% of the population are engaged in subsistence agriculture and there is widespread under-employment. The economy is closely integrated with that of South Africa.

GDP (purchasing power parity) $7.1bn. (1999 est.); GDP per capita (purchasing power parity) $4,300 (1999 est.).

2 Trade Unionism

The development of trade unionism in Namibia reflected developments in South Africa. Trade unionism was legalized for all races in 1978; previously it had been legal only for white and coloured workers and only for branches of lawful South African unions. The SWAPO-linked National Union of Namibian Workers (NUNW) was suppressed by the authorities after a short existence in 1978–79 and went into exile in Angola. 1985 regulations prohibited activity by non-Namibian trade unionists in order to prevent links between black unions in South Africa and Namibia.

The NUNW was re-launched in the mid-1980s, began to reorganize in Namibia, and was instrumental in the formation of a number of new unions after 1987. Several union leaders joined the new SWAPO government in 1989. Affiliated in the pre-independence years to the WFTU, the NUNW is now affiliated to the ICFTU and is the national centre. In addition a National Federation of Trade Unions (NFTU), comprising a number of unions less sympathetic to the government, was formed in 1998.

Namibia ratified ILO Conventions No. 87 (Freedom of Association and Protection of the Right to Organize, 1948) and No. 98 (Right to Organize and Collective Bargaining, 1949) in 1995. The 1990 constitution and the 1992 Labour Act provide for freedom of association, including for public servants, farm workers and domestic servants. About 20% of workers in the formal economy are in unions. The 1992 Act provided for the office of labour commissioner and a labour inspectorate, for a labour court supplemented by district courts, and for two tripartite bodies, the Labour Advisory Council and the Wages Commission. Minimum conditions of employment were laid down, provision for trade union recognition made and individual employment rights established. However, detailed provisions were also made for the regulation of internal union affairs.

The 1992 Act recognizes the right to bargain collectively although in practice collective bargaining is largely confined to the mining and construction sectors. There is a right to strike, subject to conciliation procedures, other than for workers involved in public health and safety or in the export processing zones. Disputes over dismissals must be referred to a labour court for arbitration.

In 1999 the government reached agreement with the NUNW to review the 1992 labour law. The NUNW said that the labour courts were ineffective, had a backlog of cases, failed to enforce rulings and were biased in favour of employers. There have also been complaints that foreign-owned companies with mining concessions in Namibia break labour legislation and penalize union members. Under 1995 legislation setting up export processing zones, workers may not go on strike but disputes must be referred to an EPZ dispute settlement panel.

3 Trade Union Centre

National Union of Namibian Workers (NUNW)

Address. Private Bag 50034, Bachbrecht, Windhoek 9000

Phone. +264 61 215 037

Fax. +264 61 215 589

E-mail. ranga@namib.com

Leadership. C. Ranga Haikali (general secretary)

History and character. The NUNW was organized by SWAPO on Apr. 24, 1971. It functioned as part of SWAPO and operated from exile in Angola. Influenced by developments in South Africa, the NUNW in the mid-1980s set up industrial affiliates inside Namibia and from 1986 these affiliates began to operate openly although police raids and detentions continued.

In 1989 the NUNW held its first consolidation congress in Windhoek, and united the internal and external leadership with John ya Otto, SWAPO Secretary for

Labour as general secretary. Several union leaders joined the new SWAPO government in 1989 and it has since then remained close to the party, nominating candidates to SWAPO's slate in elections.
International affiliation. ICFTU; CTUC

4 Other Trade Union Organization

Namibian People's Social Movement (NPSM)
Address. PO Box 2111, Windhoek 9000

Phone. +264 6121 2378
Fax. +264 6121 2828
E-mail. npsm@iafrica.com.na
Leadership. Aloysius Yon (general secretary)
Membership. 11,500
International affiliation. WCL

Nauru

Capital: Yaren district
Population: 12,000 (2000 est.)

1 Political and Economic Background

Nauru is a very small island, which became independent in 1968 as a special-status member of the Commonwealth. The Nauruan economy is almost wholly dependent on the extraction of phosphate rock derived from the country's substantial guano deposits, which until recently supported a relatively high standard of living. This resource is now virtually exhausted, however, and the exploitation of it (in the hands of a government-owned corporation) has rendered 90% of the country a wasteland. The government has instituted drastic public spending cuts, and called on

income from phosphate sales put into trust funds, to deal with this situation.

2 Trade Unionism

The 1968 constitution provides for a general right of citizens to form and belong to trade unions or other associations. However, no trade unions currently exist and efforts in the past to form unions met with government discouragement. Much of the work force has in any case been transient imported labour. There are virtually no private sector employees and in the public sector pay and working conditions are determined administratively. Nauru is not a member of the ILO.

Nepal

Capital: Kathmandu
Population: 24.7 m. (2000 est.)

1 Political and Economic Background

The Kingdom of Nepal is a monarchy in which the King exercises executive powers. All political parties were

banned in 1961 and for the next 30 years Nepal experienced direct rule by the monarchy. The 1962 constitution established a tiered, party-free system of elected village and provincial councils (panchayats). Limited reforms to this system were approved in a 1980 national referendum, which also rejected the restoration of a party system.

After social unrest a new constitution providing for

parliamentary government was adopted in 1990, and free elections were held in 1991. Since then the two leading parties have been the Nepali Congress Party (NCP), which originated in the 1940s as the Nepalese wing of the Indian National Congress, and the Communist Party of Nepal. These parties have ruled separately or in coalition, with a series of unstable administrations. In the most recent legislative elections, in May 1999, the NCP emerged with sufficient seats to form a Cabinet of its own members. There is a low-level but brutal ongoing Maoist insurgency affecting some areas.

Nepal is a poor and economically undeveloped country in which subsistence agriculture is the occupation of 80% of the workforce. Most industrial activity is concentrated on the processing of agricultural products. Production of textiles and carpets accounts for 80% of foreign exchange earnings. In recent years Nepal has sought to encourage trade and investment and reduce subsidies and many former state-owned enterprises have been privatized since 1992, although 50 public sector firms remain. There is a heavy dependence on foreign development aid and widespread underemployment.

GDP (purchasing power parity) $27.4bn. (1999 est.); GDP per capita (purchasing power parity) $1,100 (1999 est.).

2 Trade Unionism

Trade unions can be traced from 1947 at which time there was an All-Nepal Trade Union Congress (ANTUC) and the Biratnagar Labour Union, organized under the influence of the Socialist Party of India. The jute and sugar strikes of that year were the first in the history of Nepal. A split in ANTUC led to the formation of a new organization Majdur Sabha under the leadership of G. P. Koirala, (later to be NCP Prime Minister from 1991–94), but ANTUC operated underground under communist leadership, including that of Adhikari, later to succeed him. After King Birendra's coup of 1960 all unions disappeared from open activity and only the state-sponsored Nepal Labour Organization (NLO) was allowed to function. This embodied the principles of panchayat democracy; local units of the NLO were permitted to bargain collectively and to elect district committees, from which the King would nominate four representatives to the National Assembly. With the emergence of multi-party democracy in 1990 however, the NLO, which had been increasingly inactive, was disbanded.

Since 1990 there has been a proliferation of trade unions. There are two main centres, which are close to the two main political parties. The Nepal Trade Union Congress (NTUC) is ICFTU-affiliated and close to the Nepali Congress Party, while GEFONT is close to the Communist Party. The ICFTU's *Trade Union World* noted in Nov. 1999 that these two organizations claim to have a number of members "that is as impressive (because they started from nothing) as it is impossible to check (since there are no reliable statistics in Nepal)", but are certainly inflated. Continual fluctuations in the governing coalitions have also encouraged members to move from one union to another, as there are substantial perceived advantages in being linked to a union whose political party holds power. Both parties have been accused of showing favouritism towards their associated trade union centres while in power. When the Communists formed the government in 1994 they were said to have "automatically" registered their own affiliated unions but interfered in the registration of unions associated with the Nepali Congress Party's labour organization.

The different centres tend not to cooperate with each other. There are no restrictions on unions affiliating internationally.

Nepal became a member of the ILO in 1966 and ratified Convention No. 98 (Right to Organize and Collective Bargaining, 1949) in 1996. It has not ratified Convention No. 87 (Freedom of Association and Protection of the Right to Organize, 1948). However, the 1990 constitution provides for the freedom to establish and to join unions and associations. It permits restriction of unions only in cases of subversion, sedition, or similar conditions. The 1992 Trade Union Act prohibits employers from discriminating against trade union members or organizers, and there have been relatively few reports of this. However, according to GEFONT, employers anxious to eliminate activists will denounce them to the police as being Maoist sympathizers.

Trade unionism currently only involves the small minority of the workforce in the formal sector. The unions have emphasized the need to tackle issues such as child labour and debt slavery, both of which are widespread in Nepal. In debt slavery, the condition of servitude may be passed from one generation to another, with one generation of a family working to pay off the debts of the one before.

The 1992 Labour Act provides for collective bargaining, although the organizational structures to implement the Act's provisions have not been established. Collective bargaining agreements cover an estimated 20 percent of wage earners in the organized sector. Virtually all bargaining takes place at the enterprise level.

Strikes are lawful, subject to approval by 60% of the workforce in a secret ballot, other than in essential services. However, the government may order a strike to be ended and suspend a union if it disturbs the peace or adversely affects the national economic interest. In Mar. 1999 the government banned all strikes in the communications, transportation, and security sectors, pending completion of the parliamentary elections in May. This forced the ending of a strike at the state-controlled Royal Nepal Airlines.

Nepal's tripartite National Labour Advisory Board (established in 1991) registers representative unions and sets the level of the country's minimum wage.

3 Trade Union Centres

General Federation of Nepalese Trade Unions (GEFONT)

Address PO Box 10652, Putalisadak, Kathmandu.

Phone. +977 1 248072

Fax. +977 1 278073

E-mail. gefont@mos.com.np

Website. www.south-asia.com/gefont

Leadership. Bishnu Rimal (general secretary)

Membership. Claims 350,000

History and character. GEFONT was founded underground in 1989 and claims to be the country's largest and most active trade union federation. It is closely associated with the Communist Party, one of Nepal's two leading parties. It led a series of strikes against the NCP government in 1993–94, prior to Nov. 1994 elections in which the United Communist Party of Nepal (UCPN) became the largest party and formed the government. Several of the UCPN representatives elected to Parliament were GEFONT officials, including GEFONT chairman Mukunda Neupane and vice-chairman Salim Ansari, the latter becoming Minister of State for Forest and Soil Conservation. A number of other GEFONT members were appointed to advisory roles in the government.

GEFONT has formed a "Forum for Liberation from Debt Slavery" and says it has recruited 10,000 victims of debt slavery, who pay a token 1 rupee per year in membership fees. Organization of such victims has to be clandestine.

International affiliations. None

Nepal Trade Union Congress (NTUC)

Address. Central Office, PO Box 5507, Kupondol, Lalitpur, Kathmandu

Phone. +977 1 527443

Fax. +977 1 527469

E-mail. ntuc@mos.com.np

Membership. Claims 200,000

History and character. The NTUC came into being after the establishment of a multi-party system in Nepal in 1990 and is linked to the Nepali Congress Party (NCP), one of the two leading political parties in the country.

With the assistance of international donors and the government, the NTUC has set up 132 schools to provide remedial training for child labourers.

International affiliation. ICFTU

Netherlands

Capital: Amsterdam
Population: 15.9m. (2000 est.)

1 Political and Economic Background

Since 1994 Prime Minister Wim Kok has led a so-called "purple coalition" government comprising his own Labour Party (PvdA), the liberal People's Party for Freedom and Democracy (VVD) and the progressive Democrats 66 (D66). The opposition is led by the centre-right Christian Democratic Appeal (CDA), which participated in a series of coalition governments from 1977–94. The Netherlands is a member of the EU and joined the single European currency on its launch on Jan. 1, 1999.

The economy is diversified, with leading industries including food processing, chemicals, petroleum refining and electrical machinery. Although agriculture occupies only 4% of the work force, Netherlands is the world's 3rd largest exporter of food. Growth in GDP was in the range 3–4% per annum in the period 1997–2000 and the Netherlands has been successful in job creation, with labour shortages rather than high unemployment an increasing feature of recent years.

GDP (purchasing power parity) $365.1bn. (1999 est.); GDP per capita (purchasing power parity) $23,100 (1999 est.).

2 Trade Unionism

The Netherlands ratified ILO Convention No. 87 (Freedom of Association and Protection of the Right to Organize, 1948) in 1950 and Convention No. 98 (Right to Organize and Collective Bargaining, 1949) in 1993.

Before World War II trade unionism in the Netherlands was divided into three main streams, represented by the general confederation, the Netherlands Federation of Trade Unions (Nederlands Verbond van Vakverenigingen -NVV), and Roman Catholic and

Protestant federations. In the post-war period these organizations increasingly cooperated, and from the late 1950s they sought to coordinate their policies through a formal consultative framework. In Jan. 1976, the Netherlands Trade Union Confederation (Federatie Nederlandse Vakbeweging -FNV) was formed by the NVV and the Netherlands Catholic Federation of Labour (Nederlands Katholiek Vakverbond -NKV), the NVV accepting the NKV's condition that special recognition should be accorded to the role of religious inspiration in the new confederation. The (Protestant) Christian National Federation of Trade Unions (Christelijk Nationaal Vakverbond -CNV), however, proved unwilling to surrender its sovereignty, and did not join the federation.

The FNV is the leading trade union centre, reporting 1.2 million members, while the CNV claims 365,000. Both the FNV and CNV have experienced considerable reorganization in recent years as affiliates have merged or reconfigured and the trade union centres have faced budgetary pressures. There is a traditional general alignment of the FNV with the Labour Party (PvdA) and the CNV with the Christian Democratic CDA. There is also a federation of managerial and staff unions, UNIE-MHP, with 225,000 members, and there are numerous mainly small unions without affiliation to any of these centres. All employees, including members of the Armed Forces and the police, may join unions, and unions also affiliate the unemployed and (increasingly) the self-employed. Discrimination against union members is illegal and not prevalent. Trade union membership in the Netherlands declined sharply during the 1980s, when many industrial jobs were lost, but rose during the 1990s. All the trade union centres continued to report increasing memberships in the late 1990s, although this rate of increase was slower than that of the number of jobs. A contributory factor to the growth in union membership was female entry as the Netherlands' traditionally low level of female participation began to rise.

Since World War II the Dutch model of industrial relations has been that of the "Social Partnership", emphasizing the search for consensus and stability within the context of bipartite and tripartite institutions. The Social and Economic Council, created in 1950, comprises 15 representatives of the employers, 15 of the unions, and 15 independent experts nominated by government, and is the main advisory board to the government on social and economic issues. The Stichting van de Arbeid (Foundation of Labour, STAR) is a consultative body on which both sides of industry have an equal number of seats; it is a non-binding forum for the discussion of industrial issues. In 1982, in response to the high unemployment of the early 1980s, an agreement on wage restraint (the Wassenaar Agreement) was reached within the Foundation of Labour that has formed the basis for subsequent collective agreements. The unions abandoned index-linked inflationary pay claims in exchange for non-pay benefits such as reductions in working hours, training and education, and day care.

Within the centrally agreed Social Partnership framework, unions and employers negotiate detailed sectoral agreements (CAOs) that, once ratified by the Minister of Social Affairs and Employment, are binding on all employers, signatory or not. While this system has recently come under pressure from employers seeking greater flexibility, and there is a trend to more skeletal framework agreements that are then given detailed definition at enterprise level depending on circumstances, this broad approach still largely applies. One result is that while union density is about 28%, some three-quarters of workers are covered by such agreements. In practice, because of labour shortages, employers commonly pay higher wages than are provided for in collective agreements. In addition, the unions have increasingly accepted the introduction of performance-related pay linked to the individual worker's contribution. According to the Confederation of Netherlands Industry and Employers (VNO-NCW), by 2000 some 84% of employees under collective bargaining agreements also had an element of individual performance related pay in their contracts. At the enterprise level, works councils are increasingly active in defining issues such as working hours within the framework of sectoral collective agreements, although the role of works councils provided for in such agreements varies widely.

The Netherlands lacks legislation on strike issues. Indeed, the basic right to strike was ambiguous under Dutch law until the Supreme Court in 1986 ruled that it was guaranteed by application of the European Social Charter, which Netherlands had ratified in 1980. However, it is not uncommon for employers to turn to litigation to challenge individual strikes and the courts have ruled that strikes undertaken without exhausting negotiating procedures, or that adversely affect third parties, may be illegal. Claims against unions for damages rarely succeed, however. The Netherlands normally has one of the lowest rates of days lost per year to strike action of the EU member states, although there are pockets with traditions of militancy, notably the ports of Rotterdam and Amsterdam and the building trade. The civil service is covered by separate legislation and most civil servants do not have the right to strike.

3 Trade Union Centres

Christelijk Nationaal Vakverbond (CNV)
National Federation of Christian Trade Unions

Address. Postbus 2475, 3500 GL Utrecht

Phone. +31 30 2913911

Fax. +31 30 2946544

E-mail. cnv@cnv.nl

Website. www.cnv.nl (Dutch; English section)

Leadership. Doekle Terpstra (president)

Membership. 365,000

History and character. The CNV was founded in June 1909 as an inter-confessional (Christian) organization, but in practice quickly became a Protestant federation. After the formation of the FNV in 1976 some Catholic organizations affiliated. The CNV continues to emphasize its Christian base, stating that "the Christian values of justice, solidarity and stewardship give direction to the solutions for social issues of our time". It is one of the leading affiliates of the WCL. It is independent of any church or political party.

At national level the CNV participates the tripartite Social and Economic Council (SER) and, with the employers, the Foundation of Labour (STAR). Its member unions conduct collective bargaining. During 2000 the CNV underwent reorganization partly as a result of budgetary pressures, which have led to reductions in the numbers of CNV officers.

The CNV has a strongly international focus. A current key campaign for the CNV is putting pressure on multinationals and governments not to invest in countries that violate the ILO's core labour standards, and to get the WTO to adopt these standards as binding. The Actie Kom Over is a CNV organization that assists trade union organizations in Africa, Asia, Latin America and eastern and central Europe. The CNV also makes an annual award to trade union leaders worldwide who have distinguished themselves by their commitment in the face of risks.

There is a CNV youth organization, a women's union, and a study institute, and the CNV has its own holiday resorts and travel organization.

International affiliations. WCL; ETUC; TUAC

Affiliated unions. There are 11 affiliated unions as follows:

CFO
Address. Postbus 84500, 2508 AM Den Haag
Phone. +31 70 4167167
Fax. +31 70 4167100
E-mail. info@cfo.nl
Website. www.cfo.nl (Dutch; English section)
Membership. 86,000
History and character. Formed by the merger of three unions in 1983, but traces its history back to a union of Christian municipal employees founded in 1903. Represents civil servants and health care workers. Affiliated to EUROFEDOP and European Federation of Public Service Unions (EPSU).
Publications. CFO Magazine

CNV Bedrijvenbond
Address. Postbus 327, 3990 GC Houten
Phone. +31 30 6348348
Fax. +31 30 6348200
E-mail. info@cnv.net
Leadership. Bart Bruggeman (president)
Membership. 90,000
History and character. This is a general union, organizing workers in 23 sectors of industry, transport and agriculture.
Publications. Bond Nieuws

Hout- en Bouwbond CNV (Wood and Construction)
Address. Oude Haven 1, 3984 KT Odijk
Phone. +31 30 6597711

Fax. +31 30 6571101
E-mail. hout.bouwbond.cnv@tip.nl
Website. www.hbbcnv.nl (Dutch only)
Leadership. F. van der Meulen (president)
Membership. 48,000
Publication. De Opbouw

Onderwijsbond CNV (Teachers' Union)
Address. Postbus 732, Boerhaavelaan 5, 2700 AS Zoetermeer
Phone. +31 79 3202020
Fax. +31 79 3202195
Website. www.ocnv.nl (Dutch only)
Membership. 59,000
History and character. Formed in 1997 by the merger of the Catholic Teachers' Union (KOV) and the Protestant Christian Teachers' Union (PCO).

Dienstenbond CNV (Services Union)
Address. Postbus 3135, 2130 KC Hoofddorp
Phone. +31 23 565 1052
Fax. +31 23 565 0150
Website. www.cnvdibo.nl (Dutch only)
Membership. 33,000.
History and character. Has had this name since 1978 but traces its origins back to 1894. It absorbed the CNV Printing Union in 1995.

ACP Politiebond (Police Union)
Address. Postbus 290, 3830 AG Leusden
Phone. +31 33 495 2888
Fax. +31 33 496 2777
E-mail. acp.politiebond.cnv@acp.nl
Website. www.acp.nl (Dutch; English section)
Membership. 19,000
Publication. Politiebericht

ACOM CNV-bond van militairen (Military Union)
Address. Postbus 290, 3830 AG Leusden
Phone. +31 33 495 3020
Fax. +31 33 495 3005
E-mail. b.vorstermans@cnv.nl
Leadership. G. Dijkers (president)
Membership. 16,000. Includes all military ranks, military pensioners and members of the reserves.
Publication. ACOM Journaal

De Jongerenorganisatie CNV (Youth Organization)
Address. Postbus 2475, 3500 GL Utrecht
Phone. +31 30 291 3715
Fax. +31 30 296 4907
Membership. Is open to students, workers and the unemployed, up to 28 years of age.

CNV Kunstenbond (Artists' Union)
Address. Postbus 81065, 3009 GB Rotterdam
Phone. +31 10 456 8688
Fax. +31 10 455 9022
E-mail. info@continentalart.org
Website. www.continentalart.org (Dutch, English section)
Leadership. Leen La Rivière (president)
Membership. 4,000
Publication. Music + Art

Kostersbond CNV
Address. Prins Hendrikkade 5, 1165 HP Halfweg

Phone. +31 20 497 0440
Fax. +31 20 497 0440
E-mail. h.broerse-boterman@planet.nl
Leadership. J. de Visser (president)
Publication. De Koster

BKM Bond van medewerkers
Address. Lobbendijk 5, 3991 EA Houten
Phone. +31 30 637 7619
Leadership. A. van Toorn (president)
Publication. Kerkewerk

Federatie Nederlandse Vakbeweging (FNV) Netherlands Trade Union Confederation

Address. Postbus 8456, 1005 AL Amsterdam

Phone. +31 20 581 6300

Fax. +31 20 684 4541

E-mail. iz@fnv.nl

Website. www.fnv.nl (Dutch; English section)

Leadership. L.J. de Waal (president)

Membership. 1.2 million

History and character. The FNV was founded in 1976 by the partial merger of the social democratic NVV and the Roman Catholic NKV. By the end of 1981 all affiliated trade unions of NVV and NKV had merged or federated with their corresponding unions in the other federation and in 1982 the NVV and NKV were formally liquidated and the merger completed. The NVV had historically been an ICFTU affiliate, while the NKV was affiliated to the WCL. The NVV and NKV jointly sought a restructuring of the international trade union movement aimed at a linking of the ICFTU and WCL. This was not forthcoming and the NKV left the WCL in 1981, the year before its merger with the NVV was concluded.

In the early 1980s recession membership of unions declined sharply, and the FNV's share fell as it failed to keep pace with the changing composition of the workforce. FNV 2000 (1987) contained a comprehensive set of recommendations designed to make trade unionism more relevant to members and potential recruits and its findings were integrated into FNV practice pushing membership up by over 100,000 in three years from 1988. While union membership has not kept pace with the increase in jobs in the economy as a whole in the late 1990s, the FNV has nonetheless been successful in increasing its membership during this period.

There has been substantial reorganization of the FNV's affiliates in recent years. At the beginning of 1998 four FNV affiliates, the Industrial, Services, Transport, and Agriculture and Foodstuffs unions, merged to create the super-union FNV Bondgenoten ("Allied Unions"), which became the largest union in the country with 500,000 members. Further mergers are under consideration.

The FNV has a broadly social democratic alignment and is associated with the Labour Party (PvdA) although officially politically independent. Wim Kok, the Labour Prime Minister since 1994, is a former FNV president. Reflecting the role of the Catholic federation in its cre-

ation, its constitution also recognizes the place of religion as an "inspiration for trade union activities".

At national level the FNV participates the tripartite Social and Economic Council (SER) and, with the employers, the Foundation of Labour (STAR). The FNV since the early 1980s has participated in annual agreements whereby moderate wage claims have been agreed in return for steady amelioration of working conditions and benefits. Issues of working hours and stress are considered of particular importance in the Netherlands. The FNV also has a strong international focus to its work, working to support unions in developing countries.

The FNV is involved in areas such as policy development with respect to social security, economic development, labour law, international relations, etc. Other activities are research, training and education, publicity, and promotional activities. Services rendered to members include: legal aid and assistance supplied by the FNV's Legal Aid Service, expert advice through the Centre for Works Councils, advice on taxation questions, and cheap holiday opportunities in hotels or holiday parks linked to the trade union movement. Since 1999 it has been offering portfolio planning for its members, 20% of whom participate in company share option schemes.

International affiliations. ICFTU; ETUC; TUAC

Affiliated unions:
AbvaKabo (public sector)
Address. Postbus 3010, 2700 KT Zoetermeer
Phone. +31 79 353 6161
Fax. +31 79 352 1226
E-mail. post@abvakabo.nl
Website. www.abvakabo.nl (Dutch only)
Membership. 360,000. This is the major civil service union in the Netherlands.

Algemene Onderwijsbond (AOB) (Teachers' Union)
Address. Jaarbeursplein 22, 3521 AP Utrecht
Phone. +31 30 298 9898
Website. www.aob.nl (Dutch only)
Membership. 75,000
History and character. Formed by 1997 merger of teachers' unions ABOP and NGL
Publication. Onderwijsblad

Algemene Federatie van Militair Personeel (AFMP) (Military personnel)
E-mail. info@afmp.nl
Website. www.afmp.nl (Dutch only)

FNV Bondgenoten (Allied Unions)
Address. Postbus 9208, 3506 GE Utrecht
Phone. +31 30 273 8222
Fax. +31 30 273 8225
E-mail. info@bg.fnv.nl
Website. www.bondgenoten.fnv.nl (Dutch only)
Leadership. Hans de Vries (president); Fred Kagie (general secretary)
Membership. 500,000.
History and character. FNV Bondgenoten was formed in 1998 by the merger of four FNV unions, Industriebond (industrial

workers), Dienstenbond (Services), Vervoersbond (Transport) and Voedingsbond (Agriculture and Foodstuffs). The objective was to strengthen the bargaining position of the merging unions and to provide better member services. It is the largest union in the country with a diverse membership including sectors such as agriculture, retailing, financial services, information technology and electronics, textiles, chemicals, paper, metal industry, breweries, transport, and call centres. The union was structured with local branches representing all its members and in addition 15 industrial groups, including one group specifically for benefit recipients and older people, this group being the largest with 100,000 members. At its formation it had 1,000 employees, although this number was to be reduced substantially in the medium-term.

FNV Bouw (Construction Union)
Address. Postbus 520, 3440 AM Woerden
Phone. +31 34 857 5575
E-mail. info@fnvbouw.nl
Website. www.bouwenhoutbondfnv.nl (Dutch only)

FNV Horecabond (hotel and restaurant workers)
Address. Postbus 1435, 1300 BK Almere
Phone. +31 36 535 8500
Fax. +31 36 536 3397
E-mail. horecabond@fnv.nl
Website. www.horecabond.fnv.nl (Dutch only)
Leadership. Marchien Koster (president); Dick Juffermans (general secretary)
Membership. 28,500

FNV KIEM (arts, information industry and media)
Address. Jan Tooropstraat 1, Postbus 9354, 1006 AJ Amsterdam
E-mail. algemeen@fnv-kiem.nl
Website. www.q-packs.com/kiem (Dutch only)
Membership. 55,000

Nederlandse Vereniging van Journalisten (NVJ) (Journalists' Union)
Address. Postbus 75997, 1070 AZ Amsterdam
Phone. +31 20 676 6771
Fax. +31 20 662 4901
E-mail. vereniging@nvj.nl
Website. www.villamedia.nl (Dutch only)

Nederlandse Politiebond (Police Union)
Address. Postbus 393, 2700 AJ Zoetermeer
Phone. +31 79 353 6161
Fax. +31 79 352 1226
E-mail. info@politiebond.nl
Website. www.politiebond.nl (Dutch only)
Leadership. Hans van Duijn (president)

FNV Sport
Address. G. Borgesiuslaan 77, 3515 ET Utrecht
Phone. +31 30 272 2177

FNV Vrouwen (Women)
Address. Naritaweg 10, 1043 BX Amsterdam
Phone. +31 20 581 6398

Zelfstandige bondgenoten (Self-Employed)
Address. Regulierenring 6, Postbus 156, 3980 CD Bunnik
Phone. +31 30 263 7000
Fax. +31 30 263 7215

E-mail. zelfstandigen@bg.fnv.nl
Leadership. Guus Fonteijn (general manager)
History and character. Launched in June 1999 under the auspices of the general FNV affiliate Bondgenoten to organize the self-employed. It set a target to achieve a membership of 3,000 (out of 757,000 self-employed in the Netherlands) and self-sufficiency by 2000.
Publication. Eigen Baas ("Free Agent")

Kappersbond FNV (hairdressers)
Address. Nachtegaalstraat 37, 3581 AC Utrecht
Phone. +31 30 231 4221
Fax. +31 30 231 7136
Publication. De Kapper

FNV Zeevaart (Maritime)
Address. Postbus 25131, 3001 HC Rotterdam
Phone. +31 10 477 1188
Fax. +31 10 477 3846
Leadership. Ed Sarton (president)
Membership. 6,507

UNIE-MHP (Vakcentrale voor middengroepen en hoger personeel)
Address. Postbus 400, 3990 DK Houten
Phone. +31 30 637 4792
Fax. +31 30 637 8829
E-mail. uniemhp@tip.nl
Website. www.uniemhp.nl (Dutch only)
Leadership. A.H. Verhoeven (president)
Membership. 225,000
History and character. UNIE-MHP originated in 1966 and was known by the acronym NCHP until 1990 and then as Vakcentrale MHP. Its membership is primarily managerial and technical. It is independent of political parties and religious affiliations. UNIE-MHP participates in the tripartite Social and Economic Council (SER) and the Foundation of Labour (STAR).

International affiliations. ETUC; EUROCADRES

Affiliates. UNIE-MHP comprises the following organizations:

1. Unie Van Onafhankelijke Vakorganisaties (UOV)
Address. Postbus 200, 3990 DE Houten
Phone. +31 30 634 5000
Fax. +31 30 637 9811
E-mail. info@unie.nl
Website. www.uov.nl (Dutch only)
History and character. The UOV comprises some 60 independent union organizations with a total of 158,000 members. These include the 88,000-member De Unie-vakbond voor industrie en dienstverlening, the union for industry and services (*Address.* Randhoeve 221, 3995 GA Houten. *Phone.* +31 30 634 5000. *Fax.* +31 30 637 9811. *Leadership.* Jacques Teuwen (president); Harry van Herpen (secretary). *E-mail.* info@unie.nl. *Website.* www.unie.nl).

2. Centrale van Middelbare en Hogere Functionarissen (CMHF)
Address. Postbus 176, 2260 AD Leidschendam

Phone. +31 70 419 1919
Fax. +31 70 419 1940
E-mail. centrale@cmhf.nl
Website. www.cmhf.nl (Dutch only)
History and character. This is a federation of civil service unions.

3. Vereniging van Nederlandse Verkeersvliegers (VNV)
Dutch Airline Pilots' Association
Address. Postbus 192, 1170 AD Badhoeverdorp
Phone. +31 20 449 8585
Fax. +31 20 449 8588
E-mail. secr@vnvn-dalpa.nl
Website. www.vnvn-dalpa.nl (Dutch only)

4. Beroepsorganisatie Banken en Verzekeringen (BBV)
Banking and Insurance Union
Address. Postbus 1558, 3600 BN Maarsen
Phone. +31 34 655 2552
Fax. +31 34 655 2160
E-mail. bbv@bbv-vkbv.nl
Website. www.bbv-vkbv.nl (Dutch only)

NETHERLANDS DEPENDENCIES

The Kingdom of the Netherlands comprises, in addition to the Netherlands in Europe, the Netherlands Antilles and with separate status, the island of Aruba. The principal island of the Netherlands Antilles is Curaçao.

Aruba

Federación de Trabajadores Arubanos (FTA)
Aruban Workers' Federation
Address. Bernardstraat No. 23, San Nicolas
Phone. +297 8 45 448
Fax. +297 8 45 504
Leadership. José Rodolfo Geerman (president); Juan Giron (secretary-general)
International affiliation. WCL

Netherlands Antilles

The pattern of trade unionism is fragmented, with different unions operating on the various islands.

Federación Boneriana di Trabao (FEDEDBON)
Bonaire Federation of Labour
Address. Apartado 324, Kaya Korona 85, Kralenendijk, Bonaire
Phone. +597 7 8845
Fax. +597 7 8845
Leadership. Gerald Teodulo Bernabela (president)
International affiliation. WCL

Central General di Trahadonan di Corsow (CGTC)
Address. PO Box 2078, Dr. Martin Luther King Boulevard 95, Otrabanda, Willemstad, Curaçao
Phone. +599 9 462 7678
Fax. +599 462 7700
Leadership. Hubert Rojer (secretary-general)
International affiliation. WCL

Sentral di Sindikatonan di Korsou (SSK)
Central Trade Union of Curaçao
Address. Schouwburgweg 44, PO Box 3036, Willemstad, Curaçao
Phone. +599 737 0255
Fax. +599 737 5250
International affiliation. ICFTU

Windward Islands Federation of Labour (WIFOL)
Address. WIFOL Convention Center, Poundfill 91, Longwall Road, Prince Bernard Bridge, PO Box 1097, Philipsburg, St Maarten, N.A.
Phone. +599 5 227 97
Fax. +599 5 266 31
Leadership. Theophilus Thompson (president); Curtis Vanterpool (general secretary)
Membership. 3,500. WIFOL represents the majority of workers on the island of St Maarten, St Eustasius and Saba, most of whom are employed in tourism.
International affiliation. WCL

New Zealand

Capital: Wellington
Population: 3.82 m. (2000 est.)

1 Political and Economic Background

New Zealand, an independent member of the Commonwealth, is a parliamentary democracy in which the
social democratic Labour Party and the conservative
National Party have alternated in power since the
1930s. In recent years, Labour held office from 1984-
90 and the National Party from 1990–99, with the
Labour Party, led by Prime Minister Helen Clark,
again in government (in coalition with the minority
left-wing Alliance Party), following elections on Nov.
27, 1999.

Historically New Zealand's economy was built on
agriculture, with a heavy reliance on the British market.
In the last two decades, however, it has increasingly
diversified its economic base. 65% of the labour force is
now employed in services, 25% in industry (mainly
small-scale) and only 10% in agriculture. Under Prime
Minister David Lange (1984–89) Labour began to move
away from many of its traditional statist policies, introducing market deregulation, liberalization of foreign
exchange controls, the phasing out of many subsidies,
privatization, a shift to indirect taxation and reform of
industrial relations legislation. These policies were
accelerated under the National Party in the 1990s,
although the incoming Labour-led government elected
in Nov. 1999 has criticized previous "excesses" in neo-
liberalism and market deregulation.

GDP (purchasing power parity) $63.8bn. (1999 est.);
GDP per capita (purchasing power parity) $17,400
(1999 est.).

2 Trade Unionism

Trade unionism has a long history, although New
Zealand has never ratified ILO Conventions No. 87
(Freedom of Association and Protection of the Right to
Organize, 1948) or No. 98 (Right to Organize and
Collective Bargaining, 1949). The first trade union federation was formed in 1909 and became known as the
"Red Federation". Its history was one of industrial turmoil, and in 1913 the United Federation of Labour,
which was linked to the newly formed Social
Democratic Party, was formed and became the leader of
organized labour. This was superseded by the Alliance
of Labour in 1919. Following the election of a Labour
government for the first time in 1935 the New Zealand
Federation of Labour (NZFL) was formed in 1937. On
its 50th anniversary the NZFL merged with the public
sector group, the Combined State Unions, to form the

New Zealand Council of Trade Unions (NZCTU). This
is effectively the national centre, with ICFTU affiliation,
although there are several dozen unions not in affiliation
and some of these are associated with the small New
Zealand Trade Union Federation (NZTUF), set up in
1994. All sectors of workers, except members of the
armed forces, may join unions. Police officers may not
strike although they may organize and bargain collectively, with disputes referred to compulsory binding
arbitration.

There have been considerable fluctuations in the
legislation relating to trade unions within the last two
decades depending on which government has been in
power.

In 1983–84 the National Party government enacted
legislation which prohibited closed shop agreements and
made it illegal to strike over union recognition issues. In
response, in 1984 the newly elected Labour government
amended the Industrial Relations Act so as to introduce
a system of compulsory trade union membership, effective on July 1, 1985. Under it unions were granted compulsory membership rights which would be confirmed
provided that they voted within 18 months to retain the
rights. According to guidelines issued by the Ministry of
Labour, all workers on the adult wage rate were to
become union members unless they held an exemption
certificate or were apprentices. Exemption certificates
could be obtained from the Union Membership
Exemption Tribunal but only on grounds of "conscience
or any other deeply held personal conviction" and the
fee to accompany an application for exemption was set
at NZ$100. By the expiry of the deadline on Jan. 1,
1987, 193 of the country's 230 unions had voted to
retain compulsory membership, two had voted against,
and 35 others (mostly small unions representing professional or supervisory staff) had held no ballots and so
were consequently to be considered voluntary.

This regime of compulsory unionism was favoured by
the New Zealand Federation of Labour, but widely criticized elsewhere as limiting freedom of association.
Although the 1987 Labour Relations Act weakened the
positions of unions in areas such as collective bargaining, by 1988 union density in New Zealand had reached
64%. In Oct. 1990, however, the National Party was
returned to power in a landslide and this proved a water-
shed for the unions. The new government's
Employment Contracts Act (ECA) of 1991 was considered the most radical reform of New Zealand's labour
laws in the 20th Century and remained in force until
2000.

On freedom of association, the ECA banned the
requirement of membership of a trade union as a condition of employment. In the field of bargaining, the Act
underwrote the principle of individual contracts rather
than bloc collective agreements. Employees were given

the right to choose who would represent them during negotiations with the employer on an individual or collective basis, and employers could refuse to negotiate with unions. The terms of the resulting contract applied only to those who were party to it. The Act made negotiated employment contracts legally enforceable by either party during their term, and it became illegal for a union to strike while an existing contract was in force. The Act also made it illegal to strike to force an individual employer into adopting a multi-employer agreement. Other changes included an end to the situation where union membership was required for a worker to have access to grievance procedures through the labour court.

Membership in NZCTU-affiliated unions fell from 530,000 in 1988 to 350,000 in 1991 and now stands at 200,000. The fall has been attributed to the effect of the ECA, exacerbated by privatization and high unemployment. Employers at first moved cautiously to take advantage of their right to sue unions over illegal strikes, but the impact of an unregulated environment was quickly apparent in the structure of collective bargaining. National bargaining was terminated in several sectors and the unions, weakened by unemployment, found resistance difficult to organize. By 1993 there had been a 45% fall in the number of workers covered by collective agreements. Many new contracts ended check-off arrangements.

The NZCTU condemned the ECA as a blatant attempt to de-unionize the workforce and individualize the employment relationship although it was strongly welcomed by the New Zealand Employers' Federation (NZEF). However, apart from some one-day protests there was a general reluctance to take industrial action due to the very rapid rise in unemployment at that time. In 1994 the NZCTU gained a symbolic victory with an ILO ruling that the ECA breached ILO Conventions 87 and 98 in respect of freedom of association, collective bargaining and the right to strike. The government took no notice of the ILO's position, however, justifying the Act as part of a series of measures to liberalize the economy.

The overall impact of the ECA is disputed. According to the NZCTU it encouraged the growth of "poor quality jobs", with a great increase in casual and part-time work and exploitation of vulnerable workers by bad employers. It had also led to a "collapse of trust and good will" in industrial relations, as employers issued workers with "take it or leave it" contracts, without generating the productivity gains its backers expected. Whereas 48% of the work force were covered by collective agreements in 1989-90, only 24% were by 1998-99. Although days lost to work stoppages had declined to only 12,000 by 1998, compared with 331,000 in 1990, this was a continuation of a downward trend in evidence since the high point of industrial unrest in the late 1970s. The ECA contributed to a decline in union membership to one-quarter of the employed work force by the late 1990s, compared with two-thirds of the workforce in the heyday of compulsory unionism in the late 1980s. However, although under ECA choosing a union as a bargaining agent became entirely voluntary, and some employers encouraged the setting up non-union employee representative bodies for collective bargaining, the unions succeeded in retaining this role in many enterprises, 86% of collective agreements in 1998-99 being negotiated with a union.

In elections in Nov. 1999 the Labour Party returned to office on a platform that included a pledge to repeal the ECA and in Oct. 2000 it was replaced by a new Employment Relations Act (ERA). The ERA was strongly supported by the unions, with few reservations, but criticized by many employers as likely to lead to heavy compliance costs and legal disputes and as risking a return to the old days of excessive union power. The ERA did not involve a restoration of what were widely accepted as discredited past practices, such as compulsory union membership, national awards, and fixed relativities. However, while recognizing the contemporary prevalence of terms and conditions based on individual contracts, it shifted the balance back in favour of collective agreements. It gave registered unions the exclusive right to negotiate collective agreements and introduced a new concept (based on Canadian models) whereby the parties in collective bargaining must negotiate in "good faith". There were varying views on how this notion of "good faith" might work in practice, if "surface bargaining" as seen in the US was to be avoided, as there was no provision for compulsory arbitration when negotiations broke down. The ERA also restored the right to unions to take industrial action to win multi-employer contracts (but did not allow sympathy strikes); gave new employees the right to join on the same terms as those provided for in the collective contract; offered more protection for dependent contractors; and restored unions' rights of access to the workplace. It also set up new institutions to improve mediation and industrial relations.

3 Trade Union Centres

New Zealand Council of Trade Unions (NZCTU)

Address. PO Box 6645, Wellington

Phone. +64 4 3851334

Fax. +64 4 3856051

E-mail. ctu@nzctu.org.nz

Website. www.union.org.nz

Leadership. Ross Wilson (president); Paul Goulter (secretary)

Membership. 205,000 in 19 unions

History and character. The NZCTU held its founding conference at Wellington in 1987. It was formed out of the merger of the New Zealand Federation of Labour (NZFL), which comprised 150 (mainly private sector) unions, and the public sector Combined State Unions (CSU).

The NZCTU was formed at a point when, under the impact of compulsory unionism legislation introduced in 1984, two-thirds of the workforce was in unions.

However, following the election in 1990 of a National Party government, and enactment of the Employment Contracts Act (ECA) of 1991, trade union membership slumped dramatically, with the decline in membership in the decade from 1987 probably greater than for any other union centre in a developed western country. This hastened the process of consolidation of NZCTU affiliates, of which there are now only 19. Dozens of unions are unaffiliated to the NZCTU, although many of these are small. According to NZCTU president, Ross Wilson, since the return of a Labour government in Nov. 1999 the climate has changed and unions are notifying a sharp increase in membership.

In 1994 the ILO ruled in favour of the NZCTU's submission that the ECA was in violation of Conventions 87 and 98 (never ratified by New Zealand), but this did not affect government policy.

In 2000 the NZCTU focused on backing the new Labour government's legislation to repeal the ECA and replace it with the Employment Relations Act (in force from Oct. 2000). The NZCTU backed the government's bill as introduced, other than criticizing its retention of the ban on strikes undertaken for broad social and economic causes, noting the past use of action in opposition to South African sports tours and the docking of ships carrying nuclear weapons. It particularly welcomed the measure's emphasis on restoring the principle of positively endorsing and encouraging collective bargaining and on fostering an atmosphere in which negotiations would be conducted in "good faith". The NZCTU argued that the bill complemented the government's proposals to invest in skills, training and innovation, and that this rather than cutting labour costs is the key to productivity.

In the aftermath of the repeal of the ECA the NZCTU's "Fairness at Work" campaign included working to achieve improvements in workplace health and safety, a fair minimum wage, paid parental leave, more protection for contract workers and better holidays.

Publications. These include two newsletters, *CTU Work* and *CTU Health and Safety Update.*

International affiliations. ICFTU; TUAC; CTUC

Affiliates:

Association of Salaried Medical Specialists (ASMS)
Address. PO Box 10763, Wellington
Phone. +64 4 499 1271
Fax. +64 4 499 4500
E-mail. asms@asms.org.nz
Website. www.hospitals.co.nz/asms
Leadership. Ian Powell (executive director)

Association of Staff in Tertiary Education (ASTE)
Address. PO Box 27-141, Wellington
Phone. +64 4 801 5098
Fax. +64 4 385 8826
E-mail. national.office@aste.ac.nz
Leadership. Sharn Riggs (national secretary)

Association of University Staff of New Zealand Inc. (AUS)
Address. PO Box 11-767, Wellington
Phone. +64 4 382 8491
Fax. +64 4 382 8508
E-mail. national.office@aus.ac.nz
Website. www.aus.ac.nz
Leadership. Rob Crozier (executive director)
Membership. 6,200

Central Amalgamated Workers' Union (AWUNZ)
Address. PO Box 27-291, 307 Willis Street, Wellington
Phone. +64 4 384 4049
Fax. +64 4 801 7306
E-mail. centralawunz@xtra.co.nz
Leadership. Jackson Smith (secretary)

Dairy Workers' Union
Address. PO Box 9046, Hamilton
Phone. +64 7 839 0239
Fax. +64 7 838 0398
E-mail. nzdwu@wave.co.nz
Leadership. Roy Potroz (secretary)

Engineering, Printing and Manufacturing Union (EPMU)
Address. PO Box 31546, Lower Hutt, 38 Bouverie Street, Petone
Phone. +64 4 568 0086
Fax. +64 4 576 1173
E-mail. rex.jones@epmunion.org.nz
Website. www.nzepmu.org.nz
Leadership. Rex Jones (secretary)

FinSec (Financial Sector Union)
Address. P.O. Box 27-355, Wellington
Phone. +64 4 385 7723
Fax. +64 4 385 2214
E-mail. union@finsec.org.nz
Website. www.finsec.org.nz
Leadership. Don Farr (general secretary)
Membership. 13,000, in the finance and information sectors.

Flight Attendants and Related Services Association (FARSA)
Address. PO Box 78-083, Auckland Airport, Auckland
Phone. +64 9 256 1821
Fax. +64 9 256 1841
E-mail. union@farsa.co.nz
Leadership. Ann Howard (executive officer)

Meat and Related Trades Workers Union of Aotearoa
Address. PO Box 17-056, Greenlane, Auckland
Phone. +64 9 520 0034
Fax. +64 9 523 1286
E-mail. meat.union@xtra.co.nz
Leadership. Graham Cooke (secretary)

Nurses' Organization
Address. PO Box 2128, Wellington
Phone. +64 4 385 0847
Fax. +64 4 382 9993
E-mail. nzno@nurses.org.nz
Leadership. Brenda Wilson (chief executive officer)

NZ Educational Institute (NZEI)
Address. PO Box 466, Wellington

Phone. +64 4 384 9689
Fax. +64 4 385 1772
E-mail. nzei@nzei.org.nz
Leadership. Joanna Beresford (national secretary)

New Zealand Meatworkers & Related Trades Union, Inc.
Address. PO Box 13-048, Christchurch
Phone. +64 3 366 5105
Fax. +64 3 379 7763
E-mail. nzmeatworkersunion@clear.net.nz
Leadership. R.G.Kirk (secretary)
Membership. 7,700

Post Primary Teachers' Association
Address. PO Box 2119, Wellington
Phone. +64 4 384 9964
Fax. +64 4 382 8763
E-mail. gensec@ppta.union.org.nz
Website. www.ppta.org.nz
Leadership. Kevin Bunker (general secretary)

New Zealand Public Service Association (PSA)
Address. PO Box 3817, 11 Aurora Terrace, Wellington 6015
Phone. +64 4 917 033
Fax. +64 4 917 2051
E-mail. enquiries@psa.org.nz
Website. www.psa.org.nz
Leadership. Kathy Higgins (president)
Membership. 42,000

Rail and Maritime Transport Union Inc. (RMTU)
Address. PO Box 1103, Wellington 6001
Phone. +64 4 499 2066
Fax. +64 4 471 0896
Leadership. Wayne Butson (general secretary), Jim Kelly (president)
Membership. 3,735

Service Workers and Food Union of Aotearoa
Address. Private Bag 68-914, Newton, Auckland
Phone. +64 9 355 1855
Fax. +64 9 355 1854
E-mail. fent@ihug.co.nz
Leadership. Darien Fenton (national secretary)

Tertiary Institutes Allied Staff Association (TIASA)
Address. PO Box 1594, Rotorua
Phone. +64 7 346 1989
Fax. +64 7 346 3860
E-mail. tiasa@wave.co.nz
Leadership. Peter Joseph (national secretary)

Waterfront Workers' Union
Address. PO Box 27-004, Wellington
Phone. +64 4 385 0792
Fax. +64 4 384 8766
E-mail. nzwwu@paradise.net.nz
Leadership. Trevor Hanson (secretary)

Writers' Guild
Address. PO Box 47-886, Auckland
Phone. +64 9 373 2960
Fax. +64 9 373 2961
E-mail. nzwg@clear.net.nz
Website. www.wga.org/iawg/nz.html

Leadership. Alannah O'Sullivan (national president)

New Zealand Trade Union Federation (NZTUF)
Address. PO Box 11 891 Wellington
Phone. +64 4 384 8963
Fax. +64 4 384 8007
E-mail. tuf@tradeshall.org.nz
Leadership. Maxine Gay (president); Michael Gilchrist (acting secretary)
History and character. The NZTUF was founded in 1994.
International affiliations. None.

4 Other Trade Union Organizations

Several dozen, mainly small, specialized or regional, unions are unaffiliated to the NZCTU national trade union centre. The more significant among them include the following:

Footwear Workers' Union
Address. PO Box 50216, Porirura
Phone. +64 4 237 5062
Fax. +64 4 237 8157
Leadership. Robert Reid (secretary)

Manufacturing and Construction Workers' Union
Address. PO Box 11-123, Wellington
Phone. +64 4 3858 264
Fax. +64 4 3848 007
E-mail. m.c.union@tradeshall.org.nz
Leadership. Robert Reid (president); Graeme Clarke (general secretary)
Membership. 3,000

National Distribution Union
Address. Private Bag 92-904, Onehunga, Auckland
Phone. +64 9 622 8355
Fax. +64 9 622 8353
E-mail. everyone@ndunion.org.nz
Leadership. Mike Jackson (national secretary)

New Zealand Building Trades Union (NZBTU)
Address. Room 25, Trades Hall, 126 Vivian Street, Wellington
Phone. +64 4 385 1178
Fax. +64 4 385 1177
E-mail. nzbtu@tradeshall.org.nz
Leadership. Ashley Russ (national secretary)

New Zealand Firefighters' Union
Address. P.O. Box 38-213, Petone, Wellington
Phone. +64 4 568 4583

Fax. +64 4 568 3292

Leadership. Derek Best (secretary)

Membership. 1,500

New Zealand Seafarers' Union

Address. PO Box 1103, Wellington

Phone. +64 4 499 3560

Fax. +64 4 499 8872

E-mail. dmorgan@seafarers.org.nz

Leadership. Dave Morgan (national president)

Police Association

Address. PO Box 12-344, DX SX 11133, Wellington

Phone. +64 4 472 0198

Fax. +64 4 471 1309

E-mail. nzpa@nzpa.org.nz

Website. www.nzpa.org.nz

Leadership. Greg O'Connor (president)

Postal Workers' Union

Address. PO Box 11-123, Wellington

Phone. +64 4 385 8264

Fax. +4 384 8007

Leadership. John Maynard (secretary)

STAMS

Address. PO Box 56-431, Dominion Road, Auckland

Phone. +64 9 623 3993

Fax. +64 9 623 3996

History and character. STAMS (formerly APEX) covers a range of supervisors, sales, technical and office staff in both the private and public sector.

UNITE

Address. PO Box 50-216, Porirua

Phone. +64 4 237 5062

Fax. +64 4 237 8156

Leadership. Robert Reid (president)

Cook Islands

Capital: Avarua
Population: 20,000 (2000 est.)

1 Political and Economic Background

The Cook Islands have self-government in free association with New Zealand. The economy is primarily agricultural and there is a heavy dependence on aid from New Zealand. In 1996 the government declared bankruptcy and made drastic cuts to the civil service.

GDP (purchasing power parity) $112m. (1998 est.); GDP per capita (purchasing power parity) $5,600 (1998 est.).

2 Trade Unionism

Most employees in the formal economy are in the public sector, and belong to the Cook Islands Workers' Association (formerly Cook Islands Public Service Association), which is directly affiliated to the ICFTU.

3 Trade Union Centre

Cook Islands Workers' Association

Address. PO Box 403, Rarotonga

Phone. +682 24422

Fax. +682 24423

E-mail. ciwa@oyster.net.ck

Leadership. Miriama Pierre (president)

International affiliations. ICFTU; CTUC

Nicaragua

Capital: Managua
Population: 4.81 m. (2000 est.)

1 Political and Economic Background

The Frente Sandinista de Liberación Nacional (FSLN or Sandinistas) came to power in 1979 following the overthrow of the right-wing Somoza regime that had ruled Nicaragua since 1933. In the 1980s the Reagan administration's support for contra guerrillas opposing the Sandinistas, under Daniel Ortega Saavedra, for some years turned Nicaragua into a leading focus of international political attention. By the late 1980s the Sandinistas were brought to the negotiating table and in 1990 elections were held which brought victory to the National Opposition Union (UNO) led by Violeta Barrios de Chamorro, with a peaceable transfer of power. She pursued a policy of national reconciliation that after a time provoked disquiet within her own party. In 1992 charges of collusion between her administration and the Sandinistas briefly interrupted US aid but the flow was resumed. Further elections were held in Oct. 1996, resulting in victory for Arnold Aléman, the candidate of the Liberal Alliance coalition, which also became the largest group in the legislature, taking 44 of the 93 seats. The FSLN, led by Ortega, remained the main opposition, taking 37 seats.

Since the end of the 1980s military conflict Nicaragua has experienced relative stability, although there have been continuing tensions over the issue of redistribution of land and other assets seized by the Sandinistas. The Nicaraguan economy, which is based on agriculture, with coffee, cotton, sugar and bananas as the principal crops, was adversely affected by the 1980s civil war but has shown recovery in the 1990s. Post-Sandinista governments have sought to liberalize the economy in the face of opposition from the Sandinistas. Under President Chamorro, reforms had the effect of reducing the state sector to 30–40% of GDP.

In Sept. 1999 the World Bank approved Nicaragua's application to be included in the Heavily Indebted Poor Countries Initiative (HIPC), which would allow it to reduce its $6bn. external debt by 80%.

GDP (purchasing power parity) $12.5bn. (1999 est.); GDP per capita (purchasing power parity) $2,650 (1999 est.).

2 Trade Unionism

The first national trade union organization – the Organized Labour of Nicaragua (OON) – was formed in 1924, but faltered because of its support for Gen. Sandino (assassinated in 1934), who led opposition to the US military presence in the country. The position of trade unions was difficult under the rule of the Somoza family, although unions independent of the government managed to retain a degree of organizational identity for much of that period. Nicaragua ratified ILO Conventions No. 87 (Freedom of Association and Protection of the Right to Organize, 1948) and No. 98 (Right to Organize and Collective Bargaining, 1949) in 1967.

Substantial anti-government industrial unrest occurred in 1978–79, but the fall of Somoza came as result of military action. In the first three years after the Sandinista revolution, union membership quadrupled, reaching 100,000. During the 1980s civil war the right of free association and to strike was subject to suspension from time to time under emergency powers. However, opposition trade unions did continue to function through the period of Sandinista rule, while the Sandinistas attempted to organize workers and other social groups in "mass organizations".

A new labour code adopted in 1996 reinforced the right of all workers in both private and public sectors, other than the police and armed forces, to form unions and bargain collectively. It is estimated that about half the workers in the formal sector are in unions. The ICFTU reported to the WTO in Oct. 1999 that "the industrial relations climate has improved somewhat over recent years. It is now fairly easy to get a union registered and recognized". However, the labour code is not uniformly enforced and in the export processing zones (where about 20,000 are employed) some foreign-owned firms have excluded the unions. The 1996 labour code provides for a right to strike subject to extensive mediation and compulsory arbitration procedures, although there has reportedly not been a legal strike since 1990.

The trade union movement within the country is very fragmented and divided ideologically and in its attitude to the policies of the Sandinistas. Pro-Sandinista unions associate in the National Workers' Front (FNT) and non-Sandinsta unions in the Permanent Congress of Workers (CPT). Both the WCL and ICFTU are represented in the country. Estimates of memberships of unions are generally unreliable.

3 Trade Union Centres

Central Sandinista de Trabajadores (CST)
Sandinista Workers' Centre

History and character. The CST was founded immediately following the 1979 revolution, growing out of the workers' insurrectionist committees and their later form, the comités de defense de trabajadores

Sandinistas, and rapidly became the dominant labour organization in the country. The CST is closely linked to the FSLN. After Chamorro assumed office the CST led a large number of strikes, particularly in 1991. It was formerly affiliated to the WFTU.

Central de Trabajadores Nicaragüenses (CTN)
Nicaraguan Workers' Centre

Address. Calle 27 de Mayo, Pinolero 25 Varas arriba, 75 Varas Sur, Managua

Phone. +505 2 281 082

Fax. +505 2 268 3001

E-mail. ctn@apc.nicarao.org.ni

Leadership. Carlos Huembes (secretary general)

History and character. In 1962 the Christian-inspired Nicaraguan Autonomous Trade Union Movement (MOSAN) was formed, recruiting several thousand members principally in rural areas, and in 1972 this became the CTN. Members of the CTN were subjected to periods of detention without charge by the Sandinista government. During the 1980s conflict the WCL and its regional organization CLAT criticized the Sandinista government for infringements of human and trade union rights, but opposed US aid to the contra

rebels. The CTN supports the Social Christian Party (PSC).

International affiliation. WCL

Confederación de Unificación Sindical (CUS)
Confederation of Labour Unification

Address. Apartado 4845, Managua

Phone. +505 2 42039

Fax. +505 2 223139

Membership. 21,000

History and character. The CUS was formed as the Nicaraguan Trade Union Council (CSN) under the auspices of ORIT in 1964, absorbing independent and pro-government unions. Following the Sandinista take over of power it declined rapidly as a consequence of its accommodation with the previous regime. Leaders and members of CUS were detained for periods under the Sandinistas. The ICFTU opposed US aid to the Contra guerrillas and also the US economic embargo of Nicaragua imposed in 1985, arguing that the USA should maintain relations with Nicaragua linked to the observance of human and trade union rights.

International affiliations. ICFTU

Niger

Capital: Niamey
Population: 10.08 m. (2000 est.)

1 Political and Economic Background

Niger gained independence from France in 1960. A coup in 1974 was followed by 15 years of military rule. In 1988 the National Movement for a Development Society (MNSD) was formed as the sole legal party and a joint military–civilian government was formed. Multi-party elections were held in 1993 under a constitution approved in a referendum in Dec. 1992. There was a military coup in Jan. 1996, however, with a National Salvation Council taking power and its leader, Brig.-Gen. Ibrahim Barre Mainassara, becoming President the following year. A further coup took place in Apr. 1999, when Mainassara was assassinated, and an army-led National Reconciliation Council took power. Following this elections were held in Nov. 1999 resulting in victory for the MNSD and its presidential

candidate Mamadou Tandja and a return to civilian government.

Niger is an impoverished country in which 90% of the labour force are engaged in farming and herding, mostly at subsistence level. The formal economy is very small. The main export is uranium but this has been affected by depressed prices. Drought, desertification, population expansion and debt are major problems and there is a reliance on international assistance.

GDP (purchasing power parity) $9.6bn. (1999 est.); GDP per capita (purchasing power parity) $1,000 (1999 est.).

2 Trade Unionism

Niger ratified ILO Convention No. 87 (Freedom of Association and Protection of the Right to Organize, 1948) in 1961 and Convention No. 98 (Right to Organize and Collective Bargaining, 1949) in 1962.

The constitution provides for the right to establish and join trade unions. However, 95% of the workforce is engaged in subsistence agriculture and petty trading and unions represent primarily the small minority employed in formal public sector occupations such as civil servants and teachers or in state enterprises. Most unions are affiliated to the USTN trade union centre, although there are some independent unions. Several unions were suspended or closed down by the government in the late 1990s.

Collective bargaining exists in both the public and private sectors. The USTN represents civil servants in bargaining with the government. There is a legal right to strike, other than for the police and armed forces, subject to a notice period and the maintenance of essential services. The main cause of strikes in recent years has been unpaid wages in the public sector with the USTN leading many short strikes on this issue.

3 Trade Union Centre

Union des Syndicats des Travailleurs du Niger (USTN)
Union of Workers' Trade Unions of Niger

Address. BP 388, Niamey

Phone. +227 73 52 56

Fax. +227 73 52 56

Leadership. Elhadji Mahaman Mansour Daddo (secretary-general)

Membership. 70,000

History and character. A union centre, the Union Nationale des Travailleurs du Niger (UNTN), was established at independence in 1960. Its name was changed to the Union des Syndicats des Travailleurs du Niger (USTN) in 1978.

The USTN was linked to the MNSD, set up by the military regime in 1988 as the sole legal party. However, its support for the pro-democracy movement (which included mounting a general strike against austerity measures) led to police raids on its premises and the detention of secretary-general Laouali Moutari in 1990.

The President told the unions' leaders in October that their role should not extend beyond defending the workers' interests. A further general strike, this time for five days, was mounted in November in support of calls for a conference on the country's political future. It was a major factor in forcing the regime to concede multi-party democracy.

Following the military coup of Jan. 1996 the USTN faced further pressures. In Mar. 1997, Mahaman Mansour Daddo, the then USTN deputy secretary-general, was among 22 trade union leaders detained following a strike called by the USTN to protest against civil servants' pay arrears, tax increases and privatization measures. In Apr. 1997 four of those detained were convicted of sabotage and received prison sentences, but after international pressure all 22 were released in June. Since that time the USTN has continued to call numerous strikes over the issue of public sector pay arrears.

The USTN participates in a wide range of national social and economic agencies. In 1998 the USTN established a national training centre for trade unionists and has also set up a cooperative irrigation and agricultural project. There are 38 affiliated unions, in both the public and private sectors, with most members in the public sector. In addition to being affiliated to the ICFTU it participates in the work of the OATUU and its regional organization (OTAO).

International affiliation. ICFTU

4 Other Trade Union Organization

Confédération Nigérienne du Travail (CNT)

Address. Bourse du Travail, BP 10620, Niamey

Phone. +227 73 41 05

Fax. +227 73 75 15

Leadership. Seybou Issou (secretary-general)

Membership. 15,000

History and character. Founded in 1996 and affiliated to the WCL in 1998. It emphasizes education, trade union training and solidarity work.

International affiliation. WCL

Nigeria

Capital: Abuja
Population: 123.34 m. (2000 est.)

1 Political and Economic Background

Nigeria, the most populous country in Africa, became an independent member of the Commonwealth in 1960 and established a Federal Republic in 1963. It has generally been under military rule since that time, but a civilian government came into office in May 1999.

Maj.-Gen. Ibrahim Babangida seized power in 1985. After seven years he conceded legislative assembly elections which resulted in victory for the Social Democratic Party (SDP). But civilian rule was not restored and Babangida refused to acknowledge the results of the June 1993 presidential election won by Chief Mashood Abiola. He eventually resigned when unions staged a general strike, but after a confused interval, the military again seized power under General Sanni Abacha in Nov. 1993. When in June 1994 Abiola declared himself president he was charged with treason and arrested and new disturbances followed. In Nov. 1995, following the execution of the leader of the Movement for the Survival of the Ogoni People, Ken Saro-Wiwa, Nigeria's membership of the Commonwealth was suspended. Abacha died in June 1998 and was succeeded by Gen. Abbubakar, who instituted liberalization leading to elections in Feb. 1999 and the installation of a civilian government headed by President Olusegun Obasanjo in May 1999. Obasanjo is himself a former general, who headed a military government from 1976–79. He was the candidate of the People's Democratic Party, which also won a majority in the legislature.

Nigeria faces continual internal unrest on several fronts, including in the oil-producing Niger delta region. There is increasing polarization between the (mainly Christian) South and the (mainly Muslim) North; hundred died in clashes in March 2000 over the introduction of Muslim (sharia) law in the northern city of Kaduna.

Nigeria benefited from wealth generated by the oil price boom of the 1970s. However, this wealth was not effectively invested in the national infrastructure, and Nigeria became associated with rampant corruption and collapsed public services. Its largely subsistence agricultural sector has been unable to increase output to match population growth. Nigeria stood to benefit from escalating oil prices at the end of the 1990s, oil accounting for 90 per cent of export earnings and 65% of budget revenues. After soaring to high levels in the mid-1990s inflation fell to 11% by 1999. However, Nigeria's foreign debt is estimated as about $34bn and the government is seeking debt write-offs. International financial institutions believe that privatization of ineffi-

cient parastatals and better control of public finances are among the pre-conditions needed for write-offs to produce long-term benefits, although the IMF agreed a new assistance package in Aug. 2000. The government has announced plans to privatize dozens of state-controlled enterprises, but only two small privatizations involving cement companies had taken place by early 2000, and the inefficiency and cost of power, transport and telecommunications are seen as obstacles to investment in the economy generally. Manufacturing output in 1999 was 23% below 1991 levels, representing only 7% of GDP.

GDP (purchasing power parity) $110.5bn. (1999 est.); GDP per capita (purchasing power parity) $970 (1999 est.).

2 Trade Unionism

Nigeria ratified ILO Conventions No. 87 (Freedom of Association and Protection of the Right to Organize, 1948) and No. 98 (Right to Organize and Collective Bargaining, 1949) in 1960.

Nigerian trade unionism dates from the turn of the 20th century. By the 1930s a number of unions were well established and during World War II the British colonial authorities began to register them, giving organized labour official recognition for the first time. By the early 1970s there were several hundred unions and four competing trade union centres but in the mid-1970s these centres were dissolved by the military government.

The present Nigeria Labour Congress (NLC) was launched in 1978 by government decree as the sole legal organization with a large subvention of public funds. The several hundred unions and staff associations were rationalized into 42 affiliated industry-based unions. In 1989 a decree made membership of international trade secretariats illegal and under it four transport unions were fined the following year. The government also barred public employees from being members of one or other of the two legal political parties.

1993 brought a three-day general strike by the NLC in protest at the failure to restore democracy. The NLC's agreement to call off the strike angered its oil workers' affiliate NUPENG whose members stayed out for ten days. In July 1994 NUPENG, this time joined by another energy union PENGASSAN, began strikes in support of a demand to release Abiola. After six weeks of growing chaos Gen. Abacha dissolved the leadership of both unions and the NLC and put them into administration. They had been guilty, he charged, of "economic sabotage". Other unions failed to join the oil workers on strike. In early September the oil stoppage crumbled and normal working gradually resumed.

A series of decrees in 1996 forced the merger of the

41 NLC unions into 29; banned professional union organizers from holding positions in the NLC; required the inclusion of no strike clauses in collective bargaining agreements; required unions to pay 10 percent of members' dues to the NLC; and banned affiliation to non-African international organizations without government permission. Nigeria refused to accept ILO missions and in 1997 the ILO Committee on Freedom of Association condemned a "persistent deterioration of trade union rights".

Following the death of Gen. Abacha in June 1998, Gen. Abbubakar overturned the 1996 decrees. He removed the administrators running the NLC, which was allowed to form an independent executive. He also released Frank Kokori, NUPENG general secretary, and Milton Dabibi, PENGASSAN general secretary, who had been detained without charge or trial since the 1994 strike.

A new constitution adopted in May 1999 provides for freedom of association. All workers except the armed forces and those designated as being essential government employees, such as police and firefighters, are legally free to join unions. An estimated 10% of the total workforce is unionized, with members mainly in the public sector and larger enterprises in the formal private sector.

The NLC remains the national centre. However there is also a Senior Staff Consultative Association of Nigeria (SESCAN), with a membership of 600,000, which has never been officially recognized by the government.

Collective bargaining is practiced in many sectors. The right to strike has been restored and numerous strikes and other protests occurred in 1999–2000, generally over wage arrears or to demand an increase in the minimum wage.

3 Trade Union Centre

Nigeria Labour Congress (NLC)

Address. 29 Olajuwon Street, off Ojuelegba Road, PO Box 620, Yaba, Lagos

Phone. +234 774 3988

E-mail. nutg@infoweb.abs.net

Leadership. Adams Oshiomhole (executive president); John Odeh (general secretary)

Membership. Reported as about 4 million

History and character. Although formed under state sponsorship in 1978, the NLC subsequently exercised considerable autonomy and frequently opposed government policy in the 1980s on issues such as wage agreements, structural adjustment programmes and minimum wage legislation, including by strike action.

In 1988 the government dissolved the NLC executive and put its affairs in the hands of an administrator. The dissolution, presented as a move against factionalism within the NLC, prompted national and international protests. The presence of an IMF team in the country added fuel to the fire and unrest flared. Rallies were banned, universities closed and many unionists arrested. Three committees were set up to consider union grievances but detainees continued to be held, and the government established an anti-strike division, the Labour Intelligence Monitoring Unit, followed by a unit to maintain essential services during strikes. Meanwhile a promised reconstitution of the NLC was repeatedly postponed, and the tenure of the administrator extended until 1990. The administrator drew up a joint slate representative of both factions and it was returned unopposed for all offices under the presidency of Paschal Bafyau of the Nigeria National Union of Railwaymen.

The 1992 quadrennial congress re-elected most of the leadership, including Bafyau, and established a Women's Commission. A Labour Transport Corporation was set up to run buses in Lagos and Abuja, with cheaper fares for union members, and a monthly newspaper was launched. However, the events of 1993 onwards associated with the refusal of the military to accept elected civilian rulers inevitably renewed the tension between the NLC and the state. Although the NLC came under some criticism from affiliates, notably the oil workers, for being over-conciliatory, it was again put into administration in 1994, the government appointing its officers.

Following the death of Gen. Abacha in June 1998, the NLC was allowed to run its own affairs. Its right to affiliate to organizations outside Africa was also restored. In Jan. 1999, in the first major trade union election in Nigeria since 1994, Adams Oshiomhole (formerly deputy to Bafyau, and general secretary of the National Union of Textile and Garment Workers) was elected president of the NLC.

International affiliations. ICFTU; CTUC

Norway

Capital: Oslo
Population: 4.5 m. (2000 est.)

1 Political and Economic Background

Norway is a parliamentary democracy under a constitutional hereditary monarchy. Governments are usually formed by coalitions, and the Labour Party (DNA) has led the government for long periods since World War II, most recently from 1990–97. Since elections in Sept. 1997, there has been a centrist minority coalition government comprising the Christian People's Party (KRF), the Liberal Party (Venstre) and the Centre Party (SP). The Labour Party remained the largest single party, winning 65 of the 165 seats in Parliament. As the coalition parties won only 42 seats they govern on the basis of issue-by-issue cooperation with other parties. In a referendum in Nov. 1994, Norway voted not to join the European Union.

Norway has a mixed economy and a high standard of living. Since the 1960s offshore oil and gas have been a major contributor to prosperity and only Saudi Arabia exports more oil. After a downturn in the early 1990s Norway has enjoyed good growth rates, although growth fell to 0.8% in 1999, and unemployment is low at 3%. Norway is a welfare state and public sector expenditure exceeds 50% of GDP, with heavy spending on health and social services and subsidies for vulnerable sectors of the economy such as agriculture and fishing. There are concerns about the impact on the resources available for public spending of the long-term depletion of energy reserves. Some 79% of the work force are in services, and 14% in manufacturing.

GDP (purchasing power parity) $111.3bn. (1999 est.); GDP per capita (purchasing power parity) $25,100 (1999 est.).

2 Trade Unionism

Norway ratified ILO Convention No. 87 (Freedom of Association and Protection of the Right to Organize, 1948) in 1949 and Convention No. 98 (Right to Organize and Collective Bargaining. 1949) in 1955.

Union density is high in Norway compared to the European average, although below the levels seen in other Scandinavian countries. Density has not greatly altered in the last four decades. In the 1990s it declined fractionally, but the total number of union members increased because of the expansion of the number of jobs. The highest rate of organization is in the public sector, where 83% of employees are unionized, compared with 43% in the private sector. The most heavily organized private sector areas are manufacturing, banking and insurance. In Norway, occupations requiring higher levels of education tend to be more organized than those requiring lower levels.

The oldest trade union centre is the LO, founded in 1899. With 830,000 members (including pensioners and unemployed) the LO is the leading factor in most of the private sector and in many public sector areas also, outside health and education. Its membership has increased by some 60,000 since the early 1990s. LO's dominance of the Norwegian trade union movement has, however, declined since the 1970s with the formation of competing centres, the Confederation of Academic Professional Unions in Norway (AF) and the Confederation of Vocational Unions (YS). The AF was created as a confederation of unions catering for those with college and university qualifications, while the YS, although with a white-collar flavour, tended to compete more directly in LO's core areas. LO's relative position has eroded in the face of changes to the structure of the labour force, with the loss of blue-collar manufacturing jobs (LO's power base) and the rise of service industries (with lower unionization rates) and white-collar public sector jobs. Whereas the LO in 1980 organized 38% of the total workforce and other organizations only 19%, by 1997 the LO organized 30% and the others 27%.

In the late 1990s major realignments of the centres took place. In 1997–98 the AF lost nearly half its members to a new organization, Akademikerne, which capitalized on the feeling that AF was dominated by less-qualified groups such as nurses. Akademikerne was set up to cater only for those with university degrees at master's level and above and to win back positions lost in a general flattening of salary differentials. In June 2000 AF announced that plans to merge with YS had collapsed and that it would dissolve in 2001. It was unclear whether the remaining AF unions would remain independent or might ultimately join the LO.

Some unions are independent of the LO, YS, AF and Akademikerne. By far the largest of these is the 85,000-member Norwegian Union of Teachers (Norsk Laererlag), the biggest Norwegian teaching union.

The LO has historically been close to the Labour Party (DNA), which has been in office for long periods. LO leaders have served as Labour ministers and the leaders of the two organizations meet regularly. The other centres have, in contrast, stressed their political independence. The LO's leadership position in the labour movement, and its political ties, have meant that it was often the only voice of labour on government committees, a source of dissatisfaction to the growing rival confederations. In 1999 the government broadened the representative base of a number of advisory committees.

Relations between the LO and AF have generally been positive in recent years, and these two ICFTU affiliates have had a cooperation agreement. Relations between the LO and YS, in contrast, have been strained by their frequent competition to organize the same groups of workers, but have also tended to improve and the idea of a merger of the two organizations has begun to gain currency, although hindered by the LO's links to the Labour Party. On Oct. 15, 1998 the LO, AF and YS staged a 2-hour strike against budget proposals, reportedly the first time the three confederations had taken joint action in a "political" strike.

Since 1935 successive Basic Agreements (Hovedavtalen), negotiated between the LO and Confederation of Norwegian Business and Industry (NHO) have provided a detailed framework for the conduct of industrial relations and the settlement of disputes. Employers recognize the right of the unions to speak and act for the workers and their own obligation to deal with the unions, while the unions accept the constraints of submitting to highly formalized negotiating procedures. Such constraints include the "duty of peace", whereby unions will not call strikes or disrupt production while an agreement is in force (although sympathy strikes and political strikes are excluded from this ban). Collective agreements, which typically apply for two years, are submitted to referendums of the membership. Disputes over the interpretation of collective agreements can be referred to the Labour Court.

Where breakdown in negotiation of collective agreements occurs, disputes are referred for conciliation and mediation. More controversially, compulsory arbitration may be imposed by the government with the approval of Parliament. The government maintains that this occurs only where there is a serious risk to life or health or vital interests. The unions maintain that arbitration has been imposed in cases not involving such level of jeopardy. Strikes are banned in the offshore oil industry. Strikes are fairly infrequent, but because they typically take place at the national rather than enterprise level, the impact of individual strikes can be serious. Strikes over pay in several sectors in Spring 2000 were the most extensive since 1986.

3 Trade Union Centres

Akademikerne
Federation of Norwegian Professional Associations

Address. Kr. Augusts gt. 9, 0164 Oslo

Phone. +47 22 36 86 00

Fax. +47 22 36 86 10

E-mail. akademikerne@oslo.online.no

Website. www.akademikerne.no (Norwegian only)

Leadership. An-Margritt Aanonsen (president)

Membership. 114,790 (Jan. 2000) in 13 associations, including 7,460 pensioners and 13,821 students.

History and character. In Oct. 1997 seven associations within the AF (representing chartered engineers, busi-

ness economists, dentists, lawyers, architects, veterinarians and psychologists) announced they were breaking away to join the Norwegian Medical Association in the formation of Akademikerne (literally, "The Academics"). In 1998 they were joined by a further five AF affiliates, most importantly the 36,000-member Civil Engineers.

The creation of Akademikerne reflected the belief that the AF was over-centralized and too influenced by unions of lesser-qualified occupational groups and that those with high qualifications had been left out in a process of flattening differentials. Akademikerne was to admit only those with higher university qualifications, representing five years' study. The majority of members of the associations joining Akademikerne were also in the private sector or self-employed whereas those left within AF were overwhelmingly in the public sector. The declared objective of the new confederation was to seek "differentiated and market-based wage determination, as far as possible through local bargaining at the firm level".

Akademikernes Fellesorganisasjon (AF)
Confederation of Academic and Professional Unions in Norway

Address. PB 506 Sentrum, 0105 Oslo

Phone. +47 22 42 45 48

Fax. +47 22 82 33 00

E-mail. af@af.no

Website. www.af.no (Norwegian, English section)

Leadership. Aud Blankholm (president)

Membership. 115,000 in 18 associations

History and character. Founded in 1975 as a politically independent confederation to represent those with higher educational qualifications at college or university level. It grew steadily through to the mid-1990s, becoming the second centre behind the LO, with which it shared ICFTU affiliation. By 1997 it had grown to 240,000 members.

In Oct. 1997, however, seven affiliates announced their intention to break away to join a new confederation, Akademikerne. This rupture was followed by the departure of a further five unions in June 1998. These 12 unions had 90,000 members. The breakaway unions believed that AF had become dominated by public sector unions representing members with lower educational qualifications, such as nurses and teachers, and was failing to represent the needs and interests of their own higher qualified memberships. Akademikerne was to be open only to employees with master's degrees or higher.

In Jan. 1999 the Norwegian Society of Engineers (NITO), AF's second largest affiliate, said it would also leave AF at the end of 1999, saying it had become merely a bargaining cartel for teachers and nurses in the public sector and was no longer a confederation. This meant AF had lost half its membership. Those unions remaining were mainly in the public sector, including associations of librarians, tax inspectors, midwives, nurses, physiotherapists, air traffic controllers and teachers. In May 1999 newly elected AF leader Aud Blankholm agreed in principle with YS leader Randi Bjørgen on the merger of their two organizations. However, this plan ultimately foundered in the face of opposition from both AF and YS unions, which opposed the planned greater centralization in the merged organization, leading AF unions apparently believing they could survive better on their own. In June 2000, the AF council announced that the merger had been abandoned and that the AF itself would be dissolved with effect in the first six months of 2001.

International affiliations. ICFTU; ETUC; TUAC; NFS; EUROCADRES

Landsorganisasjonen i Norge (LO)
Norwegian Confederation of Trade Unions

Address. Youngsgata 11, 0181 Oslo

Phone. +47 23 06 10 50

Fax. +47 23 06 17 43

Website. www.lo.no (Norwegian; English section)

Leadership. Yngve Hågensen (president)

Membership. 830,000 (of which about three-quarters are in employment)

History and character. The LO (literally the National Organization in Norway) was founded in 1899 and was initially known as the Arbeidernes Faglige Landsorganisasjon i Norge (Workers' Federation of Trade Unions in Norway). Its status was secured during the inter-war years and entrenched in the first of the Basic Agreements in 1935. Following World War II the LO played a leading role in the building of the social state. Agreements between the LO and the Confederation of Norwegian Business and Industry (NHO) have continued to provide the basic structure for industrial relations and incomes policy in the economy as a whole. Historically, the LO has maintained considerable central power over its affiliates and has been much more centralized than the other Norwegian confederations.

The LO remains much the biggest of the Norwegian confederations although its share of the organized workforce has fallen with the rise of rival confederations, based mainly in the white collar sector, since the 1970s. In 1999 it represented 56% of the unionized work force. It dominates in manufacturing industry, where unionization rates are high. It has cooperation agreements with the AF and some independent unions, notably the large Norwegian Union of Teachers.

There is a deep historical identification with the Labour Party (DNA) although the former practice whereby trade union branches were given collective memberships in the party ended in the 1990s. The LO and Labour Party have a joint committee where the organizations' leaders (including the Prime Minister when Labour is in office) meet on a weekly basis and the LO's president, and the leaders of its largest affiliates,

are on the Labour Party executive committee. The Labour Party has been the leading party of government since the 1930s, and Cabinet ministers have commonly come from the LO ranks. In the 1997 elections the LO provided 2.5m. NOK for direct campaign support for the LO. Some of the LO's affiliates have constitutions declaring them to be politically independent, and there is also a degree of support for other parties within the LO, with some affiliates providing financial support for the Socialist Left party (SV). The close identification of the LO with the Labour Party has proved both a strength in securing union influence on government and a weakness in enabling the development of other albeit smaller confederations that emphasize their politically non-partisan position.

During the early 1990s Norway experienced an economic downturn and rising unemployment. The LO, NHO and Labour government entered a social pact, the "solidarity alternative" that provided for wage moderation in return for commitment to job creation. Unemployment dropped steadily from 6% in 1993 to 3% and the 1997 LO congress (the most recent) reaffirmed its commitment to a continuation of the solidarity alternative. Although Labour lost office in elections later in 1997 the incoming minority government retained the main outlines of the pact. Smaller union and employer confederations have been critical of the dominance of centralized bargaining and the development of industrial policy by the LO and NHO and there has been an opening up of tripartite committees to other unions since the change of government in 1997.

The LO has sought to modernize its image to reflect changes in the work place. Its image as a male-dominated blue-collar manufacturing confederation had proved problematic with the increase in services in the private sector and the rise of public sector unions with heavily female memberships. 45% of LO members are now women compared with one-third in the early 1980s. Although its 1997 congress rejected a formal policy of setting a quota for women to sit on its ruling bodies, five of the top eight leaders elected were women. The LO has also promoted active campaigns to recruit younger members and to recruit those with higher qualifications. However, its basic position remains in support of flattening pay differentials (which in Norway in any case tend to be relatively modest) and other confederations have dominated the recruitment of better-paid white-collar and professional employees.

The LO comprises 27 national unions, varying in size from under 1,000 members to the 239,000-member municipal employees' union. Their representatives meet in congress every four years. There are 15,000 local branches at enterprise level and 3,000 local unions. In 1994 the LO established four cartels grouping unions for the development of sectoral policy and bargaining purposes, covering central government (LO State), local government (LO Municipal), private sector industry (LO Industry) and services (LO Services). The objective was to provide better coordination for collective bargaining, but the individual unions still lead the bargaining process. Most blue-collar unions are, in accordance with an LO policy adopted in 1923, based on the industrial union principle (i.e. so that all workers in one plant are members of the same union); however, there are exceptions in the white-collar field.

Both the Labour Party and the LO have been divided over the issue of Norwegian accession to the EU. In 1994, a Labour conference voted two-to-one in favour of joining, but at an extraordinary congress the LO narrowly voted against. In a Nov. 1994 referendum the electorate as a whole voted not to join. The EU dimension is nonetheless seen as important by the LO, which maintains a Brussels office, and it advocates the development of framework industry agreements at the European level. In common with other Scandinavian centres it also has an active international solidarity programme, now working with unions in central and eastern Europe as well as the Third World.

Since the 1960s the LO has adopted a series of so-called Programmes of Action. The latest of these, covering the period 1997–2001, is called "Equity". It calls for work for all, equitable distribution of wealth, protection of the social state, the development of co-determination in industry, national ownership of natural resources and the development of a "strong, cost-conscious and service-minded public sector with a view to counteracting privatization of public services".

The LO operates a workers' educational association (AOF) and there is a People's Correspondence School, owned jointly by the labour movement and the cooperatives. The LO is a co-owner of an insurance company. The trade union movement has also for more than 50 years had its own bank, the Landsbanken NS. The Framfylkingen is a children's organization within the labour movement.

Publication. LO Aktuelt.

International affiliations. ICFTU; ETUC; NFS; TUAC

Affiliates. The following LO affiliates each have at least 30,000 members:

EL & IT Forbundet
Address. Youngsgata. 11, 0181 Oslo
Phone. +47 23 06 34 00
Website. www.elogit.no (Norwegian only)
Leadership. Anders Kristoffersen (president)
Membership. 41,154
History and character. Founded in 1999 by merger of the unions of Electricians and Power Station Workers and Data and Telecommunications workers.

Fellesforbundet
United Federation of Trade Unions
Address. Lilletorget 1, 0184 Oslo
Phone. +47 23 06 31 00
Fax. +47 23 06 31 01
E-mail. felesforbundet@fellesforbundet.no
Website. www.fellesforbundet.no (Norwegian; English section)

Leadership. Kjell Bjørndalen (president)
Membership. 155,000
History and character. Founded in 1988 by the merger of five unions representing workers in the clothing, building, iron and metal, paper, and forestry and land industries. It is the largest private sector union in Norway and, reflecting the breadth of occupations represented, is affiliated to several international trade secretariats (ITGLWF, IFBWW, IMF, ICEM, IUF, ITF). It is leading initiatives for the coordination of collective bargaining at the Nordic level. Fellesforbundet has staff of about 156 at head office and 18 district offices.

Norsk Arbeidsmandsforbund (NAF)
Norwegian Union of General Workers
Address. Postboks 8704, Youngstorget 0028 Oslo
Phone. +47 23 06 10 50
Leadership. Arnfinn Nilsen (president)
Membership. 32,035

Handel og Kontor I Norge (HK)
Union of Employees in Commerce and Offices
Address. Youngsgt. 11, 0181 Oslo
Phone. +47 23 06 11 80
Website. www.handelogkontor.no (Norwegian only)
Leadership. Sture Arntzen (president)
Membership. 60,111

Norsk Kjemisk Industriarbeiderforbund (NKIF)
Norwegian Union of Chemical Industry Workers
Address. Youngsgt. 11, 0181 Oslo
Phone. +47 23 06 13 40
E-mail. nkifpost@nkif.no
Website. www.nkif.no (Norwegian only)
Leadership. Olaf Støylen (president)
Membership. 31,777

Norsk Kommuneforbund (NKF)
Norwegian Union of Municipal Employees
Address. Augustsgt. 23, 0164 Oslo
Phone. +47 23 06 25 00
E-mail. post@nkf.no
Website. www.nkf.no (Norwegian only)
Leadership. Jan Davidsen (president)
Membership. 239,952
History and character. This public sector union is the largest LO affiliate.

Norsk Naerings– og Nytelsesmiddelarbeiderforbund (NNN)
Norwegian Union of Food, Beverage and Allied Workers
Address. Postbox 8719 Youngstorget, 0028 Oslo
Phone. +47 22 20 66 75
Fax. +47 22 36 47 84
E-mail. firmapost.nnn@nnn.no
Website. www.nnn.no (Norwegian only)
Leadership. Torbjørn Dahl
Membership. 36,552

Norsk Post og Kommunikasjonsforbund
Address. Møllergata 10, 0179 Oslo
Phone. +47 23 06 22 50
Website. www.postkom.org (Norwegian only)
Leadership. Odd Christian Øverland (president)
History and character. Founded 2000 by the merger of two

LO affiliates, the Norwegian Postal Organization and the Norwegian Union of Postmen.

Norsk Tjenestemannslag (NTL)
Norwegian Civil Service Union
Address. Møllergata 10, 0179 Oslo
Phone. +47 23 06 15 99
Fax. +47 23 06 15 55
E-mail. post.ntl@loit.no
Website. www.ntl.no (Norwegian only)
Leadership. Turid Lilleheie (president)
Membership. 46,599

Yrkesorganisasjonenes Sentralforbund (YS)
Confederation of Vocational Unions

Address. PB 9232, Grønland, 0134 Oslo

Phone. +47 21 01 36 00

Fax. +47 21 01 3720

E-mail. torilm@ys.no (international affairs)

Website. www.ys.no (Norwegian only)

Leadership. Randi Bjørgen (president)

Membership. 243,528

History and character. The YS was founded in 1977 as a politically independent alternative to the LO. Although recruiting especially in growing white-collar areas, it is a more general confederation than the educationally-based AF and has consequently competed more for members with the LO. A large majority of its members are in the public sector and two-thirds are women. Most of those in the private sector are in banking and insurance.

In May 1999 YS leader Randi Bjørgen proposed merger with the AF, which had suffered the defection of half its membership to the newly formed Akademikerne. The June 1999 YS conference approved the merger in principle. Ultimately, however, opposi-

tion grew within the YS to what was seen as the increased centralization involved in the planned new organization, and in June 2000 the AF announced it would dissolve. Central coordination has traditionally been much looser in the YS than in the LO. As a result of the collapse of the AF, the YS is now the leading confederation behind the LO.

Affiliates. The YS comprises 17 affiliated unions, the largest of which are:

Kommunalansattes Fellesorganisasjon (KFO, municipal employees)
Address. Brugata 19, 0134 Oslo
Phone. +47 21 01 36 00
Fax. +47 21 01 36 50
E-mail. kfo–post@kfo.no
Website. www.kfo.no (Norwegian only)
Membership. 53,495

Norsk Helse– og Sosialforbund (NHS, Norwegian Association of Health and Social Care Personnel)
Address. Postboks 151, Bryn, 0611 Oslo
Phone. +47 22 07 25 00
Fax. +47 22 07 25 10
E-mail. nhs@nhs.no
Website. www.nhs.no (Norwegian only)
Leadership. Tove Stangnes (president)
Membership. 52,337

Finansforbundet (Finance Sector Union)
Address. PO Box 9234 Grønland, 0134 Oslo
Phone. +47 22 05 63 00
Fax. +47 22 17 06 90
Website. www.finansforbundet.no
Leadership. Dag Arne Kristensen (president); Jan G. Haanaes (general secretary)
Membership. 36,000

Oman

Capital: Muscat
Population: 2.53 m. (2000 est.)

1 Political and Economic Background

The Sultanate of Oman is ruled by decree of the Sultan. There are no political parties and there is no parliament although there is an appointed Consultative Council. Most decisions are taken by the ruling family, in consul-

tation with other leading citizens. Criticism of the Sultan is forbidden by law.

Oman has a mixed economy with a heavy dependence on oil, reserves of which are modest. The government is trying to encourage private investment and diversification. Agriculture is mainly at a subsistence level, with most food imported. At least 50% of the total work force are foreigners (including an overwhelming majority in the private sector), coming mainly from South Asia, and the government is seeking to reduce the dependence on foreign labour.

GDP (purchasing power parity) $19.6bn. (1999 est.); GDP per capita (purchasing power parity) $8,000 (1999 est.).

2 Trade Unionism

Oman joined the ILO in 1993 but has not ratified ILO Convention No. 87 (Freedom of Association and Protection of the Right to Organize, 1948) or Convention No. 98 (Right to Organize and Collective Bargaining, 1949). Trade unions are illegal and do not exist inside Oman. The WFTU recognizes an exile National Committee of Omani Workers.

There is no provision for collective bargaining and wages and other conditions are set by employers within guidelines from the Minister of Labour and Social Affairs. The law requires the formation of joint labour-management committees in enterprises with more than 50 workers, but these are not authorized to discuss wages, hours, or conditions of employment. There is an absolute legal prohibition on strikes and none have been reported in recent years. Individual or (less commonly) collective grievances may be referred to the Labour Welfare Board, and this is a frequently used mechanism.

Pakistan

Capital: Islamabad
Population: 141.55 m. (2000 est.)

1 Political and Economic Background

Pakistan became an independent state following the partition of the British Indian Empire in 1947. East Pakistan seceded (as Bangladesh) in 1971. Military interventions in politics have been frequent, with the military ruling directly for 24 of the 53 years since independence.

In 1977 a military coup brought to power General Zia ul-Haq, who overthrew the Pakistan People's Party (PPP) government of Zulfiquar Ali Bhutto. Bhutto was executed by the military regime in 1979 but in elections in 1988, after Zia's death, the PPP became the largest party and Bhutto's daughter, Benazir Bhutto, Prime Minister. However, following accusations of corruption, she was dismissed in 1990 by the President in a move backed by the military. A new government under Nawaz Sharif lasted less than three years before it too was dismissed on corruption charges. New elections in 1993 brought Bhutto back to office as leader of the largest single party, but without an overall majority. Her government fell in late 1996 and elections in Feb. 1997 delivered a convincing victory to Nawaz Sharif and his Pakistan Muslim League (PML–N). However, on Oct. 12, 1999, Gen. Pervez Musharaff seized power in a bloodless coup, suspended Parliament and declared a state of emergency. Gen. Musharaff, whose coup appeared to have a measure of support within the country, said his objectives were to restore economic stability, root out corruption and build strong civil insti-

tutions. Nawaz Sharif was subsequently put on trial in connection with his efforts to stop the coup, convicted of hijacking and terrorism, and sentenced to life imprisonment, but in Dec. 2000 allowed to go into exile.

Pakistan's economy is primarily agricultural, with rice and cotton as the main agricultural exports. The modern sector of the economy is limited, and there is extensive use of child labour in some small-scale industries such as brick kilns, glass making, and carpets. In the 1990s successive governments have said they intended to liberalize the economy, attract foreign investment, privatize state enterprises and control Pakistan's perennial problems with public debt and inflation. However, the weakness of governments has been reflected in the indifferent rate of implementation of such goals and in May 1999 the IMF suspended the disbursement of structural adjustment funds for that reason. After taking power, Gen. Musharraf said he would resume the privatization programme and it was announced in Mar. 2000 that 90% of the revenues raised from sale of state assets would be used towards repaying the public debt.

GDP (purchasing power parity) $282bn. (1999 est.); GDP per capita (purchasing power parity) $2,000 (1999 est.).

2 Trade Unionism

In 1949 an All Pakistan Confederation of Labour (APCOL) was founded, with affiliates in East and West Pakistan, and which adhered to the ICFTU. In 1962 dissatisfied affiliates of APCOL, notably the Petroleum

Workers' Federation and the Cigarette Labour Union, formed the Pakistan National Federation of Trade Unions (PNFTU), with 59 member unions at that time. A further series of splits in APCOL led to it losing its ICFTU affiliation while the PNFTU gained ICFTU affiliated status in 1964. APCOL's component parts each claimed the name West Pakistan Federation of Trade Unions simultaneously until one faction changed its name to the All-Pakistan Federation of Trade Unions (APFTU) and it too affiliated to the ICFTU. The third contemporary ICFTU affiliate is the All-Pakistan Federation of Labour (APFOL).

Attempts at unity between the various national centres have been made from time to time, without success. As a result Pakistan still has three ICFTU affiliates (APFOL, APFTU, PNFTU), the WCL one (All-Pakistan Trade Union Congress, APTUC) and the WFTU claims to have five. The three ICFTU affiliates joined in an alliance as the Pakistan Workers' Confederation (PWC) in October 1994. They pledged not to compete for members and to extend their cooperation in extending recruitment. Many unions are highly politicized, reflecting divergent political streams. Other unions are not directly involved in politics.

Although the unions dispute these figures, the government estimates union members make up only about 10% of the industrial labour force and 3% of the total estimated workforce. Large sections of the labour force are in the informal sector and there is widespread use of contract labour. Where employers are opposed, the process of union registration can be extremely protracted and costly and union organizers can be victimized during the registration process.

Trade unions have been subject to periods of repression and government intervention throughout Pakistan's history, and were weakened by the loss of East Pakistan (a stronghold of militancy) as Bangladesh in the early 1970s. Numerous restrictions were placed on trade union activity under martial law from 1977, when strikes and some unions were banned, though these restrictions eased after the ending of martial law in 1985.

It remains the case that there are no, or severely restricted, trade union rights for many workers. These include teachers, radio and television, forestry, railway workers, agricultural workers, hospital workers, civil servants, supervisory and managerial staff, workers in export processing zones and those working in state enterprises such as oil and gas production, electricity generation and transmission, the state-owned airline (Pakistan International Airlines), and ports. Where workers may not form unions they can in some cases join associations, but these have limited powers and cannot engage in collective bargaining or strike. In 1997, the Supreme Court overturned a ban in force since 1978 on the right to form trade unions and bargain collectively at the Pakistan Television Corporation and the Civil Aviation Authority, but maintained a ban on strikes.

Under the Essential Services Maintenance Act of 1952 (ESA), the government can declare any service or enterprise a public service utility and limit workers' rights.

Striking in an industry or service designated under the ESMA carries a penalty of up to one year's imprisonment. Under the Act, the Government must make a finding, renewable every 6 months, on the limits of union activity. Particular controversy has arisen in respect of the application of the legislation to the Water Power and Development Authority (WAPDA), employing 140,000 workers, where all union activity was banned in Dec. 1998 after the military took control of its operations.

While the legislation prohibits employers from discriminating against union members, such discrimination occurs. Workers are discouraged from pursuing cases through the labour courts because of the cost, delays and what is perceived as widespread corruption.

Although the 1969 Industrial Relations Ordinance (IRO) provides for collective bargaining by legally constituted unions, the restrictions on forming unions mean that collective bargaining is denied to many sectors of the workforce, including most agricultural workers and those employed in the public sector.

In addition, it is not uncommon for employers to maintain their own controlled unions, and in some cases, to refuse to recognize a bargaining agent. The IRO enforces the establishment of only one 'Certified Bargaining Agent' where bargaining with management is permitted. The formal restrictions on lockouts by employers are as extensive as are those on strikes, but unions claim that practice is less even-handed. Where collective bargaining is prohibited under ESA, tripartite wage boards decide on pay, with disputes referred to the National Industrial Relations Commission.

The law formally prohibits acts of recrimination by employers against those involved in legal strikes. However, strikes are infrequent, and usually illegal and of short duration. Compulsory conciliation procedures and cooling-off periods constrain the right to strike, and the government may ban strikes that may cause "serious hardship to the community" or prejudice the national interest or have continued for 30 days.

Unions are affected by general crackdowns on opposition and dissent. The 1999 Antiterrorism Ordinance, adopted under the Sharif government, provided for sentences including imprisonment for terrorist acts, which were defined to include acts of "civil commotion", including illegal strikes, go-slows, and lockouts. On Mar. 16, 2000, the new military government announced a ban on all outdoor political rallies, strikes, processions and demonstrations.

Pakistan ratified ILO Convention No. 87 (Freedom of Association and Protection of the Right to Organize, 1948) in 1951 and Convention No. 98 (Right to Organize and Collective Bargaining, 1949) in 1952. The ILO has, however, frequently criticized Pakistan for violations of these Conventions, and others relating to forced and child labour. In 1997 the government and unions agreed to establish a committee to examine the labour laws and draft legislation to bring them into conformity with ILO conventions and the national constitution, but no changes to legislation had been made prior to the military coup of Oct. 1999. The United States revoked generalized system of preferences (GSP) trade benefits in 1996 for failure to make progress on worker rights issues. However, the European Commission has failed to take similar action despite pressure from the ICFTU and other bodies.

3 Trade Union Centres

All-Pakistan Federation of Labour (APFOL)

Address. Union Plaza, Plot No. 3, Bank Road 62, GPO Box 1709, Rawalpindi

Phone. +92 51 520 137

Fax. +92 51 513 348

E-mail. apfol@isb.paknet.com.pk

Leadership. Zahoor Awan (general secretary)

History and character. APFOL was founded in 1951 by Rahmatullah Khan Durrani ('the father of labourers'), who remained central president until his death in 1985. On his death the presidency was claimed by his son, Auranzeb. This succession was challenged and Auranzeb seceded to found a federation known as APFOL, Durrani Group, which allied with the WFTU.

International affiliations. ICFTU; CTUC

All-Pakistan Federation of Trade Unions (APFTU)

Address. Bakhtiar Labour Hall, 28 Nisbat Road, Lahore

Phone. +92 72 22192

Fax. +92 72 39529

E-mail. apftu@brain.net.pak

Leadership. Ghulam Miran Kashmiri (president); Khurshid Ahmed (general secretary)

Membership. 602,300

History and character. The West Pakistan Federation of Labour was founded in 1947, following the establishment of Pakistan, and was part of the All-Pakistan Confederation of Labour. The organization was subsequently renamed first as the West Pakistan Federation of Trade Unions and then, following the secession of East Pakistan (Bangladesh), as the All-Pakistan Federation of Trade Unions. The late president, Bashir Ahmed Bakhtiar, was a co-founder in 1947.

The APFTU describes itself as an independent trade union without political links, and seeks to unify the trade union movement to press the government to formulate labour policy in conformity with ILO Conventions No. 87 and No. 98, including the repeal of the Essential Services Act and the restoration of trade union rights to public sector employees. The APFTU joined the umbrella organization the Pakistan Workers' Confederation (PWC) on its formation in 1994 (see above) and APFTU general secretary Khurshid Ahmed is also general secretary of the PWC.

APFTU established Pakistan's first-ever Institute for Education, Training and Research in Labour Studies, which provides for the training of trade union representatives. It has set up a range of welfare projects.

The Pakistan WAPDA Hydro Electric Central Labour Union, with 140,000 members, is APFTU's largest industrially based affiliate. The union campaigned against the part privatization of WAPDA, and in Dec. 1998 the government suspended the union and handed over the management of WAPDA to the armed forces.

Publication. PAK Workers (monthly, in English and Urdu)

International affiliations. ICFTU; CTUC

All-Pakistan Federation of United Trade Unions (APFUTU)

Address. Union House, Rangpura, Sargodha Road, Gujrat

Phone. +92 4331 28736

Fax. +92 4331 525302

Leadership. Choudhry Riaz Ahmed (president); Muhammad Shakeel Janjua (senior vice–president); Pirzada Imtiaz Syed (general secretary)

Membership. 183,435.

History and character. APFUTU was founded in 1992 and registered in 1993. It affiliated to WFTU in 1993 but now has no international affiliation. Affiliates are diverse and include unions in areas such as brick kilns, textile mills, banks, sugar mills, yellow cabs, jute, and municipal offices, as well as general labour unions and the Pakistan Bonded and Child Labour Liberation Front (PBCLF).

Publications. APFUTU News (quarterly, in Urdu)

International affiliations. None

All-Pakistan Trade Union Congress (APTUC)

Address. 1st Floor, Delhi Muslim Hotel, Aram Bagh Road, PO Box 1004, Karachi

Phone. +92 21 2626142

Fax. +92 21 7780240

Leadership. A. H. Shirazi (president); Shouket Ali (secretary general)

International affiliation. WCL

All-Pakistan Trade Union Federation (APTUF)

Address. 14-N Industrial Area, Gulberg, Lahore

Fax. +92 42 751 5252

E-mail. rjapwsl@nexlinx.net.pk

Leadership. Rubina Jamil (chair)

International affiliations. WFTU; CTUC

Pakistan National Federation of Trade Unions (PNFTU)

Address. 406 Qamar House, M. A. Jinnah Road, Karachi 74000

Phone. +92 21 231 3371

Fax. +92 21 331 0981

E-mail. pnftu@cyber.net.pk

Leadership. Mohammad Sharif (president)

International affiliation. ICFTU; CTUC

Palau

Capital: Koror
Population: 19,000 (2000 est.)

GDP (purchasing power parity) $160m. (1997 est.); GDP per capita (purchasing power parity) $8,800 (1997 est.).

1 Political and Economic Background

Palau (also known in its local form as Belau) comprises 300 islands in the western Pacific and since 1994 has been an independent nation in free association with the United States. There is subsistence agriculture and fishing but the government employs half the workforce and Palau is dependent on financial assistance from the US.

2 Trade Unionism

The Constitution provides the right to organize and bargain collectively but there are no functioning trade unions. There is no constitutional provision of a right to strike. Palau is not a member of the ILO.

Panama

Capital: Panama City
Population: 2.81 m. (2000 est.)

1 Political and Economic Background

Panama has a history of political instability and military involvement in government. During the 1980s, despite a façade of civilian government, the effective ruler was Gen. Manuel Noriega, the commander of the National Guard. In 1989, however, after Noriega annulled the result of a presidential election, US troops invaded, deposed Noriega, and installed the elected President, Guillermo Endara Gallimany. Three years later Endara faced a massive crisis in the shape of riots against unemployment and official corruption, ruining a brief visit by US President Bush. The following year his administration began to disintegrate ahead of the 1994 elections. These were won by the centre–right Democratic Revolutionary Party (PRD), whose nominee, Ernesto Balladares took office as president in Sept. 1994. In the most recent elections, in May 1999, Mireya Moscoso (widow of former President Arnulfo Arias) was elected president as the candidate of the Union for Panama coalition led by her Arnulfist Party (PA). However, the unicameral legislative assembly was dominated by a coalition of opposition parties, led by the PRD. Gen. Noriega is currently serving a 40–year sentence in the USA for racketeering and drug trafficking.

The Panamanian economy is dominated by services, with shipping and port services linked to the Panama Canal pivotal. Formal ownership and control of the Canal passed from the USA to Panama on Dec 31. 1999, also ending 89 years of US military presence in the country. During the 1990s the government sought to liberalize trade, attract foreign investment, privatize state enterprises and reform the labour code.

GDP (purchasing power parity) $21bn. (1999 est.); GDP per capita (purchasing power parity) $7,600 (1999 est.).

2 Trade Unionism

Trade unions were recognized under the 1946 constitution, and Panama ratified ILO Convention No. 87 (Freedom of Association and Protection of the Right to Organize, 1948) in 1958 and Convention No. 98 (Right to Organize and Collective Bargaining, 1949) in 1966. There have been repeated revisions of the labour code. Historically, the WCL, ICFTU and WFTU have all been represented in Panama and that remains the case. The centres have cooperated with each other in a coordinating organization, CONATO.

Private sector workers are free to join unions and according to official statistics there are 80,000 union members in the private sector, with seven confederations and 250 unions. Legislation adopted in 1995 made it simpler to register unions but also introduced greater flexibility in the labour market. In 1997 a law was passed to regulate collective bargaining and provide a framework for settling disputes in the export processing zones.

Public employees may not join unions but a 1994 law allows the formation of public employee associations, which may engage in collective bargaining, although multiple associations in the same institution are not allowed. In 1998, the government refused to allow the FENASEP public service federation to affiliate to the trade union centre, Convergencia Sindical. The great majority of public sector workers do not have the right to strike. In the public sector political patronage is commonplace and wholesale dismissals of opponents occur after a change of government.

3 Trade Union Centres

Confederación General de Trabajadores de Panamá (CGTP)

Address. Av. 3, Casa n° 15, Perejil, Apartado 3370, Zona 4, Panama City

Phone. +507 2 645 101

Fax. +507 2 235287

E-mail. cgtpfu@sinfo.net

Leadership. Mariano Mena (secretary general)

International affiliation. WCL

Confederación de Trabajadores de la República de Panamá (CTRP)
Confederation of Workers of the Republic of Panama

Address. Calle 31 No. 3–50, Apartado 8929, Zona 5, Panama City

Phone. +507 225 0259

Fax. +507 221 5985

E-mail. ctrp@sinfo.net

Leadership. Aniano Pinzón Real (secretary–general)

Membership. 35,000 claimed in 13 federations.

History. Founded 1956.

International affiliation. ICFTU

Convergencia Sindical

Address. Ave Perú Final, Casa No. 3936, Apartdao 10536, Zona 4, Panama City

Phone. +507 225 6642

Fax. +507 225 6642

E-mail. converge@sinfo.net

International affiliation. ICFTU

Papua New Guinea

Capital: Port Moresby
Population: 4.93 m. (2000 est.)

1 Political and Economic Background

Papua New Guinea is a parliamentary democracy and has been an independent member of the Commonwealth since full independence from the UK in 1975. Party political allegiances are fluid, with numerous small parties represented in the legislature. Papua New Guinea comprises 1,000 tribes and the world's greatest diversity of languages (800) and there have been continuing secessionist threats from a number of provinces, especially the island of Bougainville, to which limited autonomy was granted in 2000.

Much of the country is remote and rugged with little infrastructure, and 85% of the population live in isolated villages practicing (mainly subsistence) agriculture.

Mineral extraction generates most export revenues. There is a dependence on external aid from Australia and international agencies.

GDP (purchasing power parity) $11.6bn. (1999 est.); GDP per capita (purchasing power parity) $2,500 (1999 est.).

2 Trade Unionism

Papua New Guinea ratified ILO Convention No. 98 (Right to Organize and Collective Bargaining, 1949) in 1976 and Convention No. 87 (Freedom of Association and Protection of the Right to Organize, 1948) in 2000.

The majority of the population lives in isolated villages engaged in subsistence and small-scale agriculture, but in the formal economy there is a substantial trade union presence. About half the 250,000 wage earners in the formal economy are organized in about 50 trade unions. There are legal prohibitions on discrimination against union members and organizers. Unions must be registered with the Department of Industrial Relations to enjoy legal protection, but the government has not used the denial of registration to control unions. Most of the private sector unions are in the Papua New Guinea Trade Union Congress (PNGTUC), while one-third of public sector workers are in the Public Employees' Association. Unions are independent of the government and of political parties.

The ICFTU has complained that the Department of Industrial Relations is slow or fails to investigate complaints against employers by workers who are harassed or dismissed for trying to form unions. It says that multinationals operating in areas such as forestry and plantation agriculture have refused to allow the formation of trade unions and that working conditions in these sectors are poor, with little access to health care or reasonably priced food. Provincial labour offices have few resources to investigate complaints.

The right to engage in collective bargaining is protected by the constitution and is practiced. However, the government has discretionary powers to cancel arbitration awards or wage agreements when they are considered contrary to the national interest. The government itself is a major employer but declines to negotiate, preferring to deal with pay adjustments under the minimum wage legislation. In the 1990s the government pursued labour market flexibility by declining to index-link wages under the legislation. There is increasing use by employers of individual contracts rather than registered agreements achieved through collective bargaining.

Disputes are relatively rare and secret ballots are needed to make strikes legal. In 1999 engineers working for the national airline struck; the employer dismissed the workers and selectively re-hired some of them. The courts ruled that both parties had acted illegally. To combat separatist movements, the government adopted the 1993 Internal Security Act, which limits freedom of assembly and gives broad powers of detention without trial. However, while the government has been accused of human rights abuses in its application of the Act, and the PNGTUC has called for its abolition, it does not seem to have been used against trade unions.

In Nov. 1998 the government announced that it would cut off budget funding in 1999 to its industrial relations institutions, the Arbitration Commission, the Minimum Wages Board, the Office of the Registrar of Trade Unions and the National Tripartite Consultative Council. The move was seen as effectively abolishing these institutions. However, following a work stoppage organized by the PNGTUC, the government abandoned its action.

3 Trade Union Centre

Papua New Guinea Trade Union Congress (PNGTUC)

Address. PO Box 254, Port Moresby

Phone. +675 321 2132

Fax. +675 321 2498

E-mail. daphne@dg.com.pg

Leadership. John Paska (general secretary)

Membership. 70,000

History and character. The PNGTUC was formed in 1970 after the failure of several previous attempts to establish a trade union centre. In the late 1980s the ICFTU and its regional arm APRO gave considerable assistance in turning the PNGTUC into a true national centre, and membership increased from 12 affiliates with 17,000 members in 1986 to 30 affiliates with 60,000 members by June 1988. In Nov. 1998 the PNGTUC successfully took industrial action to stop the government from withdrawing funding for industrial relations institutions.

International affiliations. ICFTU; CTUC

Paraguay

Capital: Asuncion
Population: 5.59 m. (2000 est.)

1 Political and Economic Background

Gen. Alfredo Stroessner took power in a military coup in 1954 and then ruled Paraguay under a permanent state of siege until 1989, winning successive stage-managed elections as the candidate of the right-wing Colorado party, the major force in Paraguayan politics throughout the 20th century. In 1989 Stroessner was overthrown in a "palace coup" led by Gen. Andrés Rodríguez, who in turn was elected President later that year as the Colorado Party candidate. Subsequent elections resulted in victories in 1993 for Juan Carlos Wasmosy and in 1998 for Raúl Cubas Grau, both of the Colorado Party. In March 1999, however, Vice President Luis Maria Argaña was assassinated, apparently as part of a power struggle within the government, with Cubas and former General Lino César Oviedo (who had made a coup attempt against Wasmosy in 1996, but been rehabilitated after Cubas came to power) suspected of involvement. After several days of mounting crisis, with workers on strike and an impeachment vote pending in Congress, Cubas fled to Brazil, where he was given political asylum. He was replaced as President by the leader of the Senate, Luis González Macchi, who formed a government of national unity.

The Paraguayan economy is based on agriculture, fisheries and forestry which together account for 48 per cent of the labour force. There is a large informal sector. Consistent economic policy has been undermined by political faction-fighting.

GDP (purchasing power parity) $19.9bn. (1999 est.); GDP per capita (purchasing power parity) $3,650 (1999 est.).

2 Trade Unionism

Under Stroessner Paraguay ratified ILO Convention No. 87 (Freedom of Association and Protection of the Right to Organize, 1948) in 1962 and Convention No. 98 (Right to Organize and Collective Bargaining, 1949) in 1966. In practice, however, trade unions faced considerable harassment in the Stroessner period. Many trade union activists were exiled following a 1958 general strike. According to the WFTU, Antonio Maidana, the exiled leader of the teachers' association and First Secretary of the Communist Party of Paraguay, who was a leading figure in the 1958 strike, was abducted from Argentina to Paraguay by the regime in 1980 and disappeared without trace.

Nonetheless independent trade unionism developed significantly in the 1980s and the Inter-Trade Union Movement of Paraguayan Workers (MIT–P) was founded in 1985 to unite opposition to the regime. Trade union activists were frequently detained and there were regular reports of torture at the hands of the police and armed forces; the most brutal harassment occurred in the rural areas, as in most Latin American countries.

The fall of Stroessner in 1989 brought a degree of liberalization. Basic union rights and freedoms were incorporated in the country's new constitution of 1992. Public servants, previously allowed to associate only for social and cultural purposes, were permitted to form unions. Restrictions on strikes were reduced. Under the 1993 labour code trade union leaders were given protection from dismissal for union activities, In practice, however, dismissals and harassment of union organizers have reportedly remained fairly common, and employers have sometimes disregarded court orders to reinstate unionists. Collective bargaining is said to be increasing but only involves a minority of workers. Strikes are a common occurrence.

There are an estimated 121,000 members of 1,600 trade unions. There are three trade union centres, two of them (the CNT and CPT) affiliated to the WCL and the other (the CUT) to the ICFTU. The CUT is the largest of the three. In Feb. 1998 the three centres organized a "congress of unity" to discuss the economic, social and political crisis in the country. The same month, the CUT president and Eduardo Ojeda, the general secretary of the CNT, were detained for eight days because of their involvement in a transport workers' demonstration which had closed an avenue in Asuncion.

3 Trade Union Centres

Central Nacional de Trabajadores (CNT)

Address. Calle de Piribebuy 1078 entre Hernandarias y Colón, Asuncion

Phone. +595 21 444 084

Fax. +595 21 492 154

E-mail. cnt@highway.com.py

Leadership. Eduardo Ojeda (secretary-general)

History and character. The CNT originated in 1963 as the Christian Workers' Centre (CCT), taking its present name in 1978.

International affiliation. WCL

Central Unitaria de Trabajadores (CUT)

Address. San Carlos 836, Asuncion

Phone. +595 21 443 939

Fax. +595 21 414 195

History and character. The CUT was formed in 1989 and is now reported to be the largest of the Paraguayan centres. The CUT called an indefinite strike and led demonstrations after the March 1999 assassination of Vice-President Argaña, accusing President Cubas and former General Lino César Oviedo of being behind the killing. The unrest led to Cubas fleeing the country.

International affiliation. ICFTU

Confederación Paraguaya de Trabajadores (CPT)

Address. Calle Yegros No. 1333 y Simon Bolívar, Asuncion

Phone. +595 21 443 184

Fax. +595 21 443 184

Leadership. Gerónimo López (president); Sixto Alonso Mendoza (secretary-general)

History and character. The CPT was founded in 1951 under the influence of the Colorado Party; independent elements gained control during the 1950s, however, and led a general strike in 1958. Following this many trade unionists were exiled, forming a CPT in exile (CPT–E), while the organization within the country was brought firmly under government control. The CPT is now functioning again in Paraguay after its years of exile in Mexico and elsewhere. It still associates with the Colorado Party although the ties have loosened.

International affiliation. The CPT was affiliated to the ICFTU/ORIT until 1974, when its affiliation was suspended. It is now affiliated to the WCL.

Peru

Capital: Lima
Population: 27.01 m. (2000 est.)

1 Political and Economic Background

Peru ended 13 years of military rule in 1980, but the administration of the centre-left Peruvian Aprista Party (APRA) struggled from 1985 to deal with the subversive activities of the Maoist guerrilla movement, Sendero Luminoso (Shining Path) and with economic decline. In 1990 APRA's Alan García was succeeded as President by Alberto Keinya Fujimori. However, in the face of growing internal disarray Fujimori staged a coup with military support in 1992. He thereafter ruled in an increasingly authoritarian manner. In 1993 a new constitution was approved by referendum, and the 1995 presidential elections held under its auspices resulted in Fujimori's return to office. In May 2000 Fujimori was re-elected by an apparently wide margin but a widespread belief that the result was fraudulent led to months of unrest and in Nov. 2000 Fujimori was forced from office. The president of Congress took over pending new elections in Apr. 2001. Although still in existence the Shining Path and Tupac Amarú guerrilla movements have been largely destroyed under Fujimori with key leaders arrested.

Minerals and fish products account for about two-thirds of the country's export earnings. There has been extensive privatization of state-controlled enterprises during the 1990s, including in mining, electricity and telecommunications. However, the Fujimori government confronted increasing economic difficulties at the end of the decade with economic growth lagging behind the increase in population. There is extensive underemployment and widespread poverty.

GDP (purchasing power parity) $116bn. (1999 est.); GDP per capita (purchasing power parity) $4,400 (1999 est.).

2 Trade Unionism

Trade union activities gained strength in the 1920s, assisted by the rise of the populist APRA movement, and a Marxist-influenced General Confederation of Peruvian Workers (CGTP) was established in 1929. However, the trade unions were suppressed in the 1930s, a time of violent labour unrest, and remained generally weak until the 1970s, with intervals of repression.

Peru ratified ILO Convention No. 87 (Freedom of Association and Protection of the Right to Organize, 1948) in 1960 and Convention No. 98 (Right to Organize and Collective Bargaining, 1949) in 1964.

After failing to establish a government of national unity, President Fujimori staged an army-backed presidential coup in Apr. 1992, suspending the constitution and ruling by decree. Legislation introduced by decree in 1992 allowed unions to continue to function but imposed greater restrictions and regulations on their activities. Unions were prohibited from taking part in political activities; workers were prohibited from striking over general economic and social policy issues; names of workers who attended strike meetings had to be given to employers. The law contained a broad definition of "essential" services, including health, electricity, water, gas, energy, sanitation, communications and telecommunications, and public transport, where compulsory arbitration could be imposed.

The 1992 legislation, the new national constitution adopted in Dec. 1993, and other measures such as the 1993 Employment Promotion Act, were intended to increase labour market flexibility. A 1996 measure removed guaranteed rights such as annual paid holidays and bonuses, and industrial accident compensation, and made these subject to bargaining. Procedures for laying off workers were made easier, with an increase in the use of temporary contracts. Only about 5% of the workforce (half of which is in the informal economy) are in unions. Unions are permitted and exist in both the private and public sectors. However, temporary employees may not join unions, and an increasing proportion of the workforce is hired on a temporary basis, although there is a formal (but disregarded) ceiling of 20% on the proportion of employees than can be temporary hires. No effective means exist to oblige employers to reinstate workers who have been dismissed for union activities. The law provides a framework for collective bargaining and the implementation of agreements, although this is reportedly often ignored by employers.

The ICFTU, WCL and WFTU each have an affiliated trade union centre. Many unions were active in the opposition movement that drove Fujimori out of office in the autumn of 2000.

3 Trade Union Centres

Central Autónoma de Trabajadores del Peru (CATP)

Address. Nicolás de Pierola 757, Oficina 300, Apartado 1069, Lima 1

Phone. +51 1 995 84 82

Fax. +51 1 265 37 61

Leadership. Alfredo Lazo Peralta (secretary-general)

International affiliation. WCL

Confederación General de Trabajadores del Peru (CGTP)

History and character. The CGTP was formed in 1968

under the leadership of the Peruvian Communist Party (PCP), and regards itself as the successor to the CGTP formed in 1929. It resisted the policies of Fujimori, leading a series of strikes against privatization and other policies and being involved in the demonstrations that led to his fall in 2000.

International affiliation. WFTU

Confederación Unitaria de Trahajadores del Perú (CUT)

Address. Jirón Oroya No. 224, Lima

Phone. +51 1 330 8221

Fax. +51 1 331 5415

Leadership. Julio Cuadros Manrique (secretary-general)

Membership. 300,000

History, and character. Formed in 1992. The CUT was active in the movement that led to President Fujimori's fall from office in 2000.

International affiliation. ICFTU

Philippines

Capital: Manila
Population: 81.16 m. (2000 est.)

1 Political and Economic Background

The Philippines became independent from the United States in 1946. In 1965 Ferdinand Marcos became President, imposing martial law in 1972 and thereafter ruling by decree. In Aug. 1983, Bengino Aquino, the country's foremost opposition figure, was shot dead at Manila airport upon returning from a three-year period of self-imposed exile in the USA. Aquino's death, in which the military was implicated, had the effect of unifying the growing opposition to the rule of Marcos. In 1986, in the face of a massive "people power" movement, Marcos reluctantly conceded elections, and although he claimed victory over Aquino's widow, Corazon Aquino, he was forced to stand down in the face of the defection of his senior military commanders and US pressure. A new constitution was adopted in 1987. As President, Corazon Aquino dismantled the coercive apparatus of the Marcos regime, and the institutions of the republic's American-style democracy were re-established. Her term was punctuated by unsuccessful military uprisings and growing disillusionment on the left. In 1992 she was followed as President by her Defence Secretary and chosen successor, Fidel Ramos. In May 1998 Joseph Estrada, the candidate of the opposition Struggle of the Nationalist Filipino Masses (LAMMP) party was elected President in succession to Ramos (to whom he had been Vice-President), running on a populist platform that emphasized the needs of the poor and opposition to corruption and Philippines "pork barrel" style of politics. Estrada himself became mired in accusations of corruption and was forced from office in Jan. 2001.

The Philippines economy comprises a large agricultural sector (employing 40% of the workforce) and light industry (including textiles, chemicals, electronics assembly and food processing), although manufacturing employs less than 10% of the workforce. The government has pursued policies aimed at deregulation and privatization. The availability of low-cost skilled labour has encouraged substantial inward investment from Japan and elsewhere. However, with the administration politically weak and beset by charges of cronyism and corruption, confidence in the country among foreign investors fell in 2000. Unemployment stood at 10% in 2000, with GDP growth at 3.5%. An estimated 5.5 million Filipinos, mainly unskilled, work outside the country (especially in the US, Saudi Arabia and Malaysia) and their remittances make an estimated $10bn. annual contribution to the domestic economy.

GDP (purchasing power parity) $282bn. (1999 est.); GDP per capita (purchasing power parity) $3,600 (1999 est.).

2 Trade Unionism

Trade unions were first legalized in 1908 (under US rule) and the first labour congress was held in 1913. The Philippines as an independent state ratified ILO Conventions Nos. 87 and 98 in 1957 and 1953 respectively. Following the declaration of martial law by Marcos in 1972 (when many trade union leaders were dismissed), the labour code was revised in 1974 to curb the right to strike. Unions were resurgent before the fall of Marcos in 1986, playing a role in the wave of "people power" protest that drove him from office. Under Corazon Aquino the labour laws were liberalized.

The 1987 constitution offers 'full protection to labour, local and overseas, organized and unorganized' and commits the country to 'promote full employment and equality of employment opportunities for all.' Both private and public sector workers may join unions. Unions are reported to have organized more than 12% of the total work force of 29.5 million, but according to the government's Bureau of Labor Relations, the number of new union registrations has fallen continuously since 1995. During this time, the number of firms, primarily large employers, that use non-union contract labour has grown, and was given an extra stimulus by the 1998–99 downturn caused by the Asian financial crisis. The ICFTU reports that while the right to join unions is in theory guaranteed, in practice there are many obstacles to workers joining unions and legislation is not adequately enforced in cases where employers act illegally. Employers frequently dismiss activists prior to union registration or certification elections.

Unions may federate freely but there is no united national trade union centre. The Trade Union Congress of the Philippines (TUCP) was founded under Marcos in 1975 to unify the labour movement, but its official backing ensured that it was suspect with sections of the labour movement. It is the ICFTU's sole affiliate and probably the largest centre. Also significant is the WCL's affiliate, the Federation of Free Workers (FFW), while the leading left-wing organization is the May First Labour Movement Centre (KMU). Several other organizations exist and the WFTU claims four affiliates, the National Association of Trade Unions (NATU), the Trade Unions of the Philippines and Allied Services (TUPAS), the National Congress of Workers (Katipunan) and the National Congress of Workers (Kalookan). The different organizations tend to be political and enter (fluid) alliances with each other, with frequent splits and a blurring of identity between trade union organizations and political organizations claiming to be based in the labour movement.

The election of Ramos in 1992, in succession to Aquino, polarized the union centres. The FFW and a faction of the Workers' Strength Labour Centre (LMLC) backed him and some of their leaders were appointed to government posts, among them the FFW vice-president Fil Joson, who headed the Overseas Employment Administration. In contrast the TUCP had endorsed the rival bid for the presidency of Ramon Mitra. In 1993 union campaigns were mounted against the increase in energy prices and the power crisis, the emergency powers taken by President Ramos, inflation and wage issues. But these campaigns also divided the union centres with the militant May First Labour Movement Centre (KMU) opposing the government across the policy range while the TUCP, FFW, and some members of the LMLC tended to be loyalist. In 1993 two KMU breakaway centres, the NCL and BMP, signed a Covenant of Unity with the TUCP and on May 1, 1994 formed a Caucus for Labour Unity (CCU) on a platform of industrial peace. Likewise, during 2000, the "Labour Solidarity Movement", led by the KMU, demanded the removal from office of President Estrada, while federations supporting the president organized as the Caucus for Labour Solidarity Action and Reform.

The labour code provides for the right to bargain collectively for private sector employees and for employees of government owned or government controlled corporations. However, only some 541,000 workers, or 15 percent of union members, are covered by collective bargaining agreements.

Under Marcos there were extensive limitations on strike action but Aquino made radical changes to the country's labour code and established the framework for a more liberal labour relations policy to comply with ratified ILO conventions. It became easier to call a strike in the private sector and employers could no longer recruit strike-breakers or dismiss workers for failing to comply with return-to-work orders. All means of reconciliation must be exhausted before a strike takes place and those leading illegal strikes may be sentenced to prison terms. Public sector workers, although they may form unions, may not strike. In the private sector the Secretary of Labour can intervene to impose compulsory arbitration and order strikers back to work if the strike is in an industry considered to be vital to the national interest. Such action was taken in the case of strikes at the privatized Philippine Airlines in 1998 and again in 1999 in the case of a dockers' strike at the port of Cebu. Industrial action can result in violence, sometimes involving the use of hired company security guards. Cases have been reported of employers refusing to re-hire workers dismissed for strike activities when ordered to do so by the Secretary of Labour. Following the fall of Marcos, a National Conciliation and Mediation Board (NCMB) was established in 1987. This settles most unfair labour practice disputes advanced as grounds for strikes before strikes take place. Disputes not settled by the NCMB can be referred to the quasi-judicial National Labour Relations Commission (NLRC).

The position in the export processing zones (EPZs), and other special economic zones, where 175,000 are employed, is similar to that in many other countries. Although the national labour laws nominally apply, in practice unions are systematically excluded or replaced by company unions; activists are dismissed and blacklisted; companies facing labour problems simply threaten to relocate. Local political leaders and officials generally work with employers to keep the zones union free.

Despite legal prohibitions, there is widespread use of child labour, in areas such as banana and sugar plantations, docks, quarries, and mines, and in domestic service. Forms of child bonded labour are reported.

3 Trade Union Centres

Federation of Free Workers (FFW)

Address. FFW Building, 1943 Taft Avenue, Malate 1004, Manila

Phone. +63 2 524 3150

Fax. +63 2 525 6407

Leadership. Ramon Jabar (president)

Membership. Around 400,000

History and character. The FFW was founded in 1950 and developed with the assistance of the Roman Catholic clergy. The FFW favours a managed, cooperative economy, with profit-sharing and extended social benefits. During the Marcos era it positioned itself as an independent, democratic force, distinct from the government-backed TUCP and left-wing formations such as the KMU. It is one of the WCL's leading Asian affiliates.

The FFW is campaigning to eradicate child labour, launching educational and other schemes in association with civic groups.

International affiliation. WCL

Kilusang Mayo Uno (KMU)
May First Movement Labour Centre

Address. 37-A Quinto's Compound, Tomas Morato Avenue, Quezon City

Fax. +63 2 373 1838

E-mail. kmuid@csi.com.ph

Leadership. Crispin Beltran (chairman)

History and character. Formed on May 1, 1980, the KMU describes itself as the "centre for militant unionism" standing for "freedom, democracy and socialism".

Rolando Olalia, former KMU leader and chairman of the Party of the Nation (Partido Ng Bayan–PNB), was found brutally murdered in 1986, and party leaders attributed his killing to forces within the military. The Armed Forces regarded the KMU as a communist front since its formation and the day before Olalia's assassination, the KMU had stated that it would call a general strike in the event of a military coup (which was widely expected at the time) to overthrow the Aquino government. It boycotted the 1986 elections that brought Aquino to power, but subsequently backed her government while calling for fundamental reforms. During the Aquino presidency it appeared to have increased in strength at the expense of the TUCP, which was seen by some workers as a 'Marcos union', on the basis of militant activity and organization. However it faced widespread accusations that it was provoking unrest for ideological reasons. Aquino at one point threatened to ban the KMU, which for its part complained to the ILO of violations of union rights. It claims to have lost a number of members, killed by government forces, and was the only major union centre not to sign an Industrial Peace Accord in 1990.

At the March 1993 national council a dissident group defected after protesting against the KMU's 1992 election slogan of 'revolution not election'. They subsequently formed groups known as the National Confederation of Labour (NCL) and the BMP.

The KMU campaigned for the removal from office of President Estrada, whom it accused of failing to respond to the needs of low wage earners. It opposes the privatization of state industries such as the National Power Corp. and the "unholy trinity" of the IMF, World Bank and the WTO and has called for the government to stop debt servicing.

It incorporates the militant National Federation of Labour Unions.

International affiliation. None

Trade Union Congress of the Philippines (TUCP)

Address. TUCP/PGEA Compound, Masaya Street, corner Maharlika Street, 1101 Diliman, Quezon City 3008

Phone. +63 2 921 5236

Fax. +63 2 921 9758

E-mail. tucp@easy.net.ph

Membership. Claims 1 million; otherwise reported as 450,000

History and character. The TUCP is the largest trade union centre in the Philippines and reports one million members with 28 federations and 2,544 local unions. It also claims to be the most representative labour centre, having members in private and public sectors, the cooperatives, and the peasant and informal sectors. It was formed with official backing under Marcos in 1975 in response to the implementation of the 1974 labour code, which emphasized the coordination and unification of the trade union movement. Some sections of organized labour subsequently charged the TUCP with being unduly close to the Marcos government; it did, however, mobilize 7,000 volunteers for the watchdog National Citizens' Movement for Free Elections (NAMFREL) which unofficially supervised the 1986 election that preceded Marcos's downfall.

On May Day 1990 the TUCP co-launched Labour Unity for Democracy and Peace with the FFW and LMLC and later that month was a signatory to the Industrial Peace Accord. In 1993 TUCP was in the forefront of a campaign to raise the minimum wage, review employment law and seat representatives of labour on local government councils; in 1995 it pressurized the government over the continued existence of child labour. It is generally considered the most moderate of the various trade union centres, although it expressed reservations about what it saw as a pro-business bias in the Estrada administration.

The TUCP provides a range of services, including legal assistance to affiliate federations; credit and consumer cooperative programmes; free medical and dental services for members; a primary health care program conducted by TUCP doctors and nurses; research and information dissemination for collective bargaining purposes; education and research seminars and training for trade union leaders and members; mass basic trade unionism seminars for members; and assistance to affiliates in organizing campaigns.

TUCP membership totals fell sharply in the early 1990s and it has since tried to broaden its recruitment, including in the export processing zones, where union activity faces considerable employer and official hostility.

International affiliation. ICFTU

Poland

Capital: Warsaw
Population: 38.65 m. (2000 est.)

1 Political and Economic Background

Poland was overrun by Germany and the Soviet Union in World War II and at the war's end became part of the Soviet bloc. The emergence of the Solidarity trade union, led by Lech Walesa, as a political movement in 1980 provoked a crisis in the regime and although martial law was declared in Dec. 1981 and Solidarity suppressed it remained an underground force. In the late 1980s, as part of the weakening of communist rule throughout Eastern Europe, it re-emerged to win elections in 1989 and form the government. In Dec. 1990, Walesa was elected President.

Post-communist politics were characterized by governmental instability and factionalism, with Solidarity itself fragmenting. Against this background, elections in Oct. 1993 resulted in the formation of a government led by the former communists of the Democratic Left Alliance (SLD), itself created from the alliance of the Social Democracy of the Republic of Poland (SdRP) political party and the OPZZ trade union, the official union structure set up after Solidarity was dissolved. In presidential elections in 1995 Walesa was narrowly defeated by Aleksander Kwasniewski, who was backed by the SLD. Elections to the legislature (Sejm) in Sept. 1997, however, resulted in the Solidarity Electoral Action (AWS) coalition winning 201 of the 460 seats, while the SLD came second with 164. The AWS government is led by Prime Minister Jerzy Buzek, a veteran Solidarity leader. In Oct. 2000 presidential elections, President Kwasniewski was re-elected with AWS leader Marian Krzaklewski coming only third, with 15% of the vote.

Since 1989 Poland has accomplished substantial economic reform and 70% of GDP is now generated by the private sector. State control remains in some key sectors such as coal and steel where privatization is a sensitive issue and the Solidarity movement has been divided in approach. In the early 1990s Poland experienced "shock therapy" as it faced the consequences of the dismantling of the state-controlled economy. The immediate results of the 1990 shift to the market were severe but by 1992 Poland had become the first post-communist country to show signs of recovery. By 1994 industrial production was close to the levels preceding the shock therapy of 1990. Poland's adjustment to the market has been one of the most successful in Eastern Europe, and foreign direct investment represents 40% of the total into the whole former Soviet bloc. GDP growth was between 4 and 5% per annum in 1998–99. The government is determined to join the EU at the earliest possible opportunity, although living standards remain substantially below Western European standards and entry to the EU is considered several years away. Inflation (9.8%) and unemployment (13%) continued relatively high in 1999 and the agricultural sector, which provides employment for 25% of the labour force but generates only 5% of GDP, is characterized by inefficient small farms and low investment and is the source of considerable political unrest, with regular peasant demonstrations and blockades in 1999. The opposition SLD, now broadly social democratic, favours EU entry and market-oriented reforms, but with a "social dimension".

GDP (purchasing power parity) $276.5bn. (1999 est.); GDP per capita (purchasing power parity) $7,200 (1999 est.).

2 Trade Unionism

Poland ratified ILO Conventions No. 87 (Freedom of Association and Protection of the Right to Organize, 1948) and No. 98 (Right to Organize and Collective Bargaining, 1949) in 1957.

Communist rule in Poland was punctuated by massive industrial unrest, often accompanied by attempts to establish independent unions. In 1970–71, 44 people were killed in illegal strikes and disturbances on the Baltic coast. In 1976, after huge strikes against falling real incomes, a group of intellectuals formed Komitet Obrony Robotnikow (KOR – workers' defence committee) to assist the families of those dismissed in strikes.

(KOR was subsequently renamed the committee for social self defence – KSS, and joined Solidarity in 1990.) In May 1978 a committee of free trade unions for the Baltic coast was formed under the leadership of Andrzej Gwiazda.

Official trade unionism in Poland was organized by a single body, the Central Council of Trade Unions (CRZZ). In 1980, however, the independent union Solidarity was created and, following massive popular pressure, accorded recognition by the government. At its height Solidarity had 9.5 million members (including agricultural wage earners), while the peasants' organization Rural Solidarity had 2.35 million members and there were 3 million members of branch and autonomous trade unions. For more than a year Solidarity functioned both as a union and as a vehicle for the expression of Polish national, religious and political aspirations, posing an increasingly apparent threat to the role of the ruling Polish United Workers' Party (PUWP) and by implication to the Warsaw Pact alliance. Following repeated rumours in both Poland and the West of the possibility of a Soviet invasion, martial law was declared on Dec. 13, 1981, and Solidarity banned.

The Solidarity organization was formally dissolved by the Trade Union Act of Oct. 1982, which also provided for the creation of a new structure of official trade unions that would take over the property of the dissolved unions. The All-Poland Alliance of Trade Unions (OPZZ) was formed in Nov. 1984 to coordinate the official unions. Amendments to the 1982 Trade Union Act passed by the Sejm in July 1985 confirmed a trade union monopoly by prohibiting the establishment of more than one trade union in any enterprise. Solidarity remained active underground however and in the late 1980s re-emerged as a major political force.

Amid mounting political and economic crisis the regime in Apr. 1989 was forced to agree to the re–legalization of Solidarity and to partially free elections. This process culminated in the formation of the first Solidarity-backed government in Aug. 1989. Since then Solidarity's position has been complicated by the twin identity of Solidarity as a political movement and a trade union, with a history of internal conflict, factionalism and breakaways. After the collapse of communism, the OPZZ positioned itself as opposed to government austerity policies, capitalizing on four consecutive years of falling real wages. OPZZ opposition was joined by some dissident elements within Solidarity and the period was marked by political factionalism. In Sept. 1993 the former communists of the Democratic Left Alliance (SLD, a creation of the Social Democracy (SdRP) party and the OPZZ) came to power and Solidarity returned to opposition. Their roles have again reversed since the election of the Solidarity-based government in 1997.

Solidarity and the OPZZ remain the two trade union centres, but their relative strengths are disputed. In post-communist Poland, no longer a carrier of national aspirations, Solidarity's membership fell steadily. It is now rather more than one million. The OPZZ, in common with former official unions throughout Eastern Europe, claims membership levels in excess of real participation in its structures. While the OPZZ says it has 3 million members, its real strength is considered likely to be of the order of 700,000–800,000. According to a study by the State Labour Inspectorate, out of some 27,000 local union organizations, Solidarity had 13,500 organizations, the OPZZ had 11,000 organizations, and Solidarity '80 (a breakaway from Solidarity) had 770 organizations.

Overall only some 13% of Polish employees are now thought to be in unions. There is little unionization in the emergent private sector economy although unions continue to some degree in privatized state firms.

Reflecting the origins of the OPZZ and Solidarity in the political struggles of the 1980s, unions remain highly politicized. While Solidarity's trade union strength has declined, as a political movement sharing a common origin with the trade union, it leads the government. The complex AWS coalition includes 62 deputies linked to the Solidarity union in the 460 seat Sejm and 27 Senators in the 100-seat upper house, (Senat). Likewise the OPZZ is a core element of the Democratic Left Alliance, the former communists, with 42 Sejm deputies. Hostility between the OPZZ and Solidarity has nonetheless declined with the creation of a pluralist post-communist society, and while there is a legacy of tension in practice they often agree on policy issues. Solidarity is an affiliate of the ICFTU, WCL and ETUC. The OPZZ has no international affiliation, although it has applied to join ETUC.

In July 1991 a new Trade Union Act was adopted, providing the current legal base. Trade unions have the right to bargain collectively and to make agreements and, where there is no agreement, must be consulted. The former distinction between enterprise and other unions was abandoned for the right of any ten people to form a union. Once established, unions may make their own rules subject to certain mandatory inclusions such as the aims of the organization.

The 1991 law provides for disputes to be referred to the labour courts and there are several thousand such referrals each year, while dozens of cases per year go as far as the Supreme Court. In most such cases employees were successful.

Collective bargaining typically takes place at the enterprise level. There is a right to strike except in "essential services" and only one-quarter of the workforce must vote in favour to authorize a strike. There are lengthy pre-strike procedures, however, so a majority of strikes are illegal, although meaningful sanctions are not commonly imposed against unions that call such illegal strikes. Conversely, sanctions imposed against employers who penalize strikers tend to be negligible. Strikes occur fairly regularly as do demonstrations and other forms of protest.

The Tripartite Commission for Social and Economic Issues, founded in 1994, which is chaired by the Minister of Labour, has a role in determining public sector pay, gives opinions on social policy issues, and provides a forum for the resolution of conflict. However, the OPZZ withdrew from the Commission in April 1999 claiming that the government was refusing to discuss issues seriously with it.

3 Trade Union Centres

NSZZ Solidarnosc
Solidarity

Address. ul. Waly Piastowskie 24, 80–855, Gdansk

Phone. +48 58 3010 143

Fax. +48 58 3010 143

E-mail. zagr@key.net.pl

Website. www.solidarnosc.org.pl (Polish; English section)

Leadership. Marian Krzaklewski (president)

Membership. 1,185,000

History and character. The rise, suppression, and ultimate victory of Solidarity was an historic factor in the process which eventually led to the collapse of the Communist bloc.

The elevation of the Pole Karol Wojtyla as Pope John Paul II and his visit to Poland in June 1979, encouraged the fusion of Catholic religious and nationalist sentiments with economic grievances which proved a catalyst in the rise of Solidarity. A rolling wave of strikes began in July 1980 against price rises with Lech Walesa (a Gdansk shipyard worker) emerging as the most prominent leader of the movement. Workers struck at the Lenin shipyards in Gdansk on Aug. 14, occupying the yards, which became the centre of the unrest. On Aug. 16 the inter-factory strike committee (MKS) was formed in Gdansk to coordinate activity, and as a result of negotiations with the MKS held on Aug. 23–30, the government on Aug. 31 conceded (in the "Gdansk accords") the right of workers to form free unions independent of the monolithic structure organized by the Central Council of Trade Unions (CRZZ), with the right to strike, and ancillary demands such as the broadcasting of Masses, Saturday holidays, and greater civil liberties. Government leadership changed, and on Sept. 15 it established a procedure for the registration of the new trade unions in the Court of the Voivodship of Warsaw, outside the CRZZ register, and applied the Gdansk accords nationally.

On Sept. 22, 1980, delegates from 36 regional independent unions met in Gdansk under the name of Solidarity and Walesa's chairmanship. Solidarity applied for registration with the Warsaw Court on Sept. 24.

In October the Sejm adopted an Act to amend the Trade Union Act of 1949, thereby giving statutory validity to the procedure established by the Council of State on Sept. 15, and the following month the Polish Supreme Court overruled a decision by the Warsaw Court that the charter legalizing Solidarity would be invalid without the inclusion in the union's statutes of recognition of the PUWP as the leading political force in the country (although this recognition was by compromise inserted in the annexes to the statutes). This action averted a general strike.

The CRZZ was dissolved in Jan. 1981, most of the former official trade unions having by this time dissolved or voted to become autonomous. In Apr. 1981 the government agreed to recognize the creation of Rural Solidarity, which had held its first congress on March 9; it was registered on May 12. Sept.–Oct. 1981 brought the first Solidarity delegate conference in Gdansk, revealing splits between a Walesa faction which, fearing Soviet intervention and alarmed by persistent industrial disorders and the collapse of productivity, wished to pursue a policy of greater accommodation towards the government, and militants who wished to press broad political demands. On Oct. 2 Walesa was elected chairman of Solidarity, but congress elected a radical-dominated national commission.

The conflict at the congress presaged a continuing dispute over relations with the communist regime, now led by Prime Minister Jaruzelski. In Dec. 1981, the national leadership, contrary to Walesa's advice, voted to call a national referendum in which the people would be asked if they favoured the establishment of an interim government and the holding of free elections, and whether they wished to continue to provide 'military guarantees' to the USSR. The regime responded by establishing a Military Council of National Salvation under Gen. Jaruzelski. Martial law was declared, strikes were banned, Solidarity leaders (including Walesa) arrested and all trade unions suspended; according to government figures, 7,000 persons were interned in detention camps. The representation of the interests of workers was subsequently placed in the hands of social committees set up by the military government in Jan. 1982.

According to the Polish government Solidarity had proceeded beyond the limits of the Gdansk accords and its constitution and under the influence of extremist elements had approached an attempt to seize power; martial law had been necessary to prevent this and end mounting disorder and economic disintegration which posed a threat to Poland and world peace. Particular concern was expressed at Solidarity's appeals to the population of neighbouring countries and its questioning of Poland's international alliances.

The government initially represented the suspension of the newly formed trade unions as a short–term measure. The position and role of the hierarchy of the Church had by this time become ambiguous, the Church supporting the principles of Solidarity but expressing a desire for stability and national unification.

There were no reports of violence or deaths related to the activities of Solidarity in the period from its emergence in the summer of 1980 to its dissolution under martial law, and strikes had been avoided in the health services and some other essential services. Following the imposition of martial law, nine miners died in a confrontation with security forces at the

Wujek mine near Katowice (although most protest strikes were ended relatively peacefully), and according to the ICFTU, WCL, and other reports several dozen persons were killed by the security forces in demonstrations, strikes and other incidents in the following months. There were also numerous reports of torture of detainees, dismissals from employment of previous Solidarity activists and the imposition of loyalty oaths requiring disavowal of support for or sympathy with Solidarity. Extensive purges were also carried out of Solidarity supporters in the judiciary, government service, universities and the media. In decisions of May and July 1982 the Supreme Court held that protection against dismissal under the labour code could not be applied while trade union activities were suspended. Lech Walesa was not released until Nov. 1982 and in Oct. 1983 was awarded the Nobel Peace Prize, provoking a formal complaint by the Polish government.

For four years from 1983 Solidarity maintained an underground identity through a temporary coordinating committee (TKK), while Lech Walesa remained chairman. Its strength appeared to decline steadily and calls for strikes and demonstrations against price rises in 1985 and 1986 were poorly supported. Its activists were victimized and imprisoned, and there several cases of brutal treatment including at least 15 deaths. Proceedings were also briefly brought against Walesa but abandoned. Not until early 1987 were all leading figures released.

In Sept. 1986, Walesa and other leaders formed a public Temporary Council of Solidarity (TRS), to work within the system 'to improve the country's social, political and economic conditions", and to "seek to ease the transition to legal and open undertakings.' It was announced that Walesa would remain titular chairman, but would not be a member of the TRS. Any decision to disband the underground TKK was apparently dependent on the attitude of the government to the TRS. In response, however, the Polish authorities stated that the TRS was illegal, and the Polish Supreme Court on Nov. 16 rejected an appeal by Baltic shipyard workers to create a union called Solidarity on the grounds that the creation of more than one union in an enterprise was forbidden. By Nov. 1986 temporary councils of Solidarity had sought registration in at least 10 provinces. It was reported that the Solidarity leadership was divided on the question of how far it should seek to cooperate with the authorities. In the autumn of 1986 in a gesture of international support both the ICFTU and WCL affiliated Solidarity.

On Oct. 25, 1987, a national meeting of Solidarity activists announced the creation of a National Executive Commission (KKW), with Lech Walesa as chairman. This was in response to fragmentation of the leadership between the TRS and the TKK leading to complaints that it was losing touch with grass-roots support. An application for official registration of the KKW was rejected by a Gdansk court on Nov. 9, and in late 1987 and early 1988 courts rejected several other attempts to obtain registration for Solidarity branches in individual enterprises.

The failure of the government's referendum on economic reform and limited political liberalization gave Solidarity (which had called for a boycott), its chance. In spite of the lack of majority support the government proceeded with the programme, albeit modified, from Feb. 1, 1988, when retail price rises averaging 27% took effect. Solidarity announced it would support local stoppages by workers demanding wage rises. They started almost immediately, and a major wave of strikes began on Apr. 25 when transport workers in Bydgoszcz won a 63 per cent wage increase after a 12-hour stoppage. This sparked off a strike at the Nowa Huta steelworks near Krakow on the following day, and workers at the Lenin shipyards in Gdansk began a strike on May 2. The authorities reacted by having nine members of the Solidarity KKW arrested, and on May 5 police stormed the Nowa Huta steelworks and arrested the strike coordinators. The strike at the Lenin steelworks was called off on May 10 without any concessions from the authorities. Some of those arrested remained in police custody until May 25, and 19 workers lost their jobs at Nowa Huta.

But now a further wave of strikes began on Aug. 15–18 with the occupation of mines in the Silesian coalfields, and by Aug. 22 the action had spread to enterprises in several cities, including the Lenin shipyard, prompting the declaration of a curfew in the three worst affected provinces. Following mediation by Roman Catholic Church representatives, Walesa held talks with the Interior Minister, Lt.-Gen. Kiszczak, on Aug. 31, and the strikes were called off after Walesa had received guarantees that the government would involve Solidarity in proposed round-table discussions, and was prepared to consider the union's re–authorization. However, these discussions failed to convene following arguments about procedure and participants. Doubts were cast on the sincerity of the government by a leaked PUWP document that declared that the re-legalization of Solidarity was the main danger facing the party and would not be permitted. Furthermore, Solidarity interpreted as a deliberate provocation a government decision announced on Oct. 31 to use special powers of intervention in the management of enterprises, which it had acquired under a temporary law of May 31, to close the Lenin shipyards on Dec. 1.

The final collapse of communist government was attended by further industrial and political action by local Solidarity unions. In Jan. 1989 alone there were 173 pay disputes and 39 strike situations. By this time it was clear that no solution to the crisis could be found without the involvement of Solidarity. On Feb. 6, against a background of increasing economic chaos, the government opened "round table" talks with Solidarity (which was still nominally illegal). After two months of talks with an increasingly impotent government, the seven-year ban on Solidarity was lifted and partly democratic elections were announced for June. Solidarity formally applied for registered status, declaring that the National Executive Commission (KKW) would administer the movement until a congress could be held.

In the elections of June 1989 (when 65% of Sejm seats were still reserved for communist-sponsored deputies) Solidarity swept the board, candidates it supported winning every one of the freely contested seats in the Sejm. A prolonged government crisis which found the leading communist candidate unable to form a coalition led to his displacement at the head of a new coalition by Tadeusz Mazowiecki, a Solidarity nominee, with another well known Solidarity figure, Jacek Kuron, as Minister of Labour.

The formation of this government led to a new stage in the history of Solidarity. Factions appeared such as the 'working group' of well-known leaders from 1981 (Andrzej Gwiazda, Jan Rulewski, Seweryn Jaworski) who were opposed to voluntary restrictions on the right to strike, and members of the Polish Socialist Party (Democratic Revolution) who played leading roles in some important localities.

Not until April 1990 did Solidarity finally meet in congress at Gdansk, with membership having fallen to 2.2 million and in confusion over its role because of pressure to support the Solidarity-inspired Maziowecki government. Objectors to lending support to the government included many within the union's ranks, including the "Solidarity 80" faction, and the congress heard many speeches in criticism of the Balcerowicz "shock therapy" programme, with its dismantling of the planned economy, reduction of subsidies, price liberalization, pay curbs, and escalating unemployment. The following month there were widespread strikes by Solidarity unions on the railways which disrupted the approach to local elections.

The election of Walesa as President of Poland in Dec. 1990, followed by his resignation as Solidarity chairman, compounded the movement's difficulties. It met in extraordinary congress in Feb. 1991 to review its role in the changed circumstances and elect a new leadership. Walesa's successor as chairman was Marian Krzaklewski, who had campaigned on a platform of staying free from political entanglements. President Walesa adopted a similar view: 'the union should not and will not replace political parties'.

Solidarity's fourth congress was held in Gdansk in June 1992 and re-elected Krzaklewski as president. Delegates passed a resolution expressing disapproval of the role of President Walesa in the fall of the minority government of Jan Olszewski that month. Solidarity brokered the creation of the successor government of Hanna Suchocka in July 1992 and welcomed a new Enterprise Pact with enthusiasm. Its disillusionment set in as government promises remained unfulfilled and it finally moved a vote of no confidence that brought the government down in May 1993. When at first President Walesa refused to accept Suchocka's resignation, Solidarity threatened a general strike.

The resultant elections in Sept. 1993 were a major setback. The unpopularity of shock therapy economics with the voters, and the internal divisions of the Solidarity coalition, contributed to the return to power of the reformed communists of the Democratic Left Alliance (SLD). However, the new government continued much of the general approach of previous post-communist administrations, and Solidarity entered a period of trade union opposition which gave it a new lease of life as it energetically campaigned to prevent any further falls in the real value of wages. It launched a series of selective strikes designed to force the government away from austerity policies. A nationwide day of action in Apr. 1994 against wage controls combined with disputes in the mines to force the resignation of a minister and concessions out of the government.

In Dec. 1995 Walesa narrowly lost in presidential elections to the SLD's candidate, Aleksander Kwasniewski. In June 1996 the 7th congress initiated the creation of a political coalition, comprising dozens of parties and pressure groups but rooted in mainstream Solidarity, called Solidarity Electoral Action (AWS). This came to power in coalition with the Freedom Union (UW) as a result of elections in September 1997. Dozens of Solidarity activists were elected to Parliament. Jerzy Buzek, an early Solidarity leader, became Prime Minister after Solidarity president Marian Krzaklewski had said he would not take the position.

Again Solidarity faced tensions from its dual identity as a trade union and as the base for a political movement. The identities of the Solidarity trade union and political movement remain blurred, with individuals from the union holding many political positions at national and local level. Krzaklewski, who is seen as a conservative, is an AWS member of the Sejm and president of the AWS party caucus. Solidarity as a union, however, has frequently opposed the Buzek government on economic and labour issues, warning of the adverse impact of otherwise beneficial market reforms on the unemployed and the poor, while at the same time distancing itself from the "destabilizing" activities of the OPZZ and peasant groups. One source of conflict within Solidarity has been the implementation of privatization, with a nationalist–populist wing resistant to further sales to foreign investors and Solidarity members concerned at the impact on jobs and wages. There is also resentment at the continued domination of large areas of the economy and society by the old communist nomenklatura. In Oct. 2000 Krzaklewski ran for president as the candidate of the AWS, but came only third, with the SLD's Kwasniewski being re-elected. The poor result led to renewed calls for Krzaklewski to choose between union leadership and political ambitions.

Solidarity was highly critical of OPZZ's withdrawal from the Tripartite Commission in Apr. 1999. It has criticized the government for not discussing sufficiently with the social partners but has blamed the OPZZ for making constructive dialogue between government and unions more difficult.

By the end of the 1990s the issues facing Solidarity were very different from those a decade earlier. They included the impact of deregulation and privatization, the globalization of the world economy, and the decline of traditional industries; the requirements for reform of the Polish economy and society in pursuit of accession to the EU (which Solidarity supports); and the campaign for improved healthcare, education, social insurance and other social benefits. Solidarity also confronted the problem that while it remains a political force with the voters, as a trade union it has continued to lose members as heavily organized state industries are privatized and new private sector businesses are mainly non-union.

Solidarity has 14,000 enterprise union locals, associated into 38 regions. There are in addition 16 industrially-based national branch secretariats.

Publications. Various bulletins in Polish; *Solidarnosc Newsletter* (in English, monthly)

International affiliations. Since November 1986 Solidarity has been affiliated to both the ICFTU and the WCL, and has argued for the ultimate fusion of the two bodies. It affiliated to ETUC in 1995 and TUAC in 1997. The Solidarity occupational branch unions are affiliated to the various international trade secretariats associated with the ICFTU.

Ogolnopolskie Porozumienie Zwiazkow Zawodowych (OPZZ)
All-Poland Alliance of Trade Unions

Address. ul. Kopernika 36/40, 00–924 Warsaw

Phone. +48 22 826 92 41

Website. www.opzz.org.pl (Polish; English section)

Leadership. Jozef Wiaderny (president)

Membership. Claims 3 million but is estimated at 700,00–800,00.

History and character. The OPZZ was founded in Nov. 1984 to coordinate the new official trade unions set up with government support after the suppression of Solidarity. It was formally registered on April 12, 1985, and the authorities subsequently turned over to it funds impounded upon the suspension of Solidarity in Dec. 1981. Membership in the Soviet bloc trade union international, the World Federation of Trade Unions (WFTU), was reactivated in April 1985.

The OPZZ held its second meeting on Nov. 26–30, 1986, this being declared the first congress of the Polish Reborn Trade Unions. Alfred Miodowicz, its founding chairman, was re-elected by 879 votes to 159, but the abstention of a significant minority of the 1,480 delegates was viewed as expressing dissatisfaction with his election to the communist party (PUWP) politburo in July 1986. This was seen as compromising the asserted independence of the trade union movement. The congress called for the creation of an effective system of consultation between workers and government, and adopted a final resolution which criticized government attempts to centralize control over the labour movement. The final resolution also reversed a decision taken earlier by the congress to constitute the OPZZ as the sole representative of unionized workers. This followed protests that this such a move would jeopardize the

status of the estimated 4,000 non-affiliated trade unions (mostly organized in single factories or enterprises) and would give the OPZZ a public image akin to that of its monolithic pre-Solidarity forebear, the Central Council of Trade Unions (CRZZ).

In Aug. 1987 Miodowicz stated that 'the OPZZ considered itself to be the heir to the 1980 Gdansk accords' between the government and Solidarity and had a moral obligation to ensure their realization. However, he also rejected trade union pluralism in enterprises, commenting that 'a divided workforce serves those who manipulate'. The OPZZ criticized the decision announced at the end of 1985 to reintroduce a six-day working week (the five-day working week, conceded in 1981, having been the last major surviving accomplishment of the Solidarity era), and during 1987–88 it frequently criticized other aspects of government economic policy.

The OPZZ adapted remarkably successfully to the progressive collapse of the communist regime through 1988–89, distancing itself from the regime and seeking to re-position itself as the authentic independent voice of the labour movement even as Solidarity was legalized again in the Spring of 1989. On July 29, 1989, Miodowicz resigned from the politburo of the disintegrating Polish United Workers' Party. In Dec. 1990, the OPZZ withdrew from the work of the WFTU (although all links were not finally severed until 1997). It explained this decision in terms of its modest resources, the pluralistic nature of its own movement, and the diminished coverage of the WFTU itself. Miodowicz was replaced as leader by the former Solidarity activist Ewa Spychalska in Dec. 1991. In the Sejm elections of Oct. 1991 the OPZZ joined forces with the post-communist Social Democracy of the Republic of Poland (SdRP) party (the successor to the former ruling Polish United Workers' Party) to campaign as the Democratic Left Alliance (SLD).

With Solidarity a leading force in government from 1989–93, the OPZZ adopted the position of an opposition trade union organization opposed to the impact of "shock therapy" market economics on jobs, pensioners and public services.

Following the 1993 election of a government led by the Democratic Left Alliance (SLD), the reformed former communists, the OPZZ enjoyed far better relations with the government, generally endorsing its programme but with conflicts over some issues, notably the process of implementation of privatization. The OPZZ was strongly represented among SLD deputies in the Sejm. It claimed success on issues such as the distribution of shares to workers in newly privatized industries and the adoption of a new labour code. In July 1995, OPZZ vice-president Maciej Manicki resigned to become vice-minister of labour and social policy, while Ewa Spychalska in Sept. 1996 stood down to become Ambassador to Belarus, being succeeded by Jozef Wiaderny.

Since the election of a Solidarity-led government in 1997, the OPZZ has again generally opposed government policies, and has regularly involved itself in strikes and demonstrations. It has focused on issues including unemployment, lack of employee rights in privatized industries, and the condition of the rural economy, allying itself with militant peasant groups in organizing demonstrations. It has also joined protests with breakaway Solidarity faction "Solidarity 80". A particular target was Leszek Balcerowicz, the Deputy Prime Minister and Finance Minister and leader of the pro-business Union for Freedom (UW), the junior party in the coalition with Solidarity Electoral Action (AWS) until it left the government in June 2000. Balcerowicz was the main architect of the 1990 shock therapy and an advocate of market deregulation and privatization, issues that create tensions within AWS itself. The OPZZ remains within the Democratic Left Alliance, and has 42 deputies in the Sejm, about one-quarter of the Democratic Left Alliance caucus. In Apr. 1999 it with-

drew from the Tripartite Commission claiming that the government had abandoned social dialogue.

Mirroring Krzaklewski's role in the AWS, Wiaderny chairs the SLD Group of Trade Union Deputies and Senators (42 in the Sejm and four in the Senate).

An issue for the OPZZ has been its international isolation since its withdrawal from the WFTU. The OPZZ says that it is now a social democratic organization akin to the mainstream of Western European trade unionism. It supports EU membership and integration into the wider European trade union movement and applied to join ETUC in Dec. 1998. However, it recognizes there is still considerable distrust of the role of OPZZ outside Poland, given its emergence after the suppression of Solidarity, and that admission to ETUC is unlikely to be achieved quickly.

Publication. Trade Union Chronicle (at website).

International affiliation. None

Portugal

Capital: Lisbon
Population: 10.05 m. (2000 est.)

1 Political and Economic Background

After the establishment of the quasi-fascist Salazar regime in 1933, Portugal was subject to right-wing authoritarian rule, with clerical and corporatist elements, until the overthrow of Salazar's successor, Marcelo Caetano, by the Armed Forces Movement in Apr. 1974. After an initial period when the communists were a major political force and there was considerable turmoil, Portugal has moved into the European political mainstream. The leading political parties are the Social Democratic Party (PSD) (which despite its name is a centre-right party akin to the German CDU or British Conservatives), and the social democratic Socialist Party (PS). The PSD held office most recently from 1987–95. The PS has led the government since 1995, strengthening its position in Oct. 1999 elections when it won exactly half the seats in the Assembly. The government is headed by Prime Minister António Guterres of the PS. Portugal has been a member of the EU since 1986.

Although still the poorest country in the EU (with Greece), Portugal has made progress in closing the gap between it and the other EU member states since joining in 1986. Per capita income stood at 56% of the EU aver-

age in 1986 and had risen to 74% by 1999, although growth in 2000 was below the EU average. Portugal has low unemployment at 4.1% in 2000 and inflation staying in the range 2–3% in 1999–2000. Services are the fastest growing sector of the economy, with a decreasing proportion (now only 10%) of the workforce in agriculture. Portugal joined the single European currency on its creation on Jan. 1, 1999.

GDP (purchasing power parity) $151.4bn. (1999 est.); GDP per capita (purchasing power parity) $15,300 (1999 est.).

2 Trade Unionism

In the early decades of the twentieth century the Portuguese labour movement was dominated by revolutionary trade unionism and anarcho-syndicalism. Following the creation in 1914 of the first national confederation, the União Operária Nacional (National Workers' Union), union activity led to the first revolutionary general strike in 1918. The (renamed) Confederaçao Geral de Trabalhadores (CGT, General Confederation of Workers) was dissolved in 1933 by Salazar and replaced by official trade unions within a fascist corporative structure. A revolutionary general strike in Jan. 1934 led to increased repression and the CGT gradually lost influence among the workforce. After World War II no effective trade union movement, either legal or clandestine, existed in Portugal until the emergence of an informal trade union structure, Intersindical, in 1970. This was politically pluralist, but its best organized element was the communists.

After Salazar's death in 1970, restrictions on trade unions were eased to some degree under Caetano before the armed forces took power in 1974. On April 30, 1975, the Supreme Revolutionary Council accorded recognition to the communist-led Intersindical Nacional (IN) as the sole national trade union centre (to which all unions were obliged to affiliate), despite the opposition of the Socialist Party, which had emerged as the dominant party in elections to a Constituent Assembly held on April 25. In Oct. 1976, however, the socialist government formed in July 1976 revoked the status of the IN as sole legal centre. This led to the formation of the União Geral de Trabalhadores (UGT) as an alternative centre, broadly aligned with the socialists. Portugal ratified ILO Convention No. 98 (Right to Organize and Collective Bargaining, 1949) in 1964 and Convention No. 87 (Freedom of Association and Protection of the Right to Organize, 1948) in 1977.

The two trade union centres are now the Confederaçao Geral dos Trabalhadores Portugueses–Intersindical Nacional (CGTP–IN, or CGTP), which is the renamed IN, and the UGT. These centres (of which the CGTP has been generally the stronger, except in the white–collar sector) have remained ideologically opposed to some degree, but also participate in joint actions where views converge. The CGTP–IN represents a relatively unreconstructed trade union wing that opposes most of the market liberalization process and favours state control. It has a mainstream association with the Portuguese Communist Party (PCP), which won 9% of the vote and 17 seats in the Oct. 1999 Assembly elections, but it also includes socialists and other left party elements. The UGT is more pragmatic and associated with the governing Socialist Party, but with a minority stream supporting the (centre–right) Social Democrats, the other major party. The UGT is affiliated to the ICFTU and ETUC, the CGTP to ETUC.

A government survey found that trade union membership peaked at 1.6million in the 1980s and then fell, standing at an estimated 1.15 million in 1995, giving a density of about 36%. Trade unions are numerically strong compared with most southern European countries.

Unions developed under the Trade Union Act of 1975 and trade union rights were guaranteed in general terms by the 1976 Constitution. A decree effective Apr. 1, 1999, formally extended trade union rights to the public administration, not covered by the 1975 Act, although in practice trade unionism had also become firmly established in that sector. Labour legislation is generally protectionist and employers have called consistently for more flexibility in labour markets.

Collective bargaining is widely practiced. There is little bargaining at the enterprise level, most agreements being sectoral and nationwide in character: 91% of Portuguese employees are covered by sector-level bargaining. Agreements tend to be focused on pay: only 30% of agreements in the first quarter of 2000 covered non-pay matters. A labour law commission is currently reviewing possible changes to the legal framework for collective bargaining.

Strikes occur regularly (there were 224 in the first half of 2000) and are used as a negotiating tool, a practice encouraged in the late 1990s by the relatively low level of unemployment. Most strikes are short-lived, however. Strikes affecting whole sectors or called for essentially political reasons are also a feature of the industrial relations landscape. The government has powers to order strikers back to work in essential services.

The Economic and Social Council (CES), in existence since 1992, provides an advisory forum for the social partners. Its Standing Committee for Social Dialogue (CPCS) has a specific role in industrial relations. It is chaired by the Prime Minister and includes three representatives each from the CGTP and UGT. The CPCS has provided the context for the negotiation of a series of incomes agreements and social pacts. While the CGTP has been involved in the negotiation of these pacts it has consistently fail to endorse them. Following expiry of the 1996–99 Strategic Dialogue Pact, there has been no further such comprehensive agreement, but rather individual issues are being resolved case by case. There is no new incomes policy, which will be dealt with at the level of collective bargaining.

3 Trade Union Centres

Confederação Geral dos Trabalhadores Portugueses – Intersindical Nacional (CGTP– IN)
General Confederation of Portuguese Workers

Address. Rua Victor Cordon, n. 1°–2°, 1249–102 Lisbon

Phone. + 351 21 323 6500

Fax. + 351 21 323 6695

E-mail. cgtp@mail.telepac.pt

Website. www.cgtp.pt (Portuguese only)

Leadership. Manuel Carvalho da Silva (general secretary)

History and character. The CGTP–IN, commonly referred to as the CGTP, traces its origins to the Intersindical Nacional founded illegally in Oct. 1970. Following the revolution of 1974, Intersindical, under communist leadership, became the sole national trade union centre authorized by the armed forces, inheriting the assets of the former government sponsored syndicates. When the socialists came into government in 1976, its monopoly status was revoked.

The second (1977) congress changed Intersindical's name to its present one. With the waning of the revolutionary mood, the confederation (which had supported nationalization and decolonization) lost support and faced a new rival in the UGT, which was formed in 1978.

The CGTP experienced rivalry between socialist and the (majority) communist factions, exacerbated by the reluctance of the hardline Portuguese Communist Party to respond to the changing face of the Soviet bloc in the late 1980s and early 1990s.

During the 1990s the CGTP has participated in tripartite negotiation of successive social pacts, while consistently refusing to endorse them, in contrast to the UGT. The CGTP shares the UGT's aspirations and emphasis on issues such as the need for convergence with EU average wages and conditions, the strengthening of the social dimension of the EU, and the call for full employment and good quality jobs. However, the CGTP is significantly more hostile to the process of privatization, retains a traditional belief in state ownership and control, and demands the 35–hour week while the UGT encourages its adoption. At the industrial level, the CGTP tends to be more militant, although the two centres have jointly organized strikes, as in the transport sector and civil service in the Spring of 2000. Despite significant differences in emphasis, and their antagonistic origins, the CGTP and UGT now cooperate on many issues. The CGTP's affiliation to ETUC was assisted by the UGT, which had formerly opposed it, and the CGTP has abandoned its one-time identification with the WFTU bloc.

International affiliation. ETUC

União Geral de Trabalhadores (UGT)
General Union of Workers

Address. Rua de Buenos Aires 11, 1249–067 Lisbon

Phone. +351 21 393 1200

Fax. +351 21 397 4612

E-mail. ugt@mail.telepac.pt

Website. www.ugt.pt (Portuguese; some information in English)

Leadership. Manuela Teixeira (president); João Proença (general secretary)

Membership. 400,000

History and character. The UGT was founded in Oct. 1978 with the backing of the Socialist and Social Democratic parties, in succession to the Carta Aberta (Open Letter) union grouping which in 1976 had challenged the status of the Intersindical Nacional as sole centre. It held its first congress in 1979.

The UGT is probably smaller than the CGTP–IN but resembles its rival in that there are political factions within it. The Socialists constitute the leading faction, followed by the Social Democrats (PSD, a centre-right party). In May 1992 the UGT at its sixth national congress elected a communist (Jose Bras) to its national secretariat for the first time, resulting in a secretariat comprising 28 Socialists, 21 Social Democrats and one communist. The UGT customarily maintains a balance by having a Socialist general secretary (since 1995 João Proença) and a PSD president (currently Manuela Teixeira).

After allegations of misuse (unrelated to trade union activities) of European Social Fund money by the UGT's education, training and development arm, this funding was cut off, creating a financial crisis. In March 1997 the Socialist government guaranteed a PTE 600m. bank loan to the UGT, apparently saving it from bankruptcy. The government said that the loan was intended to safeguard the continuation of democratic trade unionism, but the move attracted intense criticism from opposition parties (which united to pass vote of protest in the Assembly) and some independent unions.

The 8th UGT congress, held in May 2000, had the theme "towards development and solidarity". The congress called for full employment and the defence of the welfare state and achieving convergence of Portuguese wages and living standards with the EU average.

The UGT comprises 58 unions and two federations. It is putting particular emphasis on strengthening its representation at company level and on securing members in emergent sectors of the economy. At national level it participates with the CGTP, employers and government in the Economic and Social Council (CES) and the Standing Committee for Social Dialogue (CPCS).

International affiliations. ICFTU; ETUC; TUAC

Qatar

Capital: Doha
Population: 744,000 (2000 est.)

1 Political and Economic Background

Qatar is a monarchy in which the al-Thani family holds power, the present Amir having deposed his father in a palace coup in 1995. Amir Hamad's brother is Prime Minister. The Amir holds absolute power but legislates after consulting with leading citizens in an appointed Advisory Council. There are no political parties.

The key sectors of the economy are largely state-controlled. Oil accounts for two-thirds of government revenue and has formed the basis for a high standard of living. Qatar also has the third largest natural gas reserves in the world, which are of increasing importance. Most of the workforce are foreigners and the government has a "Qatarization" programme to try to increase the participation of citizens in the economy.

GDP (purchasing power parity) $12.3bn. (1999 est.); GDP per capita (purchasing power parity) $17,000 (1999 est.).

2 Trade Unionism

Qatar joined the International Labour Organization in 1972, but has ratified neither ILO Convention No. 87 (Freedom of Association and Protection of the Right to Organize, 1948) nor No. 98 (Right to Organize and Collective Bargaining, 1949).

Trade unions are illegal and collective bargaining is not permitted. Strikes are illegal in the public sector, but in the private sector are lawful after appeal to the Labour Conciliation Board. However, the overwhelming majority of private sector workers are foreigners, who are dependent on their employers for residency rights, and strikes are rarely recorded. There is provision for the formation of labour-management joint committees in enterprises, but these are limited in what they may discuss to issues such as health and safety and training and are not a forum for bargaining over pay.

Romania

Capital: Bucharest
Population: 22.41 m. (2000 est.)

1 Political and Economic Background

Under Nicolae Ceausescu the Romanian communists after World War II pursued a policy of some independence from the Soviet Union combined with a domestic regime of uncompromising severity, much of whose inspiration came from North Korea and China. Although communist rule ended in Romania at the same time as in other eastern European countries, it did so without a long process of increasingly organized dissidence such as occurred in Poland or the Czech Republic. Instead Ceausescu's rule ended suddenly in Dec. 1989 when mass demonstrations were joined by the army. Ceausescu was captured and summarily executed and resistance by his internal security forces was quickly crushed.

The repressiveness of the regime and the rapidity of its collapse meant there had been no real development of alternative political forces. A National Salvation Front (FSN), most of whose leaders were members of the former communist nomenklatura, assumed power after Ceausescu's overthrow. The FSN won elections in May 1990, but miner-led riots against its tentative efforts to introduce a free market precipitated its fall in Sept. 1991. Non-party government followed until Sept. 1992 when further presidential and parliamentary elections brought the Democratic National Salvation Front (FSND – a breakaway from the NSF) of President Ion Iliescu to power. Later renamed the Party of Social Democracy in Romania (PDSR), it continued in power but only by means of a coalition with the former communist Socialist Labour Party and two extreme nationalist parties. Elections in Nov. 1996 resulted in the formation of a more decisively post-communist coalition government led by the Democratic Convention of Romania (CDR), itself a coalition based on the National Peasants' Christian and Democratic Party (PNTCD), the National Liberal Party (PNL) and the National Liberal Party–Democratic Convention (PNL–CD). Further elections in Nov. 2000, however, resulted in the collapse of the centre-right coalition with the PDSR returning to government and also a strong showing by the right-wing nationalist candidates of the Greater Romania Party (PRM). In a run-off presidential election in Dec. 2000 the PDSR's Ion Iliescu defeated the PRM's Vadim Tudor.

After the collapse of the Soviet bloc Romania lost trading partners and inherited an obsolete base of heavy industry. In 1990 factories with over 2,000 workers accounted for two-thirds of those employed. The NSF government unsuccessfully sought to partly liberalize markets while retaining central control and the period 1990–92 was one of falling GDP and constant unrest. The government elected in 1996 struggled to make a successful transition to a market economy. Although the private sector now accounts for 60% of GDP and 57% of the workforce, and the new government privatized more than 4,000 enterprises in 1997–99, state control remains predominant in the heavy industry sector. The private sector comprises mainly agriculture (36% of the labour force) and service businesses. Inflation has fallen from 151% in 1997, but still stood at 56% in 1999; unemployment is high; and the economy contracted for three straight years 1997–99.

GDP (purchasing power parity) $87.4bn. (1999 est.); GDP per capita (purchasing power parity) $3,900 (1999 est.).

2 Trade Unionism

Romania ratified ILO Convention No. 87 (Freedom of Association and Protection of the Right to Organize, 1948) in 1957 and Convention No. 98 (Right to Organize and Collective Bargaining, 1949) in 1958.

Before 1989 trade unions existed on the communist model with social responsibilities and a single trade union system organized by the central UGSR. Sporadic efforts to form free trade unions had little impact and organizers were beaten and imprisoned.

The UGSR survived Ceausescu by only five days, replaced by a 'Provisional Committee for the Formation of Free Trade Unions in Romania' (later the National Confederation of Free Trade Unions of Romania, CNSLR) which inherited its assets and initially supported the new National Salvation Front (NSF) government. At the same time the independent centre Fratia (Fraternity) was formed. The CNSLR remained the country's largest centre in the post-Ceausescu era with a claimed membership of 3.5 million. In March 1990 Fratia (which claimed 800,000 members) mounted a demonstration to challenge CNSLR's right to retain the UGSR assets although this later became a demand that UGSR funds be used for unemployment benefit. Both enjoyed good relations with the ICFTU, however, and animosity gradually declined. In June 1993 the two merged to form CNSLR–Fratia, claiming to have 3.7 million members.

Under the 1991 Law on Trade Unions a confederation may be formed by as few as 60 workers, and this has contributed to the fragmentation of the labour movement. There are an estimated 18 national confederations operating, as well as many independent unions. There are two ICFTU affiliates, CNSLR–Fratia and the National Labour Bloc (BNS), and two WCL affiliates, CNS Cartel Alfa and the Democratic Trade Union Confederation of Romania (CSDR). All four are also affiliated to ETUC.

While the right to join and form trade unions is guaranteed by law, many companies prevent unions from organizing. The ICFTU says that "there are no labour courts, and workers who are unfairly dismissed, or who are victims of other violations of trade union rights, have little chance of redress, because court cases usually take one or two years, and the decisions are not usually implemented by employers."

Even under Ceausescu, strikes were reported at times in the 1970s and 1980s although they were savagely suppressed. In June 1990 the miners from the Jiu Valley marched on Bucharest to support the NSF government against demonstrators calling for the complete removal of communists from power. Six were killed and hundreds injured as the miners acted as the government's shock troops, provoking the suspension of aid by several countries. In Sept. 1991, however, with mounting dissatisfaction at economic conditions, the miners virtually occupied Bucharest, forcing the NSF government of Petre Roman to resign. The collapse of much of the Romanian economy in the early 1990s was reflected in regular strikes and demonstrations as real incomes fell 40% from 1989 to 1993. The government frequently declared strikes illegal, although it appeared to lack the means to enforce its decrees. The decline of gross domestic product and falling living standards for three straight years 1997–99 produced continuing unrest. In May 1997 unions staged a "month of the yellow card", demanding cuts in the price of food and energy and the abandonment of plans to close down or privatize state companies. In Jan. 1999 coal miners from the Jiu Valley tried to march on Bucharest to oppose mine closures and there were violent clashes when a ban on the march was enforced. On Mar. 24, 1999, up to 400,000 people supported demonstrations called jointly by the four leading centres (Cartel Alfa, the CSDR, CNSLR–Fratia and the BNS) to demand lower taxes, inflation-linked wage increases, and cuts in energy prices.

Collective bargaining was underwritten by the 1991 Law on Trade Unions. Practice is shaped by the fact that most major enterprises are in state hands and the fragmentation of the unions. Contracts are not always enforceable. Unions complain that the right to strike is heavily circumscribed, that there are excessive pre-strike procedures and that the courts have tended to rule most strikes illegal. Union officers who lead illegal strikes may under the law face fines and imprisonment. A minimum standard of coverage must be maintained during strikes in essential services, which are interpreted to include health care, education, energy, transport, telecommunications and broadcasting, and the supply of staples such as bread, milk and meat. Nevertheless, strikes are commonplace.

3 Trade Union Centres

Blocul National Sindical (BNS)
National Trade Unions Bloc

Address. Splaiul Independentei 202A, 4th Floor, Sector 6, 77208 Bucharest

Phone. +40 1 411 5184

Fax. +40 1 411 5184

E-mail. bns@bx.logicnet.ro

Membership. 350,000

International affiliations. ICFTU; ETUC

Confederatia Natională Sindicală (CNS Cartel Alfa)
National Trade Union Confederation Cartel Alfa

Address. Splaiul Independentei 202 A, Floors 2/3, Sector 6, 77208 Bucharest

Phone. +40 1 212 6638

Fax. +40 1 313 3481

E-mail. alfa@cartel–alfa.ro

Website. www.alfa.elt.ro (Romanian; English section)

Leadership. Bogdan Hossu (president); Ion Homos (secretary-general)

History and character. Founded June 1990. Affiliated to the WCL in 1990 and ETUC in 1996.

International affiliations. WCL; ETUC

CNSLR–Fratia
National Confederation of Free Trade Unions of Romania

Address. 1–3 Ministerului Street, 70109 Bucharest

Phone. +40 1 313 9457

Fax. +40 1 312 6206

E-mail. international@cnslr-fratia.ro

Website. www.fratia.home.ro (Romanian; English section)

Leadership. Pavel Todoran (president)

Membership. Reports 1.2 million

History and character. Founded from the remnants of the official centre UGSR which existed under communism, the CNSLR was able to maintain a large percentage of the original membership and held on to most of the UGSR assets. In June 1993 the CNSLR merged with its former rival, the independent centre Fratia.

In 1990 the CNSLR operated as a close ally of the NSF, but this relationship cooled. In 1992 Fratia, together with Cartel Alfa, formed a political party, the Convention for Social Solidarity (CSS) to contest the September elections. However, it polled only 30,000 votes. The unions in 1994 formed the Party of Social Solidarity, described as social democratic in orientation, chaired by Miron Mitrea, a co-president of the merged CNSLR–Fratia.

It comprises 47 professional federations and 41 regional branches. It is politically independent.

International affiliations ICFTU; ETUC

Confédération des Syndicats Démocratiques de Roumanie (CSDR)
Democratic Trade Union Confederation of Romania

Address. 1–3 Place Walter Maracineaunu, BP 1–788, Bucharest

Phone. +40 1 310 2080

Fax. +40 1 310 2080

E-mail. csdrdri@fx.ro

Leadership. Iacob Baciu (president)

International affiliations. WCL; ETUC

Russian Federation

Capital: Moscow
Population: 146.0 m. (2000 est.)

1 Political and Economic Background

From the mid-1980s Mikhail Gorbachev sought to reform the Soviet Union through the policies of "glasnost" and "perestroika" while retaining Communist Party rule. This policy culminated, first, in the collapse of Soviet hegemony and communist rule in Eastern Europe in 1989, and then, in Dec. 1991 in the dissolution of the Soviet Union itself. The Russian Federation, established as an independent state on Dec. 25, 1991, was left with half the population and a greater proportion of the economic base of the Soviet Union. Russia lacked a pre-communist democratic tradition and the communists have remained a significant minority force, sometimes in alliance with virulent ultra-nationalists, and the development of soundly based centre-right and centre-left mass parties on the Western European model has not occurred. The President has considerable executive powers, and since succeeding Boris Yeltsin (himself President since June 1991) on Dec. 31, 1999, former Federal Security Service head Vladimir Putin has consolidated his position. Elections to the Duma (legislature) in Dec. 1999 left the opposition Communists weakened but still as the largest single party, with the government supported by an anti-communist coalition including, most prominently, the Unity party set up in 1999 and associated with Putin.

Like most former Soviet bloc countries, Russia entered a deep recession in the early 1990s as its planned economy collapsed. However, it has subsequently proved less successful than some of its former Eastern European satellites in engineering a transition to free markets. Progress has been frustrated by forces including rampant corruption, the scale of obsolescent industries, lack of direction and consensus in government, the inefficiency of the workforce, and the emergence of business oligarchies enmeshed with organized crime. Real GDP probably declined by 50% or more in the period 1991–97. Tentative recovery by 1997 received a further setback with the financial crisis of Aug. 1998, resulting in a massive devaluation of the rouble and a vast emergency IMF bail-out. Russia was then helped by rising oil prices and the longer-term impact of the 1998 crisis was less than feared, with 2000 seeing the highest rate of growth since the Soviet period. Unemployment in 1999 was officially 12% but disguised unemployment (with workers remaining on the payrolls of enterprises that can not afford to pay them) and under-employment are on a much wider scale.

The Putin government faces great difficulties in attempting to restructure and rebuild Russia's industrial base. In the post-communist period there has been negative net productive investment throughout the economy. Domestic investment dried up as private capital fled abroad and the state has slashed spending to try to control public sector deficits and inflation. Foreign investors have likewise largely stayed away, regarding Russia as insecure, while much assistance from international funding agencies has been poorly monitored and siphoned off by profiteers and criminals. One objective has been to close obsolescent Soviet era heavy industry and stimulate new sectors, but this has not happened; on the contrary, consumer goods production has contracted more sharply than the economy as a whole and obsolescent industries have survived on subsidies. The investment crisis has resulted in collapsing infrastructure, exacerbated by sharp falls in government spending on education and training, which has de-skilled the work force. The devaluation of the rouble that followed the Aug. 1998 financial crisis had little beneficial impact on manufacturing exports because of the low quality of Russian products, which makes them unsaleable at any price: extractive industries produce the bulk of hard currency exports. Russia's post-communist era admission to the G-8 group of leading industrial nations was the result of political considerations rather than its economic strength. Privatization has been incompletely pursued and much inefficient industry remains in state hands, while the legitimate private sector, beset by organized crime, lack of business standards or a legal framework, and lack of affordable credit, has not become an engine of growth. Wage arrears are endemic and living standards for most of the population remain significantly below those of the Soviet era.

GDP (purchasing power parity) $620.3bn. (1999 est.); GDP per capita (purchasing power parity) $4,200 (1999 est.).

2 Trade Unionism

The USSR rejoined the International Labour Organization in 1954, having been a member from 1934 to 1940. It ratified ILO Conventions No. 87 (Freedom of Association and Protection of the Right to Organize, 1948) and No. 98 (Right to Organize and Collective Bargaining, 1949) in 1956. This ratification is considered to apply in respect of the Russian Federation.

Trade unions within the Russian Empire developed early in the twentieth century, but were of relatively little importance on the eve of the 1917 revolution. Advocates of union political autonomy had considerable influence at this time but were eliminated when the communists consolidated power. Under Soviet rule, unions were used primarily to mobilize and discipline the workers behind the objectives of the revolution and to secure greater productivity. Subsequently, all were organized within the All-Union Central Council of Trade Unions (AUCCTU). Throughout the Stalinist period of the 1930s and 1940s the unions were of little significance, collective agreements were abolished, and there was no AUCCTU congress between 1932 and 1949.

Expanded rights and obligations were accorded from the late 1950s onwards and these were consolidated, extended and codified in legislation adopted from 1970 to 1974, and also given recognition in the 1977 constitution. The Soviet government argued that its labour legislation did not prohibit the establishment of unions outside the AUCCTU and that unification reflected the workers' wishes. In practice, the AUCCTU shadowed party policy, and there was a close interlocking of party membership and trade union office-holding at all levels. Weaknesses in the operation of the trade unions as a "transmission belt" between the party and the workers arose primarily from inertia, bureaucracy, alienation and indifference, rather than any explicit conflict between the trade unions and the party in respect of this role.

Following the appointment of Mikhail Gorbachev as party General Secretary (Soviet leader) in March 1985, the trade unions were affected by the intensifying campaign against corruption and mismanagement. The AUCCTU entered a phase of "self-criticism" in which (following the party line) it said that it had in the past neglected the interests of the workers in favour of "bureaucratic formalism" and would participate in the reform process. The official unions were not prominent, however, in driving forward the Gorbachev doctrines of glasnost and perestroika.

In the summer of 1989 a strike wave in the USSR directly stimulated the establishment of workers' committees in the north (Vorkuta region), in the Ukraine (Donbass in the Don Valley), and east of the Urals (Kuzbass). Before 1990 the AUCCTU itself seemed immune to change but then massive threats to its national coverage forced internal reform. It announced far-reaching structural reform and reorganized in preparation for an October congress where it was re-launched as the General Confederation of Unions of the USSR (GCTU). Independent unions began to proliferate. With origins in the 1989 strike committees, an independent miners' union (NPG) was formed in 1990.

In Aug. 1991 communist hard-liners attempted a coup, seizing Gorbachev. Boris Yeltsin, the President of the Russian Federation, became the symbol of resistance in the defence of the Parliament (White House) and the coup crumbled. The outcome was the collapse of the Communist Party, Yeltsin's assumption of supreme authority, and the disintegration of the Soviet Union. The leader of the attempted coup, Gennady Yanaev, had been chairman of the AUCCTU until 1990. GCTU leaders attempted to meet him and apparently opposed Yeltsin's call for stoppages of production. The GCTU was accused by the Federation of Independent Trade Unions of Russia (FNPR), which organized the unions at the Russian level, of taking a position towards the coup which was 'to say the least ambiguous' although the FNPR itself did little beyond calling on workers to maintain "labour discipline." Each organization, however, claimed the responsibility for the dispatch of gas masks to the defenders of the Russian Parliament during Aug. 19–21 and some FNPR representatives were among those defending the Parliament.

Following the dissolution of the Soviet Union, the FNPR established itself as the dominant trade union organization in Russia. Since 1991, the shape of the Russian trade union movement has remained broadly unchanged. The FNPR in the late 1990s still claimed to represent 80% of Russian workers. Its active membership is a fraction of this and its sporadic efforts to mobilize workers in demonstrations and strikes have only ever produced a patchy response. However, the FNPR has inherited both the assets and many of the functions of the old official unions and it has therefore remained a powerful factor in Russian society. It has also retained many of the former bureaucrats of the old structures. In some respects, Russian social and economic organization has not greatly changed since 1991. The enterprise remains the organizing focus for much of people's lives: it provides not just work and pay, but workers' apartments, health services, holidays, even food and consumer goods. The trade unions, as in Soviet times, play a central role in the administration of the range of enterprise services, and indeed it is considered almost impossible in many cases to disentangle what assets belong to the enterprise and what to the unions. The concepts of "labour" and "management" are weakly defined. Enterprise directors are members of, and commonly lead or heavily influence, FNPR unions. Protest strikes and demonstrations are often directed at pressurizing central government to retain subsidies or tax concessions and are organized collectively by enterprise directors, unions and, sometimes, local officials. The FNPR is in effect a network of competing local and sectoral interest groups, focused more on securing benefits from the centre than on issues such as local bargaining. This phenomenon is reinforced by the lack of opportunities for workers to transfer their labour. Wage arrears are endemic, but enterprises often retain workers they cannot pay rather than lay them off; the workers in this situation continue to receive free or subsidized housing, health and other benefits.

The independent union movement has made little impact after its days of influence in 1989–91.

Independent trade unions remain largely confined to a few sectors, such as mining, air traffic controllers, the docks, and locomotive drivers, where they originally appeared. The most important independent union has remained the independent miners' union, NPG, but this is smaller than the coal miners' union linked to the FNPR. The independent unions, unlike the official unions, which were organized on the industrial union principle, have tended to be craft-based, limiting their scale. In wide swathes of the economy they do not exist and total membership may be only 500,000, a fraction of that of the FNPR (reliable membership figures do not exist for Russian unions). Most workers who have left the FNPR have joined no other union at all, while many early leaders of independent unions went on to take up official positions in the new order or to direct privatized enterprises. Organization of independent unions has been frustrated by refusal of employers to deal with them and the monopoly position and control of workers' welfare enjoyed by the FNPR in many enterprises.

Likewise, no alternative confederation has developed. The Federation of Socialist Trade Unions (Sotsprof) was founded by Moscow intellectuals in 1989, and espoused a social democratic programme. It recruited independent unions and aimed to be a confederation with contacts across the USSR. It was given a role out of proportion to its real strength by Yeltsin (whom it actively supported for several years) on the Tripartite Commission for the Regulation of Social and Labour Relations set up in 1992 but has failed to develop a mass base to rival the FNPR. This is true also of the Confederation of Labour of Russia (KTR), comprised mainly of transport sector workers, and the All-Russian Confederation of Labour (VKT), set up with backing from the NPG and Sotsprof. In the early 1990s foreign groups, such as the AFL–CIO's Free Trade Union Institute, invested considerable resources in supporting independent unions and encouraging the development of alternatives to the FNPR, but to little avail as no significant confederation has taken root. One result of this is that while the ICFTU was able to affiliate trade union centres in Eastern European countries relatively soon after the fall of communism, it was unable to recognize an affiliate in Russia. In Nov. 2000, however, the ICFTU Executive Board announced the affiliation of the FNPR (which the ICFTU claimed had 28 million members) as well as the VKT and KTR. The FNPR accordingly became the largest ICFTU affiliate, with more than twice the membership of the AFL–CIO, although its status, voluntary and active membership and legitimacy compared with other major ICFTU affiliates such as the AFL–CIO, DGB and TUC is arguable.

In the 1989–91 period the independent unions opposed the regime and after the fall of communism in 1991 mostly enthusiastically backed Yeltsin and his policies. Victor Utkin and Aleksandr Sergeyev, leaders of the NPG, became members of Yeltsin's council of advisers. As late as the autumn of 1993, Kuzbass miners offered to march on Moscow to aid Yeltsin in his confrontation with the Russian Parliament, which had blocked his programme. Years of falling living standards, and the failure of a free market economy either to take root or deliver prosperity, have produced division and confusion over aims and goals, however. NPG leaders abandoned pro-Yeltsin positions and in 1997 official and independent unions worked together to shut down the coal districts of Kuzbass and Vorkuta. In the crisis of Aug. 1998, the NPG and VKT joined the FNPR in calling on Yeltsin to resign. Sergeyev was briefly detained and NPG headquarters in Moscow was raided by Interior Ministry agents. The NPG was threatened with de-registration, although this did not happen. Overall, issues such as non-payment of wages and disillusion with the results of post-communist reforms has closed the gap between the FNPR and independent unions.

The catastrophic scale of the decline of the Russian economy in the 1990s is difficult to overstate. The real value of the average wage declined some 78% between 1991–97 and many people survive only by engaging in subsistence cultivation of small plots and because they continue to live in heavily subsidized apartments with cheap utilities. There has been a process of economic "primitivization". While local pockets (notably Moscow) are comparatively buoyant, through much of the country there is widespread privation and even malnutrition. This is reflected in indicators for health and mortality: life expectancy for adult males is now at the same level as in Tsarist times.

Wage arrears (as in many post-communist economies) as well as arrears in pensions have become endemic since the mid-1990s. Hyper-inflation in the period 1992–93 was followed by government policies aimed at taking money out of the economy. Those Russians who had cash and could send it abroad did so. Inter-enterprise debt accelerated and many enterprises abandoned the cash economy in favour of bartering. In 1997 the labour code was modified so that non-payment of wages was no longer ground for punitive damages. The problem came to a head in 1998 with the broader financial and banking crisis. From Jan.–Aug. 1998, wage arrears increased 40–50% and by this point over 20 million workers had not been paid for months, while 70% of inter-enterprise debts were being settled by barter, promissory notes or mutual cancellations of debts. The Aug. 1998 devaluation of the rouble allowed the reduction of outstanding wage arrears in the following months, before the backlogs began to increase again in 2000.

Against this background, the scale of unrest in Russia has arguably been modest. Work stoppages occur continually, and other forms of protest include blockading of railroad lines, hunger strikes, occasional hostage taking of enterprise managers or local officials, and pickets of government offices. In some areas, protesters have faced physical attack, prosecution and punishment; in others they have had the tacit support of the local authorities. Strikes are commonly declared illegal and the courts may order confiscation of union assets in compensation for losses. As a result many strikes are organized by ad hoc strike committees rather than by the unions themselves.

Major demonstrations and work stoppages occurred Russia-wide on Oct. 7, 1998, in the wake of the financial crisis, and the FNPR demanded Yeltsin's resignation. Themes of the protests were opposition to continued privatization, the payment of wage arrears, and an end to plunder by the wealthy taking money abroad. However, there has been little sustained and organized support for coherent alternatives and much protest focuses on the retention of subsidies or limited sectoral demands. Apathy characterizes much of the workforce and the trade union movement has not developed a clear and coherent unified identity to give it a role in social dialogue. In addition, Russia is geographically vast (by far the largest country in the world) and centres of opposition to the government are commonly immense distances from Moscow, isolated from each other and disregarded by the centre.

Politically, the union movement has not formed the base for a social democratic party on the Western European model. Union leaders have allied with different factions, but no party is seen as being preponderantly the party of labour. The Communists, frequently allied with ultra-nationalists and supported disproportionately by the elderly, remain the largest party in the Duma and have in some regions shared platforms with the unions, but they are also widely distrusted. The FNPR has worked to distance itself from the Communists. Other parties and coalitions are often personality-driven.

The position of the unions has deteriorated. The official unions have retained members through their role in distributing benefits, but this is declining as these functions gradually shift to the government or simply cease to exist. The unions are commonly excluded in the entrepreneurial private sector, where not joining a union can be effectively a condition of employment. Underlying these trends is the overall impoverishment of the economy. Basic functions such as collective bargaining are of limited relevance when the enterprise has no money and is in effect paying for its continuing operations by withholding wages. In such circumstances, the strike threat is an empty one. Strikes and protests are indeed directed more against the government than in pursuit of demands at the enterprise level. Meanwhile social dialogue is intermittent and often unconstructive.

3 Trade Union Centre

Federatsiia Nezavisimykh Profsoiuzov Rossii (FNPR)
Federation of Independent Trade Unions of Russia (FITUR)

Address. 42 Leninsky Prospect, 117119 Moscow

Phone. +7 95 930 89 84

Fax. +7 95 938 22 93

E-mail. fnpr@glasnet.ru

Leadership. Mikhail Shmakov (president); Andrei Isayev (secretary)

Membership. Claims 28 million.

History and character. This is the successor organization to the former communist-era official unions and is the dominant trade union centre. The FNPR says it represents 80% of all workers. The most important union to have split from it is the 1.7m-strong metalworkers' union.

The FNPR was established in 1990 in what was then the Russian component of the Soviet Union. With the dissolution of the Soviet Union in Dec. 1991 it became the Russian national trade union centre and was, with the military, virtually the only national institution to survive the Communists' loss of power. It retained a number of key assets from the Soviet period, including control over disbursement of social insurance funds, automatic deduction of dues from employee pay, and rights to veto the dismissal of workers. The FNPR also retained considerable numbers of Soviet era union officials, who retained many of their attitudes and ways of working. At the same time, prominent figures from the 1989–90 reform wave also established themselves. Mikhail Shmakov, FNPR president since 1993, came to prominence as leader of the Moscow Federation of Trade Unions (MFP), where he had brought in many new people, active in opposition during the perestroika period. The current FNPR secretary, Andrei Isayev, had organized some of the first opposition meetings in 1987–88 and revitalized the MFP's publication *Solidarnost.*

In 1992 President Yeltsin set up the Tripartite Commission for the Regulation of Social and Labour Relations, and the FNPR was given 9 of the 14 labour seats. The first general agreement to be monitored by the Commission was signed in April 1992 and outlined measures to create a social market while privatizing state property. It included measures for occupational safety and improvement of labour relations. The FNPR failed to achieve an improvement in the level of the minimum wage and opposed plans to hold back the wages of public sector workers. In autumn 1992 the government designated FNPR as its primary social partner, a step which had the effect of diminishing the status of its independent rivals. During 1992–93, however, as its members faced falling living standards and the government failed to keep commitments on wage indexation, the FNPR called many strikes, although these often had little impact. The FNPR identified with forces intent on blocking free market reform. In May 1992 the lobby of state industrial directors, the Russian Union of Industrialists and Entrepreneurs (RUIE), became co-publisher with the FNPR of the newspaper *Rabochaya Tribuna.* The RUIE warned that the government's policies would lead to the "Kuwaitization" of Russia, meaning that they would destroy Russia's industrial base and reduce the country to the status of an exporter of energy to rich Western nations. FNPR president Igor Klochvov proposed alliance with the Civic Union, an anti-reform movement set up in June 1992 and seen as controlled by directors of the big state enterprises.

Although Russian President Yeltsin had defeated Communist hardliners in the Aug. 1991 attempted coup, he continued to face determined opposition from the Russian Congress of People's Deputies (CPD), elected in 1990 in the communist era. Through 1992–93 it blocked much of his reform programme. On Sept. 21, 1993, Yeltsin dissolved the CPD and announced he would rule by decree. The CPD, led by its chairman Ruslan Khasbulatov and supported by Yeltsin's own Vice-President Aleksandr Rutskoy, refused to accept its dissolution and fortified its base in the parliament building (White House) while supporters tried unsuccessfully to seize the Moscow television facility, the Ostankino tower. On Oct. 4, Yeltsin moved against the White House with tanks, resulting in heavy casualties in hand-to-hand fighting before his forces gained control.

An FNPR plenum of Sept. 28 voted to side with the Parliament against Yeltsin and FNPR's leader Igor Klochkov called on workers to mobilize in defence of the Parliament (a call which got little support). The same day a presidential decree stripped the unions of control over social insurance funds, providing disability, child, holiday and other benefits and the source of considerable patronage. After Yeltsin's victory there were threats to end dues check-off or even dismantle the FNPR altogether. In alarm, the FNPR forced Klochkov out of office on Oct. 11 and he was replaced at an emergency congress by Mikhail Shmakov, the leader of the Moscow Federation of Trade Unions (MFP). Following this the government took no further steps against the FNPR, and although the social insurance fund was put under the nominal control of the Labour Ministry, in practice no real change was made to its administration.

A chastened FNPR did not endorse any list in the ensuing (Dec. 1993) elections). This stance confounded the hopes of opponents of the Yeltsin programme, but the lists nonetheless included a large number of individual union leaders scattered among the 26 groups taking part. Former FNPR chairman Igor Klochkov was a member of the political council of the Civic Union, although the Civic Union itself failed to make an impact in the elections.

Thenceforth, the FNPR steered an ambivalent course in relation to the Yeltsin presidency, saying that it favoured market reforms but calling for state intervention to reduce its undesirable effects on jobs and living standards. At the local level it tended to be allied with enterprise directors and local politicians demanding protectionism and subsidies. This was reflected also in the Tripartite Commission where commonly the employers and the unions combined against the government, with a resultant deadlock. In Apr. 1994 the FNPR endorsed Yeltsin's Pact on Social Accord, which offered a compromise on state budget funding in return for social peace and a promise not to campaign for early elections ahead of their due date in 1996. In July 1996 Yeltsin won a comfortable victory over the Communist candidate Gennady Zyuganov in presidential elections, but he continued to face a legislature in which the Communists were the largest party and his opponents were strongly entrenched.

In response to the Aug. 1998 financial crisis, the FNPR sent an open letter to Yeltsin declaring that his policies had led to economic collapse and calling on him to resign. In Apr. 1999 Shmakov praised Prime Minister Yevgeny Primakov (who took office with Duma backing in Sept. 1998 but was dismissed by Yeltsin in May 1999) as the "man who has really stabilized the situation in the country". Primakov's government included no prominent free market reformers. The Union of Labour, the FNPR's social–political movement, was drawn into support of the Fatherland All-Russia coalition, set up by Primakov and Moscow Mayor Yury Luzhkov.

However, Yeltsin appointed Vladimir Putin his Prime Minister in Aug. 1999 and the pro-Kremlin Unity party was set up to counter the Primakov-Luzhkov alliance. Putin launched full-scale war in Chechnya, and buoyed by his resultant popularity, Unity came a close second to the Communists in elections to the Duma in Dec. 1991, coming well ahead of the Fatherland–All Russia coalition. On Dec. 31, Yeltsin resigned and appointed Putin Acting President, following which Putin went on to win the presidential election in March 2000, with Communist Zyuganov again the main challenger. On Feb. 16, 2000, Putin told the FNPR that he wanted to work with the unions and for them to be a "renewed and progressive force". However, a draft new labour code subsequently introduced in the Duma was seen as reducing the powers of the unions, and was opposed by the FNPR. The code remained stalled in the Duma during 2000.

The FNPR represents to a considerable degree, notwithstanding the changes in Russia since 1991, a continuation of the old Soviet era trade union structures and functions. It retains a major role through its control of facilities such as summer camps, hotels, palaces of culture, sports facilities, and sanatoria. It owns a vast range of facilities. However, it has been affected by closures and sell offs of many such facilities.

Enterprise directors and managers, on the Soviet model, are commonly FNPR members and often branch leaders. With many basic industries still in state hands, the union branches tend to ally with the directors in support of the enterprise in lobbying for subsidies. Indeed, many strikes and protests have been organized on that collaborative basis. As many Russian cities are "company towns" the government has maintained subsides to avert social collapse. The FNPR has a complex structure of regional and sectoral unions that often take different positions, and this has been reinforced by the increasing fragmentation of the economy. The FNPR has little presence in the entrepreneurial private sector.

The FNPR faced considerable suspicion in Western trade union circles as the successor to the official unions of the Communist era. In the early 1990s the AFL–CIO was active in running programmes in Russia through its Free Trade Union Institute to support independent unions opposed to the FNPR. After 1995, when new leadership took over at the AFL–CIO, these programmes were wound down or became more neutral in approach. In 1997 Shmakov and FNPR international department head Alexander Sergeyen were for the first time invited to attend the AFL–CIO congress. In Apr. 2000, the FNPR had observer status at the ICFTU congress in Durban, South Africa, and ICFTU general secretary Bill Jordan said it was in the process of applying for membership. In Nov. 2000 the ICFTU Executive Board announced that the FNPR had been accepted into affiliation, alongside the smaller independent organizations the VKT and KTR. This gave the ICFTU representation inside Russia for the first time in its history.

International affiliation. ICFTU

4 Other Trade Union Organizations

All-Russian Confederation of Labour (VKT)

Address. Rozhdestvenka Street 5/7, 103031 Moscow

Phone. +7 95 925 3213

Fax. +7 95 923 3655

E-mail. vkt@vkt.org.ru

Website. www.vkt.org.ru (Russian; English section)

Leadership. Aleksandr Bugaev (president)

Membership. Reports 1.27 million.

History and character. The VKT was founded in Aug. 1995 by a coalition of independent unions including the Independent Miners' Union (NPG), regional inter-trade union federations and individual unions. By 1997–98 it was actively involved with the FNPR and KTR in the campaign of protest against unpaid wages and in the 1998 financial crisis joined the demands for Yeltsin's resignation. Its then president, NPG leader Aleksandr Sergeyev, was briefly detained at that time. Since Dec. 1999 it has participated in the Tripartite Commission for the Regulation of Social and Labour Relations. In Nov. 2000 it was admitted into affiliation to the ICFTU along with the FNPR and the KTR. It is currently working with the KTR to prepare the basis for merger of the two organizations.

International affiliation. ICFTU

Confederation of Labour of Russia (KTR)

Address. 42 Leninsky Prospect, 117119 Moscow

Phone. +7 95 938 8270

Fax. +7 95 938 8270

Membership. Claims 1.25 million.

History and character. The KTR was founded in Apr. 1995, with support from unions of air traffic controllers, doctors, seamen and railway workers. It was affiliated to the ICFTU in Nov. 2000.

International affiliation. ICFTU

Rwanda

Capital: Kigali
Population: 7.23 m. (2000 est.)

1 Political and Economic Background

Rwanda achieved independence from Belgium in 1962. Following a military coup led by Gen. Juvénal Habyarimana in 1973, the Hutu-dominated regime ran a one-party state through the National Republican Movement for Democracy and Development (MRNDD) until the adoption of a multi-party constitution in 1991. By then, however, a rebellion had been launched by the predominantly Tutsi Rwandan Patriotic Front (FPR) which by 1992 had made extensive territorial gains in northern Rwanda. A fragile peace process in 1993 collapsed in Apr. 1994 when President Habyarimana was killed in a plane crash. This triggered mass killings of genocidal proportions of Tutsi by Hutu supporters of Habyarimana (who also liquidated non-Tutsi political opponents) and this in turn led to the renewal of the FPR military offensive. In July 1994 the FPR claimed a military victory and a new government of national unity was formed, excluding the MRNDD, whose militia, the Interahamwe, had been heavily involved in the atrocities. Since then power has been held by a coalition, dominated by the FPR, which controls the (unelected) legislature, the Transitional National Assembly, and holds the presidency. Elections scheduled for June 1999 were postponed to 2003. In 1999, some 135,000 people were still detained or awaiting trial by the International Criminal Tribunal for Rwanda set up by the UN Security Council in response to the 1994 genocide and based in Arusha (Tanzania).

Rwanda is densely populated and poor. It has few natural resources and negligible industry (mainly involving the processing of agricultural products) and 90% of the population is engaged in agriculture, mainly at subsistence level.

GDP (purchasing power parity) $5.9bn. (1999 est.); GDP per capita (purchasing power parity) $720 (1999 est.).

2 Trade Unionism

Rwanda has been a member of the International Labour Organization since 1962, and ratified ILO Conventions No. 87 (Freedom of Association and Protection of the Right to Organize, 1948) and No. 98 (Right to Organize and Collective Bargaining, 1949) in 1985.

Local branches of Belgian unions existed prior to independence but a single trade union system then came into force, organized by the Centrale Syndicale des Travailleurs du Rwanda (CESTRAR). In the early 1990s, as in much of Africa, moves were made towards political pluralism, and as part of this CESTRAR formally became independent of the government and the formation of other unions was permitted. CESTRAR is now affiliated to the ICFTU, and the WCL also has a multi-industry union directly affiliated.

Workers in both private and public sectors are legally free to join unions. Only a few percent of the workforce are paid wages and salaries in the formal economy, but unionization rates are traditionally quite high in this group, especially in the public sector. The civil war and genocide of the mid-1990s devastated civil society and with it the functioning of labour legislation and unions. The ICFTU reported that trade unions resumed "limited activities" by 1997 in the aftermath of the 1994 genocide. However, there are few meaningful mechanisms in operation to enforce labour laws. There is legal provision for collective bargaining although this does not exist to any degree. Government employees may not strike.

3 Trade Union Centre

Centrale Syndicale des Travailleurs du Rwanda (CESTRAR)
Central Trade Union of Workers of Rwanda

Address. BP 1645, Kigali

Phone. +250 85 658

Fax. +250 84 012

History and character. CESTRAR was founded in 1985 under single party rule as the only national centre in Rwanda. In 1991 it declared its independence of all political parties following the proclamation of a multi-party system. Since recovering from the catastrophe that engulfed Rwanda in 1994, CESTRAR has set up branches in every prefecture and has made youth education work a priority.

International affiliation. ICFTU

4 Other Trade Union Organization

Syndicat des Travailleurs des Industries, Garages, Enterprises de Constructions, Mines et Imprimeries (STRIGECOMI)
Union of Workers in Industry, Garages, Construction Firms, Mines and Printers

Address. BP 2214, Kigali

Leadership. Emmanuel Ntegekurora (president), Dominique Bicamumpaka (national executive secretary)

International affiliation. WCL

St. Christopher and Nevis

Capital: Basseterre
Population: 39,000 (2000 est.)

1 Political and Economic Background

St. Christopher (Kitts) and St. Nevis, a federation of two islands, is an independent member of the Commonwealth. The social democratic St. Kitts–Nevis Labour Party, led by Denzil Douglas, returned to power at elections in 1995, ending 15 years of rule by the centrist People's Action Movement (PAM).

The economy is based on the cultivation and processing of sugar, and has been affected by declining world sugar prices, further aggravated by devastating hurricane damage in 1998. Tourism and an electronics industry for the US market are increasingly important.

GDP (purchasing power parity) $244m. (1998 est.); GDP per capita (purchasing power parity) $6,000 (1998 est.).

2 Trade Unionism

St. Kitts is not a member of the ILO. Trade unions were legalized in 1939 and are well established and generally recognized by employers. The St. Kitts–Nevis Trades and Labour Union (TLU) continues to dominate trade unionism on the islands, but there are also unaffiliated unions for teachers and dock workers. Collective bargaining takes place at enterprise level and there is a recognized right to strike.

3 Trade Union Centre

St. Kitts–Nevis Trades and Labour Union (TLU)

Address. PO Box 239, Masses House, Church Street, Basseterre

Phone. +1869 465 2229

Fax. +1869 466 9866

E-mail. sknunion@caribsurf.com

Leadership. Stanley Franks (general secretary)

History and character. The efforts of the St. Kitts Workers' League (founded in 1932 and later renamed as the Labour Party) were instrumental in the legalization of trade unionism in 1939, and the consequent formation of the St. Kitts–Nevis Trades and Labour Union in 1940. The union's orientation is social democratic and the relationship with the Labour party (which won all elections from 1937 to 1975 and was in power until 1980, and then again from 1995) is close.

International affiliations. ICFTU; CTUC

St. Lucia

Capital: Castries
Population: 156,000 (2000 est.)

1 Political and Economic Background

St. Lucia has been an independent member of the Commonwealth since 1979. In elections in May 1997, the centre-left St. Lucia Labour Party, led by Kenny Anthony, defeated the conservative United Workers' Party, which had held power for the previous 15 years.

The country's main export earnings come from bananas, which face heavy competition from low-cost Latin American producers and are vulnerable to storm damage. St. Lucia has been trying to diversify into tourism and services to reduce the dependence on bananas.

GDP (purchasing power parity) $656m. (1998 est.); GDP per capita (purchasing power parity) $4,300 (1998 est.).

2 Trade Unionism

St. Lucia has been a member of the International Labour Organization since 1980, and ratified ILO Conventions No. 87 (Freedom of Association and Protection of the Right to Organize, 1948) and No. 98 (Right to Organize and Collective Bargaining, 1949) in that year. Unions operate freely according to the law and in practice.

There is no trade union centre in St. Lucia. However, there are a number of unions and about 20% of the total workforce is organized, the unions being particularly strong in the public sector. Unions that gain sufficient membership at new firms may demand a ballot for recognition, but gaining this first foothold has proved difficult for them in the export processing zones. Collective bargaining is widely practiced. Police and firefighters may not strike and workers in a range of other essential services such as utilities and healthcare must give 30 days' advance notice of strike action.

3 Trade Union Centre

There is no trade union centre in St. Lucia

4 Other Trade Union Organizations

National Workers' Union (NWU)

Address. PO Box 713, 60 Micoud Street, Castries

Phone. +1758 452 3664

Fax. +1758 453 2896

Leadership. Tyrone Maynard (president)

Membership. 3,200

History and character. The NWU was founded in 1973 and is a general union with branches for each occupational sector.

International affiliation. WCL

St. Lucia Civil Service Association

Address. PO Box 244, Castries

Phone. +1758 452 3903

Fax. +1758 453 6061

E-mail. info@stluciacsa.org

Leadership. Lawrence Poyotte (general secretary)

International affiliation. CTUC

St. Lucia Seamen, Waterfront and General Workers' Trade Union (SWGWTU)

Address. 68 Micoud St, PO Box 166, Castries

Phone. +1758 452 1669

Fax. +1758 452 5452

Leadership. Crescentia Phillips (general secretary)

International affiliations. ICFTU; CTUC

St. Lucia Workers' Union (WU)

Address. PO Box 245, 3 Park Street (Reclamation Grounds), Castries

Phone. +1758 452 2620

History and character. Founded 1939 on the recommendation of a commission (appointed by the British government to investigate labour disturbances throughout the then British West Indies). Linked to the St. Lucia Labour Party, the WU is the oldest union in St. Lucia.

International affiliation. ICFTU

Vieux Fort General and Dock Workers' Union

Address. PO Box 224, Theodore Street, Vieux Fort

Phone. +1758 454 6193

Fax. +1758 454 5128

Leadership. Modeste Downes (general secretary)

International affiliation. CTUC

St. Vincent and the Grenadines

Capital: Kingstown
Population: 115,000 (2000 est.)

1 Political and Economic Background

A former British dependency, St. Vincent and the Grenadines became an independent member of the Commonwealth in 1979. Since 1984 the government has been formed by the conservative New Democratic Party (NDP), which was most recently re-elected, under Prime Minister Sir James Mitchell, in June 1998.

The economy is based on the cultivation and processing of bananas, with services, notably tourism, of increasing importance. 60% of jobs are in agriculture. The banana industry has been badly affected by competition from Latin American producers and, in some recent years, by devastating storm damage. Unemployment continues to be a major problem and unofficial estimates have put it for some years at a rate above 30 per cent.

GDP (purchasing power parity) $309m. (1999 est.); GDP per capita (purchasing power parity) $2,600 (1999 est.).

2 Trade Unionism

St. Vincent and the Grenadines joined the International
Labour Organization in 1997 and the following year ratified Convention No. 98 (Right to Organize and Collective Bargaining, 1949). It has not ratified Convention
No. 87 (Freedom of Association and Protection of the
Right to Organize, 1948). There is no compulsory recognition of trade unions and virtually no employment
legislation at all. In practice however, if there is evidence that more than 30 per cent of employees wish for
a union, the authorities intervene with the employer to
suggest recognition. Union density is about 10 per cent.
There is a legally protected right to strike.

3 Trade Union Centre

There is no national trade union centre.

4 Other Trade Union Organizations

**Commercial, Technical and Allied Workers' Union
(CTAWU)**

Address. Union House, PO Box 245, Kingstown

Phone. +1784 45 71459

Fax. +1784 45 71767

E-mail. ctawu@caribsurf.com

Membership. 2,000

International affiliations. ICFTU

National Workers' Movement (NWM)

Address. Suite 3, Burke's Building, Greenville Street,
PO Box 1290, Kingstown

Phone. +1784 457 1950

Fax. +1784 456 2858

E-mail. natwork@caribsurf.com

Leadership. Noel Jackson (general secretary)

International affiliation. WCL

**St. Vincent and the Grenadines Public Service
Union (PSU)**

Address. PO Box 875, McKie's Hill, Kingstown

Phone. +1784 457 1801

Fax. +1784 457 1705

Leadership. Glenn Jackson (general secretary)

International affiliation. CTUC

Samoa

Capital: Apia
Population: 179,000 (2000 est.)

1 Political and Economic Background

Samoa (known until 1997 as Western Samoa) achieved
full independence in 1962, having previously been
under New Zealand administration. 47 of the 49 seats in
the legislature are reserved for members of the Matai,
the traditional clan leaders. The Human Rights
Protection Party has won every election since 1982,
although politics are primarily based on personal
alliances.

The economy is predominantly agricultural. There is
a dependence on development aid and remittances from
workers abroad.

GDP (purchasing power parity) $485m. (1998 est.);
GDP per capita (purchasing power parity) $2,100 (1998
est.).

2 Trade Unionism

Workers may by law form and join unions. The Public
Service Association (PSA) is the established major local
union. There is now also a Samoa Trades Union
Congress, affiliated to the ICFTU. Collective bargaining
is not widely practiced in the private sector, but the PSA
engages in collective bargaining on behalf of government workers. There is a right to strike in both the private and public sector. Arbitration and mediation
procedures exist, although labour disputes are not
common. Samoa is not a member of the International
Labour Organization.

3 Trade Union Centre

**Samoa Trades Union Congress/Samoa National
Union of Workers**

Address. PO Box 2260, Apia

Phone. +685 22049

Fax. +685 22049

E-mail. snuw@lesamoa.net

Leadership. Tutonu Vaomua (president); Su'a Viliamu Sio (general secretary)

Membership. 1,100

History and character. Founded in 1995 and comprising unions of bank, transport, rural, forestry, public enterprises and community workers. Is campaigning for modernization of the labour laws and for Samoa to join the ILO.

International affiliation. ICFTU; CTUC

4 Other Trade Union Organization

Samoa Public Service Association (PSA)

Address. PO Box 1515, Apia

Phone. +685 24134

Fax. +685 20014

E-mail. psa@samoa.net

Leadership. Apoiliu Warren (general secretary)

International affiliations. CTUC

San Marino

Capital: San Marino
Population: 27,000 (2000 est.)

1 Political and Economic Background

San Marino is a micro-republic entirely surrounded by Italy. Legislative power is vested in a 60-member, elected Grand and General Council; two Council members are appointed every six months to act as Captains–Regent who, with a Congress of State (government) exercise executive power. Since 1992 the government has been formed by a coalition of the Christian Democratic Party (PDCS) and the Socialist Party (PS).

Tourism generates more than 50% of GDP, and there is also banking, light manufacturing and agriculture. Living standards are similar to Italy.

GDP (purchasing power parity) $500m. (1997 est.); GDP per capita (purchasing power parity) $20,000 (1997 est.).

2 Trade Unionism

San Marino joined the International Labour Organization in 1982 and ratified ILO Conventions No. 87 (Freedom of Association and Protection of the Right to Organize, 1948) and No. 98 (Right to Organize and Collective Bargaining, 1949) in 1986.

All employees, except members of the armed forces, may join trade unions and about half the workforce (which comprises some 10,000 Sammarinese citizens and 4,000 Italians) are organized. There are two long-established confederations. The Confederazione Sammarinese del Lavoro (CSdL), founded in 1943, was the only recognized union until the recognition of trade union pluralism in 1957 and the formation of the Confederazione Democratica dei Lavoratori Sammarinesi (CDLS). During the 1960s these two groups tended to adopt similar policies, and in 1976 they formed the Centrale Sindicale Unitaire (CSU – Central United Union) with the ultimate objective of creating an organic union. This goal has not yet been achieved although the CSdL and the CDLS share offices and are both now (since the CSdL joined in 1997) affiliated to the ICFTU.

Collective bargaining agreements are legally binding. A tripartite conciliation committee exists to resolve disputes and strikes tend to be infrequent and brief.

3 Trade Union Centres

Confederazione Democratica dei Lavoratori Sammarinesi (CDLS)
Democratic Confederation of San Marino Workers

Address. Via Napoleone Bonaparte 75, Citta di San Marino, I– 47890 Republic of San Marino

Phone. +378 549 879507

Fax. +378 549 992178

E-mail. info@cdls.sm

Website. www.cdls.sm (Italian only)

Leadership. Marco Beccari (secretary–general)

History and character. Founded in 1957. General orientation is Catholic and socialist, but it believes in trade union autonomy from political organizations.

International affiliations. ICFTU; ETUC

Confederazione Sammarinese del Lavoro (CSdL)
San Marino Confederation of Labour

Address. Via Napoleone Bonaparte 75, Citta di San Marino, I– 47890 Republic of San Marino

Phone. +378 549 879504

Fax. +378 549 992333

E-mail. csdl@omniway.sm

Website. www.omniway.sm (Italian only)

Leadership. Giovanni Ghiotti (secretary–general)

Membership. 2,450 in five affiliated federations.

History and character. Founded in 1943. Joined ETUC in 1991 and the ICFTU in 1997.

Publications. Argomenti; Periscopio

International affiliations. ICFTU; ETUC

São Tomé and Príncipe

Capital: São Tomé
Population: 160,000 (2000 est.)

1 Political and Economic Background

São Tomé and Príncipe achieved independence from Portugal in 1975 and was then run as a one-party state by the Marxist Movement for the Liberation of São Tomé and Príncipe (MLSTP) until a new constitution providing for a multi–party system was approved by a 1990 referendum. In 1991 legislative elections victory went to the Democratic Convergence Party–Reflection Group, whose presidential candidate, Miguel Trovoada, was also successful. In 1994, the revamped Movement for the Liberation of São Tomé and Príncipe–Social Democratic Party (MLSTP–PSD) gained control of the National Assembly (which it retained in 1998 elections). In 1995 Trovoada was temporarily removed from power in a bloodless coup by army officers, but he went on to be re-elected in 1996.

Most of the workforce are engaged in subsistence agriculture. The major cash crop is cocoa, produced in state-run plantations. There is a heavy reliance on external aid and external debt is six times GDP.

GDP (purchasing power parity) $169m. (1999 est.); GDP per capita (purchasing power parity) $1,100 (1999 est.).

2 Trade Unionism

São Tomé and Príncipe joined the International Labour Organization in 1982 and ratified Conventions No. 87 (Freedom of Association and Protection of the Right to Organize, 1948) and No. 98 (Right to Organize and Collective Bargaining, 1949) in 1992.

Trade unionism was severely curbed during Portuguese rule. In the 1980s a single trade union system was set up under the ruling party. At the beginning of the 1990s there was a move to political pluralism and the 1990 constitution provides for freedom of association. However, the modern formal economy is small and there has been little development of trade unions, with most activity in the public sector. There is constitutional provision for collective bargaining although most negotiations are with the government as the primary formal sector employer. There is a WCL affiliate but no ICFTU representation.

3 Trade Union Centre

União Geral dos Trabalhadores de São Tomé et Príncipe (UGT)

Address. Rua de Creche, BP 272, São Tomé

Phone. +239 12 22 443

Fax. +239 12 21 466

Leadership. Cosme Rita (secretary–general) `

International affiliation. WCL

Saudi Arabia

Capital: Riyadh
Population: 22.02 m. (2000 est.)

1 Political and Economic Background

Saudi Arabia is an absolute monarchy ruled according to a conservative interpretation of the laws and precepts of Islam. King Fahd has been the ruler since 1982. He is also the Prime Minister and his Council of Ministers includes family members in most key posts. The kingdom has no elected parliament and no political parties but there is a Consultative Council.

Saudi Arabia has the world's largest proven oil reserves and is the world's leading oil exporter. Oil generates 75% of government revenues. A fall in the price of oil in the late 1990s led to budget cuts in 1999, but the government enjoyed a large budgetary surplus in 2000 as a result of oil price rises. There are some four million foreign workers and since 1995 the government has promoted a campaign to increase the proportion of Saudis (only 25%) in the workforce, although in the private sector this remains negligible. There was a crackdown on illegal foreign workers in 1998–99. The government has also sought to encourage diversification and private sector investment but the economy has been generally stagnant for more than a decade with job creation not matching population growth.

GDP (purchasing power parity) $191bn. (1999 est.); GDP per capita (purchasing power parity) $9,000 (1999 est.).

2 Trade Unionism

Saudi Arabia has been a member of the International Labour Organization since 1976, but has ratified neither Convention No.87 (Freedom of Association and Protection of the Right to Organize, 1948) nor No.98 (Right to Organize and Collective Bargaining, 1949).

Trade unions are illegal and dismissal, imprisonment or (in the case of foreign workers) expulsion follow attempts at organization. Trade unions are considered to violate the principles of Islam. The WFTU recognizes an exiled "Workers' Union of Saudi Arabia" but this can not organize within the country.

Collective bargaining is forbidden under Saudi law. Wages are set directly by employers and vary according to the nationality of the worker. Strikes are illegal.

Domestic servants are not protected by labour laws. Foreign workers, who depend on their employers for residency, are reportedly sometimes victims of non-payment of wages or other abuses, and do not complain to the labour courts for fear of deportation. Employed Saudis work mainly in the public sector and private sector employers are reported to be reluctant to take on Saudis because they are difficult to dismiss if they do not do their job. Women face extensive discrimination at work and may participate in only limited areas of the economy.

Senegal

Capital: Dakar
Population: 9.99 m. (2000 est.)

1 Political and Economic Background

Senegal achieved full independence from France in 1960 and was then led by the Socialist Party of Senegal (PSS) for four decades. Senegal had a de facto one-party system in the period 1964–74. In 1974 the first opposition party was permitted, and after

1976 a greater degree of pluralism was allowed. Abdou Diouf became President in 1981 and then held the office until defeated by Abdoulayé Wade, the candidate of a coalition of opposition parties, the Front for Changeover, in presidential elections in March 2000. The hand-over of power from the PSS was reported as orderly. The PSS continued to hold the majority in the legislature, to which elections were last held in 1998 (National Assembly) and 1999 (Senate).

In recent years Senegal has sought to liberalize its

economy, privatizing state enterprises and dismantling price controls and subsidies. Real GDP grew an average 5% per annum in the period 1995–99. About 70% of the workforce are engaged in agriculture, much of it at subsistence level, and there is a limited industrial sector. External assistance is an important contributor.

GDP (purchasing power parity) $16.6bn. (1999 est.); GDP per capita (purchasing power parity) $1,650 (1999 est.).

2 Trade Unionism

Trade unions first developed prior to independence under French rule. Following independence, Senegal ratified ILO Convention No.87 (Freedom of Association and Protection of the Right to Organize, 1948) in 1960 and Convention No.98 (Right to Organize and Collective Bargaining, 1949) in 1961. In 1969 the Confédération Nationale des Travailleurs Sénégalais (CNTS) was established as the sole trade union centre, with affiliation to the only permitted party, the Union Progressiste Sénégalaise (UPS, known from 1976 as the Parti Socialiste Sénégalais – PSS). Political and trade union pluralism was re-established after 1976. At different times there have been several rival centres to the CNTS, including groupings of independent unions, but it has remained dominant, retaining its close relationship to the PSS.

Under the constitution and labour code all workers have the right of association, and there are provisions against anti-union discrimination by employers, although government approval is needed for a union to be registered. The unions are highly organized in the small formal economy and there is also some recruitment in the informal sector. There is collective bargaining and the Ministry of Labour provides mediation. There is a right to strike, subject to a period of notice, and strikes frequently occur without government interference. In 1998, however, the general secretary of the electricity workers' union was sentenced to six months imprisonment for conspiracy to disrupt law and order following industrial action against the privatization of the national electricity supplier.

3 Trade Union Centre

Confédération Nationale des Travailleurs Sénégalais (CNTS)
National Confederation of Senegalese Workers

Address. 7 Avenue du Président Laminé Gueye, BP 937, Dakar

Phone. +221 821 0491

Fax. +221 821 7771

E-mail. cnts@sentoo.sn

Leadership. Madia Diop (secretary-general)

Membership. 60,000

History and character. Founded in 1969, the CNTS has historically been allied to the Parti Socialiste du Sénégal (PSS), which has been the governing party from independence until losing the presidency in 2000.

International affiliation. ICFTU

4 Other Trade Union Organization

Union Démocratique des Travailleurs du Sénégal (UDTS)
Democratic Union of Senegalese Workers

Address. Rue 10 (face école 5), no. 1360 Pikine, BP 7124, Medina–DKR, Dakar

Phone. +221 343 897

Fax. +221 834 0595

E-mail. trintern@telecomplus.sn

Leadership. Sow Alioune (secretary–general)

International affiliation. WCL

Seychelles

Capital: Victoria
Population: 79,000 (2000 est.)

1 Political and Economic Background

Seychelles achieved independence from Britain in 1976. France-Albert René came to power in a coup in 1977 and established a one-party state with his left-wing Seychelles People's Progressive Front (SPPF) as the sole permitted party. The reform wave seen throughout much of Africa at the start of the 1990s caused the SPPF to endorse a move to political pluralism in Dec. 1991; in Apr. 1992 the President deposed in the 1977 coup returned from exile, and in 1993 multi-party elections were held. These resulted in victory for the ruling party and President René, a result repeated in the most recent elections in 1998.

Seychelles is a relatively prosperous country. Its economy is heavily dependent upon tourism, which employs 30% of the labour force and generates 70% of foreign exchange earnings. Fishing and light manufacturing are also important. There has been little movement towards privatizing state enterprises.

GDP (purchasing power parity) $590m. (1999 est.); GDP per capita (purchasing power parity) $7,500 (1999 est.).

2 Trade Unionism

Seychelles has been a member of the International Labour Organization since 1977, and ratified ILO Convention No. 87 (Freedom of Association and Protection of the Right to Organize, 1948) in 1978 and Convention No.98 (Right to Organize and Collective Bargaining, 1949) in 1999.

Following the coup which brought the SPPF to power, all previously existing trade unions were coordinated in 1978 in the National Workers' Union (Seychelles) (NWUS). According to the constitution of the SPPF the NWUS functioned under the direction of the Front, which had to approve every decision of the union. Following the move to political pluralism in the early 1990s the 1993 Industrial Relations Act ended the monopoly of the NWUS. The SPPF-associated centre is now called the Seychelles Federation of Workers' Unions (SFWU) and there is also an independent Seychelles Workers Union (SWU). Union density is estimated at 15–20%. All workers may join unions other than police and prison officers, the armed forces and firefighters. Efforts to organize an independent union in the government service have been frustrated by the government.

The Industrial Relations Act provides for collective bargaining but the government is empowered to review and approve all agreements. In the public sector, which accounts for more than half of formal employment, the government sets rates of pay.

3 Trade Union Centre

Seychelles Federation of Workers' Unions (SFWU)

Address. Maison du Peuple, PO Box 154, Victoria

Phone. +248 226 18

Fax. +248 22 53 51

Leadership. B. Adonis (general secretary)

History and character. This is the successor to the National Workers' Union (Seychelles) set up in 1978 by the ruling SPPF. The SFWU no longer has its predecessor's monopoly status but remains the leading trade union organization in Seychelles and close to the SPPF.

International affiliation. ICFTU; CTUC

Sierra Leone

Capital: Freetown
Population: 5.23 m. (2000 est.)

1 Political and Economic Background

Sierra Leone achieved independence from the United Kingdom in 1961, originally as a constitutional monarchy, but from 1971 as a republic. In 1978 the All People's Congress of President Siaka Stevens was declared the sole legal party, and the country remained a one-party state until a 1991 referendum approved the introduction of multi-party politics. In Apr. 1992, however, a military coup took place and all political activity was banned until 1995. In Feb. 1996 elections finally took place, resulting in victory for the Sierra Leone People's Party (SLPP) and its presidential candidate, Ahmad Tejan Kabbah, whose grip on power was tenuous in the face of a continuing rebellion by the Revolutionary United Front (RUF) of Foday Sankoh. A further military coup took place in May 1997, led by Lt.-Col. Johnny Paul Koroma, who gained the backing of the RUF. In Mar. 1998 Koroma was ousted by Nigerian–led forces sent under the auspices of the Economic Community of West African States (ECOWAS), and Kabbah restored as President.

In July 1999 the West brokered an agreement, notwithstanding evidence of atrocities committed by the RUF, that involved the RUF in power-sharing and allowed it to retain effective control over the country's diamond mines. UN forces sent to monitor the agreement subsequently became hostages of the RUF and in May 2000 British troops intervened, supervising an evacuation of foreign nationals and detaining the RUF's leader, Foday Sankoh.

About two-thirds of the workforce are engaged in subsistence agriculture although there is also mining, notably of diamonds. There is some light manufacturing industry but the formal private sector has been set back by persistent conflict in recent years. The country has a dependence on external assistance.

GDP (purchasing power parity) $2.5bn. (1999 est.); GDP per capita (purchasing power parity) $500 (1999 est.).

2 Trade Unionism

Trade unions were first recognized by the British colonial authorities just before World War II and were well established by the time of independence in 1961. The national trade union centre is the Sierra Leone Labour Congress (SLLC). The SLLC was active in campaigning for political pluralism in the early 1990s and was prominent in opposing the military coups of 1992 and 1997.

Sierra Leone ratified ILO Conventions No.87 (Freedom of Association and Protection of the Right to Organize, 1948) and No.98 (Right to Organize and Collective Bargaining, 1949) in 1961. The constitution provides for freedom of association other than for the police and the armed forces. Union members are found in the small manufacturing sector and in white-collar urban professions such as government and teaching. However, the great majority of the workforce are engaged in subsistence agriculture or informal activities and are not in unions. Union membership is also believed to have fallen in recent years because of the dislocation caused by conflict. The law provides a framework for collective bargaining and collective bargaining does occur in the formal sector. There is a right to strike but strikers have no protection from dismissal.

3 Trade Union Centre

Sierra Leone Labour Congress (SLLC)

Address. PO Box 1333, Freetown

Phone. +232 2 226 869

Fax. +232 2 224 439

Leadership. Uriah O.H. Davies (president); Kandeh B. Yilla (general secretary)

History and character. The SLLC was founded in 1976–77 in succession to a number of earlier centres. In 1981 it came into conflict with the government, rejecting its emphasis on external factors as responsible for the country's economic difficulties. Strikes organized by the SLLC led to looting, the detention of numerous trade union leaders, and a number of deaths. Ibrahim Langley, then SLLC president, was appointed a nominated MP by President Stevens in 1982, shortly after he had announced the dismissal as SLLC general secretary of James Kabia, the main organizer of the 1981 strikes. Sweeping emergency regulations giving the government extensive powers were introduced in 1987 following a series of strikes by public sector workers over salary non-payment. They were extended for 12 months the following year, after which the SLLC played a major part in trying to obtain a smooth transition to pluralist democracy, while guarding its political independence.

In the aftermath of the 1992 military coup, property belonging to the SLLC was taken over by the incoming regime; the passport of its general secretary Kandeh Yilla was confiscated and he was for a time ordered to report daily to the police. Two years later after continuing civil strife, Yilla was reported by the ICFTU to be in fear of his life following death threats.

Following the May 1997 coup that overthrew President Kabbah, the new regime confiscated vehicles and other property belonging to the SLLC and its affiliates. The SLLC called on workers to engage in stay-at-home protests until the elected government was restored. The SLLC has received international trade union support for its work for peace and reconciliation in Sierra Leone, which includes providing training and income generation projects for ex-combatants. After the RUF forces of Foday Sankoh attacked UN peace-keepers in Apr. 2000, the SLLC and civic groups organized a peace march on May 8. RUF fighters fired on the demonstrators, killing 22, among them the SLLC's finance officer.

International affiliation. ICFTU; CTUC

4 Other Trade Union Organization

Sierra Leone Confederation of Trade Unions (SLCTU)

Address. 8 Howe Street, Spiritus House, 1st Floor, Freetown

Phone. +232 2 222 60 82

Fax. +232 2 222 44 39

History and character. Founded in 1996. SLCTU president John P.F. Cowray was killed by RUF rebels on Jan. 22, 1999

International affiliation. WCL

Singapore

Capital: Singapore City
Population: 4.15 m. (2000 est.)

1 Political and Economic Background

Singapore achieved internal self-rule from the United Kingdom in 1959, and four years later joined the Federation of Malaysia. On leaving the Federation in 1965, the Republic of Singapore became an independent sovereign state. It has been ruled continuously since that time by the conservative and authoritarian People's Action Party, under Prime Ministers Lee Kuan Yew and (since 1990) Goh Chok Tong. There is tight censorship and opposition leaders have been fined and imprisoned in recent years for the offence of "speaking in public without a permit."

Singapore is a city–state that has developed one of the most dynamic and successful economies in Asia, serving as an international trading centre as well as possessing a substantial modern manufacturing base. It proved able to weather the 1997–98 Asian financial crisis far better than most regional economies and in 2000 GDP grew by over 10%. While Singapore has a free market economy, the government has historically played a driving role in shaping investment and economic development. The government seeks to maintain Singapore's position, in the face of high labour costs, by raising productivity through technology and focusing on high value-added industries. It is also now, in the face of globalization, moving to change the previous model of development to deregulate key sectors such as banking, power and insurance, and reducing protectionism.

GDP (purchasing power parity) $98bn. (1999 est.); GDP per capita (purchasing power parity) $27,800 (1999 est.).

2 Trade Unionism

Trade unions developed after World War II and became associated with opposition to British colonial rule. A Singapore Trades Union Congress appeared in the 1950s in association with the People's Action Party (PAP, which came to power when Singapore achieved internal self-government in 1959). The early 1960s saw the union movement divided, with strikes and unrest, over issues of post-colonial politics such as the short-lived federation with Malaysia (1963–65). In 1961 the Trades Union Congress split into the National Trades Union Congress (NTUC), allied to the PAP, and a leftist Singapore Association of Trade Unions, but the latter collapsed in 1963. Since then, with heavy guidance from the PAP, the overwhelming emphasis has come to be placed on tripartism and building and retaining a repu-

tation for labour stability and productivity. This has been reinforced by the uninterrupted success of the Singaporean model in delivering year-on-year real growth and wage increases with virtually full employment. The Asian economic crisis of 1997–98 was relatively lightly felt in Singapore and had no real impact on the tripartite consensus in favour of industrial peace. The NTUC remains closely allied with the ruling People's Action Party both ideologically and organizationally.

Singapore has not ratified ILO Convention No.87 (Freedom of Association and Protection of the Right to Organize, 1948) but domestic legislation provides for the formation of trade unions. In the private sector, workers are generally free to join unions of their own choosing and acts of anti-union discrimination by employers are prohibited. Although the Registrar of Trade Unions has extensive powers to refuse or cancel registration of trade unions, particularly where one already exists for workers in a particular occupation or industry, this power has not been exercised for more than 15 years.

In the public sector, in contrast, there is no legal right to form and join trade unions and the unrepealed colonial Trades Union Act includes a general prohibition on government employees joining trade unions. However, exemptions may be granted and the Amalgamated Union of Public Employees (AUPE) is the second largest trade union in Singapore, representing over 20,000 workers. Since 1999, all public sector employees other than some senior civil servants have been able to join a union.

NTUC affiliates account for 300,000 of the labour force of 1.9 million. Only a few thousand workers are in unions not affiliated to the NTUC. The near-monopoly position of the NTUC has been allied to the enduring domestic popularity of the PAP, which won 81 of he 83 seats in the most recent election to Parliament, in Jan. 1997, and a political culture that does not favour dissent. The NTUC and its affiliates are also able to provide a wide range of benefits and member services.

Singapore ratified ILO Convention No.98 (Right to Organize and Collective Bargaining, 1949) in 1965. Collective bargaining is widely practiced. Annual guidelines on pay are issued by the tripartite National Wages Council (NWC), set up in 1972, and provide a framework for bargaining agreements. To be enforceable, collective agreements have to be certified by the Industrial Arbitration Court, and although certification can be refused on public interest grounds, this has never happened. In theory, collective agreements in newly established enterprises cannot provide more favourable conditions than the legal minimum specified in the Employment Act, but in practice this provision is disregarded. Strikes are legal, other than in essential services and subject to a vote of 50% of all union members in favour, but no strikes are reported to have occurred since 1986. The Ministry of Manpower actively involves itself in resolving disputes, and if conciliation fails cases are usually referred to the tripartite Industrial Arbitration Court. While the law provides for compulsory arbitration in some circumstances, this has not occurred since 1981.

Non-citizens may not be union officers and union funds may not be paid out to political parties or used for political purposes.

3 Trade Union Centre

National Trades Union Congress (NTUC)

Address. NTUC Trade Union House, 73 Bras Basah Road, Singapore 189556

Phone. +65 837 8253

Fax. +65 339 6713

E-mail. wongcka@union.ntucworld.org.sg

Website. www.ntucworld.org.sg

Leadership. John De Pavya (president); Lim Boon Heng (secretary–general)

Membership. 300,918

History and character. The NTUC is the sole trade union centre, and 98.5% of union members in Singapore are in its affiliated unions. The NTUC says its membership is the highest on record and increasing, and that this was assisted by workers' realization of the value of union membership in the 1998–99 period, when the economy was under stress from the Asian economic crisis.

The NTUC's relationship with the People's Action Party (PAP), which has held power continuously since independence, is often described by both the NTUC and the PAP as "symbiotic". The unions backed the PAP when it was set up in 1954 to spearhead the country's struggle for independence from Britain. When the PAP came to power in 1959 it fulfilled its election pledges to create the conditions under which unions could operate effectively. In 1961 the labour movement split, the pro-PAP majority forming the NTUC and a pro-communist minority seceding to form a Singapore Association of Trade Unions. The latter collapsed in 1963, since when the NTUC has been the only trade union centre.

Relations between the PAP and NTUC have been cemented by office-holding. Ong Teng Cheong was simultaneously NTUC secretary-general and Second Deputy Prime Minister from 1985 until he became the country's first directly elected President (non-executive head of state) from 1993–99. His successor (and current) NTUC secretary-general, Lim Boon Heng, is Minister without Portfolio in the Prime Minister's Office. PAP Members of Parliament in the early stages of their careers commonly hold positions in the NTUC or its affiliates. NTUC policy prohibits union members who actively support opposition parties from holding office in affiliated unions, although there have been cases of local NTUC officials running as opposition candidates. However, the NTUC is financially independent of the PAP.

The NTUC works closely with the government and employers to promote industrial peace and justice. Tripartism is practiced extensively and there is cooperation at every level of industrial relations, and although in principle the strike weapon remains as part of the union armoury it has not been used since a dispute in 1986. The NTUC has supported wage flexibility as a means of adjusting to economic conditions, and argues its position on this has been a factor in ensuring Singapore has recovered quickly from its two major economic setbacks since the 1960s, the 1985–86 recession and the 1997–98 Asian financial crisis.

The NTUC is currently engaged in a variety of initiatives, often in cooperation with employers, to equip its members to deal with the impact of rapid corporate restructuring, outsourcing and technological change. It is putting more emphasis on the needs of contract workers and part-time workers. Recognizing that Singapore can only retain competitive advantage, as a high wage economy, through high productivity, and that workers with few skills will be marginalized in the labour market, it operates a Skills Redevelopment Programme, based on company participation.

Since the 1960s the NTUC has progressively developed a wide range of member services, such as consumer cooperatives, insurance services, workplace child care schemes, health facilities, and discount schemes. It provides a range of social and recreational facilities, running its own holiday resorts and country clubs.

It established the Singapore Institute of Labour Studies (SILS) as a labour college in 1990.

Publication. NTUC News (English, accessible via website)

International affiliations. ICFTU; CTUC

Slovakia

Capital: Bratislava
Population: 5.41 m. (2000 est.)

GDP (purchasing power parity) $45.9bn. (1999 est.); GDP per capita (purchasing power parity) $8,500 (1999 est.).

1 Political and Economic Background

The communist regime in Czechoslovakia collapsed in the so-called "velvet revolution" of 1989. Following this separatist sentiment developed in the eastern region of Slovakia. In June 1992 general elections resulted in victory for the nationalist Movement for a Democratic Slovakia (HZDS) in Slovakia. Agreement for the dissolution of Czechoslovakia was thereafter reached with rapidity and notable lack of conflict and on Jan. 1, 1993 two separate and independent states, the Czech and Slovak Republics, were established. Under Prime Minister Vladimir Meciar of the HZDS (in power from independence, with one short break, until Sept. 1998), Slovakia increasingly became regarded internationally as authoritarian, antireform and corrupt and its standing deteriorated compared with the Czech Republic. Whereas the Czech Republic was in the first round of former communist states to be invited by the EU to begin accession negotiations, Slovakia was excluded from the process. In elections in Sept. 1998 the HZDS remained the largest party by one seat, but a coalition government was formed by opposition parties led by the Slovak Democratic Coalition (SDK) of the new Prime Minister Mikulas Dzurinda. The new government has worked to improve Slovakia's international image and in Dec. 1999 Slovakia was invited to participate in EU entry talks. In May 1999 Rudolf Schuster defeated Meciar to become Slovakia's first popularly elected President.

The divergence of the Slovak and Czech economies after the end of communist rule encouraged the development of the Slovak independence movement. Slovakia, the location of many traditional industrial sectors and the arms industry, experienced much higher unemployment and attracted far less foreign investment than the Czech lands. Separation, however, merely served to reinforce that divergence. This fact, and the policies of the HZDS under Meciar, has influenced the relatively slow development of a free market in Slovakia. Although privatization began following 1989, much of the traditional industrial sector had not been restructured a decade later. A US Information Agency survey showed that only 38% of Slovaks were in favour of a free market economy, the lowest proportion of any central European country. Slovakia suffers high inflation (13.5% in 2000), and unemployment reached 20% by the end of 1999 against a background of austerity measures introduced by the Dzurinda government to try to control the current account deficit.

2 Trade Unionism

Slovakia ratified ILO Conventions No.87 (Freedom of Association and Protection of the Right to Organize, 1948) and No.98 (Right to Organize and Collective Bargaining, 1949) in 1993.

For four decades until 1989 the trade union movement was organized on the communist model within a unified Czechoslovakia (see country section on the Czech Republic for details of that period). Following the collapse of communist rule, the Confederation of Czechoslovakian Trade Unions (CSKOS) was founded in 1990.

The new structure of trade unionism evolved in step with nationalism and was thus fated not to last. CSKOS rested on two subordinate national bodies. Growing Czech and Slovak nationalism forced a rule change just three months into the life of the new organization (see below) and in May 1991 the Slovak Confederation threatened a general strike against the dismissal of the Slovak prime minister and his replacement by a Christian Democrat. CSKOS doubted the advantages to either nation of splitting into two separate states. A memorandum it submitted to the government in the summer of 1992 forecast economic hardship and an explosion of the black market and disputed the assumption that the Czech part of the country could expect easy expansion once economically separate from Slovakia. The Sept. 1992 general council blamed the impending division of Czechoslovakia on mistakes committed by the old regime. In speeches to the ICFTU and the ETUC on Oct. 9 its president Richard Falbr expressed the determination of CSKOS to stay united. Within a month, however, the Confederation of Trade Unions of the Slovak Republic (KOZ SR) had to be founded in acknowledgment of the new national realities.

An estimated 45% of the workforce is organized and all employees may join unions except members of the armed forces. Discrimination against union organizers and members is prohibited in law and the courts may order the reinstatement of workers dismissed for union activities. In practice anti-union discrimination does not appear to be a major issue.

Collective bargaining is protected in law as is the right to strike. However, strikers enjoy immunity from dismissal only in the case of official strikes, and a strike is official only where in pursuit of collective bargaining, when it is announced in advance, and when a list of strike participants is provided. In 1999 there were unofficial strikes over issues such as job losses but no official strikes were reported.

3 Trade Union Centre

Confederation of Trade Unions of the Slovak Republic (KOZ SR)

Address. Odborarske nam. 3, 815 70 Bratislava

Phone. +421 7 502 39109

Fax. +421 7 555 61956

E-mail. internat.dep@kozsr.sk

Website. www.internet.sk/kozsr (Slovak only)

Leadership. Ivan Saktor (president)

Membership. 752,000

History and character. KOZ SR has its origins in the formation in March 1990 of the Czechoslovak Confederation of Trade Unions (CSKOS) at a national congress whose delegates were chosen at nationwide enterprise elections. It inherited the assets of the former Central Council of Trade Unions (URO). In April 1990 a Confederation of Trade Unions was established for each nation, the Czech-Moravian Chamber (CMK CSKOS) and the Confederation of Trade Unions of the Slovak Republic (KOZ SR), and in June the name of the organization was changed to the Czech and Slovak Confederation of Trade Unions. From this point on, as separatist tendencies grew, the new organization sought to avoid a split along nationalist lines. As late as July 1992 a comprehensive CSKOS memorandum foretold dire economic and political consequences should the separation of the Czech and Slovak lands be carried through; within a few weeks however, trade unionists on both sides were forced to start preparations for the inevitable. CMKOS was formed in the Czech lands and KOZ SR in Slovakia.

KOZ SR seeks to defend trade union and individual human rights within the context of a social market economy. It has sought to steer a politically non-partisan course. Following its Oct. 1996 congress, Prime Minister Vladimir Meciar accused the Party of the Democratic Left (SDL, the reformed Communists) of seeking to exercise political power through the confederation. The SDL counter-charged that that Meciar's HZDS intended to set up its own unions if it could not get control of KOZ SR.

By 1999 KOZ SR was concerned at the impact of austerity measures and rising unemployment under the Dzurinda government. A demonstration in Bratislava called by KOZ SR on Sept. 25, 1999, to protest government policies reportedly drew 40,000 supporters. On Nov. 9, 1999, it organized a series of blockades of road junctions.

KOZ SR comprises 39 occupationally-based affiliated unions.

International affiliations. ICFTU; ETUC; TUAC (observer status)

4 Other Trade Union Organization

Independent Christian Trade Unions of Slovakia (NKOS)

Address. Jiraskova 39, Trnava

Phone. +421 805 5446837

Fax. +421 805 5446837

E-mail. centrum@nkos.sk

Leadership. Peter Novovesky (president)

Membership. 10,000

History and character. NKOS has a social Christian position. It has three affiliated unions (railways, education and industry). It is limited by Slovak legislation that gives majority trade unions a monopoly in concluding collective agreements.

International affiliation. WCL

Slovenia

Capital: Ljubljana
Population: 1.93 m. (2000 est.)

1 Political and Economic Background

Slovenia declared its independence from Yugoslavia in June 1991 and quickly consolidated its autonomy after relatively brief and small-scale fighting with Serb-led Yugoslav forces. There is no clearly dominant political party and in 2000 there was unstable and divided coalition government. Slovenia is a front-runner candidate for accession to the EU

Slovenia was the most prosperous of the former Yugoslav republics, with a diverse range of service and manufacturing industries. The initial impact of independence and loss of markets was recession, but since 1993 the economy has expanded (GDP increasing 4% in 2000) and Slovenia has increasingly oriented its market to the EU. Privatization is not yet complete.

GDP (purchasing power parity) $21.4bn. (1999 est.); GDP per capita (purchasing power parity) $10,900 (1999 est.).

2 Trade Unionism

Slovenia ratified ILO Conventions No.87 (Freedom of Association and Protection of the Right to Organize, 1948) and No.98 (Right to Organize and Collective Bargaining, 1949) in 1992. All workers, except the police and armed forces, may join unions. There are four confederations of trade unions, one of which, the Association of Free Trade Unions of Slovenia (ZSSS), has been admitted to the European Trade Union Confederation (ETUC).

In the private sector unions and employers negotiate an annual framework agreement for collective bargaining. The right to strike is guaranteed but this is restricted in some public sector areas.

The National Council (Drzavni Svet) advises government and has 40 members representing local, professional and other interest groups. It includes four representatives of labour. Dusan Semolic, the president of the ZSSS, is the leader of the Employees' Interest Group on the National Council.

3 Trade Union Centres

Konfederacija novih sindikatov Slovenije "Neodvisnost"
Confederation of New Trade Unions of Slovenia "Neodvisnost"

Address. Linhartova 13, Ljubljana

Phone. +386 1 306 1000

Fax. +386 1 230 2868

Leadership. Drago Lombar (president)

Konfederacija sindikatov Slovenije Pergam
Confederation of Trade Unions Pergam

Address. Trg OF 14/IV, 1000 Ljubljana

Phone. +386 1 231 0476

Fax. +386 1 230 2247

Leadership. Dusan Rebolj (president)

Konfederacija sindikatov 90 Slovenija
Confederation of Trade Unions 90 of Slovenia

Address. Komenskega 7, 1000 Ljubljana

Phone. +386 1 432 2256

Fax. +386 1 432 2256

Leadership. Boris Mazalin (president)

Zveza svobodnih sindikatov Slovenije (ZSSS)
Association of Free Trade Unions of Slovenia

Address. Dalmatinova 4, 1000 Ljubljana

Phone. +386 1 43 1200

Fax. +386 1 231 7298

Leadership. Dusan Semolic (president)

International affiliation. ETUC

Solomon Islands

Capital: Honiara
Population: 466,000 (2000 est.)

1 Political and Economic Background

The Solomon Islands, a South Pacific archipelago, became independent from the UK in 1978 and is a member of the Commonwealth. Political parties tend to be fluid coalitions. In 1999 conflict between the indigenous inhabitants of Guadalcanal and immigrants from elsewhere in the country led to a 4-month state of emergency and closed the nation's largest palm oil plantation.

In June 2000 there was widespread violence in Honiara involving paramilitaries of rival ethnic groups set up in response to the Guadalcanal crisis.

The majority of the population is dependent on agriculture (subsistence and commercial), forestry and fishing for a livelihood. Manufacturing industry is largely restricted to the processing of local primary commodities. The economy was affected by spillover from the 1997–98 Asian economic crisis, and thereafter by ethnic violence.

GDP (purchasing power parity) $1.21bn. (1999 est.); GDP per capita (purchasing power parity) $2,650 (1999 est.).

2 Trade Unionism

The Solomon Islands joined the International Labour Organization in 1984 but has yet to ratify ILO Conventions No.87 (Freedom of Association and Protection of the Right to Organize, 1948) or No.98 (Right to Organize and Collective Bargaining, 1949).

Trade unionism developed rapidly in the 1970s, encouraged by the creation of the Solomon Islands General Workers' Union (subsequently known as the Solomon Islands National Union of Workers – SINUW) in the mid-1970s. The right to organize trade unions and bargain collectively was provided for in the 1981 Trade Disputes Act. Some 85–90% of the workforce is outside the formal economy, but in the formal sector unionization rates are high, being estimated at 90% in the public sector and 50% in the private sector. The government has not sought to prevent the formation of unions and there are legal protections against anti-union discrimination.

Collective bargaining is practiced and unresolved disputes are referred to the tripartite Trades Disputes Panel for resolution, either before or during strikes. Unions are free to engage in political activities.

3 Trade Union Centre

Solomon Islands Council of Trade Unions (SICTU)

Address. PO Box 271, Honiara

Phone. +677 22516

Fax. +677 22516

E-mail. sictu@welkam.solomon.com.sb

Leadership. Tony Kagovai (national secretary)

History and character: The Solomon Islands National Union of Workers (SINUW) was formed in the 1970s. In 1986 the name Solomon Islands Council of Trade Unions (SICTU) was adopted, although the older name still remains in use. It is one of the few regional or Commonwealth centres still reported as an affiliate by the WFTU.

International affiliation. WFTU; CTUC

Somalia

Capital: Mogadishu
Population: 7.25 m. (2000 est.)

1 Political and Economic Background

Somalia was created by the unification of the British Somaliland Protectorate and the UN Trust Territory of Somalia at independence in 1960. In 1969 Mohammed Siyad Barre seized power and under him the Somali Revolutionary Socialist Party held power until his overthrow in a rebellion led by United Somali Congress (USC) guerrillas in Jan. 1991. The USC quickly split into factions with different groups controlling different areas of the country. A UN peace-keeping presence from 1992–95, aimed primarily at protecting relief operations, was unable to restore any degree of order and there has been no effective government since 1991, with Ethiopian and Eritrean forces also becoming embroiled in the conflict and no clan-based faction controlling more than a small part of the country. In the north-west, the self-declared Independent Republic of Somaliland (based on former British Somaliland), has de facto independence and is comparatively stable.

Somalia is an impoverished country. It is heavily dependent on the rearing of livestock, which supports up to three-quarters of the predominantly nomadic or semi-nomadic population. Food production falls far short of the country's requirements. There is little industry and much of it is closed because of civil conflict. There is a serious refugee problem and chronic external debt.

GDP (purchasing power parity) $4.3bn. (1999 est.); GDP per capita (purchasing power parity) $600 (1999 est.)

2 Trade Unionism

Somalia has been a member of the International Labour Organization since 1960 but has ratified neither ILO Convention No.87 (Freedom of Association and Protection of the Right to Organize, 1948) nor No.98 (Right to Organize and Collective Bargaining, 1949).

Under Siyad Barre a single trade union system prevailed, organized in the General Federation of Somali Trade Unions (GFSTU), founded in 1977. Under the amended 1990 constitution, promulgated in Siyad Barre's last year in power as part of the general reform wave affecting one-party states in Africa at that time, the right to form independent unions was proclaimed, though no such unions were formed prior to his fall. Before this strikes were outlawed and organizing them was punishable by death.

During the 1990s, however, civil strife led to a general collapse of all civil institutions in Somalia. The GFSTU ceased to exist as did significant trade union activity. The vast majority of the population (much of which is nomadic) is in any case not engaged in formal employment relationships. In the self-proclaimed Independent Republic of Somaliland the constitution provides for freedom of association but trade unions have not been formed.

South Africa

Capital: Pretoria
Population: 43.42 m. (2000 est.)

1 Political and Economic Background

The Union (from 1961, Republic) of South Africa was ruled by the (Afrikaaner-dominated) National Party (NP) from 1948 until May 1994. The NP created the system of apartheid (separate development) which divided the population into whites, coloureds, Indians and Africans. In general terms the system served to maintain white supremacy while providing fewest rights to the black segment of the population. Against this background, South Africa also created 10 bantustans ('homelands') as isolated islands within South Africa where blacks had a higher degree of autonomy.

In the 1980s the apartheid regime faced international isolation and sanctions and mounting unrest, although the internal politics were complex, with conflict among blacks between the African National Congress (ANC) and the (Zulu) Inkatha movement of KwaZulu homeland premier Chief Mangosuthu Buthelezi. As NP leader from 1989 State President F.W. de Klerk moved rapidly to dismantle legislative apartheid, lifting the ban on the (mainly black) ANC and the Pan-African Congress (PAC), and in Feb. 1990 releasing Nelson Mandela, deputy president and leading figure in the ANC, from jail after 26 years' incarceration. Despite further bloodshed the way was cleared for establishment (in 1993) of a new constitution and elections on a single non-racial roll. Sanctions were finally lifted in December. The first non-racial multi-party elections, held in April 1994, resulted in a clear victory for the ANC, whose leader Nelson Mandela subsequently became President, while de Klerk became Vice-President. In 1999 Mandela was succeeded as President by the ANC's Thabo Mbeki, and in legislative elections, generally conceded as fairly conducted, the ANC retained its majority, taking 66% of the vote. The government is an ANC-dominated coalition that includes members of the Inkatha Freedom Party of Chief Buthelezi.

South Africa under white rule had social and economic stratification on racial lines. The economy was the most dynamic in sub-Saharan Africa, drawing in (black) labour from neighbouring countries to work in its gold and coal mines and industries and providing a Western-style of life for the white minority. International sanctions were, however, increasingly onerous. The ANC government since 1994 has sought to achieve greater access to wealth and opportunity for the excluded majority while retaining the confidence of the white business community and international investors. In practice, although declining, considerable economic stratification on racial lines persists. President Mbeki has said there is a need to further liberalize the economy to build investor confidence in the face of unemployement estimated at 30–35%, and there has been some cautious movement towards privatization of state-owned enterprises. However, sections of the ANC are seen as hostile to this policy. Racial tension, though subdued, is persistent and AIDS and rampant crime are major problems.

GDP (purchasing power parity) $296.1bn. (1999 est.); GDP per capita (purchasing power parity) $6,900 (1999 est.).

2 Trade Unionism

Trade unions first developed among white workers in the 1880s, and a white Federation of Trade Unions was recognized in 1911. White workers were represented by the South African Confederation of Labour (SACoL), which favoured employment policies based on racial discrimination.

The Trade Union Council of South Africa (TUCSA) included white, coloured and Asian members and some blacks in dependent organizations. It was formed in 1954 and reached a peak of 500,000 members in 1983, but dissolved itself in 1986 with 120,000 members after 25 member unions had disaffiliated. TUCSA had claimed to be the only truly non-racial federation in

South Africa, believing it lost membership because of the rise of politicized unions using industrial conflict as a means to broader political change. It became fully open to all races in 1980, while remaining white-run, but foundered despite the use of closed shop agreements with employers designed to discourage the defection of blacks to other independent unions. It opposed economic sanctions against South Africa and had a system of 'parallel unions', under which black workers were recruited into separate subsidiary sections of white unions. These parallel black unions still had 32,000 members in 1984.

The first trade union organizing blacks appeared as early as 1917, followed in two years by the Industrial and Commercial Workers' Union of Africa. During the 1930s some black unions affiliated to the white-dominated South African Trades and Labour Council (SATLC), and after 1941 other black unions joined the Council of Non-European Trade Unions, which claimed 119 unions with 158,000 members in 1945. However, black trade union activity was suppressed after the National Party came to power in 1948, and in 1954 SATLC was disbanded and replaced by TUCSA, which excluded independent black unions from affiliation. 14 former SATLC members founded the South African Congress of Trade Unions (SACTU) the following year and immediately merged with the Council of Non-European Trade Unions. SACTU developed thereafter as the highly politicized trade union arm of the ANC, claiming 53,000 members by 1961. It was then driven underground by state repression and black unionism lost all internal expression until the 1970s.

The Soweto riots of 1976–77 contributed to the development of black trade unionism. Black unionists opposed to TUCSA had formed the non-racial Federation of South African Trade Unions (FOSATU) in 1979; the Council of Unions of South Africa (CUSA), which stressed black leadership, followed in 1980. Several important unions remained outside these federations. Largely regionally based, they, like FOSATU, were non-racial but opposed to registration: among their number were the Cape-based Food and Canning Workers' Union, the Western Province's General Workers' Union, and the South African Allied Workers' Union, organized mainly in East London and Durban.

In the period from 1979 black union activists emphasized the goal of building effective industrial strength, with strike action built around issues specifically concerning trade unions. The unrest of 1984 onwards began predominantly with community and student groups, but soon several hundred thousand black Transvaal workers were mobilized by FOSATU and CUSA as well as student and community leaders in a two-day stoppage against police action in the townships. In 1985 FOSATU joined the newly formed Congress of South African Trade Unions (COSATU), and in 1986 CUSA merged with the small Azanian Confederation of Trade Unions (AZACTU) to form the National Council of Trade Unions (NACTU). In 1986 Chief Buthelezi formed a Zulu-based organization the United Workers' Union of

South Africa (UWUSA), to oppose disinvestment from South Africa by foreign companies and the other black unions.

1.5 million black workers 'stayed away' from work on May 1, 1986, to demand an official May Day holiday (the largest strike in South African history). Under the renewed state of emergency of June 1986, 'statements calculated to encourage or promote disinvestment or the application of sanctions or foreign action against the Republic' or 'calculated to incite any person to take part in any unlawful strike' were defined as subversive. In July 1986, 200 trade union officials were reported as being among 4,500 detained under the state of emergency, while others were in hiding. Among those detained for periods were the COSATU leaders Elijah Barayi and Jay Naidoo, and Phiroshaw Camay, the CUSA general secretary.

Repression of the labour movement escalated in the later 1980s. Seven strikers were shot in 1987 during a railway strike. COSATU headquarters in Johannesburg were raided and many officials arrested; the office was later bombed. Another mass one-day stay-away followed to mark the 11th anniversary of the Soweto riots; it was followed by further repression. Ten miners were killed in clashes with the police and vigilantes in 1987 and that October Moses Mayekiso, general secretary of the recently formed National Union of Metalworkers (NUMSA), was brought to trial for treason under the emergency regulations and detained until 1989.

In 1988, the NP government severely restricted and in some cases banned the activities of COSATU and 17 other organizations; raids and detentions of unionists followed. The draconian powers taken by government under that year's Labour Relations Amendment Bill, drafted to curb 'politically-motivated' strikes, were described by the ILO as 'probably the most serious attack on the emerging unions since the early 1970s.'

Widespread union protests followed, with numerous work stoppages and demonstrations. Opposition united the rival union centres COSATU and the National Council of Trade Unions (NACTU) which in June mobilized 1.3 million in a protest general strike. The unions negotiated expanded recognition agreements with employers to by-pass the new legal restrictions: COSATU and NACTU reached an agreement with the South African Employers' Consultative Committee on Labour Affairs (SACCOLA) which by implication specifically excluded several of the law's provisions. Faced later with interest of some employers in using the new law, the unions broke off talks with SACCOLA: COSATU and NACTU called a summit at the end of 1988 to discuss further action against the new legislation.

The next year the unions entered a tripartite Labour Commission in surrogate fashion via an umbrella organization, the South African Trade Union Coordination Council (SATUCC), but they continued to press for agricultural, public sector and domestic workers to be covered by the new Act. To protest at exclusion of blacks from the 1989 election unions helped launch the

Mass Democratic Movement (MDM) which organized a two-day 'stay-away' from work. It was distinguished from the contemporaneous township revolt of the United Democratic Front (UDF) by its greater discipline, and received widespread support.

The struggle between the labour movement and the government continued in other areas. The unions accused the authorities of using 'dirty tricks' to discredit them, by sowing divisions between the COSATU and NACTU, and between the leadership and rank and file of individual unions. Alfred Makeleng, a COSATU and UDF official, died in police custody in suspicious circumstances after 26 months' detention under the emergency regulations. A 1989 anti-apartheid conference called by COSATU for September was hamstrung by the arrest and detention of 28 union leaders together with other anti-apartheid activists. Leaders of the Post and Telecommunications Workers' Association were detained, the union's offices burgled and another official died in suspicious circumstances, against the background of negotiations to secure the reinstatement of postal workers dismissed during a 1987 strike. Twenty members of the COSATU affiliate, the Paper, Wood, Printing and Allied Workers Union (PPWAWU), were detained under the emergency regulations while involved in strikes in the Transvaal. Striking municipal workers in Soweto also entered serious conflict with the police. 31,000 metalworkers went on strike for two weeks in the same month and won improved benefits from employers. The unions also gave tacit support to the boycott of October's municipal elections; they were banned under the emergency regulations from campaigning openly.

The most significant sectoral organization of blacks occurred in mining, where the National Union of Mineworkers (NUM) developed to become the largest black union. In contrast, blacks working on farms, as domestic servants, and as state employees, were almost entirely unorganized. Mass dismissals occurred after industrial action, and many employers were active in attempting to frustrate trade union activities, in some cases hiring their own company security forces to break up meetings. The threat of deportation to the homelands or neighbouring states was a potent weapon to curb strikes. Numerous activists were also detained incommunicado without charge under the Internal Security Act, and a number of trade union officials died in police custody.

As restrictions on union activity lapsed, COSATU thrived, pushing its membership towards one million. In 1990 it joined in a 'revolutionary alliance' with the ANC and the South African Communist Party (SACP). NACTU's membership grew at a lower rate, partly because of its emphasis on black exclusivism and partly because of factional fighting between supporters and opponents of the Pan-Africanist Congress.

After the Soweto riots of 1976–77 SACTU (from exile) had urged unions to affiliate to the United Democratic Front (UDF – the principal grouping of community groups opposing the South African govern-ment), arguing that the class struggle must progress within a national struggle against apartheid. It also called for the unification of the progressive trade union movement, opposed 'collaboration' with TUCSA, and welcomed the 1985 formation of COSATU, calling for a truly democratic centre of organized activity for all workers who are determined to 'liberate our country from its existing oppressive and exploitative social system'. SACTU added that 'as long as the oppressive apartheid regime exists, where the above-ground trade unionists face detention without trial, torture and murder at the hands of the police ... there will always be a need for the SACTU' , which would 'continue to maintain its underground structures'. After 1990, however, SACTU lost its raison d'être, and at a meeting with COSATU it dissolved and advised its members to join COSATU's affiliates.

The collapse of official apartheid stimulated a nationwide wave of celebratory strikes, but COSATU and NACTU called for the maintenance of sanctions. They met the Manpower Minister to discuss changes to employment legislation, and complained of intimidation at the hands of Inkatha and its union wing UWUSA. After the deaths of members of its affiliate the National Union of Mineworkers (NUM), COSATU pressed for freedom of association in Natal which, in its view, would destroy the basis of Inkatha. It also alleged police collusion in Inkatha attacks and called for an independent inquiry: there were later revelations that UWUSA had been funded by the security forces, and that some employers had worked with it to evict COSATU and NACTU affiliated unions, sustaining a campaign of dirty tricks and killings.

In 1991, following three years' negotiations between COSATU, NACTU and SACCOLA, a new Labour Relations Amendment Act repealed the 1988 restrictions, restored the pre-1988 definition of an unfair labour practice and abolished Labour Court powers to ban lawful strikes and lock-outs. It also lifted union responsibility for illegal, unofficial strikes and eased the conciliation process.

The 1991 Act cleared the way for union entry into the National Manpower Commission (NMC). COSATU argued for enhancement and broadening of its powers, compelling the Minister to ratify decisions jointly reached by the unions and the employers. Like NACTU it believed that places should be allocated proportionally to size thus reducing the influence of white right-wing unions. Both pressed for new legislation on collective bargaining rights, extension of the right to strike and recognition of rights for unions at companies. After protracted negotiations expedited by COSATU with a nationwide protest strike, it was finally agreed to transform the NMC into a tripartite forum for negotiations on all employment matters. In 1992 it incorporated ten members each from employers, unions and government.

From 1992 onwards the Ministry, unions and employers worked together to bring South Africa broadly in line with the standards of the ILO. An earlier ILO commission to South Africa (at COSATU's request) had made sweeping recommendations. (South Africa had joined the ILO in 1919 but left in 1966). Freedom of association was promulgated by the 1991 amendment but public sector collective bargaining was still restricted. A 1992 ILO commission encountered a very different atmosphere. A Labour Appeal Court was agreed and promised for 1993, with judges to be appointed by the Chief Justice following NMC consultation. The 1983 Employment Act was then extended to cover both domestic and farm workers, and plans announced to bring them within the 1956 Labour Relations Act and the 1957 Workmen's Compensation Act.

Apart from the NMC the other key tripartite institution of the new South Africa was the tripartite National Economic Forum (NEF). Labour was represented on it by COSATU, NACTU, and the Federation of South African Labour Unions (FEDSAL). COSATU wished to see the NEF given mandatory powers, while business preferred advisory status, but COSATU also advocated that NEF be merged with the NMC. In 1994 it succeeded in persuading the government to establish the National Economic, Development and Labour Council (NEDLAC) to supersede both. This has become the principal vehicle for tripartite social dialogue.

With the end of apartheid in sight, many leading union figures moved into the political sphere, led by the NUM general secretary Cyril Ramaphosa, who became secretary of the ANC. After the 1994 elections prominent COSATU figures occupied positions of power within the new administration. No less than 20 were elected to the new Parliament. Former COSATU general secretary Jay Naidoo became Minister without Portfolio; another COSATU figure Alec Erwin became Minister of Finance, and Sydney Mufamadi, also of COSATU, was appointed Minister of Safety and Security. Many others were appointed to civil service positions. But the election of an ANC government also showed that COSATU could act independently. On assuming power the ANC called for a moratorium on strikes, but COSATU demurred. Its affiliates were in mounting conflict with a number of private firms, notably in the mines where NUMSA was engaging international conglomerates. In 1994 disputes in the metal, paper, mining, oil, and road freight industries, led President Mandela to appeal to the COSATU congress for industrial peace.

By mid-1994 aggregate union membership was estimated at 3.5 million, an increase of over 500,000 from two years earlier. This figure corresponded to 26 per cent of the economically active population. COSATU affiliates accounted for perhaps 1.3 million of this number.

The Zulu-based UWUSA, launched by Chief Butehelezi in 1986 in opposition to COSATU and sanctions, was affected by revelations in July 1991 that it had received funds from the security police for most of its existence, amounting to at least 1.5 million Rand. Operation Omega (as it was known) brought together UWUSA and anti-union employers in a campaign of dirty tricks that in some cases were said to have resulted in the deaths of COSATU and NACTU activists. After

the decision of Chief Buthelezi to participate in the 1994 elections UWUSA fell into obscurity.

The Labour Relations Act, implemented in 1996 after being negotiated by employers, unions and government through NEDLAC, provided a detailed framework for industrial relations and gave statutory effect to the provisions in the constitution on freedom of association. All private sector workers and all in the public sector except those involved with national security may join unions, and the Act enforces rights which enable unions to function in practice, such as access to workplaces, the check-off and paid leave for union officials. The Act guarantees the right to strike except for the security services and essential public services, and strikes may be staged in pursuit of broad 'socio-economic protest'. In practice, since the end of the apartheid area, the government has not interfered in union recruitment or the internal affairs of unions or generally in collective bargaining. The Act also provided for the establishment of workplace forums in larger enterprises, but these have not taken root.

The Labour Relations Act also set up a Commission for Conciliation, Mediation and Arbitration (CCMA), which has been involved in the settlement of many disputes, and a Labour Court, to which disputes can be referred after failure of the CCMA to achieve a resolution. However, somewhat on the British model, the emphasis has been primarily on employers and unions achieving agreement directly between them without quasi-judicial intervention. In 1996 South Africa ratified ILO Conventions No.87 (Freedom of Association and Protection of the Right to Organize, 1948) and No.98 (Right to Organize and Collective Bargaining, 1949). In 1997 the Basic Conditions of Employment Act set a framework, generally in accordance with union wishes, for such areas as working hours, maternity leave and Sunday pay.

In Apr. 1997 the current structure of main trade union centres crystallized when the Federation of Unions of South Africa (FEDUSA), a non-political multi-racial (but majority white) organization, was formed by the merger of the Federation of South African Labour Unions (FEDSAL) and other smaller unions. On its formation it claimed 515,000 members in 25 affiliated unions, making it the second most important confederation after COSATU, and ahead of NACTU. All three are now affiliated to the ICFTU, NACTU having been the first to affiliate, in 1994. By 1998, according to official estimates, union membership had declined from about 3.5 million in 1994 to 2.9 million, with 248 registered trade unions and between 30 and 40 unregistered unions.

COSATU's continued alliance with the ANC, though not without tensions, has been a stabilizing factor in the new South Africa. However, in his state-of-the-nation address to Parliament on Feb. 5, 2000, President Mbeki announced that his government would amend the Labour Relations Act and Basic Conditions of Employment Act, which business leaders had criticized as discouraging employment and investment. In Dec. 1999 the government had also announced plans to privatize the four largest state industrial enterprises, in telecoms, electricity, defence and transport (together employing 77 per cent of state industrial sector employees), notwithstanding COSATU's opposition to previously announced sell-offs.

3 Trade Union Centres

Congress of South African Trade Unions (COSATU)

Address. PO Box 1019, Johannesburg 2000

Phone. +27 11 339 4911

Fax. +27 11 339 5080

E-mail. cosatu@wn.apc.org

Website. www.cosatu.org.za

Leadership. Willy Madisha (president); Zwelinzima Vavi (general secretary)

Membership. Reports 2 million, of which 1.8 million are paid-up.

History and character. COSATU was formed in 1985 by 33 mainly black unions with 558,000 members as a federation that would emphasize opposition to apartheid on a non-racial basis. It absorbed the non-racial Federation of South African Trade Unions (FOSATU), which had nine affiliates, and incorporated the 180,000-member National Union of Mineworkers (NUM), which had left the Council of Unions of South Africa (CUSA). Although membership is open to whites, it is overwhelmingly black.

The founding congress made the following demands: (i) the repeal of the pass laws; (ii) the repeal of the state of emergency; (iii) withdrawal of troops and police from the townships; (iv) unconditional release of Nelson Mandela and all political prisoners, and the repeal of all banning orders; (v) the dismantling of the bantustan (homelands) system; and (vi) an end to the migrant labour system. COSATU committed itself to worker control, representation based on paid-up membership, broad-based industrial unionism, and non-racial recruitment, the demand for a national minimum wage, an end to overtime, sexual equality, and support for disinvestment by foreign firms and economic sanctions against South Africa.

COSATU suffered serious harassment from 1987 onwards. Officials were detained, and offices were raided and sabotaged. With other anti-apartheid groups repressed under the State of Emergency, COSATU was impelled further into the political arena. It was prominent in the organization of the 1986 and 1987 May Day strikes and the June 1987 'stay away'. In 1987 it adopted the Freedom Charter and reaffirmed its support for international sanctions against South Africa. In response the government proscribed it from engaging in a wide range of specified political activities, as part of a package of still greater restrictions on anti-apartheid organizations introduced early in 1988.

Before 1989 a 'workerist' faction argued for a concentration on industrial activities but the leadership,

against a background of escalating change in South Africa, retained support for its political focus. Following the dissolution of SACTU, the ANC's trade union front, in 1990, COSATU replaced it in a tripartite 'revolutionary alliance' with the ANC and the South African Communist Party (SACP).

A special congress of Sept. 1993 elected 20 officials to stand on the ANC list in the forthcoming national and regional elections. Nelson Mandela told the Congress: 'The ANC will never betray the cause of democracy, and the cause of the workers. You must support the ANC only if it delivers the goods. If it does not, do to it what you have done to the apartheid regime!' Congress also adopted a Platform of Workers' Rights on the basis of which it negotiated to commit the ANC in the elections: the platform included basic organizing rights, collective bargaining, workplace empowerment, human resource development, and national industry-based provident funds.

In a 1994 conference COSATU developed special proposals for the reform of industrial relations structures, which to a considerable degree were reflected in the subsequent creation of NEDLAC.

Great symbolism was attached to the attendance of Nelson Mandela, now President, at the fifth (Sept. 1994) congress, but he brought an unappetizing message. He appealed to delegates to think of the unemployed rather than of pay demands. Little greater encouragement came from Jay Naidoo (former COSATU general secretary) and Alec Erwin (former COSATU education officer), now key economic ministers. The SACP general secretary Charles Nqakula warned that the new government was in danger of representing only the employers.

Despite tensions, the triple alliance of COSATU, ANC and the SACP has nonetheless continued. It is reflected in political affiliations: SACP members hold government posts and former COSATU general secretary Mbhazima Shilowa is premier of the key industrial province of Gauteng, which includes Johannesburg. Likewise, the current COSATU general secretary Zwelinzima Vavi is an SACP member. COSATU claims credit for securing the enactment of measures such as the 1997 Basic Conditions of Employment Act, which covered issues such as working hours (providing for a 45-hour maximum week), maternity leave and child labour and was relevant to many of South Africa's most vulnerable workers.

At the same time, COSATU has found itself opposed to some key government initiatives, including plans to sell off a range of public assets. In alliance with the SACP, COSATU has attacked the government's Growth, Employment and Redistribution strategy (GEAR), which aims to cut the budget deficit by curbing public spending, claiming it has produced poor growth and increased unemployment. On Jan. 31, 2000 COSATU announced a programme of 'mass action' in protest at an estimated unemployment rate of 35%. A few days later President Mbeki, in his state-of-the-nation address underlined the need for further 'restructuring' (privatization) of state assets and warned that labour laws would be amended.

On May 10, 2000 COSATU called a one-day strike against unemployment, with a response described as patchy. Through 2000 COSATU kept up political pressure against government plans to make it easier for employers to lay off workers. COSATU has also sought to make a practical contribution to easing unemployment by establishing a Job Creation Trust and is working with others to develop coherent alternatives to GEAR.

COSATU has 19 affiliates in all main sectors of the economy, ranging in size from the powerful National Union of Mineworkers to the 450 members of the South African Football Players' Union. It is attempting to build membership in areas such as domestic service and temporary and casual work.

International affiliations. ICFTU; CTUC

Affiliates. The following are the major affiliates in order of size:

1. National Union of Mineworkers (NUM)
Address. PO Box 2424, Johannesburg 2000
Phone. +27 11 833 7012
Fax. +27 11 836 6051
E-mail. numres@num.org.za
Website. www.num.org.za
Leadership. Gwede Mantashe (general secretary)
Membership. 290,070
History and character. Founded in 1982, the NUM grew with great rapidity among black mineworkers and won recognition for bargaining purposes from the employers' organization, the Chamber of Mines, in 1983. It campaigned effectively in the 1980s for the end of the job reservation system whereby the best-paid jobs were reserved for whites. It has been the biggest COSATU affiliate since COSATU was formed in 1985 and has members in mining, energy, engineering and construction. In Dec. 1993 it opened the first union-owned training centre in South Africa; in 1996 the Mine Health and Safety Act, which it had backed, became law. It offers a wide range of member services. It is affiliated internationally to the ICEM.

2. National Education, Health and Allied Workers' Union (NEHAWU)
Address. PO Box 10812, Johannesburg 2000
Phone. +27 11 833 2902
Fax. +27 11 834 3416
E-mail. nehawu@wn.apc.org
Website. www.nehawu.org.za
Leadership. Fikile Majola (general secretary)
Membership. 234,607
History and character. NEHAWU was founded in 1987 and is the largest public sector union in South Africa. It provides a range of member services including scholarships, medical assistance, provident funds, and group insurance.

3. South African Democratic Teachers' Union (SADTU)
Address. PO Box 6401, Johannesburg
Phone. +27 11 334 4830
Fax. +27 11 334 4836
E-mail. sadtu@wn.apc.org
Website. www.sadtu.org.za
Leadership. Thulas Nxesi (general secretary)
Membership. 218,747

4. National Union of Metalworkers of South Africa (NUMSA)
Address. PO Box 260483, Excom 2023

Phone. +27 11 832 2030
Fax. +27 11 833 6330
E-mail. dumisa@numsa.org.za
Website. www.numsa.org.za
Leadership. Silumko Nondwangu (general secretary)
Membership. 200,000

5 Southern African Clothing and Textile Workers' Union (SACTWU)
Address. PO Box 1194, Woodstock 7915
Phone. +27 21 447 4570
Fax. +27 21 447 4593
E-mail. lynnt@sactwu.co.za
Leadership. Ebrahim Patel (general secretary)
Membership. 119,930

6. South African Municipal Workers' Union (SAMWU)
Address. Private Bag X9, Athlone 7760
Phone. +27 21 697 1151
Fax. +27 21 696 9175
E-mail. samwu@wn.apc.org
Website. www.cosatu.org.za/samwu
Leadership. Roger Ronnie (general secretary)
Membership. 119,792

7. Food and Allied Workers' Union (FAWU)
Address. PO Box 1234, Woodstock 7915
Phone. +27 21 637 9040
Fax. +27 21 638 3761
E-mail. fawu@wn.apc.org
Leadership. Derrick Cele (general secretary)
Membership. 119,302

8. South African Commercial, Catering and Allied Workers' Union (SACCAWU)
Address. PO Box 10730, Johannesburg 2000
Phone. +27 11 403 8333
Fax. +27 11 403 0309
E-mail. saccawu@wn.apc.org
Leadership. Bones Skulu (general secretary)
Membership. 103,296

9. South African Transport and Allied Workers' Union (SATAWU)
Address. PO Box 9451, Johannesburg 2000
Phone. +27 11 331 9321
Fax. +27 11 331 5418
E-mail. hana@tgwusa.co.za
Leadership. Randall Howard (general secretary)
Membership. 103,218

10. Chemical, Energy, Paper, Printing, Wood and Allied Workers' Union (CEPPWAWU)
Address. PO Box 3219, Johannesburg 2000
Phone. +27 11 331 6861
Fax. +27 11 331 5263
E-mail. cwiuinfo@cwiu.wn.apc.org
Leadership. Muzi Buthelezi (general secretary)
Membership. 73,720

11. Police and Prisons Civil Rights Union (POPCRU)
Address. PO Box 8657, Johannesburg 2000
Phone. +27 11 403 0406
Fax. +27 11 403 9377
E-mail. popcru@wn.apc.org

Leadership. Abbey Witbooi (general secretary)
Membership. 70,618

12. SASBO: The Finance Union

Address. Private Bag X84, Bryanston 2021
Phone. +27 11 467 0192
Fax. +27 11 467 0188
E-mail. research@sasbo.org.za
Leadership. Shaun Oelschig (general secretary)
Membership. 63,046

13. Communication Workers' Union (CWU)

Address. PO Box 10248, Johannesburg 2000
Phone. +27 11 333 451
Fax. +27 11 333 4527
E-mail. cwu@wn.apc.org
Leadership. Seleboho Kiti
Membership. 35,008

Federation of Unions of South Africa (FEDUSA)

Address. PO Box 2096, Northcliff 2115

Phone. + 27 11 476 5188

Fax. +27 11 476 5131

E-mail. fedusa@fedusa.org.za

Website. www.fedusa.org.za

Leadership. Mary Malete (president); Chez Milani (general secretary)

Membership. 555,600 paid-up members in 26 affiliated unions.

History and character. FEDUSA was launched on Apr. 1, 1997 and ranks second to COSATU among South Africa's trade union centres, although much smaller and far less influential. Its leading founder was the Federation of South African Labour Unions (FEDSAL). FEDSAL's membership was 80% white-collar and this meant that, reflecting South African employment patterns, FEDSAL membership was about 70 per cent white. Thus, although both COSATU and FEDUSA are explicitly non-racial in recruitment, FEDUSA differs in its composition from COSATU, which is heavily black.

Also unlike COSATU, FEDUSA has no political alliances. It emphasizes moderation and participates fully in the range of tripartite institutions, such as NEDLAC and the Commission for Conciliation, Mediation and Arbitration set up after the end of apartheid. Its membership dipped initially after formation but rose from 454,719 in Jan. 1998 to 555,600 by July 1999 as a majority of its affiliates increased their numbers, against the general trend in South African trade unionism.

Its affiliates include the South African Typographical Union, founded 1898 and reportedly South Africa's oldest union.

FEDSAL had cordial relations with the WCL, without being affiliated. In 1998, however, FEDUSA was accepted into affiliation by the ICFTU.

International affiliation. ICFTU; CTUC

Affiliates. FEDUSA has 26 affiliates; the following are the largest, with more than 30,000 members each:

1. Hospital Personnel Trade Union of South Africa (HOSPERSA)

Address. 2nd Floor, Glen Galleries, Glen Manor Avenue, Menlyn, Pretoria 0181
Phone. +27 12 365 2021
Fax. +27 12 365 2043
E-mail. hospers1@acc.co.za
Website. www.hospersa.co.za
Membership. 60,357

2. Independent Municipal and Allied Trade Union (IMATU)

Address. PO Box 35343, Menlo Park 0102
Phone. +27 12 466 2762
Fax. +27 12 325 3272
E mail. imatu@icon.co.za
Website. www.imatu.org.za
Membership. 67,249

3. Public Servants Association of South Africa (PSA)

Address. PO Box 40404, Arcadia 007
Phone. +27 12 303 6500
Fax. +27 12 303 6652
E-mail. psacas@mweb.co.za
Website. www.psa.co.za
Membership. 202,000

4. United Association of South Africa (UASA)

Address. PO Box 565, Florida 1709
Phone. +27 11 472 3600
Fax. +27 11 674 4057
E-mail. admin@uasa.org.za
Website. www.uasa.org.za
Membership. 34,159

National Council of Trade Unions (NACTU)

Address. PO Box 10928, Johannesburg 2000

Phone. +27 11 833 1040

Fax. +27 11 833 1032

E-mail. nactrec@netactive.co.za

Leadership. Cunningham Ngcukana (general secretary)

History and character. NACTU was formed in 1986, by the merger of the former Council of Unions of South Africa (CUSA) and Azanian Confederation of Trade Unions (AZACTU).

NACTU's position was that blacks should always hold the leadership positions in unions even if (as was the case with some CUSA unions) they had some non-black members (AZACTU unions admitted only blacks). While AZACTU was affiliated to the Azanian People's Organization, CUSA had sympathies with the Pan-Africanist Congress (PAC). The new federation was weakened by the disaffiliation from CUSA of the National Union of Mineworkers, the major element in CUSA, to become a founding member of COSATU. NACTU faced divisions in its attitude to the ANC, which had established a clear leadership position in the struggle against apartheid.

In 1994 NACTU became the ICFTU's first post-apartheid South African affiliate. However, it is dwarfed in significance by COSATU.

International affiliation. ICFTU; CTUC

Spain

Capital: Madrid
Population: 40.0 m. (2000 est.)

1 Political and Economic Background

Following his victory in the Spanish Civil War of the 1930s, Gen. Franco maintained authoritarian right-wing rule until his death in 1975. There then followed a political transition with the establishment of a constitutional monarchy and democratic political structures. Under the social democratic Spanish Socialist Workers' Party (PSOE), in office from 1982, Spain gained entry to the European Communities in 1986. In 1996 the PSOE lost power to a coalition government led by the conservative Popular Party (PP). In elections in March 2000, the PP under Prime Minister José Maria Aznar obtained an absolute majority, winning 183 of the 350 seats in the Congress of Deputies, with the PSOE remaining the major opposition party, with 125 seats. There is a decentralized regional government structure with elected local parliaments.

Spain has enjoyed economic growth above the EU average over the last five years. It joined the single European currency at its launch on Jan. 1, 1999. The economy is based on private enterprise and the Aznar government is committed to further market deregulation and increased competition although some major enterprises remain in state hands. The government's approach is to sell profitable public companies and use the proceeds to meet the costs of closing loss-making companies. Although Spain has the highest rate of job creation in the EU, its unemployment rate, at nearly 15% in 2000, is also still the highest in the EU and there is a high rate of transient temporary employment. Inflation was 2.5% in 2000.

GDP (purchasing power parity) $677.5bn. (1999 est.); GDP per capita (purchasing power parity) $17,300 (1999 est.).

2 Trade Unionism

Spain has been a member of the ILO since 1956, having earlier been a member from 1919 to 1941. It ratified ILO Conventions No.87 (Freedom of Association and Protection of the Right to Organize, 1948) and No.98 (Right to Organize and Collective Bargaining, 1949) in 1977.

The anarchist Confederación Nacional del Trabajo (CNT) and the socialist Unión General de Trabajadores (UGT) were the largest centres before the civil war of 1936–39, although the trade union movement was highly fragmented. Under Franco a corporatist vertical trade union structure was imposed, and employers were incorporated in the membership of the trade unions. The unions predominantly provided social services and strikes were illegal. The UGT, CNT and the Basque union, ELA-STV, maintained some underground activity, with headquarters in exile, and workers' commissions developed at shop-floor level in the 1960s, contributing to the weakening of the official trade union structure in the latter part of Franco's rule. In 1977, following the return to democratic government, the Francoist trade union structure was dissolved and free trade unionism has since developed. The 1985 Law of Trade Union Liberty superseded legislation of 1977. It guarantees full freedom to almost all employees (excluding the armed forces and those in the judicial system) to join and form unions; the self-employed, unemployed and the retired may join established unions but not set up unions of their own. Unions are free to draw up their own rules and may not be dissolved or suspended except through the courts in the event of a serious breach of the law. They may engage in collective bargaining, organize activities both on and off working premises, strike, and put forward candidates for election as workers' delegates in enterprises. Discrimination by employers against trade union members and organizers is prohibited and such cases have priority in the labour courts.

During the 1980s trade union membership declined sharply. This reflected factors such as the loss of jobs in traditional industries, increasing unemployment, growth in temporary employment, and conflict between the unions, which were also slow to adjust to the changing nature of work and society. At the start of the 1990s, total union membership stood at 1.7m. (14.5% of the workforce), a decline of 750,000 compared with 1978, the year following the legalization of free unions. During the 1990s, however, the unions have increased their strength, with membership totaling 2.25m. (18.2% of the workforce) by 1997, and continuing to grow thereafter. In part this growth reflected the rate of job creation (the fastest in the EU) but the unions also proved more successful in focusing on bargaining to improve the wages and conditions of their members.

While the strength of the unions is still concentrated in the industrial areas, especially Catalonia (which includes the second largest city, Barcelona), the capital Madrid, and the Basque country, growth has occurred in other traditionally less organized areas, particularly in the public or semi-public services sector. About 30–35% of union members are in the public sector. Some 60% of workers are employed in businesses with fewer than ten employees and the unions are weak in these small enterprises. Involvement of women in unions also still lags behind their participation in the labour force.

During the transition period of the late 1970s the union movement was fragmented, but its organizational structure has since solidified. The two main centres are the UGT and the Workers' Commissions (CCOO), both now affiliated to the ICFTU. They are of similar strength and together account for three-quarters of union members. Since 1978 workplace elections have been held (every two years before 1982, and then every four years) to elect workers' delegates (in companies with more than 50 members these forming works committees), with responsibility for collective bargaining. The elections, in which turnouts of over 70% are normal, also have a broader significance. Only organizations winning 10% of all seats nationwide are considered representative at sectoral or national level, and only the UGT and CCOO qualify on that basis. At regional level, the cut-off is 15%. Two regional unions are also considered representative in the Basque country (Basque Workers' Solidarity, ELA/STV and the Assembly of Basque Workers, LAB), while in Galicia the Confederación Intersindical Galega (CIG) is considered representative. One effect of the system of workplace elections is that it has tended to marginalize smaller unions unable to cross the 10% threshold, and to consolidate the position of the UGT and CCOO. In addition to the main national centres, the civil service union confederation CSI-CSIF is of influence in its sector.

Relations between the UGT and CCOO were formerly combative, reflecting political differences and the fact that they competed in the same workplaces. The two centres have retained a rough parity in workplace elections since democratization. In the 1998 elections, the CCOO came first with 81,314 representatives (38% of the total) while the UGT gained 76,382 (36%). While the CCOO and UGT compete nationwide and in all main sectors there are some regional variations in strength: the CCOO is stronger in Catalonia and Madrid, the UGT in Aragon, Asturias, Galicia, Murcia and Valencia. The UGT is also stronger in much of the public administration. In third place in 1998 came the locally powerful Basque regional organization, ELA/STV with 7,267. These electoral results closely mirrored the unions' own reported membership figures for 1997. These showed that the CCOO had 790,000 members (35.2% of the total), the UGT 775,000 (34.4%), and ELA/STV 82,000 (3.6%). The 3rd largest national centre, the Unión Sindical Obrera (USO) had only 80,000 members (3.5%). The former anarchist unions have ceased to be of significance.

In its early stages the CCOO was strongly associated with the Communist Party of Spain (PCE) while the socialist UGT up to the 1980s functioned almost as the alter ego of the PSOE. Nicolas Redondo, UGT leader until 1994, was an architect of the PSOE's post-Franco revival and proposed Felipe González as party leader in the 1970s. However the unions' traditional political alignments were disrupted as the UGT came into conflict with the PSOE, in office after 1982, which adopted cautiously free market policies. In effect the UGT swapped partners, embracing the CCOO as an industrial ally to replace the PSOE. The rapprochement began in 1986 and by Feb. 1988 they were able to sign a pact to 'work together for a social shift' in the government's policy. The two centres worked together henceforth (with minor hiccups) jointly calling general strikes in 1988, 1992 and 1994.

The CCO has adopted centrist positions and the two confederations now emphasize their closeness in perspectives, generally working together to create common positions. They have tended to take similar viewpoints, and with a similar weight of emphasis, on issues such as privatization, tax reform, job creation and defending public services. Both have in recent years generally supported the policy of moderation in wage claims in exchange for measures to promote employment. While they have similar agendas, the CCOO has during the Aznar period adopted a slightly more moderate line, emphasizing the achievement of goals through negotiation with employers rather than legislation. This has been a point of difference over achievement of the 35-hour week. In the event, the government has emphatically refused to legislate a 35-hour week, and the first examples of its introduction in 2000 (in the Basque public administration and in a provincial sectoral agreement) were achieved through local bargaining. In Oct. 1997 the CCOO signed a sectoral collective bargaining agreement for the construction industry one day before the UGT was due to hold a general strike in the industry over the high rate of industrial accidents. The issue was finally resolved three months later when the UGT signed the agreement with an annexe on health and safety added. Such breakdowns are unusual, however.

Of particular concern to the Spanish unions are the issues of unemployment and temporary employment. Spain has created more jobs than any other EU country since 1996, but unemployment although declining, remains the highest in the EU, at close to 15%. The problem of unemployment is exacerbated by the fact that, while unemployment benefits are comparable to elsewhere in the EU, half of the unemployed do not qualify for benefits. During the late 1990s associations of the unemployed appeared in many parts of Spain, and these commonly criticized the unions for focusing on their (employed) members. In response, the unions have emphasized their concern for the position of the unemployed. Both the CCOO and UGT were highly critical of the 1999 governmental National Action Plan on jobs (as required by the EU), adopted in May 1999, saying that they had not been consulted on its content. The unions argue for adoption of the 35-hour week, as well as for positive government intervention in depressed areas, as a means to stimulate extra jobs. However, the employers emphasize the need to remove rigidities in the labour market and reduce Spain's traditional job security.

Following deregulation in 1994, aimed at increasing labour market flexibility, there has been a major increase in forms of temporary employment. This accounts for 33% of all employment, the highest rate of transient temporary employment in the EU. Nearly two-thirds of temporary contracts are for a period of less than one month, and in Spain temporary work is associated not just with insecurity but poor working conditions and low wages. The rate of temporary employment is twice as high among women as among men, affecting particularly areas such as retailing, catering and domestic service. The unions say that the high proportion of workers on temporary contracts is a deterrent to union organizers, as such workers are unlikely to wish to jeopardize their employment prospects. In July 1999 the Law on Temporary Employment Agencies was adopted obliging employers to pay the same rates to workers on contract from such agencies (responsible for about 15% of temporary recruitment) as to their other workers.

The unions also see the issue of temporary employment as linked to Spain's high incidence of industrial accidents, the highest in the EU and with fatalities double the EU average. According to government statistics more than half of all such accidents involve temporary workers. Lack of training of temporary workers, and the prevalent lack of a health and safety culture, are blamed by the unions for this situation. In 1996 a Law on the Prevention of Occupational Risks came into force but since then the number of industrial accidents has increased each successive year and the unions say the law has not been effectively enforced. Despite the emphasis on the issue at national level, collective bargaining agreements adopted in 1999 rarely referred to it.

Collective bargaining is widely practiced in both the private and public sectors. Bargaining tends to be decentralized, with much bargaining at provincial sectoral levels, although there has been some increase in company agreements, sometimes achieved without union involvement. Sectoral collective agreements nominally apply to all in that sector, signatories or not, and collective agreements cover some 60% of private sector workers, but the dominance of small and medium-seized enterprises, and the high incidence of transient and precarious employment, reduces their real impact. Spain has complex and multi-layered conciliation and arbitration mechanisms with the system processing some 500,000 conciliation cases and 250,000 judicial cases each year. In 1996 these mechanisms were added to when the employers and unions agreed to set up (effective 1998) the Intersectoral Mediation and Arbitration Service (SIMA). Notwithstanding these systems for dispute resolution, strikes are fairly common: there were 521 in 1999, involving 834,000 workers, although this is much lower rate than earlier in the decade. The most hard fought strikes in 1999 were in shipyards and coal mines where the union demands related to the continuation of subsidies to save jobs and more government support for diversification in depressed areas. The right to strike has been interpreted by the Constitutional Court to include general strikes called in opposition to government policy.

In March 2000 the conservative PP government was re-elected, this time with an absolute majority. Prime Minster Aznar has emphasized that he wishes to see continuing labour market reform but is seeking consensus on measures with the social partners and wishes to make social dialogue a priority.

3 Trade Union Centres

Confederación Sindical de Comisiones Obreras (CCOO)
Trade Union Confederation of Workers' Commissions

Address. Fernández de la Hoz 12, 28010 Madrid

Phone. +34 91 702 80 00

Fax. +34 91 310 48 04

E-mail. ccoo@ccoo.es

Website. www.ccoo.es (Spanish; English and French sections)

Leadership. José Maria Fidalgo (secretary-general)

Membership. 790,000

History and character. The workers' commissions developed in the 1960s as a shop floor movement, mounting frequent (although illegal) strikes and industrial action. In Nov. 1967 the Supreme Court declared the CCOO illegal as an instrument of the (outlawed) Communist Party of Spain (PCE) and hundreds of members were imprisoned.

Following the death of Franco in 1975 there was a gradual liberalization. In 1976 the CCOO was established as a trade union confederation, and it and other trade unions were formally legalized in Apr. 1997. It held its first congress in June 1978, with Marcelino Camacho elected secretary-general. The veteran Camacho made way at the fourth (1987) congress for the 37 year-old Antonio Gutiérrez. His election represented a victory for the *gerardistas*, supporters of the moderate PCE leadership of Gerardo Iglesias, who favoured a broad left alliance, against the candidate of the previously influential hardline *carrillistas* supporting the former PCE leader, Santiago Carrillo, purged in 1985. Camacho became president in 1987, but was not re-elected in 1996 having 'joined minority and critical positions'. Under Gutiérrez PCE members were sidelined from key positions in the CCOO. In Apr. 2000 José Maria Fidalgo, a bone surgeon seen as a pragmatist able to do business with the Aznar government (which won a substantial victory in elections the previous month), was elected secretary-general in succession to Gutiérrez.

Since legalization in 1977 the CCOO has been of a similar size to the other principal trade union centre, the UGT. In the 1998 workplace elections, the CCOO came first with 81,314 representatives (38% of the total) compared with 76,382 for the UGT (36%). The CCOO's close relationship with the PCE, and that of the UGT with the PSOE, contributed to adversarial relations in the post-Franco period, but the two centres progressively developed a more cooperative relationship in response to PSOE policies from the mid-1980s. The CCOO now emphasizes its political independence and has adapted to the realities of a political system dominated by the social democratic PSOE and the (now governing) conservative PP. Its policy positions are close to that of the UGT in most areas and the two centres generally work closely together.

The CCOO supported Spanish accession to the European Communities (which took effect in 1986) and calls for the development of a 'social Europe'. Domestically its priorities include Spain's high rates of unemployment, temporary employment and industrial accidents, defence of welfare services, extension of unemployment benefits, and achieving the 35-hour week. It sees the Spanish economy as facing problems of lack of social cohesion, fragmented labour relations, unfair competition, and low quality jobs and work, and rejects further deregulation as the solution for these ills. However, Fidalgo has also emphasized the need to engage with younger sections of the population, who are not attracted by old-style industrial trade unionism, and for the unions to recognize that the labour market has changed, and the issue is no longer tying to retain jobs for life, but employability.

Along with the UGT, the CCOO is recognized as representative at the national level and participates in tripartite negotiations with the government and employers. At the international level, the CCOO was finally admitted to the ETUC in 1991, after many years delay. The 1996 congress decided to apply for membership of the ICFTU and this was subsequently granted.

International affiliations. ICFTU; ETUC; TUAC

Unión General de Trabajadores (UGT)
General Union of Workers

Address. Horteleza 88, 28004 Madrid

Phone. +34 91 589 7691

Fax. +34 91 589 7813

E-mail. internacional@cec.ugt.org

Website. www.ugt.es (Spanish only)

Leadership. Cándido Méndez (secretary-general)

Membership. 775,000

History and character. Founded in 1888, the UGT claimed 2 million members on the eve of the Spanish Civil War in 1936. Its leadership was in exile in France during the Franco period. In 1976 the UGT held its 30th congress in Spain, and in 1977 it was legalized.

For many years the UGT was very closely linked to the socialist PSOE and its fortunes mirrored that of the PSOE: the PSOE took power for the first time in 1982, the same year that the UGT came first in workplace elections, having previously trailed the CCOO. However, the 1980s were marked by the gradual disillusionment of the UGT with the PSOE government and its social and economic policies. Early in the decade it was prepared to enter into tripartite pacts, but the last centralized wage round, the social and economic agreement (AES) lapsed in 1986. After the breakdown of negotiations over the renewal of a social pact in 1987, relations between the UGT and PSOE became increasingly acrimonious. Rival factions within the Catalonian metal workers' federation of the UGT attacked each other with bottles and iron bars in March 1988 during a meeting to choose delegates for the union's congress. Antonia Puerta, the leader of the metal workers and a government supporter,

even led a breakaway congress though this attracted only a small minority of delegates. The agreement between the UGT and the CCOO in support of a Dec. 1988 general strike over social security reform hardened the rift as the PSOE attempted to mobilize its supporters within the UGT against the leadership of the union.

At its 35th congress, held in Madrid in April 1990 the UGT symbolized its estrangement from PSOE by inviting all groups represented in the Parliament to attend. After being unanimously re-elected secretary-general, Nicolás Redondo reported that the UGT had consolidated its understanding with the CCOO and the Basque Union ELA-STV, leaving behind the 'confrontational relationship of previous years'. Relations with the PSOE government remained difficult into the 1990s as the government adhered to policies to control public deficits and inflation to harmonize with the leading EU economies. In 1993 the UGT rejected the government's call for a social pact involving below-inflation wages for three years and reform of the labour market, and joined in a 24-hour general strike in Jan. 1994.

In 1993 the UGT finance arm IGS and its property cooperative PSV, went into receivership. The ventures had been launched in 1988 with the aim of delivering cheap housing for the masses, and it was thought that as many as 50,000 investors had participated. In fact, only 1,100 homes of a planned total of 20,000 had been completed. Only the extension of government credits prevented outright bankruptcy.

Even before this Redondo had announced his intention to retire, an announcement which proved a signal for the disgruntled construction, metal worker and transport affiliates to call for a total change of leadership. At a Feb. 1994 meeting the UGT executive moved to defuse discontent by proposing to the April congress the compromise name of Cándido Méndez as Redondo's successor.

Since 1996 the UGT has had to deal with an increasingly strong conservative PP government. The 38th congress, held in March 1998, saw a relaxation of past tensions with the PSOE and the UGT calling for the creation of a common front of the social and political left. The UGT is one of only two confederations (the other being the CCOO) regarded as representative at national level. It participates in bilateral and tripartite negotiations with the employers' organizations and the government. While it competes for members in the same sectors as the similarly-sized CCOO, relations between the two centres are generally cordial and constructive and there is active coordination in formulating policies. For both key issues are employment security; extending unemployment benefit cover; achieving the 35-hour week; improving regulation of temporary employment; reducing industrial accidents; adoption of a more progressive tax policy; and seeking more public investment in job creation. Both are committed to seeking the development of the social dimension of the European Union. They also organize jointly, as on Dec. 3, 1998, when the two centres joined to call a day of action in opposition to government policy on unemployment benefit cover, working hours and tax reform. Differences have appeared over the 35-hour week. The UGT has called for legislation, on the French model, to impose a 35-hour week, which it says will help create jobs, but on this it differs from both the CCOO and the PSOE, which have argued for achieving shorter hours through collective bargaining.

The UGT operates nationwide and in all sectors, although it is not as strong as the CCOO in Madrid and Catalonia. It leads in much of the public administration. Women are underrepresented, and the 1998 congress adopted a resolution that union management bodies should aim to have 20% women on their management boards. In Jan. 2000 a Union of Professionals and Self-Employed Workers (UPTA) was formed within the UGT. There are an estimated 1.8 million self-employed in Spain. There is also a Union of Small Farmers linked to the UGT.

International affiliations. ICFTU; ETUC; TUAC

4 Other Trade Union Organizations

Euzko Langilleen Alkarasuna/Solidaridad de Trabajadores Vascos (ELA/STV)
Basque Workers' Solidarity

Address. Consulado 8, Apartado 971, 20080 San Sebastian

Phone. +34 943 46 16 88

Fax. +34 943 47 08 58

E-mail. eladonosti@maptel.es

Leadership. José Miguel Leunda Etxeberria (president); José Elorrieta Aurrekoetxea (secretary-general)

Membership. 82,000

History and character. The ELA/STV was founded in Bilbao in 1911, and operated underground in the Franco period. It is politically independent but Basque nationalist in orientation and close to the Basque Nationalist Party (PNV), which favours full regional autonomy but opposes the violence of the ETA movement. The ELA/STV and Polish Solidarity are unique in Europe in that they hold dual ICFTU/WCL affiliation.

ELA/STV is the leading union in the Basque country, and has representative status at the regional level based on workplace elections. In the 1990s ELA/STV's principal strength lay in the white-collar sector, where it had considerable success in achieving higher salaries for public sector professionals than their counterparts received in Madrid. In July 2000 it reached agreement with the Basque regional government on introduction of the 35-hour week in the public administration, the first Spanish province to agree this.

International affiliations. ICFTU; WCL; ETUC; TUAC

Unión Sindical Obrera (USO)
Workers' Union

Address. Príncipe de Vergara 13 7°, 29001 Madrid

Phone. +34 91 577 41 13

Fax. +34 91 577 29 59

E-mail. s.general@uso.es

Leadership. Manuel Zaguirre (secretary-general)

Membership. 80,000

History and character. Founded in 1961, the USO is politically independent and pluralist.

International affiliation. WCL

Sri Lanka

Capital: Colombo
Population: 19.24 m. (2000 est.)

1 Political and Economic Background

Sri Lanka gained its independence from the United Kingdom in 1948. The Sri Lanka Freedom Party (SLFP) dominates the left-wing People's Alliance coalition which has held power since 1994 elections, when it defeated the conservative United National Party (UNP), which had been in office since 1977. Since elections in Oct. 2000 the People's Alliance forms a minority gov-

ernment. The President is SLFP leader Chandrika Bandaranaike Kumaratunga, who was re-elected in Dec. 1999. The President's mother, Sirimavo Bandaranaike, held the (now largely ceremonial) role of Prime Minister until her death in Oct. 2000. Since the mid-1980s the dominant issue facing the country has been the conflict between the majority Sinhalese and minority Tamil populations, with continuing military action against with the Tamil Tiger rebel movement. Political life is conducted under the shadow of regular assassinations and attempted assassinations.

Sri Lanka's economy is primarily agricultural, with tea, rubber and coconuts as the main crops, although plantation crops now make up only 20% of exports compared to 93% in 1970. A range of industries has also been developed, with textiles and garments now contributing 63% of exports. After 1977 the UNP reversed much of the previous SLFP government's policy of state interference in the economy and the incoming SLFP-led People's Alliance government elected in 1994 committed itself to proceed with some privatization while retaining state ownership of a large number of enterprises. Growth has averaged 5–6% per annum for most of the 1990s.

GDP (purchasing power parity) $50.5bn. (1999 est.); GDP per capita (purchasing power parity) $2,600 (1999 est.).

2 Trade Unionism

Sri Lanka ratified ILO Convention No.98 (Right to Organize and Collective Bargaining, 1949) in 1972 and Convention No.87 (Freedom of Association and Protection of the Right to Organize, 1948) in 1995. Trade unions were given legal recognition under colonial rule in 1935, by which time substantial development had occurred. Since independence, trade union freedoms have been substantial but subject to periodic modification or suspension according to political conditions. The historical stronghold of the labour movement is the plantations, where over 70% of the workforce, which is predominantly 'Indian' Tamil, are organized. In total there are approximately 900,000 union members, 650,000 of whom are women, reflecting the role of women in the plantations.

Unions exist in most large private sector firms, but have little presence in the small business sector or small-scale agriculture. The public sector is highly organized. Members of the police force, the judiciary and armed forces may not join unions, and unions in government services may not confederate. Amendments to the Industrial Disputes Act, adopted in Dec. 1999, imposed an obligation on employers to recognize trade unions and prohibited anti-union discrimination. Employers found guilty of such discrimination are required to reinstate workers dismissed for union activities, but have the right to transfer them to different locations. While workers in the export processing zones are in theory free to join unions, in practice union organizers are kept out of the zones and union membership is negligible.

Only seven persons are needed to form a union and this factor in combination with ethnic, linguistic and ideological divisions has fragmented the labour movement. In 1998 the Department of Labour reported a total of 1,678 functioning unions. Many leading unions in the private (but not the public) sector are affiliated with political parties and are politically active. The Department may cancel the registration of any union that does not submit an annual report, although this is the only legal basis for cancellation of registration.

There is no national trade union centre. The ICFTU-affiliated Ceylon Workers' Congress (CWC) is based primarily in the plantations. The WCL is represented by the National Workers' Congress (NWC), while the WFTU claims to have five affiliates, the Ceylon Federation of Trade Unions, the Democratic Workers' Congress, the Sri Lanka Mahajana Trade Union Federation, the Sri Lanka Nidakas Sewaka Sangamaya, and the Progressive Workers' Congress.

Collective bargaining is extensively practiced in the private sector, although complicated by the multiplicity of unions in individual enterprises. Worker councils exist in non-union enterprises and the export processing zones as a forum for negotiations, but according to the unions these are ineffective.

All workers, other than public employees and those in essential services, have the right to strike and the law prohibits retribution against strikers. Strikes are common. Under the conservative UNP administration (1977–1994), the government used a broad interpretation of 'essential services' to control strikes and made use of emergency powers. Up to 100,000 employees were dismissed after a 1980 general strike supported by the opposition (most of these were later reinstated). The People's Alliance government has, however, generally shown a more liberal approach to strike action while retaining the power to declare industries to be essential services. In 1998 an essential services designation was used to try to end industrial action in the postal service, leading to the arrest of the general secretary and other leaders of the UPTO postal workers' union. However, the dispute was ultimately settled by negotiation with agreement that strikers would not be victimized. In 1999 the government also attempted to end a doctors' strike in this way, although the dispute was resolved with the government agreeing to consider the doctors' grievances. While public employees may not legally strike, but only submit their grievances to the Public Service Commission, in practice government workers in the transportation, medical, educational, power generation, financial, and port sectors have all staged brief strikes and other work actions in recent years. There were 128 strikes in the public sector during 1999.

Sri Lanka has some tripartite elements in its industrial relations system, primarily the Wages Boards. These Boards determine minimum terms and conditions of employment. Conciliation and arbitration services are available through the Department of Labour.

3 Trade Union Centres

There is no recognized trade union centre.

4 Other Trade Union Organizations

Ceylon Workers' Congress (CWC)
Address. 72 Ananda Coomarasamy Mawatha, PO Box 1294, Colombo 3
Phone. +94 1 574 452

Fax. +94 1 301 358

E-mail. cwcctuc@slt.lk

Leadership. Arumugan Thondaman (president)

Membership. 180,000.

History and character. From its foundation the CWC recruited mainly among plantation workers of Indian Tamil descent, who had for decades suffered institutionalized discrimination. Although CWC membership is drawn from teachers, mercantile and commercial employees, the bulk comes from the tea and rubber plantations.

The Ceylon Indian Congress Labour Union was founded in 1940 as the labour wing of the Ceylon Indian Congress (CIC), itself formed in 1939 by Shri Nehru as the envoy of Mahatma Gandhi. In its early years the principal objective of the CIC was to secure independence from British rule, and following the achievement of this in 1948, the Labour Union was renamed as the Ceylon Workers' Congress. It became a trade union with a separate political wing, rather than vice versa, in 1950. In 1977 the CWC's political wing became a political party (also called the Ceylon Workers' Congress, and in effect indivisible from the union) and the union/party president, Sovumiyamoorthy Thondaman, was returned to parliament, taking office in 1978 for the first time as Minister for Rural Development in the UNP government of Junius Jayewardene. Using this position within the government coalition, the CWC was able to secure constitutional revisions that extended basic rights to so-called 'stateless' persons, most of whom were of Indian descent. S. Thondaman, often regarded as the leader of the people of Indian descent in Sri Lanka, retained a Cabinet post after the change of government in 1994 but died in Oct. 1999. His successor as CWC president, Arumugan Thondaman, became Minister for Livestock Development and Estate Infrastructure.

The CWC opposes all discrimination based on race, creed, caste or religion. It has established a vocational training complex and a construction consortium with the help of the ICFTU, and has launched credit schemes and a project to create a number of small dairy farm cooperatives on plantations.

International affiliations. ICFTU; CTUC

Lanka Jathika Estate Workers' Union (LJEWU)

Address. 60, Bandaranayakepura, Sri Jayawardenepura Mawata, Welikada, Rajagiriya

Phone. +94 1 865138

Fax. + 94 1 862262

E-mail. ctucljeu@sri.lanka.net

Leadership. Ranil Wickremesinghe (president); Rajah Seneviratne (general secretary)

Membership. 398,000

History and character. The LJEWU was founded in 1958. It has a collective agreement with the Employers' Federation of Ceylon which represents the 23 privatized plantation companies.

Publications. *Jathika Jeevaya* (in Sinhala) and *Murasoli* (in Tamil)

International affiliations. CTUC

National Workers' Congress (NWC)

Address. 94 1/6 York Building, York Street, Colombo 1

Phone. +94 1 431 847

Fax. +94 1 470 874

E-mail. nwccmb@itmin.com

Leadership. Marcelle Rajahmoney (president); Antony Lodwick (general secretary)

Membership. 80,000.

History and character: Founded in 1952; politically independent and non-sectarian. Emphasizes worker education and is focusing on trying to organize in the free trade zones.

International affiliation. WCL

Sudan

Capital: Khartoum
Population: 35.08 m. (2000 est.)

1 Political and Economic Background

Since its establishment in 1956, the Republic of Sudan has experienced political instability, division between the Arab, Muslim north, including the capital, Khartoum, and the mainly Christian and animist, African south. The current President, Omar Hassan Ahmad al-Bashir, seized power in a military coup in 1989. Political parties have been illegal since then, and the National Islamic Front has operated as the sole political organization. In 1999 a new constitution provided for the formation of political 'associations', but these were required to abide by Islamic Sharia law. In Dec. 1999, in response to calls in the National Assembly for changes to reduce his powers, Bashir declared a state of emergency and dissolved the Assembly. He was re-elected as President in Dec. 2000 in a poll boycotted by opposition forces. A state of rebellion continues in the Christian south. There is a large refugee population, from Sudan's wars and those of its neighbours.

Sudan has been impoverished by decades of civil war, the burden of military spending, drought and rapid population increase. Some 80% of the workforce are engaged in agriculture and herding, much of it at subsistence level, and there has been little investment in modern industries and services, although an oil sector is under development with foreign investment. The country is heavily indebted.

GDP (purchasing power parity) $32.6bn. (1999 est.); GDP per capita (purchasing power parity) $940 (1999 est.).

2 Trade Unionism

Sudan ratified ILO Convention No.98 (Right to Organize and Collective Bargaining, 1949) in 1957, but has not ratified Convention No. 87 (Freedom of Association and Protection of the Right to Organize, 1948).

Trade unions originally developed after World War II. In the late 1980s there were two centres, the blue-collar Sudanese Workers' Trade Union Federation (SWTUF) – which at that point claimed to have 1.5 million members – and the white-collar Sudanese Federation of Employees and Professional Trade Unions (SFEPTU). After Bashir came to power in 1989 he dissolved the trade unions. The SWTUF leaders kept their personal freedom following the coup but their activities were outlawed; most members of the SFEPTU were arrested however. In the summer of 1990, Dr. Ali Fadul of the Sudan Doctors' Union died in prison as the result of torture.

In 1989 General Bashir set up preliminary committees to run union affairs and other steering committees were

announced. In 1991 a Trade Union Dialogue Conference was convened in Khartoum, ostensibly intended to secure agreement of trade unionists to new laws conforming to ILO Conventions. From this conference a tripartite committee was chosen which drafted the 1992 Trade Union Law establishing a new system of enterprise unions.

Under the 1992 Act, which still applies, a single trade union system was set up, in which the government dictates the sectors and enterprises in which unions can exist. The reorganized SWTUF according to its rules functions to 'mobilize the masses for production and to defend the authenticity of the Islamic state.' In 1992, elections to union office were held, prior to which many union activists had been asked for written undertakings that they would not stand for office or work in opposition. Since by this time a number of union members had also been imprisoned and tortured, a number of leading figures withdrew from the country to organize abroad.

The SWTUF continues to exist as a government-sponsored trade union organization. Following a 1996 merger it now mobilizes 13 unions and claims to have 800,000 members. It remains the case that independent trade unions may not be organized in Sudan and there are continuing reports of the arrest and torture of activists who try to organize independently. The SW(L)TUF, which sees itself as the successor to the SWTUF abolished in 1989, operates in exile and to some degree underground in Sudan. Following the adoption of a new constitution in Jan. 1999, which embodied a right of association, the SW(L)TUF said this appeared to allow a small margin of freedom. However, when it attempted to hold a meeting in Khartoum on July 6, 1999, the authorities arrested 14 members of the executive committee, including the president and secretary-general.

There is a nominal right to engage in collective bargaining but in practice the government dominates the process of setting wages in the formal sector. Strikes are banned but took place in 1998–99 over the impact of privatization on jobs and salary arrears.

Surinam

Capital: Paramaribo
Population: 431,000 (2000 est.)

1 Political and Economic Background

Formerly Dutch Guiana, Surinam achieved complete independence from the Netherlands in 1975. In Feb. 1980, the government was overthrown by Sgt.-Maj.

Désiré ('Desi') Bouterse. Since then its politics has been characterized by periods of direct or indirect military intervention, with close relationships between military commanders and civilian politicians. The current President, Jules Wijdenbosch, became Prime Minister and Vice-President after a coup (sponsored by Bouterse) in 1990, lost power in elections in 1991, and was elected President (by a United People's Conference) in 1996. The government is a coalition of parties, led by

Wijdenbosch's National Democratic Party (whose leader is Bouterse), and including parties based in Surinam's Indonesian and Indian communities

The largest section of the Surinam workforce is employed by the government and by para-statal industries such as the state oil company, sugar estate, rice farm, banana and palm oil plantations and others. The economy is dominated by the mining of bauxite and its processing into alumina and finished aluminium. The country has been associated with gun running, international drug trafficking and money laundering. After coming into office in Sept. 1996 the Wijdenbosch government ended participation in a structural adjustment programme, saying it was unfair to the poorer elements in society.

GDP (purchasing power parity) $1.48bn. (1999 est.); GDP per capita (purchasing power parity) $3,400 (1999 est.).

2 Trade Unionism

Surinam ratified ILO Convention No.87 (Freedom of Association and Protection of the Right to Organize, 1948) in 1976 and No.98 (Right to Organize and Collective Bargaining, 1949) in 1996. The unions are well established with some 60% of the workforce organized. The labour movement is also highly fragmented: there are six federations and the ICFTU has three affiliates in a country of less than half a million people. There is a tradition of active union involvement in politics and the unions have been politically influential.

About 50% of the workforce are covered by collective bargaining agreements. There is a constitutional right to strike in both private and public sectors and strikes are common. It is difficult for employers to dismiss workers and the Ministry of Labour reviews each dismissal individually, with powers to order reinstatement.

3 Trade Union Centre

There is no recognized trade union centre.

4 Other Trade Union Organizations

Algemeen Verbond van Vakverenigingen in Surinam 'De Moederbond' (AVVS or Moederbond)
General Alliance of Labour Unions in Surinam

Address. PO Box 2951, Coppenstraat 134, Paramaribo

Phone. +597 463 501

Fax. +597 465 116

History and character. De Moederbond was founded in 1951. In Dec. 1982 the military declared a state of martial law, destroyed the union's offices and summarily executed its president, Cyrill Daal, and other opponents of the regime. Following this other leaders of De Moederbond went into exile. The ICFTU suspended De Moederbond's affiliation in 1986 but restored it in 1988, when the ICFTU executive board found that it had now been restored to democratic principles.

International affiliation. ICFTU

Centrale van Landsdienaren Organisaties (CLO)
Federation of Civil Service Organizations

Address. Verlengde Gemene Landsweg 74, Paramaribo

Phone. +597 49 98 39

International affiliation. ICFTU

Organisatie van Samenwerkende Autonome Vakbonden (OSAV)
Organization of Cooperating Autonomous Trade Unions

Address. Keizerstraat 218, Paramaribo

Phone. +597 476 921

Fax. + 597 474 866

Leadership. Waldo Bijnoe (chairman)

History and character. OSAV was founded in 1985 after a dispute over the leadership of De Moederbond, of which most of its officers were members.

International affiliation. WCL (extraordinary member)

Progressieve Vakcentrale 47 (C-47)
Progressive Labour Federation 47

Address. PO Box 9331, Paramaribo

Phone. +597 401 044

Fax. +597 490 915

International affiliation. ICFTU

Swaziland

Capital: Mbabane
Population: 1.08 m. (2000 est.)

1 Political and Economic Background

The Kingdom of Swaziland achieved full independence from the United Kingdom in 1968. The present King, Mswati III, acceded to the throne in 1986 and enjoys considerable executive powers, ruling through a Cabinet appointed by him. Emergency powers have been in force since 1973 and political activity is banned under the 1978 Constitution although a number of political associations developed in the 1990s. The majority of members of the lower house of Parliament are elected, on a non-party basis, as representatives of the tribal assemblies (Tinkhundla).

About 60 per cent of the population are supported by (mainly subsistence level) agriculture, and manufacturing is based largely on the processing of agricultural products. The domestic mining sector has declined but an estimated 20% is added to national income by remittances from Swazi workers employed in the mines of neighbouring South Africa.

GDP (purchasing power parity) $4.2bn. (1999 est.); GDP per capita (purchasing power parity) $4,200 (1999 est.).

2 Trade Unionism

Swaziland joined the ILO in 1975 and ratified ILO Convention No.87 (Freedom of Association and Protection of the Right to Organize, 1948) and Convention No.98 (Right to Organize and Collective Bargaining, 1949) in 1978.

Unions are relatively well organized in the formal sector and there is a national centre, the Swaziland Federation of Trade Unions (SFTU). The SFTU is affiliated to the ICFTU. Since the mid-1990s it has been in constant conflict with the government over labour legislation and restrictions on political and civil rights.

Industrial relations legislation provides a framework for trade union activities, requiring employers to recognize unions with 50% membership among the workforce and permitting collective bargaining. However, there is also a range of restrictions on unions, including a ban on engaging in political activity and a restriction on the role of federations to the provision of advice and services. Severe penalties may be imposed in case of illegal strikes and strikes in broadly defined essential services, and sympathy strikes and strikes not considered in the national interest are banned. Trade union federations may not lead or incite work stoppages, and their officials can be sentenced to up to five years' imprisonment for

violations. Despite this, and regular arrest of its officials, the STFU has called numerous strikes, demonstrations and other protests as part of a broad campaign for democratization.

3 Trade Union Centre

Swaziland Federation of Trade Unions (SFTU)

Address. PO Box 1158, Manzini

Phone. +268 50 56 575

Fax. +268 50 56 575

Leadership. Jan Sithole (general secretary)

Membership. 80,000 in 21 affiliates

History and character. Founded in 1973, the SFTU became the central trade union organization in the mid-1980s, with members from both the public and private sectors, and including agricultural workers.

Since 1994, the SFTU has stepped up its campaign, in alliance with civic and opposition groups, for repeal of restrictive labour legislation, for a democratic and pluralist society and the end of emergency powers legislation. It has called regular strikes and demonstrations and this has led to continual harassment. In 1995 general secretary Jan Sithole was threatened with deportation when the authorities challenged his right to Swazi citizenship, and this threat has recurred in subsequent years. In Aug. 1995 Sithole was kidnapped, according to the SFTU by government agents, and abandoned in the boot of a car on the outskirts of Manzini. In Feb. 1997 armed police broke up an SFTU general council meeting after the SFTU called a national stay-away. Council members were reportedly beaten by police and the death of SFTU treasurer, Mxolisi Mbata, in Oct. 1998 was attributed to injuries sustained at that time. Sithole and three other officials were arrested in connection with the stay-away. They subsequently stood trial on charges of intimidating bus operators into not running services during the stay-away, but were acquitted by a judge.

The SFTU called for a boycott of the most recent legislative elections in Oct. 1998 on the ground that they were not democratic. On Nov. 17, Sithole was held for questioning in connection with an explosion, but released the following day, and over the following months other SFTU officials were subject to arrests and police raids on their homes. In Nov. 2000 Sithole was put under house arrest after the SFTU, in alliance with civic and opposition groups, called a two day strike, banned by the government, on a platform demanding the legalization of political parties and trade union and human rights. The SFTU's campaign is receiving the active support of COSATU in South Africa.

International affiliation. ICFTU

Sweden

Capital: Stockholm
Population: 8.87 m. (2000 est.)

1 Political and Economic Background

The Social Democratic Labour Party (SAP) has been in office continuously since 1936, other than for periods in 1976–82 and again in 1991–94. In elections in Sept. 1998 the SAP declined to 36.4% of the vote but remained in office under Prime Minister Göran Persson with support from the Left Party and the Green Ecology Party, although there is no coalition. The opposition is led by the Moderate Alliance Party, which itself formed a centre-right coalition government in the period Sept. 1991–Sept. 1994 under Prime Minister Carl Bildt. After a referendum in Nov. 1994, Sweden joined the EU on Jan. 1, 1995 but it did not adopt the single European currency at its inception in 1999.

Sweden is a prosperous country that combines a welfare state with a strong private sector. Sweden is notable for its international orientation, reflected in the fact that a country with a population of less than nine million is home to an array of major international companies. The 'Swedish model' of consensus involving a high degree of social organization, centralized bargaining between employers and unions, and generous social provision came under strain in the late 1980s and early 1990s. Manufacturing jobs were lost and Sweden experienced recession for the first time since the 1930s, with GDP falling year-on-year 1991–93. The centre-right Bildt government of 1991–94 was a period of austerity measures and there was a financial crisis in 1992. Since the mid-1990s however there has been strong economic growth led by areas such as pharmaceuticals, computers and telecommunications and a wide range of private-sector services. Unemployment, which reached close to 15% at mid-decade, had fallen to 4% by late 2000. Since 1997, 190,000 new jobs have been created. This has been achieved with inflation of only 1% in 2000.

GDP (purchasing power parity) $184bn. (1999 est.); GDP per capita (purchasing power parity) $20,700 (1999 est.).

2 Trade Unionism

Sweden ratified ILO Convention No.87 (Freedom of Association and Protection of the Right to Organize, 1948) in 1949 and Convention No.98 (Right to Organize and Collective Bargaining, 1949) in 1950.

Numerous socialist-inclined trade unions appeared in the 1880s and in 1889 these were influential in the formation of the Social Democratic Labour Party (SAP), which functioned both as a political party and as a trade union centre. This in turn led to the formation of the Swedish Trade Union Confederation (LO) in 1898. In 1906 the newly formed Employers' Confederation (SAF) recognized the LO and the right of workers to bargain collectively. In 1938 the two sides concluded their first Basic Agreement.

The structure of the Swedish trade union movement is similar to that in other Scandinavian countries. The trade union centres form a pyramid. At the base is the largest centre, the LO, which represents blue-collar workers and has about 2.1 million members. In the middle of the pyramid is the 1.3 million-strong Swedish Confederation of Professional Employees (TCO). This represents the white-collar sector, where unionization began in the 1930s. At the apex is the Swedish Confederation of Professional Associations (SACO) with 479,000 members, which represents employees and professionals with graduate qualifications. In general (and again reflecting a pattern seen in other Scandinavian countries) the LO and the TCO have maintained a cooperative relationship, which has been enhanced by the trend to equalization of pay and conditions between the manual and white-collar sectors. The LO and the TCO have demarcation agreements to reduce intrusions on their various areas of recruitment, but there are few such agreements between the TCO and SACO.

Union density in Sweden is the highest achieved voluntarily anywhere in the world, with the overwhelming majority of employees in unions. Density declined slightly from the mid-1980s, standing at 81% in 1990, but then recovered to its previous level of 83% by mid-decade. Density peaks at 94% for municipal employees but even in the weakest area – white-collar workers in private sector service industries – density is close to 70%. Overall, there is little difference in density as between white-collar and blue-collar employees. The proportion of self-employed in Sweden, 8% of the labour force, is also the lowest in the EU. The LO has considered but not agreed the principle of recruiting among the self-employed, while SACO freely recruits the self-employed into its member associations.

The exceptional organizational success of Swedish trade unions has been variously explained. The persistence of social democratic government for most of the period since the 1930s undoubtedly provided a favourable environment for trade unionism. However, while the LO has been close to the Social Democratic Labour Party (SAP) the TCO and SACO have grown without political allegiance. The closed shop does not exist and the unions enjoy few exceptional privileges in law: indeed, the whole basis of the industrial relations system is free bargaining between unions and employers, with relatively light state intervention.

The trade unions have benefited to some degree from their role in the administration of unemployment insurance funds. Most workers automatically become members of an unemployment insurance scheme (97% of funding for which comes from the government) by joining a union. On the other hand, union membership is not obligatory to be a member of an unemployment insurance fund, and the number of workers who have joined such funds directly rather than through a union has increased in the 1990s at the same time as union density has risen.

Factors that in other countries have generally been seen as weakening the trade unions seem to have had no or the opposite effect in Sweden. Thus union density increased in the period 1990–94 notwithstanding there being a centre-right government in office, the worst recession since World War II, and loss of manufacturing jobs. The Swedish economy has experienced the same movement out of blue-collar manufacturing and into services as other developed countries, but the unions have succeeded in increasing their strength in the services sector. The most rapid growth in union membership in the 1990s came in the blue-collar private services sector, an area with a high incidence of low-paid part-time female working; in many countries such workers have proved difficult or impossible to organize, but in Sweden this is not the case.

In Swedish society there is a traditional emphasis on achieving consensus and a general commitment to maintaining a social safety net. The unions have played a role for decades as social partners and adopted positions in which they have considered the broad national interest as well as their members' sectional interests. In that sense, they have been seen as acceptable and even desirable by the broader community and as a force for social stability. Symptomatically, higher-paid managers and professionals are highly organized. Similarly, the employers have accepted the place of unions and been prepared to accept them as legitimate representatives of the workforce. These features of Swedish society should not be exaggerated, however. Strikes have always been a an element of industrial relations and the conflict between free market deregulators and advocates of the welfare state has continued in Sweden since the 1980s.

Swedish unions have avoided the political and religious polarization seen in many European countries. The LO identifies with the SAP, but the TCO and SACO are politically neutral rather than anti-SAP. They have also generally avoided conflict over recruitment, not least because the three confederations recruit in distinct areas. Where there are potential overlaps the unions have generally worked to ensure strict demarcation. The continued blurring of distinctions between white-collar and blue-collar, the basic division between the LO and TCO, and between rank-and-file white-collar employees and those with graduate qualifications, the dividing line between the TCO and SACO, has produced remarkably little friction. However, it seems possible that this blurring will produce major changes in the medium-term. The TCO has floated the prospect of an eventual merger with SACO, in view of the increasingly graduate nature

of the white-collar workforce, although SACO has seemed less enthusiastic.

The high degree of organization of Swedish employers has also worked to strengthen the role of the unions. In many countries the absence of representative employer organizations to deal with seriously undermines national level trade unions, which cannot negotiate national or sectoral agreements that are deliverable at the enterprise level. In Sweden most employers are members of employer organizations and adhere to the agreements these organizations reach. This is the case despite the lack of any legislation binding employers to such agreements.

Swedish collective bargaining arrangements famously express a cooperative spirit and have done so since the 1938 Saltsjobaden Agreement of the Swedish Employers' Confederation (SAF) and the LO. In 1952, they signed their first major national collective pay agreement, which was widely observed even though the participants were not legally or constitutionally bound by it. For several decades thereafter the pattern was one in which the LO and SAF negotiated a central agreement which was then translated into detail in sectoral and in some case company-level agreements. From the 1970s the 'Swedish model' came under strain and finally collapsed at the end of the 1980s under the impact of growing white-collar trade unionism, increasing employer unease over legislated rights for employees in the enterprise, and gathering economic difficulty. From 1983 onwards individual LO and SAF affiliates had sought separate agreements with their counterparts rather than the usual umbrella arrangements, but the main framework survived (with some structural changes) until 1989. That year's central agreement proved to be the last.

Since that time the pattern has been one of sectoral bargaining, with the LO and other confederations playing a looser coordinating role. However, while a return to the old centralized system is no longer even on the LO's agenda there has been movement to introduce more structure to the bargaining process. In the period 1994–99 wage increases were generally ahead of the average in Sweden's major competitors and the government is concerned that wage drift should not damage Sweden's competitiveness. In 1997 the government set up a committee to review the options for changing the bargaining structure. However, the unions showed themselves divided on the issue. While the LO was keen to strengthen centralized bargaining, the TCO and SACO were against imposed pay norms and any form of incomes policy. In the event the social partners could not produce a consensus and the government went ahead with legislation in Dec. 1999 which embraced a number of the committee's recommendations but fell short of creating a rigid system for centralized incomes policy. Under this legislation a new Mediation Authority (Medlingsinstitute) was established effective June 2000. This was to be responsible for drawing up an annual report on wage determination, which is expected to bear heavily on the thinking of employers and trade unions in future bargaining rounds (the next major bargaining round is in 2001). With the consent of the parties the Mediation Authority will be able to appoint mediators to lead collective bargaining. The unions have generally welcomed the creation of the Mediation Authority and are not unresponsive to the government's anxieties about Swedish firms becoming uncompetive if wage costs soar, or to the risk of increasing unemployment if inflation triggers rises in interest rates. A panel of employers' and unions' economists has proposed a benchmark whereby wages should rise at the EU average.

The trade union movement is relatively decentralized and is vigorous at the local level. Union branches within companies maintain a bargaining role and there is no parallel system of works councils. Collective agreements are binding on signatories (but not on those employers who are not members of the signatory organization). There are virtually no restrictions on strikes in either the public or private sector, beyond a duty to give notice. There is no provision for compulsory mediation or arbitration and no legislation on strikes in essential services. SAF has called for a ban on sympathy strikes and on strikes directed against small traders and family firms; it has also called for a principle of proportionality to be legislated, whereby unions could not undertake lightly strikes destroying other people's interests. These calls have been ignored by the government, but the new Mediation Authority has been given powers to force the postponement of industrial action, and the notice period has been extended from 7 to 14 days. Strikes tend, however, to be at a generally low level in Sweden. Successive governments have generally avoided intervening in industrial disputes leaving these to be resolved by the parties.

The Co-determination Act of 1977 requires employers to advise and consult employees before making any significant changes in company operation. Under the Board Representation Act employees have the right to be represented on the boards of all companies with 25 or more employees. The unions appoint the employee representatives on boards. Employee representatives do not participate in discussions relating to issues such as collective bargaining and are in effect excluded from most critical decision-making, but both unions and the majority of employers believe the system is a beneficial one.

Like Swedish institutions generally, the unions have a strong international focus. The LO and the TCO cooperate with the Swedish International Development Authority (SIDA) and distribute SIDA funds to unions in developing countries through the LO/TCO Secretariat for Trade Union Development.

3 Trade Union Centres

Landsorganisation i Sverige (LO)
Swedish Trade Union Confederation

Address. Barnhusgaten 18, S-105 53 Stockholm

Phone. +46 8 796 25 00

Fax. +46 8 796 28 00

E-mail. info@lo.se

Website. www.lo.se (Swedish; English)

Leadership. Wanja Lundby-Wedin (president)

Membership. 2,066,500

History and character. The LO is the organization of blue-collar workers in Sweden. Its membership splits 61% private sector and 39% public sector. A small majority (54%) of its membership is male, in contrast to the white-collar TCO, which has a female majority. During the 1990s the LO has had success in increasing the organization of blue-collar women workers in services.

The LO sees its role as providing central coordination and national-level policy direction on behalf of its affiliated unions. The individual unions are responsible for sectoral bargaining and for managing unemployment insurance funds.

The LO was created in 1898 by the Social Democratic Labour Party (SAP), and it has remained close to the party. The SAP first came to power in 1932, applying Keynesian policies to counter the depression. In 1938 the LO reached the first 'Basic Agreement' with the employers' confederation SAF and thereafter pursued in conjunction with the SAP (in office for most of the rest of the century) 'middle way' policies of social and industrial reform. Despite strains in the 1980s over government austerity policies, the relationship remains close and explicit, with a general convergence over policy positions, and the LO is represented on the SAP executive committee.

From the 1950s to the late 1980s collective bargaining was highly centralized with the LO reaching a series of Basic Agreements providing a detailed framework. This system, which the LO very much favoured, did not survive into the 1990s as the increasing influence of free market economics, the election of a centre-right government in 1990, and the desire of both the SAF and the white-collar union centres for increased decentralization, undermined it. Even the SAP, back in office since 1994, has not supported a return to the old highly centralized system. However, the desire for a more controlled process for wage determination was reflected in the establishment of the new Mediation Institute, with effect from June 2000, a move welcomed by the LO. The LO has accepted that future bargaining should take place mainly at the sectoral level but emphasizes that achieving pay awards that do not stoke inflation or damage competitiveness, as the government wishes, demands a degree of national coordination.

Historically the LO used centralized bargaining to promote a policy of 'wage solidarity' whereby differentials between different industries, and different occupations in the same industry, were to be leveled out. It still through its coordinating role seeks to encourage this approach, though it has met declining support from individual unions and members in successful areas of the economy.

Most LO affiliates work on the principle of organizing

all blue-collar workers in a workplace in the same union regardless of trade. Exceptionally, the building trades unions are craft-based. The majority of LO affiliates organize about 80–90% of the workers in their fields, except in retailing and services. The LO's role includes the resolution of demarcation disputes between its member unions, although the affiliates are independent.

The LO has generally been unenthusiastic about admitting the self-employed to membership, in contrast to SACO and some TCO unions. A 1998 LO report concluded that 'helping members who have been forced into self-employment is a trade union task, while helping those who want to become self-employed is not'. The LO unions for builders, painters and transport workers have all decided against admitting the self-employed. The forestry workers' union has taken a different position, however, reflecting industry changes that pushed many former employees into tied forms of self-employment.

The LO has allied itself with SAP in saying that introduction of the 35-hour week, while a goal, should be introduced by industry agreement on a case-by-case basis and not legislated for. The normal statutory working time is 40 hours.

Sweden joined the EU in 1995 and building the social dimension of the EU is an increasingly important priority for the LO. Wanja Lundby-Wedin, the LO's first woman president, elected in Sept. 2000, had previously held responsibility for European-level trade union issues.

The LO has a traditionally strong involvement in international trade union development. Its assistance programmes for central and Eastern Europe and developing countries take place through the LO-TCO Secretariat for Trade Union Development and the Olof Palme International Centre.

The LO favours the extension of worker participation and co-determination in the workplace. It is represented on numerous governmental bodies such as the National Labour Market Board, the National Board of Occupational Safety and Health, and the National Social Insurance Board.

Pensions are a major issue in Sweden, which has an aging population. In 1996 the SAF and LO signed a new pension agreement to provide a supplementary pension scheme for blue-collar workers.

Enterprises linked to the LO include the Workers' Educational Association (ABF), the Correspondence School (Brevskolan) and insurance company Folksam.

Publications. LO-tidningen

International affiliations. ICFTU; ETUC; TUAC; NFS

Affiliated unions. There are 18 affiliates, as follows:

1. Building Workers' Union (Byggnads)

Address. Hagagatan 2, S-106 32 Stockholm
Phone. +46 8 728 48 00
Fax. +46 8 34 50 51
E-mail. forbundert@byggnads.se
Website. www.byggnads.se (Swedish only)
Leadership. Ove Bengtsberg (president)

Membership. 133,000
History and character. Absorbed the small Sheet Metal Workers' Union in Jan. 2000.

2. Electricians' Union (SEF)

Address. PO Box 1123, S-111 81 Stockholm
Phone. +46 8 412 82 82
Fax. +46 8 412 82 01
Membership. 22,993

3. Building Maintenance Workers' Union (Fastighets)

Address. PO Box 70440, S-107 25 Stockholm
Phone. +46 8 696 11 50
Fax. +46 8 24 46 90
E-mail. info@fastighets.se
Website. www.fastighets.se (Swedish; English section)
Leadership. Barbro Palmerlund (president)
Membership. 44,302

4. Social Insurance Employees' and Insurance Agents' Union (FF)

Address. PO Box 3466, S-103 69 Stockholm
Phone. +46 8 402 94 00
Fax. +46 8 21 10 44
E-mail. ff@ff.nu
Website. www.ff.nu (Swedish only)
Leadership. Börje Johansson (president)
Membership. 13,760

5. Graphic Workers' Union (Grafiska Fackförbundet, GF)

Address. PO Box 1101, S-111 81 Stockholm
Phone. +46 8 791 16 00
Fax. +46 8 411 41 01
E-mail. gf@gf.se
Website. www.gf.se (Swedish only)
Membership. 31,278

6. Commercial Employees' Union (Handels)

Address. PO Box 1146, S-111 81 Stockholm
Phone. +46 8 412 68 00
Fax. +46 8 10 00 62
Website. www.handels.se (Swedish; English section)
Membership. 170,000. Represents workers in retail and wholesale trades, clerical workers, etc. 74% of members are women.

7. Hotel and Restaurant Workers' Union (HRF)

Address. PO Box 1143, S-111 81 Stockholm
Phone. +46 8 781 02 00
Fax. +46 8 411 71 18
Website. www.hrf.net (Swedish; English section)
Membership. 61,000

8. Industrial Workers' Union (Industrifacket)

Address. PO Box 1114, S-111 81 Stockholm
Phone. +46 8 786 85 00
Fax. +46 8 10 59 68
E-mail. postbox.fk@industrifacket.se
Website. www.industrifacket.se (Swedish; English section)
Leadership. Leif Ohlsson (president)
Membership. 96,000
History and character. Founded in 1993 by merger of the Factory Workers' Union and the Textile, Garment and Leather Workers' Union. This is a general industrial union with members in industries including textiles, clothing, leather, chemicals, rubber, plas-

tics, oil-refining, glass, gas, pharmaceuticals, sugar, concrete, laundry and others, and it organizes 95% of blue-collar workers in the industries it covers. It has an active international trade union development programme. Affiliated to ICEM and ITGLWF.

9. Municipal Workers' Union (Kommunal)

Address. PO Box 19039, S-104 32 Stockholm
Phone. +46 8 728 28 00
Fax. +46 8 31 87 45
E-mail. kommunalinfo@kommunal.se
Website. www.kommunal.se (Swedish; English section)
Leadership. Ylva Thörn (general secretary)
Membership. 600,000
History and character. Founded in 1910 and the largest union in the LO. It organizes blue-collar employees in local government, members including care workers, workers in parks, street cleaning, schools, leisure facilities, waters and sewage, fire stations and urban transit. 80% of its members are women, 65% are part-time and 10% are unemployed. Kommunal emphasizes skills development and partnered in founding the Municipal University in collaboration with Göteborg and Linköping Universities and Jönköping University College. It plays an active role in helping members find jobs through its Job Points, which act as employment agencies. It is affiliated to PSI and ITF.

10. Agricultural Workers' Union (Svenska Lantarbetare förbundet, SLF)

Address. PO Box 1104, S-111 81 Stockholm
Phone. +46 8 796 29 70
Fax. +46 8 796 29 88
E-mail. info@sv-lantarb.se (Swedish only)
Membership. 17,000

11. Food Workers' Union (LIVS)

Address. PO Box 1156, S-111 81 Stockholm
Phone. +46 8 796 29 00
Fax. +46 8 796 29 03
E-mail. post.fk@livs.se
Website. www.livs.se (Swedish only)
Leadership. Åke Södergren (president)
Membership. 49,346

12. Metal Workers' Union (Metall)

Address. Olof Palmes Gata 11, S-105 52 Stockholm
Phone. +46 8 786 80 00
Fax. +46 8 24 86 74
E-mail. post.fk@metall.se
Website. www.metall.se (Swedish only)
Membership. 422,000
History and character. Founded in 1888. Absorbed the small Mineworkers' Union in 1994. It is the second largest LO affiliate and organizes workers in engineering, the auto industry, mining and similar.

13. Musicians' Union (Musikerförbundet)

Address. PO Box 43, S-101 20 Stockholm
Phone. +46 8 587 060 00
Fax. +46 8 16 80 20
E-mail. info@musikerforbundet.se
Website. www.musikforbundet. se (Swedish only)
Leadership. Roland Almlén (president)
Membership. 5,643

14. Painters' Union (Malareforbundet)

Address. PO Box 1113, S-111 81 Stockholm

Phone. +46 8 587 274 00
Fax. +46 8 587 274 99
E-mail. post@malareforbundet.a.se
Website. www.malareforbundet.a.se (Swedish; English section)
Leadership. Kjell Johansson (president)
Membership. 20,000

15. Paper Workers' Union (Pappers)

Address. PO Box 1127, S-111 81 Stockholm
Phone. +46 8 796 61 00
Fax. +46 8 411 41 79
E-mail. info@pappers.se
Website. www.pappers.se (Swedish only)
Membership. 27,985

16. Union for Service and Communications Employees (SEKO)

Address. PO Box 1105, S-111 81 Stockholm
Phone. +46 8 791 41 00
Fax. +46 8 21 89 53
E-mail. internationella@seko.se
Website. www.seko.se (Swedish; English section)
Leadership. Sven-Olof Arbestål (president)
Membership. 190,000
History and character. In 1995 the Swedish National Union of State Employees (SF) was reorganized as SEKO. It absorbed the Seamen's Union in 1996. SEKO organizes public and private sector workers in areas including telecoms and IT, postal services, public administration, transport, energy, the prison service, and defence. It is the 3rd largest LO affiliate.

17. Forest and Wood Workers' Union (Skogstrafacket)

Address. PO Box 1152, S-111 81 Stockholm
Phone. +46 8 701 77 00
Fax. +46 8 20 79 04
E-mail. postbox.fk@skogstrafacket.org
Website. www.skogstrafacket.org (Swedish only)
Leadership. Kjell Dahlström (president)
Membership. 70,000
History and character. Founded in 1998 by merger of the Wood Workers' Union and the Forest Workers' Union.

18. Transport Workers' Union (Transportarbetareförbundet)

Address. PO Box 714, S-101 33 Stockholm
Phone. +46 8 723 77 00
Fax. +46 8 24 03 91
Website. www.transport.se (Swedish only)
Membership. 93,000. Organizes truck, taxi and bus drivers.

Sveriges Akademikers Centralorganisation (SACO)
Swedish Confederation of Professional Associations

Address. Box 2206, S-10315 Stockholm

Phone. +46 8 613 48 00

Fax. +46 8 24 7701

E-mail. kansli@saco.se

Website. www.saco.se (Swedish; English section)

Leadership. Anders Milton (president)

Membership. 479,000 in 26 member associations

History and character. SACO traces its origins back to

1947, and absorbed the National Federation of Civil Servants (SR) in 1975. It has more than doubled its membership since the mid-1980s. SACO members are holders of university degrees or other higher educational qualifications, an expanding section of the workforce. An estimated 70–80% of Swedish graduates are members. Students comprise 15% of the membership. Its affiliated organizations are characteristically both trade unions, engaging in collective bargaining and defending members' interests as employees, and professional associations.

SACO functions to coordinate the activities of member unions on matters of common concern. 40% of members are in local government, 26% in central government and 31% in the private sector. Some 9% of members are fully or partly self-employed, and the proportion of members who are self-employed is rising.

SACO members include senior managers who negotiate with SACO unions. SACO states that it as 'an unspoken but self-evident rule' that such managers do not participate in aspects of SACO activities that have a bearing on such negotiations. Managers in such positions are not covered by collective bargaining agreements but will receive individual support and advice in situations such as redundancy. Negotiations on salaries and other conditions of employment are conducted through two cartels. SACO-S represents members in central government service; the Federation of Salaried Employees in Industry and Services (PTK) negotiates for private sector salaried employees as well as representing the corresponding membership of TCO. There is a mixed pattern of collective and individual negotiation by unions with members employed in municipalities and counties.

SACO has a joint office with the LO and TCO in Brussels.

All SACO members are in the Graduate Employees' Unemployment Benefit Society (AEA), established by SACO in 1970 as a state-supported scheme. It launched a supplementary unemployment insurance scheme in June 2000.

International affiliations. ICFTU; ETUC; TUAC; NFS
Affiliated unions.

1. Agrifack (Swedish Association of Graduates in Agricultural, Horticultural, Forestry, Environmental and Nutrition Sciences)
Address. Box 2062, S-103 12 Stockholm
Phone. +46 8 613 49 00
Fax. +46 8 20 20 81
E-mail. agrifack@saco.se
Website. www.agrifack.com (Swedish only)
Leadership. Göran Bäckstrand (president)
Membership. 6,895

2. Akademikerförbundet SSR (Swedish Association of Graduates in Social Science, Personnel and Public Administration, Economics and Social Work)
Address. Box 12 800, S-112 96 Stockholm
Phone. +46 8 617 4400
Fax. +46 8 617 4401
E-mail. kansli@akademssr.se

Website. www.akademssr.se
Leadership. Agneta Bygdell (president)
Membership. 38,000
Publications. SSR Journal, Socionomen

3. Arkitektförbundet (Swedish Association of Architects, Interior Designers and Landscape Architects)
Address. Box 9097, S-102 72 Stockholm
Phone. +46 8 556 06 700
Fax. +46 8 556 06 729
E-mail. kansli@arkitektforbundet.se
Website. www.arkitektforbundet.se (Swedish; English section)
Membership. 7,000

4. Civilekonomerna (Swedish Association of Graduates in Economics and Business Administration)
Address. Box 4720, S-116 92 Stockholm
Phone. +46 8 783 2750
Fax. +46 8 783 2751
E-mail. kontakt@civilekonomerna.se
Website. www.civilekonomerna.se (Swedish only)
Leadership. Benny Johansson (president)
Membership. 25,000
Publications. Civilekonomen

5. Civilingenjörsförbundet (CF) (Swedish Association of Graduate Engineers)
Address. Box 1419, S-111 84 Stockholm
Phone. +46 8 613 8000
Fax. +46 8 796 7102
E-mail. info@cf.se
Website. www.cf.se (Swedish only)
Leadership. Gerhard Raunio
Membership. 79,200
Publications. Civilingenjören Civilingenjörsförbundet

6. DIK-förbundet (Swedish Federation of Employees in the Documentation, Information and Cultural Fields)
Address. Box 760, S-131 24 Nacka
Phone. +46 8 466 24 00
Fax. +46 8 466 24 04
E-mail. dik@akademikerhuset.se
Website. www.dik.se

7. Förbundet Sveriges Arbetsterapeuter (FSA) (Swedish Association of Occupational Therapists)
Address. Box 760, S-131 24 Nacka
Phone. +46 8 466 24 40
Fax. +46 8 466 22 24
E-mail. fsa@akademikerhuset.se
Website. www.fsa.akademikerhuset.se

8. Ingenjörsförbundet (TLI) (Swedish Society of College Engineers)
Address. Box 30225, S-104 25 Stockholm
Phone. +46 8 619 51 70
Fax. +46 8 656 36 70
E-mail. epost@ing.se
Website. www.ing.se (Swedish only)

9. JUSEK (Swedish Federation of Lawyers, Social Scientists and Economists)
Address. Box 5167, S-102 44 Stockholm
Phone. +46 8 665 29 00
Fax. +46 8 662 79 23

E-mail. jusek@jusek.se
Website. www.jusek.se (Swedish only)

10. Kyrkans Akademikerförbund (Association of Church Employees)
Address. Box 19609, S-104 32 Stockholm
Phone. +46 8 441 85 60
Fax. +46 8 441 85 77
E-mail. kansli@kyrkansakademikerforbund.a.se
Website. www.kyrkansakademikerforbund.a.se (Swedish only)

11. Legitimerade Sjukgymnasters Riksförbund (LSR) (Swedish Association of Registered Physiotherapists)
Address. Box 3196, S-103 63 Stockholm
Phone. +46 8 567 06 100
Fax. +46 8 567 06 199
E-mail. kansli@lsr.se
Website. www.lsr.se (Swedish only)

12. Lärarnas Riksförbund (LR) (National Union of Teachers in Sweden)
Address. Box 3529, S-103 69 Stockholm
Phone. ++46 8 613 27 00
Fax. +46 8 21 91 36
E-mail. lr@lr.se
Website. www.lr.se (Swedish only)

13. Officersförbundet (Swedish Association of Military Officers)
Address. Box 5338, S-102 47 Stockholm
Phone. +46 8 440 83 30
Fax. +46 8 440 83 40
E-mail. kansliet@officersforbundet.se
Website. www.officersforbundet.se (Swedish only)

14. SACO – förbundet Trafik och Järnväg, TJ (Transport and Railways)
Address. Munkbron 9, S-111 28 Stockholm
Phone. +46 8 14 29 65
Fax. +46 8 10 80 67
E-mail. kansli@trafikochjarnvag.a.se
Website. www. trafikochjarnvag.a.se (Swedish only)

15. SACO:s Tjänstemannaförbund SRAT (SACO's General Group)
Address. Box 38401, S-100 64 Stockholm
Phone. +46 8 442 44 60
Fax. +46 8 442 44 80
E-mail. kansli@srat.se
Website. www.srat.se (Swedish only)

16. Skogsakademikerna
Address. Box 2088, S-103 12 Stockholm
Phone. +46 8 613 49 40
Fax. +46 8 10 55 15
E-mail. skogsakademikerna@saco.se
Website. www.skogsakademikerna.saco.se (Swedish only)

17. Skolledarna (Swedish Association of Heads and School Principals)
Address. Box 3266, S-103 65 Stockholm
Phone. +46 8 567 06200
Fax. +46 8 567 06299
E-mail. info@skolledarna.se
Website. www.skolledarna.se (Swedish; English section)

Leadership. B. Andreasson
Membership. 6,500

18. Sveriges Farmacevtförbund (Swedish Pharmacists' Association)
Address. Box 3215, S-103 64 Stockholm
Phone. +46 8 507 999 00
Fax. +46 8 507 999 99
E-mail. post@farmacevtforbundet.se
Website. www.farmacevtforbundet.se

19. Sveriges Fartygsbefälsförening (Swedish Ships Officers' Association)
Address. Gamla Brogatan 19, 2 tr, S-111 20 Stockholm
Phone. +46 8 10 60 15
Fax. +46 8 10 67 72
E-mail. info@sfbf.a.se
Website. www.sfbf.a.se (Swedish; English section)
Membership. 2,700

20. Sveriges Läkarförbund (Swedish Medical Association)
Address. Box 5610, S-114 86 Stockholm
Phone. +46 8 790 33 00
Fax. +46 8 20 57 18
E-mail. info@slf.se
Website. www.slf.se (Swedish only)

21. Sveriges Naturvetareförbund (Swedish Association of Scientists)
Address. Box 760, S-131 24 Nacka
Phone. +46 8 466 24 80
Fax. +46 8 466 24 04
E-mail. sn@akademikerhuset.se
Website. www.naturvetareforbundet.se (Swedish; English section)
Membership. 11,000

22. Sveriges Psykologförbund (Swedish Psychological Association)
Address. Box 3287, S-103 65 Stockholm
Phone. +46 8 567 06 400
Fax. +46 8 567 06 499
E-mail. post@psykologforbundet.se
Website. www.psykologforbundet.se (Swedish; English section)

23. Sveriges Reservofficersförbund (SROF) (Swedish Reserve Officers' Association)
Address. Box 2138, S-103 14 Stockholm
Phone. +46 8 613 4932
Fax. +46 8 791 7966
E-mail. srof@algonet.se
Leadership. Lars Ekeman
Membership. 6,000
Publications. Reservofficeren

24. Sveriges Tandläkarförbund (STF, Swedish Dental Association)
Address. Box 5843, S-102 48 Stockholm
Phone. +46 8 666 15 00
Fax. +46 8 662 58 42
E-mail. kansli@tandlakarforbundet.se
Website. www.tandlakarforbundet.se (Swedish; English section)
Membership. 11,500

25. Sveriges Universitetslärarförbund (SULF, Swedish Association of University Teachers)

Address. Box 1227, S-111 82 Stockholm

Phone. +46 8 698 36 10

Fax. +46 8 216 182

E-mail. kansli@sulf.se

Website. www.sulf.se (Swedish; English section)

Leadership. Prof. Staffen Hellberg

Membership. 16,600

Publications. Universitetsläraren

26. Sveriges Veterinärförbund (SVF, Swedish Veterinary Association)

Address. Box 12709, S-112 94 Stockholm

Phone. +46 8 654 2480

Fax. 1 46 8 651 70 82

E-mail. erik.kjellgren@svf.se

Tjänstemännens Centralorganisation (TCO)
Swedish Confederation of Professional Employees

Address. Linnégatan 14, S–114 94 Stockholm

Phone. +46 8 782 91 00

Fax. +46 8 663 75 20

E-mail. tco@tco.se

Website. www.tco.se (Swedish; English)

Leadership. Sture Nordh (president)

Membership. 1.3 million in 18 member organizations

History and character. The TCO is the principal trade union centre representing white-collar employees in Sweden. Its members include teachers, engineers, police officers, secretaries, bank clerks and nurses as well as white-collar workers throughout industry. Women have constituted a majority of the membership since 1977.

Unions of salaried employees did not exist in Sweden before the 1920s. In 1931 a white-collar centre, DACO, was formed in the private sector. This won rights of association and collective bargaining for private sector white-collar employees in 1936, and in 1937 the TCO was created to campaign for such rights in the public sector. The DACO merged with the TCO in 1944, and freedom of association for white-collar workers was won progressively in the public sector from the 1940s to 1966. The membership of the TCO includes members of the police and armed forces, who are not barred from union membership or industrial action.

Some TCO unions are organized on the principle of recruiting all white-collar workers in a given enterprise, while others are occupationally-based.

Unlike the LO, the TCO has never aligned itself politically, and opinion surveys indicate that its membership is broadly representative of the Swedish population as a whole in its political balance. It has a cooperation agreement with the LO and their member unions have avoided conflicts in recruitment. However, as the proportion of graduates in the white-collar workforce continues to rise, there is thought to be scope for conflict with SACO, which organizes only graduates and with which the same degree of cooperation does not exist. There have been suggestions of eventual merger with SACO from within the TCO,

although this has met with little apparent enthusiasm from SACO. The TCO has also sought to enforce demarcation among its own member organizations. In 1997 the TCO congress voted, fairly narrowly, to expel its affiliate representing supervisors in the private sector after this changed its name to Ledarna ('Leaders') and announced its intention to recruit managers at all levels across the entire workforce, in opposition to other TCO unions.

The TCO emphasizes the need to achieve professional development and training for its members, a good working environment and job and income security. It seeks the development of a social Europe. In early 2000 its economists argued in favour of adoption of the single European currency, although this position has not been adopted officially by the TCO.

The TCO shares SACO's opposition to a return to the centralized bargaining led by the LO that dominated until the late 1980s. It prefers a devolved system such as now exists. It generally welcomed the creation of the new Mediation Institute in 2000, however, given that this body has a role in influencing but not constraining pay negotiation.

TCO's information services include a web-TV service in English.

Affiliated unions. The TCO has 18 affiliates; those with at least 10,000 members are listed below:

1. SIF (Swedish Union of Clerical and Technical Employees)

Address. Olof Palmes Gata 17, S-105 32 Stockholm

Phone. +46 8 50 89 70 00

Fax. +46 8 791 77 90

E-mail. postservice@sif.se

Website. www.sif.se (Swedish; English section)

Leadership. Mari-Ann Krantz (president)

Membership. 349,251

History and character. SIF is the largest TCO affiliate, with members in areas including manufacturing, construction, computing and consulting.

2. Lärarförbundet (Swedish Teachers' Union)

Address. Box 12 229, S-102 26 Stockholm

Phone. +46 8 737 65 00

Fax. +46 8 56 04 15

E-mail. lararforbundet@lararforbundet.se

Website. www.lararforbundet.se (Swedish; English)

Leadership. Christer Romilson (president)

Membership. 208,903

History and character. This is the largest Swedish teachers' union, with members in all branches of education. Its headquarters, the Teachers' House, has a staff of 145 and there are 12 regional offices. It organizes union training courses for 30,000 teachers per year.

3. Union of Local Government Officers (SKTF)

Address. Box 7825, S-103 97 Stockholm

Phone. +46 8 789 63 00

Fax. +46 8 21 52 44

E-mail. k.ottosson@sktf.se (international department)

Website. www.sktf.se (Swedish only)

Leadership. Inger Efraimsson (president)

Membership. 177,500

4. Tjänstemannaförbundet (HTF, Salaried Employees' Union)

Address. Box 30102, S-104 25

Phone. +46 8 737 80 00

Fax. +46 8 618 77 19

E-mail. htf@htf.se

Website. www.htf.se (Swedish; English section)

Leadership. Holger Eriksson (president)

Membership. 155,765

History and character. The HTF organizes in commerce, transport and services, with a substantial majority (63%) of women members. It organizes on the vertical principle and members are in a broad range of occupations and salary levels. It has 280 employees and 18 regional offices.

Publication. HTF-tidningen

5. Vårdförbundet (Swedish Association of Health Professionals)

Address. Box 3260, S-103 65 Stockholm

Phone. +46 8 14 77 00

Fax. +46 8 411 42 29

E-mail. mailbox@vardforbundet.se

Website. www.vardforbundet.se (Swedish; English section)

Leadership. Eva Fernvall (president)

Membership. 112,236. Represents 93% of those in its area, including nurses and midwives, the great majority of whom work for county councils and municipalities.

6. Statstjänstemannaförbundet (ST, Union of Civil Servants)

Address. Box 5308, S-102 47 Stockholm

Phone. +46 8 790 51 00

Fax. +46 8 21 32 82

E-mail. st@stmf.se

Website. www.stmf.se (Swedish only)

Leadership. Annette Carnhede (president)

Membership. 89,191

7. Finansförbundet (Bank and Finance Employees' Union)

Address. Box 7375, S-103 91 Stockholm

Phone. +46 8 614 03 00

Fax. +46 8 611 38 98

E-mail. finansforbundet@finansforbundet.se

Website. www.finansforbundet.se (Swedish only)

Leadership. Lillemor Smedenvall (president)

Membership. 43,901

8. Polisförbundet (Police Union)

Address. Box 5583, S-114 85 Stockholm

Phone. +46 8 676 97 00

Fax. +46 8 23 24 10

E-mail. ulrika.wallden@polisforbundet.se

Website. www.polisforbundet.se (Swedish only)

Leadership. Jan Karlsen (president)

Membership. 23,307

9. Svenska Journalistförbundet (SJF, Swedish Union of Journalists)

Address. Journalisternas Hus, Box 1116, S-111 81 Stockholm

Phone. +46 8 613 75 00

Fax. +46 8 21 26 80

E-mail. kansliet@sjf.se

Website. www.sjf.se (Swedish; English section)

Leadership. Håkan Carlson (president)

Membership. 17,626

10. Union of Swedish Insurance Employees (FTF)

Address. Kammakargatan 38, S-103 54 Stockholm

Phone. *+46 8 791 17 00*

Fax. +46 8 20 87 95

E-mail. ftf@fors-tjm.se

Website. www.fors-tjm.se (Swedish only)

Leadership. Ingolf Lundin (president)

Membership. 12,560

Switzerland

Capital: Bern

Population: 7.26 m. (2000 est.)

1 Political and Economic Background

The Swiss Confederation is a republic comprising 23 cantons. The cantons enjoy considerable autonomy and the style of government that has evolved out of Switzerland's linguistic and religious diversity is one that emphasizes consensus and caution in adopting change. Symptomatically, the four leading political parties (the Social Democratic Party, SPS; the Swiss People's Party, SVP; the Radical Democratic Party, FDP; and the Christian Democratic People's Party, CVP), although representing different political currents, have together formed a governing coalition continuously since 1959. Following elections in Oct. 1999, the SPS held 51 seats in the National Council, the SVP 44, the FDP 43, and the CVP 35. Smaller parties outside the government held only 27. Switzerland has a tradition of combining internationalism in business, and providing a base for international organizations, with neutrality and isolationism in its domestic and foreign policy. In 1992 Swiss voters approved by referendum a proposal backed both by employers and unions to join the IMF and the

World Bank, but Switzerland is not a member of the EU.

The Swiss economy is prosperous with strong manufacturing and service sectors (notably banking and offshore financial services). Switzerland imports labour and there are nearly one million foreign workers, mainly Italians. In 1999 it had modest growth of 1.4%, but inflation was low (1%) and unemployment remained negligible (2.8%).

GDP (purchasing power parity) $197bn. (1999 est.); GDP per capita (purchasing power parity) $27,100 (1999 est.).

2 Trade Unionism

Switzerland ratified ILO Convention No.87 (Freedom of Association and Protection of the Right to Organize, 1948) in 1975, but did not ratify Convention No.98 (Right to Organize and Collective Bargaining, 1949) until 1999.

The trade union movement is long established and all workers may form and join unions of their own choosing. Some 775,000 of the labour force of 3.8 million (which includes 956,000 foreign workers) are unionized. Union density of 20% is at the lower end of the European range. Unionization rates are higher in the public than private sectors.

Women were politically enfranchised at the federal level only in 1971 and the trade unions also have a traditional male dominance. In the private sector, 35% of the workforce are women, but women constitute only 15% of union members; in the public sector, the comparable figures are 51% and 31%. Foreign workers may join unions but have a low rate of participation. There are few foreign workers in the more highly unionized white-collar public sector areas.

The trade union movement has divisions between blue-collar and white-collar unions and on a political and religious basis. There are two general trade union centres. The leading centre, the Swiss Trade Union Confederation (Schweizerischer Gewerkschaftsbund, SGB/USS), dates back to 1880 and is close to the Social Democratic Party (SPS). It is affiliated to the ICFTU and has the support of about half of Switzerland's trade unionists. The smaller Swiss Confederation of Christian Trade Unions (Christlichnationaler Gewerkschaftsbund der Schweiz, CNG/CSC), is a WCL affiliate and close to the Christian Democratic People's Party (CVP). There is in addition a white-collar confederation, the Vereinigung Schweizerischer Angestelltenverbände (VSA). All three confederations are affiliated to ETUC.

At the end of 1998 there were 775,601 union members, of whom 387,249 were in unions affiliated to the SGB, 116,323 in the VSA, and 105,375 in the CNG. In addition, there are about 30 independent unions, most of them long established, and based particularly in white-collar and public sector occupations. The most important of the independent unions are the Association of Banking Staffs (SBPV), with 19,000 members; the Association of Swiss Teachers (LCH), with 46,000 members; the Swiss Central Federation of State and Community Employees (ZV), with 31,000 members; the Swiss Association of Nurses (SBK), with 16,000; the Union of Federal Civil Servants (PVB) with 16,000; and Association of Swiss Policemen (VSPB), with 19,500.

The devolved style of Swiss society is reflected in the lack of strong central control by the trade union centres. They represent their member unions in respect of social and economic policy formulation and debate at national level, but the individual unions are highly autonomous. There is also little systematic cooperation between the different centres and they compete for members. A previous Cooperation Agreement in force between the SGB and VSA from 1928 was terminated by the VSA in 1992, reflecting increasing competition in recruiting white-collar workers. In response to the impact of privatization in the public sector, the unions set up a framework for discussion of common problems following the 1995 Ebenrain Conference. However, this has not led to any basic changes in the established relationship between the centres.

The trade unions lost members during the 1990s. Between them the three confederations lost 11% of their members from 1992–97. The major losses were in the manufacturing area, reflecting a shake-out of jobs in older industries. This impacted primarily on SGB and CNG affiliates. The independent unions, based mainly in white-collar public sector areas, in contrast lost only 1.5%. The unions overall have their strength in manufacturing industry and public sector areas and have had little impact in private sector services. Until the formation of Unia in 1996, the SGB had virtually no representation in this area. The loss of members has triggered considerable restructuring among the affiliates of the SGB and CNG.

The emphasis on consensus and conservative values that pervade Swiss society are reflected in industrial relations. The willingness of employers to reach compromise agreements has reflected the involvement of unions in running public affairs – through consultation machinery, through socialist participation in government, and through direct democracy.

Switzerland's reputation as an almost strike-free economy is often traced back to an historic 1937 agreement between the employers and unions in the watch making and metal trades. It established collectively agreed industrial relations on the basis of mutual good faith, each party undertaking, for the length of the contract, to forgo any industrial action, with provision for disputes to be resolved through an arbitration panel. Most Swiss agreements remain local, however. Only a minority provide for arbitration in the event of a dispute on the model of the 1937 agreement, and most leave differences to be resolved in bargaining. Strikes can take place (though they rarely do) on expiry of an agreement if it is not immediately renewed. On average there have only been ten strikes per year since 1975.

3 Trade Union Centres

Christlichnationaler Gewerkschaftsbund der Schweiz (CNG)
Confédération des Syndicats Chrétiens de Suisse (CSC)
Swiss Confederation of Christian Trade Unions

Address. Hopfengweg 21, Postfach 5775, 3001 Bern

Phone. +41 31 370 21 11

Fax. +41 31 370 21 09

E-mail. info@cng-csc.ch

Website. www.cng-csc.ch (German; French)

Leadership. Hugo Fasel (president)

Membership. 105,375

History and character. The CNG/CSC was founded in 1907 by the Catholic trade union movement. In 1982 it absorbed the smaller Swiss Association of Protestant Workers (SVEA). The orientation is social Christian and it is close to the Christian Democratic People's Party (CVP).

The CNG faced significant loss of members in the 1990s with the decline of traditional manufacturing industries. This encouraged a radical process of restructuring of the member unions. In 1998 the major CNG unions in the private sector joined with the small Landesverband Freier Schweizer Arbeitnehmer/ Union Suisse des syndicats autonomes (LFSA/USSA, Swiss Union of Free Trade Unions) to form a new Christian-oriented private sector union SYNA. This represents more than three-quarters of CNG membership.

The CNG's four public sector unions group together as the Public Sector Federation (VGCV). This leading component of this is the union Transfair. The CNG also includes unions representing Hungarian workers in Switzerland (VUCAS) and Czech and Slovak workers (VCTSA).

International affiliations. WCL; TUAC; ETUC

Affiliated unions.

1. SYNA, die Gewerkschaft/SYNA, syndicat interprofessionnel
Address. Josefstrasse 59, CH-8031 Zurich
Phone. +41 1 279 71 71
Fax. +41 1 279 71 72
E-mail. zue@syna.ch
Website. www.syna.ch (German; French; Italian)
Leadership. Peter Allemann, Hugo Fasel (co-presidents)
Membership. 80,000
History and character. SYNA was formed in 1998 by the merger of the two main CNG private sector unions, the construction workers' federation (FCTC) and the industry and commerce union (FCOM), together with the Swiss Union of Free Trade Unions (LFSA/USSA) and the graphic arts unions (SAG). SYNA's intention was to target particularly areas where the unions are weak, notably private sector services and women workers.

2. Transfair
Address. Hopfengweg 21, Postfach, 2000 Bern 14
Phone. +41 31 370 21 21

Fax. +41 31 370 21 31
E-mail. zentralsecretariat@transfair.ch
Leadership. Peter Bollinger
Membership. 10,500
Website. www.transfair.ch (German; French)
History and character. Transfair was created in the late 1990s to bring together smaller public sector CNG unions.

Schweizerischer Gewerkschaftsbund (SGB)
Union Syndicale Suisse (USS)
Swiss Trade Union Confederation

Address. Monbijoustrasse 61, 3007 Bern

Phone. +41 31 371 5666

Fax. +41 31 371 0837

E-mail. info@sgb.ch

Website. www.uss.ch (German; French)

Leadership. P.Rechsteiner (president); Christine Luchsinger, Serge Gaillard (co-secretaries)

Membership. 387,249

History and character. The SGB was founded in 1880 and is the largest Swiss trade union centre, with about half of Swiss trade unionists in its affiliated unions.

The SGB is close to the Social Democratic Party (SPS). In 1992 former SGB official Ruth Dreifuss was elected as a cabinet member, only the second woman in Switzerland to become a Federal Councillor. In Dec. 1998 she became Switzerland's first woman President. In 2000, Christiane Brunner, previously president of SGB's Industry, Construction and Services affiliate (SMUV/FTMH), became party chair.

After being fairly stable in the 1980s, membership declined in the 1990s (from 443,885 in 1990), reflecting primarily the loss of jobs in manufacturing industry and falling below 400,000 for the first time since 1953. Despite some shift in the gender balance, membership remains 80% male. The SGB is seeking to increase its presence in private sector services, an ambition reflected in the creation of Unia to target this area in 1996. There were a number of mergers during the 1990s, notably leading to the creation of the GBI, the largest affiliate, in 1992. The objective of the SGB is to reduce the traditional isolation of individual unions and create a more integrated and influential trade union movement.

Public sector affiliates form the Public Services Federation (Föderativverband des Personals öffentlicher Verwaltungen und Betriebe, FöV), together with some non-SGB unions, but efforts to convert this into a unitary organization for public sector workers have not come to fruition.

International affiliations. ICFTU; TUAC; ETUC

Affiliated unions. Leading SGB affiliates are:

1. Comedia (Swiss Media Union)
Address. Monbijoustrasse 33, 3001 Bern
Phone. +41 31 390 66 11
Fax. +41 31 390 66 91
E-mail. sekretariat@comedia.ch
Website. www.comedia.ch (French; German; Italian)
Membership. 20,000

History and character. Comedia was formed in Dec. 1998 by four unions. The Swiss Association for Mass Media Workers (SSM) with about 3,000 members and the 6,000-member Swiss Association of Journalists (SVJ) stayed outside.

2. Gewerkschaft Bau und Industrie (GBI)/Syndicat Industrie et Bâtiment (SIB)
Union of Construction and Industry
Address. Postfach 915, 8021 Zurich
Phone. +41 1 295 15 15
Fax. +41 1 295 17 99
E-mail. info@gbi.artemis.ch
Website. www.gbi.ch (German; French; Italian)
Membership. 100,276
History and character. The GBI is the largest SGB affiliate. It was formed in 1992 by the merger of the Union of Textile, Chemical and Paper Industry Workers (GTCP) and the Union of Construction and Wood Workers (GBH).

3. Schweizerischer Eisenbahn- und Verkehrspersonal-Verband/Syndicat du personnel des transports (SEV)
Transport Workers' Union
Address. CP 186, 3000 Bern
Phone. +41 31 357 57 57
Fax. +41 31 357 57 58
E-mail. info@sev-online.ch
Website. www.sev-online.ch (German; French; Italian)
Membership. 55,000

4. Gewerkschaft Industrie, Gewerbe, Dienstleitungen (SMUV)/Syndicat de l'industrie, de la construction et des services (FTMH)
Address. Weltpoststrasse 20, 3000 Bern 15
Phone. +41 31 350 2111
Fax. +41 31 350 22 55
E-mail. mail@smuv.ch
Website. www.smuv.ch (French; German)
Leadership. Renzo Ambrosetti (president)

5. Unia
Address. Monbijoustrasse 61, CP3000, Bern 23

Phone. +41 31 376 09 00
Fax. +41 31 376 09 04
E-mail. unia@access.ch
Website. www.uniacontreubs.ch (French; German; English)
History and character. Unia was founded by the GBI and SMUV in 1996 to cater for employees in services, such as sales people, restaurant and hotel staff, and office workers, with a special emphasis on recruiting women members. These were areas previously little catered for in the SGB.

6. Verkauf, Handel, Transport, Lebensmittel (VHTL)/Fédération suisse des travailleurs du commerce, des transports et de l'alimentation (FCTA)
Commerce, Transport and Food Workers
Address. Birmensdörferstrasse 67, 8004 Zurich
Phone. +41 1 242 35 76
Fax. +41 1 242 94 05
E-mail. vhtl@limmat.ch
Website. www.vhtl.ch (German)
Membership. 20,000

7. Verband des Personals Öffentlicher Dienste (VPOD)/Syndicat suisse des services publics (SSP)
Public Service Union
Address. Sonnenbergstrasse 83, case postale, 8030 Zurich
Phone. +41 1 266 52 53
Fax. +41 1 266 52 53
E-mail. central@ssp-vpod.ch
Website. www.vpod.ethz.ch (German; French; Italian)

8. Gewerkschaft Kommunikation/Syndicat de la Communication
Communication Workers' Union
Address. Oberdorfstrasse 32, 3072 Ostermundigen
Phone. +41 31 939 52 11
Fax. +41 31 939 52 62
E-mail. zentralsekretariat@syndicom.ch
Membership. 45,000

Syria

Capital: Damascus
Population: 16.31 m. (2000 est.)

1 Political and Economic Background

The Ba'ath Arab Socialist Party took power in a coup in 1963 and has been the ruling party since that time, with a state of emergency almost continually in force. Lt.-Gen. Hafez al-Assad gained control of the party in 1970, and then led the country as President from 1971. Assad was unanimously re-elected as President by the People's Council (Majlis) for a fifth term in Jan. 1999, this being confirmed by 99.9% of the vote in a popular referendum in March. He died in June 2000, however, and his son, Bashar al-Assad, succeeded him as President. Only candidates from the Ba'ath party or its supporters may stand for election to the Majlis and there is no organized political opposition.

The state still exercises control over large areas of the

economy, including much of manufacturing. About 40% of the labour force are engaged in agriculture. Although efforts have been made in recent years to encourage the private sector, these have been hampered by factors including poor infrastructure, corruption, bureaucracy, political interference by Ba'ath party officials, and lack of skilled labour. Growth stagnated in the late 1990s.

GDP (purchasing power parity) $42.2bn. (1999 est.); GDP per capita (purchasing power parity) $2,500 (1999 est.).

2 Trade Unionism

Syria ratified ILO Convention No.87 (Freedom of Association and Protection of the Right to Organize, 1948) in 1960 and Convention No.98 (Right to Organize and Collective Bargaining, 1949) in 1957.

Under a decree of 1968 a single-trade-union system is in force, organized by the General Federation of Trade Unions, which has powers to dissolve the executive committee of any union and is closely tied to the ruling Ba'ath party. No unions may be formed outside this structure. A decree of 1969 gave the Ministry of Labour extensive powers of supervision over the financial affairs of the unions.

There is some collective bargaining in both the public and private sectors. The Ministry of Labour and Social Affairs can veto any collective agreement on the grounds of national economic interest. Most disputes are settled directly between labour and management representatives, although there is the possibility of resort to binding arbitration.

Strikes are specifically prohibited in the agricultural, military-industrial and public service sectors and are in any case rare. In the case of the military-industrial sector they are classed as treasonable activity and are punishable by death. The last major strike was in 1980, in protest at emergency powers, and resulted in wholesale detention of strikers, some of whom were still believed to be imprisoned two decades later. In 1992 Syria's eligibility for tariff preferences under the US Generalized System of Preferences was suspended because of violations of workers' rights.

3 Trade Union Centre

General Federation of Trade Unions (GFTU)

Address. PO Box 2351, Damascus

History and character. Founded in 1948. The GFTU is controlled by the ruling party. No unions may exist outside it. The GFTU advises the government on relevant legislation. Its president is a senior member of the Ba'ath Party. He and his deputy may attend cabinet meetings on economic affairs.

International affiliation. WFTU

Taiwan

Capital: Taipei
Population: 22.12 m. (2000 est.)

1 Political and Economic Background

Following the establishment in 1949 of the People's Republic of China on the Chinese mainland, the Nationalist Kuomintang (KMT) forces relocated to the island of Taiwan, which they called the Republic of China. The Taipei and Beijing governments have thenceforth continued to describe China as one country, of which they are respectively the rightful rulers. Although Taiwan was expelled from the UN on China's admission in 1971, the Chinese government has de facto accepted the existence of Taiwan provided that it did not declare itself a separate and independent state.

The end of martial law in 1987 brought significant political liberalization with several independent political parties being formed and a greater political role being accorded to the indigenous Taiwanese population as opposed to the Nationalist elite. During the 1990s the KMT's former virtual monopoly on political power steadily eroded. Relations with China also tended to improve (with Taiwan also being a major investor in the Chinese economy). However, the election in March 2000 of Chen Shui-bian of the Democratic Progressive Party (DPP) as Taiwan's first non-KMT President, triggered a spate of hostile rhetoric from Beijing as the DPP had traditionally called for independence. The KMT remains the largest party in the legislature, where it won 123 seats in the Dec. 1998 elections compared with 70 for the DPP.

Taiwan's free market economy, based on manufacturing, has achieved an average real growth rate of 8.5% p.a. in the last three decades, and it has also become a major investor in other economies. Unemployment is low. Government direction of trade and investment has lessened although the government still retains a stake in major banks and industrial companies. Taiwan is seeking to develop capital and technology-intensive industries to retain a competitive edge. It was little affected by the Asian financial crisis of 1997–98.

GDP (purchasing power parity) $357bn. (1999 est.); GDP per capita (purchasing power parity) $16,100 (1999 est.).

2 Trade Unionism

The Chinese Federation of Labour (CFL), which has close links with the KMT, has been the sole trade union centre since the establishment of Taiwan. In 1988, in response to the climate of increasing liberalization, reflected in the formation of the Democratic Progressive Party in 1986 and lifting of martial law in 1987, a number of unions organized into 'voluntary associations' in order to challenge the CFL's role as the sole legal labour centre. The two main such associations were the Brotherhood of Unions and the Labour Union Alliance. In 1987 a Labour Party was formed, which looked to the country's workers to become its principal support base. During 1988 the Labour Party worked within individual unions, attempting to weaken traditional KMT control. In some unions, members rejected KMT candidates for leadership posts, voting instead for non-partisan or opposition figures. In 1988 Kang Yi-yi, a Labour Party member, was elected Chairman of the China Petroleum Corporation Union, the first non-KMT member to head a major union. However, independent unions declined in 1990 in concert with the regression in the fortunes of the Labour and Workers' Parties, both of which did poorly in the 1989 legislative elections.

The monopoly position of the CFL is entrenched by the requirement that no administrative district may have competing labor confederations. In 1994, 12 unions in state-run enterprises said they would withdraw from the CFL and establish a national federation of unions in state-run enterprises. However, their attempt to register a new organization was rejected by the government's Council of Labour Affairs (CLA). The National Federation of Independent Trade Unions (NAFITU) comprises some 20 unions, but it has a total membership of less than 5,000 and is considered illegal. Overall the demand to create a trade union centre independent of the CFL declined during the 1990s, reflecting good economic conditions and the limited scale of most unions, as well as the hostile legislative and regulatory regime.

Under the Trade Union Law, employers may not discriminate against workers on the grounds of union membership, although there are no specific penalties for violation. Cases of such discrimination are reported and NAFITU says that over 400 activists have been dis-

missed since the lifting of martial law. Nonetheless, union density is relatively high. In the new climate of liberalization, the unionized proportion of the workforce rose from 26.4% in 1988 to 34.9% by 1992. The absolute number of union members has since stabilized at around 3 million, with density declining slightly to about 31% in 1999. Most unions are small and there has been no effective consolidation: there were 3,657 registered unions in 1992 and this figure had actually increased to 3,710 by 1999.

Some groups, including teachers, civil servants and defence industry workers, are not permitted to form trade unions. Trade unions may be dissolved if they fail certification requirements or if their activities are held to disturb public order. However, these powers are not currently being exercised. Union leaders must be elected by secret ballot, and, in recent years, workers have sometimes rejected KMT- or management-endorsed union slates.

Collective bargaining is governed by the Collective Agreements Law, which provides for voluntary collective bargaining. In practice, collective bargaining occurs only in large firms. Under Martial Law provisions, strikes were forbidden, as were demonstrations, marches or picket lines. After martial law ended in 1987 the law was amended in 1988, so as to allow workers to legally resort to strike action after one round of mediation, but requiring that they return to work if a second arbitration phase was called. During the same period the country's first labour courts were established, under the aegis of the Judicial Yuan, to deal with labour-management disputes. Strikes remained prohibited in four 'essential' industries (power, water, gas, and medical services). Strikes are in practice relatively uncommon, with the CLA reporting only 34 from 1990–98, 23 of which affected bus companies.

Taiwan was expelled from the ILO as a consequence of the admission of China to the UN, hence ILO Conventions are not applicable.

3 Trade Union Centre

Chinese Federation of Labour (CFL)

Address. 11th Floor, Back Building 201–18, Tung Hua. N. Road, Taipei

Phone. +886 2 2713 35111

Fax. +886 2 2713 35116

E-mail. cfl@ma10.hinet.net

Leadership. Lee Cheng Chong (president); Pan Shih Wei (general secretary)

Membership. 1 million

History and character. The CFL originated in a Kuomintang labour organization founded in mainland China in 1948 and is still closely enmeshed with the KMT. It is the only legal confederation of unions and has 11 affiliated federations and unions.

Publication. CFL News

International affiliation. ICFTU

4 Other Trade Union Organization

National Federation of Independent Trade Unions (NAFITU)

Address. No. 95, 4th Floor, Sec. 1, Han-Chou South Road, Taipei

Phone. +886 2 2392 3670

Fax. +886 2 2351 7580

E-mail. nafitu@mail.ht.net.tw

Leadership. Wang Yao-Tze (president); Wuo Young-Le (general secretary)

History and character. Comprises 20 affiliates with 4,700 members and is technically illegal.

International affiliation. WCL

Tajikistan

Capital: Dushanbe
Population: 6.44 m. (2000 est.)

GDP per capita (purchasing power parity) $1,020 (1999 est.).

1 Political and Economic Background

Tajikistan declared its independence from the dissolving Soviet Union in 1991. A civil war broke out in 1992 pitching the former communist establishment against Islamic forces, with the conflict complicated by tribal allegiances. Imomali Rakhmanov has been President since 1992, winning elections in 1994 and 1999 that were generally seen as unfair. He is identified with the communist old guard but his power is also regionally based and the government does not hold sway over all parts of the country. Russian forces are present as peace-keepers and under a 1997 peace agreement opposition groups have places in government.

Tajikistan is the poorest and most backward of the former Soviet republics and its economy deteriorated with the loss of the former Soviet market and the impact of civil strife. It has some mineral resources but little industry. Agriculture (which remains partly collectivized), with cotton the main crop, is the dominant means of livelihood. It depends on international aid for basic subsistence. Privatization of larger-scale enterprises has made little progress.

GDP (purchasing power parity) $6.2bn. (1999 est.);

2 Trade Unionism

Tajikistan ratified ILO Conventions No.87 (Freedom of Association and Protection of the Right to Organize, 1948) and No.98 (Right to Organize and Collective Bargaining, 1949) in 1993. Legislation provides for the right to join and form unions. The trade union centre is the Tajikistan Federation of Trade Unions which is the continuation of the old Soviet official trade union structure. It claims to have 1.5 million members, but many of the enterprises in which its members are located are not operating. There is also an independent Trade Union of Non-State Enterprises, which claims 37,000 members, scattered in 3,000 small and medium-sized enterprises. Both organizations are consulted by the Council of Ministers in the drafting of labour and social welfare legislation.

The right to organize and bargain collectively is codified in law. However, the collapsed state of the economy has made meaningful collective bargaining a rarity. Compulsory arbitration must precede a strike, but both trade union organizations have said that they will not use the strike weapon in view of the social crisis.

Tanzania

Capital: Dodoma
Population: 35.31 m. (2000 est.)

1 Political and Economic Background

The United Republic of Tanzania was established in 1964, when the newly independent states of Tanganyika and Zanzibar merged. The leftist Revolutionary Party of Tanzania (Chama Cha Mapinduzi, CCM) was the sole legal party until 1992. Multi-party elections were held in 1995, resulting in the CCM gaining a substantial majority in the legislature and the election of its presidential candidate, Benjamin Mkapa. Further elections in Oct. 2000 resulted in Mkapa and the CCM retaining power.

Under President Julius Nyrere Tanzania pursued a policy of socialism and self-reliance. Under his successors from 1985, the government has sought to liberalize the economy but Tanzania remains a poor country with a continuing dependence on external assistance. About 90% of the labour force work on the land, mainly at subsistence level and the limited manufacturing sector is based mainly on agricultural processing. By the late 1990s there was substantial foreign investment in gold mining and increasing revenues from tourism.

GDP (purchasing power parity) $23.3bn. (1999 est.); GDP per capita (purchasing power parity) $550 (1999 est.).

2 Trade Unionism

Tanganyika and Zanzibar ratified ILO Convention No.98 (Right to Organize and Collective Bargaining, 1949) in 1962 and 1964 respectively, and this ratification now applies in respect of Tanzania. Tanzania ratified Convention No.87 (Freedom of Association and Protection of the Right to Organize, 1948) in 2000. There are some variations in labour legislation as between mainland Tanzania (Tanganyika) and the islands of Zanzibar.

Most of the workforce is engaged in subsistence agriculture, but unions represent an estimated 10–15% of the two million wage earners. Workers in both the private and public sectors may lawfully join unions although in practice this is often difficult.

A single-trade-union system has applied since independence, although direct political control by the ruling party eased in the early 1990s. The trade union organization has been known as the Tanzania Federation of Free Trade Unions (TFTU) since 1995. The 1998 Trade Unions Act came into force on July 1, 2000. Prior to its enactment only one of the 11 member unions of the TFTU formally had legal status and the Act provided a basis for the legal registration of unions as well as repealing the single-trade-union system. It also gave the Registrar of Trade Unions extensive powers to supervise, suspend and de-register unions. Under its terms the TFTU was formally dissolved and put into administration, apparently as a prelude to a restructuring of the organization. This action came despite Tanzania's ratification of ILO Convention No.87, which specifically bars dissolution of unions by the state, earlier in the year.

Collective bargaining is limited to the private sector. Collective agreements are generally negotiated by the TFTU with the employers and must be submitted for the approval of the Industrial Court, which is required to take account of the needs of the national economy. Strike action is only legal following long drawn-out mediation and conciliation procedures. Generally, there is a hostile official attitude to industrial action.

3 Trade Union Centre

Tanzania Federation of Free Trade Unions (TFTU)

Address. PO Box 15359, Dar es Salaam

Phone. +255 51 116572

Fax. +255 51 113555

E-mail. tftu.educ@cats-net.com

Leadership. Bruno Mpangala (general secretary)

Membership. Reports 360,000

History and character. In 1964 the Tanganyika Federation of Labour was dissolved and replaced as the sole union central organization by the National Union of Tanganyika Workers (NUTA), which was linked by law to the ruling party. NUTA was expanded in 1978 to incorporate trade unions in Zanzibar and was renamed as the Union of Tanzania Workers (JUWATA), a designated mass organization of the ruling CCM. In line with the move to greater pluralism (as in most of Africa) at that time, a 1991 conference of JUWATA resolved to assert its independence from the ruling party. In 1991 the Tanzania National Assembly, while affirming the organization as the sole union representative of workers in the country, recognized it under a new name, the Organization of Tanzania Trade Unions (OTTU). This in turn became the Tanzania Federation of Free Trade Unions in 1995, gaining affiliation to the ICFTU in 1996.

The 1998 Trade Unions Act was represented as providing a means for formal registration of the TFTU and its 11 member unions (only one of which was legally recognized) to take place. Under it, however, the TFTU was itself put into administration, and its leadership stood down, when the law came into effect in July 2000.

International affiliation. ICFTU; CTUC

Thailand

Capital: Bangkok
Population: 61.23 m. (2000 est.)

1 Political and Economic Background

Thailand is the only south-east Asian country not to have been colonized by a European power. The military has staged 17 coups since absolute monarchy ended in 1932, most recently in 1991. In Sept. 1992 elections resulted in victory for opposition parties, and a new government was formed under the Democrat Party leader Chuan Leekpai, the first Prime Minister since the mid-1970s with no military background. Elections in Jan. 2001 resulted in victory for the populist Thai Rak Thai ("Thais Love Thais") party of billionaire Thaksin Shinawatra.

More than half the labour force is engaged in agriculture, but Thailand also has a diverse industrial sector. By the late 1980s Thailand had one of the fastest growing economies in the world, and this rapid growth continued into the 1990s, with growth rates of 7–8% per annum. Thailand was severely affected by the late 1990s Asian economic recession, however, the economy contracting 8.5% in 1998, before recovering in 1999–2000.

GDP (purchasing power parity) $388.7bn. (1999 est.); GDP per capita (purchasing power parity) $6,400 (1999 est.).

2 Trade Unionism

Thailand has been a member of the ILO since 1919 but has ratified neither Convention No.87 (Freedom of Association and Protection of Right to Organize, 1948) nor No.98 (Right to Organize and Collective Bargaining, 1949).

All unions were dissolved in 1958 and workers were not permitted to associate again until 1972. The Labour Relations Act, providing for the registration of trade unions, was enacted in 1975. However, by 1991 the number of registered union members was only 330,000, in 732 unions. The strongest unions were in the public sector, which accounted for more than half of union membership but only 6% of all employment. A number of small trade union centres had developed, among them the ICFTU-affiliated Labour Congress of Thailand (LCT) and Thai Trade Union Congress (TTUC), and the WCL-affiliated National Congress of Thai Labour (NCTL).

Following a military coup in 1991, the unions again faced extreme adversity. Agricultural workers and civil servants had always been excluded from coverage of the Labour Relations Act but now public sector unions were effectively dissolved by rescinding its coverage of state employees. Little secret was made of the regime's wish for removal of the state sector unions in order for privat-

ization to succeed. State enterprise workers were now placed under an entirely different and separate employment law, the 1991 State Enterprise Labour Relations Act (SELRA), and allowed only to form State Enterprise Employees' Associations (SEEAs) which had no collective bargaining rights. The number of union members was severely reduced by the state enterprise ban and by Jan. 1992 was put at 194,681, all of them in the private sector.

A period of severe repression of the two main centres, the LCT and the TTUC, followed the 1991 coup during which the president of the LCT disappeared, presumed killed. Despite this, unions were prominent in demonstrations that led up to the fall of the military government in June 1992, although some union leaders supported the military coup. Conditions have eased since the restoration of democracy in 1992.

By the late 1990s, according to the ICFTU, about 3.5% of the total private sector workforce belonged to trade unions. Estimates suggest that less than 2% of the total workforce, but nearly 11% of industrial workers, are unionized. Under the 1975 Labour Relations Act, still in force, ten workers may form a union but there are few protections for workers who are dismissed when they attempt to form a union. The 1975 Act also requires that every union official must be a full time employee at the workplace where they are elected, making it difficult to have full-time officials. A measure brought in under the military government in 1991 requires the registration and approval of union advisers and this has been used to restrict the support that can be given by federations. The formation of federations is also restricted by complex legal requirements. Company-controlled unions are common in the private sector.

The right to collective bargaining in the private sector is recognized by the 1975 Act, which also provides for government-assisted conciliation and arbitration. In practice, real collective bargaining exists in only a small number of enterprises. Wage increases for most workers come as a result of increases in the minimum wage, rather than as a result of collective bargaining. Minimum wages are now set through provincial tripartite committees, but it is reported that many of these tripartite committee have brought in company managers to represent labour. The private sector is covered by a labour courts system and disputes may also be referred to a tripartite Labour Relations Committee.

In the private sector a proposed strike must be approved by the majority of the union members in a secret ballot, and registered with the Ministry of Labour, to be legal. The government has powers to ban strikes that it considers may 'affect national security or cause severe negative repercussions for the population at large,' and striking illegally may result in imprisonment.

Civil servants are prohibited from joining trade unions by the 1975 Labour Relations Act. In other areas of the public sector, including health and education, the 1991 SELRA legislation banning unions remained in force through 1999. The state enterprise employees' associations had an advisory role and could not bargain collectively or strike, form federations or join private sector trade union centres. Workers trying to form unions in the public sector in 1999 were reported to have been dismissed.

The civilian Chuan government appointed in 1992 said that it would reform SELRA and allow workers in state enterprises to form unions. This commitment proved sufficient to achieve suspension of petitions then being filed by the AFL-CIO under the General System of Preferences (GSP). In the event the government failed to bring about reform. In Feb. 2000, however, in the face of the threat of loss of US trade privileges, the Thai legislature finally adopted legislation to revise SELRA so as to allow the 330,000 workers in state enterprises to change their enterprise associations into functioning trade unions. Such unions would not, however, be permitted to federate with unions in the private sector.

There are many migrant workers – primarily Burmese, Laotian and Cambodian – and they are not permitted to join trade unions. Child labour is widespread in Thailand, in both rural and urban areas, and although there are formal legal protections these are inadequately enforced. Women and children are victims of bonded labour and this has attracted international condemnation.

3 Trade Union Centres

Labour Congress of Thailand (LCT)

Address. 420/ 393–394 Tipawal No. 1 Village, Theparak Road, Muang, Samutprakan 1020

Phone. +66 2 758 3300

Fax. +66 2 384 6789

History and character. The LCT was created in 1978. Following the 1991 coup, LCT president Thanong Po-arn disappeared, feared dead. The LCT subsequently lost 65% of its membership as a result of the ban on unions in the public sector.

International affiliation. ICFTU

National Congress of Thai Labour (NCTL)

Address. 1614/876 Samuthprakan Government Housing Estate, Sukhumvit Road (KM30), T. Aaiban, A. Mang, 10270 Samuthprakan

Phone. +66 2 3857 162

Fax. +66 2 3857 162

Leadership. Panus Thailuan (president); Jumrus Chailungga (secretary general)

International affiliation. WCL

Thai Trade Union Congress (TTUC)

Address. 420/ 393–394 Tipawal No. 1 Village, Theparak Road, Muang, Samutprakan 1020

Phone. +66 2 221 2182

History and character. The TTUC was founded in 1982 by Paisal Thawatchainant, who had earlier founded the Labour Congress of Thailand (LCT). It affiliated to the ICFTU in 1987. The 1991 State Enterprises Labour Relations Act, dissolving public sector unions, cost the TTUC the bulk of its membership, which fell from 123,150 in July 1990 to 42,748 in Jan. 1992.

International affiliation. ICFTU

Togo

Capital: Lomé
Population: 5.02 m. (2000 est.)

1 Political and Economic Background

President Gnassingbé Eyadéma has ruled since seizing power in a coup in 1967. For the first 25 years of his rule the sole legal party was the Rassemblement du Peuple Togolais (RPT). In Sept. 1992 a constitution providing for political pluralism was approved in a referendum and the following year President Eyadéma was confirmed in power in an election. Legislative elections of 1994 led to

a victory for a coalition of opposition parties. In June 1998 Eyadéma was again elected President, although opposition groups alleged electoral malpractice. In March 1999 the RPT won a large majority in legislative elections, which were boycotted by most other parties.

Togo's economy is based on agriculture, both subsistence and commercial, which accounts for 65% of the workforce. There is also phosphate mining, some industry, and Togo has a regional commercial and service role. There has been some economic liberalization in the 1990s but many enterprises remain in state hands.

GDP (purchasing power parity) $8.6bn. (1999 est.); GDP per capita (purchasing power parity) $1,700 (1999 est.).

2 Trade Unionism

Togo ratified ILO Convention No.87 (Freedom of Association and Protection of the Right to Organize, 1948) in 1960 and Convention No.98 (Right to Organize and Collective Bargaining, 1949) in 1983. Under the constitution all workers except those in the emergency and security services are free to join unions. About two-thirds of workers in the formal waged economy are reported to be in unions.

All previously existing trade unions were dissolved in 1972 and the Confédération Nationale des Travailleurs du Togo (CNTT) was established by the ruling RPT in the following year. Even at the height of the one-party state, there was no formal establishment of a single-trade-union system. But union contributions were deducted automatically from all wages and salaries, and for many years no unions existed outside the structure of the CNTT.

With Togo affected by the democratic wind of change blowing through Africa in the early 1990s, pressure grew for independent trade unionism. This was reflected in the creation of new organizations, such as the Union Nationale des Syndicats Indépendants du Togo (UNSIT), alliances of unions with civic groups, and a reform movement within the CNTT, which took positions critical of the government. There was appreciable labour unrest in the period 1992–94. In Nov. 1992 unions launched a general strike to protest at the failure to implement democratic reforms. Three strikers were shot dead by police and the secretary-general of UNSIT was among those who fled abroad. In Nov. 1994 a number of unionists were arrested and imprisoned on treason charges in connection with two attacks on army barracks. Among them was Komi Dackey, leader of the principal transport workers' union. The unionists were released in January 1995.

Conditions have been more settled since the mid-1990s. However, on Jan. 31, 2000 the government arrested the secretary-general of UNSIT and the secretary-general of the teachers' federation, and issued a warrant for the arrest of the secretary-general of the WCL-affiliated CSTT. The union leaders were accused of spreading false information and injuring the honour of the Education Minister. President Eyadéma ordered the union officers to be released after a few days following international trade union protests.

The labour code provides for collective bargaining. In practice, there is one national tripartite agreement that sets wages for the whole formal sector. The government itself is the largest employer in the formal sector and the dominant voice in defining agreements.

3 Trade Union Centres

Confédération Nationale des Travailleurs du Togo (CNTT)
National Confederation of Togolese Workers

Address. Bourse du Travail, 160 Boulevard-13 Janvier, BP 163, Lomé

Phone. +228 21 4833

Fax. +228 22 0255

Membership. Previously reported as 35,000

History and character. The CNTT was created in Jan. 1973, absorbing the previous Union Nationale des Travailleurs du Togo (UNTT), founded in 1962, and the Confédération Syndicale des Travailleurs du Togo (CSTT), which was founded in 1946 and was affiliated to the WCL. In the period of single party rule by the RPT, the CNTT's role was defined as the defence of the workers' interests 'within the context of responsible participation' in the overall development of the country, with representation on the RPT central committee and in the National Assembly.

In the early 1990s the CNTT increasingly allied itself with independent unions calling for democratic reform, calling strikes on the issue in 1992, while not breaking its alliance with the ruling party. Since that time it has remained the confederation considered closest to the government.

International affiliation. ICFTU

Confédération Syndicale des Travailleurs du Togo (CSTT)
Trade Union Confederation of Togolese Workers

Address. BP 3058, Lomé

Phone. +228 22 11 17

Fax. +228 22 44 41

E-mail. cstt@café.tg

Leadership. Adrien Akouété Beliki (secretary-general)

International affiliation. WCL

Union Nationale des Syndicats Indépendants du Togo (UNSIT)
National Union of Independent Trade Unions of Togo

Address. BP 30082 Tokoin-Wuiti, Lomé

Phone. +228 21 6565

Fax. +228 21 6565

Leadership. Tétévi Gbikpi-Benissan (secretary-general)

History and character. UNSIT emerged as part of the democratic movement of the early 1990s. Its participation in a Nov. 1992 general strike resulted in its general secretary, Tétévi Gbikpi-Benissan, fleeing the country for a period. The union said the murder in Aug. 1998 of the UNSIT deputy secretary-general could have been the result of his opposition to the privatization of a state-owned pharmaceutical company. The ICFTU asked the government to set up an independent investigation but this did not happen.

International affiliation. ICFTU

Tonga

Capital: Nuku'alofa
Population: 102,000 (2000 est.)

1 Political and Economic Background

Tonga, comprising 169 small islands in the South Pacific, became fully independent from the UK in 1970 and is a monarchy. The legislature comprises the King and his Privy Council, nine nobles, and nine popularly elected representatives. The current Prime Minister is the King's third son.

Tonga's economy is primarily agricultural, but food production is mostly on a subsistence basis. There is a limited light industrial sector and tourism generates foreign exchange earnings. There is a dependence on external aid.

GDP (purchasing power parity) $238m (1998 est.); GDP per capita (purchasing power parity) $2,200 (1998 est.).

2 Trade Unionism

The authorities refused to allow trade unions until the formation of the Friendly Islands Teachers' Association and Tonga Nurses' Association in 1990. Tonga is not a member of the ILO.

3 Trade Union Centre

There is no trade union centre.

4 Other Trade Union Organizations

Friendly Islands Teachers Union (FITA)
Address. c/o Tonga High School, Nuku'alofa
Phone. +676 23972
Fax. +676 23972
International affiliations. ICFTU; CTUC

Tonga Nurses' Association (TNA)
Address. PO Box 150, Nuku'alofa
Phone. +676 23200
Fax. +676 24291
E-mail. sela@tongatapu.net.to
Leadership. Pisila Sovaleni (general secretary)
International affiliations. ICFTU; CTUC

Trinidad and Tobago

Capital: Port of Spain
Population: 1.18 m. (2000 est.)

1 Political and Economic Background

Trinidad and Tobago achieved independence from the United Kingdom in 1962. The centre-right People's National Movement (PNM) won every election from its formation in 1956 until 1986, when it was defeated by the centre-left National Alliance for Reconstruction (NAR). In 1988 the NAR split, leading to the formation of the United National Congress (UNC) party under Basdeo Panday. The PNM won back power in 1991, but elections in 1995 resulted in the formation of a coalition government, led by Panday and dominated by the UNC.

Panday, the first Trinidadian of Indian extraction to be Prime Minister, had built his career in the trade union movement.

Trinidad and Tobago's economy is based on oil and natural gas production and downstream activities, but the government is seeking to diversify the economy and foreign investment has been attracted into other sectors including tourism.

GDP (purchasing power parity) $9.41bn. (1999 est.); GDP per capita (purchasing power parity) $8,500 (1999 est.).

2 Trade Unionism

Trade union activity dates back to the formation of the

Working Man's Association in 1919. Following independence, Trinidad and Tobago ratified ILO Conventions No.87 (Freedom of Association and Protection of the Right to Organize, 1948) and No.98 (Right to Organize and Collective Bargaining, 1949) in 1963. The Trinidad and Tobago Labour Congress (TTLC) was formed in 1966, and affiliated to the ICFTU. The 1972 Industrial Relations Act (IRA) replaced the Industrial Stabilization Act (1965) and from then on was the principal legislation under which unions operated.

In 1975, Basdeo Panday, the leader of the All Trinidad Sugar and General Workers' Trade Union (ATS/GWTU), the most important union on the islands, formed the United Labour Front (ULF) in opposition to the ruling conservative People's National Movement (PNM). In the 1976 elections the ULF took 10 of the 36 seats in the House of Representatives, campaigning on a programme which included worker participation, nationalization of key enterprises, and land reform. The ULF later joined the moderate socialist National Alliance for Reconstruction (NAR), which won the 1986 general election. In 1988 the NAR split and Panday and other former ULF members in 1989 founded the United National Congress (UNC), which in 1995 achieved power as the dominant party in coalition with the much-weakened NAR, with Panday as Prime Minister. Panday campaigned in 1995 on the issues of unemployment and crime. The ATS/GWTU has remained close to the UNC.

Until 1994 there were two trade union centres, the Trinidad and Tobago Labour Congress (TTLC) and the Council of Progressive Trade Unions (CPTU). The ICFTU-affiliated TTLC was the larger of the two confederations by a ratio of about 2:1 against the WFTU-affiliated CPTU. In June, however, the two centres united to form the National Trade Union Centre of Trinidad and Tobago (NATUC) with a combined membership of some 50,000. The ATS/GWTU remained independent and affiliates to the WCL. Union density is estimated at 28%, with 14 active unions in existence.

Under the 1972 Industrial Relations Act all workers may join or form unions of their own choosing and anti-union acts by employers are prohibited. The Act also provides for collective bargaining and all workers except those in essential services have the right to strike. Where bargaining is deadlocked the issue in dispute is referred to the Ministry of Labour and may progress to a strike or a lock-out only when the Minister himself declares it unresolved. 'Essential services' has been defined to include teaching. There is an Industrial Court, which is empowered to penalize employers and reinstate workers in cases of anti-union discrimination.

3 Trade Union Centre

National Trade Union Centre of Trinidad and Tobago (NATUC)

Address. 91 Abercromby Street, Port of Spain

Phone. +1868 625 3023

Fax. +1868 627 7588

E-mail. natuc@carib-link.net

Leadership. Vincent Cabrera (general secretary)

Membership. 80,000

History and character. Formed in June 1994 by merger of the Trinidad and Tobago Labour Congress (TTLC) and the more left-wing but smaller Council of Progressive Trade Unions (CPTU).

International affiliations. ICFTU; CTUC

4 Other Trade Union Organizations

All Trinidad Sugar and General Workers' Trade Union (ATS/GWTU)

Address. Rienzi Complex, Exchange Village, Couva

Phone. +1868 636 2354

Fax. +1868 636 3372

E-mail. atsgwtu@opus.co.tt

Leadership. Rudranath Indarsingh (general secretary)

Membership. 7,700

History and character. Established in 1937 as a Sugar Workers' Union. Constitution changed in 1978 to represent workers in other industries, recruiting in diverse areas such as rum production, contracting, construction, entertainment, air line, transport, food processing, garment manufacturing, and animal food production. In 1981 membership was 18,000 but has declined to less than half that. Basdeo Panday, the former ATS/GWTU President, now leads the United National Congress Party and is Prime Minister.

Publication. Battlefront.

International affiliation. WCL

National Union of Government and Federated Workers (NUGFW)

Address. 145–147 Henry Street, Port of Spain

Phone. +1868 623 4591

Fax. +1868 625 7756

E-mail. headoffice@nugfw.org.tt

Leadership. Jacqueline Jack (general secretary)

International affiliation. CTUC

Tunisia

Capital: Tunis
Population: 9.59 m. (2000 est.)

1 Political and Economic Background

Tunisia achieved independence from France in 1956. One party has held power continuously since independence, although it has had different names: the Neo-Destour Party, the Destourian Socialist Party, and the Democratic Constitutional Rally. The current name, the Democratic Constitutional Rally (RCD) was adopted in 1988 and intended to reflect a greater political openness under President Zine El Abidine Ben Ali, who deposed 'President-for-Life' Habib Bourguiba in Nov. 1987. The democratic opening has been limited and opposition parties are weak, while the government is reportedly generally popular. In elections in Oct. 1999, President Ben Ali was re-elected with 99.44% of the vote, despite facing opposition candidates for the first time, while the RCD won all 148 directly-elected seats in the 182-member legislature, the Chamber of Deputies (the remaining 34 seats being reserved for opposition parties). There have reportedly been several thousand victims of torture in the 1990s (mainly 1990-95), and political prisoners are primarily Islamists or supporters of the outlawed Communist Workers' Party.

Tunisia has a relatively developed economic base and a high per capita income by African standards. Petroleum exports and tourism are the main sources of foreign exchange. The government controls significant portions of the economy but its structural adjustment programme, including modest privatization, is considered to have been generally effective and the economy has grown at an average 5% per annum since 1987.

GDP (purchasing power parity) $52.6bn. (1999 est.); GDP per capita (purchasing power parity) $5,500 (1999 est.).

2 Trade Unionism

Tunisia ratified ILO Conventions No.87 (Freedom of Association and Protection of the Right to Organize, 1948) and No.98 (Right to Organize and Collective Bargaining, 1949) in 1957, following independence. The right to form unions is protected by the constitution and the labour code and discrimination against union members is prohibited. However, the unions say that in some sectors, such as textiles and construction, employers employ mainly temporary workers to make union organization more difficult.

Trade unions developed under French rule and were associated with nationalist politics. The ICFTU-affiliated UGTT has been the sole or only significant trade

union centre since independence, although this status is not entrenched in law. After 1978, UGTT relations with the government and the ruling party deteriorated and it experienced severe harassment from the state. At the 1989 (Sousse) congress it was re-organized and has recovered its position since that time, with its leadership seen as allied to the government. An estimated 10–15 percent of the work force are in member unions, although the UGTT says that 30% of the economically active are members. According to the UGTT 60% of its members are in the public sector.

Collective bargaining is widely practiced. 80% of the private sector workforce are covered by three-year sectoral framework agreements (most recently negotiated in 1999) which are negotiated directly by the UGTT member unions and employers' representatives. The government must approve these agreements, which then apply to all employees in the relevant industry. The UGTT also negotiates wages and work conditions of civil servants and employees of state-owned enterprises.

There are tripartite conciliation and arbitration mechanisms. Unions in both the private and public sectors may call strikes, in theory provided they give 10 days' advance notice and have the approval of the UGTT, although in practice this restriction is commonly ignored. Strikes over pay and conditions, usually of brief duration, are relatively frequent.

3 Trade Union Centre

Union Générale Tunisienne du Travail (UGTT)
Tunisian General Labour Union

Address. 29 Place Mohamed Ali, Tunis

Phone. +216 1 332 400

Fax. +216 1 354 114

E-mail. ugtt.tunis@email.ati.tn

Website. www.ugtt.org.tn (French only)

Membership. About 300,000

History and character. The UGTT was founded under French rule in 1946 by Fahrat Hached (assassinated by French agents in 1952) and was involved in the struggle for independence in association with the Neo-Destour Party (renamed the Destour Socialist Party – PSD – in 1964, and the Democratic Constitutional Rally in 1988) of Habib Bourguiba. In Jan. 1978 the UGTT (the only organized grouping in Tunisia outside the PSD and the armed forces, and hitherto allied with the PSD government) called a general strike during which several dozen people were killed in clashes between strikers, police and troops. Following this, Habib Achour, the UGTT secretary-general and a vice-president of the ICFTU, who had already resigned from the political bureau and central committee of the PSD, was removed from his post at the UGTT, being replaced by Tijani Abid. In Oct. 1978 the State Security Court sentenced Achour and other former UGTT leaders to imprisonment with forced labour following conviction on charges of plotting to overthrow the government and incitement to violence, looting and murder. In 1979 Achour, who had been released into house arrest, was re-elected a vice-president of the ICFTU at the ICFTU's 12th congress, causing the new leadership of the UGTT to suspend relations with the international body.

All other detained members of the former UGTT leadership were released during 1980. The new UGTT leadership to failed to win international recognition or support within the Tunisian labour movement, and when a unity congress of the UGTT was held in 1981 it elected a new 13-member executive bureau which included 11 members of the executive arrested in 1978. One of these, Taieb Baccouche, became secretary-general, leaving Achour the only former UGTT leader still barred from office.

All seats in the 1981 multi-party National Assembly elections were won by a PSD–UGTT alliance, the UGTT share being 27. After this President Bourguiba granted a full pardon to Achour, who was immediately appointed UGTT chairman and a member of the executive bureau. Two years later the UGTT administrative commission dismissed seven of the 14 members of the executive bureau after they had charged Achour with anti-democratic methods, poor financial management and use of UGTT funds for bribery and secret deals. In Feb. 1984 they formed the Union Nationale des Travailleurs Tunisiens (UNTT), with Abdelaziz Bouraoui as secretary-general, while at the end of 1984 the 16th regular congress of the UGTT elected a new executive committee with Achour succeeding Baccouche as secretary-general.

During 1985 relations with the government again deteriorated following a UGTT campaign of strikes for public sector pay increases after a two-year wage freeze. This was a time of acute economic difficulties which caused widespread unrest and bread riots. Trade union meetings were banned, strikers dismissed, the UGT newspaper *Ach Chaab* suspended, and the check-off system for union dues ended. By November Achour and 100 UGTT activists were in detention, and regional offices had been occupied by so-called provisional committees, assisted by the police. An agreement to end the crisis proved ineffective, and on Dec. 31, Achour was sentenced to one year's imprisonment (later reduced to eight months) on charges of breaking and entering the premises of a fishing cooperative in a case originally dating from 1982. On Jan. 21, 1986, control of the national headquarters of the UGTT in Tunis was handed over by the police to a provisional committee, and on Jan. 29 the UGTT administrative commission, meeting under the supervision of a national coordination bureau at the Tunis headquarters, announced that it had ceased to recognize the executive bureau and endorsed the work of the national coordination bureau towards the reconstruction of the trade union movement.

In April 1986, Achour was sentenced to a further two years' imprisonment for mismanagement of a union-funded insurance company, after which the provisional committees held an extraordinary UGTT congress and elected a new executive bureau with Ismail Lajeri as secretary-general. In September the UGTT absorbed the UNTT. In December a new executive bureau was formed and Lajeri was replaced by Abdelaziz Bouraoui; the next month the UGTT held an extraordinary congress from which it addressed a 'message of faithfulness' to President Bourguiba and pledged itself to responsible participation in the tasks of national recovery. This congress, boycotted by most of the bodies elected under Achour but attended by Bourguiba, elected a new executive bureau comprising five representatives of the former provisional committees, four representatives of the former UNTT, and four representatives of the old UGTT leadership who had broken recently with Achour. Bouraoui was confirmed as secretary-general, on the recommendation of President Bourguiba.

After the fall from power of Bourguiba in Nov. 1987 factionalism declined, and Achour, still recognized by the ICFTU as the legitimate secretary-general, was freed from house arrest. In May 1988, ICFTU general secretary John Vanderveken visited Tunisia for talks with government officials and unionists and reported that normalization of trade unionism was making good progress. A National Trade Union Commission was set up to organize a new UGTT congress and the government undertook that all public sector workers sacked for involvement in the strikes of 1984 and 1985 would be reinstated. In addition, dismissed private sector workers were to be the subject of talks between the government and employers' federation.

Regional elections were held in early 1989 at which those leaders deposed by President Bourguiba ('legitimistes') were mostly returned to office. The UGTT then held a special congress at Sousse in April 1989 at which a unified list of delegates was put forward for election, and Ismael Sahbani, the metalworkers' union leader, was elected secretary-general. Following the congress, the 50 UGTT federations held elections which, like those of the regions, led to the return of those officers deposed earlier in the decade.

According to the UGTT leadership the Sousse congress marked the 'rehabilitation' of the UGTT, since when it has re-built its influence and has been able to secure a succession of benefits for its members. The UGTT avoided further damaging conflict with the state and in Oct. 1999 secretary-general Sahbani said that a vote for President Ben Ali in the forthcoming national elections would be a 'vote for stability, security and national solidarity'.

It is reported that the UGTT receives substantial government subsidies to assist its work. Internal opponents of the leadership have received the hostile attention of the state. About 20 UGTT officials and members, including the secretaries-general of affiliates representing bank workers, posts and telecommunications workers, and teachers in higher education, were detained and questioned by police after circulating a petition critical of the leadership in Apr. 1997. The petition charged that the UGTT had lost its credibility with the people and created a 'state of indifference and discouragement' among the workers by failing to defend democracy, human rights and social justice and becoming the tool of a group around the secretary-general. In May 1999, ten activists were briefly detained after circulating a petition during the UGTT congress that criticized Sahbani and threatened to set up an independent union. According to the government, the activists were detained on suspicion of threatening the public order and violating the Publications Code, which requires prior approval of publications by the state.

Habib Achour died in March 1999. In Oct. 2000 the ICFTU announced it would send a delegation to Tunisia to investigate the circumstances surrounding the resignation of Sahbani, who had only recently been unanimously re-elected secretary-general.

Publication. Ach-Chaab

International affiliations. ICFTU

Turkey

Capital: Ankara
Population: 65.67m. (2000 est.)

1 Political and Economic Background

Modern Turkey was founded from the remnants of the Ottoman Empire in 1923. Civil conflict in the 1970s culminated in a military coup in Sept. 1980 staged with the objective of ending what was seen by the military as a slide into anarchy through terrorist violence of both the right and the left. A new military-backed constitution approved by referendum in Nov. 1982 began a gradual process of return to a democratic system of government. The formation of political parties was re-authorized in 1983 (although extreme left- and right-wing parties remained banned), and elections to a new Grand National Assembly in Nov. 1983 were won by the conservative Motherland Party (ANAP) led by Turgut Ozal. Since then successive governments have sought to improve Turkey's poor image for human rights and orient the country more to Europe while confronting ongoing problems such as Kurdish insurgency in the south-east of the country, a significant Islamist movement, and extremist political groups of the right and left. Following elections in Apr. 1999, the government is led by Prime Minister Bulent Ecevit, whose Democratic Left Party (DSP) is the largest in the Grand National Assembly and forms a fractious coalition government with the Nationalist Action Party (MHP) and the Motherland Party (ANAP). The Islamist Virtue party (FP) is the leading opposition party. Ecevit was first Prime Minister in the 1970s, and was formally banned from political activity for ten years under transitional provisions of the 1982 constitution until this was overturned in a 1987 referendum.

Turkey's economy combines an industrial sector, with textiles, iron and steel as the main exports, and a large agricultural sector, much of it traditional, which occupies close to half the workforce. The proportion of the workforce in industry was lower at the end of the 1990s than in the early 1980s. There is still a substantial state involvement in the economy in areas such as basic industries, banking, transport and communications. Although the incoming Ecevit government declared its aim to accelerate privatization, curb inflation and tackle the public deficit this policy has lacked consistent political support even within the cabinet. Lack of market confidence in the government's commitment to reform was seen as behind a financial crisis in Dec. 2000 that forced an emergency IMF bail-out. Unemployment was officially 7% in 2000, but there is considerable underemployment and a low (and declining) rate of workforce participation. Turkey aspires to join the EU and was formally accepted as a candidate state in Dec. 1999, although it remains underdeveloped and poor by Western European standards, with a highly skewed income distribution and a lack of skills in the workforce. It has had minimal success in attracting foreign investment.

GDP (purchasing power parity) $409.4bn. (1999 est.); GDP per capita (purchasing power parity) $6,200 (1999 est.).

2 Trade Unionism

Turkey ratified ILO Convention No.98 (Right to Organize and Collective Bargaining, 1949) in 1952 but did not ratify ILO Convention No.87 (Freedom of Association and Protection of the Right to Organize, 1948) until 1993.

Only about 2.75 million, or some 12% of the 23 million workforce, are unionized. However, Turkey has large informal and farm sectors (46% work on the land) and the proportion of union members in industry is much higher; the majority of workers in member firms of the Turkish Confederation of Employer Associations (TTSK) are in unions.

There are three trade union centres affiliated to the ICFTU. Turk-Is, the Confederation of Trade Unions of Turkey, is the largest and organizes about 73% of all trade unionists. It was founded in 1952. DISK, the Confederation of Progressive Trade Unions of Turkey, originated as a left-wing breakaway from Turk-Is in 1967, while Hak-Is, the Confederation of Real Turkish Trade Unions, was founded in 1976. The ICFTU also affiliates the public sector Confederation of Public Workers' Unions, KESK. All four of these are also affiliated to ETUC. There is no WCL or WFTU affiliate. The small Confederation of Nationalist Trade Unions (MISK) was revived in 1994. In the 1970s there were widespread rumours of links between MISK and extreme right-wing groups and it was suspended from 1980–84 and subsequently went into dissolution. There are also about 27 independent unions.

The 1961 constitution guaranteed the right to form trade unions and to engage in collective bargaining. Trade union activities were severely restricted after the military coup in 1980. The 1961 constitution, partially suspended after the 1980 coup, was superseded by a new constitution in 1982. Under its various provisions and labour legislation adopted in 1983, the right of association was guaranteed subject to considerable restrictions. Unions could be closed by a court order or (in case of emergencies) by the Minister of the Interior, and trade unions could not pursue political ends or cooperate with political parties. In 1986 a military court ordered the dissolution of the leftist Confederation of Progressive Trade Unions of Turkey (DISK), whose activities had been suspended since 1980, and the ban was not lifted until 1991. Civil servants and workers in public services (including banks, schools, electricity, water and petroleum) could not organize.

The 1990s brought greater liberalization. This was reflected in Turkey's ratification of ILO Convention No.87, together with a number of other ILO conventions, in 1993. During the 1990s unofficial unions developed in the public sector and in 1997 the law was changed in line with amendments to the 1995 constitution to officially allow public sector workers, such as teachers, municipal workers, and nurses, the right to join unions, although not to bargain collectively or strike.

From 1988 unions were allowed to make political statements while still barred from having links with political parties or other organizations. Restrictions on political activity by unions were finally lifted in 1997. However, a state of emergency in the southeast, where there is a Kurdish insurrection, has led to curbs on trade unions in five provinces, including the closure by the courts in Dec. 1998 of three union branches that had called for a cessation of military action against the Kurds. There are complaints that anti-terrorist measures, brought in to counter Kurdish insurgency, are used to intimidate and suppress trade unions in the southeast and that union activists have faced arbitrary detention and torture.

Considerable restrictions remain on trade union activity in both law and practice. Legislation restricts the forms trade union organization may take: the first level of organization must be at sectoral level, so enterprise and occupational unions are not permitted. Union officers must have worked for ten years in the industry covered by the union. This latter provision was used to ban the DISK affiliate in the leather industry. Workers must notify a public notary if they wish to join or leave a trade union.

While discrimination against union members and organizers is prohibited in law, the unions claim that it is widespread. According to the Turkish unions, some 40,000 workers in 2,000 workplaces lost their jobs for union activities in the period 1992–98, with no protection from the courts or authorities. Union organizing campaigns and strikes are not infrequently surrounded by violence between union members and hired security guards and police. Many employers are hostile to union organization in their plants. The unions have also been hampered by an increase in sub-contracted or other precarious forms of employment.

Collective bargaining resumed in 1984 but is circumscribed. To be recognized as a bargaining agent a union must not only represent more than 50% of employees in the bargaining unit but also 10% of all workers in that industrial sector. This provision has been used to deny bargaining rights especially to smaller unions. However, while the ILO has urged Turkey to abolish the 10% requirement, its continuation has been favoured by both Turk-Is, as by far the largest confederation, and the employers' confederation. Although the government told the ILO in 1994 that it would propose abolition of the rule to the social partners, it has taken no action to change the law. Collective bargaining does not take place in the public sector.

From 1984 unions were no longer required to seek official permission to start a strike: the first legal strike since 1980 occurred that year in the docks. By the end of the 1980s industrial action had become widespread, as a newly strengthened trade union movement sought pay increases to offset the impact on real incomes of rampant inflation. During the 1991 Gulf Crisis all collective bargaining and strikes were banned by decree for a period, although this was overturned by the Council of State in Feb. 1991. Unions must obtain permission to hold meetings or rallies. There is a constitutional right to strike, but this is subject to significant restrictions. General strikes, political strikes and sympathy strikes are prohibited, as are strikes in the public sector. The government may suspend strikes for 60 days for reasons of national security or public health, and may impose binding arbitration at the end of this period. Sectors in which strikes are not allowed include the production and distribution of water, gas, electricity, coal, and oil, in transport, and in banking. Strikes are banned in the free trade zones for the first ten years, although Turkey has had little success in attracting foreign investment and only a few thousand workers are employed in the nine zones. In sectors where strikes are banned binding arbitration is to be employed. However, employers may not dismiss workers who take part in legal strikes or hire strikebreakers to replace them.

During 1999 the main confederations combined to wage a campaign including demonstrations against government legislation intended to raise Turkey's retirement age closer to international norms (from 43 to 60 for men and from 38 to 58 for women). The legislation was adopted in Sept. 1999, however.

3 Trade Union Centres

DISK (Confederation of Progressive Trade Unions of Turkey)

Address. Nakiye Elgun Sokak No: 117, Kat: 5-6-7, Sisli, Istanbul

Phone. +90 212 2310 408

Fax. +90 212 234 2075

E-mail. disk-f@tr-net.net.tr

Leadership. Ridvan Budak (president)

Membership. 327,000

History and character. DISK was formed by leftist unions in 1967 as a breakaway from Turk-Is, and nearly all its founder were linked to the Turkish Workers' Party (TIP). It assumed the character of a militant socialist labour organization with a Marxist wing, and operated primarily in the private sector, where it organized many strikes. Before 1980 it was the second largest centre, claiming to have 800,000 members.

DISK was often a target for right-wing terrorism in the violent 1970s. Its president and founder, Kemal Turkler, was assassinated in July 1980, shortly before the military seized power, and DISK was suspended and many of its leaders detained following the army coup. A mass trial of members was initiated before a military court in 1981, continuing until 1986. At its peak the trial involved close to 3,700 defendants, and resulted in the conviction of 264 leaders and members of DISK for terms of up to 15 years' imprisonment under Article 141 of the Penal Code relating to intending to overthrow the social and economic order of the country. In addition the court ordered the dissolution of DISK and 28 of its 30 affiliated unions and confiscation of their assets. The case attracted international trade union pressure, the ICFTU, WCL and ETUC opposing the increasing normalization of relations between Turkey and Western Europe while trade union rights continued to be infringed. DISK leaders maintained throughout the trial that they adhered to Turkey's 1961 constitution and the principles of free, democratic trade unionism, and rejected violence as a means. The defendants were subsequently allowed out of prison and DISK president

Abdullah Basturk and general secretary Fehmi Isiklar won seats in parliament in the 1987 elections.

The ban on DISK was lifted in July 1991. In March 1992 the Constitutional Court ordered that DISK should have its sequestered assets returned; it actually received them following the passage of enabling legislation by Parliament in Dec. 1992. Its international status was secured when, in Dec. 1992, it was admitted to the ICFTU as a full affiliated member. In May 1993 the authorities permitted it to organize a May Day rally in Istanbul. During the course of 1993 some 11 DISK affiliates received the authority to engage in collective bargaining activities. Its current president, Ridvan Budak, was first elected in 1994.

DISK has moved closer to the European trade union mainstream, being a member of ETUC as well as the ICFTU. Notwithstanding this, and the relative liberalization within Turkey, DISK continues to report widespread harassment of its officials and activists. In March 1999, Suleyman Yeter, an official of the DISK dockworkers' union, died in police custody after interrogation, having previously been arrested and tortured in 1997.

International affiliations. ICFTU; ETUC; TUAC

Hak-Is (Confederation of Turkish Real Trade Unions)

Address. Tunus Cad. No: 37, 06690 Kavaklidere, Ankara

Phone. +90 312 417 1630

Fax. +90 312 425 05 52

E-mail. info@hakis.org.tr

Website. www.hakis.org.tr (Turkish; English under construction)

Leadership. Salim Uslu (president); Huseyin Tanriverdi (vice-president); Recai Baskan (general secretary)

Membership. 340,000

History and character. Hak-Is was founded in 1976. In its early days it had close relations with the Islamist National Salvation Party (MSP), which was banned under military rule. Its founding charter emphasized 'partnership at the workplace' and opposition to communism, Zionism and fascism.

Hak-Is was suspended briefly after the 1980 military coup but allowed to continue in operation from Feb. 1981. It subsequently gave its support to the Welfare Party (RP), set up in 1983 in succession to the National Salvation Party. In Dec. 1995 elections, Necati Celik, who had been Hak-Is president for 14 years, was elected to the Grand National Assembly on the RP ticket and the RP became the largest party. It formed a coalition government in which RP leader Necmettin Erbakan became Turkey's first Islamist government leader since the end of the Ottoman Empire, defining a position that mixed Turkey's established secularist and Western-leaning state ethos with closer cooperation with Islamic countries. Celik became Minister of Labour in June 1996. He was succeeded as Hak-Is president by Salim Uslu.

Hak-Is now describes itself as politically independent. It applied to join the ICFTU and ETUC in 1993 but this was rejected after opposition from Turk-Is and DISK. In 1995 Hak-Is adopted a revised charter that incorporated a commitment to 'pluralist and liberal democracy'. Affiliation to both ICFTU and ETUC was finally granted in Dec. 1997.

Publications. Hak-Is magazine; statistical handbook

International affiliations. ICFTU; ETUC

KESK (Confederation of Public Workers' Unions)

Address. Abdulhak Hamit Caddesi, Kucukpalas Apt. No: 32, Taksim, Istanbul

Phone. +90 212 297 5552

Fax. +90 212 297 5552

History and character. KESK was founded in Dec. 1995 and organizes in the public sector, the most unionized sector of the workforce, its policies including opposition to privatization. It was admitted to the ICFTU and ETUC in Dec. 1997. It is politically independent.

International affiliations. ICFTU; ETUC

Turk-Is (Confederation of Turkish Trade Unions)

Address. Bayindir Sokak 10, Yenisehir, Ankara

Phone. +90 312 433 31 25

Fax. +90 312 433 6809

Leadership. Beyram Meral (president)

Membership. About 1.75 million

History and character. Turk-Is was formed in 1952 during a phase of liberalization in Turkey's social and political conditions, and developed as the general confederation of the labour movement. Some of its membership formed the more left-wing DISK in 1967, but Turk-Is remained the larger centre. It adopted a politically centrist character.

Turk-Is was the only trade union centre not suspended following the 1980 military coup, and its general secretary Sadik Side took office as Minister of Social Security, leading to the suspension of Turk-Is by the ICFTU (it is now re-admitted to full membership). The position taken by Turk-Is during the mass trial of DISK members from 1981–86 was criticized by trade unionists inside and outside Turkey as being one of relative indifference. In 1986, however, it organized its first demonstration since the 1980 coup, calling for economic reforms and a restoration of trade union freedoms and as the 1980s wore on, relations with the Ozal government came under increasing strain and Turk-Is led a revival of trade union activity. Its head office was wrecked by a bomb in 1990 but the motive for the attack was not established. In Jan. 1991 about 90% of the Turk-Is membership stopped work to demand a democratic system and the respect of civil and trade union rights, but the response of the government was to open legal proceedings against union leaders, a number of whom were detained in custody.

In 1996 the trial began of Turk-Is officials accused of violating the law when Turk-Is announced support for political parties during the 1995 election. All the defendants were acquitted in 1999. On Aug. 6, 1999, the Turk-Is general secretary, Semsi Denizer, was assassinated during the congress of the miners' union, of which he was also president. He had first been elected general secretary on a reform ticket at the 1992 congress.

Owing to the criteria for representativeness, whereby a union must represent 10% of the workers in a particular sector, as well as 50% in a work place, to have collective bargaining rights, Turk-Is is by far the major force in collective bargaining in Turkey. It has been described as dominated by a few large conservative unions.

International affiliations. ICFTU; ETUC; TUAC

Turkmenistan

Capital: Ashkhabad
Population: 4.52 m. (2000 est.)

1 Political and Economic Background

Turkmenistan is a former republic of the USSR that declared its independence in Oct. 1991. President Saparmurad Niyazov, the leader of the Democratic Party of Turkmenistan (the reformed Communist Party) has ruled since independence. No election for President has been held since 1992 (when Niyazov was the sole candidate) and in Dec. 1999 the legislature, the Majlis, unanimously voted to remove the limit on his term of office. All the members of the Majlis are members of the President's party or his supporters and no opposition parties are permitted. Human rights abuses are widespread.

Turkmenistan is largely a semi-desert country with nomadic agriculture, but with intensive agriculture (notably cotton) in irrigated areas and extensive oil and gas reserves. The economy remains under substantial state control.

GDP (purchasing power parity) $7.7bn. (1999 est.); GDP per capita (purchasing power parity) $1,800 (1999 est.).

2 Trade Unionism

The former Soviet single-trade-union system survives, with unions organized under the umbrella Colleagues' Union trade union centre. This claims a membership of 1.3 million. Turkmenistan joined the International Labour Organization in 1993 and ratified ILO Conventions No.87 (Freedom of Association and Protection of the Right to Organize, 1948) and No.98 (Right to Organize and Collective Bargaining, 1949) in 1997. However, there are no legal guarantees enabling workers to form or join unions of their own choosing and while there is no specific legal bar to the formation of independent trade unions, none exist.

Wages and other conditions are determined administratively, with some flexibility at the enterprise level. In practice, pay is in arrears in many enterprises. Strikes are neither allowed nor banned by law, but strikes are rare and there were none reported in 1999.

Tuvalu

Capital: Funafuti
Population: 11,000 (2000 est.)

1 Political and Economic Background

Tuvalu, formerly the Ellice Islands, became independent from the UK in 1978 and is a 'special member' of the Commonwealth. The country comprises nine small but densely populated coral atolls in the south Pacific. It has parliamentary government but informal groups rather than political parties.

Tuvalu is exceptionally dependent upon foreign aid and remittances from workers abroad. Subsistence farming and fishing are the primary economic activities.

GDP (purchasing power parity) $7.8m. (1995 est.); GDP per capita (purchasing power parity) $800 (1995 est.).

2 Trade Unionism

Tuvalu is not a member of the International Labour Organization. Workers are free to organize and join unions of their own choosing, but few work in waged employment, and the only registered union is the Tuvalu Overseas Seamen's Union. There are several hundred civil servants, teachers and nurses, who are enrolled in professional associations. Strikes are legal, but none has been recorded.

3 Trade Union Centre

There is no trade union centre.

4 Other Trade Union Organization

Tuvalu Overseas Seamen's Union

Address. GPO Box 99, Vaiaku, Funafuti

Phone. +688 20609

Fax. +688 20610

E-mail. tuvalutus@aol.com

Leadership. Tommy Alefaio (general secretary)

Membership. 600, who work on foreign vessels. The union affiliates to the ITF.

International affiliation. CTUC

Uganda

Capital: Kampala
Population: 23.32 m. (2000 est.)

1 Political and Economic Background

Uganda achieved independence from the United
Kingdom in 1962. As an independent state successive
governments were overthrown by military coups, but the
current President, Yoweri Museveni, has remained in
power since 1986, when his National Resistance
Movement triumphed after a five-year guerrilla war. As
in most African states, a degree of political pluralism
was introduced in the early 1990s, and political parties
are now permitted, although a system of non-party elections and government has been retained. In the most
recent elections, in 1996, Museveni retained the presidency with 74% of the vote, while his supporters won a
majority in the National Assembly. There is continuing
rebellion and acts of terrorism in the north and west of
the country.

Uganda's economy is based on agriculture (which
generates virtually all export earnings and accounts for
90% of the workforce) with only a small industrial
sector. It became the first country to receive debt relief
under the Initiative for Heavily Indebted Poor Countries
(HIPC), after being declared eligible in Apr. 1997. In
Mar. 2000 donor countries approved a further major aid
package and praised Uganda's efforts to reduce poverty,
while criticizing the level of military spending, which
escalated in 1998-99 as a result of Uganda's involvement in the war in the Democratic Republic of Congo.

GDP (purchasing power parity) $24.2bn. (1999 est.);
GDP per capita (purchasing power parity) $1,060 (1999
est.).

2 Trade Unionism

Uganda ratified ILO Convention No.98 (Right to
Organize and Collective Bargaining, 1949) in 1963, but
it has not ratified Convention No.87 (Freedom of
Association and Protection of the Right to Organize,
1948). Trade unions developed after 1940 under British
colonial rule and were given legal recognition in 1952.
Under the 1976 Trade Union Decree 1,000 members are
required to form a union, and 51% of the workforce
must be in membership in order for it to be recognized
for collective bargaining purposes. In 1993 Parliament
enacted legislation amending the 1976 decree to permit
unionization of the public service (including teaching)
and the Bank of Uganda, although the police, armed
forces, school heads and senior civil servants may not
join unions. Two new unions, the Uganda Civil Service
Union and the Uganda Medical Workers' Union, were

formed after the 1993 amendment bringing the total
number to 17.

The National Organization of Trade Unions (NOTU)
is the single centre to which all unions are by law affiliated. However, recently formed trade unions of public
servants and teachers have according to the ICFTU not
been required to affiliate to NOTU. The vast majority of
the workforce is engaged in (mainly subsistence) agriculture and NOTU has only about 100,000 members in
the small urban formal economy. There is negligible
unionization of workers engaged in the commercial agriculture sector. Privatization of state textile companies
has been followed by withdrawal of union recognition.
New investors in hotels and other enterprises have in
many cases refused to recognize unions as bargaining
agents.

Where the majority of the workforce are in a union, it
may engage in collective bargaining. The government is
the major employer in the formal sector, in the civil
service and state-owned enterprises. Uganda has a tripartite framework, which brings together NOTU with
the Federation of Ugandan Employers (FUE) and the
Minister of Labour. Bargaining has tended to be highly
centralized. There is an Industrial Court but the FUE has
charged it with bias and appealed decisions to the High
Court, where unions have often lost cases because they
could not afford the legal costs.

Notice of strike action must be given to the Labour
Minister, who generally refers the matter to the
Industrial Court. In practice, in the absence of rulings
from the Court, strikes have often been declared illegal,
although they have still occurred, sometimes being
broken up by police action. Under the Trades Dispute
(Arbitration and Settlement) Act of 1964, workers in
'essential services' may be prevented from terminating
their contracts of service and strikes may be prohibited.

Under the electoral system, representatives for special
interest groups have reserved places in the National
Assembly, and the unions have three seats.

3 Trade Union Centre

National Organization of Trade Unions (NOTU)

Address. PO Box 2150, Plot 94, William Street,
Kampala

Phone +256 41 256295

Fax. +256 41 259833

Leadership. L.O. Ongaba (general secretary)

Membership. 100,000

History and character. The Uganda Trade Union
Congress (UTUC), the first national trade union centre,
was formed in 1955 with the assistance of the ICFTU. In

1964, however, a Federation of Uganda Trade Unions (FUTU), affiliated to the WFTU, was formed as a splinter from the UTUC. In 1966 the trade unions reunited in the Uganda Labour Congress (ULC), and this was succeeded in 1974 by NOTU. NOTU comprises 17 unions in both private and public sectors. NOTU states that it is non-political and seeks to build a strong labour movement in Uganda without interference in the internal affairs of other organizations. It is represented on a number of government bodies such as the Industrial Court, Social Security Fund and the Industrial Training Council.

International affiliation. ICFTU; CTUC

Ukraine

Capital: Kiev
Population: 49.15 m. (2000 est.)

1 Political and Economic Background

The Ukraine achieved independence with the dissolution of the Soviet Union in 1991. The Communist Party was banned in Aug. 1991 but restored by 1993 and has remained largely unreformed and a considerable force. In subsequent parliamentary elections, most recently in March 1998, it has been the largest single party.

Ukraine steered an uncertain course after independence with a lack of a clear mandate for or commitment to major political and economic reform. Initial efforts at deregulation of prices and markets met resistance and were stalled. President Leonid Kuchma was first elected in 1994, as the candidate of the Inter-Regional Bloc for Reform, on a platform including a cautious programme of free market reform. However, he was also supported by the Communists, and the continued influence of communists and former apparatchiks throughout the bureaucracy has been reflected in the slow pace of change, notwithstanding a continuing growth in the private sector. Kuchnik was re-elected in Nov. 1999.

The Ukraine was the breadbasket of the former Soviet Union as well as an industrial stronghold and it has struggled to maintain its economy since independence. It has yet to grow its economy in any year since independence although there was virtually no further decline in 1999. Industrial output declined during the 1990s to only 40% of its 1991 level and many industrial enterprises are engaged only in part-time working or are virtually closed, although official unemployment in 1999 was only 4%. Wage arrears are widespread and there is a large informal sector. Foreign investment has been discouraged by corruption, opaque regulatory and licensing regimes, and arbitrary and onerous taxation, and most enterprises remain controlled by individuals with political links. There is a persistent budget deficit caused by relatively high spending on social programmes and subsidies to industry against a background of economic decline.

GDP (purchasing power parity) \$109.5bn. (1999 est.); GDP per capita (purchasing power parity) \$2,200 (1999 est.).

2 Trade Unionism

Independent Ukraine has inherited the Soviet era ratification in 1956 of ILO Conventions No.87 (Freedom of Association and Protection of the Right to Organize, 1948) and No. 98 (Right to Organize and Collective Bargaining, 1949).

Under the law all employees are free to form and join unions of their own choosing. There was no major development of opposition to the regime within the trade unions prior to the collapse of the Soviet Union in 1991, however, and since independence the reorganized official trade unions have retained their dominance. The Federation of Trade Unions of Ukraine (FPU), the successor to the Soviet unions, has the great majority of the workforce in membership, and claims 20 million members. In contrast, although independent unions exist in a number of sectors, their total membership is variously estimated at only between 100,000 and 300,000. As in Russia, membership of the official unions is generally passive and linked to their administration of a range of benefits through the social insurance fund. The official unions retained the property and other assets of the Soviet era unions. In practice giving up membership in the official unions is difficult. Similarly, the official unions include enterprise managers and directors as members and the unions have retained much of their former character of working closely with management. They have come into conflict with the government, however, over the problem of unpaid wages. In 1997 the FPU created a political party, the All-Ukrainian Party of Workers.

The most influential of the independent unions is the Independent Miners' Union of Ukraine, which is affiliated to the ICEM. Mikhail Volynets, the president of the miners' union, is also president of a Confederation of Free Trade Unions of Ukraine. The All-Ukrainian Organization of Solidarity of Working People (VOST) is affiliated to the WCL but there is no ICFTU affiliate in Ukraine.

In Sept. 1999 Ukraine adopted a new trade union law that independent unions saw as weakening their position by setting high barriers to achieving 'national status', which confers a range of privileges including participation in national-level bargaining. The legislation also made registration with the Justice Ministry compulsory and provoked fears that the government might refuse to register unions it did not favour. However, the Constitutional Court subsequently ruled the key clauses of the law unconstitutional.

Wage levels are set in the state sector through agreement between the government and the official unions. The independent unions have little access to or involvement in collective bargaining. The value of agreements is undermined by the widespread problem of wage arrears. Many enterprises retain workers on their books who are effectively redundant. This is preferable for the enterprise as it avoids paying compulsory redundancy of three months' salary, while workers also prefer to retain their jobs in hope of a recovery and to maintain pension and other benefits. The Law on Disputes Resolution, which came into force in March 1998, provided for the creation of national arbitration and mediation services, though these were not in practice immediately set up.

There is a constitutional right to strike but the constitution also says that strikes must not jeopardize national security, public health, or the rights and liberties of others. Public servants, the military and those engaged in the administration of justice, may not strike. Strikes aimed at overturning the constitutional order are banned. The leading recent cause of strikes and other forms of unrest, such as occurred in the mines and nuclear power plants in 1999, is wage arrears, mostly caused by inter-enterprise debt. As of July 1999, unpaid wages in the mining sector alone were the equivalent of $532 million, resulting from the situation that the power generation industry was only able to pay 5% of its obligations in cash, with the rest bartered or unpaid.

United Arab Emirates

Capital: Abu Dhabi
Population: 2.37 m. (2000 est.)

1 Political and Economic Background

The UAE is a federation comprising seven skeikhdoms, each of which is governed by an hereditary ruler with absolute power over non-federal matters. The highest federal authority is the Supreme Council of Rulers, comprising the seven hereditary rulers of the sheikhdoms. There are no political parties or democratic institutions.

The economy is based on oil and gas production, which provides a high standard of living for citizens, with plentiful reserves. The UAE is a huge importer of labour. Nationals represent only 20 per cent of the population, and a lesser proportion of the workforce. Unskilled workers come primarily from South Asia.

GDP (purchasing power parity) $41.5bn. (1999 est.); GDP per capita (purchasing power parity) $17,700 (1999 est.).

2 Trade Unionism

The UAE has been a member of the International Labour Organization since 1972, but has ratified neither Convention No.87 (Freedom of Association and Protection of the Right to Organize, 1948) nor Convention No.98 (Right to Organize and Collective Bargaining, 1949).

There is no legal right to form trade unions and they do not exist. About 85–90% of the workforce are migrant workers who could be deported if they formed unions. There is likewise no provision for or practice of collective bargaining or a right to strike.

Conciliation committees organized by the Ministry of Labour and Social Affairs, and labour courts, consider grievances on an individual basis. However, fear of reprisals and deportation are a deterrent. Labour laws do not apply to government employees, agricultural workers and domestic servants.

United Kingdom

Capital: London
Population: 59.51 m. (2000 est.)

1 Political and Economic Background

The United Kingdom comprises Great Britain (England, Scotland and Wales) and the province of Northern Ireland. The leading political parties are the Conservative Party and the Labour Party. Since World War II, the Conservatives have generally formed the government, but with periods of Labour government in 1945–51, 1964–70, 1974–79, and again since 1997. New regional assemblies for Scotland, Wales and Northern Ireland opened in 1999.

During the long period of Conservative government from 1979–97 major steps were taken to liberalize the economy, with privatization of state enterprises and measures to encourage the private sector. The process of 'Thatcherism' was seen as parallel to that of 'Reaganism' in the United States. Despite this, the rate of new business formation is much lower than that in the United States and the overall social and economic model remains closer to that of the European mainland than the United States. The Labour Party has since the 1980s largely abandoned socialist doctrine and instead adopted what Prime Minister Tony Blair calls the 'third way', emphasizing free markets tempered by a developed social welfare system. There has been no attempt to re-nationalize privatized industries. The UK is a member of the EU, but opted not to join the single European currency at its launch in 1999.

A deep economic downturn at the beginning of the 1980s accelerated the closure of wide swathes of traditional industry in areas such as coal mining and iron and steel. Three has been an accompanying diversification into services but this process has not aligned geographically with the closure of older industries, with a resultant divide between more dynamic service-based areas, especially in the South-East corner, and less prosperous older industrial zones, especially in the North and Wales. The UK experienced a sharp recession in the period 1990–92, but since then has produced steady growth, with falling unemployment and inflation maintained below 4% for nine successive years. Unemployment fell fractionally to 6.3% in 1999, continuing the decline from the 10.7% level reached in 1993. Inflation fell to an average 2.1% in 2000.

Publicly owned industries such as gas, water and electricity have been privatized, leaving only one major enterprise (the Post Office) in state hands. Apart from this public sector employment is now concentrated in national and local administration, education, welfare and health, and between the mid-1980s and mid-1990s declined from 29% to 22% of the workforce.

Since coming into office in 1997 the Labour government has emphasized partnership in industry, and prioritization of education and training, to foster innovation and meet what it sees as a productivity gap between the UK and its competitors.

GDP (purchasing power parity) $1.29 trillion; GDP per capita (purchasing power parity) $21,800.

2 Trade Unionism

The UK trade union movement is the oldest in the world and emerged in three phases. First came the mid-19th century emergence of skilled craft unions in industries such as engineering and printing. Then in the 1890s began the formation of major general unions of unskilled or semi-skilled workers. Finally came the early-20th century emergence and consolidation of white-collar and professional organizations, in areas such as public administration, education and health. In 1871 the Trades Union Act permitted collective bargaining and laid the foundation for the UK's system of 'immunities', in which unions had no positive legal right to act but enjoyed legal immunities, for example against claims for damages by employers. The shape and scope of these immunities were developed over the following decades by judicial rulings and Acts of Parliament, with a general tendency for them to be extended through to the 1970s. The UK ratified ILO Convention No. 87 (Freedom of Association and Protection of the Right to Organize, 1948) in 1949 and Convention No. 98 (Right to Organize and Collective Bargaining, 1949) in 1950.

The Trades Union Congress (TUC), founded in 1868, has never had a serious rival as Britain's trade union centre. It has no direct role in bargaining and its powers over affiliated unions are limited, but its longevity and cohesion give it considerable authority as the voice of British trade unions: since 1918 it has rarely represented less than three-quarters of all union members. Occasionally unions have been expelled but they have usually sought to return to the fold.

In the 1970s, and especially during the Labour government of 1974–79, the unions in general and the TUC in particular reached a peak of influence through their involvement in setting pay policy against a background of high inflation. Key leaders such as Jack Jones of the Transport and General Workers' Union, Hugh Scanlon of the Amalgamated Union of Engineering Workers and Lionel (Len) Murray of the TUC, assumed a public prominence comparable to that of senior members of the government. The government consulted the TUC on many issues and it had representatives on economic planning, industrial, training, educational, community, and health bodies. However, as pay policy collapsed the unions became embroiled in a series of pay disputes, especially in the public sector. The 1978–79 'winter of discontent' of industrial action by low-paid refuse, hospital, transport and cemetery workers contributed to disenchantment with the Labour government, opening the road to the election in May 1979 of a Conservative administration under Prime Minister Margaret Thatcher that was pledged to curb union power. The early 1980s brought deep recession and wholesale closures and unemployment in 'smokestack' industries like coal, steel, shipbuilding and the docks. The double impact of job losses in areas of union strength and a series of increasingly restrictive anti-union laws contributed to a rapid decline in the position of the unions. Continuing conflict in some sectors, notably the miners' strike of 1984, provided momentum for a sustained anti-union policy. Through successive Conservative administrations, consultation of the unions virtually ceased and many tripartite bodies were abolished. Trade union membership plummeted from over 13 million at the start of the 1980s to just over 9 million in the early 1990s. The number of unions shrank and the number of TUC affiliates fell from 109 in 1981 to 72 in 1992 as many merged under financial pressure.

The initial reaction of the unions to restrictive legislation, including measures that would later be accepted as reasonable, such as the introduction of secret postal ballots in place of show of hands to elect officials or call industrial action, was unwaveringly hostile. From the later 1980s, however, unions in dispute generally sought to ensure compliance with the law, made greater efforts to win public support, and tried to minimize the cost to their organizations and members. Union-government relations eased somewhat after the 1992 general election (the fourth in succession won by the Conservatives) but it was not until 1997, with the election of the first Labour government since 1979, that the position of the unions changed significantly. The new Labour administration was elected on a manifesto that emphasized there was no question of a return to the 'bad old days' of the 1970s. There would be no return of the closed shop (outlawed by a series of measures in the 1980s) under which some employees had lost their jobs for refusing to join a union. Nor would old-style methods of calling a strike through a 'show of hands', or 'disciplining' members who declined to participate, be allowed to return, while Conservative restrictions on industrial action, such as the ban on secondary 'sympathy' action taken against other workers' employers, would remain in place. While protection for employees was to be improved, a distinction was drawn between protecting the rights of employees as individuals and increasing the rights of the trade unions, which had traditionally seen themselves as the main guarantors of employee terms and conditions.

At the same time, the manifesto also endorsed the right of workers to union representation as 'promoting orderly industrial relations'. Following the election there was a revival of social dialogue and union leaders had renewed access to government. The government repealed harassing 1993 legislation requiring unions to run (costly) workplace ballots every three years for

members to renew check off arrangements for paying union dues, on the ground that this regulation was 'unnecessary and burdensome for employers and unions'. In a significant symbolic gesture the government immediately after the election also restored trade union rights, withdrawn in 1984, to staff at the GCHQ intelligence agency. The issue had been the subject of a long-running union campaign and the ILO had upheld a complaint by the TUC that the dismissals had been a violation of Convention No. 87.

The Employment Relations Act of 1999 was the first piece of legislation assisting trade union organization since the 1970s. Under it procedures were put in place (effective from June 2000) to allow the independent Central Arbitration Committee (CAC) to compel employers (with more than 20 employees) to recognize a union (or more than one union acting cooperatively) for collective bargaining purposes where the union can demonstrate that it enjoys the support of the workforce. If the CAC is satisfied that a union represents a majority of workers in a bargaining unit, it can compel recognition without further action. Where union membership is less than 50%, it can compel recognition where the union wins the votes of a majority of those voting, and at least 40% of those entitled to vote, in a recognition ballot. The new procedure, while similar to that in place in the US since the 1930s, represents a new development in terms of British trade unionism, which has been built up on the voluntarist principle that a union would be recognized where the employer chose to recognize it, or where the union was strong enough to be able to force the employer to do so. The 1999 Act, in other provisions, gave the government power to prohibit the compilation of 'blacklists' of union activists, banned employers from discriminating against union members in awarding benefits, and strengthened protections against dismissal in the aftermath of an industrial action.

From 1980 trade union membership showed a continuous year-on-year decline, falling to a mere 54% of its 1980 level by 1998. Trade union density declined from its 1979 peak of 56% to 31% in 1996, the last full year of Conservative government. By 1998 some 47% of workplaces had no union members at all, compared with only 36% as recently as 1990.

A major factor in the decline of union membership was the loss of jobs in traditional manufacturing sectors from the early 1980s, and the declining number of union members in firms that survived. At same time unions have proved comparatively unsuccessful in organizing the expanding private sector service industries that have driven economic growth, and involvement of young people in the unions has dropped particularly fast. As in Germany, the pattern of union organization tends to reflect the employment patterns of a generation ago. While few employers have staged aggressive drives to weed out unions (cases of union de-recognition are not common), the changed style of management has also undermined the unions. Management has increasingly sought to communicate with staff without union involvement, collective bargaining has declined, and unions have come to seem less relevant to the lives of increasing numbers of employees. Union density shows a pronounced geographical bias, in 1997 ranging from 42% in the older industrial areas of Northern England and Wales to only 23% in the economically more dynamic and prosperous, service-oriented economy of London and the South-East. Excluding older manufacturing industries, the main strength of the unions is in the public sector, where white-collar unionism (among groups such as teachers, social workers and civil servants) is high. In 1998 public sector density was 60%. In contrast density in the private sector was only 19%. Both white-collar and blue-collar jobs are weakly organized in most service industries where private sector jobs are increasingly congregated.

In some countries, unions have been particularly undermined by failure to organize women workers, but this is not broadly true in the UK. Some 46% of trade unionists are women, comparable to women's overall participation in the workforce. This, however, to some degree reflects the preponderance of women in highly-unionized public sector areas such as teaching, and low-skilled women in private services are often not unionized. Part-time and temporary workers are less often in unions than full-timers, but (unlike in much of the EU) the proportion of such workers in the labour force has shown little increase. The proportion of jobs defined as permanent fell only 1% from 1984–99 and average length of time spent in any one job also changed little. In 1999 temporary workers constituted only 6% of the workforce, compared with an EU average of 13%, while the growth in part-time work from 1993–99 was only 1%, the least of any EU country. Similarly, the loss of union members cannot be attributed to factors in operation in some other countries, such as increasing self-employment (the number of self-employed grew in the 1980s but actually fell by 400,000 from 1990–99), or increasing employment in smaller enterprises (the proportion of employees in large firms grew in the 1990s).

In June 2000, the TUC reported that official Labour Force Survey figures showed that union membership had grown 100,000 from 1998 to 1999, rising to nearly 7.3 million, while union density had remained steady. The TUC, while warning that 2000 could see a drop of 16,000 in union membership as a result of job losses in manufacturing, hailed the development as a turning point. It predicted that 1 million new members could be added by its affiliates over the next five years, to take total TUC membership to 7.8 million. The improvement (which paralleled that in the USA) was attributed in part to new recruitment campaigns aimed especially at temporary and part-time workers. In the run up to implementation of the trade union recognition provisions of the Employment Relations Act in 2000, there had also been a reported trend for employers to enter voluntarily into recognition agreements rather than wait for this to be compelled. The TUC said 267 such agreements were signed in 1999, compared with between 85 and 104 in each of the previous four years. At the same time, union leaders portrayed the reversal of fortunes as

a success for a moderate policy, that combined defence of employee rights with awareness of the competitive challenges and need for labour flexibility that confronted employers. This trade union approach placed emphasis on partnership rather than confrontation. In Jan. 2001 the TUC reported there had been 158 new recognition agreements, covering 58,000 workers, signed in 2000.

Patterns of union organization have traditionally varied considerably, largely reflecting bargaining systems. The craft unions have typically had a well-developed local workplace representative (shop steward) system; they tend to give considerable authority to elected lay officials, and often have strong branches or regions. General unions, whose membership turnover is often higher, tend to have larger branches with relatively little negotiating authority but often with substantial funds and a major role in members' welfare. Shop stewards may rely more on the help of professional full-time union officials who have relatively greater authority. White collar unions are usually organized along semi-craft lines, although there is often less emphasis on pay bargaining and the unions have traditionally offered a wider range of membership benefits such as travel, legal advice and insurance, as well as actively developing members' professional interests.

One aspect of declining union strength in the 1980s and 1990s was the weakening role of union shop stewards. By the late 1990s employee work place representation through trade union representatives was largely confined to the public sector, the privatized utilities and manufacturing. Where unions are not established, alternative formal structures for employee representation and consultation are unusual, the UK having no system to parallel that of the works councils found in most other EU countries, and with management tending to discuss with employees on an individual basis or not at all. With companies commonly seeking to by-pass the unions, employees have come to feel that the union has little real influence, and therefore not worth joining.

During the 1990s many unions have put an emphasis on 'partnership' as the new model for industrial relations. Where partnership agreements have been struck with employers, the scope of collective agreements has typically been widened to include matters such as job security and employee training and development. At the same time the union has formally recognized that employee security can only be achieved by contributing to the success and profitability of the company, a concept that has traditionally been less acknowledged in the UK than in countries such as Germany and Japan. To some degree, the unions' emphasis on partnership also reflects the reality that they need to find ways to re-establish themselves at grass-roots level in working environments where organizational militancy is ineffective.

Employers see that partnership, while having advantages in building a consensus behind company strategies, can be a two-edged sword. In June 1999 CBI president Sir Clive Thompson warned that the concept of partnership could be masking a 'damaging build-up of trade union influence'. He warned that: 'we mustn't fall into the trap of thinking that partnership means unions. Of course it can and sometimes does, but what's right for one company is by no means right for all'. At the same time, the employers (in this case backed by the government) are opposed to any extension to UK 'national' companies under EU directives of consultation rights to employees in works council-type structures, as proposed by the European Commission. (These are currently required only in multi-national companies, where they are called European Works Councils). The unions have come to favour such an extension as not only providing opportunities for enhanced employee consultation but as providing a starting point for unionization. While in the past unions often looked upon European-style works councils as potentially a way for employers to by-pass unions, in practice formalized consultation structures of that sort rarely exist in the UK other than in unionized environments.

Until the late 1970s, most collective bargaining was typically conducted nationally at industry level: for example, in engineering, chemicals or the health service. Major companies or organizations often bargained independently. On top of these rates local establishments commonly negotiated top-up rates, bonuses, etc. Such two-tier bargaining was prevalent in manufacturing and the private sector; single-tier national agreements were the public sector norm. Collective bargaining covered over three-quarters of all employees: the service sectors and professional occupations were not usually covered. In the voluntarist tradition agreements were not backed by legal sanctions.

During late 1980s and 1990s the scope of private sector industry-wide collective bargaining declined. The major surviving national sectoral agreement, covering 600,000 workers, is the building and engineering agreement. At the same time, company-level agreements also became fewer. In 1998 trade unions had collective bargaining rights in 45% of workplaces with at least 25 employees, compared with 53% in 1990. Only 37% of employees were covered by collective bargaining by 1997, although a tendency remained for rates set in collective bargaining to be reflected as the 'going rate' in non-union companies. In addition, the collective bargaining agenda has tended to narrow, primarily to issues of pay, grievance procedures and heath and safety. The new pattern reflects the weakening of the unions nationally, the increasing importance of service sectors where unions are weak, the reassertion of managerial authority and government hostility to national bargaining with its connotations of an annual pay round.

Some 1.3 million public sector workers, including nurses, teachers, doctors, the armed forces and senior civil servants, are covered by a system of independent pay review boards. These make annual pay recommendations for the government to decide upon, and government decisions can be highly sensitive and politicized in terms of the lead they set for other workers, including nearly 4 million other public sector workers covered by collective bargaining.

The UK has no tradition of state-mandated minimum wages, other than for specific groups of vulnerable workers for whom minima were set by wages councils. In the 1980s the scope of wages councils was reduced before (in 1992) their role was abolished except in respect of agricultural workers. Following the election of the Labour government, however, legislation was enacted (with effect from Apr. 1999) to provide for a national minimum wage. It was estimated that this would affect the position of 7–9% of the workforce.

The Advisory, Conciliation and Arbitration Service (ACAS) had a prominent role in dispute resolution in the 1970s. However, under Conservative government it shifted its emphasis from crisis management to more advisory work. Under the 1992 Employment Act its remit altered from a duty to promote collective bargaining (thus necessarily involving unions) to a duty to promote good industrial relations (improving personnel practice but not necessarily involving unions). In Oct. 2000 ACAS reported that it had provided collective conciliation in 1,247 disputes in the last financial year. 52% of cases involved pay and terms and conditions of employment while 12% related to union recognition and redundancy. These figures for collective conciliation compared with a record high of 164,000 individual claims in the same period.

The UK has never had a formal legal 'right to strike', and indeed strikers are considered in breach of contract and may be dismissed. However, historically official and unofficial strikes were a commonplace feature of British industrial relations, with union participation protected by immunities built up by legislation and legal precedent, and employers rarely dismissing individual workers. Union power was in effect the main guarantee of the right to strike. A series of Acts passed by the Conservative government after 1979 were aimed at curbing the sort of industrial action seen in the 'winter of discontent'. Through successive Employment Acts in 1980, 1982, and 1988 secondary action was prohibited, mass picketing curbed, balloting of union members before industrial action introduced, and union legal immunities reduced.

The 1990 Employment Act made unions liable for any form of industrial action (including unofficial action not sanctioned by union ballots and procedures) which had been organized or supported by officers or members, unless the union explicitly repudiated the action. It gave employers the right to selectively dismiss anyone taking part in unofficial action (previously employers had normally been able to dismiss all those taking part in action, or none). The Act was widely seen as a return to the famous 1900 Taff Vale judgment (reversed by the 1906 Trade Disputes Act) which found that a union could be held liable for acts done by any of its members, authorized or not. The 1992 Trade Union Reform and Employment Rights Act increased public rights to seek redress for injury caused by strike action. A further statute, the Trades Union Reform and Employment Rights Act 1993, required that pre-strike ballots (a requirement of an earlier Conservative statute) should be postal.

Unions are required to ballot their members before taking industrial action. Such ballots are not uncommon: in an 11-month period in 1997–98, for instance, the two main providers of balloting services supervised 1,759 ballots on industrial action, 75% of which resulted in majorities in favour of action. However, such ballots tend to be used mainly as a bargaining tool. The incidence of actual strikes has declined markedly since the 1970s, falling in the 1990s to lower levels than at any time since records began in 1891. In 1998 only 282,000 days were lost to strike action, compared with the 29.5 million lost in 1979. The UK is now seen as a country with a low rate of industrial action, with the number of days lost per employee running at half the EU average.

The degree to which the cumulative body of Conservative legislation curbed strikes is disputed. Traditionally strike prone industries such as mining, engineering and the docks, once major employers, have declined greatly in significance and many newer service sectors are without any culture of industrial action. Some employers have shown more willingness to dismiss strikers, although this has not been a general phenomenon. In the 1980s, and especially the 1990s, industrial action also declined in many other European countries that did not enact punitive anti-strike laws, reflecting greater control over inflation and consequent wage moderation and an increase in partnership between unions and employers. The election of a Labour government has not led to a union campaign to restore lost immunities, or indeed to any increase in strike action of the sort predicted by the Conservatives. Only relatively minor changes have been made to the law surrounding industrial action. These have included ending the requirement for unions to give employers advance notice of the names of individual employees intending industrial action (although notice must be given of the action itself) and increasing protections against dismissal in the aftermath of industrial action.

The issue of working time has not achieved the same prominence that it has in countries such as Spain, France and Germany. Historically, working time has not been regulated by law in the UK, but in 1999 an EU working time directive setting a limit of an average 48 hours per week came into force in the UK. However, there are some exclusions, such as for junior doctors, and individuals may opt out. The average normal working time in 1999 collective agreements was 38.4 hours. In practice actual working hours are generally longer than those in other European countries, especially for groups such as white-collar middle managers.

3 Trade Union Centre

Trades Union Congress (TUC)

Address. Congress House, 23–28 Great Russell Street, London WC1B 3LS

Phone. +44 20 7636 4030

Fax. +44 20 7636 0632

E-mail. info@tuc.org.uk

Website. www.tuc.org.uk

Leadership. John Monks (general secretary)

Membership. 6.8 million in 77 unions

History and character. The TUC was founded in 1868, since when it has been the sole national trade union centre. More than 90% of British trade unionists are in unions affiliated to the TUC. There is also a Scottish Trades Union Congress (STUC), and unions may affiliate to both the STUC and TUC. Trade unions in Northern Ireland are represented by the Irish Congress of Trade Unions (Northern Ireland Committee), although most organized workers in Northern Ireland are members of British-based unions which are affiliated to the TUC. There is also a Wales TUC within the TUC structure. Regional committees within England help organize education, research and campaigning. At the local level, trades councils are the TUC's local bodies. The TUC works to coordinate the activities of its affiliates and represents the trade union movement to government and internationally. Its member unions are autonomous, however, and the TUC does not instruct them or negotiate on their behalf. The TUC also has a National Education Centre, based in London, and an office in Brussels.

The TUC was one of the leading British institutions for much of the twentieth century. While never a mass political organization in the manner of many continental European centres (the TUC has only once participated in a general strike, in 1926, and that in pursuit of an industrial dispute), the TUC and its affiliates have historically had a political voice through the Labour Party, which the unions were instrumental in founding. TUC leaders were especially prominent in the 1960s and 1970s (under both Conservative and Labour governments) as participants in the tripartite formulation of economic policy. The TUC assumed great power and status and successive general secretaries were household names. By the end of the 1970s its membership had reached over 12 million. Following the 1979 election of a Conservative government under Margaret Thatcher with a radical free-market anti-union agenda, however, it was largely excluded from access to government policy-making. The TUC also seemed to some to compound its problems by refusing in the early years of the Thatcher government, when anti-union legislation was somewhat tentative and the Cabinet divided, to offer any cooperation or accept any sort of reform even in those areas (such as extended balloting of members or curbs on mass secondary picketing) where there was evidence of widespread public support for the government's position. In addition, the TUC's rhetoric in that period was not matched by an ability to mobilize its own membership. In terms of national political and economic decision-making the TUC became a fringe organization, and its capacity for influence declined as its membership fell year on year and the labour market was progressively deregulated. At the same time, the TUC re-evaluated its own position and by 1993 had moved to a position of 'new unionism' which sought to position the unions as a force for consensus and partnership in society.

In 1997 Labour returned to power for the first time since 1979, leading to an immediate warming of relations between government and unions. 'New' Labour, pursuing its 'third way' policies, was anxious not to appear tied to the unions, reflecting the view that the association of Labour with the unions had been a primary cause of its loss of office in the aftermath of the 'winter of discontent' of 1979. A new generation of Labour leaders, in contrast to those at the time of the last Labour government, has far less by way of roots in the trade union movement and some are inclined to view it more as another interest group rather than as the historic bedrock of the party. Financial ties have also lessened. In 1996, for the first time in history, union donations accounted for less than half the party's annual income. In this context, the relationship between party and TUC has become more of an arm's length one. Nonetheless there are continuing strong organizational, ideological and emotional linkages. The unions have retained a powerful position in the (nominally) sovereign party conference and on the party's national executive committee. Although individual members inevitably have diverse political views, and a majority of TUC affiliates are now politically non-aligned, no prominent union leader is a supporter of any other political party and no TUC union is affiliated to any other party.

Britain has a tradition of numerous unions with ill-defined organizational boundaries, and at one time demarcation disputes between unions were common, with the TUC commonly acting as mediator. Provisions in the 1992 Trade Union Reform and Employment Rights Act that prevent unions refusing membership applications deprived the TUC of its traditional role as adjudicator between affiliates in such disputes. As a result the 'Bridlington rules' which once enforced spheres of membership were replaced by a voluntary code.

The TUC has also had a role in brokering mergers of unions, a process encouraged by the difficulties faced by some unions as membership dues declined. In 1993 three TUC affiliates merged to create the public sector union UNISON, which became the TUC's largest affiliate. In March 1999, the TUC said it would develop proposals for 'fewer unions, organized more logically' and new procedures to minimize inter-union competition in seeking recognition agreements under the 1999 Employment Relations Act. In Nov. 1999 two major unions, the AEEU and MSF, announced plans to merge, which would create the second largest British union, with 1,150,000 members. Despite this, the number of affiliated unions had actually increased to 77 by 2000, compared with 68 in 1994, as a result of new affiliations by white-collar unions in areas such as financial services. Half (38) of the TUC's affiliates have fewer than 10,000 members. Most of these small unions fall into three groups. Firstly, long-established craft unions representing old industrial trades that have dwindled in sig-

nificance. These unions are based typically in the industrial North or Midlands, often with a very localized membership, and include unions such as the Card Setting Machine Tenters' Society, which has 88 members, all men, or the General Union of Loom Overlookers, with 322 members, also all men. A second group comprises single employer staff associations, mainly in financial services (banks and building societies). Finally, there are associations representing specific white-collar professional groups, such as the Association of Educational Psychologists and the Society of Chiropodists and Podiatrists. A special case is the National Union of Mineworkers (NUM), which in the 1970s era of industrial militancy and high dependence on coal, was arguably the most powerful union in Britain. Following a disastrous strike in 1984–85, and the wholesale closure of pits as alternative sources of energy were found or coal imported, the NUM now has only 5,000 members, although it has retained the same president (Arthur Scargill) throughout.

The TUC has lost more than four million members since the end of the 1970s. While the decline of the unions in the period from 1980 was driven mainly by structural changes in the economy and the new political climate, it was exacerbated by the fall in dues to fund full-time officials, as these carried the burden of recruiting members in non-union work places. Under John Monks (general secretary since 1993) the TUC has sought to re-shape its public image and rebuild its base. In Dec. 1993 the TUC stated its intention to become a campaigning organization, abolishing its complex committee structure and setting up a series of task groups focused on specific campaign issues. A 'New Unionism Task Group' was set up in 1996 with the objective of halting the decline in union membership by assisting the unionization of growth sectors in the economy and trying to win over groups with low density, such as young people. As an outcome of this Task Group, the TUC, in concert with member unions, set up an Organizing Academy in 1998. Unions are also trying to free up more of their full-time officers' time for organizational work by providing training for lay workplace representatives in how to represent employees in grievance and disciplinary proceedings, which consume officials' time. Member unions commonly provide a wide range of services, such as specially negotiated insurance and discount schemes. However, these are generally considered to contribute to retaining members rather than in attracting new ones, and the focus in winning new members is on achieving benefits in terms of collective bargaining on wages and conditions and protecting individual employee rights. The TUC welcomed the Employment Relations Act of 1999, which increased trade union organizing rights by providing for a system of workplace recognition ballots, but is aware that legislation without grass roots organizational activity is likely to have only marginal impact.

The TUC hailed a small increase in union membership totals in 1999, after two decades of decline, as a turnaround. This success, and with a Labour government in office and a generally buoyant economy, led John Monks to tell the Sept. 2000 TUC congress that they were meeting in the most favourable political and economic context for over 30 years.

The TUC has actively promoted its concept of 'partnership' at the work place, advocating this as the way to improve flexibility, training, competitiveness and employment security. In May 1999 it staged a conference on this theme with the participation of government ministers and the CBI. John Monks has argued that unionized workforces are the most content, the best trained, have the lowest rate of industrial tribunal cases and are more likely to show high productivity growth. Monks says that flexibility must be shown by employers as well as workers, in areas such as child care provision, flexible working hours that help the employee, skills training, and giving proper rights to part-time workers. Job security is also viewed as an element of partnership. While partnership has been advanced as a tripartite cause, it is nonetheless viewed with suspicion by some employers as an entering wedge for increasing union power in the workplace. In Jan. 2001 the TUC launched a new Partnership Institute to foster the development of partnership.

The TUC has moved over time to an increasingly positive view of the EU, especially its social dimension and potential for establishing Europe-wide labour standards. It identifies the European Commission's plan (proposed in a draft directive of Nov. 1998) to extend information and consultation rights (on the model of European works councils) to all companies of 50 or more workers as the most important of the current EU legislative proposals. However, both employers and government are opposed to any such measure as an interference in national-level arrangements, and this issue was described by John Monks in Oct. 1999 as the one on which there is the 'sharpest divide' between the government and the unions. The leading issue in British politics generally in respect of the EU has been the UK's decision not to participate in the single European currency, launched in Jan. 1999, and this has produced some division among the unions. In March 2000 a group of TUC affiliates, including the AEEU, the GMB and the Iron and Steel Trades Confederation, launched 'Trade Unions for Europe' (TufE) in support of joining the single currency. The unions represented mainly manufacturing sectors hit by the strength of the pound relative to the European single currency (the Euro). In contrast, some public sector unions, including the TUC's largest affiliate, UNISON, fear that achieving the convergence criteria for joining the currency could impact on public spending. The Sept. 2000 TUC congress backed the Labour government's line that the UK should adopt the single currency but only at an undefined future date when circumstances are appropriate.

The TUC participates in tripartite bodies including ACAS, the Health and Safety Commission and the Low Pay Commission. In the 1960s and 1970s the National Economic and Development Council (NEDC) had considerable prominence as a tripartite forum for wide-ranging economic issues, but under the Conservatives from 1979 its role was curtailed and it was finally abolished in 1992. Following the election of a Labour government in 1997 there has been a renewal of tripartism. In Oct. 2000 the Chancellor of the Exchequer (Finance Minister) Gordon Brown asked the TUC and CBI to participate in a series of working parties on six topics identified by the Treasury as contributing to a 'productivity gap' between Britain and other industrialized countries. These were restrictive practices, low skills, underinvestment, resistance to innovation, under-use of technology, and poor management. The TUC warmly welcomed the initiative although CBI reaction was cooler.

The **Wales TUC** (David Jenkins, general secretary. *Address.* 1 Cathedral Road, Cardiff CF11 9SD. *Phone.* +44 29 20 372 345. *Website.* www.wtuc.org.uk.) is an integral part of the TUC and was set up in 1974 to strengthen the role of the TUC in Wales, where there is partially devolved government. It works with and represents union views to, the Welsh Office, the CBI Wales and the Welsh Development Agency and coordinates the trade unions' interface with the elected National Assembly of Wales, set up in 1999.

International affiliations. ICFTU; ETUC; CTUC; TUAC

Affiliates. There are currently 77 affiliated unions. Only those with 10,000 members or more are listed below. (Note: many unions also have affiliation to the Irish Congress of Trade Unions, based in the Republic of Ireland – see ICTU entry under Ireland.)

1. Amalgamated Engineering and Electrical Union (AEEU)

Address. Hayes Court, West Common Road, Hayes, Bromley, Kent BR2 7AU
Phone. +44 20 8 462 7755
Fax. +44 20 8 315 8234
E-mail. j.steed@headoffice.aeeeu.org.uk
Website. www.aeeu.org.uk
Leadership. Sir Ken Jackson (general secretary)
Membership. 730,000
History and character. Formed in 1992 by merger of the Amalgamated Engineering Union (AEU) and the electricians' union EETPU. This is the largest manufacturing sector union in the UK. It represents both blue-collar and white-collar workers, the latter being represented through the AEEU Staff Section. Its members are in a wide range of industries including engineering, energy, construction, IT, defence, aerospace, motor industry, chemicals, pharmaceuticals, civil air transport, steels and metals, and shipbuilding. It is affiliated to the Labour Party and 20 AEEU members sit in the House of Commons.

The AEEU is a leading member of the 'Britain in Europe' campaign, that supports deepening UK integration with the EU. It has also been a leading proponent of partnership agreements with employers, which it sees as a mechanism for expanding union membership. In Feb. 2000 general secretary Sir Ken Jackson forecast that membership could increase by 300,000 by mid-2001: the union said that 100 recognition agreements had been signed with employers since the 1997 election, and there had been 60 partnership agreements. Among the union's facilities are two training colleges.

In 1999 the AEEU agreed in principle to amalgamate with the MSF in a new union on a 50/50 parity basis, to create the UK's second largest union. The merger was seen as unlikely to be completed until 2003.

2. Associated Society of Locomotive Engineers and Firemen (ASLEF)

Address. 9 Arkwright Road, Hampstead, London NW3 6AB
Phone. +44 20 7317 8600
Fax. +44 20 7794 6406
E-mail. info@aslef.org.uk
Website. www.aslef.org.uk
Leadership. Mick Rix (general secretary)
Membership. 15,250
History and character. Founded in 1880. It has members in all British train operating companies and reports that 'membership is growing for the first time in a generation'. Affiliated to Labour Party.
Publications. *Locomotive Journal* (content accessible via website).

3. Association of First Division Civil Servants (FDA)

Address. 2 Caxton Street, London SWIH OQH
Phone. +44 20 7343 1111
Fax. +44 20 7343 1105
E-mail. head-office@fda.org.uk
Website. www.fda.org.uk
Leadership. Jonathan Baume (general secretary)
Membership. 10,000
History and character. Politically independent; represents senior grades in the civil service. It is affiliated to PSI.
Publications. *Public Service Magazine*

4. Association of Teachers and Lecturers (ATL)

Address. 7 Northumberland Street, London WC2N 5DA
Phone. +44 20 7930 6441
Fax. +44 20 7930 1359
E-mail. info@atl.org.uk
Website. www.askatl.org.uk
Leadership. Peter Smith (general secretary)
Membership. 113,760
History and character. Founded in 1978 as the Assistant Masters and Mistresses Association through the merger of separate men's and women's teachers' unions. It emphasizes professionalism, and won many members from the main teachers' unions when they staged a series of strikes in the mid-1980s. It changed its name to the ATL in 1993 to help recruitment in the further education sector. It affiliated to the TUC for the first time on 1 January 1999.
Publications. Report

5. Association of University Teachers (AUT)

Address. Egmont House, 25–31 Tavistock Place, London NW1H 9UT
Phone. +44 20 7670 9700
Fax. +44 20 7670 9799
E-mail. hq@aut.org.uk
Website. www.aut.org.uk
Leadership. David Triesman (general secretary)
Membership. 41,758
History and character. Members include a wide range of staff in institutions of higher education and research, including administrators, academics, computer staff and librarians.
Publications. Members' news magazine accessible via website.

6. Bakers, Food and Allied Workers' Union (BFAWU)

Address. Stanborough House, Great North Road, Stanborough, Welwyn Garden City, AL8 7TA
Phone. +44 1707 260150
Fax. +44 1707 261570
E-mail. bfawu@aol.com
Website. www.bfawu.org.uk
Leadership. Joe Marino (general secretary)
Membership. 29,962
History and character. Founded in 1849. Represents mainly manual and technician bakery workers.

7. British Actors' Equity Association (EQUITY)

Address. Guild House, Upper St. Martins Lane, London WC2H 9EG
Phone. +44 20 7379 6000
Fax. +44 20 7379 7001
E-mail. info@equity.org.uk
Website. www.equity.org.uk
Leadership. Ian McGarry (general secretary)
Membership. 36,563

8. Broadcasting Entertainment, Cinematograph and Theatre Union (BECTU)

Address. 111 Wardour Street, London WIF 0AY
Phone. +44 20 7437 8506
Fax. +44 20 7437 8268
E-mail. info@bectu.org.uk
Website. www.bectu.org.uk
Leadership. Roger Bolton (general secretary)
Membership. 29,000
Publications. *Stage, Screen and Radio*

9. Ceramic and Allied Trades Union (CATU)

Address. Hillcrest House, Garth Street, Hanley, Stoke-on Trent ST1 2AB
Phone. +44 1782 272755
Fax. +44 1782 284902
Leadership. Geoff Bagnall (general secretary)
Membership. 18,677
History and character. Founded in 1827. Represents pottery workers, almost all in Staffordshire.

10. Chartered Society of Physiotherapy (CSP)

Address. 14 Bedford Row, London WC1R 4ED
Phone. +44 20 7306 6666
Fax. +44 20 7306 6611
Leadership. Phil Gray (chief executive)
Membership. 31,351

11. Communication Workers' Union (CWU)

Address. 150 The Broadway, London SW19 1RX
Phone. +44 20 8971 7200
Fax. +44 20 8971 7300
Website. www.cwu.org
Leadership. Derek Hodgson (general secretary)
Membership. 287,000
History and character. Formed in 1994 from the merger of the Union of Communication Workers (UCW) and the National Communications Union (NCU). Members work in posts, telecommunications, cable TV and related areas. The CWU is the largest communications union in the UK and the second largest in the EU. It is affiliated to the Labour Party and internationally to UNI.
Publications. *Voice*

12. Connect: The Union for Professionals in Communications

Address. 30 St. George's Road, TW9 4BD
Phone. +44 20 8971 6000
Fax. +44 20 8971 6002
E-mail. union@connectuk.org
Website. www.connectuk.org
Leadership. Simon Petch (general secretary)
Membership. 16,747
History and character. Represents managerial and professional staff in telecoms; changed name from Society of Telecom Executives in Jan. 2000.

13. Educational Institute of Scotland (EIS)

Address. 46 Moray Place, Edinburgh EH3 6BH
Phone. +44 131 225 6244
Fax. +44 131 220 3151
Website. www.eis.org.uk
Leadership. Ronald A. Smith (general secretary)
Membership. 49,994
History and character. Founded in 1847, and possesses a royal charter. Represents teachers, lecturers and associated staff in Scotland.

14. Engineers' and Managers' Association (EMA)

Address. Flaxman House, Gogmore Lane, Chertsey, Surrey KT16 9JS
Phone. +44 1932 577011
Fax. +44 1932 567166
E-mail. gs@ema.org.uk
Website. www.ema.org.uk
Leadership. Tony Cooper (general secretary)
Membership. 29,517. Members are managers, engineers and scientists in industries such as aerospace, electricity supply, engineering, oil and shipbuilding.
Publications. EPE (Electrical and Power Engineer)

15. Fire Brigades Union (FBU)

Address. Bradley House, 68 Coombe Road, Kingston-upon Thames, Surrey KT2 7AE
Phone. +44 20 8541 1765
Fax. +44 20 8546 5187
Leadership. Andy Gilchrist (general secretary)
Membership. 53,000
History and character. Founded 1918. Represents almost all firefighters and control staff and many managers. Affiliated to the Labour Party.
Publications. Firefighter

16. GMB

Address. 22/24 Worple Road, Wimbledon, London SW19 4DD
Phone. +44 20 8947 3131
Fax. +44 20 8944 6552
E-mail. daniel.hodges@gmb.org.uk (communications dept.)
Website. www.gmb.org.uk
Leadership. John Edmonds (general secretary)
Membership. 712,010
History and character. The GMB is a general union that has been shaped by numerous mergers since the formation of the National Union of General and Municipal Workers in 1924. Among the more notable of these in recent times was the absorption of the white-collar Association of Professional, Executive, Clerical and Computer Staff (APEX) in 1989. The initials 'GMB' were adopted as the

union's official title in 1989, and were derived from the previous name of General, Municipal, Boilermakers and Allied Trades Union. The GMB has members in public sector areas such as the National Health Service and local government, and the diversity of its private sector membership is reflected in the fact that 34 of the top 50 British companies employ GMB members. Its membership is approximately 60% male.

The GMB has eight sections, covering clothing and textiles; commercial services; construction, furniture, timber and allied; energy and utilities; engineering; food and leisure; process workers; and public services. It has 10 regional offices, 300 full-time regional organizers and 25,000 workplace shop stewards. It was the first British union to set up a permanent office in Brussels.

The GMB is affiliated to the Labour Party and over 80 of the Labour MPs elected in the most recent general election in May 1997 are GMB members. General secretary John Edmonds has been prominent in recent years in arguing that the pound's strength against European currencies is damaging manufacturing exports, and the GMB says that 250,000 manufacturing jobs have been lost since the 1997 election.
Publications. Wide range of publications accessible via website.

17. Graphical Paper and Media Union (GPMU)

Address. Keys House, 63-67 Bromham Road, Bedford, MK40 2AG
Phone. +44 1234 351521
Fax. +44 1234 270580
E-mail. general@gpmu.org.uk
Website. www.gpmu.org.uk
Leadership. Tony Dubbins (general secretary)
Membership. 204,822
History and character. Formed in 1991 from merger of NGA and SOGAT, the two major print and paper unions, and includes clerical, administrative and production workers in printing, publishing, multi-media and IT. Affiliated to the Labour Party.
Publications. GPMU Direct; GPMU@Work

18. Independent Union of Halifax Staff (IUHS)

Address. Simmons House, 46 Old Bath Road, Charvil, Reading, RG10 9QR
Phone. +44 118 934 1808
Fax. +44 118 932 0208
Leadership. Ged Nichols
Membership. 25,652. This is the largest of the single-company staff associations in the finance sector affiliated to the TUC.

19. Institution of Professionals, Managers and Specialists (IPMS)

Address. 75–79 York Road, London SE1 7 AQ
Phone. +44 20 7902 6600
Fax. +44 20 7902 6667
E-mail. ipmshq@ipms.org.uk
Website. www.ipms.org.uk
Leadership. Paul Noon (general secretary)
Membership. 74,000
History and character. Founded in 1919 as union for middle-ranking professional and scientific civil servants; changed name to IPMS in 1989 as privatization had moved many members to the private sector. The union is campaigning against proposed further privatizations affecting air traffic controllers,

the Defence Evaluation and Research Agency and the Royal Mint. Affiliated to PSI.
Publications. IPMS Bulletin

20. Iron and Steel Trades Confederation (ISTC)

Address. Swinton House, 324 Gray's Inn Road, London WC1X 8DD
Phone. +44 20 7239 1200
Fax. +44 20 7278 8378
E-mail. istc@istc-tu.org
Website. www.istc-tu.org
Leadership. Michael Leahy (general secretary)
Membership. 50,001
History and character. Represents process, craft, technician, contractors' staff and middle management in metal manufacture and related industries. Affiliated to Labour Party.

21. Manufacturing, Science, Finance (MSF)

Address. MSF Centre, 33-37 Moreland Street, London EC1V 8HA
Phone. +44 20 7505 3000
Fax . +44 20 7505 3030
Website. www.msf.org.uk
Leadership. Roger Lyons (general secretary)
Membership. 425,000
History and character. Formed in 1988 by the merger of the Technical, Administrative and Supervisory Staffs union (TASS) and the Association of Scientific, Technical and Management Staffs (ASTMS). TASS represented mainly technicians and management in engineering, having formerly been the white-collar section of the Amalgamated Union of Engineering. ASTMS, itself formed by merger in 1969, had grown with great rapidity under the leadership of its high-profile general secretary (from 1969–88) Clive Jenkins. It had absorbed more than 30 staff associations and become the leading force in multi-sector white-collar trade unionism.

MSF members are employed in a wide range of white-collar occupations in both the public and private sectors. Nearly half its members work in manufacturing industry as engineers, scientists, technicians, supervisors, researchers and managers. The other half are employed in areas such as universities, health services, sales and finance. The MSF absorbed the TUC-affiliated, 6,000-member, National Union of Insurance Workers with effect from the beginning of 2000.

The MSF is affiliated to the Labour Party, and has a parliamentary group of 82 members. In addition 12 British and Irish Members of the European Parliament are MSF members.

In the 1990s the MSF was forced to make major cutbacks in an attempt to balance expenditure with its reduced income as membership fell. In Nov. 1999 it agreed in principle to merge with the Amalgamated Engineering and Electrical Union (AEEU) to form a new union on a 50/50 parity basis. Roger Lyons said that the new union's structure and rule book were unlikely to be completed before 2003. On Nov. 11, 2000 an MSF conference voted to proceed to a full ballot of the membership on the proposed merger.
Publications. MSF Report (accessible at website)

22. Musicians' Union (MU)

Address. 60-62 Clapham Road, London SW9 OJS
Phone. +44 20 7582 5566
Fax. +44 20 7582 9805
E-mail. info@musiciansunion.org.uk
Website. www.musiciansunion.org.uk
Leadership. Dennis Scard (general secretary)

Membership. 30,500
History and character. Founded in 1893, this is the second largest musicians' union in the world.
Publications. Musician

23. National Association of School Masters/Union of Women Teachers (NASUWT)

Address. 5 King Street, London WC2E 8HN
Phone. +44 20 7420 9670
Fax. +44 20 7420 9679
E-mail. nigel.degruchy@nasuwt.org.uk
Website. www.nasuwt.org
Leadership. Nigel de Gruchy (general secretary)
Membership. 185,000
History and character. Formed 1975 by merger of separate teaching unions for men and women. It competes for members with the National Union of Teachers (NUT), and has grown in membership and influence at the expense of the NUT through an approach that combines political moderation with strong campaigning for teacher interests on issues such as work loads and pupil indiscipline and violence. It has no political affiliation.

24. NATFHE (National Association of Teachers in Further and Higher Education) – The University and College Lecturers Union

Address. 27 Britannia Street, London WCIX 9JP
Phone. +44 20 7837 3636
Fax. +44 20 7837 44403
E-mail. hq@natfhe.org.uk
Website. www.natfhe.org.uk
Leadership. Paul Mackney (general secretary)
Membership. 65,000
History and character. Formed by merger in 1976, this is the largest lecturers' union.

25. National Union of Journalists (NUJ)

Address. Acorn House, 314-320 Gray's Inn Road, London WCIX 8DP
Phone. +44 20 7278 7916
Fax. +44 20 7837 8143
E-mail. acorn.house@nuj.org.uk
Website. www.gn.apc.org/media/nuj/html
Leadership. John Foster (general secretary)
Membership. 19,436

26. National Union of Knitwear, Footwear and Apparel Trades (KFAT)

Address. 55 New Walk, Leicester, LEI 7EB
Phone. +44 116 255 6703
Fax. + 44 116 254 4406
E-mail. head-office@kfat.org.uk
Website. www.poptel.org.uk/kfat
Leadership. Paul Gates (general president)
Membership. 20,000
History and character. Formed by a merger in 1991 between two 19th century footwear and clothing unions. It has suffered severely from the decline of the industries in which its members work. Affiliated to the Labour Party.
Publications. KFAT News

27. National Union of Marine, Aviation and Shipping Transport Officers (NUMAST)

Address. Oceanair House, 750–760 High Road, Leytonstone, London E11 3BB
Phone. +44 20 8989 6677

Fax. +44 20 8530 1015
E-mail. info@numast.org
Website. www.numast.org
Leadership. Brian Orrell (general secretary)
Membership. 18,759
History and character. Represents all officer ranks and cadets in the merchant navy and those in related shore-based employment. Numbers employed in the British merchant fleet have fallen with many more now employed under foreign flags, and NUMAST has been active in securing government initiatives to arrest this decline and support seafarer training. It is also involved in international initiatives to combat piracy. Affiliated to ETF and ITF.
Publications. *Numast Telegraph* (monthly newspaper)

28. National Union of Rail, Maritime and Transport Workers (RMT)
Address. Unity House, 205 Euston Road, London NW1 2BL
Phone. +44 20 7387 4771
Fax. +44 20 7387 4123
E-mail. info@rmt.org.uk
Website. www.rmt.org.uk
Leadership. Jimmy Knapp (general secretary)
Membership. 56,476
History and character. Formed in 1990 by merger of seamen's and rail unions, each dating from the late-19th century.

29. National Union of Teachers (NUT)
Address. Hamilton House, Mabledon Place, London WC1H 9BD
Phone. +44 20 7388 6191
Fax. +44 20 7387 8458
Website. www.teachers.org.uk
Leadership. Doug McAvoy (general secretary)
Membership. 194,259
History and character. Founded in 1870, affiliated to TUC in 1970. Represents all teachers, although strongest in primary schools. Traditionally the most militant of the teaching unions and previously lost members to less militant rivals AMMA (now ATL) and NASUWT, both of which are stronger in secondary schools. The NUT is currently actively opposing government plans to link teachers' pay to pupils' test results. Affiliated to EI.
Publications. *The Teacher* magazine; *Education Review* (accessible at website)

30. Nationwide Group Staff Union (NGSU)
Address. Middleton Farmhouse, 37 Main Road, Middleton, Cheney, Banbury, OX17 2QT
Phone. +44 1295 710767
Fax. +44 1295 712580
Website. www.ngsu.co.uk
Leadership. Tim Poli (general secretary)
Membership. 10,000

31. Prison Officers' Association (POA)
Address. Cronin House, 245 Church Street, Edmonton, London N9 9HW
Phone. +44 20 8803 0255
Fax. +44 20 8803 1761
Leadership. David Evans (general secretary)
Membership. 29,563
History and character. Founded 1919. Absorbed the Scottish Prison Officers' Association in Apr. 2000.

32. Public and Commercial Services Union (PCS)
Address. 160 Falcon Road, London SW11 2LN

Phone. +44 20 7924 2727
Fax. +44 20 7924 1847
Website. www.pcs.org.uk
Leadership. Barry Reamsbottom, John Sheldon (joint general secretaries)
Membership. 260,000
History and character. PCS is the result of mergers of civil service unions and has members mainly in government departments and agencies and other public bodies, but also includes members in private sector IT and other service companies. It represents mainly lower and middle-level staff, and two-thirds of members are women.

33. Society of Radiographers (SoR),
Address. 207 Providence Square, Mill Street, London SE1 2EW
Phone. +44 20 7740 7200
Fax. +44 20 7740 7204
Leadership. Stephen Evans (general secretary)
Membership. 13,725

34. Transport and General Workers' Union (TGWU)
Address. 128 Theobald's Road, Holborn, London WC1X 8TN
Phone. +44 20 7611 2500
Fax. +44 20 7611 2555
E-mail. tgwu@tgwu.org
Website. www.tgwu.org.uk
Leadership. Bill Morris (general secretary)
Membership. 871,512
History and character. Founded 1922 by merger of three large late-19th century dock, transport and general unions; represents employees in almost every sector and at every level, although predominantly manual workers in manufacturing and public services, transport, construction and agriculture. Historically the TGWU ('T&G') has been the single most influential and important union in the British labour movement, but it lost its long-standing position as Britain's largest union when the public sector super-union UNISON was created in 1993. The TGWU lost membership heavily from the early 1980s, and a large financial deficit forced it to shut some 60 offices and merge regional organizations in the early 1990s. However, at end-decade income and expenditure were in balance. The T&G, like other British unions, is run on the basis of membership dues, without subventions from the state or other sources.

The TGWU has four industrial sectors, each headed by a national organizer. (1) *Food and agriculture* includes food retailing and distribution. (2) *Manufacturing* includes vehicle building and automotive trades, power, engineering, textiles, chemicals, oil and rubber. (3) *Services* covers 300,000 workers in public services, such as refuse collectors, librarians and leisure attendants, as well as construction and other sectors. (4) *Transport* covers 200,000 members on buses, in the freight industry, the docks and water transport. There is a strong emphasis on workplace shop steward organization. There is also a sector for women, race and equality. The TGWU has a range of educational programmes for members, including a National Members' School.

The TGWU is affiliated to the Labour Party and traditionally had an important voice in party policy. The TGWU was the most reluctant major union to endorse the revision of Labour Party objectives in 1995. Bill Morris, the first black leader of a European union, gained re-election in 1995 after a hard-fought contest with national officer Jack Dromey.

The T&G has a predominantly (81%) male membership. In 1998 it introduced a rule change to reserve six seats on its gen-

eral executive council for women after attempts to increase women's representation on a voluntary basis failed.
Publication. T&G Record

35. Transport Salaried Staffs' Association (TSSA)

Address. Walkden House, 10 Melton Street, London NW1 2EJ
Phone. +44 20 7387 2101
Fax. +44 20 7383 0656
E-mail. enquiries@tssa.org
Website. www.tssa.org.uk
Leadership. Richard Rosser (general secretary)
Membership. 28,940

36. UNIFI

Address. Sheffield House, 1b Amity Grove, London SW20 0LG
Phone. +44 20 8879 4259
Fax. +44 20 8879 3728
E-mail. info@unifi.org.uk
Website. www.unifi.org.uk
Leadership. Ed Sweeney/Rory Murphy (joint general secretaries)
Membership. 190,000
History and character. Formed by the merger in May 1999 of three unions in the finance sector, the largest of which had been the Banking, Insurance and Finance Union (BIFU). The new organization intended to target company-based employee associations in the finance sector.
Publications. Fusion (accessible via website)

37. Union of Construction, Allied Trades and Technicians (UCATT)

Address. UCATT House, 177 Abbeville Road, London SW4 9RL
Phone. +44 20 7622 2442
Fax. +44 20 7720 4081
E-mail. info@ucatt.org.uk
Website. www.ucatt.org.uk
Leadership. George Brumwell (general secretary)
Membership. 111,804
History and character. Founded 1971 on merger of several craft building unions each dating from early-19th century. Represents all building workers but mainly semi-skilled and skilled. Affiliated to Labour Party.

38. Union of Shop, Distributive and Allied Workers (USDAW)

Address. Oakley, 188 Wilmslow Road, Fallowfield, Manchester M14 6LJ
Phone. +44 161 224 2804
Fax. +44 161 257 2566
E-mail. enquiries@usdaw.org.uk
Website. www.usdaw.org.uk
Leadership. Bill Connor (general secretary)
Membership. 303,060
History and character. Founded 1947 on merger of two early-20th century unions. Represents shop workers as well as having members in areas including food processing, laundries, catering, home shopping, insurance agents and milk rounds. 60% of members are women, with a high proportion of lower-paid, part-time and ethnic minority members. USDAW is a strong proponent of partnership agreements with employers and reports a growing membership. Affiliated to Labour Party.

39. UNISON

Address. 1 Mabledon Place, London WC1H 9AJ
Phone. +44 20 7388 2366
Fax. +44 20 7387 6692
E-mail. direct@unison.co.uk
Website. www.unison.org.uk
Leadership. Rodney Bickerstaffe (general secretary)
Membership. 1.2 million
History and character. This public sector super-union was formed out of the Confederation of Health Service Employees (COHSE), the National Union of Public Employees (NUPE) and the National Association of Local Government Officers (NALGO) in 1993. It is the largest TUC affiliate. Its members are both manual and white-collar workers. Half the membership is in local government, including schools, and UNISON has the largest education membership of any union. One-third is in health, making UNISON the largest health union, with the remainder mainly in the utilities (electricity, gas and water). It includes some private sector employees who work for contractors providing public services and utilities. About two-thirds of members are women, and 44 of the 67 seats on the National Executive Committee are reserved for women.

UNISON has 13 regions, each with its own delegate council, and six 'service groups', covering local government, health care, higher education, energy, water and transport. It also has 'self-organized groups', representing women, black members, disabled members and lesbians and gay men.

Uniquely, UNISON gives members the option of choosing whether to subscribe to its Affiliated Political Fund, which supports the Labour Party, or its General Political Fund, which is politically non-aligned.

It has opposed entry into the single European currency because of what it fears would be the impact on public spending and welfare provision of meeting convergence criteria. Internationally it is affiliated to PSI.
Publications. Focus newspaper; UNISON magazine

4 Other Trade Union Organizations

General Federation of Trade Unions (GFTU)

Address. Central House, Upper Woburn Place, London WC1H OHY
Phone. +44 20 7387 2578
Fax. +44 20 7383 0820
Website. www.gftu.org.uk
Leadership. Mike Bradley (general secretary)
Membership. 252,000 in 34 unions
History and character. The GFTU was founded at a special congress of the TUC in 1899. Its role today is to provide a service to specialized unions, for which it carries out research and provides education and training for union officials. Membership overlaps with that of the TUC. Its 23 full members are mainly (although not exclusively) small unions with only a few thousand members, and its associate members are mainly specialist sections within major unions such as the GMB, MSF and TGWU.
Publications. Federation News (quarterly); *Federation Journal* (quarterly); *Union Reps Briefing*

National Association of Head Teachers (NAHT)

Address. 1 Heath Square, Boltro Road, Haywards Heath, West Sussex, RH16 1BL

Phone. +44 1444 472 472

Fax. +44 1444 473 473

E-mail. info@naht.org.uk

Website. www.naht.org.uk

Leadership. David Hart (general secretary)

Membership. 30,000

History and character. Represents heads and deputies; emphasizes professionalism.

Professional Association of Teachers (PAT)

Address. 2 St. James' Court, Friar Gate, Derby, DEI 1BT

Phone. +44 1332 372 337

Fax. +44 1332 290 310

E-mail. hq@pat.org.uk

Website. www.pat.org.uk

Leadership. Kay Driver (general secretary)

Membership. 35,000

History and character. Founded in 1970, PAT has members in all parts of the UK from nursery schools to tertiary institutions, in both the maintained and independent sectors. It is strictly non-political and has a no-strike rule. In 1999 it established the PAT (Education and Learning) Charity.

Publications. Professionalism in Practice: the Pat Journal (quarterly); miscellaneous other materials.

Royal College of Nursing of the United Kingdom (RCN)

Address. 20 Cavendish Square, London W1M OAB

Phone. +44 20 7872 0840

Fax. +44 20 7355 1379

Leadership. Christine Hancock (general secretary)

Membership. 310,000

History and character. Founded in 1916; became a certified, independent trade union in 1977. Grew rapidly thereafter. In 1995 it voted to drop its 'no strike' rule. It provides professional, labour relations and higher educational services for its members.

Scottish Trades Union Congress (STUC)

Address. 16 Woodlands Terrace, Glasgow G3 6DF

Phone. +44 141 332 4946

Fax. +44 141 332 4649

Leadership. Campbell Christie (general secretary)

Membership. 700,000 in 44 affiliated unions

History and character. The STUC is an independent centre, founded in 1897, separate from but having reciprocal arrangements with the British TUC. It serves to provide a representative voice for the trade union movement at the Scottish level. Most of its affiliates are also affiliated to the British TUC. It traditionally stands on the left of the labour movement. It was active in the movement to establish a Scottish Parliament, which opened in 1999.

United Road Transport Union (URTU)

Address. 76 High Lane, Chorlton-cum-Hardy, Manchester M21 9EF

Phone. +44 161 882 2706

Fax. +44 161 862 9127

E-mail. info@urtu.com

Website. www.urtu.com

Leadership. David Higginbottom (general secretary)

Membership. 17,000

History and character. An independent union that represents road haulage drivers and offers various specialist services including a 24-hour call centre and distance learning for lorry drivers.

United Kingdom Dependency

Bermuda

Capital: Hamilton
Population: 63,000 (2000 est.)

1 Political and Economic Background

Bermuda is a British dependency with a system of internal self-government introduced in 1968. It rejected independence in a referendum in 1995. The two major political parties are the multi-racial United Bermuda Party and the predominantly black Progressive Labour Party (PLP). Following elections in Nov. 1998 the government has been formed by the PLP.

Bermuda has a high standard of living based on financial services and tourism. There is little agriculture and only a small manufacturing sector.

GDP (purchasing power parity) $2bn. (1999 est.); GDP per capita (purchasing power parity) $31,500 (1999 est.).

2 Trade Unionism

Unions have existed since World War II. The principal unions are the Bermuda Industrial Union, traditionally the largest on the island, and the Bermuda Public Services Association.

Bermuda Industrial Union (BIU)
Address. 49 Union Square, Hamilton HM 123
Phone. + 1441 292 0044

Fax. +1441 295 7992

E-mail. biu@ibl.bm

Leadership. Molly Burgess (general secretary)

History and character. The BIU was founded in 1946. It is a general union and has collective agreements in both the private and public sectors. It generally supports the PLP and expects it to support the union on all social legislation and other political issues. It supported independence in the 1995 referendum in which the majority of the electorate voted to remain a British dependency.

International affiliation. ICFTU; CTUC

Bermuda Public Services Association (BPSA)
Address. PO Box HM 763, Hamilton HMCX

Phone. +1441 292 6985

Fax. +1441 292 1149

E-mail. beepsa@ibl.bm

Leadership. Betty I. Christopher (president); Edward G. Ball Jr. (general secretary)

History and character. Originated in 1952 as the Bermuda Civil Service Association, adopting the present name in 1971. It is affiliated to the Union Network International (UNI) and Public Services International (PSI) trade secretariats.

Publication. Feedback (newsletter)

International affiliation. CTUC

United States of America

Capital: Washington DC
Population: 275.56 m. (2000 est.)

1 Political and Economic Background

Following 12 years of Republican Presidents (Ronald Reagan, 1981–89; George Bush, 1989–1993) the Democrat Bill Clinton took office in 1993 and was re-elected for a second four-year term in 1996. The Nov. 2000 presidential election resulted in unprecedented controversy with Republican George W. Bush ultimately emerging as the winner through vote of the Electoral College, although he had gained a lesser share of the popular vote than the Democratic candidate, Vice-President Al Gore. The closeness of the result was also reflected in Congress where the two parties were left evenly balanced in both Houses, the Senate being tied with 50 seats each. Considerable powers are devolved to the 50 states, where there is a mixed pattern of control.

The USA's market-based economy is the largest in the world and in most innovation-based sectors it has a clear and in some cases increasing lead over competitor nations. Services now generate 80% of GDP. After a shallow recession in the early 1990s the USA has enjoyed sustained growth led by investment in technology, with buoyant stock markets, low inflation, falling government debt, and large-scale creation of new jobs. Since 1995 growth has averaged 4% per annum. The economy is characterized by a high level of flexibility, low taxes and light regulation, and an emphasis on risk-taking and innovation. New business start-ups run at a far higher level than in Europe. Falling unemployment (reaching a 30-year low of 3.9% by Oct. 2000) has been reflected since 1995 in a slight increase in the proportion of regular full-time jobs, previously in decline, from 73.6% in 1995 to 75.1% in 1999. Despite a tight labour market there has been no inflationary pressure from wage increases. Most of the gains in household income in the last quarter century have gone to the top 20% of households. There is also a distinct underclass of under-qualified people in low-wage jobs or without jobs, many of them from minorities, who lack many of the social safety nets common in Western Europe. However, after 15 years of stagnation and decline inflation-adjusted wages have begun to rise since 1995. The USA is a member of the NAFTA free trade area with Mexico and Canada, and 35% of its export and 29% of its import trade is with those two countries.

GDP (purchasing power parity) $9.255 trillion (1999 est.); GDP per capita (purchasing power parity) $33,900 (1999 est.).

2 Trade Unionism

Trade unions which organized on a national scale developed in the middle decades of the nineteenth century, and the American Federation of Labor-Congress of Industrial Organizations (AFL-CIO), today the sole union centre, has a continuous history dating back (through the AFL) to the early 1880s. The strength of trade unionism was consolidated under the New Deal of the 1930s, especially through the National Labor Relations Act (NLRA), or Wagner Act, of 1935. This Act affirmed the right to organize and engage in collective bargaining, prohibited "unfair labour practices", and established the National Labor Relations Board (NLRB) to supervise and protect trade union activities and conduct representation ballots. The NLRA proved an influential factor in assisting the rapid development in the late 1930s of what became the Congress of Industrial Organizations (CIO), which unlike the craft-based AFL, organized on the industrial union principle. The unions further strengthened their position in the boom economy of World War II and although they faced some reverses in the Cold War period, notably the Taft-Hartley Act of 1947, they retained most of the gains made in the 1930s. In 1955 the AFL and CIO united to form the AFL-CIO, and this represents today more than 13 million of the 16 million union members.

The position of trade unions under federal labour legislation has changed little for several decades, although the rights of individuals in the workplace have been greatly affected by a sequence of laws on equality and discrimination. The states have had little role in shaping private sector labour relations and the courts have generally struck down efforts by states to legislate in this area. The 1935 NLRA defined the basic process for union recognition that still applies today. Once a union has achieved a significant level of workplace support (signed union cards), which in practice usually means a substantial majority, it may (assuming the employer denies recognition, which is usual) ask the National Labor Relations Board (NLRB) to conduct a certification election. If the union then wins 50% of the vote the employer must recognize it for collective bargaining purposes. No further election may be held for a year. The Act also prohibits employers from setting up company unions or favouring one union at the expense of another and defines illegal "unfair labour practices".

The 1947 Labor Management Relations Act (LMRA, or Taft-Hartley Act) put some limitations on union rights under the NLRA. It authorized "employer free speech" to campaign against union representation and defined unfair labour practices by unions. It weakened the right to strike by prohibiting secondary actions against employers or others not directly involved in a dispute. It also enabled individual states to enact "right-to-work" laws, prohibiting the use of agency shops (in which non-union employees are required to pay, as a condition of employment, agency fees to the union for its role as bargaining agent). In other states agency shops remain common, although the Supreme Court held in 1988 that fee payers could not be forced to pay for services other than those related directly to the union's role as bargaining agent. Taft-Hartley also set up the Federal Mediation and Conciliation Service (FMCS) to assist in conflict resolution, and most states also have set up mediation and conciliation offices.

The Labor Management Reporting and Disclosure Act (LMRDA, Landrum-Griffin Act) of 1959 enhanced the rights of individual union members by requiring democratic elections of union officers, free from intimidation and fraud, and transparency in union finances and collective agreements. The Act required unions to file annual detailed reports on their financing with the Department of Labor. Unions complain that this latter provision is onerous and costly, although it is also a measure against racketeering.

These three statutes, as interpreted through the courts and by rulings, underpin the position of unions in most of the private sector. However, 230,000 workers in the railroad industry and 590,000 in the airline industry are covered by the separate provisions of the Railway Labor Act (RLA) of 1926, which provided for collective bargaining and was aimed at providing mechanisms for resolving conflict without strike action. These highly unionized industries have their own National Mediation Board. Farm workers are excluded from the provisions of the NLRA and consequently from the right to collective bargaining (although this right is extended in some states, notably California, by state legislation). Ironically, it was the exemption of farm workers from federal labour law that allowed Cesar Chavez's United Farm Workers (UFW) so effectively to mount secondary boycotts of supermarkets selling non-union grapes in the 1960s and 1970s. The UFW is a small, mainly California union, however, and overall, farm workers have the lowest union density of any important sector. Managerial staff have commonly been excluded from union rights and this has become a significant issue with changes in the composition of the workforce. In the public sector trade union rights to represent workers are more circumscribed. Federal employees were only extended the right to join unions in 1962. The position at state level varies. However, much of the public sector is highly organized.

Trade unions were at their peak strength in the two decades after passage of the NLRA, a period which included the rise of industrial unionism and boom conditions and labour scarcity arising from World War II. Union density hit a peak of 35% in 1945–46, and again in 1954, since when it has declined continuously. Only in the 1990s did the decline in density begun to slow, but density at the end of the century was back at the levels of the mid-1930s, before the NLRA and the creation of the CIO.

Total union membership, while lagging behind the growth in the workforce, continued to increase to the late 1970s, rising from 17 million in 1954 to 20.2 million by 1978. It then fell quickly during the early 1980s recession, to 17.7 million by 1983, and thereafter declined more slowly. In 1998, however, union membership increased by 100,000 and in 1999 there was a net gain of 265,000 (the biggest annual increase in 20 years), taking total membership to 16.48 million. Private sector union membership increased by 112,000 in 1999, only the second increase in 20 years. Despite these encouraging trends for the unions, the main driver of expanded union rolls has been the huge increase in number of jobs as the economy has expanded unrelentingly, and density has continued to decline.

There has been a strikingly different experience in the public and private sectors over the last two decades. Union density in government employment has risen steadily and by 1999 stood at 37%. In contrast, non-farm private sector density has slumped from 17% to only 9.5% in the period 1983–99 (density in agriculture is even lower, at 2.5%). The result is that, although the US has overwhelmingly a private sector workforce, 43% of union members (7.1 million) are now in the public sector. Even in traditional private sector union strongholds, such as construction (19.1%), transportation (25.5%) and manufacturing (15.6%), density is well below that in the public sector, and wide swathes of private sector services are non-union. In finance, insurance and real estate (highly organized areas in some European countries) density is only 2%, a similar figure to agriculture where there are no NLRA protections, while density is only 5% in retail trades. The changes in the composition of union membership are also reflected in the gender balance: blue-collar trade unionism was heavily male-dominated, but with the shift to white-collar and public service employment women now make up 40% of union membership. Women trade unionists increased from 5.9 million in 1983 to 6.5 million by 1999.

There is also a pronounced geographical variation in density. Average union density is 7.9% in the "right-to-work" states compared with 16.1% in what the unions call the "free" states, with a national average of 13.9%. Although the basic federally-guaranteed right to organize and bargain collectively applies in all the states, union organizers tend to face a more hostile political and judicial climate in the right-to-work states: all those states are in the South and West and have predominantly conservative Republican politics. The largest of the right-to-work states, Texas, has a density of only 6.0%. The map of union density correlates closely with the pattern of voting in presidential elections, the low-density states having mainly backed George W. Bush in the 2000 elections and the high-density states having backed Al Gore. Two upper Midwestern states with a special tradition of progressive politics, Minnesota and Wisconsin, have high densities, of 19.2% and 18.1% respectively. High-density states are mainly urban and industrial states like Michigan (21.5%), New Jersey (20.7%), and New York (25.3%), with a high proportion of traditional manufacturing jobs. In the South and West "sunrise" industries are mostly non-union, and agriculture, the sector with the lowest density of all, is also much more significant. Exceptions exist for specific local reasons: high density in Nevada (19.6%), for example, reflects the strong position of the unions in Las Vegas construction work and in the leisure industry.

Structural changes in the economy have undoubtedly been the main driver of falling union density, and in this respect the US mirrors the record of many other industrialized countries. In addition to the fundamental shift to a private sector service economy, there has been a long-term (though at the end of the 1990s reversed) increase in part-time and non-standard working. Employees in such arrangements are significantly less likely than are full-time permanent employees to belong to unions. At the same time, the unions' problems have been exacerbated, especially since the end of the 1970s, by the implacable hostility of many employers to unionization efforts. Whereas in many (Western) industrialized countries employers, and particularly major employers, have to a greater or lesser degree accepted the role of unions as negotiating partners, there is no such consensus in the United States. This is reflected in an ambivalence in the US, the NLRA notwithstanding, concerning basic trade union rights. The United States has, for example, ratified neither ILO Convention No. 87 (Freedom of Association and Protection of the Right to Organize, 1948) nor Convention No.98 (Right to Organize and Collective Bargaining, 1949), which have been ratified by every member state of the European Union. The 1999 ICFTU survey of labour violations accused the US of "massive, ongoing and appalling labour rights violations". In the absence of a collective contract, many workers have few protections in areas such as dismissal, so that conceding union recognition is seen by many employers as likely to lead to significant restrictions on their freedom to act.

In an atmosphere where many employers are overtly hostile, winning union recognition is itself difficult, despite the protective framework established by the NLRB. Trade unions can secure representation rights by winning the support of a majority of the workforce in a ballot. However, hostile employers can and do interfere in this process and "union-busting" is a highly professional industry with its own consultants, private detectives and security firms deployed to undermine union organizers. According to the unions, one in three employers facing organizing campaigns dismisses union activists; nine out of ten employers require workers to attend meetings where they receive anti-union propaganda; half threaten to shut down operations if a union is formed; and 80% hire union-busting consultants. Whereas in Europe, supervisory staff are often themselves union members, in the US four in five employers require supervisors to attend union-busting training sessions and seek to persuade workers not to join. In 1994 a Commission on the Future of Worker-Management Relations concluded that "the United States is the only major democratic country in which the choice ... to be

represented by a union is subject to such a confrontational process".

The unions charge that NLRB procedures to protect union organizers from discrimination are ineffective; it takes the NLRB an average of 557 days to resolve a case and there is backlog of 25,000 cases. Even where reinstatement is ordered, only a minority of workers ever return on a permanent basis. Challenges and litigation are also used to delay or prevent implementation of ballots where the union has won. The NLRB cannot itself enforce its decisions and must resort to the courts, and as many employers believe the courts to be less sympathetic to the unions than is the NLRB they commonly ignore NLRB rulings and let matters go into the legal system. In this way recognition may be bogged down for years. As the only sanction against employers for ignoring NLRB rulings is to have the ruling enforced (there is no other penalty) there is little incentive for employers to concede defeat prematurely. Even in cases where unions win recognition (which occurs in about half of cases), determined employers may work hard to bring about de-certification, or fail to negotiate in good faith (so-called "surface bargaining"). In one-third of cases where the union has won a representation election, they have been unable to secure a collective agreement, even though that is the fundamental right secured under the NLRA election process. Furthermore, in a quarter of cases where unions have won a first collective agreement, they have been unable to secure a second agreement. While the law says that the parties must negotiate in good faith, it does not compel them to reach agreement.

As union density declined, and the unions concentrated on defending their core areas, the number of representation elections fell from an average 7,000 per year in the 1960s and 1970s to 3,800 per year by the 1990s. In addition by the 1980s, de-certification elections (to expel a union from the workplace), occurred with increasing frequency as did termination of workers trying to organize a union. Union members were also more likely to cross picket lines. Against this background employers proved more resistant to union demands. The unions also claimed that appointments to the NLRB and the courts under successive Republican presidents had led to anti-union bias.

The NLRA does not apply to public employees, of whom there are some 19.4 million. Some 2 million federal employees fall under the 1978 Federal Labor Relations Act, which prevents meaningful collective bargaining and bans strikes. Only postal workers have bargaining rights at the national level. For federal employees the principal weapon is direct lobbying of Congress. There are considerable variations at the state level. Nearly half of the 14.9 million state and local government employees may not bargain collectively and 14 states do not allow collective bargaining at all for public employees. In the private sector collective agreements are typically negotiated at the local level, with the national level unions providing coordination, research, support, and legislative activity. Few unions bargain on an industry-wide basis; only rarely do several combine to coordinate their bargaining proposals while nonetheless concluding separate agreements. It is more common for negotiations to be de-centralized, covering a single plant, corporation or area. Most unions' constitutions require approval of agreements by ballot of the members before they can be ratified. Other than for the conciliation services provided by the FMCS and in case of declared emergencies there is no government intervention.

In the private sector (other than in areas covered by the RLA) there are few legal restrictions on strikes, which are seen as essentially a private matter between employers and workers. No vote is required to authorize a strike (although in practice most unions do ballot their members to ensure they have support). The main restrictions are the Taft-Hartley ban on secondary action and the right of the federal government under the LMRA to seek an injunction where a strike threatens a national emergency. This latter provision has been used at different times in respect of disputes in the steel, coal, atomic energy, maritime transport and telecommunications industries. At the same time, there are few protections for strikers. The US Supreme Court has ruled that employers may permanently replace workers engaged in an economic strike, and there is only protection for strikers where a strike is the result of an unfair labour practice. Unions commonly allege that individual strikes are the result of unfair labour practices. However, this can be a hazardous course because if its members are dismissed and replaced and the courts subsequently (and often long after the strike) decide that the strike was not in response to an unfair labour practice, the dismissed employees have no retrospective protection. These are not theoretical concerns as from the 1980s employers increasingly employed non-union strikebreakers to defeat unions in disputes, reviving a once-common tactic little seen in the post-World War II period. Disputes may be settled with only a proportion of the strikers being taken back, to work alongside replacements who had broken the strike. As in other labour relations matters, the individual states have not had an important role in shaping the right to strike as federal law has taken precedence. In 1992 Wisconsin enacted legislation prohibiting the permanent replacement of strikers, but this was struck down in the federal courts. However, state and local administrations and state courts do exert an influence because they have powers in areas such as controlling pickets: both employers and unions complain of bias depending on the political flavour of the local administration and courts.

While individual strikes can be protracted and bitter, overall the US has a low rate of industrial action. Most bargaining results in agreement without conflict, sometimes through use of the Federal Mediation and Conciliation Service (FMCS). Most collective agreements (which typically have a 3–4 year life span) also have a provision in which the union agrees that there will be no strikes for the duration of the agreement. Disputes during that time are normally referred to an independent arbitrator. There is no government arbitration service and arbitrators are private individuals, with lists of qualified personnel maintained by the FMCS and the American Arbitration Association (AAA).

Unions have long had a somewhat mixed image in public perception. The tradition of business unionism has tended to be one in which broader social issues have had little consideration, while the interests of members have been pursued with single-minded determination. Unlike in many Western European countries, where tripartism is highly developed, the unions have not benefited from a perceived role in social and economic development and in building national consensus. The lack of a labour party has not allowed the unions to participate nationally in the process of government and in so doing consolidate a position as a core component of society. The image of unions in the period from the 1940s was also shaped to a considerable degree by the history of racketeering and intimidation that affected some unions and locals in blue-collar industries such as transport, construction and sanitation and by the unions' involvement in picket-line violence. Symptomatically, the best-known union leader in the US in modern times was Jimmy Hoffa, the Teamsters' leader (and father of the current IBT president) who disappeared, presumed murdered, in the 1970s and was linked to organized crime. In recent years, however, many unions have put emphasis on improving and softening their public image. To some degree this has been driven by the changing nature of the labour movement itself. As in European countries, trade union membership is increasingly female (women now making up 40% of union membership) and white-collar (density in the areas covered by the AFL-CIO professional employees' department has increased since the department was created in 1977). A related factor is that membership is also increasingly concentrated in the public sector, where industrial relations are without the history of strikebreaking, intimidation, and use of security guards that have scarred some private sector areas. The AFL-CIO now seeks to portray unions as active communitybuilders that are good for the whole community not just their own members, and encourages local unions to work closely with other civic groups. The unions' agenda has broadened to embrace broad social issues, such as Medicare, social security (pensions), education and child care, which are meaningful to broad sections of the population that are resistant to the conflictual, workplace-based culture of traditional unionism.

Historically the major US political parties have been coalitions, and in the early part of the twentieth century the progressive wing of the Republican Party was the most significant ally of labour. Since the 1930s New Deal, however, the Democrats have come to be seen as the more pro-labour party, with the Republicans identified as a conservative business party. In many Western European countries the unions and the social democratic parties have an organic unity born of common origins and shared values. There is not this depth of relationship between the unions and the Democrats. The AFL-CIO is officially non-partisan and candidates for office tend to be supported on an individual basis. Nonetheless at national level the weight of union support is for the Democratic Party. While Bill Clinton was not seen as a particularly pro-labour nominee for president, he enjoyed the support of the unions once nominated. On taking office Clinton made various pro-union gestures, including withdrawing an order that federal contractors must post notices informing all non-union members that they did not have to join unions and had the right to stop unions collecting money in lieu of union dues for political purposes. He appointed a chairman of the NLRB, Bill Gould, who was criticized by business as pro-union and whose ratification by the Senate took seven months. However, legislation to end the hiring of permanent replacements for strikers was filibustered in the Senate in July 1994 and in Nov. 1994 the Republicans won control of both Houses of Congress.

The US has itself ratified only one (the Abolition of Forced Labour Convention, No.105, in 1991) of the seven so-called core labour standards of the ILO. In 1995, US Labour Secretary Robert Reich described the failure to ratify ILO Conventions No.87 and No.98 as "a source of shame". However, during the Clinton presidency the US sought to some degree to exert a reforming influence on the labour practices of some other countries through denial of tariff concessions under the Generalized System of Preferences.

The unions feared the extension of the North American Free Trade Agreement (NAFTA) to Mexico would lead to loss of US jobs as employers relocated lower-wage plants south of the border. However, President Clinton pushed ahead with the treaty, criticizing the use of "strong-arm" tactics by the unions to try to persuade members of Congress to vote against it. As adopted, the treaty includes a side agreement on workers' rights called the North American Agreement on Labour Co-operation (NAALC). Under the NAALC labour offices are established in each member country, and have the responsibility of receiving and reporting on breaches of employment law. Compliance is not mandatory, however, except in the case of non-observance of the minimum wage, child labour or health and safety law. The unions tested the NAALC when the AFL-CIO filed complaints against General Electric, Honeywell, and Sony for violating the employment rights of Mexican workers; in each case the charge was that the company had disciplined employees for union membership. However, the findings in these cases did not lead to reinstatement of the workers concerned. At the same time the booming state of the US economy has tended to minimize union anxieties about the impact of NAFTA.

3 Trade Union Centre

American Federation of Labor -Congress of Industrial Organizations (AFL-CIO)

Address. 815 16th Street, NW, Washington, DC 20006

Phone. +1 202 637 5000

Fax. +1 202 637 5058

E-mail. feedback@aflcio.org

Website. www.aflcio.org

Leadership. John J. Sweeney (president); Richard Trumka (secretary-treasurer); Linda Chavez-Thompson (executive vice-president)

Membership. 13 million

History and character. The origins of the AFL-CIO lie in the formation of the Federation of Organized Trades and Labor Unions of the United States and Canada in 1881: five years later the American Federation of Labor was born. It grew by emphasizing craft-based organization and trade unionism directed towards immediate bargaining over wages and conditions rather than broader political and social objectives. In the mid-1930s, however, under the impact of the Great Depression and the favourable political climate of the New Deal, some AFL unions sought to organize in the mass-production industries on the industrial union principle, forming the Committee for Industrial Organization within the AFL and becoming involved in many strikes. This led to the creation of the separate Congress of Industrial Organizations (CIO) in 1938. The two streams of the trade union movement were re-united in 1955, at the high tide of the organized labour movement. There is no other trade union centre and AFL-CIO affiliates represent about 80% of the unionized workforce.

The AFL-CIO seeks to coordinate the activities of its affiliates, and to represent the union movement to government. It also settles jurisdictional disputes between its affiliates. The AFL-CIO is a loose federation with no power to instruct its affiliates. Policy is made by the biennial convention, which last met in 1999, and the AFL-CIO executive council (comprising the president, secretary-treasurer, executive vice-president and 51 vice-presidents) is elected by the convention every four years. The executive council guides the day-to-day work of the federation. In addition there is a general board, which deals with matters referred to it by the executive council, and this comprises the executive council members, a chief officer from each affiliate and the AFL-CIO trade and industrial departments, and four regional representatives of the state federations. There are AFL-CIO state federations in each of the 50 states and in Puerto Rico, and 590 central labour councils chartered by the AFL-CIO at community level.

Many of the affiliated unions belong to one or more of the AFL-CIO's seven trade and industrial departments, which group them together around specific areas of interest. These departments are: building and construction trades; food and allied services trades; maritime trades; metal trades; professional employees; transportation trades; and the union label and service trades department, which seeks to promote consumer interest in union-made products and union services and discourage purchases of products on the AFL-CIO boycott list. The departments have their own executive bodies and hold their own conventions.

The AFL-CIO's day-to-day work is carried on

through 13 programme departments. *Organizing,* supports the affiliates in membership drives and also runs the Organizing Institute to train activists. *Field mobilization,* coordinates the state federations and the central labour councils. *Corporate affairs,* carries out and disseminates research in areas such as collective bargaining and best practice. *Legislative,* promotes the federation's "Working Families Agenda" in Washington. *Political,* includes non-partisan voter registration and provision of information on political candidates' positions. *Public policy,* provides analysis in the areas of social, economic and trade policy. *Education,* promotes labour education and maintains academic links. *Public affairs,* is responsible for a range of publications and also carries out public opinion research. *Civil and human rights,* works to ensure full participation in the union movement and economic life of minorities. *Working women,* campaigns on issues such as pay equality and affordable child care. *International affairs,* includes the Solidarity Center, supporting independent unions around the world. *Safety and health,* works with affiliates on health and safety issues. *General counsel,* whose work includes assisting in the internal dispute resolution procedure for jurisdictional conflicts between affiliates.

"Constituency groups" include the A. Philip Randolph Institute, the Asian Pacific American Labor Alliance, the Coalition of Black Trade Unionists, the Coalition of Labor Union Women, and the Labor Council for Latin American Advancement. The AFL-CIO Working for America Institute works in partnership with employers, government and community groups to foster training, education and job creation.

During the 1980s, under Lane Kirkland, substantial efforts were made to reintegrate unions beneath the AFL-CIO umbrella. At the 1987 biennial convention the decision was taken to readmit the Teamsters to membership (despite some evidence of misgivings arising from the Teamsters' long history of racketeering). Apart from the Teamsters (America's biggest union), other unions rejoining the AFL-CIO in the 1980s included the United Auto Workers (UAW), United Transportation Union, Brotherhood of Locomotive Engineers, the International Longshoremen's and Warehousemen's Union, the Writers' Guild of America-East, and the Union of Mine Workers.

These successes in consolidating the union movement were, however, overshadowed by the unrelenting deterioration in the unions' position overall. The Reagan (1981–89) and Bush (1989–1993) presidencies saw the unions on the defensive politically and rapid structural changes in the economy eroding their strength. Total trade union membership fell from over 20 million at the end of the 1970s to below 16.7 million in 1994, despite a great increase in the workforce. The AFL-CIO reported a loss of 634,000 members between the 1991 and 1993 conventions and the number of workers voting in NLRB certification elections in 1994 was down to only one-quarter of the level of 25 years earlier. The union movement was losing influence not just in the workplace but also politically and the decline was

reflected in increasing dissatisfaction with the style of leadership. For four decades from its foundation as a unified movement in 1955, the AFL-CIO had had only two presidents, the founding president George Meany being succeeded by Lane Kirkland in 1979. By the mid-1990s criticism of the national leadership had built up and intensified after a Republican landslide in congressional elections in Nov. 1994 that resulted in Republican majorities in both House and Senate. Discontent focused on declining density, down to levels not seen since the 1930s, and the unrepresentative character of an executive council that contained only two blacks and three women. It culminated in a May 1995 announcement by secretary-treasurer Thomas R. Donahue that he would resign, a move which seemed at first to open the way to a direct challenge to president Kirkland, who had declared his intention to seek a ninth term. However, Donahue's announcement precipitated a statement by Kirkland that he himself would retire in August and endorse Donahue as his successor. Donahue was appointed president by the executive council in Aug. 1995 but then faced a challenge from a reform slate headed by John J. Sweeney, the president of the Service Employees' International Union (SEIU).

The SEIU had greatly increased its membership under Sweeney, and he urged a new focus on grass-roots organization, charging that the AFL-CIO had become a "Washington-based institution instead of a worker-based movement". Organized labour was, Sweeney said, "the only voice of American workers and their families and the silence is deafening". Sweeney was elected AFL-CIO president at the Oct. 1995 convention, bringing with him Mine Workers' president Richard Trumka as secretary-treasurer, while Linda Chavez-Thompson, vice-president of the AFSCME, filled the new post of executive vice-president.

Donahue warned in 1995 that militancy would not appeal to the great mass of working people and that the Sweeney programme would "marginalize us and consign us to the fringes of society for generations to come". However, under Sweeney the emphasis has been less on "militancy" than on intensive work to recruit new union members and build the role of unions in their communities (such as through the "Union Cities" programme). The objective has been to emphasize through campaigning in the workplace and on the streets and in community meeting places that union jobs are better paid, more secure, and contribute more to building strong communities. The AFL-CIO argues that 98% of collective bargaining agreements are reached without conflict. It says that union workers have higher productivity and are more likely to be loyal to their employer, 48% of unionized workers having been with the same employer for more than ten years, compared with 22% of non-union workers. In Aug. 1999 the executive council unveiled plans to build a "new alliance" to energize the unions at the local level, on the grounds that "the political, legislative and organizational battlegrounds are sited increasingly at the state and local level". This would involve creating a new tier of area federations in those urban areas with sufficient critical mass to support full-time organizers. Smaller communities would continue to be represented through labour councils but their role and that of the state federations of labour would be revitalized, with the cooperation of the national unions.

Since 1995 AFL-CIO membership has stabilized at a little over 13 million, and the century ended positively. In 1999 total union membership rose 265,000 and a number of unions recorded their most successful years in recent history: the UAW and IBEW recorded 50,000 new members each and the SEIU gained 150,000 members. A renewed confidence and buoyancy was evident among union leaders and Sweeney said that the increases showed "our renewed emphasis on helping working people form unions is having an impact". Reflecting this confidence, in Aug. 2000 the executive council adopted an ambitious target of adding new members at the rate of one million per annum. At the same time, the union movement has not yet found solutions for the erosion in union density that has gone on since the mid-1950s or for how to organize private sector services where most jobs are now created. Indeed, the executive council concluded in May 1999 that although unorganized areas remained the prize long-term, in the short term resources would have to be focused on major industries that already had relatively high density and on the unions' traditional power base in rust-belt states where their political strength was under immediate attack. Many employers are determined not to surrender unilateral management control of their businesses and concepts of "partnership" with employers, with which the unions have sought to consolidate their position in European countries with problems of declining density, are difficult to realize in the United States.

In 1985 an AFL-CIO report urged consolidation of member unions, 50 of the then 96 affiliates having fewer than 50,000 members. To some degree, this process has occurred and is continuing and there are now only 68 affiliates. However, the US, like Britain has a strong tradition of craft unionism, and there remain many relatively small unions serving discrete occupational communities. For members of such organizations the benefits of representation specifically focused on their particular needs may well seem to outweigh the benefits of absorption into large unions with theoretically more muscle but in practice less interest in or understanding of niche areas. In addition, also like Britain and in contrast (for example) to Germany, demarcation lines between unions are often ill-defined. A notable example is the area of health care, which has been organized only in the last two to three decades. Numerous unions, including many which in their core areas are totally unrelated to health care, now have a presence in this growing sector. The AFL-CIO has sought to police demarcation issues, and in 1999 the executive council ruled that unions should develop organizing strategies that focused on their core industries and occupations. Where individual unions wished to pursue a policy of diversification this had to be with a long-term strategy in view rather than organizing on an ad hoc basis.

The AFL-CIO has no political affiliation. It gives financial support to individual congressional candidates of both parties (reflecting the status of the parties as diverse coalitions), but mostly favours Democrats. In presidential elections it consistently supports the Democratic candidate. Following the election of Bill Clinton in 1992, many AFL-CIO key personnel as well as officers of affiliates found places in the transition team or in the incoming administration, although concrete measures to assist the unions were limited and frustrated by the Republican-dominated Congress. The AFL-CIO has in recent years emphasized voter registration drives to ensure that union members get out to vote. It reported that in the 1998 mid-term elections union households accounted for 17% of the population but 23% of those who went to the polls, and that 71% of union members who voted did so on behalf of union-backed candidates. It believed that (although the Republicans retained control of both Houses of Congress) this effort had reduced the "anti-worker majority" in the House of Representatives. The AFL-CIO has also promoted the idea of union members themselves running for office and in 1998 identified 626 candidates for state, local and national office as union members. It then set a goal of backing 2,000 union members for office in the year 2000. In the nomination process for the 2000 presidential election campaign there was evidence of some minority support in union ranks for John McCain, contender for the Republican nomination. However, the AFL-CIO announced its backing for Democratic candidate Al Gore from the outset, and George W. Bush, seen as no friend of labour, got the Republican nomination. The union movement made considerable efforts to bring out the vote for Gore in the Nov. 2000 election, one of the factors reflected in the large pluralities for Gore in the more heavily unionized states, which resulted in him winning the popular vote nationally while losing the election.

The relationship between the AFL-CIO and the mainstream of Western trade unionism has at times been an uneasy one. The AFL and the CIO both participated in the formation of the ICFTU in 1949, but never fully accepted its heavily socialist and social democratic orientation, and the AFL-CIO withdrew in 1969. (The AFL-CIO remained a member of, and the dominant factor in, the ICFTU's regional organization for the Americas, ORIT, and individual affiliates remained within ICFTU-linked international trade secretariats). Only in 1981 did it return. The active role of the AFL-CIO in supporting anti-communist worker organizations, with US government funding, caused concern in some socialist European circles. In the 1990s, however, there has been a far greater convergence between European unions and the AFL-CIO. In part this reflects the end of the Cold War and the fading of left-wing sentiment in European unions; in that respect socialist-influenced unions in Europe and elsewhere have moved closer to the AFL-CIO. But it also reflects a new emphasis from the AFL-CIO under Sweeney. In international affairs the main concerns of the AFL-CIO today are in areas such as universal fair labour standards and the impact of globalization. It organized protests against the World Trade Organization (WTO) and its "heedless rush towards further trade liberalization" at the 1999 Seattle conference, calling for core labour standards to be built into WTO rules, and has a "Campaign for Global Fairness" to protest unfair labour practices. In this its positions are close to those of unions in other developed countries. The particular target of the US unions is China, and although that reflects the fact that China is the sole surviving significant country with a communist government, and seen as engaging in numerous abuses of labour and human rights, it relates mainly to China's position as a vast producer of cheap goods that the unions see as undermining US jobs and wages. US administration support for admitting China to the World Trade Organization has been strenuously attacked by the unions.

The **George Meany Center for Labor Studies** is an AFL-CIO attached national training college for trade union activists. It also hosts the George Meany Memorial Archives, preserving the records of the AFL-CIO, and George Meany Memorial Archives Library.

Address. 10000 New Hampshire Avenue, Silver Spring MD 20903

Phone. +1 301 431 6400

Fax. +1 301 434 0371

E-mail. info@georgemeany.org

Affiliates. There are 68 national affiliates. The following list excludes some smaller unions.

1. Associated Actors and Artists of America ("4 As")

The 4As is an umbrella for seven member unions. These include **(1) Actors' Equity** Association, AEA (www.actorsequity.org), 165 West 46th Street, 15th Floor, New York, NY 10036, phone +1 212 869 8530; (2) **American Federation of Television and Radio Artists, AFTRA** (www.aftra.org); and (3) **Screen Actors' Guild, SAG** (www.sag.org), 5757 Wilshire Blvd, Los Angeles, CA 90036–3600. Phone +1 323 954 1600.

2. Air Line Pilots Association, International (ALPA)

Address. 535 Herndon Parkway, Herndon, VA. 20170

Phone. +1 703 481 4440

Website. www.alpa.org

Leadership. Captain Duane E. Woerty (president)

Membership. Represents 55,000 pilots at 51 US and Canadian airlines

Publication. Air Line Pilot

3. Amalgamated Transit Union (ATU)

Address. 5025 Wisconsin Avenue, NW, Washington, DC 20016-4139

Phone. +1 202 537 1645

Fax. +1 202 244 7824

Website. www.atu.org

Leadership. Jim La Sala (international president); Warren S. George (international executive vice-president); Oliver W. Green (international secretary-treasurer)

Membership. 162,000 in 280 local unions in the US and Canada. The union represents bus, subway, light rail, and school bus workers.

Publication. Transit News

4. American Federation of Government Employees (AFGE)

Address. 80 F Street, NW, Washington, DC 20001

Phone. +1 202 737 8700

Website. www.afge.org

Leadership. Bobby L. Harnage (national president); Rita R. Mason (national secretary-treasurer)

Membership. 200,000 (active and retired)

History and character. AFGE is the largest union of federal employees. Collective bargaining is limited for federal employees and for this reason a particular emphasis is on political action and lobbying. Half of AFGE members are in agency-wide bargaining units.

Publications. Government Standard; *AFGE Bulletin*

5. American Federation of Musicians (AFM)

Address. Suite 600, 1501 Broadway, New York, NY 10036

Phone. +1 212 869 1330

Website. www.afm.org

Leadership. Steve Young (president); Thomas F. Lee (secretary-treasurer)

Membership. 110,000

6. American Federation of State, County and Municipal Employees (AFSCME)

Address. 1625 L Street, NW, Washington DC 20036-5687

Phone. +1 202 429 1000

Fax. +1 202 429 1293

E-mail. pubaffairs@afscme.org (public affairs department)

Website. www.afscme.org

Leadership. Gerald W. McEntee (international president); William Lucy (international secretary-treasurer)

Membership. 1.3 million

History and character. Founded in 1936, during the New Deal era that saw a major expansion of state and local public employment, the AFSCME has grown steadily to become one of the most powerful players in the US labour movement, with members in the public services and health care. It is the largest public sector AFL-CIO affiliate. AFSCME explains its rapid growth in the 1960s and 1970s as due in large measure to its reputation for fighting for equal treatment for minorities, a significant element of the workforce in the areas in which it organizes.

Current reported membership of 1.3 million compares with 1.2 million in the early 1990s and AFSCME continues to affiliate independent associations and to organize aggressively, claiming to win 90 per cent of representation elections. About 52% of the membership are women. AFSCME seeks a high media profile and has a staff of 30 in its public affairs department producing news releases, broadcasts, video and other communications. AFSCME was heavily committed to a Clinton-Gore victory in the 1992 presidential elections and seven of its officers joined the incoming president's transition team. Vice-President Gore told the 1994 AFSCME convention that the union's role in his and President Clinton's 1992 victory had been 'pivotal', while Labour Secretary Robert Reich called AFSCME 'the best grass-roots organization in the country'. It campaigned strongly for Al Gore in the 2000 presidential race, and both Clinton and Gore addressed the 2000 AFSCME convention. Politically a key focus for AFSCME is opposition to the privatization of public services, which it feared would accelerate with the election of George W. Bush.

Publications. These include *AFSCME Public Employee* (magazine to all members, 6 per year); *The Leader* (monthly newsletter to 31,000 AFSCME leaders). Publications content accessible via website.

7. American Federation of Teachers (AFT)

Address. 555 New Jersey Avenue, NW, Washington, DC 20001

Phone. +1 202 879 4400

E-mail. iad@aft.org (international affairs)

Website. www.aft.org

Leadership. Sandra Feldman (president)

Membership. 1.1 million. Members are teachers, schools support staff, higher education faculty and staff, health care professionals and state and municipal employees.

Publications. American Teacher; Inside AFT; Healthwire; On Campus, PSRP Reporter and others. Content can be accessed via website.

8. American Postal Workers' Union (APWU)

Address. 1300 L Street, NW, Washington, DC 20005

Phone. +1 202 842 4200

Website. www.apwu.org

Leadership. Moe Biller (president); William Burrus (executive vice-president); Robert Tunstall (secretary-treasurer)

Membership. 366,000 in 11,600 locals

History and character. The APWU represents employees of the US postal service who are clerks, maintenance employees, motor vehicle operators, and non-mail processing professional employees. It says it is the world's largest postal union. Postal workers first won the right to bargain collectively under the Postal Reorganization Act of 1970 and APWU was founded in 1971 with the merger of five postal unions. It is affiliated internationally to UNI.

Publications. APWU News Service Bulletins (content accessible via website)

9. Asbestos Workers, International Association of Heat and Frost Insulators and Asbestos Workers (AWIU)

Address. Suite 301, 1776 Massachusetts Avenue, NW, Washington DC 20036-1989

Phone. +1 202 785 2388

Fax. +1 202 429 0568

Website. www.insulators.org

Leadership. William G. Bernard (general president); James A. Grogan (general secretary-treasurer)

10. Association of Flight Attendants (AFA)

Address. 1275 K Street, NW, Suite 500, Washington DC 20005-4090

E-mail. afatalk@afanet.ore

Website. www.flightattendant-afa.org

Leadership. Patricia A. Friend (international president); George M. Donahue (international vice-president); Paul G. MacKinnon (international secretary-treasurer)

Membership. 47,000

History and character. AFA says it is the world's largest union of flight attendants and membership has grown from 36,000 in 1995. All its officers are themselves flight attendants and the union has a strong involvement with safety issues.

Publications. Flightlog (quarterly); *AFA Interactive* (e-mail newsletter)

11. Bakery, Confectionery, Tobacco Workers and Grain Millers' International Union (BCTGM)

Address. 10401 Connecticut Avenue, Kensington, Maryland 20895

Website. www.bctgm.org

Leadership. Frank Hurt (president); David B. Durkee (secretary-treasurer)

Membership. 120,000 in US and Canada

History and character. Formed Jan. 1999 by merger of the Bakery, Confectionery and Tobacco Workers' International Union and the American Federation of Grain Millers.

12. Brotherhood of Locomotive Engineers (BLE)

Address. Standard Building, 1370 Ontario Street, Mezzanine, Cleveland, Ohio 44113-1702

Phone. +1 216 241 2630

E-mail. pr@ble.org (public relations department)

Website. www.ble.org

Leadership. Ed Dubroski (international president); Jim McCoy (1st vice-president); Russell Bennett (general secretary-treasurer)

Membership. 55,000. Includes 30,000 active members in the US and 8,000 in Canada.

History and character. BLE calls itself the "senior national labour organization in the United States", dating back to 1863. Its members now include other types of railway employees, in addition to locomotive engineers, and it says its membership is growing despite industry consolidation. Also affiliated to the Canadian Labour Congress.

Publications. Locomotive Engineers' Journal; Locomotive Engineers' Newsletter

13. Brotherhood of Maintenance of Way Employees (BMWE)

Address. 26555 Evergreen Road, Suite 200, Southfield, Michigan 48076

Phone. +1 248 948 1010

Fax. +1 248 948 9140

E-mail. sue@bmwe.org (Susan Creswell, Director of Communications)

Website. www.bmwe.org

Leadership. Mac A. Fleming (president); William E. LaRue (secretary-treasurer)

Membership. 60,000

History and character. Founded in 1887, this is the union of workers who maintain the tracks, bridges and buildings on US and Canadian railways. At its height it had 360,000 members but factors such as automation, the development of road freight and airlines, and sell-offs of railroad assets have depleted its membership. Also affiliated to the Canadian Labour Congress.

Publications. BMWE Journal

14. Brotherhood of Railroad Signalmen (BRS)

Address. PO Box U, Mount Prospect, Illinois 60056

Phone. +1 847 439 3732

Fax. +1 847 439 3743

E-mail. signalman@brs.org

Website. www.brs.org

Leadership. W.D.Pickett (president); W.A. Barrows (secretary-treasurer)

Membership. 10,000 in US and Canada

Publications. Signalman's Journal (content accessible via website).

15. Communication Workers of America (CWA)

Address. 501 3rd Street NW, Washington, DC 20001-2797

Phone. +1 202 434 1100
Fax. +1 202 434 1279
Website. www.cwa-union.org
Leadership. Morton Bahr (president); Barbara Easterling (secretary-treasurer); Larry Cohen (executive vice-president)
Membership. 740,000
History and character. The CWA is the largest US communications and media union and now represents workers in a wide swathe of the information industry including broadcast media (e.g. ABC and NBC), telecoms (e.g. AT&T) and information technology companies such as Microsoft and IBM. It also has some members in other areas including airline customer service, health care and education. It has eight regional district headquarters, 50 field offices and 1,200 local unions in the US, Canada and Puerto Rico. The CWA is party to some 2,000 collective agreements and says that in areas such as training and education and child and family care its contracts are considered pacesetters. Its affiliations include the Canadian Labour Congress, and the trade secretariats UNI, IMF and IFJ.

The CWA has since 1995 incorporated **The Newspaper Guild, TNG** (501 Third Street, NW, Suite 250, Washington DC 20001. *Phone.* +1 202 434 7177. *Fax.* +1 202 434 1472. *E-mail.* guild@cwa-union.org.
Website. www.newsguild.org.
Leadership. Linda K. Foley (president)).
Publications. CWA News

16. Graphic Communications International Union (GCIU)

Address. 1900 L Street, NW, Washington, DC 20036
Phone. +1 202 462 1400
Fax. +1 202 721 0600
Website. www.gciu.org
Leadership. James J. Norton (international president); Gerald H. Duneau (international secretary-treasurer)
Membership. 150,000 active and retired members in Canada and the USA; the largest union representing printing and publishing workers in North America.
Publications. Graphic Communicator (content accessible via website)

17. Hotel Employees' and Restaurant Employees' International Union (HERE)

Address. 1219 28th Street, NW, Washington DC 20007
Phone. +1 202 393 4373
Fax. +1 202 333 0468
E-mail. pbarry@hereunion.org (news and information)
Website. www.hereunion.org
Leadership. John H. Wilhelm (general president); Ted T. Hansen (general secretary-treasurer)
Membership. 300,000 in the US and Canada
History and character. HERE dates back to 1891. Its members work in hotels, motels, restaurants and cafeterias, taverns, cocktail lounges, clubs, casinos, riverboats, hospitals, schools, airports, bus terminals and similar. Its membership includes some clerical and university employees not in the hospitality trades. It has 118 locals, the largest of which is Las Vegas, with 40,000 members; general president John Wilhelm led the Las Vegas union through most of the 1980s and the 1990s, when its membership increased by 20,000. A strike begun in 1991 by 550 members at the Frontier Hotel and Gambling Hall in Las Vegas ended after more than six years when new owners agreed to recognize the union. Union locals negotiate most collective bargaining agreements with HERE providing coordination, research, support and political action.

Publications. Catering Industry Employee (content accessible via website)

18. Glass, Molders, Pottery, Plastics and Allied Workers' International Union (GMP)

Address. 608 East Baltimore Pike, PO Box 607, Media, Pennsylvania 19063-0607
Phone. +1 610 565 5051
E-mail. gmpiu@ix.netcom.com
Website. www.gmpiu.org
Leadership. James H. Rankin (international president); Joseph Mitchell, Sr. (international secretary-treasurer)
Membership. 62,000 in US and Canada
Publications. GMP Horizons (content accessible via website)

19. International Association of Bridge, Structural and Ornamental Iron Workers

Address. 1750 New York Avenue NW, Suite 400, Washington, DC 20006
Phone. +1 202 383 4800
Leadership. Jake West (general president); James Cole (general secretary); Joseph Hunt (general treasurer)

20. International Association of Firefighters (IAFF)

Address. 1750 New York Avenue, NW, Washington DC 20006
Phone. +1 202 737 8484
Fax. +1 202 737 8418
Website. www.iaff.org
Leadership. Alfred K. Whitehead (general president)
Membership. 230,779 (including 17,038 retired) in 2578 locals across the US and Canada. Members are fire fighters and employees in emergency medical or rescue service activities.
Publication. International Fire Fighter; IAFF Leader

21. International Association of Machinists and Aerospace Workers (IAM)

Address. 9000 Machinists Place, Upper Marlboro, Maryland 20772-2687
Phone. +1 301 967 4500
Website www.iamaw.org
Leadership. R. Thomas Buffenbarger (international president); Donald E. Wharton (general secretary-treasurer)
History and character. The IAM dates its origins back to 1888 and has members active in 200 industries. Its members work in many of the major US industrial corporations such as Boeing, United Airlines and General Electric. It absorbed the woodworkers' union in 1994 and has discussed (unrealized) unification plans with the auto and steelworkers to create the largest union in North America. It is affiliated to the ITF, IMF, and IFBWW international trade secretariats, and the to the Canadian Labour Congress.
Associated education centre. The William W. Winpisinger Education and Technology Center provides members with education and training in labour history and skills in leadership as shop stewards, local or district officers or grand lodge representatives. (*Address.* 24494 Placid Harbor Way, Hollywood, Maryland, 20636. Phone +1 301 373 3300. *Fax.* +1 301 373 2860)
Publications. IAM Journal

22. International Association of Operative Plasterers' and Cement Masons of the United States and Canada (OPCMIA)

Address. 14405 Laurel Place, Suite 300, Laurel, Maryland, 20707
Phone. +1 301 470 4200
Fax. +1 301 470 2502
Website. www.opcmia.org

Leadership. John J. Dougherty (general president); Patrick D. Finley (general secretary-treasurer)

23. International Brotherhood of Boilermakers, Iron Ship Builders, Blacksmiths, Forgers and Helpers (IBB)

Address. 753 State Avenue, Suite 570, Kansas City, KS 66102
Phone. +1 913 371 2640
Fax. +1 913 281 8101
E-mail. dcaswell@boilermakers.org (Donald Caswell, Director, Communications Dept.)
Website. www.boilermakers.org
Leadership. Charles W. Jones (international president); Jerry Z. Wilburn (international secretary-treasurer)
Membership. 100,000 in US and Canada
History and character. The Boilermakers' union was founded in 1893. Its members are in diverse industries including construction, repair, maintenance, manufacturing and professional emergency medical services. In 1994 it absorbed the 5,800 member Stove, Furnace and Allied Appliance Workers' international union and in 1996 the 4,000-member Metal Polishers, Buffers, Platers and Allied Workers' international union.
Publication. Boilermaker Reporter (content accessible via website)

24. International Brotherhood of Electrical Workers (IBEW)

Address. 1125 15th Street, NW, Washington, DC 20005
Phone. +1 202 833 7000
Fax. +1 202 778 6056
E-mail. ibewnet@compuserve.com
Website. www.ibew.org
Leadership. J.J.Barry (international president); Edwin D. Hill (international secretary-treasurer)
Publication. IBEW Journal

25. International Brotherhood of Painters and Allied Trades (IBPAT)

Address. 1750 New York Avenue, NW, Washington, DC 2006
Website. www.ibpat.org
Leadership. Michael E. Monroe (general president); James A. Williams (general secretary-treasurer)
Membership. 130,000
History and character. This is a craft union whose members include painters, paperhangers, glaziers, carpet installers, sign painters, display decorators, paint and brush makers, and related trades. It reports a growing membership. Through its district councils and local unions it offers a range of training programmes in craft skills for its members with the objective of ensuring that employers who sign agreements with the union have access to the most skilled workers. It also has an agreement with Marshall University in West Virginia which gives college credits for union apprenticeship programmes. IBPAT's COMET programme educates union members in leadership and bargaining skills. Also affiliated to the Canadian Labour Congress.
Publication. IBPAT Union Journal (content accessible via website)

26. International Brotherhood of Teamsters (IBT)

Address. 25 Louisiana Avenue, NW, Washington, DC 20001
Phone. +1 202 624 6800
Website. www.teamster.org
Leadership. James P. Hoffa (general president); Tom Keegel (general secretary-treasurer)

Membership. 1.5 million in US, Canada and Puerto Rico
History and character. The IBT (or Teamsters) is the largest and most powerful single union in the United States. Its position was weakened in the 1980s by the de-regulation of the trucking industry which introduced many small non-union companies; by 1986 only about 200,000 truckers worked under the IBT master agreement compared with 400,000 a decade earlier. It sustained its membership by organizing in other sectors, including clerical, service and high technology workers, and in that respect benefited from not being subject to AFL-CIO demarcation restrictions at that time. Its greatest asset historically has been its reputation for winning high wage settlements and it continues to be an aggressive bargainer, backing up its demands with industrial action.

It has divisions for airlines; automobile transportation; bakeries and laundries; breweries and soft drinks; building material and construction trades; dairy; freight; industrial trades; motion pictures and theatrical trades; newspaper, magazine and electronic media workers; parcels and small packages; ports; public employees; tank haul; trade shows and convention centres; and warehouses.

The Teamsters has for decades been seen as the US union most affected by racketeering. The President's Commission on Organized Crime, reporting in March 1986, found IBT leaders had been 'firmly under the influence of organized crime since the 1950s'. These criminal associations, which included the use of the union's multi-billion dollar Central States Pension Fund to finance activity controlled by the Mafia, had led to expulsion from the AFL-CIO in 1957. In 1967 IBT president James R. ('Jimmy') Hoffa was imprisoned for involvement in misuse of pension funds. He was released in 1971 (in exchange for an agreement that he would stand down as president) but disappeared in 1975 and is generally presumed to have been murdered. A later president, Roy L. Williams, was convicted in 1982 of conspiracy to bribe a US senator in return for favourable trucking legislation. Williamns stood down in favour of Jackie Presser, who was in turn indicted by a Cleveland grand jury on embezzlement and racketeering charges in May 1986 (but was reelected as IBT president at the national convention five days later). Many local and regional IBT officials also served prison terms in this period.

After 15 years of talks, the Teamsters finally re-affiliated to the AFL-CIO in Oct. 1987, but readmission occurred as the Justice Department was about to present a civil lawsuit aimed at removing the entire executive and placing the union under a trustee appointed by the Court. The IBT's increased respectability as an AFL-CIO affiliate did not thwart legal proceedings: the suit was duly filed in June 1988 under federal racketeering laws with the Department charging that Mafia figures had played a part in the election of Presser and his predecessor. Presser himself died in hospital a few days later.

The AFL-CIO, with some congressional support, responded that the government was interfering with the right of union members to choose their own leaders. A new organization, Americans Against Government Control of Unions, was launched with support from such diverse figures as Jesse Jackson and Alexander Haig. However, in 1989 the case was settled with the IBT's affairs coming under federal government supervision, which still remains in force. Some 200 IBT officials accused of corruption have been forced out of office under federal supervision.

On Presser's death in July 1988, William McCarthy had been elected as president. McCarthy dismissed a number of key union figures associated with the now discredited regime. McCarthy declined to run for re-election. When elections for the general presidency and leading union posts were finally held in Dec. 1991 the victors were a reform slate headed by Ron Carey, principal officer of local 804 in New York City.

Carey pledged that the IBT would say 'good-bye to the Mafia ... corruption ... and give-back contracts.' The Feb. 1992 general executive board established a grievance panel committee, an ethics sub-committee and other reforms. His first executive act was to reduce his own salary by $50,000. 46 people who made 'outrageous salaries' were removed from the payroll, and the union's luxury jets and limousine were sold. A special pension fund for 22 top officials was wound up. The new leadership argued that the old had exceeded its income for many years, covering shortfalls on its general fund by making withdrawals from the strike fund.

The Carey regime itself, however, in turn faced charges of corruption. William Hamilton, the director of the IBT's government affairs department, was indicted on charges of funneling union funds into Carey's 1996 re-election campaign, when Carey beat James P. Hoffa (Jimmy Hoffa's son) in a disputed contest in which Hoffa pledged to remove organized crime from the union. In a further election in Dec. 1998, Hoffa was elected president. (He was not sworn in until March 22, 1999, after four months of delays amid allegations of voting irregularities). Between then and year's end, five union locals were placed under direct control by the international union on charges of racketeering, typically involving misappropriation of funds and non-enforcement of collective bargaining contracts. In July 1999, Hoffa announced a new internal anti-corruption programme (Project RISE – Respect, Integrity, Strength and Ethics), to be headed by a former US attorney, and linked this to the IBT's quest to bring to an end the decade-long government oversight of the union's affairs. In Nov. 1999 Hamilton was convicted in federal court on embezzlement charges, and Hoffa praised the verdict as "an important step towards closing a dark chapter in Teamster history" while calling on the government to prosecute others involved with Hamilton.

DRIVE (Democratic, Republican, Independent Voter Education) is the Teamsters' politcal action committee. It was launched in 1963 and became the most powerful labour political action fund. It has supported both Democratic and Republican candidates but the IBT was the only union that supported Republican President Ronald Reagan in both his election campaigns (1980, 1984). In an important switch, following a nationwide survey of members' attitudes that revealed 53.35 per cent backing for the Democratic candidate, the IBT endorsed Democrat Bill Clinton in the 1992 campaign. In 1999 there was press speculation that Hoffa might be a running mate with Pat Buchanan, a maverick right-wing Republican aligned with the IBT's views on protecting American jobs from low-cost foreign competitors, but Hoffa stated in Sept. 1999 that he would not be involved "at this time" in presidential politics. The IBT was slow to endorse any presidential candidate for 2000, and Hoffa attended both the Democratic and Republican conventions, being honoured with a reception at the latter, and even held a joint press conference with Ralph Nader of the Green Party. In Sept. 2000, however, after polling its members, the IBT endorsed Democratic candidate Al Gore, Hoffa declaring that the Teamsters "will not stand idly by while the forces of reaction try to roll back the gains achieved over the past century".

Politically the Teamsters have strongly opposed trade liberalization under NAFTA and the WTO, and the proposed admission of China to the WTO. Active IBT hostility was a factor in the Clinton administration's decision to maintain controls on US-Mexico cross-border trucking beyond the Jan. 1, 2000 deadline for opening the borders under NAFTA. The administration officially attributed the decision to concerns about the safety standards of Mexican trucking operators.
Publications. Teamster; also sectoral publications for the various divisions of the union.

27. International Federation of Professional and Technical Engineers (IFPTE)
Address. 8630 Fenton Street, Suite 400, Silver Spring, Maryland 20910
Phone. +1 301 565 9016
Fax. +1 301 565 0018
Website. www.ifpte.org
Leadership. Paul E. Almeida (international president); Gregory J. Junemman (secretary-treasurer)
Membership. 75,000. Membership covers a diverse range of occupations- accountants, administrative assistants, laboratory staff, public relations personnel, computer programmers, among them- in both the public and private sectors.
Publication. The Outlook (quarterly, all members*); Organizing Bulletin* (monthly to locals)

28. International Longshoremen's Association (ILA)
Address. 17 Battery Place, Suite 930, New York, NY 10004
Phone. +1 212 425 1200
Fax. +1 212 425 2928
E-mail. jmcnamara@ila2000.org
Website. www.ila2000.org
Leadership. John Bowers (international president); Robert E. Gleason (international secretary-treasurer)
History and character. The ILA, which has about 60,000 members, in 1996 entered a five-year master agreement, covering all ILA ports from Maine to Texas (the eastern and southern seaboards). In March 2000 ILA president Bowers and James Hoffa, president of the much larger Teamsters' union, pledged to "respect one another's jurisdiction" in an effort to end "festering differences."
Publications. ILA Newsletter (content accessible via website)

29. International Longshore and Warehouse Union (ILWU)
Address. 1188 Franklin Street, San Francisco, California 94109
Phone. +1 415 775 0533
Fax. +1 415 775 1302
E-mail. info@ilwu.org
Website. www.ilwu.org
Leadership. Brian McWilliams (president); Joe Ibarra (secretary-treasurer)
Membership. There are 42,000 members in the western seaboard states of California, Washington, Oregon and Alaska, and Hawaii. An additional 3,500 members belong to the Inland Boatmen's Union of the Pacific and 14,000 to the autonomous ILWU Canada.
Publications. Dispatcher

30. International Union of Bricklayers and Allied Craftworkers (BAC)
Address. 815 15th Street, NW, Washington, DC 20005
Phone +1 202 783 3788
Website. www.bacweb.org
Leadership. John J. Flynn (president); James Boland (secretary-treasurer)

History and character. With its signatory employer contractors, this craft-based union operates the International Masonry Institute (IMI) as a joint labour-management trust; the IMI has a national training centre in craft skills at Fort Ritchie, Maryland.

Publication. Journal (content accessibkle via website)

31. International Union of Electronic, Electrical, Salaried, Machine and Furniture Workers (IUE)

Address. 1126 16th Street, NW, Washington DC 20036
Phone. +1 202 785 7200
Fax. +1 202 785 4563
E-mail. iuenews@iue.org
Website. www.iue.org
Leadership. Edward L. Fire (president); Thomas J. Rebman (secretary-treasurer)
Membership. 180,000, active and retired. The 125,000 active members work in a miscellaneous group of industrial enterprises, including electronics factories, breweries, and furniture manufacturers.

32. International Union of Elevator Constructors (IUEC)

Address. 5565 Sterrett Place, Suite 310, Columbia, MD 21044
Phone. +1 410 997 9000
Fax. +1 410 997 0243
E-mail. info@iuec.org
Website. www.iuec.org
Leadership. Dana A. Brigham (general president); Richard W. Scariot (general secretary-treasurer)
Membership. 25,000

33. International Union of Operating Engineers (IUOE)

Address. 1125 17th Street, NW, Washington DC 20036
Phone. +1 202 429 9100
Website. www.iuoe.org
Leadership. Frank Hanley (general president); Budd Coutts (general secretary-treasurer)
Membership. 400,000 in 170 locals in the US and Canada
History and character. Members are primarily employed in operating and maintaining heavy equipment and plant such as diesel engines, generators, air conditioning, electric- and steam-powered systems in the construction industry and in locations such as factories, hospitals, utilities, offices, hotels, and shopping malls. The union also has a minority of members in other areas, such as nurses and other health workers. The union offers apprenticeship and skills development programmes jointly sponsored by IUOE local unions and their contract signatory employers.
Publication. International Operating Engineer Magazine (content accessible via website)

34. International Union of Police Associations (IUPA)

Address. 1421 Prince Street, Suite 330, Alexandria, Virginia 22314
Website. www.sddi.com/iupa
Leadership. Sam A. Cabral (international president); Richard A. Estes (international secretary-treasurer)
Membership. 80,000 in 480 locals (includes 8,000 in Puerto Rico)
History and character. The IUPA was chartered by the AFL-CIO in 1979, giving law enforcement officers an independent voice within organized labour for the first time. It represents federal, state and local law enforcement officers, deputy sheriffs, corrections officers and law enforcement support staff. Membership grew from under 17,000 in 1990 to over 80,000 by the end of the decade.

Publication. Police Union News (content accessible via website)

35. Laborers' International Union of North America (LIUNA)

Address. 905 16th Street, NW, Washington DC 20006
Phone. +1 202 737 8320
Fax. +1 202 737 2754
Leadership. Terence M. O'Sullivan (general president); Carl E. Booker (general secretary-treasurer)
Membership. 750,000 in 650 locals in the US and Canada
History and character. Founded in 1903, LIUNA has a diverse membership including Alaska pipeline workers, airline machinists and mechanics, park rangers, Disneyland maintenance workers, poultry workers, nurses and many construction trade workers. LIUNA's "tri-funds" are "labour-management cooperatives" where union members and contracting employers discuss common concerns.

LIUNA also incorporates as an affiliate the National Federation of Independent Unions (NFIU) (Francis J. Chiappardi, president). This organization was founded in 1963 to give a voice to independent union members, but membership has declined to 10,000. As a division of LIUNA the NFIU maintains an element of independence, and still recruits in its own name, while its members benefit from the AFL-CIO union privilege programme.
Publications. The Laborer magazine

36. National Association of Letter Carriers (NALC)

Address. 100 Indiana Avenue, NW, Washington DC 20001-2144
Phone. +1 202 393 4695
Fax. +1 202 737 1540
E-mail. nalcinf@nalc.org
Website. www.nalc.org
Leadership. Vincent R. Sombrotto (president); William R. Yates (secretary-treasurer)
Membership. 315,000 (220,000 active)
History and character. Founded 1889 and with 2,800 local branches. Under US law postal employees are prohibited from going on strike and are subject to a system of binding arbitration should bargaining and mediation fail to produce agreement. Affiliated to Union Network International (UNI).
Publications. The Postal Record; The Activist; NALC Bulletin; NALC Retiree

37. National Air Traffic Controllers' Association (NATCA)

Address. 1325 Massachusetts Avenue, NW, Washington DC 20005
Phone. +1 202 628 5451
Website. www.natca.org
Leadership. Mike McNally (president); James R. (Randy) Schwitz Jr. (executive vice-president)
Membership. 14,000
History and character. NATCA was certified in 1987 as the sole bargaining agent for air traffic controllers employed by the Federal Aviation Administration.
Publications. Newsletter (accessible via website)

38. Office and Professional Employees' International Union (OPEIU)

Address. 265 West 14th Street, 6th Floor, New York, NY 10011
Phone. +1 800 346 7348
E-mail. opeiu@opeiu.org
Website. www.opeiu.org

Leadership. Michael Goodwin (international president)
Membership. 140,000 in US and Canada
History and character. The union was the first specifically chartered by the AFL to represent white-collar employees, in 1935. The OPEIU has a highly diverse membership in both the public and private sectors in the US and Canada, including computer programmers, engineers, secretaries, nurses, accountants, attorneys, transit supervisors, security guards, bank tellers and others. It embraces a number of specialist associations, the Models' Guild, the American Guild of Appraisers, the Pennsylvania Nurses' Association, the National Union of Chiropractic Physicians and the National Guild of Medical Professionals, the first trade union for doctors, founded in 1996.

39. Paper, Allied-Industrial, Chemical and Energy Workers' International Union (PACE)

Address. PO Box 1475, Nashville, TN 37202
Phone. +1 615 834 8590
Fax. +1 615 834 7741
Website. www.paceunion.org
Leadership. Boyd Young (international president); Robert Wages (executive vice-president); James Dunn (secretary-treasurer)
Membership. 320,000 in US and Canada
History and character. PACE was formed in January 1999 by the merger of the United Paperworkers' International Union (UPIU) with the smaller Oil, Chemical and Atomic Workers' International Union (OCAW). About half the membership is in the paper industry, 10% in oil and 7% in chemicals.
Publication. Pacesetter (content accessible via website)

40. Seafarers' International Union (SIU)

Address. 5201 Auth Way, Camp Springs, Maryland 20746
Phone. +1 301 899 0675
Fax. +1 301 899 7355
Website. www.seafarers.org
Leadership. Michael Sacco (president)
History and character. This is the largest North American union representing merchant mariners. It represents unlicensed mariners on US-flag vessels in the deep sea, Great Lakes and inland waterway sectors, and licensed mariners in the Great Lakes and inland waterway sectors. In March 2000 membership referenda approved the absorption of the National Maritime Union (NMU) by the SIU.
Publication. *Seafarer's Log* (accessible via website)

41. Service Employees' International Union (SEIU)

Address. 1313 L Street, NW, Washington, DC 20005
Phone. +1 202 898 3200
E-mail. info@seiu.org
Website. www.seiu.org
Leadership. Andrew L. Stern (president); Betty Bednarczyk (secretary-treasurer)
Membership. 1.2 million
History and character. SEIU has doubled its diversified membership over the past two decades. Its two main areas are federal, state and local government, and health care. It was the first union to organize the health care sector and is now the largest health sector union in North America, with 475,000 members working in hospitals, HMOs, clinics, nursing homes and blood banks. SEIU also has members in other miscellaneous areas including race tracks and ball parks. 185,000 members are in building services, in occupations such as janitors, window cleaners and security guards. A majority (58%) of its members are women and one-third are black, Hispanic or other minorities.

42. Sheet Metal Workers' International Association (SMWIA)

Website. www.smwia.org
Leadership. Michael J. Sullivan (general president); A.T. "Ted" Zlotopolski (general secretary-treasurer)
Membership. 150,000 in the sheet metal industry in the US and Canada.

43. Transportation Communications International Union (TCU)

Address. 3 Research Place, Rockville, MD 20850
Phone. +1 301 948 4910
Fax. +1 301 948 1872
Website. www.tcunion.org
Leadership.. Robert A. Scardelletti (international president); L.E. Bosher (internatonal secretary-treasurer)
History and character. Originated in 1899 as the Order of Railroad Clerks of America, adopting present name in 1987. Members work in a wide range of occupations in transportation, including clerks, skycaps, service workers, truck drivers, supervisors, accountants, police officers, grain handlers and reservations agents.
Publication. Interchange

44. Transport Workers' Union of America (TWU)

Address. 80 West End Avenue, New York, NY 10023
Phone. +1 212 873 6000
Fax. +1 212 721 1431
Website. www.twu.com
Leadership. Sonny Hall (international president); John J. Kerrigan (international secretary-treasurer); Frank McCann (international executive vice-president)
Membership. 110,000 in mass transportation, airlines, railroads, utilities and other areas.

45. Union of Needletrades, Industrial and Textile Employees (UNITE)

Address. 1710 Broadway, New York, NY 10019
Phone. +1 212 265 7000
E-mail. jmort@uniteunion.org
Website. www.uniteunion.org
Leadership. Jay Mazur (president)
History and character. UNITE was formed in 1995 by the merger of the Amalgamated Clothing and Textile Workers' Union (ACTWU) and the International Ladies' Garment Workers' Union (ILGWU)
Publications. UNITE Magazine

46. United Association of Journeymen and Apprentices of the Plumbing, Pipefitting and Sprinkler Fitting Industry of the United States and Canada (UA)

Address. 901 Massachusetts Avenue, NW, Washington, DC 20001
Phone. +1 202 628 5823
Fax. +1 202 628 5024
Website. www.ua.org
Leadership. Martin J. Maddaloni (general president); Thomas H. Patchell (general secretary-treasurer)
Membership. 291,000 in 418 local unions across North America
History and character. The UA operates more than 360 training centres across the US and Canada, owned by local joint training committees, and it spends more than $1m per week on training, with 17,000 apprentices being trained at any one time.
Publications. UA Journal (content accessible via website)

47. United Automobile, Aerospace and Agricultural Implement Workers of America International Union (UAW)

Address. Solidarity House, 8000 East Jefferson Avenue, Detroit, MI 48214

Phone. +1 313 926 5000

Fax. +1 313 823 6016

E-mail. uaw@uaw.org

Website. www.uaw.org

Leadership. Stephen P. Yokich (president); Ruben Burks (secretary-treasurer)

Membership. 760,000 active and 500,000 retired members

History and character. The UAW was founded in 1935. More than 400,000 of the active membership are production workers, engineers and draftsmen in the big three automobile companies, General Motors, Ford, and DaimlerChrysler. The UAW is also present in automotive parts, aerospace, defence and a wide range of other manufacturing industries. Its membership includes a growing number of technical, office and professional employees in manufacturing companies, the public sector, health care, schools and universities and telecommunications, including 48,000 state employees in Michigan and Indiana, 5,000 members of the National Writers' Union, and 3,000 members of the Graphic Artists' Guild. It comprises 1,000 local unions and has contracts with 1,000 employers. It is affiliated internationally to the International Metalworkers' Federation (IMF).

Publication. Solidarity

48. United Brotherhood of Carpenters and Joiners of America (UBC)

Address. 101 Constitution Avenue, NW, Washington DC 20001

Phone. +1 202 546 6206

Leadership. Douglas J. McCarron (general president); Douglas Banes (general vice-president); Andris Silins (secretary-treasurer)

Membership. 400,000 in woodworking and allied trades

49. United Farm Workers of America (UFW)

Address. PO Box 62, Keene, California 93531

E-mail. euranday@ufwmail.com

Website. www.ufw.org

History and character. The UFW was founded in the early 1960s by Cesar Chavez and built its reputation in the course of campaigns against exploitation of Californian grape workers. In 1970 for the first time, grape growers signed contracts that ended the most brutal period in the vineyards and Chavez became a revered and inspirational figure on the left. He died in 1993 at a time when the union's membership had declined to less than half the 1970 level of 50,000. Many parks, schools, streets and other public facilities have been named after Chavez and he was awarded the Medal of Freedom by President Clinton.

50. United Food and Commercial Workers' International Union (UFCW)

Address. 1775 K Street, NW, Washington DC 20006

Phone. +1 202 223 3111

Fax. +1 202 466 1562

Website. www.ufcw.org

Leadership. Douglas H. Dority (international president)

Membership. 1.4 million

History and character. The UFCW was the only private sector union to grow during the 1980s, to rival the International Brotherhood of Teamsters as the largest US private sector union. It has one million members in the food sector, including retail food, meat packing, poultry, and other food processing industries. Other members work in health care (where its 100,000 members include nurses, assistants, pharmacists, technicians and caretakers), insurance, department stores, garment manufacturing, chemicals and textiles. More than half its members are women. It has 13,000 collective bargaining agreements. Its services include a Worker Advisory Project that helps workers who are not members of the union when their rights are being violated. It also emphasizes political action and every local union is directed to set up a grass-roots lobbying programme.

The UFCW incorporates:

(1) Retail, Wholesale and Department Store Union (RWDSU)

Address. 30 East 29th Street, New York, NY 10016

Website. www.rwdsu.org

Leadership. Stuart Appelbaum (president)

Membership. 100,000 in US and Canada

History and character. Affiliated to UFCW in 1993

(2) International Chemical Workers' Union Council (ICWUC)

Address. 1655 West Market Street, Akron, OH 44313

Phone. +1 330 867 2444

Website. www.icwuc.org

Leadership. Frank D. Martino (president); Larry V. Gregoire (secretary-treasurer)

History and character. Affiliated to UFCW in 1996.

51. United Mine Workers' of America (UMWA)

Address. 8315 Lee Highway, Fairfax, VA 22031

Phone. +1 703 208 7200

Website. www.umwa.org

Leadership. Cecil Roberts (president); Jerry Jones (vice-president); Carlo Tarley (secretary-treasurer)

History and character. In addition to mineworkers now includes health care workers, truck drivers and school board employees.

Publication. UMW Journal (accessible at website)

52. United Steelworkers of America (USWA)

Address. Five Gateway Center, Pittsburgh, Pa 15222

Website. www.uswa.org

Leadership. George Becker (international president); Leo W. Gerard (international secretary-treasurer)

Publication. Steelabor (content accessible via website)

53. United Transportation Union (UTU)

Address. 14600 Detroit Avenue, Cleveland, Ohio 44107-4250

Phone. +1 216 228 9400

Fax. +1 216 228 5755

Website. www.utu.org

Leadership. Charles L. Little (international president); Paul C. Thompson (general secretary and treasurer)

Membership. 125,000 active and retired railroad, bus and mass transit workers in the US and Canada. It is the largest railroad union with 700 locals; members are mainly from the "operating crafts", such as conductors, brakemen, switchmen and locomotive engineers.

Publications. UTU News (accessible via website)

54. United Union of Roofers, Waterproofers and Allied Workers

Address. 1660 L Street, NW, Suite 800, Washington DC 20036

Website. www.unionroofers.com
Leadership. Earl J. Kruse (international president); Kinsey M. Robinson (international secretary-treasurer); John C. Martini (international executive vice-president)
Membership. 22,000

55. Utility Workers' Union of America (UWUA)
Address. 815 16th Street, NW, Washington, DC 20006
Phone. +1 202 347 8105
Fax. +1 202 347 4872
Website. www.uwua.org
Leadership. Donald E. Wightman (national president); Gary M. Ruffner (national secretary-treasurer); James P. Keller (executive vice-president)
Membership. 50,000 in the electricity, gas and water industries.

4 Other Trade Union Organizations

The National Alliance of Postal and Federal Employees (NAPFE)

Address. 1628 11th Street, NW, Washington, DC 20001

Phone. +1 202 939 6325

Fax. +1 202 939 6389

E-mail. napfe@patriot.net

Leadership. James McGee (president)

International affiliation. WCL

National Education Association (NEA)

Address. 1201 16th Street NW, Washington, DC 20036-3290

Phone. +1 202 833 4000

Website. www.nea.org

Leadership. Robert Chase (president); Reg Weaver (vice-president); Dennis Van Roekel (secretary-treasurer)

Membership. 2.4 million

History and character. The NEA was founded as a professional body in 1857. It works to advance the cause of quality public education while providing assistance and representation for its members in areas such as employee protection, legal assistance and collective bargaining. The NEA has affiliates in every US state, plus the Federal Education Association and the Associación de Maestros de Puerto Rico. There are 14,000 local affiliates and members include teachers in both schools and colleges as well as educational support personnel. It is affiliated to Education International.

Publications. NEA Today; specialist publications

United Electrical, Radio and Machine Workers of America (UE)

Address. One Gateway Center, Suite 1400, Pittsburgh, PA 15222-1416

Phone. +1 412 471 8919

Fax. +1 412 471 8999

E-mail. ue@ranknfile-ue.org

Leadership. John H. Hovis (president); Robert L. Clark (secretary-treasurer)

Membership. 35,000

History and character. At the end of World War II, UE was the third largest CIO union with 500,000 members but it withdrew in 1949 and was subsequently expelled by the CIO on the grounds that it was communist dominated. It continues to adopt positions to the left of the mainstream labour movement in the US and emphasizes that it is a rank-and-file union. Members are in a range of sectors but mostly in electrical manufacturing, metalworking and plastics.

United States Dependency

Puerto Rico

Capital: San Juan
Population: 3.92 m. (2000 est.)

1 Political and Economic Background

Puerto Rico is under its constitution a "free state associated with the USA". Its economy includes industries such as textiles, petrochemicals and pharmaceuticals, and there is a tourism sector. It is heavily dependent upon the USA, its main trading partner.

GDP (purchasing power parity) $38.1bn. (1999 est.); GDP per capita (purchasing power parity) $9,800 (1999 est.).

2 Trade Unionism

US unions have branches in Puerto Rico and the AFL-CIO is represented by the Federación del Trabajo de Puerto Rico.

Federación del Trabajo de Puerto Rico AFL-CIO

Address. Apartdao 19689, Fernandez Juncos Station, Santurce 00910-9689

Phone. +1809 722 13 43

Fax. +1809 725 0907

International affiliation. ICFTU

Uruguay

Capital: Montevideo
Population: 3.33 m. (2000 est.)

1 Political and Economic Background

Historically, Uruguayan politics have been dominated by the conflict between the (dominant) liberal Colorado (red) and conservative Blanco (white) parties. In 1971, however, laws drastically curtailing civil liberties were introduced to give the army a free hand in fighting the Tupamaro guerrilla movement, and in 1973 the armed forces took power, initiating 11 years of military government noted for wide-scale repression and "disappearances". Civilian government was restored in 1984, with the Colorado candidate being elected president in 1984, 1994 and 1999, and the Blanco candidate in 1989. The current president is Jorge Batlle, in office from March 2000, and his government includes both Colorados and Blancos.

Uruguay has a mixed economy built primarily on commercial agriculture and the processing of farm products. In the 1990s governments sought to pursue free market policies, control spending and combat inflation, which was in excess of 80% at the start of the decade but down to 4% by 1999. The economy was badly affected in 1999 by knock-on from financial difficulties in Argentina and Brazil, its main trading partners. Uruguay has a relatively even income distribution and its welfare state is considered the most extensive in Latin America.

GDP (purchasing power parity) $28bn. (1999 est.); GDP per capita (purchasing power parity) $8,500 (1999 est.).

2 Trade Unionism

Uruguayan trade unionism dates from the 1880s; the first national confederations appeared early in the twentieth century. Trade union activities continued under generally constitutional rule and in notably favourable conditions by Latin American standards until the early 1970s, when civil liberties were undermined by the conflict between the army and the Tupamaro guerrillas. The leftist Convención Nacional de Trabajadores (CNT) was dissolved in 1973 when it staged a general strike, following which independent trade unionism was crushed. The Confederación General de Trabajadores del Uruguay (CGTU, founded in 1951 as the Confederación Sindical del Uruguay), which was an ICFTU affiliate, came firmly under government control and was eventually suspended by and disaffiliated from the ICFTU.

After the restoration of democracy, the PIT-CNT emerged as a unified centre supported by all sections of the labour movement. During 1987–88 it organized a series of strikes, in both the public and private sectors, to oppose President Sanguinetti's austerity policies and his programme of restructuring the economy, especially through the development of free trade zones. It continued to stage general strikes at intervals in the 1990s, against privatization and other policies.

The PIT-CNT remains the sole trade union centre with 90% of unionized workers in its affiliated unions, although its membership at 120,000 is only half the mid-1980s level. It is unaffiliated to any of the three world centres. The WCL-affiliated Uruguayan Trade Union Action (ASU) does not rival the PIT-CNT but rather seeks to gain influence within it. Workers in both the private and public sectors, including civil servants, may join unions but only about 13% of the workforce are unionized.

Uruguay ratified ILO Conventions No.87 (Freedom of Association and Protection of the Right to Organize, 1948) and No.98 (Right to Organize and Collective Bargaining, 1949) in 1954. Following the restoration of democracy the repressive industrial relations laws of the 1973–84 period were repealed but not replaced.

Although it has a considerable amount of protective legislation, Uruguay lacks a comprehensive labour code; indeed the conduct of industrial relations is almost entirely unregulated. There are few rules governing union or management behaviour in conflict apart from a few general constitutional guidelines. In the present unregulated situation, where there are no legal procedures, many employers recognize unions and accept the principle of collective bargaining, though a minority does challenge the principle that such accords are legally binding. Although there is no law prohibiting anti-union discrimination, a 1993 executive decree established fines for employers engaging in anti-union activities. The ICFTU says, however, that where union organizers are dismissed "the companies concerned are often able to succeed in fabricating explanations which avoid the penalties under the law". In general governments have sought to encourage consensus, with the Ministry of Labour acting a mediator where disputes arise. The right to strike is generally observed, although the government may order workers in essential services back to work. Strikes were frequent in the early 1990s but have had less worker support in more recent years. National labour legislation applies in the free trade zones but the unions have not been able to establish a base in the zones.

3 Trade Union Centre

Plenario Intersindical de Trabajadores-Convención Nacional de Trabajadores (PIT-CNT)

Address. 18 de Julio 2190, Montevideo

Phone. + 598 2 409 6680

Fax. + 598 2 400 4160

Membership. 120,000

History and character. The communist-influenced CNT was founded in 1964, bringing together all the major unions, but was dissolved under military rule in 1973, following which 18 members of the CNT central council 'disappeared'. Trade union activities re-emerged in 1983 under the name of the PIT, which was banned in Jan. 1984 when it led a general strike. The fused PIT-CNT was restored to legal status in March 1985 and convened its congress later that year under the slogan 'Consolidating Democracy' with attendance by representatives of the ICFTU, WCL and the WFTU.

Since its legalization, the PIT-CNT has led numerous general strikes, especially in the period 1990–92 against the administration of the right-wing (Blanco) President Luis Alberto Lacalle, on issues such as the impact of structural adjustment programmes, proposals to restrict the right to strike, unemployment benefits, wages, and privatization. Frequent as these strikes were they left much of the private sector relatively unscathed. Industrial action subsided after the election of the Colorado Party's President Sanguinetti in 1994. In June 2000 the PIT-CNT called a one-day strike against the policies of the new president, Jorge Batlle, calling for action against 12% unemployment and for more spending on health and education, but the strike call was little observed outside Montevideo. Left-wing leadership persists in the PIT-CNT but by statute it is not affiliated to any political party. Most unions support the Frente Amplio (FL, Broad Front), a disparate coalition including moderate socialists, communists and even some former Tupamaros. The FL's 1999 candidate for president, Tabaré Vázquez, came a close second to Jorge Batlle of the Colorados in a run-off election.

Although the PIT-CNT represents perhaps 90% of union members, its total membership has fallen considerably in recent years, and its influence has declined.

International affiliation. None

4 Other Trade Union Organization

Acción Sindical Uruguaya (ASU)
Uruguayan Trade Union Action

Address. Calle José E. Rodó n° 1836, Casilla de Correo 1466, 11200 Montevideo

Phone. +598 2 400 4235

Fax. +598 2 408 5684

E-mail. inesasu@chasque.apc.org

Leadership. Alberto Melgarejo (secretary-general)

History and character: Supports the PIT-CNT and does not consider itself as a trade union centre or as a trade union but as an organization to promote trade union autonomy and industrial peace.

International affiliation. WCL

Uzbekistan

Capital: Tashkent
Population: 24.76 m. (2000 est.)

1 Political and Economic Background

Uzbekistan is a former republic of the USSR that became independent in Aug. 1991. It has a predominantly Muslim population. In Dec. 1991, the chair of the Supreme Soviet, Islam Karimov, was elected President and he continues to hold that office, being re-elected most recently in Jan. 2000. The legislature, the Oly Majlis, is comprised solely of the members of Karimov's People's Democratic Party (the reformed Communist Party) and its allies.

Uzbekistan is an arid country with irrigated areas, with agriculture and agricultural processing the predominant form of livelihood. It is also a major exporter of cotton, produces gold and gas and has heavy industry. Restructuring of the economy has been limited, with state control remaining paramount.

GDP (purchasing power parity) $59.3bn. (1999 est.); GDP per capita (purchasing power parity) $2,500 (1999 est.).

2 Trade Unionism

Uzbekistan ratified ILO Convention No.98 (Right to Organize and Collective Bargaining, 1949) in 1992, but it has not ratified Convention No.87 (Freedom of Association and Protection of the Right to Organize, 1948). A 1992 trade union law provides that workers have the right to form and join unions of their own choosing, and that unions should be independent of interference by the state. In practice, however, the former Soviet single trade union structure has largely survived, known as the Federation of Trade Unions of Uzbekistan (FTUU). The FTUU is formally accorded a consultative role in the preparation of legislation concerned with labour and social issues. The unions have, however, lost their previous role in state planning and in the management of enterprises. Government officials and representatives of the management of state enterprises sit on union executive committees.

In the still dominant state sector of the economy wages and conditions are determined administratively by the government, albeit with consultation with the unions. While collective bargaining is allowed for in the private sector, this does not yet appear to have developed to any degree. There is no specific right to strike, and reports of strikes are rare.

Vanuatu

Capital: Port Vila
Population: 190,000 (2000 est.)

1 Political and Economic Background

Vanuatu, the former Anglo-French condominium of the New Hebrides, became an independent republic within the Commonwealth in 1980. There have been frequent changes of government in recent years. In Nov. 1999, Barak Sope, leader of the Melanesian Progressive Party, became Prime Minister in a coalition government.

Vanuatu is a poor country with the majority of the population engaged in subsistence and small-scale agriculture and fishing. Most formal sector employment (estimated at 29,000) is in government, tourism and off-shore financial services, with some light manufacturing.

GDP (purchasing power parity) $245m. (1999 est.); GDP per capita (purchasing power parity) $1,300 (1999 est.).

2 Trade Unionism

The first trade unions were formed in 1984 and soon organized the Vanuatu Council of Trade Unions (VCTU). The law does not require an employer to recognize a union, but acts of anti-union discrimination are prohibited once a union has been recognized. Collective bargaining exists, with arbitration by a tripartite arbitration board as a backstop, although this is not often used.

There was considerable conflict between unions and government in the period 1993-94, with a series of strikes spearheaded by the Vanuatu Public Services Association (VPSA) and backed by the VCTU. Trade union officials were detained, international trade union observers refused access to the country, and hundreds of public servants and teachers were dismissed in 1994 as a result of strike action that the courts declared illegal. In 1995 legislation was enacted requiring unions to give 30 days' notice of intent to strike, with a list of the names of intending strikers. Combined private and public sector membership in unions has reportedly fallen from more than 4,000 to less than 1,000 in the aftermath of the 1994 unrest.

Vanuatu is not a member of the International Labour Organization.

3 Trade Union Centre

Vanuatu Council of Trade Unions (VCTU)

Address. PMB 089, Port Vila

Phone. +678 24517

Fax. +678 26034

E-mail. synt@canuatu.com.vu

Leadership. Ephraim Kalsakau (general secretary)

Membership. Less than 1,000

History and character. The VCTU held its first national congress in Dec. 1985. In 1993-94 it came into bitter conflict with the government of Maxime Carlot, backing a series of public sector strikes which were met by wholesale dismissals of strikers and new anti-strike legislation in 1995. All five unions in Vanuatu are in the VCTU but membership has fallen sharply since 1994.

International affiliations. ICFTU; CTUC

Vatican City

1 Political and Economic Background

The state of the Vatican City (the Holy See) which came into being in 1929, is the seat of the central government of the Roman Catholic Church. Employees are engaged in administration and communications.

2 Trade Unionism

The Vatican City has about 3,000 employees, the majority of whom are now members of the Association of Vatican Lay Workers (ADLV), which achieved recognition in 1993. The Vatican City is not a member of the International Labour Organization.

Associazione Dipendenti Laici Vaticani (ADLV)
Association of Vatican Lay Workers

Address. Arco del Belvedere, I-00120 Citta del Vaticano

Phone. +39 6 6988 4400

Fax. +39 6 6988 5343

History and character. The ADLV originated in 1985. According to its president, workers' requests had hitherto been met "with silence" by the Vatican authorities, wages had been seriously eroded by inflation, and there were no internal Vatican labour regulations. The ADLV was set up to secure labour regulations based on international standards that should also reflect 'the social doctrine of the Church and serve as an example to the world'. The ADLV organized the first ever strike in the Vatican in 1988. In 1992 the union organized a mass resignation, which led to a Vatican commitment to a pension scheme. In Dec. 1993, after achieving its long-standing aim of recognition, the ADLV announced it would extend its membership to those working for institutions dependent on the Vatican.

International affiliation. ICFTU

Venezuela

Capital: Caracas
Population: 23.54 m. (2000 est.)

1 Political and Economic Background

Venezuela achieved independence from Spain in 1830 and has a history of rule by caudillos ("strong men") and army intervention in politics. The dominant political parties since the 1950s have been Democratic Action (AD) and the Social Christian Party (COPEI). Economic austerity measures introduced by AD's President Carlos Andrés Pérez in 1989 led to unrest put down by the army with the loss of 600 lives. Discontent continued, and in Apr. 1992 Lt.-Col. Hugo Chávez led an unsuccessful attempted military coup against Pérez; Chávez was jailed, but in Nov. 1992 his supporters staged a second abortive coup. The presidential election in 1993 was won by Rafael Caldera (who had broken with COPEI) as an independent. Elections in Nov.–Dec. 1998 resulted in Chávez being elected President on a nationalist-populist so-called "Bolivarian" platform, in which he offered himself as the opponent of the ruling elites, as the candidate of the Patriotic Front movement. He formed a government with a strong military presence. The election results were seen as disastrous for the AD and COPEI. In Dec. 1999 a new constitution was approved which concentrated more power in the hands of the President. Chávez was re-elected in a landslide victory under the new constitution, for a six-year term, in July 2000.

Venezuela's political instability in the 1990s, culminating in the election of Chávez, was exacerbated by the decline in oil prices, petroleum accounting for more than 80% of exports and more than half of government operating revenues. The country has faced persistent problems of fiscal deficits, high interest rates and inflation, and the economy went into recession in 1998, with GDP contracting 7.2% in 1999 and unemployment escalating. Welfare programmes and cuts in the working week included in the 1999 constitution were, on some estimates, likely to cost the equivalent of 10% of GDP.

GDP (purchasing power parity) $182.8bn. (1999 est.); GDP per capita (purchasing power parity) $8,000 (1999 est.).

2 Trade Unionism

The first Venezuelan unions began to make an impact after the death in 1936 of the dictator Gómez: that year saw a 43-day strike in the oil fields. But the development of trade unions was restricted by predominantly military rule until from 1945-48 the founder of Democratic Action (AD), Rómulo Betancourt, headed a revolutionary junta with wide labour support which became organized in the Venezuelan Confederation of Workers (CTV).

The AD government was overthrown and replaced by a military dictatorship under Pérez Jiménez in 1948, and trade unions were dissolved. Pérez Jiménez fell from power in 1958, and AD candidates served as elected presidents form 1959 to 1969. During this period the re-founded CTV consolidated its position as the dominant trade union centre, maintaining a close relationship to the AD, which provided it with financial assistance. It has since retained that position, and affiliates up to 90 per cent of union members. The CTV has at times in its history been almost indistinguishable from the AD party but from the late 1980s it adopted a more critical stance in the face of economic austerity packages. Social and economic unrest, including strike action called by the CTV, contributed to the atmosphere which led to the abortive 1992 Chávez coup against the AD government.

Since his election at the end of 1998 Chávez, as part of his campaign against entrenched institutions, has targeted the CTV from a populist position, accusing it of corruption and not serving the needs of the people. In Aug. 1999, a draft decree was issued threatening the dissolution of the CTV and its 3,000 affiliated unions, the confiscation of their assets, and a ban on trade union leaders traveling abroad, pending an "audit" of the unions by the government. The ICFTU warned that if this happened, it would complain not just to the ILO but to the IMF and World Bank, as Venezuela's funders. The WCL regional affiliate CLAT (which is based in the Venezuelan capital), in contrast, issued an ambiguous statement in Oct. 1999 saying that caution was required in assessing the situation brought about by the Chávez programme. This programme would, according to CLAT, lead to the appearance of new political, social and trade union actors, and seemed to be a "favourable evolution" though with "a number of uncertainties". The proposal was subsequently dropped but Chávez resumed his attacks in 2000, and on Dec. 3 a referendum approved powers to allow the dissolution of existing federations and confederations and replacement of their leaders within 180 days. The ICFTU and international trade secretariats subsequently put out a statement warning that they would not recognize any trade union organization that was created as a result of implementation of the referendum.

Venezuela was a founding member of the International Labour Organization, but withdrew briefly in 1957-58. It ratified ILO Convention No.98 (Right to Organize and Collective Bargaining, 1949) in 1968 and Convention No. 87 (Freedom of Association and Protection of the Right to Organize, 1948) in 1982. All workers, except the armed forces, may join unions.

Collective bargaining has a history dating back to the

1930s. Indeed, the country was one of the first in Latin America to allow public employees to bargain collectively. However, collective agreements are largely to be found at the plant level. There is a right to strike but this is restricted in cases involving a serious threat to the population, where the President may order a return to work and compulsory arbitration. Although there is a strong legislative tradition governing employment conditions, largely designed to protect the worker, it applies only to large enterprises; small and medium-sized workplaces operate outside legal constraints in what is a large informal sector.

3 Trade Union Centre

Confederación de Trabajadores de Venezuela (CTV)
Venezuelan Confederation of Workers

Address. Av. Andres Eloy Blanco, Edificio José Vargas, Piso 17, Los Caobos, Caracas 1050

Phone. +58 2 576 4616

Fax. +58 2 575 1920

E-mail. ctvpresidencia@cantv.net

History and character. The CTV was reorganized in 1947 in close association with the ruling Democratic Action (AD) party, though it traces itself back to the CTV that held its first congress in 1936. It was dissolved under the dictatorship of Pérez Jiménez, but reformed in 1959, since when it has been the principal Venezuelan trade union centre. Its relationship with the AD has always been close, but it criticized the AD governments' adoption of austerity measures in the 1980s, the CTV

arguing that a disproportionate share of the burden of the debt crisis was being borne by labour.

Its closeness to government received a severe jolt with the popular unrest of 1989 against the retrenchment programme of President Pérez. Nonetheless the centre's reaction to the government privatization programme was muted and tended to take the form of constructive involvement rather than outright criticism. While the CTV's leadership includes members of a number of parties, the majority are supporters of AD.

During 1999 President Chávez attacked the CTV as a corrupt institution and threatened to dissolve it. That threat further intensified following a referendum in Dec. 2000 (see above).

International affiliation. ICFTU

4 Other Trade Union Organization

Movimiento Nacional de Trabajadores Para La Liberación (MONTRAL)

Address. Av. Las Palmas, Edificio Montral, Urbanización Las Palmas, La Florida, Apartado 6058, Caracas 1010

Phone. +58 2 781 3511

Fax. +58 2 793 6230

Leadership. Dagoberto González (president)

History and character. Founded in 1974 and is a coordinating body for Christian-influenced unions.

International affiliations. WCL

Vietnam

Capital: Hanoi
Population: 78.77 m. (2000 est.)

1 Political and Economic Background

Vietnam, divided from 1954, was reunified in 1975 after the communist forces of the North defeated the US-backed South. Since that time, power has been held by the Communist Party of Vietnam (CPV), which is the only legal party.

Since 1987 there has been some movement away from rigid communist economic orthodoxy towards a more reformist line, including recognition of private enterprise as legitimate, and efforts to attract foreign

investment. However, despite the growth of a vigorous small business sector, the state continues to dominate the economy, with a lack of political commitment to privatization. Foreign investment declined sharply in the late 1990s. 65% of the labour force is engaged in agriculture and Vietnam remains a poor country.

GDP (purchasing power parity) $143.1bn. (1999 est.); GDP per capita (purchasing power parity) $1,850 (1999 est.).

2 Trade Unionism

In the former Democratic Republic of Vietnam (North Vietnam) unions were organized on the communist model in the Vietnam Confederation of Trade Unions (VCTU). In former South Vietnam unions were affiliated to the anti-communist Confédération Vietnam miene du Travail (CVT), founded in 1949, which in its latter years was affiliated to the WCL.

After the North's military victory and unification of the country the VCTU was established throughout Vietnam, changing its name to the Vietnam General Confederation of Labour (VGCL) in 1988. The former secretary-general of the CVT, Nguyen Van Phong, spent 10 years in a 're-education camp' following the fall of South Vietnam, and died in 1986. The ICFTU reported at that time that 20 former CVT officials were still detained in re-education camps. While there has been some liberalization of the labour laws in the 1990s in parallel with developments in the structure of the economy, Vietnam did not experience a reform movement parallel to that which swept through most Soviet-influenced states in the early 1990s. The CVT still exists in exile, based in France.

Vietnam has not ratified ILO Conventions No. 87 (Freedom of Association and Protection of the Right to Organize, 1948) or No.98 (Right to Organize and Collective Bargaining, 1949). Under the 1992 constitution the VGCL must cooperate with state organs, take part in state affairs and supervise the work of state bodies. Unions cannot be set up without approval from the VGCL. The labour law requires provincial trade union organizations to establish unions within 6 months at all new enterprises with more than 10 employees as well as at existing enterprises that operate without trade unions. Company managers are required by law to accept and cooperate with these unions. However, while the law states that all unions must be affiliated to the VGCL, there has been a growth of hundreds of unaffiliated "labour associations" recruiting occupations such as taxi drivers, cooks, and market porters.

Collective bargaining is provided for under the 1995 labour code but in practice is limited. There is a system of labour arbitration councils. Unions have the right to appeal a council decision to the provincial people's court. The 1995 code also provides a right to strike. While strikes had previously been illegal, they did occur and were tolerated, at least in the non-state sector; there were 32 strikes in 1994, mainly in foreign-owned enterprises. Approximately 250 strikes were reported in the period from Jan. 1995–Sept. 1999. Of these, the majority (132) were in enterprises with foreign investment, and most (80) of the rest in private enterprises. Many strikes began as wildcat actions and were techni-

cally illegal, having not completed conciliation and arbitration procedures, although the government tolerated the strikes and did not take action against the strikers. While the VGCL or its affiliated unions did not sanction these strikes officially, they were supported unofficially at the local and provincial levels of the VGCL on an informal basis. Strikes have occurred over issues such as non-enforcement of the labour code, unpaid wages, working conditions, unfair dismissals and allegations of repressive management techniques in foreign-owned enterprises. In 1997, the government claimed that most labour disputes took place at small-scale enterprises owned or partly owned by companies from South Korea, Singapore and Taiwan, while statistics issued in 1998 showed that half of all strikes in the previous three years took place at Korean-owned companies.

Strikes are prohibited in a wide range of sectors including public services, defence industries, water, electricity generation, posts and telecommunications, railways, maritime and air transportation, banking, and the oil and gas industry. The government may also order an end to a strike considered detrimental to the national economy or public safety.

3 Trade Union Centre

Vietnam General Confederation of Labour (VGCL)

History and character. The Vietnam Confederation of Trade Unions (VCTU) was established in communist-controlled North Vietnam and then extended to the whole country after the collapse of the South in 1975. It adopted its present name in 1988. No unions may legally exist outside its structure. The VGCL has sought to achieve a presence in the new private and foreign-owned sectors. A 1992 conference on building and developing organizations in the emergent non-state sector stressed that this was the foremost task ahead of the VGCL. The VGCL says that it now represents 95% of public sector workers, 90% of workers in state-owned enterprises, and nearly 70% of private sector workers.

The VGCL emphasizes the need to secure national economic objectives, while ensuring a tripartite approach to problem-solving and appreciation of the value of labour. Its unions generally work to avoid industrial unrest, but have retrospectively supported some strikes, especially in foreign-owned enterprises.

International affiliation. WFTU

Yemen

Capital: Sana'a
Population: 17.48 m. (2000 est.)

1 Political and Economic Background

The Republic of Yemen was established in May 1990 by the unification of the Yemen Arab Republic (North Yemen) and the People's Democratic Republic of Yemen (South Yemen). Lieutenant-General Ali Abdullah Saleh, the former President of North Yemen, has been President of the unified state since its creation. In 1994 his Vice-President, who had been the leader of the ruling party in South Yemen, declared the secession of the South, but this rebellion was quickly crushed by Northern forces. President Saleh was re-elected in Sept. 1999 with 96.3% of the vote and his General People's Congress party has a large majority in the legislature.

Yemen is the poorest Arab country, its problems compounded by a high population growth rate. In the early 1990s it suffered the return of 850,000 migrant workers by Saudi Arabia and other Gulf States dissatisfied with its lack of support for military action against Iraq. Unemployment is estimated at 40% and development of its small private sector economy is hampered by lack of resources, poor infrastructure, government interference, corruption and political instability.

GDP (purchasing power parity) $12.7bn. (1999 est.); GDP per capita (purchasing power parity) $750 (1999 est.).

2 Trade Unionism

North Yemen ratified ILO Conventions No.87 (Freedom of Association and Protection of the Right to Organize, 1948) and No.98 (Right to Organize and Collective Bargaining, 1949) in 1976. South Yemen ratified only Convention No. 98 (in 1969). The unified country is considered to have ratified both Conventions.

Trade unions first appeared in the 1960s in North Yemen but workers' organization there was strictly regulated by the labour code. There was a national con-federation but little indication of significant trade union activity. In South Yemen, the ICFTU-affiliated Aden Trades Union Congress participated in the struggle for independence from the UK. After independence in 1967, the South's unions were reorganized into the General Confederation of Workers' Trade Unions, which joined the WFTU. With the unification of North and South in 1990, the two national confederations merged in 1990 to form the Yemeni Confederation of Labour Unions, but differences persisted as the more militant trade unionists of the South saw continued cause for protest, particularly against the extension of Islamic law.

Existing labour laws were intended to apply in their respective areas until the enactment of a new national code, but this had not been addressed by the time civil war erupted again in 1994. At the time of unification there were no collective agreements in force and bargaining did not take place.

A new labour law was enacted in 1995 that brought a degree of liberalization. Workers, other than those in the public sector or agricultural workers, may form and join unions. While this right exists in practice, the government also ensures that loyalists hold responsible positions in the unions. Employers may not dismiss workers for union activities and cases of anti-union discrimination may be taken to the Ministry of Labour or the labour courts, which are reportedly often sympathetic to workers, especially where foreign companies are involved.

The Yemeni Confederation of Labor Unions (YCLU) is the sole trade union centre, claiming to have 350,000 members in 15 unions. Its legal monopoly was repealed by the 1995 labour law but no alternative organization has been formed. It tends to work closely with the government to avoid labour disputes and is affiliated to the World Federation of Trade Unions.

Collective agreements must be reviewed and registered by the Ministry of Labour and may be rejected if considered contrary to the national economic interest. Strikes are lawful provided there has been an irreversible breakdown of negotiation and arbitration, and subject to permission being obtained from the YCLU, although none were recorded in 1999. Political strikes are banned.

Yugoslavia

Capital: Belgrade
Population: 10.66 m. (2000 est.)

1 Political and Economic Background

The former Socialist Federal Republic of Yugoslavia (SFRY) collapsed in the period 1991–92 when the constituent republics of Slovenia, Croatia, Bosnia-Herzegovina and Macedonia, with more than half the population, declared their independence. This was a consequence both of each republic's own respective national aspirations and the rise of a domineering nationalism among the Serbian population (the largest single group) within Yugoslavia. In Apr. 1992 creation of the Federal Republic of Yugoslavia (FRY) was proclaimed but as this comprised only two of the former republics (Serbia and Montenegro), and was entirely dominated by Serbia, it failed to achieve universal recognition as the legitimate successor to the SFRY. Throughout the 1990s power was held by Slobodan Milosevic, the leader of the Socialist Party of Serbia (SPS, the descendant of the former ruling League of Communists), who was successively President of Serbia and then (from 1997) President of Yugoslavia. Under him from 1991–95 a series of wars was waged against all the former Yugoslav republics other than Macedonia. In 1999 Serbian efforts to crush the rebellious Albanian majority in the Serbian province of Kosovo triggered a massive intervention by NATO, and in June 1999 control of Kosovo passed to the United Nations Interim Administrative Mission in Kosovo (UNMIK). In addition, under President Milo Djukanovic (elected in 1997) Montenegro effectively became detached from Yugoslav federal structures and threatened to break away altogether.

In Oct. 2000 Milosevic initially sought to hang on to the presidency after apparently suffering defeat in elections but was forced to concede to opposition leader Vojislav Kostunica after mass demonstrations throughout the country. In Dec. 2000 opposition parties overwhelmingly defeated Milosevic's SPS in elections in Serbia.

The FRY was created against a background of war and economic collapse as the inter-dependent economic structure of the former SFRY fell apart. Under Milosevic the economy was characterized by corruption and cronyism (with key posts in state enterprises held by Milosevic supporters), the lack of a transparent and equitable framework for private investment, and chronic inefficiency and under-employment. These problems were exacerbated by the application of international sanctions. Plummeting output, unemployment, widespread wage arrears, shortages, and anxieties about the forthcoming winter in the face of international sanctions

were factors that led to Milosevic's loss of the presidency in Oct. 2000.

GDP (purchasing power parity) $20.6bn. (1999 est.); GDP per capita (purchasing power parity) $1,800 (1999 est.).

2 Trade Unionism

Yugoslavia joined the International Labour Organization in 1919, but withdrew from 1949 to 1951. It ratified ILO Conventions No.87 (Freedom of Association and Protection of the Right to Organize, 1948) and No.98 (Right to Organize and Collective Bargaining, 1949) in 1958. These ratifications are considered to apply to the FRY.

The trade unions of the former SFRY were essentially the product of the establishment of communist rule after World War II and the subsequent re-modelling of the economy and political and social relations through the principle of self-management. The unions were organized through the Confederation of Trade Unions of Yugoslavia (Savez Sindikata Jugoslavije, SSJ). Neither the national constitution nor the law formally prohibited the formation of unions outside the structure of the SSJ, although as a named organization it had various rights and responsibilities, but no unions outside it appeared before 1988. In Slovenia and Croatia independent unions developed in 1989 and the official union councils there endorsed the principle of freedom of association. The June 1990 (11th) SSJ congress withdrew from the Socialist Alliance of Working Peoples of Yugoslavia, the coordinating body for all communist institutions in the country, and accepted that it would have to function in a pluralistic environment. Thereafter the former federal structure collapsed with the rise of nationalism in the constituent republics. Much of the panoply of industrial relations institutions and practices, including the self-management system for enterprises, dissolved in the face of war, secession and economic collapse.

The official unions are now organized as the Confederation of Autonomous Trade Unions of Serbia (Savez Samostalnih Sindikata, SSS), which retained the assets of the former SSJ and benefits from automatic check-off of union dues in state enterprises. The SSS claims 1.8 million members although its membership is considered closer to one million. The official unions from the early 1990s generally supported Milosevic's mix of strident Serbian nationalism and unreformed socialism and subsidization of inefficient state enterprises, although there was periodic unrest caused by inflation, unemployment and wage arrears. On occasions workers in official unions joined with members of independent unions in protest strikes. In Aug. 1999 the government concluded an agreement with the SSS whereby its members would get fuel at subsidized prices in the winter of 1999–2000.

The leading independent union is Nezavisnost (Independence), formed in 1991, which has about 180,000 members. Most other independent unions operate in individual sectors of the economy but formation of independent unions has generally faced opposition from enterprise directors.

Collective bargaining is dominated by the SSS. However, effective collective bargaining is undermined by widespread unemployment and the inability of enterprises to pay wages. In wide areas of the economy strikers are required to maintain a minimum service level. Strikers are not permitted to gather outside workplaces. The criminal code provides for prison penalties for "abuse of the right to strike".

In **Kosovo**, the Confederation of Independent Trade Unions of Kosovo (BSPK) was founded in 1990 and developed among the Albanian workforce in opposition to the official unions. It claimed to have organized 250,000 members in 24 unions. In March 1999, however, BSPK president Agim Hajrizi was arrested by the Yugoslav authorities and murdered, and union records were destroyed. Following the establishment of a UN protectorate under UNMIK, BSPK began to reconstruct itself. It is working with the ILO to establish a Solidarity Centre office in Pristina, the capital of Kosovo.

In **Montenegro**, the Confederation of Independent Trade Unions split in 1998 between a majority group, led by president Danielo Popovic, broadly supporting the line of Montenegrin President Milo Djukanovic in seeking greater autonomy from Serbia, and a pro-Milosevic minority. However, the confederation has criticized the Montenegrin government for adopting labour legislation without consulting the unions. The main concerns are mass unemployment, wage arrears, and the impact of nationalism on regional stability.

3 Trade Union Centre

Nezavisnost
Independence

Address. Nusiceva 4/V, 11000 Belgrade

Phone. +381 11 323 8226

Fax. +381 11 324 4118

E-mail. office@nezavisnost.org.yu

Website. www.nezavisnost.org.yu (Serbian; English)

Membership. 180,000

History and character. Nezavisnost is a federation of 13 member unions, in all the main sectors of the economy, and says that it is active in over 1,000 companies throughout Serbia. Its oldest affiliates are the Metal Workers' Union and the Independent Media Union (founded 1991) and the Teachers' Union (founded 1992). It has regional offices in 10 provincial cities. Nezavisnost organizers have faced problems including job suspensions or downgrading, barring from workplaces, compulsory leave, disciplinary proceedings and dismissal.

Nezavisnost led strikes of teachers and health workers in 1998 but in 1999–2000 focused on political action campaigns. Nezavisnost demanded constitutional and legal protection of human and trade union rights and a genuine multi-party democracy. It accused the official trade unions of the SSS of supporting the Milosevic regime and itself participated in the opposition Yugoslav Action Group (Jugoslovenska Akcija) with other civic groups. It played a role in the fall of Milosevic in Oct. 2000, campaigning for the opposition and a high turnout in the elections, and subsequently backing strikes when Milosevic at first refused to accept defeat.

Publication. Monthly Bulletin (Serbian only) on website.

International affiliation. ICFTU

Zambia

Capital: Lusaka
Population: 9.58 m. (2000 est.)

1 Political and Economic Background

Zambia gained its independence from the United Kingdom in 1964, and its President from then until 1991 was Kenneth Kaunda, whose socialist United National Independence Party (UNIP) was declared the sole legal political organization in 1972. Zambia shared in the early 1990s movement to political pluralism and reform that affected much of Africa. In Oct. 1991, elections were held on a multi-party basis, and resulted in victory for the Movement for Multiparty Democracy (MMD) and its presidential candidate Frederick Chiluba, the chairman of the Zambia Congress of Trade Unions. In Nov. 1996 Chiluba was re-elected President (in an election in which Kaunda had been barred from standing), while in simultaneous legislative elections (which the

UNIP boycotted in protest at the bar on Kaunda) the MMD retained control of the National Assembly.

Some 85% of the workforce are engaged in agriculture, much of it at subsistence level. Copper mining and processing dominate in the formal economy. Zambia derives around 90% of its export earnings from copper (and most of the balance from other minerals) and was severely affected by the fall in world copper prices which occurred from the late 1970s onwards. Discontent with the economic condition of the country was a major factor in Kaunda's 1991 election defeat. The Chiluba administration has implemented an IMF-backed programme of privatization and deregulation but efforts to privatize the copper mines took seven years to 2000, with output falling to less than half 1970s levels. There is a continuing dependence on international economic assistance.

GDP (purchasing power parity) $8.5bn. (1999 est.); GDP per capita (purchasing power parity) $880 (1999 est.).

2 Trade Unionism

Trade unions first developed under British rule in the copper belt in the 1930s. The Zambia Congress of Trade Unions (ZCTU) is the national trade union centre, although traditionally some unions have operated outside it. The 1993 Industrial and Labour Relations Act is based on the "one industry, one union" principle, and new unions have found it difficult to achieve recognition where an existing union is already established. By African standards, the labour movement is large, independent and influential, and the principle of collective bargaining is well established. An estimated 60% of the 300,000 workers in the formal economy are unionized.

The unions' influence was reflected in the transition to political pluralism. Frederick Chiluba, the chairman of the ZCTU, became the leader of the Movement for Multiparty Democracy, set up in 1990 to oppose Kaunda's UNIP party. In Oct. 1991 Chiluba won 75% of the vote to defeat Kaunda for the presidency in the first elections under a new multi-party constitution. Chiluba also appointed the ZCTU secretary-general, Newstead Zimba, to his Cabinet. In 1996 the Chiluba government ratified ILO Conventions No.87 (Freedom of Association and Protection of the Right to Organize, 1948) and No.98 (Right to Organize and Collective Bargaining, 1949).

The new Chiluba government sought to involve the unions in the restructuring of the economy on the basis of tripartite consultations. Ahead of privatization the reduction of the copper mines workforce by 10,000 was agreed with the unions in 1994. But despite supporting the MMD, the ZCTU was critical of its economic policies and willingness to implement IMF-inspired structural adjustment programmes.

Collective bargaining is well established and tends to be centralized, with employers and unions in each industry negotiating agreements through joint councils without government involvement. Public service employees such as civil servants and teachers negotiate directly with the government. In the event of a breakdown of negotiations, conciliation and arbitration disputes can be referred to the Industrial Court. The Court also provides protection for workers victimized for union activities. All workers other than those in essential services and the police, judicial and security services have the right to strike, but because strike action can be taken only after lengthy procedures, most strikes are in practice illegal.

Many local government workers have been affected by lengthy pay arrears. The Public Order Act, which requires police permission for public meetings and demonstrations, has been used to arrest workers protesting against such arrears.

3 Trade Union Centre

Zambia Congress of Trade Unions (ZCTU)

Address. Baynards Building, PO Box 20652, Kitwe

Phone. +260 2 224 765

Fax. +260 2 228 284

E-mail. zctu@zamnet.zm

Leadership. Silvester Tembo (secretary-general)

History and character. The ZCTU was formed in 1965 in succession to the United Trades Union Congress (UTUC). It affiliates all but one of the major unions in the country.

During single-party rule under Kenneth Kaunda and UNIP, the ZCTU sought to assert its independence of the government. The ZCTU leaders Frederick Chiluba and Newstead Zimba, and 15 other prominent trade unionists, were expelled from UNIP in 1981 following a wave of strikes that the government linked to a thwarted plot to stage a coup. The expulsions were followed by protest strikes in the copper-belt and other sectors, and after three months the expelled trade unionists were re-admitted to the party. Chiluba, Zimba and others were detained a second time in 1981 after further industrial unrest, when President Kaunda stated that they were instigating illegal strikes with the aim of toppling the UNIP leadership. All detained union leaders were released on the order of the courts by Nov. 1981.

Early in 1985, in response to a wave of wildcat strikes triggered by the imposition of austerity measures required by the IMF, the government banned strikes in various sectors of the economy and ordered employers to end the statutory check-off of union dues for illegal strikers. These measures were revoked in 1986, but the labour movement still complained that it was hamstrung by legal restrictions, censorship and pressure to succumb to the demands of the ruling party. The passports of Chiluba and Zimba were withdrawn in 1987. At the end of that year Chiluba was expelled from his own union, the National Union of Building, Engineering and General Workers (NUBWEGW), amid charges of constitutional irregularities. However the ZCTU alleged that this internal discord was engineered by the government as part of its campaign to disable the labour movement. Chiluba retained his position as ZCTU chairman-general and the courts later ruled that the ZCTU could over-rule his expulsion from the NUBWEGW.

In the late 1980s living standards continued to fall and there was growing pressure for political change. In July 1990 Chiluba was prominently involved in the launch of the Movement for Multiparty Democracy (MMD) as a new opposition party. At the end of the year the ZCTU severed all ties with UNIP. In Oct. 1991 multi-party elections Chiluba, as the candidate of the MMD, defeated Kaunda for the presidency. Of seven ZCTU leaders who stood for election, six were successful and all joined the government, including ZCTU secretary-general Zimba.

After Chiluba's election the ZCTU sought to act as an independent force, insisting that, despite the presence of trade unionists within it, the MMD was not a labour party. In May 1993 ZCTU leaders visited IMF headquarters to put their views on the need for leniency in imposition of restructuring programmes on Zambia. Simultaneously they proposed to the government a solidarity pact to work out an equitable distribution of the burden through tripartite bodies.

In Oct. 1994 defeated candidates in ZCTU leadership elections complained of government interference in the elections. This culminated in five of the ZCTU's affiliates, most prominently the Mineworkers' Union, breaking away and setting up a rival federation for a period. With the re-affiliation of the Mineworkers in 1999, however, the Zambia Union of Financial and Allied Workers remained the only one of the country's 19 major national unions outside the ZCTU.

In 1997 the government announced a wage freeze for public sector workers and plans to make tens of thousands of public sector workers redundant. In Feb. 1998 the ZCTU warned it would stage a one-day strike on Mar. 9 unless the government agreed to negotiate, leading former ZCTU secretary-general Zimba to threaten to de-register the ZCTU and any of its affiliates that took such action. Workers in essential services were warned that they could not take part in work stoppages under emergency regulations introduced in Oct. 1997. The strike went ahead nonetheless and the unions were not de-registered.

International affiliations. ICFTU; CTUC

Zimbabwe

Capital: Harare
Population: 11.34 m. (2000 est.)

1 Political and Economic Background

The white minority regime in Rhodesia, which had declared unilateral independence from the United Kingdom in 1965, ended in 1979. In 1980 the country achieved full independence as the Republic of Zimbabwe and has been ruled since then by the Zimbabwe African National Union-Patriotic Front (ZANU-PF) of Robert Mugabe, who was Prime Minister until 1987 and thereafter President. In 1991 Mugabe announced he had abandoned plans to introduce a one-party state structure and the party deleted references to Marxism, Leninism and scientific socialism from its constitution. In elections in 1995 ZANU-PF won all but two of the 120 elective seats (with the President also being able to himself appoint a further 30 MPs), while in 1996 Mugabe was re-elected as President with 93% of the vote after other candidates withdrew. In further parliamentary elections in June 2000, marked by widespread intimidation by ZANU-PF supporters of

their opponents, ZANU-PF narrowly retained its majority of elected seats but 58 opposition MPs were elected, 57 of them from the Movement for Democratic Change founded in 1999.

About three-quarters of the population depend on agriculture for a livelihood, with the majority engaged in subsistence cultivation. The highly developed commercial agriculture sector, which contributes 10% of GDP, is dominated by a few thousand white farmers, and in 1999–2000 ZANU-PF supporters staged occupations of white-owned land saying this should be redistributed to landless black "war veterans". Zimbabwe also has mining, manufacturing and service sectors, with the non-farm sector dominated by state monopolies. The economy continued to deteriorate in the late 1990s, with rising inflation and unemployment, an escalating budget deficit, and underlying chronic mismanagement and corruption. In Oct. 2000 the World Bank announced that it would cease lending to Zimbabwe because of its failure to meet its debt-servicing obligations. Zimbabwe is thought to have the highest incidence of HIV/AIDS in the world, affecting one-quarter of the adult population and threatening the country's future prospects.

GDP (purchasing power parity) $26.5bn. (1999 est.);

GDP per capita (purchasing power parity) $2,400 (1999 est.).

2 Trade Unionism

Zimbabwe has not ratified ILO Convention No.87 (Freedom of Association and Protection of the Right to Organize, 1948) and only ratified Convention No. 98 (Right to Organize and Collective Bargaining, 1949) in 1998. However, under the 1985 Labour Relations Act, private sector workers (but not managers) are free to join and form unions of their own choosing and employers are prohibited from discriminating against union members. Public servants, teachers and nurses are not covered by the Labour Relations Act; their conditions of employment are covered by the constitution, and they may only join associations, which cannot bargain collectively or strike. Also excluded from the scope of the Labour Relations Act are domestic and agricultural workers and workers in export processing zones.

After independence, previously competing centres representing European and African workers were merged into the Zimbabwe Congress of Trade Unions (ZCTU). About 20% of the workforce in the formal sector are members of the 33 unions affiliated to the ZCTU. While the government may de-register individual unions the High Court has ruled it may not suspend or de-register the ZCTU. In Oct. 1996 a Zimbabwe Federation of Trade Unions (ZFTU) was launched with the objective of working in collaboration with the government, but it has gathered little support. The ICFTU reported in 1999 that the ZFTU's "origin, leadership and membership remain unclear".

Under the 1992 Labour Relations Amendment Act a framework is provided for collective bargaining. Negotiations generally take place on an industry-wide basis between unions and employer bodies meeting in joint national employment councils. The government does not involve itself in these negotiations but retains the right to veto agreements it considers contrary to the national interest. The 1985 Labour Relations Act also provided for works councils to be set up (in parallel with trade unions) to negotiate with management on various plant-level issues, excluding wages. Under the 1992 Labour Relations Amendment Act the role of works councils was extended and they were given powers to negotiate collective agreements overriding industry-wide agreements, a development opposed by the unions. In the public sector, wages are determined by the government, subject to the review of an independent Public Service Commission, which also consults the employees' associations.

Strikes are illegal in "essential services" and these have been given a broad definition. All public servants are considered by the government to be involved in essential services and barred from striking, but in practice from 1996 onwards civil servants, teachers, and health service staff have all been involved in strikes. Although this has led to wholesale dismissals, most were rehired at the end of the disputes.

Relationships between the ZCTU and the government deteriorated sharply in the late 1990s. Industrial action over declining living standards began to gather pace in 1997 as the economy continued to deteriorate. On Dec. 9, 1997, the ZCTU led the biggest protest strike yet seen in Zimbabwe. The strike was triggered by a 5% levy imposed on workers to finance compensation projects for "war veterans", the imposition of sales taxes and increases in fuel and electricity costs. This was followed by a succession of "stay-aways" and other protests through 1998. In the aftermath of two successive widely supported general strikes in Nov. 1998, on Nov. 27, 1998 Mugabe used emergency powers to ban national strikes for six months. Employers were encouraged to dismiss any worker taking part in a banned strike. By this time the ZCTU and the Institute of Directors were united in blaming Mugabe and the mismanagement and corruption of ZANU-PF for the collapse of the economy. However, the government abandoned plans to convert the six-month ban into permanent restrictions in the face of legal and political challenges.

In Sept. 1999, the ZCTU and civic groups formed the Movement for Democratic Change (MDC), with ZCTU secretary-general Morgan Tsvangirai as its leading figure, to oppose ZANU-PF in elections due to be held in 2000. The MDC called for a "people's constitution", with open, accountable government. The MDC's policies included: the withdrawal of Zimbabwean troops from the Democratic Republic of Congo; negotiation on the foreign debt; restrictions on unnecessary imports and incentives for exports; removal of the managers of non-performing state enterprises; the distribution of unused agricultural land to subsistence farmers; and the declaration of a national emergency over AIDS.

The MDC's support base was seen as largely urban, and in escalating conflict in the months preceding the June 2000 elections, Mugabe sought to mobilize his rural support with a campaign of occupations of white-owned commercial farms by ZANU-PF "war veterans". Mugabe claimed the ZCTU and the MDC were being used by white farmers as a front for their own opposition to his land re-distribution policy. In the elections, the MDC won 57 of the 120 elected seats in Parliament, emerging as the strongest party in the capital and other urban areas, and enabling it to create a viable parliamentary opposition to ZANU-PF for the first time since independence. Tsvangirai, who had stood down from the ZCTU but was not elected to Parliament, announced his intention was to contest the presidential election due in 2002.

3 Trade Union Centre

Zimbabwe Congress of Trade Unions (ZCTU)
Address. PO Box 3549, Harare
Phone. +263 4 794742
Fax. +263 4 728 484
E-mail. zctu@mango.zw

Leadership. Isidore Zindoga (acting secretary-general)

Membership. 400,000 in 33 affiliated unions

History and character. The ZCTU was founded after independence in Feb. 1981. In its early years it adopted the characteristic position of many African trade union centres at that time, associating closely with the ruling party and emphasizing its role in assisting national social and economic development.

From the late 1980s the ZCTU became more outspoken in criticism of the government, and in 1989 secretary-general Morgan Tsvangirai was arrested after condemning the closure of the University of Zimbabwe, under powers inherited from the previous white regime. He was held for two months in defiance of High Court orders to free him and refused to join other ZCTU officials in endorsing Mugabe's 1990 re-election.

In the 1990s the ZCTU continued to be an irritant to the government, and sharply critical of its interference in industrial relations matters. Since 1997 the ZCTU has emerged as a major source of opposition to the Mugabe government, leading a succession of strikes and protests which have had considerable support in the urban areas and provoked government harassment and use of emergency powers legislation. Two days after the protest strike of Dec. 9, 1997 (see above), Tsvangirai was attacked and beaten unconscious by armed men; the ZCTU reportedly provided the police with names of suspects but no action was taken. In Jan. 1999, Isidore Zindoga, the then deputy secretary-general, was beaten unconscious in an attack linked to the police.

In Sept. 1999, the ZCTU was the leading force in the formation of the Movement for Democratic Change (see above), and at its first congress in Jan. 2000 Tsvangirai was elected MDC president and ZCTU president Gibson Sibanda became MDC vice-president.

In Aug. 2000 the ZCTU staged a one-day protest strike against the breakdown of law and order.

International affiliation. ICFTU; CTUC

INTERNATIONAL AND REGIONAL ORGANIZATIONS

Caribbean Congress of Labour (CCL)

Address. NUPW Complex, Dalkeith Road, St. Michael, Barbados

Phone. +246 427 5067

Fax. +246 427 2496

E-mail. cclres@caribsurf.com

Leadership. Lloyd Goodleigh (president); George De Peana (general secretary)

Membership. 500,000 in 33 affiliates

History and character. Founded in 1960, the CCL now has 33 affiliates in 17 countries in the English and Dutch-speaking Caribbean (including the mainland nations of Belize, Guyana and Surinam).

The CCL provides research, educational and campaigning support to its affiliates and works to encourage the development of trade unionism and national centres in the region. It represents trade union concerns to the Caribbean Community (CARICOM), the Organization of Eastern Caribbean States (OECS) and the Association of Caribbean States (ACS) and works closely with the ICFTU and its regional organization ORIT.

Commonwealth Trade Union Council (CTUC)

Address. Congress House, Great Russell Street, London WC1B 3LS, United Kingdom

Phone. +44 20 7631 0728

Fax. +44 20 7436 0301

E-mail. info@commonwealthtuc.org

Website. www.commonwealthtuc.org

Leadership. Gibson Sibanda (chairperson); Annie Watson (director)

Membership. 30 million members in Commonwealth countries

History and character. The CTUC was established in 1979. It provides a representative voice for trade unions in dealing with the institutions of the Commonwealth and Commonwealth governments. It also fosters cooperation among members unions and assists in trade union education, training and solidarity activity. Campaigns in more recent years in the area of human rights and trade union freedoms have covered countries such as South Africa (now re-admitted to the Commonwealth), Nigeria, Fiji and Sierra Leone. It holds an annual general session for member organizations to set policy.

Publications. Include news service accessible at website.

Affiliates. The CTUC has members (which are usually national trade union centres) in the following independent states (see country sections for details): Antigua; Australia; Bahamas; Bangladesh; Barbados; Belize; Botswana; Cameroon; Canada; Cyprus; Dominica; Fiji; Gambia; Ghana; Grenada; Guyana; India; Jamaica; Kenya; Kiribati; Lesotho; Malawi; Malaysia; Malta; Mauritius; Mozambique; Namibia; New Zealand; Nigeria; Pakistan; Papua New Guinea; St. Christopher and Nevis; St. Lucia; St. Vincent; Samoa; Seychelles; Sierra Leone; Singapore; Solomon Islands; South Africa; Sri Lanka; Swaziland; Tanzania; Tonga; Trinidad and Tobago; Tuvalu; Uganda; United Kingdom; Vanuata; Zambia; Zimbabwe. There are also affiliates in the following dependent territories: Bermuda and Montserrat (UK); Cook Islands (New Zealand).

Confédération Européene des Syndicats Indépendants (CESI)
European Confederation of Independent Trade Unions

Address. Avenue de la Joyeuse Entrée 1–5, B–1040 Brussels, Belgium

Phone. +32 2 282 1860

Fax. +32 2 282 1872

E-mail. cesi.akad.eur@skynet.be

Website. www.cesi-bxl.be

Membership. Reports 7 million members in independent unions in Europe.

History and character. CESI was founded in 1990 and represents the views of minority, independent unions. Its affiliates are a mix of European umbrella organizations, including the International Confederation of Public Servants (CIF), national multi-sector organizations, and national industry-level unions and professional associations. It has affiliates in Belgium, Bulgaria, Czech Republic, Denmark, France, Germany, Hungary, Italy, Luxembourg, Poland, Portugal, Romania, Serbia, Slovakia, Spain and Switzerland. Its more significant affiliates include the CGSLB in Belgium, the CGB and DBB in Germany, the MOSz in Hungary and CISAL in Italy. The membership is diverse, but with particular strength in public administration, as well as several unions of train drivers. CESI has an education institute, "Academy Europe".

Confédération Internationale des Fonctionnaires (CIF)
International Confederation of Public Servants

Address. 59/63 rue du Rocher, 75008 Paris, France

Phone. +33 1 40 85 08 98

Fax. +33 1 41 21 46 47

Website. www.cif-net.org (French; English)

Leadership. Pierre Trausch (president); Christian Chapuis (general secretary)

Membership. 11 member unions in eight countries.

History and character. The CIF was founded in 1955. It is independent of political and religious organiz-ations. Its membership of affiliated unions overlaps to some degree with that of the European Confederation of Independent Trade Unions (CESI) but is smaller. It has an annual summer academy in association with CESI. All its affiliates are in Western Europe.

Education International (EI)

Address. 5 boulevard du Roi Albert II (8th), B–1210 Brussels, Belgium

Phone. +32 2 224 0611

Fax. + 32 2 224 0606

E-mail. educint@ei-ie.org

Website. www.ei-ie.org

Leadership. Mary Hatwood Futrell (president); Fred van Leeuwen (general secretary)

Membership. 23.7 million teachers and workers in edu-cation in 294 unions in 152 countries or territories

History and character. EI is an international trade sec-retariat. It was created in 1993 by the merger of the International Federation of Free Teacher Unions (IFFTU), one of the international trade secretariats associated with the ICFTU, and the World Conference of Organizations of the Teaching Profession (WCOTP).

EI is in formal associate relations with UNESCO and the ILO and works closely with the ICFTU. It is rep-resented on the board of the European Trade Union Committee for Education (ETUCE)

Publications. Include *EI Monthly Monitor; Education International,* quarterly magazine (both published in English, French and Spanish). Content accessible via website.

European Trade Union Confederation (ETUC)
Confédération Européene des Syndicats (CES)

Address. 5 Boulevard Roi Albert II, B–1210 Brussels, Belgium

Phone. +32 2 224 0411

Fax. +32 2 224 0454

E-mail. etuc@etuc.org

Website. www.etuc.org

Leadership. Fritz Verzetnitsch (president); Emilio Gabaglio (general secretary)

Membership. 67 national trade union centres throughout Europe in full membership.

History and character. ETUC was formed in 1973 by the merger of the previous European Confederation of Trade Unions in the European Community with the European Free Trade Area Trade Union Committee. In 1974, the members unions of the WCL's former European organization also joined.

Over the last decade ETUC's membership has increased significantly in the wake of the general col-lapse of communism in Europe. In part, this has resulted from the admission of formerly communist-led centres from Western Europe. The Spanish Workers' Commissions (CC.OO) joined in 1991, to be followed by the Portuguese CGTP-IN. Finally, in 1999, 25 years after it first applied for membership, the French CGT was admitted, its application approved by all member organizations except the CGT-FO. In addition, there has been a measured process of extend-ing ETUC's membership eastward into the former communist bloc. There are now full ETUC members from Bulgaria, Czech Republic, Hungary, Poland, Romania, Slovakia, and Slovenia, while observer status has been given to organizations in the Baltic States (Estonia, Latvia and Lithuania) and the former Yugoslav republics of Croatia and Macedonia. There are as yet no full members or observers from the former Yugoslav republics of Serbia, Montenegro, or Bosnia-Herzegovina, or from Albania, or from any of the successor states to the Soviet Union, other than the Baltic republics.

In addition to expanding its reach eastwards, the ETUC has also increased its role in line with the deep-ening of social and economic integration among the EU member states. Its position as the representative cross-sectoral European-level trade union voice is reflected in its access to the EU's core institutions and it is an active lobbyist for trade union rights and more broadly for enhancing the social dimension and democ-ratization of the EU. It campaigned for the European Works Council Directive on Information and Consultation rights. The ETUC is increasingly regarded as the pan-European voice of the union move-ment.

It also works with employers at the European level in developing social dialogue and has reached two cross-sectoral framework agreements (on parental leave and part-time work) with the employers' representative pan-European body UNICE and CEEP (the state employers' organization). These agreements have the force of law in the EU.

In the 1990s there was a growth in significance of the ETUC's affiliated industrial committees, which are expected by some observers ultimately to be the cutting edge of European-wide collective bargaining.

ETUC works closely with the ICFTU, which does not have a separate regional organization for Europe.

The Council of European Professional and Managerial Staff (EUROCADRES) works under the auspices of ETUC (EUROCADRES: Rue Joseph II 3, B–1000, Brussels, Belgium. *Phone* +32 2 230 7455. *Fax.* +32 2 230 7566. *Website.* www.etuc.org/euro-cadres), as does the European Federation of Retired and Elderly Persons (FERPA).

The ETUC's research arm is the European Trade Union Institute (ETUI, 5 Boulevard du Roi Albert II, B–1210 Brussels, Belgium. *Phone* +32 2 224 04 70. *Fax.* +32 2 224 05 02. Director, Reiner Hoffmann).

Affiliated national trade union organizations: Austria (ÖGB); Belgium (ABVV/FGTB, ACV/CSC); Bulgaria (CITUB; Podkrepa); Cyprus (SEK; Turk-Sen); Czech Republic (CMKOS); Denmark (AC; FTF; LO); Finland (AKAVA; SAK; STTK); France (CFDT-UNSA combined representation; CFTC; CGT; CGT-FO); Germany (DAG; DGB); Greece (ADEDY; GSEE); Hungary (ASzSz; LIGA; MOSz; MSzOSz; SZEF); Iceland (ASI; BSRB); Ireland (ICTU); Italy (CGIL; CISL; UIL); Luxembourg (CGT-L; LCGB); Malta (CMTU; GWU); Netherlands (CNV; FNV; UNIE-MHP); Norway (AF; LO); Poland (NSZZ Solidarnosc); Portugal (CGTP-IN; UGT-P); Romania (BNS; Cartel Alfa; CNSLR-Fratia; CSDR); San Marino (CDLS; CSdL); Slovakia (KOZSR); Slovenia (ZSSS); Spain (CC.OO; STV-ELA; UGT-E); Sweden (LO; SACO; TCO); Switzerland (CNG; SGB; VSA); Turkey (DISK; HAK-IS; KESK; TURK-IS); United Kingdom (TUC). *Observer status*: Croatia (SSSH); Estonia (EAKL; TALO); Latvia (LBAS); Lithuania (LDS; LPSS); Macedonia (SSM).

Affiliated European Industry Federations. The ETUC structure embraces European-wide industry federations and European committees of international trade secretariats. The exact relationships between these bodies and ETUC and the international secretariats varies. Individual federations include:

European Federation of Agricultural Workers' Unions (EFA/ECF)

Address. Rue Fossé-aux-Loups 38, B–1000 Brussels, Belgium

Phone. +32 2 218 5308

Fax. +32 2 219 9926

E-mail. efa.weipert@skynet.be

Website. www.efa-ecf.org

Leadership. Wolfgang Weipert (secretary-general)

European Federation of Building and Wood Workers (EFBWW/FETBB)

Address. Rue Royale 45 bte 3, B–1000 Brussels, Belgium

Phone. +32 2 227 1040

Fax. +32 2 219 8228

E-mail. efbh.fetbb@skynet.be

European Federation of Journalists (EFJ/FEJ)

Address. Rue Royale 266, B–1210 Brussels, Belgium

Phone. +32 2 219 2528

Fax. +32 2 219 2976

E-mail. efj@ifj.org

Membership. 200,000 in 29 countries

History and character. The EFJ is constituted as the regional organization of the International Federation of Journalists (IFJ), with a close working relationship with ETUC.

European Mine, Chemical and Energy Workers' Federation (EMCEF)

Address. Av. Emile de Béco 109, B–1050 Brussels, Belgium

Phone. + 32 2 626 2180

Fax. +32 2 646 0685

E-mail. info@emcef.be

Leadership. Hubertus Schmoldt (president); Reinhard Reibsch (general secretary)

Membership. 3 million in 100 unions in 27 countries

History and character. EMCEF relates at the international sectoral level to ICEM but is separate from it.

European Metalworkers' Federation (EMF/FEM)

E-mail. emf@emf-fem.org

Website. www.emf-fem.org

European Federation of Public Service Unions (EPSU/FSESP)

Address. Rue Royale 45, B–1000 Brussels, Belgium

Phone. +32 2 250 1080

Fax. +32 2 250 1099

E-mail. epsu@epsu.org

Website. www.epsu.org

Leadership. Herbert Mai (president); Carola Fischbach-Pyttel (general secretary)

History and character. Represents 10 million public service workers in 180 trade unions in national and local public administration, health and social services and public utilities; this is the largest of the ETUC industry federations and works with PSI at the international level.

European Transport Workers' Federation (ETF/FEST)

Address. Rue de Pascale 22, B–1040 Brussels, Belgium

Phone. +32 2 285 4660

Fax. +32 2 280 0817

E-mail. etf@etf.skynet.be

Website. www.itf.org.uk/etf/be

Leadership. Wilhelm Haberzettl (president); Doro Zinke (general secretary)

Membership. 3 million in 34 countries

History and character. The ETF held its founding congress June 14–15, 1999 in Brussels.

It operates both as the European regional organization of the International Transport Workers' Federation (ITF) and as the transport federation of ETUC and replaced the former Federation of Transport Workers' Unions in the European Union (FST). Its membership comes from both the EU member states and from the states of central and Eastern Europe.

European Trade Union Committee for Education (ETUCE/CSEE)

Address. 5 Boulevard du Roi Albert II, B–1210 Brussels, Belgium

Phone. +32 2 224 0691

Fax. +32 2 224 0694

E-mail. secretariat@csee.etuce.org

Website. www.ei–ie.org/etuce

Membership. 81 teaching unions in 19 countries

Union Network International–Europa

Address. Rue de l'Hôpital 31, B–1000 Brussels, Belgium

Phone. +32 2 234 5656

Fax. +32 2 235 0870

E-mail. uni-europa@union-network.org

Website. www.uni-europa.org

Leadership. Bernadette Tesch-Ségol (regional secretary)

History and chaacter. This is the regional organization of the international trade secretariat Union Network International (UNI), created in 2000.

Federation of International Civil Servants' Associations (FICSA)

Address. Pavillon Le Bocage, Office BOC.74, 10 Route de Pregny, CH–1211 Geneva 10, Switzerland

Phone. +41 22 917 3150

Fax. +41 22 917 0660

E-mail. fisca@ficsa.org

Leadership. Alvaro J. da Silva Durão (general secretary)

History and character: FICSA was established in 1952 and promotes the interests of the staff of the United Nations and its specialized agencies. It has 27 member organizations.

Publications. FICSA Quarterly, and other reports

International Confederation of Arab Trade Unions (ICATU)

Address. PO Box 3225, Damascus, Syria

Leadership. Hacène Djemam (general secretary)

History and character. ICATU was founded in 1956, and based in Egypt until it moved in 1978 in protest against the international policies of President Sadat. Its role and international status is limited by the low level of development of trade unions in much of the Arab world and the close government control under which most of them operate. It tended to have close ties in the past with WFTU. Its 10th congress, held in Damascus Nov.29–Dec. 2, 1999, aimed to strengthen relations with WCL, ICFTU, ETUC and OATUU, and also to restore historical links with unions in Eastern Europe.

International Confederation of Free Trade Unions (ICFTU)
Confédération Internationale des Syndicats Libres (CISL)
Confederación Internacional de Organizaciones Syndicales Libres (CIOSL)
International Bund Freier Gewerkschaften (IBFG)

Address. 5 Boulevard Roi Albert II, B–1210 Brussels, Belgium

Phone. +32 2 224 0211

Fax. +32 2 201 5815

E-mail. internetpo@icftu.org

Website. www.icftu.org

Leadership. Bill Jordan (general secretary)

Membership. 155 million members in 221 organizations in 148 countries

History and character. The ICFTU is a worldwide confederation of national trade union centres. It is one of three such confederations, but is of immensely more importance than the other two (World Confederation of Labour, WCL; and World Federation of Trade Unions, WFTU). The ICFTU today represents nearly all the leading national centres worldwide that operate independently of governments. While overwhelmingly a confederation of national centres, it does permit some individual union affiliations where no such centres exist or for other specific reasons. Affiliates must be free of the control of any other (outside) body, although in practice a few of them operate in countries where social organizations are effectively controlled by a single party. They must also derive their authority only from their members, have a freely and democratically elected leadership, and voluntarily accept the aims and constitution of the ICFTU.

The ICFTU provides leadership and a representative voice for its affiliates at international level. It participates in the work of the International Labour Organization (ILO) and has consultative status with the various specialized agencies of the UN system. Increasingly, it is seeking to build an interface with the International Monetary Fund (IMF), World Bank and World Trade Organization (WTO). It sends regular missions to investigate violations of trade union freedoms in individual countries and makes representations on behalf of its members to international agencies and governments.

The ICFTU originated in the early days of the Cold War when in 1949 unions in Western countries broke away from the WFTU. The principal founding organizations were the AFL and the CIO from the United States, the British TUC and the Dutch NVV, which in a manifesto stated that the WFTU was 'completely dominated by communist organizations, which are themselves controlled by the Kremlin and the Cominform'. For four decades thereafter the ICFTU represented most of the leading Western trade union centres, most of the centres in the newly industrializing countries of Asia, and competed with the WFTU, and to a lesser extent the WCL, for the allegiance of unions in Africa and Latin America.

The general collapse of communism and disintegration of the Soviet Union in the period 1989–91 gave the ICFTU an opportunity to transcend the divisions of the Cold War. It gained the affiliation of new independent confederations, or reformed former official trade union centres, through much of Eastern Europe, where the national centres had previously affiliated to the WFTU. This process, slowed by the uncertain development of authentic independent unions in some parts of the region, is not yet complete, but reached a climax in 2000 with the affiliation of the Russian FNPR. The early 1990s also saw a parallel process in Africa, where much of sub-Saharan Africa, previously dominated by one-party states, saw a movement (in some cases not long sustained) towards political pluralism. Many African centres, previously affiliated only to the Organization of African Trade Union Unity (OATUU) or in some instances also to the WFTU, moved into the ICFTU camp. The ICFTU also recorded important gains with the end of apartheid in South Africa, which brought the affiliation of COSATU, and added the three national centres in Brazil. As a result of this process the ICFTU by the end of 2000 claimed 155 million members, compared with 87 million in 1988. This numerical gain had come about entirely through affiliation of new organizations, and a broadening of the number of countries represented, because most of its established affiliates in the developed world had experienced little growth, and in most cases membership losses, during the same period.

From the 1940s to the 1980s the stronghold of the ICFTU was clearly Western Europe. It was founded in London, had its headquarters in Brussels, and the majority of its most influential and biggest members were European. While never monolithic, its predominant values were those of democratic socialism, and its leading European affiliates were closely allied with the democratic socialist parties in their own countries, such as the DGB in West Germany, the TUC in Britain and the LO in Sweden. In this the ICFTU stood in antithesis to the Prague-based WFTU, which was dominated by communist party-controlled official unions in the Soviet bloc, with a tail of independent leftist unions and unions linked to national liberation movements or one-party states in the developing world. The Western European democratic socialist identification also created tension at times with ICFTU affiliates, more conservative in focus or working within authoritarian political structures, in other parts of the world, especially Asia and Latin America. The ICFTU's regional organization for the Americas, ORIT, for long reflected this tension with the ICFTU centre. From 1969–81 the United States AFL-CIO withdrew from participation in the work of the ICFTU because of its socialist orientation, but continued to participate in and dominate ORIT. There was persistent unhappiness among some European unions at the emphasis of the AFL-CIO, with financial support from the US government, on supporting anti-communist unions even in situations where those unions might seem compromised in their relationships with right-wing regimes. Only in the 1990s, with the end of the Cold War, has the AFL-CIO moved from the sidelines to a position closer to the centre ground of the ICFTU.

Despite the fall in union density in much of the region since the early 1980s, Western Europe remains the leading single base for free and developed trade unionism, with its well-organized unions having an established and significant role in industrial relations and more broadly as social partners. However, the huge increase in ICFTU membership outside Western Europe in the last dozen years has influenced, and is likely increasingly to influence, the organization's development. The largest affiliate, nominally at least, is now the Russian FNPR. However, its origins in (only partly reformed) official Soviet era trade unionism, the uncertain identification of much of its membership with the FNPR and its goals, and the intensely difficult economic and political environment in which it works, clearly present issues and challenges not faced by the Western European centres. Into the 1980s a high proportion of ICFTU affiliates were in countries in which basic rights of association and trade union freedoms were broadly accepted and established. In contrast, most of the affiliates added since 1990 – whether in Eastern Europe and Russia, Africa, or Latin America – are in countries where only a decade or so ago free trade unionism was met with repression, imprisonment, or even murder and "disappearances". For these new affiliates, the building of sound trade union structures, and working to guarantee their survival in political circumstances that are still not yet entirely secure and settled, are great challenges. While, at one level, as reflected in the swelling number of ICFTU members, the position of free trade unionism has never been stronger, it is also the case that the proportion of ICFTU members facing very real threats to the free exercise of trade union rights is greater than ever before. The ICFTU's *Annual Survey of Trade Union Rights* covers two-thirds of the countries in the world, and whereas the infringements of rights described in some countries may seem relatively marginal, in many other cases trade unions affiliated to the ICFTU face serious attack. The ICFTU's commitment to, and involvement in, international solidarity work in support of its more hard-pressed affiliates is a major part of its work, and an area that seems likely only to increase.

The globalization of the ICFTU's membership has also marched in step with the increasing globalization of the world economy. Economic globalization has had two consequences. On the one hand, it is opening up the labour practices of unseen corners of the world to scrutiny in ways that were previously unknown. The casual ratification of core ILO conventions by one-party states that entirely ignored them in practice, and the unchallenged participation of such countries in the ILO, served only to undermine the ILO's credibility. At the same time, the onward rush of globalization, beginning with the structural adjustment programmes introduced by many countries at the behest of the IMF from the 1980s, and gaining pace with the creation of the World Trade Organization in the 1990s, has pushed forward social and economic models in which the claims of the free market, and not those of organized labour, have been paramount. The theme of the 2000 world ICFTU congress was "globalizing social justice". Accepting that globalization is inevitable, the ICFTU is pressing for the values embodied in ILO conventions (but often ignored by autonomous, insulated states in practice) to be given vitality through integration into the agenda of the Bretton Woods institutions (the IMF and World Bank) and the WTO. While the ICFTU continues to emphasize its belief in the importance of the ILO, with its mandate to create conditions of dignity and equality for workers, in practice the focus is increasingly on the campaign for ILO values to be incorporated in the programmes and rulings of the now much more powerful IMF, World Bank and WTO. These bodies have real powers over governments because they control the purse strings, whereas the ILO is in this respect essentially toothless. In this, and alongside the WCL and the international trade secretariats, the ICFTU has put its emphasis on achieving adoption of the so-called ILO "core labour standards", covering trade union rights of association and collective bargaining, equality of opportunity, and abolition of child and forced labour.

While to some extent these standards may be seen as providing only a minimum safety net, securing their implementation remains a massive uphill struggle. Neither of the world's two biggest economies, the USA and China, have ratified the basic ILO conventions covering trade union freedoms, No.87 (Freedom of Association and Protection of the Right to Organize, 1948) and No.98 (Right to Organize and Collective Bargaining, 1949). Furthermore, in many countries, whether or not they have ratified the conventions on paper, neither the spirit nor the letter of the conventions is properly observed. In developing countries, cheap and "flexible" labour is seen as a critical element in competitive advantage and the development of strong unions as an impediment to national progress. Even in middle-income countries, especially in Asia, the view is often taken that unions are not beneficial unless they play a role in ensuring labour discipline and productivity. ICFTU affiliates in these countries inescapably work within a different set of assumptions and rules than do those in Europe.

Supreme authority in the ICFTU is vested in the congress, held every four years (most recently in Durban, South Africa, in 2000), composed of delegates from the member federations in proportion to the size of their membership. The congress elects an executive board, which directs activities between congresses. Day-to-day authority is exercised by the Brussels-based secretariat, under the direction of the general secretary. The ICFTU is financed solely by its member organizations. In 1988 it was resolved that a Women's World Conference should meet every four years between congresses; it most recently convened in 1998.

ICFTU offices. The ICFTU has offices in a number of countries to provide support at a more localized level or liaise with international agencies. Of these, the most important are the offices in Geneva (the site of the ILO), New York (United Nations) and Washington (IMF and World Bank).

Geneva Office

Address. Avenue Blanc 46, CH–1202, Geneva, Switzerland

Phone. +41 22 738 4202

Fax. +41 22 738 1082

E-mail. icftu.ge@geneva.icftu.org

UN Office

Address. 104 East 40th Street, Room 404, New York, NY 10016, USA

Phone. +1 212 986 1820

Fax. +1 212 972 9746

E-mail. icftuny@igc.org

Washington Office

Address. 1925 K Street, NW, Suite 425, Washington DC 20006, USA

Phone. +1 202 463 8573

Fax. +1 202 463 8564

E-mail. icftu@mnsinc.com

Regional Organizations of the ICFTU. The ICFTU has regional organizations for Asia-Pacific (APRO), Americas (ORIT), and Africa (AFRO). It has no European regional organization, but has close relations with the European Trade Union Confederation (ETUC), which also affiliates the ICFTU's member national centres.

1. ICFTU Asian and Pacific Regional Organization (ICFTU–APRO)

Address. 73 Bras Basah Road NTUC Trade Union House, Singapore 189556

Phone. +65 222 6294

Fax. +65 221 7380

E-mail. gs@icftu-apro.org

Website. www.icftu-apro.org

Leadership. Noriyuki Suzuki (general secretary)

Membership. 32 million in 43 affiliates in 29 countries.

Publications. Asian and Pacific Labour; Labour Flash (content accessible via website)

2. Inter-American Regional Organization of Workers (ORIT)

Address. Avda. Andrés Eloy Blanco (Este 2), Edificio José Vargas, Piso 15, Los Caobos, Caracas, Venezuela

Phone. +58 2 578 3538

Fax. +58 2 578 1702

E-mail. secgenorit@cantvnet

Leadership. Luis Anderson (general secretary)

3. ICFTU African Regional Organization (AFRO)

Address. PO Box 67273, Ambank House (14th Floor), University Way, Nairobi, Kenya

Phone. +254 2 221 357

Fax. +254 2 215072

E-mail. icftuafro@form-net.com

Leadership. Andrew Kailembo (general secretary)

International Trade Secretariats associated with the ICFTU. There are ten international trade secretariats (ITSs), providing a global voice for unions on a sectoral basis by industry. These all originated in Western Europe, and all still have their headquarters in European countries (including four each in Belgium and Switzerland), although all now act globally and (like the ICFTU) have increased their worldwide representation over the last decade. The ITSs are fully autonomous and in most cases have a history pre-dating the formation of the ICFTU, but are associated with the ICFTU and in general work closely with it in coordinating campaigns. In a major re-organization, which took effect at the start of 2000, a new international secretariat, Union Network International (UNI) was formed by the merger of Communications International (CI), the International Federation of Commercial, Clerical and Technical Employees (FIET), the International Graphical Federation (IGF) and Media and Entertainment International.

The ITSs (see separate entries for each) are: Education International (EI); International Federation of Building and Wood Workers (IFBWW); International Federation of Chemical, Energy, Mine and General Workers' Unions (ICEM); International Federation of Journalists (IFJ); International Metalworkers' Federation (IMF); International Textile, Garment and Leather Workers' Federation (ITGLWF); International Transport Workers' Federation (ITF); International Union of Food, Agricultural, Hotel, Restaurant, Catering, Tobacco and Allied Workers' Associations (IUF); Public Services International (PSI); and Union Network International (UNI).

National affiliates. The ICFTU has affiliates in the following independent countries (see country sections for details): Algeria; Angola; Antigua; Argentina; Australia; Austria; Azerbaijan; Bahamas; Bangladesh; Barbados; Belgium; Belize; Benin; Botswana; Brazil; Bulgaria; Burkina Faso; Cameroon; Canada; Cape Verde; Central African Republic; Chad; Chile; China (Hong Kong); Colombia; Congo, Democratic Republic of; Congo, People's Republic of; Costa Rica; Côte d'Ivoire; Croatia; Cyprus; Czech Republic; Denmark; Djibouti; Dominica; Dominican Republic; Ecuador; El Salvador; Eritrea; Estonia; Fiji; Finland; France; Gabon; Gambia; Georgia; Germany; Ghana; Greece; Grenada; Guatemala; Guinea; Guinea-Bissau; Guyana; Honduras; Hungary; Iceland; India; Indonesia; Ireland; Israel; Italy; Jamaica; Japan; Jordan; Kenya; Kiribati; South Korea; Latvia; Lebanon; Liberia; Lithuania; Luxembourg; Madagascar; Malawi; Malaysia; Mali; Malta; Mauritania; Mauritius; Mexico; Moldova; Mongolia; Morocco; Mozambique; Namibia; Nepal; Netherlands; New Zealand; Nicaragua; Niger; Nigeria; Norway;

Pakistan; Panama; Papua New Guinea; Paraguay; Peru; Philippines; Poland; Portugal; Romania; Russia; Rwanda; St. Kitts-Nevis; St. Lucia; St. Vincent; Samoa; San Marino; Senegal; Seychelles; Sierra Leone; Singapore; Slovakia; South Africa; Spain; Sri Lanka; Surinam; Swaziland; Sweden; Switzerland; Taiwan; Tanzania; Thailand; Togo; Tonga; Trinidad and Tobago; Tunisia; Turkey; Uganda; United Kingdom; United States; Vanuatu; Vatican City; Venezuela; Yugoslavia; Zambia; Zimbabwe.

Publications. The ICFTU has a wide range of publications, variously available in hard copy or on its website, including the *Annual Survey of Trade Union Rights* and its monthly journal *Trade Union World*. Its press and publications department can be contacted by e-mail at: press@icftu.org

International Federation of Building and Wood Workers (IFBWW)

Address. 54 route des Acacias, PO Box 1412, CH–1227 Carouge GE, Switzerland

Phone. +41 22 827 37 77

Fax. +41 22 827 37 70

E-mail. info@ifbww.org

Website. www.ifbww.org

Leadership. Roel de Vries (president); Ulf Asp (general secretary)

Membership. 11 million members in 281 unions in 124 countries

History and character. The IFBWW is an international trade secretariat. It was established in 1934 by the merger of the Building Workers' International and the Wood Workers' International. Its membership is in the building wood, forestry and allied trades.

The IFBWW has regional offices for Latin America, Africa and Asia–Pacific. At the European level it cooperates with the ETUC-affiliated European Federation of Building and Wood Workers (EFBWW), as well as the Nordic Federation of Building and Wood Workers. It runs project offices in several regions.

IFBWW members commonly work in hazardous occupations and health and safety is a prominent issue. It is campaigning for ratification of ILO Conventions 167 (safety in construction) and 162 (asbestos). It is also campaigning for sustainable development in forestry.

It supports 90 projects worldwide giving educational support to trade unionists in developing countries and the former communist countries of Eastern Europe.

Publications. Building and Wood (English, French, German, Spanish, Swedish); *IFBWW Fax News* (English) (content accessible via website)

International Federation of Chemical, Energy, Mine and General Workers' Unions (ICEM)

Address. Avenue Emile de Béco 109, B–1050 Brussels, Belgium

Phone. +32 2 626 2020

Fax. +32 2 648 4316

Website. www.icem.org

Leadership. John Maitland (president); Fred Higgs (general secretary)

Membership. 20 million in 390 unions in 107 countries

History and character. The ICEM is an international trade secretariat and was founded in 1995 by the merger of the International Federation of Chemical, Energy and General Workers' Unions (ICEF) and the Miners' International Federation (MIF). Members are blue- and white-collar workers in energy (including electricity, oil and gas), all types of mining, plastics, petrochemicals, chemicals, pharmaceuticals, pulp and paper, rubber, glass, ceramics, cement, environmental services such as waste disposal, and miscellaneous other industries not covered by other international trade secretariats. On Nov. 1, 2000, the ICEM also absorbed the Universal Alliance of Diamond Workers (UADW).

The ICEM's activities include support for union-building in countries where unions are weak or non-existent; solidarity work on behalf of member unions; information and services for member unions in areas such as collective bargaining and health and safety; and trade union skills training. It is developing networks of trade unions to coordinate their activities in negotiating with transnational corporations.

The ICEM believes it is necessary to engage with bodies such as the International Monetary Fund, World Bank and World Trade Organization which are now more influential in shaping the position of workers than traditional UN agencies like the ILO. It has called for these bodies to be made democratically accountable.

The ICEM has a Global Health and Safety Initiative focused on the mining industry. This aims to win changes in national health and safety legislation, ratification by ILO Member States of ILO Convention No. 176 (1995) on safety and health in mines, and inclusion of health and safety in collective agreements. It supports the campaign of the IUF international trade secretariat to protect workers from misuse of pesticides. The ICEM says that fear of job losses in the sectors it represents has often kept workers quiet over environmental issues, but that it is necessary for unions to engage with environmental organizations and industry in solving problems "or suffer from someone else's solutions later that take no account of workers or their communities."

The 1999 congress heard that there had been "positive improvements" in relations with the European Mine, Chemical and Energy Workers' Federation (EMCEF), which is affiliated to the ETUC, and the issue of ICEM's organizational structure in Europe was deferred.

Publications. ICEM Info (three per annum); *ICEM Global* (two per annum); content accessible via website.

International Federation of Journalists (IFJ)

Address. 266 rue Royale, B–1210 Brussels, Belgium

Phone. +32 2 223 2265

Fax. +32 2 219 2976

E-mail. ifj@ifj.org

Website. www.ifj.org

Leadership. Chris Warren (president); Aidan White (general secretary)

Membership. 450,000 journalists in 105 countries

History and character. The IFJ is an international trade secretariat. It originated in 1926. It speaks for journalists within the UN system and cooperates with other international trade secretariats and the ICFTU. It has consultative status with UNESCO, the ILO, World Intellectual Property Organization (WIPO) and the UN Centre for Human Rights.

Issues for the IFJ include women's rights in the media, concentration of ownership, authors' rights, and attacks on press freedom. It has an International Safety Fund to support journalists in need. A sombre feature of its website is an annual "Killed List", dating back to 1990, giving details of journalists killed during or because of their work. The list included 62 names for the year 2000.

Publications. IFJ Directline (monthly bulletin, content accessible via website); regular reports

International Metalworkers' Federation (IMF)

Address. 54bis, route des Acacias, Case Postale 1516, CH–1227 Geneva, Switzerland

Phone. +41 22 308 5050

Fax. +41 22 308 5055

E-mail. info@imfmetal.org

Website. www.imfmetal.org

Leadership. Klaus Zwickel (president); Marcello Malentacchi (general secretary)

Membership. Nearly 23 million in 193 unions in 101 countries

History and character. Founded in Zurich in 1893; membership collapsed to only 190,00 on eve of World War II; re-built in post-War period. Membership increased from 12.7 million in 1989 to 18 million in 1993 as a result of affiliation of unions in Eastern Europe.

The IMF has regional offices worldwide. Union development projects are underway in particular in former Eastern Europe and Mexico. Its structure includes the IMF World Auto Council, with company councils for major manufacturers.

Publications. Metal World and range of others (content accessible via website)

International Textile, Garment and Leather Workers' Federation (ITGLWF)

Address. 8 rue Joseph Stevens, B–1000 Brussels, Belgium

Phone. +32 2 512 2606

Fax. +32 2 511 0904

E-mail. itglwf@compuserve.com

Website. www.itglwf.org

Leadership. Peter Booth (president); Neil Kearney (general secretary)

Membership. 220 unions in 110 countries with over 10 million members

History and character. The ITGLWF is an international trade secretariat. It works to represent unions in its sector in international organizations, provide solidarity support for member unions, and carry out education and development work to build unions in countries where they are weak or do not exist. It has regional organizations for the Americas, Europe, Asia and Africa.

The theme of the 8th (June 2000) congress was "global solidarity in a global industry". The ITGLWF has particular concerns about the impact of globalization because it represents workers in industries which "because they are labour intensive ... are among the easiest to relocate, making it easy for companies to shift production as soon as national governments impose restraints on their operations, or as soon as workers organize for better wages and working conditions."

Publications. ITGLWF Newsletter

International Transport Workers' Federation (ITF)

Address. ITF House, 49–60 Borough Road, London SE1 1DS, United Kingdom

Phone. +44 20 7403 2733

Fax. +44 20 7357 7871

E-mail. mail@itf.org.uk

Website. www.itf.org.uk

Leadership. David Cockroft (general secretary)

Membership. Over 5 million in 533 unions in 136 countries

History and character. The ITF was founded in 1896 in London by European seafarers' and dockers' leaders. It subsequently expanded to embrace railways, road transport and civil aviation. The ITF represents the interests of its affiliates to transport-specific bodies such as the International Maritime Organization and the International Civil Aviation Organization as well as to the ILO. It has regional offices for Africa, Asia-Pacific, North America and Latin America. In Europe it works closely with the Brussels-based European Transport Workers' Federation (ETF), which is made up primarily of ITF affiliated unions.

At international level key issues for the ITF include the use of flags of convenience in the maritime sector; working hours in road transport; and the impact of globalization, which it sees as undercutting national laws, regulations and collective agreements.

The ITF has eight industrial sections, each of which has its own committees and conferences, as follows: road transport, railways, seafarers, civil aviation, docks, fisheries, tourism, inland navigation.

Publications. *ITF News; Seafarers' Bulletin*

International Union of Food, Agricultural, Hotel, Restaurant, Catering, Tobacco and Allied Workers' Associations (IUF)

Address. Rampe du Pont-Rouge 8, CH-1213 Petit-Lancy, Switzerland

Phone. +41 22 793 2233

Fax. +41 22 793 2238

E-mail. info@iuf.org

Website. www.iuf.org

Leadership. Frank Hurt (president); Ron Oswald (general secretary)

Membership. 10 million members in 326 unions in 118 countries

History and character. The IUF traces its origins back to 1920, when it was initially known as the International Union of Food and Drink Workers. The current name was adopted as the outcome of a series of mergers with the International Federation of Tobacco Workers (1958), the International Union of Hotel, Restaurant and Bar Workers (1961), and the International Federation of Plantation, Agricultural and Allied Workers (1994).

The IUF operates in sectors where trade union organization is often difficult. In the agricultural sector (where the IUF represents 3 million waged workers) unions are weak or banned or actively persecuted in many countries. Leading issues for IUF include agricultural child labour and the exposure of farm workers to dangerous pesticides, which the World Health Organization says leads to 40,000 deaths per annum. In 1998 the IUF launched a Global Pesticides Project to provide education and training on pesticide safety issues for activists, and it is calling for an ILO convention specifically on health and safety in agriculture. At the international level it seeks to intervene directly with transnational corporations on behalf of its national member unions.

The IUF structure includes regional secretariats for Africa, Asia-Pacific, the Caribbean, Latin America and North America. In Europe it works through the ETUC-affiliated European Committee of Food, Catering and Allied Workers' Unions within the IUF (ECF-IUF). It also has a number of local offices worldwide, including Moscow. Three IUF sectors (agricultural workers; hotel, restaurant and catering workers; and tobacco workers) – hold their own conferences in addition to the IUF congress held every four years.

Publications. News Bulletin (accessible via website). Also a range of regional, sectoral (e.g. *Banana Workers' Bulletin*, *Brewery Bulletin*) and company-level (e.g. *Nestlé Bulletin*) publications.

Nordens Fackliga Samorganisation (NFS)
Council of Nordic Trade Unions

Address. Barnhusgatan 16, S-111 23 Stockholm, Sweden

Phone. +46 8 209 880

Fax. +46 8 789 8868

Membership. 8 million

History and character. The NFS is a coordinating organization for unions in the Nordic countries. Its member organizations consist of blue-collar, white-collar and academic unions in Denmark, Finland, Iceland, Norway and Sweden. Nordic unions have a history of cooperation dating back to the nineteenth century. For a long time this cooperation was informal and irregular, but at the beginning of the 1970s greater formality was introduced leading to the formation of the NFS in 1972.

Organization of African Trade Union Unity (OATUU)
Organisation de l'Unité Syndicale Africaine (OUSA)

Address. PO Box M 386, Aviation Road, Accra, Ghana

Phone. +233 21 508 851/55

Fax. +233 21 508 851/53

E-mail. oatuu@ighmail.com

Leadership Hassan Adebayo Sunmonu (secretary-general)

Membership. 30 million in 53 national trade union centres

History and character. The OATUU is a specialized agency of the Organization of African Unity (OAU) and provides a collective voice for African trade union centres. It is independent of other international trade union confederations.

The first pan-African trade union organization was the All-African Trade Union Federation (AATUF), founded in Casablanca in May 1961. In an attempt to exclude the influence of the ICFTU and the Christian unions, which were seen as dampening militancy and 'revolutionary zeal', the AATUF insisted on the principle of disaffiliation of all its member national centres from any non-African union organizations. National centres which maintained affiliation to the ICFTU or the International Federation of Christian Trade Unions (IFCTU, the forerunner of the World Confederation of Labour), or which were unwilling to accept this policy, formed the African Trade Union Confederation (ATUC) in Jan. 1962. In 1973 these two rival federations, and a third smaller grouping known as the Pan-African Workers' Congress, were merged into the Organization of African Trade Union Unity (OATUU), under the auspices of the Organization of African Unity (OAU). The OATUU suffered a split in 1986 in which different countries backed opposing camps. This ended in a reconciliation in which Hassan Sunmonu, a former president of the Nigeria Labour Congress, became secretary-general in Oct. 1986, a position he continues to hold.

The OATUU long advocated the position that African trade unions should not affiliate to global trade union centres. In part this reflected a wish to avoid damaging conflict between African unions arising from competition between the ICFTU, WFTU and WCL, although some African governments were also actively hostile to their national unions having non-African alliances. In practice, however, many national centres did form such affiliations. With the end of the Cold War and the movement to greater pluralism in many African countries in the early 1990s, most of the more firmly established and freely functioning centres are now affiliated to the ICFTU.

OATUU's activities include representing the interests of its affiliates before African governments and in international organizations, and it has consultative status with the ILO, the UN Economic and Social Council (ECOSOC), UNESCO and FAO. It has engaged in campaigns on issues such as strengthening the African Economic Community, promoting the African Alternative Framework to Structural Adjustment Programmes, and calling for debt cancellation. It believes that globalization and the policies of the IMF, World Bank and WTO are undermining the ability of African nations to protect domestic industries and develop fair labour standards and opposes the growing influence of these agencies.

OATUU runs worker education programmes on trade union and broader social and economic issues. It also has a health, safety and environment programme.

OATUU's regional organizations are: the Organization of Trade Unions of West Africa (OTUWA); Organization of Trade Unions of Central Africa (OTUCA); Southern Africa Trade Union Coordinating Council (SATUCC); and the Organization of Trade Unions of Arab Maghreb (OTUAM). In addition it has a series of specialized agencies for each industrial sector.

Public Services International (PSI)

Address. 45 Avenue Voltaire, BP 9, Ferney-Voltaire Cedex, 01211 France

Phone. +33 4 50 40 64 64

Fax. +33 4 50 40 73 20

E-mail. psi@world-psi.org

Website. www.world-psi.org

Leadership. Hans Engelberts (general secretary)

Membership. 20 million in 528 affiliated unions in 144 countries

History and character. PSI is an international trade secretariat (ITS) that works in association with other ITSs and with the ICFTU. It dates its origins back to 1907. Its membership is in all public sector areas, including administration, utilities, public works, health and social services, police, the law, leisure and taxation, with the principal exception of teaching, which is covered by Education International (EI).

PSI is an officially recognized non-government organization for the public sector within the ILO and has consultative status with ECOSOC and observer status with other UN bodies such as UNCTAD and UNESCO. Its has regionally based committees with executive powers for the Inter-Americas, Asia-Pacific, and Africa and Arab Countries and Europe. In Europe it works closely with the European Federation of Public Service Unions (EPSU), which is affiliated to ETUC.

The key issues for PSI include "the new challenges of globalization, the threats from ideological privatization, commercialization and contracting out of public services... attacks on services through structural adjustment polices and the intrusion of transnational corporations into public services". It runs an education programme to train trade union activists.

Publications. Regular publications include *Focus* (magazine); *PSI Women*; *Research Network News*; *World News*; *Africa Flash*; *Asia-Pacific News*; *Euroflash*; *Inter-American Flash*. (Content accessible via website).

Trade Union Advisory Committee to the OECD (TUAC)

Address. 26 avenue de la Grande Armée, 75017 Paris, France

Phone. +33 1 47 63 42 63

Fax. +33 1 47 54 98 28

E-mail. tuac@tuac.org

Website. www.tuac.org

Leadership. Bob White (president); John Evans (general secretary)

Membership. 55 trade union organizations in OECD countries

History and character. TUAC originated as a trade union advisory committee to the Organization for European Economic Cooperation (OEEC), set up in 1948 to implement the post-War European Recovery Programme (the Marshall Plan). It brought together most of the non-communist union national centres in Western Europe. Under a convention in force from Sept. 1961, the OEEC became the Organization for Economic Cooperation and Development (OECD), with a broad role in promoting sound economic development, and adding the USA and Canada as full members alongside the European membership.

TUAC has consultative status with the OECD and regularly meets the OECD secretariat and specialist committees as well as member governments. It also coordinates trade union input to the G-7 economic summits and works closely with the ICFTU, WCL, ETUC and international trade secretariats. Its membership has expanded with the OECD and now comprises 55 organizations in 29 countries.

Plenary sessions, involving representatives of all the affiliates and the international organizations, are held twice yearly and make policy decisions and approve the budget. An administrative committee oversees administration and draws up the budget; it currently comprises representatives of the DGB (Germany), TUC (United Kingdom), AFL-CIO (United States of America), FO and CFDT (France), CISL (Italy), Rengo (Japan), ÖGB (Austria), STTK (Finland), and CSC (Belgium), together with the president, vice-presidents and general secretary. There are also various working groups. Decision-making is generally by consensus. There is a small secretariat based in Paris.

Affiliated unions. (See under country sections for detailed entries). Australia, ACTU; Austria, ÖGB; Belgium, CGSLB, CSC, FGTB; Canada, CLC, CSN; Denmark, AC, FTF, LO; Finland, AKAVA, SAK, TVK; France, CFDT, CFTC, CGC, CGT-FO, UNSA; Germany, DGB; Greece, GSEE; Hungary, LIGA, MSZOSZ; Iceland, ASI, BSRB; Ireland, ICTU; Italy, CGIL, CISL, UIL; Japan, Rengo; South Korea, FKTU, KCTU; Luxembourg, CGT-LG, LCGB; Mexico, CTM, FESEEBES; Netherlands, CNV, FNV; New Zealand, NZCTU; Norway, AF, LO; Poland, NSZZ Solidarnosc; Portugal, UGT-P; Spain, CC.OO, ELA-STV, UGT; Sweden, LO, SACO, TCO; Switzerland, CNG, USS; Turkey, DISK, Turk-Is; United Kingdom, TUC; United States of America, AFL-CIO.

Union Network International (UNI)

Address. Avenue Reverdil 8-10, CH-1260 Nyon 2, Switzerland

Phone. +41 22 365 2100

Fax. +41 22 365 2121

E-mail. contact@union-network.org

Website. www.union-network.org

Leadership. Kurt Van Haaren (president); Philip Jennings (general secretary); Philip Bowyer (deputy general secretary)

Membership. 5.5 million in 900 unions in 140 countries

History and character. UNI is an international trade secretariat. It was formed on Jan. 1, 2000 as "a new international for a new millennium". The founding partners were:

International Federation of Commercial, Clerical, Professional and Technical Employees (FIET), dating back to 1904 and with 10 million members in 435 affiliated unions in 136 countries.

Communications International (CI), itself formerly known as Postal, Telegraph and Telephone International (PTTI) and with origins in 1911, with 4.5 million members in posts and telecommunications, broadcasting and electricity, in 281 unions in 127 countries.

International Graphical Federation (IGF), with 1 million members in 103 unions in 76 countries.

Media and Entertainment International (MEI), with 200,000 members in 130 unions in 65 countries. MEI was the smallest of the international trade secretariats and was itself founded only in 1993 by merger of the International Secretariat for Arts, Mass Media and Entertainment Trade Unions (ISETU) and the International Federation of Audiovisual Workers (FISTAV).

The general secretary of UNI, Philip Jennings, was formerly general secretary of FIET, and his deputy, Philip Bowyer, was general secretary of Communications International. Jennings stated as a reason for the formation of UNI that "workers across the service, communications and entertainment sector increasingly face the same employers and the same issues and are increasingly lobbying the same international organizations." Bowyer stated that "communications companies like Sprint, MCI-WorldCom, Cable and Wireless and UPS strenuously oppose union organization. We are bringing unions together everywhere such companies operate in the world to force them to listen to their workers and to allow them to organize."

UNI is organized into the following sectors: Casino Employees; Commerce; Electricity; Finance; Graphical; Hair and Beauty; IBITS (white collar, professional and IT staff); Media, Entertainment and Arts; Postal; Property Services; Social Insurance and Private Health Care; Telecommunications; and Tourism. There are also three cross-sectoral groups, for Women, Youth, and Professional and Managerial Staff.

UNI has four regional organizations, for Africa, Americas, Asia-Pacific, and Europe (UNI-Europa also being the sectoral federation of ETUC).

Publications. UNInet.news (accessible at website)

World Confederation of Labour (WCL)
Confederación Mundial del Trabajo (CMT)
Confédération Mondiale du Travail (CMT)

Address. Rue de Trèves 33, B-1040 Brussels, Belgium

Phone. +32 2 285 47 00

Fax. +32 2 230 87 22

E-mail. info@cmt-wcl.org

Website, www.cmt-wcl.org

Leadership. Fernand Kikongi (president); Willy Thys (secretary-general)

Membership. The WCL reports that its affiliates have 26 million members, in 113 countries

History and character. The WCL was founded in 1920 as the International Federation of Christian Trade Unions (IFCTU), with a mainly European membership. Following World War II it lost ground as the European trade union movement became polarized between the WFTU, representing the trade union centres of the communist countries, and the ICFTU, representing most of the centres in Western Europe. To counter these losses the IFCTU began in the 1950s to establish contacts with unions in the Third World. The interchanges with unions sharing similar values, although not coming from the same (European) Christian tradition, contributed to overstepping the borders of narrow denominationalism and laid the basis of a more ecumenical approach. In 1968 the IFCTU changed its name to the World Confederation of Labour, ending the explicit association with the Christian Church. The changing geographical composition of its membership may be gauged by the way a total of only three non-European delegates at the 1952 congress had increased to 82, predominantly from the Third World, by the 1977 congress. Its core European and Latin American membership remains mainly Christian, however, whereas that of its affiliates elsewhere is more diverse.

The WCL represents an alternative and distinctive voice to the ICFTU for free trade unions, but operates on a much smaller scale. Overall the WCL claims to have some 26 million members in its affiliated organizations, although reliable membership figures for many of its affiliates are not available and some of them have a tenuous or marginal position. In some countries its affiliates are small organizations focused mainly on training, education and solidarity work rather than fully developed trade union centres.

It has minimal presence in the major countries of the developed world. In the G-7 group of leading industrialized countries (USA, Japan, Germany, UK, France, Italy, and Canada) there is a WCL affiliated national-level confederation only in France and Italy, and in both cases these are minor organizations. In Europe the WCL-affiliated centres of most significance are the CSC/ACV in Belgium and the CNV in Netherlands. With 1.5 million members, the Belgian Confederation of Christian Unions (CSC/ACV) is the only case in the member states of the European Union of the WCL affiliate being larger than the ICFTU affiliate.

In contrast, the WCL has more presence in the developing world, especially (but not exclusively) in countries with a Christian tradition. It is influential in South and Central America although this is usually from a minority position, with the big trade union centres in the major economies such as Argentina, Brazil, Chile and Mexico all affiliated to the ICFTU. It is represented on a more fragmentary basis in Africa and Asia and made few gains when many trade union centres joined the ICFTU in the early 1990s as part of a widespread move to greater pluralism in sub-Saharan Africa. A notable new affiliate in recent years has been the SBSI, which grew to prominence in the late 1990s in (mainly Muslim) Indonesia.

The WCL (jointly with the ICFTU) affiliated Polish Solidarity (which had a heavy Catholic influence) in 1986, when it was a banned organization. However, the WCL's efforts to build its position in the former communist countries of Eastern Europe since then have not overall had much success, although it has assisted in trade union development and training. To the degree that trade unionism has not just collapsed, or remained dominated by communist-era structures, the more significant organizations in Eastern Europe have preferred to join the world trade union mainstream by seeking affiliation to the ICFTU. In some cases the WCL has complained that national laws in post-communist countries effectively encourage a single-trade-union system, or limit trade union pluralism, for example by confining collective bargaining rights to most representative national unions, thereby assisting ICFTU affiliates at the expense of its own smaller member organizations. The WCL has also confronted the difficulty of validating the authenticity and independence of new union structures in countries with no tradition of independent trade unionism.

The WCL historically adopted a non-aligned position in global power politics, and emphasized the right to national self-determination of the countries of the Third World. The WCL believes that human fulfilment must have a spiritual as well as a material dimension, and that workers possess individual human rights in addition to their collective rights. This individualistic and spiritual dimension has meant that in Europe its affiliates have often been seen as standing to the political right of the socialist-led union mainstream, whereas in authoritarian regimes in developing countries its affiliates have often had a radical campaigning edge. The WCL favours the development of forms of worker participation in the management of enterprises. Like the ICFTU it currently emphasizes issues arising from globalization, calling in particular for adoption and enforcement of fair labour standards worldwide and a globalization of social justice to match that of the globalization of capital and trade. The WCL's "Norm" programme is aimed at promoting the universal observance of international human rights instruments and especially the ILO's core minimum labour standards (Conventions 87 and 98 on freedom of association, 100 and 111 on equality of opportunity and treatment, 29 and 105 on the abolition of forced labour, and 138 on the minimum age of employment).

The WCL's work with other trade union bodies is coordinated by the International Solidarity Foundation. The Foundation provides resources, funds campaigns and backs projects intended to promote independent trade unionism. The WCL enjoys consultative status with the ILO, the Economic and Social Council of the United Nations, and the other agencies of the UN system, and with the OECD. It has permanent representatives in Geneva, Rome, Paris, Vienna and Washington.

The congress is the ruling body, comprising delegates from national centres, regional organizations and the associated international trade federations. The congress, which meets every four years, sets overall policy and elects the confederal board. The confederal board, consisting of 38 members (representing the national confederations, the continents and the trade sections) and elected for four-year terms, meets annually and is the ruling body between congresses. The nine-member executive committee, composed of the president, the secretary-general, the six vice-presidents, and the treasurer, is responsible for the concrete implementation of policies laid down by the congress and the confederal board and meets at least twice a year. The secretariat in Brussels (led by the secretary-general and assisted by three confederal and two executive secretaries) is responsible for day-to-day affairs.

The WCL is based upon affiliations of national centres or confederations or other broad-based organizations. Exceptionally it accepts direct affiliations of individual unions, as was the case in Africa before the democratization wave of the mid-1990s.

Publications. Include *Tele-Flash* (every two weeks), *Labour* (four per annum), accessible via website.

Regional organizations. The WCL has had no regional organization for Europe since 1973. Instead its main European affiliates are members of the European Trade Union Confederation (ETUC). The WCL has little presence in North America, where it is represented in the USA by a small union (the National Alliance of Postal and Federal Employees) and in Canada by the Christian Labour Association of Canada and the Centrale des Syndicats Démocratiques (CSD), a minority union based on the province of Quebec.

1 Central Latinoamericana de Trabajadores (CLAT)

Address. Apartado 6681, 1010A Caracas, Venezuela

Phone. +58 32 72 07 94

Fax. +58 32 72 04 63

E-mail. clat@telcel.net.ve

History and character. CLAT is the WCL's regional organization for Latin America and the Caribbean, a region in which the WCL is traditionally relatively strong. Historically it has been the most important regional component of the WCL. It was founded in 1954. Much of its success lay in the establishment of new independent unions, sometimes in collaboration with the worker-priest movement. Many of its affiliates have faced severe difficulties arising from the prevalence of military rule and death squad activities in various parts of the continent over several decades, although the 1990s brought an amelioration of conditions in many countries. It campaigns for trade union organization, for the defence of human and civil rights, against dictatorship, and for the political, social and economic integration of the countries of the continent (it favours the creation of a Latin American Community of Nations). CLAT has sub-regional organizations for the Southern Cone (CTCS), Central America (CCT), Caribbean (CTC) and Andes (CSTA), and it also maintains the Workers' University of Latin America (UTAL), based in Caracas. Emilio Maspero, CLAT's long-standing secretary-general, died on May 31, 2000.

2. Brotherhood of Asian Trade Unionists (BATU)

Address. 1943 Taft Avenue, Malate 1004, Manila, Philippines

Phone. +63 2 50 07 09

Fax. +63 2 52 18 335

E-mail. batunorm@iconn.com.ph

Leadership. Juan Tan (president)

History and character. Asian sub-regional structures include liaison offices in Tokyo and Singapore, a project development office in Manila, and the Rerum Novarum Labour Centre in Taiwan.

3. Democratic Organization of African Workers' Trade Unions (DOAWTU/ODSTA)

Address. Route Internationale d'Atakpamé, Lomé-Agoenyive, Togo

Phone. +228 25 07 10

Fax. +228 25 61 13

Leadership. Fernand Kikongi (president); Alioune Sow (general secretary)

History and character. DOAWTU has member unions in 24 countries and four pan-African federations in the following sectors: agriculture, building and wood workers, education, industry and public service. It also has three sub-regional offices.

International Trade Federations. The WCL's structure includes a number of international trade federations, the more important of which are listed below. These lack the scale or autonomous significance of the international trade secretariats associated with the ICFTU. There are also regional-level trade groups affiliated at industry level to the international trade federations and at regional level to WCL's regional organizations such as CLAT.

1. International Federation of Employees in Public Service (INFEDOP)

Address. Rue de Trèves 33, B–1040 Brussels, Belgium

Phone. +32 2 230 38 65

Fax. +32 2 231 14 72

E-mail. info@infedop-eurofedop.com

Leadership. Guy Rasneur (president); Bert Van Caelenberg (secretary-general)

2. International Federation Textile-Clothing (IFTC)

Address. Koning Albertlaan 27, B-9000 Gent, Belgium

Phone. +32 9 222 57 01

Fax. +32 9 220 45 59

E-mail. acvtextiel@acv-csc.be

Leadership. Jacques Jouret (president); Bart Bruggeman (secretary-general)

3. International Federation of Trade Unions of Transport Workers (FIOST)

Address. Rue de Trèves 33, B-1040 Brussels, Belgium

Phone. +32 2 285 47 35

Fax. +32 2 230 87 22

E-mail. Freddy.Pools@cmt-wcl.org

Leadership. Michel Bovy (president); Jaap Wienen (secretary-general)

4. World Confederation of Teachers (WCT/CSME)

Address. Rue de Trèves 33, B–1040 Brussels, Belgium

Phone. +32 2 285 47 29

Fax. +32 2 230 87 22

E-mail. csme@cmt-wcl.org

Leadership. Louis Van Beneden (president); Gaston de la Haye (secretary-general)

5. World Federation of Agriculture, Food, Hotel and Allied Workers (FEMTAA/WFAFW)

Address. Rue de Trèves 33, B–1040 Brussels, Belgium

Phone. +32 2 285 47 753

Fax. +32 2 230 87 22

E-mail. femtaa@cmt-wcl.org

Leadership. Adrian Cojocaru (president); José Gomez Cerda (secretary-general)

6. World Federation of Building and Woodworkers' Unions (WFBW)

Address. Rue de Trèves 31, B–1040 Brussels, Belgium

Phone. +32 2 230 85 70

Fax. +32 2 230 74 43

E-mail. piet.nelissen@cmt-wcl.org

Leadership. Jacky Jackers (president); Dick Van De Kamp (secretary-general)

7. World Federation of Clerical Workers (WFCW/FME)

Address. Rue de Trèves 33, B–1040 Brussels, Belgium

Phone. +32 2 285 47 33

Fax. +32 2 230 87 22

E-mail. piet.nelissen@cmt-wcl.org

Leadership. Roel Rotshuizen (president)

8. World Federation of Industry Workers (WFIW/FMTI)

Address. Rue de Trèves 33, B–1040 Brussels, Belgium

Phone. +32 2 285 47 33

Fax. +32 2 230 87 22

E-mail. piet.nelissen@cmt-wcl.org

Leadership. Jaap Wienen (president); Alfons Van Genechten (secretary-general)

National affiliates. The WCL reports that it has affiliates in the following independent countries (details of most are included under individual country entries): Antigua; Argentina; Austria; Bangladesh; Belgium; Belize; Benin; Bolivia; Brazil; Burkina Faso; Cameroon; Canada; Central African Republic; Chad; Chile; China (Hong Kong); Colombia; Congo, Democratic Republic of; Congo, Republic of; Costa Rica; Côte d'Ivoire; Cuba; Cyprus; Dominica; Dominican Republic; Ecuador; El Salvador; France; Gabon; Gambia; Ghana; Guatemala; Guinea; Guyana; Haiti; Honduras; Hungary; India; Indonesia; Italy; Liberia; Liechtenstein; Lithuania; Luxembourg; Madagascar; Malaysia; Malta; Mauritania; Mauritius; Morocco; Namibia; Netherlands; Nicaragua; Niger; Pakistan; Panama; Paraguay; Peru; Philippines; Poland; Romania; Rwanda; St. Lucia; St. Vincent; Sao Tome and Principe; Senegal; Sierra Leone; South Africa; Spain; Sri Lanka; Switzerland; Taiwan; Thailand; Togo; Trinidad; United States; Ukraine; Uruguay; Venezuela; Vietnam; Zimbabwe.

World Federation of Trade Unions (WFTU)
Fédération Syndicale Mondiale (FSM)

Address. Branicka 112, Branik, 14700 Prague 4, Czech Republic

Phone. +42 2 4446 2140

Fax. +42 2 4446 1378

E–mail. wftu@login.cz

Website.: www.wftu.cz

Leadership. K.L.Mahendra (president); Alexander Zharikov (secretary-general)

Membership. Claims 120 million, but this is undoubtedly a considerable exaggeration. Reported membership fell from 208 million at the time of the 12th (1990) congress to the 120 million level by the time of the 14th congress in 2000.

History and character. The WFTU was formed in 1945, as a reflection of the unity of purpose among the trade union centres in the countries of the anti-fascist coalition during World War II. It fractured in the Cold War period, most of the major Western trade union centres leaving to create the ICFTU in 1949. Those that remained in the WFTU after the split included the CGT (France), CGIL (Italy), AUCCTU (Soviet Union), CTC (Cuba), AITUC (India), and a number of centres in newly independent states of Asia, Africa, and Latin America as well as the communist states of Eastern Europe.

There have been major changes in the WFTU's composition over the decades. In the 1970s the Italian CGIL (along with the French CGT its most important Western affiliate), reflecting the shift of the Italian Communist Party (PCI) to Eurocommunism, downgraded its relationship with the WFTU and then left altogether in 1978. However, the basic Cold War polarization between the ICFTU and WFTU remained in place through to the beginning of the 1990s, when the situation was transformed by the collapse of communism in Eastern Europe and the dissolution of the Soviet Union. This led to the dissolution or breakaway of WFTU affiliates in much of the former Soviet bloc and the creation of new centres, mostly affiliating to the ICFTU. The French CGT, the main remaining bastion of the WFTU in the West, disaffiliated, while the movement of many one-party states in Africa to more pluralist forms of government also led to numerous affiliations to the ICFTU of centres which had previously been either unaffiliated at a global level or linked to the WFTU.

Since the early 1990s the WFTU has lost all significant influence in Europe, although a number of industrial federations are affiliated with the WFTU's associated trade union internationals (TUIs). It has no presence in North America, and in Latin America, Africa and most of the Asia-Pacific region it has been eclipsed by the ICFTU. The Chinese ACFTU, the world's largest trade union centre, has not participated as an affiliate of the WFTU since the 1960s, although it has since 1994 attended the WFTU's 13th and 14th congresses as an observer. At the global level the WFTU remains divorced from the mainstream of trade unionism now clearly represented by the ICFTU. Although the WCL attended the WFTU's 14th congress (New Delhi, March 2000) as an observer, the ICFTU was not represented.

The 12th (Moscow, 1990), 13th (Damascus, 1994) and 2000 world congresses made changes in strategy, policy and structure to take account of the changing context in which the WFTU found itself. Past excessive centralization was heavily criticized and greater emphasis was placed on regional activity and the specific needs of industrial and service sectors. The 13th congress resolved that the WFTU was to become a "flexible, light and operational structure".

The reports presented at the 2000 congress attacked the impact of globalization, liberalization and privatization. Support was reiterated for the commitments and programme of action adopted by the World Summit for Social Development held in Copenhagen in 1995, including the commitment to take positive action to promote full employment. The report said that this programme had been nullified by the policies imposed by the IMF, World Bank and WTO. The WFTU called for the implementation of the UN Declaration for a New International Economic Order which was adopted by the UN General Assembly in 1974, upholding international economic cooperation based on equality of rights of all countries and an end to unequal trade and economic exchanges. The WFTU declared that the drive for neo-liberal globalization undermined the national sovereignty and economic independence of individual states while it introduced elements of neo-colonialism. Monopoly control of the information media, particularly the electronic media, was strongly criticised as transforming the emerging "information society" into a virtual "misinformation" society.

The detailed resolutions of the 14th congress, while reflecting shared concerns of the ICFTU and WCL with the impact of globalization and the general triumph of free markets, were perhaps most notable for the similarity with congresses prior to the collapse of communism. The "anti-capitalist" and "anti-imperialist" rhetoric and endorsement of states such as North Korea, Iraq and Yugoslavia in their "struggles", demonstrated the degree to which the WFTU remains ideologically unreconstructed and fundamentally hostile to the framework of beliefs espoused by the ICFTU and WCL. With the defection of former centres in the developed world, the WFTU has been left primarily as a representative of the controlled trade union systems of one-party states and of mostly marginal left-wing centres elsewhere. Its roster of vice-presidents includes leaders of the controlled trade unions of such countries as Cuba, Vietnam, North Korea, Libya and Syria. The WFTU accepts a contradiction between its own freedom of action and that of many of its affiliates. According to principles adopted at the 1994 congress, the WFTU's position is that: "as an international organization, and notwithstanding the relations established at national level by member organizations, the WFTU maintains its independence from governments, political parties and employers".

The ruling body is the congress, which last met in March 2000 after a six-year gap, and this elects the general council. The general council is made up of representatives of the affiliated national centres and trade union internationals, and this meets between congresses, establishes plans of work, decides on the composition of the presidential council, and elects the general secretary, vice-presidents and secretaries as well as the auditing commission. The presidential council elects the president from among its members annually. The secretariat is composed of the secretary-general and deputy secretaries-general elected by the general council. The WFTU's trades union internationals (TUIs), covering specific industrial sectors, have been restructured in recent years and consolidated into six organizations.

Regional offices. The WFTU has the following regional offices:

Asia

Address. 4 Windsor Place, New Delhi 110 001, India

Phone. +91 11 3311829

Fax. +91 11 3311849

E-mail. aitucong@bol.net.in

Leadership. Debkumar Ganguli (regional secretary)

Africa

Address. Villa No. 2016 Talli Boumag, Pikine, Dakar, Senegal

Phone. +221 346522

Fax. +221 225863

Leadership. Djibril Diop (vice-president)

Americas

Address. Oficina regional de la FSM, Calle 32, No.1, entre la y Mar, Miramar, Municipio Playa, Havana, Cuba

Phone. +53 7 294531

Fax. +53 7331614

E-mail. secamfsm@ceniai.inf.cu

Leadership. Jose Ortiz (regional secretary)

Middle East

Address. PO Box 30383, Damascus, Syria

Phone. +963 11 452513

Fax. +963 11 4454214

Leadership. Ibraham Rangos

Trade union internationals. The WFTU has the following associated trades union internationals (TUIs):

1.TUI of Energy, Metal, Chemical, Oil and Allied Industries

Address. Antonio Caso No.45, Colonia Tabacalera, CP 06470 Mexico, D.F., Mexico

E-mail. sinmexel@infosel.net.mx

Website. www.uis-ui.org

Leadership. Rosendo Flores (general secretary)

TUI of Agriculture, Food, Commerce, Textile and Allied Industries

Address. Case 428, 93514 Montreuil Cedex, France

Fax. + 33 1 48 51 57 49

Leadership. Freddy Huck (president)

TUI of Workers in the Building, Wood and Building Materials Industries

Address. PO Box 281, 00101 Helsinki, Finland

Fax. +358 9 6931020

Leadership. J. Dinis (general secretary)

E-mail. rguitbb@kaapeli.fi

TUI of Public and Allied Employees

Address. 10A, Shankharitola Street, Calcutta 700014, India

Fax. +91 33 246 9593

E-mail. aisgef@cal2.vsnl.net.in

Leadership. Sukomal Sen (general secretary)

World Federation of Teachers' Unions (FISE)

Address. 6/6 K.C.Ghose Road, Calcutta 700050, India

Fax. +91 33 557 1293

Leadership. Mrinmoy Bhattacharyya (general secretary)

TUI of Transport Workers

Address. Tengerszem u. 21 B, 1142 Budapest, Hungary

Fax. +36 1 189 0413

Leadership. Josef Toth (general secretary)

National affiliates. The following list shows affiliates (in independent states) as reported by the WFTU in 2000. The list should not be regarded as in all respects reliable.

In some instances these affiliates have little or no current organizational identity, while in others the organizations themselves no longer recognize their affiliation.

Afghanistan: National Workers' Union of Afghanistan

Albania: Confederation of Trade Unions of Albania

Angola: União Nacional dos Trabalhadores Angolanos (UNTA)

Argentina: Coordinadora Nacional de Agropaceres Agustin Tosco (CONAT); Movimiento Politico Sindical "Liberación" (MPSL)

Austria: Fraktion des Gewerkschaftlichen Linksblocks im ÖG B

Bahrain: Bahrain Workers' Union

Bangladesh: Bangladesh Trade Union Kendra (BTUK); Jatio Sramik Jote; Jatio Sramik League; Ganotantrik Sramik Federation; Jato Sramik Federation

Bolivia: Central Obrera Boliviana

Brazil: Central Geral dos Trabalhadores (CGT)

Bulgaria: National Council of Independent Trade Unions "EDINSTVO"

Burkina Faso: Union Syndicale des Travailleurs du Burkina

Cambodia: Cambodia Federation of Trade Unions

Colombia: Federación Nacional Sindical Unitaria Agropecuaria; Federación Nacional de Trabajadores de la Alimentacion, Bebidas, Afines y Sim.; Sindicato Unitario de Trabajadores de la Industria de Materiales de Construccion

Congo, Democratic Republic of: Confédération Générale du Travail

Congo, Republic of: Confédération Syndicale Congolaise (CSC)

Costa Rica: Confederación Unitaria de Trabajadores (CUT); Confederación de Trabajadores de Costa Rica; Asociacion de Servicios de Promocion Laboral; Sindicato de Trabajadores de la Universidad Nacional (SITUN)

Cuba: Central de Trabajadores de Cuba (CTC)

Cyprus: Pancyprian Federation of Labour; Dev-Is

Czech Republic: Trade Union Association of Bohemia, Moravia and Silesia

Djibouti: Union Générale des Travailleurs de Djibouti

Dominican Republic: Corriente Unitaria de Trabajadores

Ecuador: Confederación de Trabajadores del Ecuador (CTE)

Eritrea: General Union of Eritrean Workers

Ethiopia: Confederation of Ethiopian Trade Unions

Gambia: Gambia Labour Congress (GLC)

Guatemala: Federación Autónoma Sindical Guatemalteca (FASGUA)

Guinea-Bissau: União Nacional dos Trabalhadores da Guiné-Bissau (UNTG)

Guyana: Guyana Agricultural and General Workers Union (GAWU)

Haiti: Confédération Ouvrière des Travailleurs Haitiens

Honduras: Federación Unitaria de Trabajadores de Honduras (FUTH)

India: All-India Trade Union Congress (AITUC); United Trade Union Centre (Lenin Sarani)

Iran: Commission de Liaison des Syndicats Iraniens

Iraq: General Federation of Trade Unions of Iraq

Jamaica: Independent Trade Unions Action Council (ITAC)

Japan: WFTU Japanese affiliates council

Jordan: General Federation of Jordanian Trade Unions (GFJTU)

North Korea: General Federation of Trade Unions of Korea

Kuwait: Kuwait Trade Union Federation

Laos: Fédération des Syndicats du Laos

Lebanon: Fédération Nationale des Syndicats des Ouvriers et des Employés du Liban (FENASOL)

Libya: General Federation of Professional and Productive Trade Unions

Madagascar: Fédération des Syndicats des Travailleurs de Madagascar (FISEMA); Confédération des Syndicats des Travailleurs Malagasy Révolutionnaires (FISE-MARE)

Mauritius: General Workers' Federation (GWF)

Nepal: Nepal Trade Union Federation

Oman: National Committee of Omani Workers

Pakistan: All-Pakistan Federation of Labour (Durrani Group); All-Pakistan Trade Union Organization; Pakistan Trade Union Federation (PTUF); All-Pakistan Trade Union Federation (APTUF); Pakistan National Federation of Trade Unions (Malik Group)

Panama: Central Nacional de Trabajadores de Panama (CNTP)

Peru: Confederación General de Trabajadores del Péru (CGTP)

Philippines: National Association of Trade Unions (NATU); Trade Unions of Philippines and Allied Services (TU-PAS); National Congress of Workers (KATIPUNAN); National Congress of workers (Kalookan)

St. Vincent and the Grenadines: Progressive Trade Union Centre

Saudi Arabia: Workers' Union of Saudi Arabia

Senegal: Union des Travailleurs Libres du Sénégal (UTLS)

Solomon Islands: Solomon Islands National Union of Workers (SINUW)

Sri Lanka: Democratic Workers' Congress; Ceylon Federation of Trade Unions; Sri Lanka Mahajana Trade Union Federation; Sri Lanka Nidakas Sewaka Sangamaya; Progressive Workers' Congress

Sudan: Federation of Sudanese Professionals and Technicians Trade Union; Trade Union Front of Sudan

Syria: General Federation of Trade Unions

Togo: Union Générale des Syndicats Libres

Trinidad and Tobago: Council of Progressive Trade Unions

Venezuela: Central Unitaria de Trabajadores de Venezuela (CUTV)

Vietnam: Vietnam General Confederation of Labour

Yemen: General Federation of Yemen Trade Unions

Index

This is an index based on trade union acronyms or short names. It does not include defunct unions, merged unions (other than in exceptional cases of very recent mergers of important unions), or previous names of existing unions. International trade union organizations are indexed to their main entry only.